Maturity, Marriage, Motherhood, Mortality

Maturity, Marriage, Motherhood, Mortality

Women's Life-Cycle Rituals in Ancient Israel

SUSAN ACKERMAN

Oxford University Press is a department of the University of Oxford.
It furthers the University's objective of excellence in research, scholarship,
and education by publishing worldwide. Oxford is a registered trade mark of
Oxford University Press in the UK and in certain other countries.

Published in the United States of America by Oxford University Press
198 Madison Avenue, New York, NY 10016, United States of America.

© Oxford University Press 2025

All rights reserved. No part of this publication may be reproduced, stored in a retrieval system, transmitted, used for text and data mining, or used for training artificial intelligence, in any form or by any means, without the prior permission in writing of Oxford University Press, or as expressly permitted by law, by license or under terms agreed with the appropriate reprographics rights organization. Inquiries concerning reproduction outside the scope of the above should be sent to the Rights Department, Oxford University Press, at the address above.

You must not circulate this work in any other form
and you must impose this same condition on any acquirer.

Library of Congress Cataloging-in-Publication Data
Names: Ackerman, Susan author
Title: Maturity, marriage, motherhood, mortality : women's life-cycle rituals
in ancient Israel / Susan Ackerman.
Description: 1. | New York, NY : Oxford University Press, [2025] |
Includes bibliographical references and index. |
Identifiers: LCCN 2025020344 (print) | LCCN 2025020345 (ebook) |
ISBN 9780197809655 hardback | ISBN 9780197809686 | ISBN 9780197809662 epub
Subjects: LCSH: Women in Judaism | Judaism—Customs and practices |
Jewish way of life | Life cycle, Human—Religious aspects—Judaism
Classification: LCC BM729.W6 A27 2025 (print) | LCC BM729.W6 (ebook)
LC record available at https://lccn.loc.gov/2025020344
LC ebook record available at https://lccn.loc.gov/2025020345

DOI: 10.1093/9780197809686.001.0001

The manufacturer's authorized representative in the EU for product safety is
Oxford University Press España S.A., Parque Empresarial San Fernando de Henares,
Avenida de Castilla, 2 – 28830 Madrid (www.oup.es/en or product.safety@oup.com).
OUP España S.A. also acts as importer into Spain of products made by the manufacturer.

To my sister Laura, whose love and support have sustained me beyond measure during the many life-cycle events and life passages that we have journeyed through together

Contents

List of Figures	ix
Acknowledgments	xi
List of Abbreviations	xiii

Prologue: Of Universals and Not	1
Introduction: The Nature of Women's Life-Cycle Rituals	6

PART I. A GIRL'S BIRTH AND COMING INTO MATURITY

1. The Birth of a Female Child	51
2. Women's (and Men's) Coming of Age	70

PART II. MARRIAGE

3. Israelite Betrothal Rituals	89
4. A Young Woman's Wedding	119

PART III. MOTHERHOOD

5. Pregnancy and Childbirth	143
6. Naming a Child	170
7. Nursing and Weaning a Child	200

INTERLUDE

8. Menopause	223

PART IV. MORTALITY

9. Ritually Marking a Woman's Death — 239

Epilogue: Of Fragments and (W)holes — 261

Notes — 267
Bibliography — 325
Index of Subjects — 367
Index of Scripture and Other Ancient Sources — 383

Figures

5.1 Lapis Lazuli Taweret Amulet. Egyptian, Eighteenth Dynasty (ca. 1539–1292 BCE). 3.5 cm high, 1.5 cm wide. From the collection of the Metropolitan Museum of Art, New York. Accession no. 17.194.2477.   145

5.2 Single-Strand Necklace with Taweret Amulets. Egyptian, ca. 1332–1292 BCE. Faience, 1.9 x 20.5 x 0.4 cm. Brooklyn Museum, Gift of Mrs. Lawrence Coolidge and Mrs. Robert Woods Bliss, and the Charles Edwin Wilbour Fund, 48.66.42. Creative Commons-BY. Photo: Brooklyn Museum, 48.66.42_PS2.jpg.   146

5.3 Calcite ointment jar, for holding anointing oil used by pregnant and parturient women. From Abydos, Egypt, ca. 1479–1352 BCE. 19 cm high. From the collection of the British Museum, London. BM no. EA65275. © Trustees of the British Museum.   150

5.4 Limestone ostracon depicting an Egyptian woman in a birth arbor after delivery, as a maid offers a mirror and kohl. From Deir el-Medina, Ramesside period (ca. 1292–1075 BCE). 14.5 cm high, 11.2 cm wide. From the collection of the Musée du Louvre, Paris. Inv. no. E 25333. Photo: Christian Decamps. © RMN-Grand Palais/Art Resource, New York.   153

5.5 Queen Mutemwiya giving birth to Amenhotep III after his divine conception by Amun-Re, with Isis and Nephthys serving as midwives. Birth room of Amenhotep III, Luxor Temple, Egypt, first half of the fourteenth century BCE. Photograph by the author.   154

5.6 Bes amulets, from (left to right) Iron IA Azekah, Iron IIB Megiddo, and Iron IIB Lachish. After Herrmann, *Ägyptische Amulette aus Palästina/ Israel* IV, 345 (Azekah: 0214.2006) and 347 (Megiddo: 0409: 1994; Lachish: 0393: 1994). Drawing by Dorothea Ulrich.   158

6.1 Limestone ostracon that may depict the celebration after an Egyptian woman's period of postpartum impurity ends, with female attendants offering flowers and perfume while a figure above the new mother's left shoulder (the demigod Bes?) dances. From Deir el-Medina, Ramesside period (ca. 1292–1075 BCE). 8.5 cm high, 12 cm. wide. From the collection of the Musée du Louvre, Paris. Inv. no. E 25318. Photo Christian Decamps. © RMN-Grand Palais/Art Resource, New York.   183

7.1 Egyptian tomb relief depicting an agricultural scene, including a woman with a baby stacking fruit, ca. 670–650 BCE. Limestone, 9 7/16 x 11 5/16 in.

	(23.9 x 28.7 cm). Brooklyn Museum, Charles Edwin Wilbour Fund, 48.74. Creative Commons-BY. Photo: Brooklyn Museum, 48.74_SL1.jpg.	204
7.2	Terracotta Judean Pillar Figurine, from Lachish, ca. eighth–seventh century BCE. 18.4 cm high. From the collection of the Metropolitan Museum of Art, New York, gift of Harris D. and H. Dunscombe Colt, 1934. Accession no. 34.126.53.	211
7.3	Late seventh-/early sixth-century BCE model shrine from the Edomite site of Ḥorvat Qitmit, as reconstructed by Pirhiya Beck. From Beck, "Catalogue of Cult Objects," 103. Drawing by Yoseph Kapelyan. Courtesy of the Institute of Archaeology of Tel Aviv University.	214
7.4	Judean Pillar Figurine, with a figure of a child applied to the figurine's back, from Tell Beit Mirsim, Iron Age II. From Albright, *Excavation of Tell Beit Mirsim III*, Pl. 32:1. Courtesy of the American Society of Overseas Research.	216
9.1	Judahite Rock-Cut Bench Tomb. A. Bench; B. Repository. From Suriano, *History of Death*, 41. Courtesy of Matthew J. Suriano.	244

Acknowledgments

I have been at work on this book for many years, and there are thus years' worth of colleagues and friends to whom I owe my thanks for their encouragement and support. Rainer Albertz and Rüdiger Schmitt provided me with my first opportunity to present my then-nascent ideas about Israelite women's life-cycle rituals at the conference they organized on "Household Religion—Towards a Synthesis of Old Testament Studies, Archaeology, Epigraphy, and Cultural Studies" in Münster in April 2009. They also provided me with the opportunity to publish my presentation, and I am grateful to Pennsylvania State University Press for permission to include here revised and significantly expanded materials from that essay, "Women's Rites of Passage in Ancient Israel: Three Case Studies (Birth, Coming of Age, and Death)," which appeared in *Family and Household Religion—Toward a Synthesis of Old Testament Studies, Archaeology, Epigraphy, and Cultural Studies* (ed. Rainer Albertz, Beth Alpert Nakhai, Saul M. Olyan, and Rüdiger Schmitt; Winona Lake, IN: Eisenbrauns, 2014), 1–32.

As the years went by, I also had opportunities to present my work-in-progress at the 2010 annual meeting of the Society of Biblical Literature, at the 2022 and 2023 annual meetings of the American Society of Overseas Research, at multiple meetings of the Colloquium of Biblical Research and the Biblical Colloquium, and at a 2022 conference hosted by Renewed Philology at Yale University and the Hebrew Union College–Jewish Institute of Religion. My colleagues at these various gatherings have been extremely generous with their help and advice, as have colleagues at various academic institutions where I was invited to speak about my research: Baylor University, Colby College, Cornell University, Duke University, and the University of California, Los Angeles. The faculty in the Department of Religion at my own institution, Dartmouth College, have continued to provide the same warm and sustaining environment they have throughout my career, and the Department's administrative staff, including Meredyth Morley, Caroline Latta, and Marcia Welsh, kept me going throughout my interminable fights with computers, copiers, printers, and scanners—or, really, anything that plugs into an electrical outlet. The Dartmouth College librarians are remarkable, and I—along with every researcher at Dartmouth—owe them a particular thanks for their herculean efforts to keep our scholarship on track even while the library was closed during the early months of the COVID pandemic.

I am also grateful to Steve Wiggins at Oxford University Press, who has embraced this project with enthusiasm ever since I pitched it to him over a decade ago, and I also thank Professors Jennie Ebeling and Karel van der Toorn, who vetted the project on behalf of Oxford and whose comments made my manuscript a better piece of work. At Oxford, I have in addition been privileged to work with editorial team leader Cathryn Steel and Senior Project Editor Zara Cannon-Mohammed.

Finally, I extend thanks to the many people in my life whose friendship and care nurture me, including Kate Conley, Anna Covici, Sheila Culbert, Bill Dever, Mona Domosh, Steve and Elizabeth Dycus, Pam Gaber, Tim Harrison, Sharon Herbert, Ann-Marie Knoblauch, Peter Lanfer, Frank Magilligan, Dee Michel, the late Deborah Nichols, Bill Propp, Saul Olyan, Fred Schockaert, Bruce, Gabey, and Jason Smoller, Richard Stamelman, Rachel Starr, Andy Vaughn, Richard Voos, John Watanabe, Ed Wright, and Richard Wright. Writing a book about life-cycle events and rituals has also caused me to think deeply about the families with whom these events and rituals are most typically shared, especially since, during the years I worked on this project, my own family celebrated two weddings and the birth of my great-nephew Ben, even as we mourned the deaths of my beloved parents, George and Peggy Ackerman. There every step of the way, throughout happy times and sad, was my dear sister Laura, and it is to her—in acknowledgment of the sixty-five years of life's path that we have traveled together—that this book is lovingly dedicated.

Abbreviations

AASOR	Annual of the American Schools of Oriental Research/Annual of the American Society of Overseas Research
ABD	*Anchor Bible Dictionary*. Edited by David Noel Freedman. 6 vols. New York: Doubleday, 1992.
ABS	Archaeology and Biblical Studies
AIL	Ancient Israel and Its Literature
AJPA	*American Journal of Physical Anthropology*
ANEM	Ancient Near Eastern Monographs
AOAT	Alter Orient und Altes Testament
AOS	American Oriental Series
AYB	Anchor Yale Bible
AYBRL	Anchor Yale Bible Reference Library
BA	*Biblical Archaeologist*
BAM	Franz Köcher, *Die babylonisch-assyrische Medizin in Texten und Untersuchungen*. 6 vols. Berlin: de Gruyter, 1963-80.
BASOR	*Bulletin of the American Schools of Oriental Research/Bulletin of the American Society of Overseas Research*
BDB	Francis Brown, S. R. Driver, and Charles A. Briggs, *A Hebrew and English Lexicon of the Old Testament*. Oxford: Clarendon, 1907.
BHS	*Biblia hebraica stuttgartensia*. Edited by K. Elliger and W. Rudolph. Stuttgart: Deutsche Bibelgesellschaft, 1983.
Bib	*Biblica*
BibInt	*Biblical Interpretation*
BJS	Brown Judaic Studies
BN	*Biblische Notizen*
BZAW	Beihefte zur Zeitschrift für die alttestamentliche Wissenschaft
CAD	*The Assyrian Dictionary of the Oriental Institute of the University of Chicago*. Edited by A. Leo Oppenheim, Erica Rainer, et al. 26 vols. Chicago: The Oriental Institute, 1956–2010.
CANE	*Civilizations of the Ancient Near East*. Edited by Jack M. Sasson. 4 vols. New York: Scribner's, 1995. Reprinted ed. Peabody, MA: Hendrickson, 2000.
CBC	Cambridge Bible Commentary
CBQ	*Catholic Biblical Quarterly*
CHANE	Culture and History of the Ancient Near East

COS	*The Context of Scripture*. Edited by William W. Hallo. 3 vols. Leiden: Brill, 2003.
DDD	*Dictionary of Deities and Demons in the Bible*. Edited by Karel van der Toorn, Bob Becking, and Pieter W. van der Horst. 2nd ed. Leiden: Brill, 1999.
FAT	Forschungen zum Alten Testament
HALOT	Ludwig Koehler, Walter Baumgartner, and Johann J. Stamm, *The Hebrew and Aramaic Lexicon of the Old Testament*. Translated and edited under the supervision of Mervyn E. J. Richardson. 4 vols. Leiden: Brill, 1994–1999.
HAR	*Hebrew Annual Review*
HSM	Harvard Semitic Monographs
HSS	Harvard Semitic Studies
HUCA	*Hebrew Union College Annual*
ICC	International Critical Commentary
JANER	*Journal of Ancient Near Eastern Religions*
JAOS	*Journal of the American Oriental Society*
JBL	*Journal of Biblical Literature*
JCS	*Journal of Cuneiform Studies*
JEA	*Journal of Egyptian Archaeology*
JESHO	*Journal of the Economic and Social History of the Orient*
JFSR	*Journal of Feminist Studies in Religion*
JHS	*Journal of Hebrew Scriptures*
JNES	*Journal of Near Eastern Studies*
JNSL	*Journal of Northwest Semitic Languages*
JSOT	*Journal for the Study of the Old Testament*
JSOTSup	*Journal for the Study of the Old Testament: Supplement Series*
KAI	Herbert Donner and Wolfgang Röllig, *Kanaanäische und aramäische Inschriften*. 3 vols. 2nd ed. Wiesbaden: Harrassowitz, 1966.
KTU	*Die keilalphabetischen Texte aus Ugarit, Ras Ibn Hani und anderen Orten*. Edited by Manfried Dietrich, Oswald Loretz, and Joaquín Sanmartín. 3rd ed. Münster: Ugarit-Verlag, 2013.
LHBOTS	Library of Hebrew Bible/Old Testament Studies
LXX	Septuagint
MC	Mesopotamian Civilizations
MT	Masoretic Text
NEA	*Near Eastern Archaeology*
NICOT	New International Commentary on the Old Testament
NRSV	Bible, New Revised Standard Version
OBO	Orbis biblicus et orientalis
OEAE	*The Oxford Encyclopedia of Ancient Egypt*. Edited by Donald Redford. 3 vols. Oxford: Oxford University Press, 2001.
OIP	Oriental Institute Publications

Or	*Orientalia*
OTL	Old Testament Library
RB	*Revue biblique*
RBS	Resources for Biblical Study
RS	Ras Shamra
SBLDS	Society of Biblical Literature Dissertation Series
SBLWAW	Society of Biblical Literature Writings from the Ancient World
SEL	*Studi epigrafici e linguistici sul Vicino Oriente antico*
SFSHJ	South Florida Studies in the History of Judaism
SJOT	*Scandinavian Journal of the Old Testament*
StBibLit	Studies in Biblical Literature
STDJ	Studies on the Texts of the Desert of Judah
SWBA	Social World of Biblical Antiquity
TDOT	*Theological Dictionary of the Old Testament.* Edited by G. Johannes Botterweck, Helmer Ringgren, and Heinz-Josef Fabry. 15 vols. Grand Rapids, MI, and Cambridge, UK: Eerdmans, 1974-2006.
UF	*Ugarit-Forschungen*
VT	*Vetus Testamentum*
VTsup	Supplements to Vetus Testamentum
WBC	Word Biblical Commentary
WIS	*Women in Scripture: A Dictionary of Named and Unnamed Women in the Hebrew Bible, the Apocryphal/Deuterocanonical Books, and the New Testament.* Edited by Carol Meyers, with Toni Craven and Ross S. Kraemer. Boston: Houghton Mifflin, 2000.
ZA	*Zeitschrift für Assyriologie*
ZAW	*Zeitschrift für die alttestamentliche Wissenschaft*

Prologue

Of Universals and Not

"It is a truth universally acknowledged," as Jane Austen's *Pride and Prejudice* famously begins, "that a single man in possession of a good fortune, must be in want of a wife."[1] In the context of the novel, the work this opening statement does is enormous, for in the pages that follow, plot twists and turns concerning money, marriage, and the nonnegotiable relationship between the two are the subject of practically every scene. Already in the novel's third sentence, we are introduced to our first marriage—the rather unhappy union of Mr. and Mrs. Bennet—and we are made privy to the couple's bickering about their new neighbor, Mr. Bingley, and what should take place (Mrs. Bennet) but seemingly will not be done (Mr. Bennet) to bring Mr. Bingley, with his fortune of "four or five thousand a year," to wed one of the Bennets' five marriage-age daughters.[2] Scant pages later, we are introduced to another single man of an even greater fortune (ten thousand pounds a year) and the novel's male protagonist, Mr. Darcy, who joins the Bingley party, the Bennets, and others of the neighborhood at a local ball, an event that is then meticulously dissected by various characters in conversation upon conversation as they consider the attributes and qualities (read: suitability for marriage) of the various attendees. Soon thereafter, Mr. Collins, a distant cousin of the Bennets who, as the nearest male heir, is due to inherit from Mr. Bennet, comes to visit, with the intent, we learn, of marrying one of the Bennet daughters in an attempt to make right the financial injury that stems from the terms of the inheritance. Yet the novel's main female character, Miss Elizabeth Bennet (the second daughter), refuses him, even as she is attracted to another newcomer in their town, Mr. Wickham. But no matter: Mr. Collins quickly—within two days!—shifts his attention and proposes to a different young woman of the region, Miss Charlotte Lucas, who willingly agrees to marry him and whose parents just as willingly proffer their consent. In short order, Volume I of *Pride and Prejudice* ends, although with much more to come of marriage and the interdependent matter of money in Volumes II and III.

Yet however important the first sentence of *Pride and Prejudice* is for setting forth the action of the novel that is to follow ("under any circumstances, marriage, marriage!"),[3] my interest in *Pride and Prejudice*'s opening line in the context of this book, which is about women's life-cycle events in ancient Israel and the rituals associated with them, is the way that Austen (or more accurately speaking, *Pride and Prejudice*'s omniscient narrator), in claiming a "truth universally acknowledged" about marrying, might be said to voice more generally a conviction about the universality of events and rituals that define the human life cycle across cultures, and even a conviction about the universal commemoration of many of the same life-cycle events. After all, all of us are born, and all of us will die, and thus our biology might suggest that these moments in the life cycle are something to be universally marked. Biology might also suggest that we all might mark our coming into sexual maturity in some way, and it is in addition commonly supposed that sexual maturation is followed sooner or later, as Austen (or her novel's narrator) suggests, by entering into a union (such as marriage) with which sexual maturity is associated.

That said, it is as universally acknowledged as anything can be among scholars that the famous opening line of *Pride and Prejudice* is laden with irony, for the very fact that Austen identifies the "truth" of which she speaks to be "universally acknowledged" signals that it is neither: neither true, that is, nor universal. Rather, we learn already in the novel's second sentence that the "truth" Austen's narrator claims as "universal" is "nothing more than one of the fixed opinions of the 'neighborhood' of 'surrounding families' amidst which the novel's action is to take place."[4] As such, it is an opinion very much governed by the particulars of these neighbors' and families' circumstances, which is to say: the particulars of rank, class, and sex as they were manifest in what one of Austen's characters describes as England's "polished societ[y]" during the period of the late eighteenth and early nineteenth centuries in which the novel is set.[5] It was within England's "polished society" of this era, for example, that good fortunes were to be had for at least some single men (typically, older sons who were made rich through inheritance); it was also within that society that such men had choices about a marital partner (as opposed, say, to younger sons, "who may suffer from the want of money ... [and] cannot marry where they like").[6] The real "truth" about marriage in England's eighteenth- and nineteenth-century "polished society" turns out to be, moreover, not that a single man in possession of a good fortune is inevitably in want of a wife, but that "dowerless young women ... are desperately in want of wealthy single men."[7] Or, as the novel's omniscient narrator reports in explaining Charlotte Lucas's reasons for marrying the "conceited, pompous, narrow-minded, [and] silly" Mr. Collins:[8] "marriage ... was the only honourable provision for well-educated young women of small fortune, and however uncertain of giving happiness, must be their pleasantest preservative from want."[9]

As with Austen's novel, so too with life-cycle events and their attendant rituals, for just as Austen's irony calls into question *Pride and Prejudice*'s "truth universally acknowledged" about marriage, we might as well question whether the ritual marking of life-cycle events is really as universal a truth as we might sometimes suppose. Even the commemoration of seemingly fixed biological happenings such as birth and death can "vary significantly between cultures and over time,"[10] so that physical birth may not be identical to a child's "social birth," the moment when a newborn is "properly identified and accepted as a member of the social group."[11] The British anthropologist Janet Carsten reports, for example, that "among Malays in Pulau Langkawi, an infant does not 'come into existence' as a member of the community until the umbilical cord is cut,"[12] and it was only on the fifth day after birth (or even, according to some sources, the seventh or tenth day) that an infant in classical and Hellenistic Greece was formally accepted (or rejected) by its father and marked (or dismissed) as a new member of the family.[13] We can similarly ask, as we will in Chapters 1 and 6, when, exactly, an Israelite neonate was accorded full-fledged membership within its family unit and larger household and village community, just as the title of archaeologist Ron Tappy's review article on burial practices in ancient Israel's Southern Kingdom—"Did the Dead Ever Die in Biblical Judah?"—urges us to consider whether an individual's physical death really marked that person's social death in the Israelite worldview.[14]

The age at which a society recognizes its members as coming into maturity can also vary widely and need not be coordinated with physical markers such as "a swelling of the breasts, an enlargement of the pelvis, the appearance of pubic hair, and ... the first menstrual flow" (for girls) and "the development of facial hair, the deepening of the voice or the first nocturnal emission" (for boys).[15] For example, J. S. La Fontaine has argued that among the Gisu people of eastern Uganda, it is only when a female gives birth that she achieves "full feminine maturity" and "is entitled to the honorific '*umugyerema*', nowadays translated as 'Mrs.' or 'Madam,'"[16] even though menarche as a marker of biological maturity and marriage as a marker of at least some degree of social maturity had preceded—and perhaps long preceded—parturition. Nancy C. Lutkehaus has suggested a similar understanding holds among the Manam islanders of Papua New Guinea, as it does elsewhere in Oceania, according to M. G. Swift, among the Malay people of Sumatra.[17] Conversely, Vincent Crapanzano has demonstrated that circumcision in the Moroccan villages he studied in the late 1960s,[18] which was performed as soon as a boy was deemed old enough to remember the event (usually between three to six years of age), was understood at some level to declare that the boy had become a man, even though the boy was in fact neither "physically a man" nor "treated as a man."[19] Rather, circumcision was only a "necessary prerequisite" for and an "anticipation" or "preview" of the manhood that was to come significantly later.[20] As for marriage, we well know that the specifics of this institution—however common it may be across cultures—can vary widely: among cultures that practice polygamous marriage, for example, as opposed to those cultures in which marriage is monogamous.[21] Moreover, the most prevalent type of polygamous marriage, polygyny (in which a man has more than one wife), is obviously experienced differently by the marriage's wives than it is by their husband.

Indeed, students of life-cycle events have come increasingly to argue that life-cycle events and the rituals associated with them are experienced differently by women than by men (much more on this in the Introduction). In this study of women's life-cycle events and rituals in ancient Israel, I seek to demonstrate that such differences manifest themselves, and profoundly so, in the Israel of the so-called Iron Age (ca. 1200–586 BCE) and the first century or so of the Persian period (ca. 539–450 BCE), or what biblical scholars would describe as the preexilic and early postexilic periods of Israelite history. More specifically, my goal is to describe women's life-cycle events and rituals in preexilic and early postexilic Israel, highlight the ways in which women's experiences during these life-cycle events and rituals differed from those of men, and offer a theoretical model that seeks to explain these distinctions. I begin, in the Introduction, by discussing the analytical paradigms that illuminate my study of Israelite women's life-cycle events and rituals, before turning in Chapters 1–9 to look at several specific moments within an Israelite woman's life-cycle: a girl child's birth and her coming into sexual maturity; a young woman's betrothal and marriage; then, events regarding motherhood: pregnancy, parturition, and two signal events in the life of a new mother—the naming of her newborn child and weaning. Next, I consider features that may have characterized the lives of menopausal women, before concluding with observations regarding the rituals marking an ancient Israelite woman's death.

Introduction

The Nature of Women's Life-Cycle Rituals

Among scholars of life-cycle events, the groundbreaking work of the French ethnographer and folklorist Arnold van Gennep (1873–1957) is as iconic as is the first line of *Pride and Prejudice* among Jane Austen aficionados. Van Gennep, moreover, was as emphatic in his claims as was Austen—albeit without the irony—about the universality of ritually marking life-cycle events, through what van Gennep called *rites de passage*, or rites of passage: "rites that accompany every change of state, place, social position and age."[1] Indeed, as David I. Kertzer notes in his introduction to the 2019 English edition of van Gennep's 1909 monograph *Les rites de passage*, "van Gennep opens the book by noting the *universality* of rites of passage in the life course," and the Danish anthropologist Bjørn Thomassen similarly begins his 2014 review of van Gennep's work by writing: "Throughout the inhabited world, *in all times and under every circumstance*, rites of passage have flourished."[2] Or, in van Gennep's words, "The life of an individual *in any society* is a series of passages from one age to another and from one occupation to another" (emphasis in all three quotes is mine).[3]

Moreover, and more important, van Gennep maintained that life-cycle events were universally observed according to a common ritual pattern, or what he called a *schéma*, with "a wide degree of *general similarity* among ceremonies of birth, childhood, social puberty, betrothal, marriage, pregnancy, fatherhood, initiation into religious societies, and funerals" (emphasis again mine).[4] Van Gennep described this common pattern as tripartite in form: (1) separation from "an earlier fixed point in the social structure or from an earlier set of social conditions"; (2) a transition, or threshold, or liminal period (from the Latin *limen*, meaning, among other things, threshold), "when the state of the ritual subject is ambiguous: he is no longer in the old state and has not yet reached the new one"; and (3) the stage of (re)incorporation, (re)integration, or (re)aggregation, "when the ritual subject enters a new stable state with its own rights and obligations."[5] For example, in Hopi childbirth rites as reported by van Gennep, the pregnant woman, while attended by her mother during labor, is isolated (or separated) at the moment of delivery itself, during which no one is allowed to be present. After the baby arrives, there is a twenty-day period during which the new mother is subject to various dietary restrictions, and the woman is also proscribed from leaving her house before sundown: for the initial five days postpartum if she had previously borne children and for the entire twenty-day period if the child is her first. Then, on the twentieth day after the birth, whatever constraints that have been imposed on the new mother during this transitional or liminal period end, as her infant is named and a special ritual meal is served to the entire community. "From that day [of (re)incorporation/(re)integration/(re)aggregation] on," van Gennep writes, "everything in the house goes its usual way for the mother, the child, the family, and the pueblo."[6]

Yet even though van Gennep went on to say of this Hopi rite, "Therefore the sequence is (1) separation, (2) a transitional period with gradual removal of barriers, and (3) reintegration into ordinary life,"[7] he insisted throughout *Les rites de passage* that his tripartite pattern was not to be applied mechanically, without due attention to any given ritual's particularities.[8] He argued, for example, that the various elements of his tripartite pattern were not necessarily realized to the same degree in different life-cycle rituals. Thus, while marriage rites might focus on the stage of incorporation (the incorporation of the newly married couple into the combined community of their natal and marital families, or, in cultures that practice patrilocality, the incorporation of the bride into the groom's household structure and organization), transition rites "may play an important part . . . in pregnancy, betrothal, and initiation; or they may be reduced to a minimum in adoption, in the delivery of a second child, [or] in remarriage."[9]

Van Gennep was also careful to note that rituals that mark life-cycle events need not function only as rites of passage: "marriage rites, for example, are also likely to include rites aimed at ensuring the couple's fertility," and "pregnancy ceremonies . . . are likely to include rites aimed at protecting mother and child from evil forces and ill health."[10] "Nonetheless," as Catherine Bell writes in her important monograph on ritual, "van Gennep was still very much concerned to demonstrate the *universality* of certain patterns," with "an appeal to *universal patterns* within examples from many disparate traditions" (emphases mine).[11] Or, as van Gennep himself puts it, "since the goal is the same" ("to enable the individual to pass from one defined position to another which is equally well defined"), "it follows of necessity that the ways of attaining it should be at least analogous, if not identical in every detail ... the underlying arrangement is always the same."[12]

Van Gennep's most famous follower, the Scottish-born anthropologist Victor Turner (1920–1983), was no less sweeping than his predecessor in his claims of universality, which Turner put forward in a wide-ranging series of works that sought to develop van Gennep's concept of the rite of passage's threshold or liminal phase. Originally, in his first essay on the topic, "Betwixt and Between: The Liminal Period in *Rites de Passage*," published in 1964, Turner's focus was exactly what his title might suggest: to elaborate on van Gennep's prior account of rites of passage in order to describe more thoroughly the features that Turner believed defined these rituals' intermediate stage.[13] As his essay's title also suggests, it was therein that Turner first articulated the phrase "betwixt and between" that has become practically synonymous with Turner's sense of "liminal *personae*": "their condition is one of ambiguity and paradox," he writes; they are "at once no longer classified and not yet classified," "neither one thing nor another; or may be both; or neither here nor there; or may even be nowhere."[14]

Turner also described how liminal persons, as "structurally invisible" (that is, "betwixt and between" the set identities and classificatory systems of their society), are often secluded and hidden away (as in van Gennep's description of the Hopi parturient noted above), as well as treated as if they have nothing: "no status, property, insignia, secular clothing, rank, kinship position."[15] Accordingly, these liminal persons are placed in a position of subordination, even "complete submission," which requires that they acquiesce passively and in full obedience to whatever authorities are administering or have jurisdiction over the rites of passage that are being undertaken—although these authorities (typically, community elders) might impose "ordeals and tests ... that amounted to tortures."[16] Turner argued, moreover, that because liminal persons are "neither living nor dead from one aspect, and both living and dead from another," "the symbols that represent them are, in many societies, drawn from the biology of death, decomposition, catabolism, and other physical processes that have a negative tinge."[17]

Yet even as Turner detailed these negative features of the liminal experience (motifs of ambiguity, invisibility, seclusion, submission, suffering, and death), he took pains to "draw attention to certain positive aspects of liminality": for example, the "symbols modeled on processes of gestation and parturition ... embryos, newborn infants, or sucklings" that can be paired with the more ominous symbols that come from "the biology of death."[18]

Indeed, he suggested that liminal persons, precisely because of their negatively connoted attributes of structural invisibility and lack of social identity, are perfectly positioned to die to their old selves and be reborn, and not just reborn into a new state or social role, as van Gennep would have it. Rather, in Turner's account, liminal persons are deconstructed and reconstructed, or "ground down" and subsequently "fashioned anew" in the sense of being inwardly, morally, and ontologically transformed, acquiring what Turner called an "arcane knowledge or *gnosis*" that alters a liminal person's "innermost nature," "impressing him, as a seal impresses wax," and so effecting "a change in being."[19] Turner furthermore argued that because during a rite of passage's liminal period, the ritual's subjects are without the differentiating markers of "rank, status, and corporate affiliation," they experience among themselves "complete equality." The result is a "comity of comrades" that can extend beyond the liminal phase to create lifelong ties of deep friendship.[20]

Turner's 1964 essay was republished, almost without alteration, in his 1967 monograph *The Forest of Symbols*.[21] At about the same time, he undertook his next major foray into the study of liminality: the essay "Liminality and Communitas," given as one of the Lewis Henry Morgan lectures that Turner delivered at the University of Rochester in 1966 and subsequently published in his 1969 monograph *The Ritual Process*.[22] In this work, Turner began by reiterating some of the key points of his 1964 "Betwixt and Between" article, but he quickly moved to expand upon them, first by elaborating on his ideas about the "comity of comrades" that he had previously suggested existed among liminal persons. More specifically, Turner introduced the term *communitas*—a feeling of "intense social togetherness" and "of union with one's fellow human beings"[23]—to "distinguish this modality of social relationship."[24]

More important for our purposes, Turner suggested that liminality need not be understood only as a transitional period manifest during the intermediate stage of a rite of passage. Instead, he proposed that in increasingly specialized societies and cultures, characterized by "progressive complexity in the social division of labor," liminality can be present as a permanent way of being, so that "what was in tribal society principally a set of transitional qualities 'betwixt and between' defined states of culture and society has become itself an institutionalized state."[25] Turner cited as a preeminent example the monastic and mendicant communities "in the great world religions," such as Christian monks who commit to live permanently in an institutionalized context of liminal-like austerity and in liminal-like submission to the abbot who has authority over them.[26] He also identified individual figures within certain societies whom he took to embody liminal-like characteristics as a permanent way of being: for example, court jesters, whom Turner described as personifying the liminal attributes of inferiority and marginality within monarchical societies and thereby symbolized, in Turner's reckoning, "common humanity" in the face of authoritarian and potentially unjust agents (kings and other "supreme political rulers").[27] Turner, writing in the latter half of the 1960s, even used the language of liminality to describe the hippies of his own day, who had "'opt[ed] out' of the status-bound social order," to take on "the stigmata of the lowly" and to "stress personal relationships rather than social obligations."[28]

Yet as the noted scholar of medieval European Christianity Caroline Walker Bynum trenchantly suggested in a 1984 essay titled "Women's Stories, Women's Symbols: A Critique of Victor Turner's Theory of Liminality," Turner fails to exploit the potential of these insights regarding the permanently liminal in order to consider how they might be much more extensively applied:[29] not just, say, to certain subcommunities of monastics or hippies living within specialized and increasingly complex societies, and not just to certain individuals, such as jesters within a royal court, but instead to a significant portion of the world's population throughout time—namely, women during many periods in history and in many cultures. After all, during many periods in history and in many cultures—including both tribal cultures and the cultures Turner characterized as more specialized and complex—women, as part of their *normal* course of existence, have manifested many of the attributes that Turner associated with a rite of passage's liminal phase.

For example, during many periods in history and in many cultures, women, as part of their *normal* course of existence, have been unable to hold property, much as, according to Turner, "liminal entities" during a rite of passage are often represented "as possessing nothing." Turner then goes on to say, as I have intimated already, that this lack of possessions illustrates liminal persons' lack of "rank or role" and "position in a kinship system" and so, in Turner's account, demonstrates the structural invisibility of liminal entities and their lack of social identity as they move through the intermediate or transitional stage of a rite of passage.[30] Yet women, during many periods in history and in many cultures, have often been without rank or role in the *normal* course of their existence, especially rank or role independent of some male in their lives (most frequently, the woman's father, husband, or son).[31] So too are women, as part of their *normal* course of existence, often deemed peripheral or irrelevant in the delineation of kinship systems. Biblical scholars might consider in this regard the almost complete absence of women in the genealogical texts—or the "begat" lists—that punctuate the book of Genesis and comprise the first eight chapters of 1 Chronicles.[32] Overall, what is suggested, as above, is that women, during many periods in history and in many cultures, were inherently, permanently, or standardly liminal—or liminal as part of the *normal* course of their existence.

Indeed, at some level, Turner seems to articulate such an understanding: as Bynum writes, "in many places he [Turner] suggests that women are liminal."[33] She cites, for example, Turner's "Liminality and Communitas" essay that I discussed just above, where Turner describes, among other things, the installation rite of a senior chief of the Ndembu, a tribal people of northwestern Zambia among whom Turner, while a doctoral student, conducted fieldwork for fifteen months in 1950–1952 and again for fourteen months in 1953–1954.[34] According to Turner, the most significant actor during this installation rite is an agent called Kafwana, who—in addition to taking on other responsibilities—delivers a homily during the ritual's liminal phase that reviles the chief-to-be as "mean, selfish, and bad-tempered." Also during the installation rite's liminal phase, Kafwana periodically strikes his buttocks against the chief-to-be "insultingly" and is otherwise said to "manhandle" the incipient chief and his wife and order them to perform menial tasks.[35] Turner takes this to be part and parcel of the ritual submission and subjugation that the chief-to-be, as a liminal entity, is required to endure,[36] while also making note of the fact that Kafwana, though biologically male, is positioned in the Ndembu worldview as "symbolically feminine."[37] Concerning this, Turner writes, "there is a certain homology between the 'weakness' and 'passivity' of liminality in diachronic transitions between states and statuses, and the 'structural' or synchronic inferiority of certain personae, groups, and social categories in political, legal, and economic systems."[38]

Which is to say: Turner posits a homology between the liminal submissiveness of the chief-to-be during his installation rite and the structural inferiority of the "symbolically feminine" Kafwana and, by extension, all females in the Ndembu political, legal, and economic systems. A decade or so later, in a 1979 essay where Turner considers, among other things, Natalie Z. Davis's work on the carnival tradition in France in the later Middle Ages and the sixteenth century, he is even more explicit.[39] There he writes of the female participants in these carnival traditions as "*quintessentially* liminal, since they represent persons who, even in the mundane 'indicative' world, by reason of their status inferiority and marginality, have a 'subjunctive' penumbra."[40]

Again, though, Turner fails fully to grasp the implications of these observations regarding the "'structural' or synchronic inferiority" of the "symbolically feminine" Kafwana and regarding, more generally, women as "*quintessentially* liminal . . . even in the mundane 'indicative' world." Thus, he fails to ask the sorts of questions that arguably should follow in his analysis of life-cycle rituals: what happens, for example, when women, for whom liminal features and characteristics are inherent and quintessential aspects of their normative, day-to-day identity, participate in a rite of passage whose very structure, as Turner would have it, requires movement *into* and then *out of* liminality as a central and constitutive part? Instead, according to Bynum, Turner takes the male experience to epitomize the universal nature of rites of passage and of liminality that I have previously suggested characterizes his work, in order "to look at women" (or the "symbolically feminine" Kafwana) in relation to men (for example, the Ndembu chief-to-be), rather than "to stand with women" and ask what effect women's inherently and normative liminal existence might have on the structure and nature of women's life-cycle events and rituals.[41]

Bynum notes a further irony in this regard: that despite Turner's failure to grasp the implications of his observations regarding women's inherent and normative liminality, and what this might mean for analyzing women's life-cycle events and rituals, Turner actually had the data to address these issues ready to hand, for, as the iconic anthropologist Mary Douglas observed in her obituary of Turner written for Britain's Royal Anthropological Institute, Turner was "an unrivalled ethnographer." In fact, "no one," according to Douglas, "has produced a fuller account of the life and work of an African civilisation" than did Turner in his "four major studies on the Ndembu."[42] Indeed, Turner's Ndembu ethnographies are so renowned that, still today, the American Anthropological Association commemorates them by awarding an annual Victor Turner Prize in Ethnographic Writing.[43] Furthermore, as Bynum (of all people!) points out, Turner's descriptions of *women's* rituals among the Ndembu are "both extensive and subtle."[44] For example, in Chapter 3 of his 1968 book *The Drums of Affliction*, Turner offers a long and detailed account of the Ndembu's *Nkula* ritual, whose "aim is to remove a ban imposed by a shade of a deceased relative" on a woman's fertility—a ban that might manifest itself in the woman's life in the form of "menstrual disorders of various kinds," "abnormal parturition, such as breech-delivery, still-birth, and abortion," "marital frigidity," or a "protracted incapacity to conceive."[45] More important for our purposes: in Chapters 7 and 8 of this same volume,[46] Turner provides an even longer report of what he elsewhere describes as one of the three most important life-cycle rituals in Ndembu culture, the ritual of *Nkang'a*.[47] This is the rite that transforms a pubescent girl into both a woman and a wife.[48]

Indeed, Turner's description of the *Nkang'a* ritual is so rich and fulsome that I propose to identify within it six features that can characterize women's life-cycle rituals. As we will see, some of these features parallel, at least to some degree, what we find in men's life-cycle rituals: in *Nkang'a*, for example, we will see evidence of the tripartite structure that van Gennep originally argued was typical of all rites of passage. We will also see many of the features of liminality that, in Turner's account, distinguish any rite of passage's intermediate or transitional phase. Still, I will suggest that van Gennep's rite-of-passage pattern may not be as fully realized in *Nkang'a* as his convictions regarding this pattern's universality presume. Likewise, I will argue that the specific ways in which liminality and some of its associated attributes (for example, Turner's "comity of comrades") are expressed during *Nkang'a*, and more generally in women's life-cycle rituals, differ in significant respects from the liminal experiences of men, and I will put forward a theoretical model that explains why these differences occur. Then, following on the analyses offered by Bynum in the essay I cited above, as well as by the historian of religion Bruce Lincoln, I will present an account that explains another significant difference between men's and women's life-cycle rituals that is demonstrated by *Nkang'a*: the presence (for men), as opposed to the absence (for woman), of dramatic reversals or ruptures in terms of status or social position within life-cycle events. Finally, I will consider a particular moment within *Nkang'a* and within similar young women's puberty rites as catalogued by Lincoln that seems anomalous—a moment during the ritual when the woman subject's typically abject status is temporarily enhanced—and I will conclude by discussing why, and under what conditions, this seeming peculiarity can be manifest within some (although not all) women's life-cycle rituals.

I turn, then, to use Turner's account of the *Nkang'a* ritual, together with three accounts of the *Nkang'a* rite published by Turner's wife and "his principal collaborator,"[49] Edith L. B. Turner,[50] to do what Turner did not: to consider the distinctive features of women's life-cycle events and rituals by describing how women's life-cycle rituals can differ from (as well as sometimes appear similar to) men's and by offering theoretical analyses that account for these differences.

The *Nkang'a* Ritual of Guinea Fowl: Its Structure and Liminal Features

According to Turner, the *Nkang'a* rite that marks a Ndembu girl's transformation into a woman and is also the occasion of her marriage is divided into three parts: *kwing'ija*, or "causing to enter"; *kunkunka*, or "seclusion in a grass hut"; and *kwidisha*, or "bringing out."[51] *Kwing'ija*, or "causing to enter," is initiated at a point before the onset of the girl's menses. Instead, according to Turner, the "main biological reference is the development of breasts," so much so that "in Ndembu ritual idiom, *Nkang'a* is a 'white' not a 'red' ritual, or a ritual of 'milk' rather than 'blood.'"[52] At the time of *Nkang'a*, which Turner at one point suggests took place when its ritual subject was about age fifteen or sixteen,[53] the girl is already betrothed, something that may have happened when she was seven or eight.[54] Her bridegroom is thus an important player in *Nkang'a*. *Kwing'ija*, or "causing to enter" begins, for example, with the bridegroom and the girl's mother exchanging arrows that will be used as the ritual progresses: toward, say, the end of *Nkang'a*, when these arrows are placed at either end of the couple's bridal bed.[55]

After the arrows are exchanged, and after some other preliminary matters that take place on the ritual's eve are enacted (for example, the invocation of ancestral shades, to be discussed further below), the girl is brought the next morning, before sunrise, to a *mudyi* tree that is in the bush outside her village. The *mudyi* tree, or really shrub, has dark green leaves that exude a brilliant white sap when broken off;[56] its symbolic significance in the "milk" ritual of *Nkang'a* is obvious. Also symbolically significant is the name given to the site of the *mudyi* tree—*ifwilu* or *chifwilu*, "the dying place," or *ihung'u*, "the suffering place"—for once brought there, the girl figuratively dies.[57] She lies on the ground, curled on her side and nearly naked—she wears only a cloth covering her genitalia—while otherwise wrapped in a blanket that covers her from head to toe. As such, in the words of Edith Turner (who had access to moments within this women's ritual that Victor Turner did not), she looks "like a corpse in the Ndembu grave."[58] The precepts of the ritual accordingly dictate that, like a corpse, she cannot move, nor can she speak or eat for the entire day while rites at the *mudyi* tree (women's dances in the morning; a ritual meal later in the day) take place around her.[59]

In the afternoon, the ritual's locus expands, as the girl's bridegroom and his younger brother build a rudimentary structure on the opposite side of the village from the *mudyi* tree.[60] This building, which consists of three poles that form a tripod that is thatched with grass, is called the *nkunka*, which Turner refers to as the girl's "seclusion hut"; according to Edith Turner, however, the woman designated as the *Nkang'a* girl's ritual instructress described it to her as the "hut of humility."[61] At sunset, the girl's humble and even abased status is vividly enacted, as she is lifted from the ground and draped over the instructress's back; as she hangs there limply, arms around the instructress's neck, she is carried to the hut. As one of Edith Turner's Ndembu colleagues tells her, at the *mudyi* tree, "the Place of Death," the girl "has lost everything, there she has suffered, and there she has died." Thus, "she cannot walk," but must be carried to the hut of humility, which will be her home for the next three months.[62] Within it, the girl is to be "reborn" to her new stage in life—a woman who, given her breasts' development, has reached a significant moment in terms of her physical maturity and so is now, according to Ndembu tradition, of marriageable age.

Indeed, already at the *mudyi* tree, images of the girl's rebirth have been evoked: for instance, the blanket that was wrapped around her as if it were a shroud is said also to have "enclosed her like a womb," as, "like a baby . . . she lies in the foetal position."[63] Many more images of rebirth then characterize the girl's three months in her seclusion hut. For example, on the night when she is first brought to the hut, the girl is put to bed by her instructress "as though she were a baby," and during the three months that she remains in the hut, she is completely naked—even the cloth that covered her genitalia when she lay beneath the *mudyi* tree is removed.[64] This, in the words of Victor Turner, "symbolizes her ritual infancy. She is as though newly born."[65] What's more, in Edith Turner's accounts of *Nkang'a*, the instructress is called the girl's "midwife."[66] Just as a midwife might feed a newborn baby, moreover, the girl is fed by hand by her instructress.[67] And not only is the girl prohibited from feeding herself; all her food is brought to her. Although there is a fire in the hut, the girl cannot use it for cooking, nor can she even tend it. She is also forbidden to undertake any other kind of work. In addition, she cannot sing, cannot laugh, cannot speak loudly, and cannot become angry, and she is supposed only to look down, with her fists pressed against her temples.[68]

It is a curiosity here that neither of the Turners, in their accounts of these ritual events, applies the language of liminality, the aspect of life-cycle rituals with which Victor Turner, as we have seen, is most famously associated. As best I can tell, this is—at least in the case of Victor Turner—an issue of chronology: while Turner published a sustained study of the *Nkang'a* rite only in his 1968 monograph *The Drums of Affliction*, a decade and a half after his time living among the Ndembu, he hints in the "Acknowledgements" of that book that the two chapters on *Nkang'a* were drafted already in the late 1950s, when Turner was a Simon Research Fellow at Victoria University of Manchester, and in 1961–1962, when Turner was resident at the Center for Advanced Studies in the Behavioral Sciences in Palo Alto, California. This was before Turner had read Arnold van Gennep's work on rites of passage (he read van Gennep in 1963, although he knew of his work at least a year earlier) and thus before Turner had used van Gennep's analysis to author his two foundational essays on liminality: "Betwixt and Between" in 1964 and "Liminality and Communitas" in 1966.[69]

Nevertheless, van Gennep's propositions regarding rites of passage and Turner's proposals regarding liminality lurk just below the surface of both Victor and Edith Turner's accounts of *Nkang'a*. For example, Victor Turner reflects van Gennep's conviction that rites of passage have a tripartite structure when he describes the *Nkang'a* ritual as divided into three parts. More specifically: van Gennep's description of the three parts of rites of passage— (1) separation from "an earlier fixed point in the social structure or from an earlier set of social conditions"; (2) a transition, or threshold, or liminal period, "when the state of the ritual subject is ambiguous: he is no longer in the old state and has not yet reached the new one"; and (3) (re)incorporation, (re)integration, or (re)aggregation, "when the ritual subject enters a new stable state with its own rights and obligations"[70]—clearly seems to be echoed in Turner's account of the tripartite structure of *Nkang'a*, as he calls *kwing'ija*, or "causing to enter," "the rite of separation"; stresses, as noted above, the sort of seclusion both he and van Gennep associate with liminality as the central feature of *kunkunka*; and describes *kwidisha*, "bringing out," as "reaggregation."[71]

Likewise, were either of the Turners to have applied the lens of liminality to the *Nkang'a* ritual, they surely would have described the rite's second or intermediate phase of *kunkunka* as characterized by many more liminal features than the seclusion that I just noted. As the very name that the girl's instructress uses to describe the seclusion hut—the "hut of humility"—implies, it is a place where, as one of Edith Turner's Ndembu colleagues puts it, the girl is "low,"[72] or, in Victor Turner's classic description of liminal beings, where she is without "status, property, insignia, secular clothing, rank, kinship position."[73] The girl must also endure other hardships—for example, relative silence (no singing, no laughter)—that Turner describes as characteristic of liminality.[74] The hut itself, as Turner's classic description of liminality would have it, is "betwixt and between," as it is located, according to Turner's account, at "the boundary between the village and the bush."[75]

While in the hut, the girl is arguably "betwixt and between" as well, as the hut, in the words of Edith Turner's Ndembu colleague, is the place where the girl is "set-on-one-side" and where she will "change into something else," not a place where she is "an ordinary person."[76] The girl's "change into something else," moreover, is—as noted above—repeatedly described in terms of death and rebirth. So too in Turner's account, symbols that come from the "biology of death" are paired in liminality with "symbols modelled on processes of gestation and parturition," rendering the liminal subject "neither living nor dead from one aspect, and both living and dead from another."[77] Or, as her instructress tells the girl at one point, "Not born yet, still dead, little one!"[78] Regarding the instructress, moreover, we can note that all the commands that she, as well as other elders, gives the girl are to be obeyed,[79] just as liminal persons generally, in Turner's account, are placed in a position of "complete submission" to whatever authorities have jurisdiction over the rites of passage these liminal beings undertake.[80]

Indeed, as one would expect in a rite of passage's liminal phase, the girl must endure a certain amount of physical suffering at the hands of her instructress and other elders. The instructress uses various techniques to widen the girl's vagina and lengthen her labia, for example; more notably, the girl undergoes scarification, with incisions made around the navel, during which "the novice is said to experience much pain." For those who can bear still more pain, cuts are also made mid-chest, "above the line of the breasts."[81] The teaching the instructress delivers is also the sort of special and somewhat secret knowledge that again, in Turner's account, is typically conveyed during a rite of passage's liminal phase:[82] in the case of *Nkang'a*, this involves the girl learning several traditional dances and being trained in various sexual techniques.[83] Note, moreover, that through all this, the Ndembu girl is presented as nameless, known during the course of the *Nkang'a* rite only as "Guinea Fowl"[84]—just as "anonymity" is one of the features Turner identifies in his 1966 Lewis Henry Morgan lectures as characteristic of liminality.[85]

In short, from what we have seen so far, we can identify two of the six characteristics that I suggest can define women's life-cycle rituals, and, in this case, two characteristics where women's life-cycle rituals can, at least to some degree, parallel men's: first, evocations of the basic tripartite structure that van Gennep suggested already in 1909 characterized *all* life-cycle rituals ("ceremonies of birth, childhood, social puberty, betrothal, marriage, pregnancy, fatherhood, initiation into religious societies, and funerals");[86] second, experiences of seclusion, humiliation, abjection, deprivation, submission, suffering, and ambiguity—especially ambiguity in terms of one's identity—that Turner described as characterizing life-cycle rituals' middle or liminal phase.

Still, a number of caveats regarding this assessment need to be raised. Indeed, some scholars would reject entirely my claim that van Gennep's rites-of-passage pattern and Turner's work on liminality can be relevant in the study of female life-cycle rituals. For example, in a 2013 article regarding Jiezhu, "a local ritual for Hakka women of menopausal age in Fujian Province," which is located on the southeastern coast of mainland China, ritual studies scholar Lesley A. Northup argues that Jiezhu, though identified as a rite of passage and more specifically as a "once-in-a-lifetime ritual done to rectify the life crisis of menopause" in Neky Tak Ching Cheung's book-length study of the rite,[87] does not have a tripartite structure, "nor does it stress transition to liminality."[88] Rather, according to Northup, "the pattern of Jiezhu appears as separation INCORPORATION transition INCORPORATION separation." "This is clearly a different pattern," Northup goes on to say, "from our customary expectation of a rite of passage."[89] She offers some evidence to suggest that the differences may be attributable to cultural context ("investigation of Asian life-cycle rituals has yielded several theoretical patterns that differ substantially from the three-part accepted norm"),[90] but the variable that more compels her is gender: "examination of Jiehzu . . . reinforces the conclusion that rites of passage for women do not necessarily follow the tripartite structure closely."[91]

In an article from 2000, anthropologist and archaeologist Lynn Meskell, drawing on her extensive study of materials from the New Kingdom village of Deir el-Medina, makes an even more dramatic argument regarding ancient Egypt. At Deir el-Medina—which was inhabited by the families of the workmen who built Egypt's royal tombs during the Eighteenth to the Twentieth Dynasties (ca. 1539–1075 BCE), especially the tombs in the nearby Valley of the Kings—Meskell suggests that the whole notion of rites of passage and its attendant sense of transitions between life stages does not apply. Nor, she proposes, does the "the model of *rites de passage*" apply more generally in ancient Egypt. Rather, Meskell writes, "in Egypt it appears that the concept of the lifecycle is a more accurate template for life experience rather than the model of *rites de passage*, with its specific European lineage and intellectual baggage."[92] Unfortunately, Meskell does not explicitly indicate the aspects of its "European lineage and intellectual baggage" that derail, in her mind, "the model of *rites de passage*," nor does she clearly define what she means by "the concept of the lifecycle." What she appears to have in mind, however, is something similar to what the noted feminist archaeologist Roberta Gilchrist has defined as a "life-course perspective," which "attempts to understand the experience of human life as a continuum," instead of focusing on what we might take "the model of *rites de passage*" to highlight: the "successive stages of the lifecycle in isolation, such as childhood, adolescence, old age, and so on."[93]

That said, Gilchrist, especially in her 2012 book *Medieval Life: Archaeology and the Life Course*, carefully integrates her notion of the "life-course perspective" with discussions that use van Gennep's and Turner's concepts of "rites of passage," "thresholds," "transformative rites," and "liminality," in order to describe life-cycle rituals (both men's and women's) that take place at particular moments throughout the extended sweep of an individual's "life course" in medieval Christian Europe.[94] For example, in a section of her book on clothing and its significance during the medieval life course that is titled, notably, "*Rites de passage*: Marking Life Course Transitions," Gilchrist writes: "Thresholds in the medieval life were marked by transformative rites in which clothing played a pivotal role." She then goes on to note that "females entering puberty celebrated their new status by wearing their hair loose and their heads uncovered"; then, at marriage, "a new or best gown of red was sometimes worn," while "a woman's transition to motherhood was [also] marked by special apparel . . . a white veil and maternity wear," and widowhood, too, had its own "appropriate . . . clothing."[95] Gilchrist likewise traces ways in which bodily adornment and various accoutrements might mark transitions in the lives of medieval Christian men: "young boys," for example, "underwent hair-cutting ceremonies in some regions"; "drinking vessels connected with medieval guilds" were likely used during ceremonies when a young man finished the "occupational apprenticeship that was associated with skilled trades in medieval towns" and thereby became a full-fledged member of a guild hall; and "a boy's first hunt or first kill," and so his "initiation into the masculine hunting culture," may have been marked by the acquisition of a leather scabbard "designed for hunting knives."[96]

Somewhat similarly, Meskell eventually backs away from the substantive critique of van Gennep's rites-of-passage model that she suggests in her 2000 article will appear in her then-forthcoming book, *Private Life in New Kingdom Egypt*.[97] Instead, in the index of *Private Life in New Kingdom Egypt* (published in 2002), the heading "Rite of Passage Ceremonies" is used, apparently with approval, to point readers to a discussion of Egyptian traditions that may have "marked the passing from adolescence to adulthood," such as circumcision and the end of shaving children's heads.[98] More notably, in her discussion of Egyptian funerary rites and other mortuary practices in *Private Life in New Kingdom Egypt*, Meskell writes: "It is usual to divide Egyptian rituals of death into a mourning period, preparation of the corpse, interment, and regular cultic practices for the deceased." She then goes on to say: "Most scholars see a project of three stages: separation and bereavement, recovery and readjustment, and maintenance, where the dead are incorporated into the world of the living via continuing rituals. This tripartite model is based on the influential model formulated by ... Arnold van Gennep."[99] And while one could argue that Meskell's use of the passive voice ("it is usual") and her account of "most scholars" in these quotes indicate that she disagrees with the "usual" scholarly consensus, in point of fact, she immediately turns to offer a description of Egyptian death rituals that follows the pattern she has attributed to van Gennep: a "first stage" of mourning; the "recovery" stage of the funeral, including the "postmortem transitions" that enabled the deceased—"both women and men"—to "become an Osiris"; and the ongoing rituals the living were required to perform "to maintain the deceased in the afterworld."[100] Then, as her discussion of Egyptian death rites continues, Meskell again cites van Gennep's work with approval—more specifically van Gennep's arguments regarding the transitional or liminal stage in his rites-of-passage paradigm, as well as Turner's elaborations of van Gennep's concept of liminality—to describe the dangerous period during Egyptian death rituals (the stage of "postmortem transitions") when the soul of the deceased transfers from the realm of the living to the afterlife.[101]

I am left to conclude that whatever doubts Meskell raised in her 2000 article, she subsequently became persuaded that van Gennep's and Turner's work regarding rites of passage and liminality could be relevant and, more important, useful—as Gilchrist likewise suggests—for understanding both male and female life-cycle rituals. I thereby reiterate my conviction, noted already above, that some of van Gennep's and Turner's key contentions can apply to women's life-cycle rituals: first, women's life-cycle rituals can follow, at least to some degree, the basic tripartite structure that van Gennep suggested already in 1909 characterized all life-cycle rituals; second, women's life-cycle rituals can exhibit many of the features that Turner described as characterizing these rituals' intermediate or liminal phase. Nevertheless, I do take seriously Northup's argument that van Gennep's rites-of-passage model may not hold in Chinese menopausal rites, although unlike Northup, I suggest that the factor that underlies this disconnect is neither the Jiezhu ritual's Asian context nor the participants' gender, but rather the occasion: menopause. Indeed, I have designated my discussion of menopause in Chapter 8 as an "Interlude" in this study of Israelite women's life-cycle rituals, precisely because I do not think ancient Israelite menopause can be analyzed using the methodologies I will otherwise deploy to consider Israel's life-cycle rituals of birth, coming of age, betrothal, marriage, motherhood, and death.

I also take seriously Gilchrist's and Meskell's efforts to define continuities, or a continuum within what Meskell calls the "lifecycle" and Gilchrist the "life course." I particularly take seriously Meskell's arguments that the life-cycle model she advocates is appropriate for analyzing the life experiences of ancient Egyptian women and, by implication, women more generally[102]—so much so that, in the discussion that follows, I consider the presence of continuities, or a continuum within the female life cycle to constitute a major difference between the way male and female life-cycle events and the rituals associated with these life-cycle events are manifest. A focus on continuities or a continuum in the female life cycle also has led the historian of religion Bruce Lincoln, whose work I mentioned above, to question whether there can "truly be . . . a process of reincorporation" in at least some women's life-cycle rituals (the female puberty rituals he has studied).[103] Toward the end of my discussion of *Nkang'a*, I will raise similar questions regarding the nature of reincorporation during that rite. Thereby, I question whether *Nkang'a*—and by extension all women's life-cycle rituals—can be said fully to correspond to the tripartite structure of a rite of passage as conceived by van Gennep. Likewise, as I have previously indicated, I will suggest that Turner's understanding of a rite of passage's liminal phase is differently expressed in *Nkang'a* and, more generally, in the life-cycle rites of women than it is in the life-cycle rituals of men.

In other words, and as stated above, women's life-cycle rituals can correspond to van Gennep's tripartite structure and Turner's descriptions of liminality at least to some degree, but they diverge in important respects from van Gennep's and Turner's models. I thus move to discuss differences between men's and women's life-cycle rituals by returning to Turner's description of *Nkang'a* and comparing—as Turner does at several points[104]—the *Nkang'a* ritual to *Mukanda*, the boys' circumcision rite practiced by many West Central Bantu peoples, including the Ndembu.[105] As we will see, these two rituals, while analogous in some fundamental respects, deviate from one another in ways that illuminate crucial means by which women's life-cycle rituals can differ from men's.

Mukanda and Nkang'a: Illuminating the Differences Between Men's and Women's Life-Cycle Rituals

Turner describes the *Mukanda* circumcision rite as being, like *Nkang'a*, a ritual of death and rebirth. He begins his extensive study of *Mukanda*,[106] for example, by quoting from C. M. N. White's work on circumcision among the Luvale tribes of northwestern Zambia, who are closely related to the Ndembu. There, White writes of Luvale circumcision rituals as "typical *rites de passage* in which the novices are reborn as men after a symbolic death."[107] Turner likewise cites A. M. Vergiat's description of circumcision among the Manja of northern Congo and his account of how Manja boys, at the end of their circumcision rites, paint themselves white, just as do initiates in Ndembu circumcision, for "the color white is that of rebirth ... and these are new men."[108] The place where Ndembu circumcisions take place, moreover, is called *ifwilu*, "the dying place," or *ihung'u*, "the suffering place," just as is the site under the *mudyi* tree where the initial "dying" stage of a girl's *Nkang'a* ritual occurs.[109]

The ritual stages of *Mukanda* that Turner describes also parallel closely the three stages he described for the *Nkang'a* ritual.[110] Like *Nkang'a*, *Mukanda* begins with the rites of *kwing'ija*, or "causing to enter," which, in the case of *Mukanda*, lasts two days, during which, on the second day, the actual circumcision takes place. This is followed by *kung'ula*, or "at the circumcision lodge," a period of seclusion that lasts approximately two to four months, during which newly circumcised boys heal and are initiated into the lore of Ndembu manhood.[111] Finally comes *kwidisha*, which Turner, in discussing *Nkang'a*, translated as "bringing out," but which, in his analysis of *Mukanda*, he renders as "to take outside," although *kwidisha* also, according to Turner, "has the additional sense of 'to approve publicly.'"[112] As these variant renditions imply, this is the period when recently circumcised boys are brought out from the circumcision lodge and presented to their community to be acclaimed as newly made men.

Yet despite the similar tripartite structures of *Nkang'a* and *Mukanda*, and despite also the two rites' similar imagery of death and rebirth, female initiates during *Nkang'a* arguably experience the intermediate or liminal phase of the ritual differently than do *Mukanda*'s male initiates—more specifically, I submit, the female initiates in the *Nkang'a* ritual experience liminality in a more intense or exacerbated form. For example, while the preliminary events of both *Nkang'a* and *Mukanda* include an invocation of the participants' ancestral shades, the shades in *Mukanda* are beseeched only to protect the boys who are entrusted to the elders' care during the course of the ritual. In *Nkang'a*, however, "the novice is felt to be not only in personal danger but also dangerous to her kin," so much so that if she "breaks one of her taboos, a kinsman is thought to fall sick, or even die."[113] The shades invoked at the beginning of the *Nkang'a* rite are thus asked to protect not just the ritual's girl subject but also the occupants of her village. In other words, what Mary Douglas describes as the dangers incurred by "the person who must pass from one [state] to another," and the dangers that person "emanates ... to others," are expressed in an intensified and exacerbated form during the preliminary phase of a girl's *Nkang'a* ritual when compared to the otherwise parallel preliminaries that take place during the boys' rite of *Mukanda*.[114]

More notably, as the two rituals are fully engaged, the nature of the seclusion that is part of both *Nkang'a* and *Mukanda* is intensified and exacerbated within *Nkang'a*, as newly circumcised boys live and are initiated into Ndembu manhood collectively during their two to four months at the circumcision lodge, whereas a Ndembu girl lives alone during the three months she resides in her seclusion hut.[115] To be sure, a *Nkang'a* girl's seclusion is not absolute. She is served by a "handmaid" (usually the initiate's younger sister) and attended regularly by her instructress, and the girl is also able to receive other visitors and even (with restrictions) go visiting herself.[116] Still, a girl is "alone" when it comes to enduring the various obligations and physical ordeals imposed upon her, and she is also alone in enduring her symbolic death at the *mudyi* tree.

Ndembu boys, conversely, are circumcised, or they "die" to their childhood within a cohort that includes, ideally, boys of the same family.[117] Practically speaking, this means that Ndembu circumcisions happen infrequently, only every eight years according to Edith Turner, when there is a large enough group of boys of appropriate ages:[118] Victor Turner suggests a company of nineteen or so boys, whose ages range from seven to seventeen.[119] Experientially, though, the group context of *Mukanda* means that the suffering and the symbolic dying by circumcision with which the ritual begins, as well as the various restrictions imposed on male initiates during the two to four months at the circumcision lodge that follow, are made easier to bear due to what Turner called in his 1964 "Betwixt and Between" essay the "comity of comrades"[120]—including (in those cases when brothers are, in fact, circumcised together) a family comity. Accordingly, *Mukanda* initiates are able to effect among themselves the comfort and care that friends and family members can offer to one another. It is furthermore the case that the "shepherds" or "guardians" of the seclusion lodge where *Mukanda* initiates are housed after their circumcisions are "often their own fathers, their circumcised older brothers, or 'just special friends'":[121] these "shepherds" or "guardians," that is, are yet again close intimates of the boys who can be expected to offer them sympathetic comfort and care as they heal.

Turner in addition remarks on the protective comfort and care a boy's father offers his son during the circumcision proper: "in the past," he was told, "a novice's father would stand with an ax or spear in his hand, at no great distance behind a circumciser when he was cutting, and if the circumciser 'made a mistake,' the father would wound him in the shoulder."[122] And while that custom had disappeared by the time of Turner's time among the Ndembu, Turner still documented episodes of fathers' close engagement with their sons during the course of the circumcision. He notes, for example, that "one of the most striking and touching features" of the period immediately after the circumcision was "the concern showed by fathers for their sons ... expressed in solicitous and encouraging words and gestures."[123] Conversely, during *Nkang'a*, "it is absolutely taboo for the novice's mother to be present" at the moments when the girl is arguably at her most vulnerable—for example, at the beginning of *Nkang'a*, when the girl is brought to the *mudyi* tree, and subsequently as she lies there "dead" while women, excluding her mother, dance around her; then again later, during the three months in the seclusion hut, at the points when the girl is being specially trained in sexual techniques.[124] More generally, "there is a strong taboo against mothers acting as instructresses of their novice-daughters." Nor should the *Nkang'a* initiate's instructress be her uterine sister or her maternal grandmother.[125] Moreover, while the *Nkang'a* initiate is required to obey all the commands of her instructress during her period of seclusion, the guardians of the *Mukanda* seclusion lodge are forbidden to bully the novices unduly (although obedience to and respect for the elders is still expected).[126]

Over and over, then, we see evidence that the liminal experiences of girls during the *Nkang'a* ritual are intensified and exacerbated when compared to the experiences of their *Mukanda* counterparts. To explain, I can cite once more Turner's observation that I noted earlier in this Introduction—"in many places . . . women are liminal" as part of the *normal* course of their existence[127]—even as I note again that Turner did not realize the significance of this insight. More specifically, I submit that we are now in a position to answer, at least in part, the question regarding Turner's observation that I previously raised: what happens when a woman, for whom liminal features and characteristics are inherent and quintessential aspects of her identity, undergoes a life-cycle ritual or participates in a life-cycle event whose very structure, as van Gennep and Turner would have it, demands a move into liminality? The answer that our comparison of *Nkang'a* with *Mukanda* suggests is that during women's life-cycle events, the rituals' already liminal women become still more liminal, or that a woman's normal liminal experience is exacerbated or intensified.

More specifically, a woman's liminal experience during a life-cycle ritual must necessarily be exacerbated or intensified to a degree greater than the liminal experience of a male, for if a male, symbolically speaking, must go down one rung of a ladder during the liminal phase of a life-cycle ritual, by giving up, say, status and/or rank, women, who already begin at least one rung down, must go down at least one rung more. Thus, while the hardships that the isolation of liminality imposes on *Mukanda*'s male initiates can be mitigated by *Mukanda*'s group context, the isolation these boys' female counterparts must endure during *Nkang'a* must be significantly heightened.[128] I would take this intensification of liminal features and experiences to be the third feature of women's life-cycle rituals that I wish to highlight.

Our comparison of *Nkang'a* with *Mukanda* also illustrates a second difference between men's and women's life-cycle rituals, and, concomitantly, the fourth feature of women's life-cycle rituals that I have identified: the way in which men's life-cycle rituals tend to signal dramatic ruptures in terms of their ritual subject's social identity or status position within his community, whereas women's life-cycle rituals, as I suggested above (citing Lynn Meskell), often need to be read in terms of continuity or a continuum. Indeed,

Turner specifically describes *Mukanda* as marking a breach in the structural position of a boy within the Ndembu community, as he is "sever[ed]" from being a "part of the social personality" of his mother and the "effeminacy" of childhood, in order to join the "masculine politico-religious sphere."[129] The ritual attends to this reclassification of the boy's identity in several ways. For example, a boy's uncircumcised penis can be compared negatively to female genitalia, which are considered "wet" and "polluting": a state circumcision corrects by making the *glans penis* "dry" and, more generally, making "manhood visible."[130] In addition, Turner reports being told by the Ndembu that "if during circumcision a boy cried out for his father, this was all right, but if he appealed to his mother, he was reckoned to be a coward and might be made *Kajika*" ("the dunce," or the lowest-ranked among the initiates).[131] Also, after participating in the *Mukanda* ritual, circumcised men are rigorously differentiated from others in their community: for example, they are forbidden to eat food from a fire used to cook for the uncircumcised. Nor may they use a platter from which the uncircumcised have eaten; instead, they "eat from one plate and from one fire."[132] Once circumcised, males are also "privileged . . . to sit in the village men's shelter and hear cases being discussed."[133]

For women, though, as Turner notes, "the transition between infancy and adulthood is less sharply marked."[134] For example, *Nkang'a*, as I have already indicated, marks not just a stage in a young woman's pubescence (breast development), but also the moment of the woman's marriage, as well as being the culmination of her long betrothal. During this long betrothal, moreover, the girl may have been visited frequently by her bridegroom, and he may even have had intercrural intercourse with her. Intimations and adumbrations of marriage are thus present in the girl's life well before matrimony actually happens, even though there is no penetrative intercourse until the wedding night.[135] Turner also argues that a Ndembu woman's complete and full maturation is a longer process still: thus, after *Nkang'a*, which, recall, is meant to take place before the onset of a young woman's menses, she further "'matures' at her first menstruation; she 'matures' at her first pregnancy. She 'matures' at her first parturition; she 'matures' yet again when she has borne several healthy children, and 'matures' finally when she has passed the menopause."[136]

Many other scholars have likewise identified a woman's movement through various stages within her life cycle as a continuum of interconnected and enmeshed events, or what the anthropologist Paul B. Roscoe has described in his edited volume *Gender Rituals* as "an extended ritual context."[137] I noted already in this book's Prologue, for example, J. S. La Fontaine's observation that among the Gisu people of eastern Uganda, a female's movement into full maturity is a gradual process, extending from the onset of menstruation, through marriage, and then childbirth.[138] I also cited the similar conclusions reached by the co-editor of *Gender Rituals*, Nancy C. Lutkehaus, regarding the Manam islanders of Papua New Guinea and by M. G. Swift about the Malay people of Sumatra.[139]

Of even greater significance in this book about ancient Israelite women are the kindred arguments that scholars of the ancient Near East and eastern Mediterranean have advanced. For example, in her 1998 PhD dissertation on women's life-cycle events in classical Greece, Heather Ann Thompson describes how an Athenian girl's journey from childhood to *gyne*, "meaning a fully-fledged adult woman," is an extended process, that—much like the cases of Uganda's Gisu women, the women of Manam Island, and the Sumatra Malay—is realized only when a female gives birth, and not, say, at the onset of menstruation as a marker of a woman's sexual maturity or even at marriage as a marker of social maturity.[140] Meskell likewise uses data from the New Kingdom village of Deir el-Medina to argue that in this ancient Egyptian community, "life stages were more marked for men, as opposed to women."[141] More specifically, Meskell writes that "girls participated in domestic life from an early age, and were depicted in both iconography and material culture as sexual beings from an early age onwards." "Young men," however, "may have experienced more marked experiences, moving from the domestic sphere of their mothers to the world of work, specifically the prestigious work of preparing pharaoh's tomb."[142]

The similarity of Meskell's analysis to Turner's observations regarding the less dramatic structural transitions of *Nkang'a*, as opposed to the dramatic change in social position and social identity that is effected in a boy's life by *Mukanda*, is striking. Yet even though Turner notes that among the Ndembu, women's life stages and the transitions between them are less forcefully marked than are men's, he fails, once again, to exploit the potential of this insight in order to theorize regarding *why*: what might it be about women—their lives, their experiences, their position in a social order—that drives the different nature of transitions in women's life-cycle rituals?[143] Nor does La Fontaine, Lutkehaus, Swift, Thompson, or Meskell really address this question. Yet this is exactly the task Caroline Walker Bynum sets herself in her 1984 essay "Women's Stories, Women's Symbols: A Critique of Victor Turner's Theory of Liminality" that I cited earlier in this Introduction.

To be sure, Bynum begins by grounding her analysis in data, much like the data presented by La Fontaine, Lutkehaus, Swift, Thompson, and Meskell regarding continuities in a female's life cycle and in a woman's identity across various life stages. More specifically, Bynum's interest is continuity in the stories that she evokes in the first words of her essay's title "Women's Stories, Women's Symbols"—that is, given Bynum's academic interests, medieval European stories about women saints and other female religious figures. She demonstrates—much as did Turner, in his discussion of *Nkang'a* versus *Mukanda*, and much as did Meskell in her discussion of girls' versus boys' life cycles at Deir el-Medina—that the medieval accounts she examines lack the pronounced language of structural rupture that van Gennep's and Turner's tripartite model of separation–liminality–reintegration presumes. "Women's stories," Bynum writes, "are in fact less processual than men's; they don't have turning points ... the themes are less climax, conversion, reintegration ... than continuity."[144] The early fifteenth-century Englishwoman Margery Kempe, for example, "achieves spiritual growth" not by breaking with her previous social position (a wife whose husband is annoyed by her asceticism) but by living an increasingly pious life within the context of her married life—in Bynum's words, "being more fully herself with Christ" by imagining, for instance, that she feels Jesus's toes in her hand as she lies in her marital bed.[145]

Bynum also cites a 1982 study of medieval saints' lives authored by Donald Weinstein and Rudolph M. Bell, which reports that "women's saintly vocations often grew slowly through childhood and into adolescence," whereas "male saints were far more likely to undergo abrupt adolescent conversions, involving renunciation of wealth, power, marriage, and sexuality."[146] Consider, for example, the story of the woman saint Marie d'Oignies (1177–1213), who, although born to wealthy parents, eschewed fashionable clothes and ornaments even as a child before committing herself to a religious vocation when she became an adult.[147] Then contrast the dramatic repudiation of material well-being and worldly garb found in the story of Marie's male contemporary St. Francis of Assisi (1181/82–1226), who in his mid-twenties, as he turned his back on his life as the cosmopolitan son of an affluent textile merchant in order to take up a religious calling, "took off his clothes ... even took off his underwear, stripping himself completely naked before all."[148] In addition, Francis, in taking up his religious calling, renounced marriage and sexuality, whereas Marie was married but persuaded her husband to join her in a life of celibacy and in charitable work nursing lepers.[149] Indeed, Bynum suggests that, like Marie, "a strikingly large number of the women saints of the thirteenth and fourteenth centuries . . . were simply women in the world (in their fathers', uncles', or husbands' homes), being religious." These women, that is, "simply continued their ordinary lives" in taking on a religious vocation, and their religious work—"weaving, embroidery, care of the sick and small children"—similarly "continued women's ordinary work."[150]

As to *why* women's life cycles are less characterized by dramatic reversals and ruptures in terms of social identity and more by continuity, the key, as Bynum sees it, is Turner's understanding of the liminal phase of a rite of passage as a period of "anti-structure."[151] According to Turner, that is, liminality is a time during a life-cycle event when "normal rules and roles" are suspended, and even more so, it is a period when the liminal subject escapes from "social and normative structures" and structural "roles."[152] The Ndembu chief-to-be, for example, gives up the leadership role that he brings into his initiation ritual and will fully achieve at its end to become, during this rite of passage's liminal phase, subordinate and submissive. More generally, Turner argues, as we have seen, that rites-of-passage participants leave behind normative structures and roles by being stripped of "status, property, insignia, secular clothing, rank, kinship position" during the ritual's liminal phase.[153]

Yet who are those within a society, Bynum asks, who have "status, property . . . rank, [and] kinship position" that can be stripped away; ditto, who are those who are embedded within, and so might temporarily escape from, "social and normative structures" and structural "roles"? Her answer is "elites"—"educated elites, aristocratic elites, and *male* elites" (emphasis mine).[154] Liminality, that is, or at least liminality as classically defined by Turner in, say, his 1964 and 1966 essays "Betwixt and Between" and "Liminality and Communitas," "may be less a universal," Bynum theorizes, "than an escape for those who bear the burdens and reap the benefits of a high place in the social structure."[155] In other words, Turner, having defined liminality as a release from structure, has described a phenomenon that is relevant only for those who "*are* the structures"—that is, a society's (male) elites.[156]

Turner, Bynum thus suggests, yet again fails to understand that his notion of liminality must be differently realized with regard to women. More specifically, Turner fails to understand that women do not and cannot experience the ruptures and reversals in the structural order that are effected during a life-cycle event's liminal phase for the "elites" who "are the structures." To put the matter another way: "women could not take off all their clothes and walk away from their fathers or husbands" during liminality, in order to take on some new role or structural position within their society by liminality's end, because women have no role or structural position within their society that they can abandon and no new place within their society into which they can be received.[157] Instead, liminality, for women, who are outside their communities' "social and normative structures" and structural "roles,"[158] can only "continue or enhance in image . . . what the woman's ordinary experience is";[159] it is to be understood "as continuity with, not as reversal of . . . women's ordinary experience."[160] Consequently, a woman's movement through any specific life-cycle event, or through progressive stages of her life cycle, lacks the dramatic breeches and breaks in social identity that characterize men's life-cycle rituals.

Interestingly and importantly, another major religious studies scholar, Bruce Lincoln, presented a similar (although not identical) analysis about women and liminality at roughly the same time (1981) that Bynum's 1984 essay critiquing Turner was published, in his monograph *Emerging from the Chrysalis* (reissued in 1991, with a new Afterword). As this volume's subtitle—*Rituals of Women's Initiation*—makes clear, Lincoln's focus is to some degree circumscribed, as he considers only rituals that, in his words, mark "the moment at which a girl becomes a woman" and thus effect the "transformation of an immature female into an adult."[161] In other respects, however, Lincoln's enterprise is wide-ranging, as it is broadly comparative: he examines (1) the rite of *Tālikettukalyānam*, or the rite of the "*tāli*-tying marriage" of the Tiyyar caste of India's North Kerala Province, which lies on the southern tip of India's west coast; (2) the Navajo ritual of the Kinaaldá, which he indicates means either "first menstruation" or perhaps "house sitting, with reference to the initiand's stay within her family hogan" (more on this below);[162] (3) the scarification of pubescent girls among the Tiv of Nigeria; and (4) the ceremony of Festa das Moças Novas, or the "Festival of the New Maiden," enacted by the Tukuna of the northwest Amazon; as well as (5) the myth of Demeter and her daughter Persephone from classical antiquity, which Lincoln follows Henri Jeanmarie in reading as a "description of a woman's initiation."[163]

After describing each of these traditions individually, Lincoln turns, in his concluding chapter, "On the Nature of Women's Initiations," to offer some synthetic comments, including (and of greatest interest to us) an analysis of the morphology, or form, of women's initiation rituals. He begins, not surprisingly, with van Gennep's attempts to define the tripartite form, or structure, of all life-cycle rituals, including the initiation rites that Lincoln's study examines, before turning to focus on van Gennep's "use of a spatial model."[164] Other commentators have drawn attention to this point as well, for while van Gennep is most famously associated with describing passages in an individual's life, as the individual moves, or passes, from one stage of life to another, his interests in *Les rites de passage* were far broader and included rituals related to seasonal and calendrical change (again, more on this below), as well as what van Gennep called "le passage matériel" (rendered in his book's English translation as "the territorial passage"). Indeed, the first major chapter of van Gennep's *Les rites de passage*, after the introduction, is about these territorial passages, such as the crossing of mountain passes, the crossing of rivers, and, in what van Gennep described as a time "not so long ago" in Europe, "the passage from one country to another, from one province to another within each country . . . even from one manorial domain to another."[165]

"It is far from coincidental," Bjørn Thomassen writes in his 2014 comments on van Gennep's work, that van Gennep began *Les rites de passage* with a chapter on the territorial passage,[166] as van Gennep asserts in the chapter's first sentence that "territorial passages can provide a framework for the discussion of rites of passage which follows."[167] In van Gennep's view, this is because "transition from one social situation to another is identical with physical transition."[168] Indeed, in his conclusion to *Les Rites de passage*, van Gennep identifies this point as one of the crucial insights of his overall analysis: "It seems important to me that the passage from one social position to another is identified with a *territorial passage*, such as the entrance into a village or a house, the movement from one room to another, or the crossing of streets or squares." As this summary statement continues, van Gennep writes even more emphatically that "phrases and events" such as "passage under a portal" and "opening of the doors" within rites of passage that mark social transitions are "seldom meant as 'symbols'": "the passage is actually a territorial passage." Thus, "a change of social categories involves a change of residence, and this fact is expressed by the rites of passage in their various forms."[169]

As Lincoln points out, van Gennep's convictions regarding territorial passages as the framework for all rites of passage, including those that mark social transitions, motivate van Gennep's frequent use of spatially inflected language: terms like "border" and "position," as well as "threshold" (to describe his tripartite pattern's middle phase) and the term "passage" itself. Yet Lincoln suggests that the examples of female initiation that he surveys "point to a very different use of spatial language."[170] More specifically, Lincoln argues that only in the Demeter and Persephone myth, if that myth is to be read as somehow depicting a woman's initiation, is there a sense of significant physical movement: Persephone, having been seized by the god Hades while dancing in a meadow, picking flowers, is taken by him to his underworld domain. Conversely, "the Tiv girl," when scarified at the time of puberty, "never leaves her mother's side and stays entirely within the bounds of her village."[171] Similarly, the Tiyyar initiate is confined to an inner room reserved for menstruating women that is located within her matrilineal ancestral home for three of the four days of her initiation ritual; the Tukuna initiate is moved for three months or longer into a very small and sparsely furnished "seclusion chamber" that is specially constructed for the ritual inside her family's dwelling; and the Kinaaldá initiate, on the fourth and climactic night of her initiation ritual, must stand in a specifically designated space within her family's hogan.[172] Yet Lincoln, following van Gennep, indicates that there is typically a more dramatic change in spatial locus in male initiation rites (Ndembu boys, for example, withdraw from their village during *Mukanda*),[173] and Lincoln proposes that stemming from this distinction between male and female initiation rites are "important theoretical repercussions."[174]

More specifically, Lincoln argues that for males to move spatially within, say, their tribe's territory and its nearby environs during initiation rituals is emblematic of their movement into an enhanced status within the sociopolitical arena of their community that the initiation rite makes possible. For men, Lincoln writes, "initiation is . . . a change from one level of authority and responsibility to a higher one, and as such it involves a spatial transition."[175] Conversely, while women can and do move through "a number of differentiated stages such as girl, marriageable woman, wife, mother" during their lifetimes, and while "women may be intimately involved in status distinctions within a domestic hierarchy" ("a mother-in-law . . . set above her daughters-in-law or a senior wife . . . set above junior wives"), these stages and distinctions, according to Lincoln, "have few ramifications beyond the immediate household" and do not "carr[y] significant weight in the sociopolitical arena of men."[176] Rather, when it comes to "sociopolitical power or prestige . . . a woman remains always a woman." Thus, there is no spatial movement in a girl's initiation rite; rather, "she remains where she has always been" in terms of her position (or lack thereof) within her community's sociopolitical hierarchy and thus in terms of her domicile.[177]

In other words, a girl, during an initiation rite, and women generally, in the course of life-cycle events, do not really go anywhere in terms of a change in social status, especially a change in social status within their larger community. Thus, as Lincoln sees it, they do not go anywhere spatially in the course of their life-cycle rituals. Or we might cite again van Gennep's argument—"transition from one social situation to another is identical with physical transition"[178]—and suggest, following Lincoln, that the magnitude of the social transition is coordinate with the degree of the physical transition. For women, because the transition in terms of social status is minimal, so is the physical relocation. As Lincoln concludes regarding the Tiyyar, Kinaaldá, Tiv, and Tukuna initiants he studies: "This is why she is secluded within her normal living space, rather than separated from it at the outset of initiation."[179]

Like Bynum, moreover, Lincoln invites us to consider what men do, according to Turner's classic formulation of liminality, when they move not only from one space to another but from "one level of authority and responsibility to a higher one" during an initiation rite:[180] they temporarily relinquish "status, property, insignia, secular clothing, rank, kinship position," only to claim a new and higher status and rank—and often new property, insignia, clothing, and even a new kinship position—once the ritual has been completed.[181] Yet again, Lincoln asks whether these features really apply to the women's initiations he has surveyed, for if women are not "a part of the social hierarchy," and if they cannot "have any significant independent status," then there is nothing in terms of rank and position that they might "be deprived of" in a liminal state. Nor is there, as noted above, any "sociopolitical power or prestige" for them to gain. Rather, to quote again Lincoln's assessment of this situation, "a woman remains always a woman." Because of this, "one is forced to conclude," Lincoln states, "either that there can be no liminal state for women or that women exist always in a liminal state."[182] The similarity to Bynum's language regarding the female religious figures she studied is striking—"one either has to see the woman's religious stance as permanently liminal or as never quite becoming so"[183]—just as Lincoln's overall conclusions, regarding liminality as classically defined by Turner as the province of a society's (male) elites, echo Bynum's analysis.

The *Nkang'a* Ritual of Guinea Fowl: More Differences within Women's Life-Cycle Rituals

Interestingly, however—and significantly—Lincoln describes at least one instance of a somewhat different phenomenon than those I have just reported in his study of women's initiations, regarding clothing. In male initiation rites, one feature of the liminal experience—concomitant with the loss of status, property, rank, kinship position—can be nudity, or the removal of insignia and clothing that might identify the initiate's place in the social structure. Nudity can also mark men's experience during other life-cycle transitions (as in the story of Francis of Assisi, where nudity marks his taking on a religious vocation). But in the female initiation rites that Lincoln surveys, "the symbolism of clothing is entirely different," as "we find the *addition* of new clothing or bodily adornment" (emphasis mine).[184] The "new clothing or bodily adornment," moreover, can be quite elaborate: a golden ornament, hung around the girl's neck on a white silk thread, in the case of the Tiyyar initiate; a special sash and special turquoise and white shell jewelry, in the case of the Navajo Kinaaldá ritual; a complex iconography of scarification, in the Tiv initiation; and highly embellished ceremonial regalia, including a spectacular feather headdress, in the case of the Tukuna girl.[185]

A very similar motif characterizes the beginning of the third phase of the Ndembu *Nkang'a* ritual: the *kwidisha*, translated by Turner as the "bringing out."[186] The initial feature of this "bringing out," as the name implies, is the novice's leaving her seclusion hut in order to be brought, first, to a place outside the village where she is bathed and the hair around her hairline and her pubic hair is shaved. The *Nkang'a* initiate is also at this point elaborately adorned: the hair that remains on her head is plaited; oil and red earth are massaged into her skin; she is bedecked with strings of beads; and she is clothed in a skirt and girdle made of two large cloths.[187]

What happens next is even more striking. The initiate is brought to the village dancing place, where she performs the various dances that she has been taught during her time in the seclusion hut. These dances, not surprisingly for a "milk" ritual, highlight the young woman's adorned yet uncovered breasts, which Edith Turner (Victor Turner is more circumspect) describes as "ripe" and "flashing up and down."[188] As she dances, moreover, the young woman "is given the eland-tail switch of authority belonging to the village headman."[189] Then, as the dancing continues, she seizes a gun and performs a hunters' dance that is normally the prerogative of men. Indeed, according to Turner, "in the idiom of Ndembu ritual, hunting and masculinity or virility are symbolically equivalent, and the symbols and gear of huntmanship are reckoned to be symbolically dangerous to females."[190] Yet here, a *woman* dances as a hunter and wields a gun. Finally, consider what happens that night, when the *Nkang'a* initiate is taken to the hut in her village where the bridegroom has been staying. As I have previously noted, it is at this point that the two have penetrative intercourse for the first time, and, indeed, for "as many times as the bridegroom can manage."[191] Then, as the night comes to an end, the young woman's instructress returns, and the bride gives her a signal in order to indicate whether or not the bridegroom has performed satisfactorily. Turner describes this, as well as the events of her bringing-out dances, as "an outlet . . . given to her [otherwise] suppressed individuality": as he puts it, that day, "she holds the switch of male political authority in her hand . . . and that night she can pronounce sentence on her husband's virility."[192]

Yet again, though, I suggest that Turner fails to grasp the significance of his own observations. More specifically, Turner fails to consider an argument he put forward in his final Louis Henry Morgan lecture, this one titled (at least in its 1969 published version) "Humility and Hierarchy: The Liminality of Status Elevation and Reversal."[193] There, Turner begins by discussing what is now familiar ground to us: rites of passage in which an individual is conveyed not just from one stage in life to another (from, say, girlhood to womanhood), but—as in the initiation ritual of the Ndembu chief—"irreversibly from a *lower* to a *higher* position in an institutionalized system of such positions" (emphasis mine). Turner then continues by returning to the claims he had made in his 1964 "Betwixt and Between" article to argue that in such rites of passage, liminality "usually involves a putting down or humbling . . . as its principal cultural constituent," through, for example, structural invisibility and absolute submissiveness.[194] Then, from that position of humiliation and submission, liminal persons are built back up by being "endowed with additional powers to enable them to cope with their new station in life."[195] Thus, they are prepared to assume the "higher position in an institutionalized system of such positions" at which the rite of passage is directed.

Again, for us, this is all familiar ground. But as Turner's exposition in "Humility and Hierarchy" continues, he identifies, by way of contrast to these rites of passage in which subjects permanently attain a higher status, something new: what he calls "rituals of status reversal." In Turner's account, these "rituals of status reversal" correspond to certain "cyclical and calendrical ritual[s],"[196] which, we will recall, were among the "other types of rites of passage" (the passage, say, from one season to another) originally catalogued by Arnold van Gennep.[197] As rites of passage, cyclical and calendrical rituals should, in van Gennep's and Turner's understanding, have a liminal phase, although according to Turner, when cyclical and calendrical rituals manifest as "rituals of status reversal" (and not all do), these rites of passage have a different type of liminal expression than do rites of passage that culminate with the ritual subject's acquiring a higher status. More specifically, Turner describes the liminal phase of those cyclical and calendrical rites of passage that manifest as "rituals of status reversal" as a time characterized by the "liminality of the permanently structural inferior," and this liminality's "key element," he goes on to say, is "a symbolic or make-believe elevation of the ritual subjects to positions of eminent authority," where "the weak act as though they are strong."[198] Indeed, he suggests that in the liminal phase of these cyclical and calendrical "rituals of status reversal," "groups or categories of persons who habitually occupy low status positions in the social structure are *positively enjoined* to exercise ritual authority over their superiors" (emphasis mine).[199] To illustrate, Turner discusses the traditions associated with Halloween, "when the powers of the structurally inferior are manifested in the liminal dominance of pre-adolescent children,"[200] and the anthropologist's McKim Marriott's 1966 account of an Indian village's celebration of the annual Hindu festival of Holi.[201] During that Holi celebration, low-caste women beat the shins of high-caste men; a bullying older boy, also high caste, was forced to ride backwards on a donkey; and the village landlord had a gallon of diesel oil poured over his head.

But Lincoln's description of the elaborate clothing donned by the Tiyyar, Kinaaldá, and Tukuna initiates, as well as his description of the Tiv initiate's elaborate scarification, invite us to consider how "a symbolic or make-believe elevation" might be temporarily experienced not only during certain cyclical and calendrical rites such as Halloween and Holi, but also during some women's life-cycle rituals. Turner's description of the elaborate decoration of the *Nkang'a* girl's body and also of her wielding symbols of male and even chiefly authority during her bringing-out dances, along with her ability to pronounce judgment on her husband on her wedding night, invite consideration of "a symbolic or make-believe elevation" as well. Indeed, I take the temporary status elevation that Lincoln and Turner have documented within female puberty rites and during *Nkang'a*—where women, despite their role as "permanently structural inferiors," can momentarily rise to "positions of eminent authority"[202]—to be the fifth feature of women's life-cycle rituals that I wish to highlight.

Bynum too allows that in the world of medieval Christian Europe that she studies, occasionally—"although only very occasionally"—the eucharistic ritual and the symbol of the raised host can result in hierarchical reversals that "for women . . . express status elevation." "Women occasionally . . . feel empowered to act in a priestly capacity by their reception of the eucharist, or see themselves (or other women) as priests," she writes, and they can thus find in the eucharist "the power to preach, teach and criticize, to hear confessions and pronounce absolution, to administer the eucharist to others."[203] Nevertheless, Bynum is clear, as we should also be, that these incidents of hierarchical reversal do not mark any permanent change in women's status: eucharistic ritual "ultimately . . . integrates the woman more fully into clerically controlled structures" rather than elevating her to a position equal to or even above the male officials who had charge of the church. That is, even though a woman's vision can "project women into power through reversed images" (of, say, the host flying away from a corrupt priest into the mouth of a deserving nun), Bynum maintains that this is not a true reversal of status positions, in terms of either gender or authority, given that the woman, in order to have such a vision, "must attend the liturgy, controlled by exactly that clergy her visions might seem to bypass or criticize."[204]

Lincoln reports much the same, for although he originally argued that elaborate dress donned by the initiates he surveyed represented an "expansion of powers, capabilities, experiences," as each was "endowed with symbolic items that make of her a woman, and beyond this a cosmic being,"[205] in his 1991 "Afterword" to his book's second edition, Lincoln left behind these claims of cosmic and also ontological significance to focus only on the extremely deleterious effects of women's "sociopolitical deprivation." As he writes in that 1991 essay, "women's initiations . . . have not always served women very well," as they are "performed on *and against* women," in order that society might "consistently and effectively assert its interest in and control over women's sexual and reproductive capacities, while also asserting that women's primary sphere of activity is to be located within domestic space."[206] Even more telling are Lincoln's comments in an article on "The Initiatory Paradigm" that was published in 2003. There, he appears fully to repudiate his 1981 "cosmic claim" by writing, "we should put an end to any lingering notions that initiatory rituals can produce transformation that is properly called ontological."[207]

Likewise, Turner is clear that despite the incidents of status enhancement that take place during *kwidisha*, the *Nkang'a* initiate does not become a hunter or take over the office of the village headman. Nor does any authority she might have in her marriage endure. Rather, her gun- and switch-bearing dances and her wedding-night pronouncements take place within the larger context of submission that she has experienced during the previous phases of the *Nkang'a* ritual; in addition, submission is interspersed with the moments of status elevation the young woman experiences during her bringing-out dances and the intercourse that follows that night. After the bringing-out dances are finished, for example, Edith Turner writes that the woman "is led away, rendered passive again," as "the midwife takes her to the door of her husband's hut." There, according to Edith Turner's report, the new bride is to say, upon achieving orgasm during intercourse with her husband that night, "'*Nafwi*,' 'I am dying.' "[208] And so, symbolically, she does (her ability to render judgment on her husband's virility notwithstanding), especially after the two-week period that follows the wedding night comes to an end. At that point, the bridegroom takes the *Nkang'a* woman to his home village, so that, in Turner's words, "she 'dies' as an active member of her own family group, and is 'born' into membership of her husband's village and the adult tribe."[209]

Indeed, while Turner's description of the *kwidisha* phase of *Nkang'a* suggests that it represents "reaggregation,"[210] the "re-" is in fact notably absent, as the young woman, as we have just seen, is not *re*turned to life within her community. Earlier, I quoted Lincoln, who asked "whether," in the female puberty rites that he studied, "there can truly be ... a process of reincorporation" as van Gennep's rites-of-passage model predicts,[211] and the answer here, regarding *Nkang'a*, must be no. Rather, many of the features and experiences that more typically characterize the liminal phase of women's life-cycle rituals reassert themselves during *kwidisha*: for example, the intensification and exacerbation of liminality's negative aspects, as evidenced by the young woman's submission that I just noted, and also the notion that a woman's life cycle is a continuum, in which, again to quote Lincoln, the woman, in terms of her "authority and responsibility," or "sociopolitical power or prestige," "remains where she has always been."[212] In fact, the *Nkang'a* initiate arguably remains in the permanently liminal state that Lincoln, Bynum, and even Turner identify as normative within a woman's life. Accordingly, after some brief moments of status elevation, the *Nkang'a* ritual ends more or less where it began, with the woman being separated from the people and the place that had defined her life heretofore in order to be taken away to live with a family and in a village that she does not know.

Nevertheless, it is worth noting that in both the initiation rituals that Lincoln discusses and *Nkang'a*, the passing episodes of status elevation that occur within those rites take place at the moments most closely associated with the initiates' nascent sexuality and their prospective reproductive fertility. In each case, moreover, one can argue that the attributes of sexuality and fertility are central to the woman's identity within her culture. In Ndembu tradition, for example, just as hunting, as we saw above, is symbolic of Ndembu masculinity and virility, sexuality and reproductive fertility are symbols of Ndembu females.[213] As Turner reports, a common Ndembu saying is "for the man, huntsmanship; for the woman, procreation," and a Ndembu folktake likewise recounts how a man, when his village is raided, snatches up his hunting gear and gun and flees, whereas his wife runs into the bush with her child.[214] This womanly priority is not unrelated, I suggest, to the temporarily enhanced status the woman subject experiences during the *Nkang'a* ritual. Rather, as I intimated above, *the precise moments* when the *Nkang'a* initiate experiences status elevation and enhancement are those where her sexuality and reproductive fertility are most on display: during the dances where she first presents to her community her newly sexualized body and during the night when she first engages with her husband in penetrative and so potentially reproductive intercourse. Here, then, is the sixth and final point I wish to make about women's life-cycle rituals: that on the occasions when status elevation happens within some women's life-cycle rituals, this status elevation signals and moreover celebrates the attributes of the woman the society most values. Typically, these attributes are her sexuality and her reproductive capability.

In conclusion, then, I have identified six features that can characterize women's life-cycle rituals:

1. Women's and men's life-cycle rituals can share, at least to some degree, the same tripartite structure originally defined by van Gennep in his 1909 book *Les rites de passage*: separation; a transitional or liminal period; and the stage of (re)incorporation, (re)integration, or (re)aggregation;
2. Women's and men's life-cycle rituals can share, at least to some degree, the same basic features of liminality that Turner identified in his

foundational 1964 and 1966 essays as characteristic of van Gennep's second, or transitional/liminal phase, when "liminal *personae*" are "betwixt and between" the identities defined as normative in their society: for example, status inferiority, structural invisibility, marginalization and disenfranchisement, subordination and even complete submission;

3. However, liminality in women's life-cycle rituals often manifests markers of exacerbated or intensified liminality as compared to liminality as manifest in men's life-cycle rituals (a more pronounced expression of marginalization and disenfranchisement, for example, or a tendency to identify status inferiority as a permanent, as opposed to a transitional state);

4. In addition, men's life-cycle rituals tend to be marked by dramatic ruptures that substantively redefine (and typically elevate) a man's status, power, prestige, and social position within his community, whereas women's life-cycle rituals—and, indeed, women's life cycles in general—are more typically characterized by continuity, especially continuity in terms of a persistent liminal identity of status inferiority;

5. Occasionally in women's life-cycle rituals, the "liminality of the permanently structural inferior"[215] can express itself in terms of hierarchical reversals that occur in the midst of the ritual and temporarily elevate or enhance the status of the otherwise persistently inferior female subject;

6. This status enhancement or elevation during certain women's life-cycle rituals arguably takes place when women are most being recognized for their primary value within their society, most typically, their reproductive capability.

In the chapters that follow, on women's life-cycle rituals in ancient Israel, I consider how these various characteristics manifest themselves within Israelite rituals of birth, coming of age, betrothal, marriage, motherhood, and death.

A Few Comments on Terminology

In a book on women's life-cycle events and rituals, and especially a book that considers how women's life-cycle rituals can differ from men's and thus, at least by implication, considers how life-cycle rituals might differentiate women from men, it is reasonable to ask how categorizations such as "woman" and "man," which define an individual's biological sex, were understood in the ancient world. Moreover, it is reasonable to ask how biological classifications based on sex were understood in relation to culturally determined designations of gender. After all, it has become increasingly common in many contemporary communities, especially those within the Euro-American cultural orbit, to reject classificatory systems that presume a male–female model of sexual and gender binarism, and especially to reject the binarist notion that a male or female gender identity, which is socially determined, must align with one's biological sex (or at least the sex that one was assigned at birth). It is also well understood that many other cultures do not presume sexual and gender binarism (for example, those Native American communities that hold there are four genders).[216]

Ancient Near Eastern tradition generally assumes, however, a binary of male and female. For example, regarding biological sex, we can cite the Mesopotamian Epic of Atraḫasis, where the first human beings are created when Mami, or Bēlet-ili, the midwife of the gods, pinches off fourteen pieces of clay, from which seven birth goddesses create (presumably seven) males and seven other birth goddesses create (presumably seven) females.[217] A similar motif is found in the Bible, in the story of creation attributed by biblical scholars to the Priestly, or P source, where humans are created as "male and female" (Gen 1:27).

Mesopotamian sources also indicate that an infant's biological sex and gender identity were understood to be correlate at the time of birth,[218] even though there is a rich corpus of evidence from Mesopotamia concerning older individuals who came into identities "of composite, intersectional, transitional, multiple, fluid, ambiguous or modified genders."[219] One verse in the Bible, Deut 22.5, which speaks of women who use a man's "implement" or "weapon" (kĕlî) and men who dress in women's clothes, also suggests that at least some modes of ambiguous gender presentation were known in ancient Israel. Yet Deuteronomy, by excoriating in God's name those who position themselves in ways other than is deemed normative for their biological sex, gives voice to the Bible's overwhelming conviction that sex and gender identity were inherently interconnected. As Marc Zvi Brettler states, "the notion of gender demarcation . . . is encoded throughout the Bible" and "gender . . . should be immediately evident," which is to say that, according to biblical understanding, "males should act and look like males, and females should act and look like females."[220] Similarly, Kristine Henriksen Garroway writes, "Unlike today, when we make a distinction between sex and gender, the Hebrew Bible understands the two as one and the same. Thus, a child with a penis is a boy and will grow up to be gendered as an Israelite man; a child with a vagina, likewise, is a girl who will grow up to be an Israelite woman."[221]

But who is a child? Just as identities regarding sex and gender can be understood differently across and also within cultures, so too can the identity of "child" vary across time and space.[222] Nevertheless, scholars of ancient Israelite childhood tend to agree that childhood begins with birth or very shortly thereafter.[223] Thus, I have referred to the newly born who are my interest in Chapter 1 and who in addition are a considerable focus of my attention in Chapters 5 and 6 as "children," and more specifically as "neonates," "newborns," "babies," and "infants." This initial period of a child's life ends, Garroway argues, "when the baby is weaned,"[224] which in the ancient world could take up to three years (much more on this in Chapter 7). Still, while the Hebrew terms *ôlēl, ôlāl,* and *yônēq,* each of which means "suckling child," clearly indicate, as Garroway suggests, that the ancient Israelites understood all nursing children, whether newborns or three-year-olds, as a collective who belonged to the same "suckling" stage of life,[225] I have sometimes chosen to use terms that are more rooted in our own culture's sense of distinctions within early childhood in order to differentiate children who are at the beginning of the nursing period from those near the end. For example, I have used the term "infant" to denote a child in its first year or so of life, as opposed to "toddler" to denote a child who has become both mobile and verbal.[226]

At the end of the suckling stage of life, a newly weaned individual enters fully into the childhood years (more on this also in Chapter 7),[227] which end, in my estimation, when a boy child becomes a *bāḥûr,* a young man, and a girl child becomes a *bĕtûlâ,* or a young woman. For girls especially, as I will suggest in Chapter 2, this transition is associated with biological puberty. Biblical scholars generally take female biological puberty to be marked, moreover, by a young woman's first menses, given that the *bĕtûlâ* seems to be reproductively able (or is at least moving toward reproductive capability),[228] although she has not yet borne a child.[229] This view of puberty stands in contrast to, say, the Ndembu sensibility that I outlined above, where biological puberty for a young woman, as we have seen, is marked by her breast development, which preceded the onset of menstruation by about two years.[230] Nevertheless, in both Israel and among the Ndembu, a young woman's biological puberty, whether marked by the onset of menstruation or the development of breasts, is closely coordinated with and, indeed, almost identical to, the occasion of the woman's marriage (more on this in Chapters 1, 2, and 3), so much so that we might as readily say that a young woman's entry into married life is the point when her childhood ends.[231]

I thus disagree with those who suggest that for ancient Israelite women, there was a significant period between puberty and marriage.[232] Even more so, as I will argue in Chapter 1, I disagree with the suggestion many scholars make regarding the chronological age—twelve—at which menstruation for an Israelite woman began.[233] As we will see, this is a mistaken retrojection of data from modern industrialized societies, where high standards of health care and nutrition tend to promote early menstruation, back into the often marginal agrarian-pastoralist economy of ancient Israel. Indeed, we might recall that even in Central Africa in the 1950s, according to Victor Turner's reports, the *Nkang'a* ritual that marked a girl's breast development but that took place before menarche was only enacted when a girl was about fifteen or sixteen.[234]

Because of these data, I eschew in this volume the terms "adolescent" and "adolescence," unless they appear in material I directly quote, based on my conviction that our association of an early- to mid-teens adolescent life stage that is coordinate with biological puberty is precisely that, ours, and not applicable to the ancient world. Emiel Eyben, in his work on youth in ancient Rome, quotes the sociologist Frank Musgrove in order to capture perfectly this sentiment: "The adolescent as a distinct species is the creation of modern social attitudes and institutions. A creature neither child nor adult, he is a comparatively recent socio-psychological invention, scarcely two centuries old."[235]

One might also note here that in contrast to, say, Vincent Crapanzano, whom I quoted in this book's Prologue as describing a model of social rather than biological puberty in his work on circumcision in Morocco in the late 1960s,[236] I have suggested puberty is biologically defined, at least for women, in ancient Israel. As we will see in Chapter 3, however, it is not so clear that puberty—or, more specifically, biological puberty as the immediate prologue to marriage—plays the same role in an Israelite male's life cycle as it does in the life cycle of his female counterpart. Rather, social considerations seem to take priority over biological. Likewise, we will see in Chapter 8 that when it comes to identifying menopausal women in ancient Israel and elsewhere in the southern Levant, social considerations take priority: a woman, that is, seems able to be defined as menopausal if she has lost the potential to bear children (because, for example, her husband has died), whether or not she has actually ceased to menstruate and so has become incapable of conception.

The other stages of the Israelite woman's life cycle that I will examine in this volume—motherhood and death—seem to me more straightforward, although I will define whatever terms are necessary there and elsewhere.

A Note on Sources

As my repeated evocation of religious studies scholars in the preceding discussion of women's life-cycle rituals might imply, I understand a community's life-cycle events and rituals to be a part of that community's religious culture. I thus consider ancient Israel's life-cycle events and rituals to be a part of ancient Israelite religion, even though I acknowledge that not all life-cycle events and rituals "had direct religious associations or connotations."[237]

I furthermore consider the three sources most useful for an examination of any aspect of ancient Israelite religion to be

1. archaeological remains, both archaeological remains from ancient Israelite sites and remains that come from the many peoples of the Near Eastern and eastern Mediterranean world with whom the Israelites interacted and with whom, in many cases, the Israelites shared certain cultural and, more specifically, religious conventions: preeminently, the peoples of second- and first-millennium BCE Mesopotamia and Egypt, second-millennium BCE Anatolia, and first-millennium BCE Greece; the Canaanite peoples of the Late Bronze Age (ca. 1550–1200 BCE) and their first-millennium BCE Phoenician, Ammonite, Moabite, and Edomite descendants; and other non-Canaanite Semites of the first millennium BCE, such as the Aramaeans;
2. written texts that come from these same peoples of the Near Eastern and eastern Mediterranean world; and
3. the Bible.

In my study of Israelite women's life-cycle events and rituals, however, I have found the utility of archaeological remains to be limited: there is some evidence regarding funerary and other mortuary rituals that can be derived from burial sites (see Chapter 9), and I will consider an artifact found in many Israelite archaeological excavations, the Judean pillar figurine, when discussing rituals having to do with a mother's weaning her child in Chapter 7. I will also cite some archaeological evidence in my study of pregnancy and parturition in Chapter 5. Overall, though, archaeological remains are not well positioned to reveal the features and elements of ancient Israel's life-cycle events and rituals, and they are especially not well positioned to illuminate the issues that I have indicated are of particular interest to me: how Israelite women experienced life-cycle events and the enactment of life-cycle rituals, and especially the ways in which Israelite women experienced these events and ritual enactments differently than did Israelite men. Consequently, I will draw on archaeological evidence only sporadically in this study.

Conversely, written texts from ancient Israel's Near Eastern and eastern Mediterranean neighbors can be a very helpful source for understanding both men's and women's life-cycle events and rituals. I suggested in the Prologue, for example, that classical and Hellenistic-era Greek traditions about a father's acceptance of a neonate into his family on the fifth day after birth (or perhaps the seventh or tenth day) can tell us something about how "social birth" as opposed to "physical birth" may have been understood in the eastern Mediterranean world.[238] The father's role in this Greek ritual will also be of interest to us in Chapter 6, when we consider the responsibility ancient Israelite mothers often assumed in bestowing on their children a name. In fact, throughout the chapters that follow, I will draw to a considerable degree on evidence that comes from Near Eastern and eastern Mediterranean written sources. My primary source, though, for describing Israelite women's life-cycle events and rituals in the preexilic and early postexilic periods on which I focus in this study will be the Bible.

Implicit here are certain assumptions about the nature of the Bible as a source. First and foremost, I assume that the biblical texts on which my analysis relies can be used to reveal accurate historical data about the ritual lives of Israelite women during the preexilic and early postexilic periods. I assume this because I contend these biblical texts must have made sense to their ancient audiences, which is to say: the Bible's descriptions of—or, somewhat more typically, its allusions to—Israelite women's life-cycle events and rituals must have "rung true" to their ancient audiences and so must have corresponded to those audiences' experiences of life-cycle events and rituals that took place in the society in which they actually lived. In other words, as Philip J. King and Lawrence E. Stager have written in their book *Life in*

Biblical Israel, "It matters little whether the biblical accounts are true in the positivistic sense of some historians and biblical scholars. It is enough to know that the ancient Israelites believed them to be so. The stories must have passed some test of verisimilitude, that is, having the appearance of being true or real."[239]

This assumption that texts "rang true" to ancient audiences implies a further assumption: that the biblical texts on which my analysis relies would have "rung true" to their ancient audiences and corresponded to those audiences' experiences because these texts are contemporaneous in date with those audiences—that is, contemporaneous in date with the preexilic and early postexilic Israelite communities that are my focus in this study. While I therefore acknowledge that in the past few decades, a number of scholars have argued that significant blocks of the biblical text date only to the late Persian or even the Hellenistic periods of Israelite history (the fourth, third, and second centuries BCE), I identify as more or less a traditionalist when it comes to dating many biblical corpora to the second half of the preexilic period, to the time of the exile, and to the early years of the postexilic era.[240] For example, I take the Bible's so-called J or Yahwistic writer and the kindred E or Elohistic writer, whose texts are found interspersed within the books of Genesis and Exodus and the last two-thirds of the book of Numbers, to date from somewhere within the ninth or, more probably, the eighth century BCE.[241] I further hold that one of the other major sources found in Genesis-Numbers, the work of the Priestly authors, or P, depends on core traditions that are preexilic, although I agree with many that P comes together in its final form only in the late exilic or early postexilic period (the late sixth or even early fifth century BCE).[242] In addition, while I agree with the conclusion initially put forward by Israel Knohl that the related materials of the so-called H or Holiness source found preeminently in Leviticus 17–26 postdate P,[243] the affinities between H and the prophet Ezekiel suggest to me that while the precise relationship of H and Ezekiel is a matter of debate,[244] H materials must, to some degree, be contemporaneous with Ezekiel's ministry, which took place between ca. 593 and 571 BCE.

I assign a roughly similar date to the so-called Deuteronomistic History that runs from Joshua through Judges, 1–2 Samuel, and 1–2 Kings, which is to say: I agree with a major strand of American biblical scholarship that this Deuteronomistic History was originally rendered in a "first edition" at the end of the seventh century BCE, in ca. 620–610 BCE, and in a "second" or "revised edition" a few decades later, in ca. 580 BCE.[245] From this it follows that the book of Deuteronomy, which serves the Deuteronomistic History as prologue and on whose theology the Deuteronomistic History in large part depends, dates from the preexilic period, and, more specifically, from the same general period during the late seventh century BCE in which the Deuteronomistic History was originally promulgated.[246]

Finally, I note that in suggesting, say, a ninth- or (better) eighth-century BCE date for J or the Yahwistic writer and the kindred E or Elohistic writer, and in also suggesting that these corpora are useful sources for my examination of women's life-cycle events and rituals of the preexilic and early postexilic periods, I signal my conviction that whatever era any given source purports to describe—for example, in J's and E's case, events that are said to have taken place during the second millennium BCE—these sources in fact reflect the social conditions of their own day. I thus reject arguments that suggest sources such as J and E can accurately transmit oral traditions that go back hundreds of years. In making this claim, I am particularly influenced by the classicist Ian Morris and his analysis of the great Homeric epics of the *Iliad* and the *Odyssey*. As Morris argues, it is methodologically flawed to posit that these eighth-century BCE poems contain accurate accounts of the Greeks' exploits from the thirteenth-twelfth centuries BCE, the putative period of the Trojan War that they purport to describe. In Morris's words, "The much-vaunted oral tradition was not in any sense a 'chronicle,' a repository of antiquated institutions and world-views."[247]

Still, while this means for Morris that the Homeric epics are "of little use to the historian" of the thirteenth and twelfth centuries BCE, this does not mean they are of no use at all.[248] Rather, "the institutions, attitudes, and conditions of action that we find in the *Iliad* and the *Odyssey* must of necessity be derived in some way from those of the functioning societies that Homer himself knew": that is, the Greek societies of the eighth century BCE from which the Homeric epics date. More specifically, Morris argues that we should search the *Iliad* and the *Odyssey* for their "unintended evidence" concerning the eighth century BCE during which they were composed.[249] The *Iliad* and the *Odyssey*, that is, "are scrutinized not for what their authors wished to say [regarding the Greeks' purported exploits against Troy in the thirteenth-twelfth centuries BCE], but for the unarticulated assumptions they carry with them [regarding the Greek world of the eighth century BCE]."[250]

Likewise, I maintain, "the institutions, attitudes, and conditions of action" that we find in biblical texts "must of necessity be derived in some way from" the Israelite society that those texts' authors themselves knew: that is, the

Israelite society contemporaneous with the authors themselves. Thus, while the accounts in, say, Genesis are, like the Homeric epics, "of little use to the historian" with respect to documenting their purported second-millennium BCE milieu, they are nevertheless, again like the Homeric epics, of considerable use for the evidence they provide regarding the time during the preexilic period in which they were composed. In particular, these accounts, yet again like the Homeric epics, are of considerable use when it comes to their "unintended evidence," as we can read between the lines, and sometimes against the grain, to uncover their "unarticulated assumptions" about women's life-cycle events and rituals. Indeed, because the Bible is not particularly interested in women in general, nor, therefore, in women's religious lives, including women's life-cycle rituals, the effort to read for "unintended evidence" and "unarticulated assumptions" will be particularly important, in order to identify and analyze what as I described above as the biblical text's "allusions to" women's life-cycle events and rituals.

So now let us turn to these life-cycle events and rituals. Unless otherwise noted, all translations of biblical and other ancient texts in the chapters that follow are my own.

PART I
A GIRL'S BIRTH AND COMING INTO MATURITY

1
The Birth of a Female Child

There is a large corpus of ancient Near Eastern texts that address matters of pregnancy and labor, especially ritual texts that detail how to protect the well-being of a delivering mother at a time when childbirth put her at great risk.[1] We also know of many texts that describe ritual means for protecting the mother's newly born and equally vulnerable child.[2] I will discuss a few of these rituals that protected newborns in the latter part of this chapter, and I will catalog others, along with rituals meant to protect an expectant mother, in Chapter 5, where I consider pregnancy, parturition, and the period immediately postpartum as key moments within an Israelite woman's life cycle. My primary focus in what follows, though, as I address traditions concerning the birth of a baby girl, is a special subset of the rituals that pertain to newborn children: those that are sex- and gender-specific. In particular, I aim to follow the program I have set out in the Introduction by identifying and explaining features in the rites that mark the beginning of a girl child's life that are characteristic of, and distinctive to, female life-cycle rituals.

I begin with a Hittite ritual text from the second half of the second millennium BCE that describes how the midwife of a newly delivered mother confers "the goods of a male child" or "the goods of a female child" upon a newborn in order to demarcate the child's sex and gender.[3] Unfortunately, this text offers no further information about what these "goods" might be, but we can perhaps get some idea from the more elaborate, and also the oldest sex- and gender-specific birth rituals known from the Near Eastern world, which come from ancient Mesopotamia: from third-millennium BCE Sumer and the Old Babylonian period of second-millennium BCE Akkad (ca. 1894–1595 BCE). There, according to both Sumerian and Old Babylonian birth incantations, newborn girls and boys could be associated with certain colored gemstones (carnelian and lapis lazuli), although scholars debate whether carnelian was assigned to girl infants and lapis lazuli to boys, or whether it was the other way around.[4]

It is undisputed, however, that according to both Sumerian and Old Babylonian texts, the birth of a child could be marked by bringing the newborn into contact with specific objects that signified the infant's sex and gender identity: a baton or club (Sumerian *tukul*) and an axe (Sumerian *ḫa-zi*; Akkadian *ḫaṣṣinnu*) for a newborn boy, and a spindle (Sumerian *bala*; Akkadian *pilakku*) and a pin or clasp (or perhaps a "distaff," according to some interpreters; Sumerian *kirid*; Akkadian *kirissu*) in the case of a newborn girl.[5] The choice of objects here is not coincidental. According to a birth incantation from the Ur III period (ca. 2112–2004 BCE) that details these items associated with newborns, a boy's baton or club and his axe represent strength and heroism, which were attributes Mesopotamian culture connoted as masculine and which the newborn boy was expected someday to embody.[6] Likewise, we know from second-millennium BCE Hittite and Ugaritic sources and first-millennium BCE Phoenician-Luwian and biblical materials that the spindles associated in Mesopotamia with infant girls were characteristic markers of femininity in the ancient world, as they symbolized the work of textile production that was a significant part of a woman's labor in life.[7]

Indeed, Tikva Frymer-Kensky has noted that "producing cloth" was the "basic economic task" of Mesopotamian women and their "most important and characteristic nonprocreative function."[8] Carol Meyers has similarly stressed the important role women played in textile production in ancient Israel, especially in the self-sufficient agrarian-pastoralist households that were the characteristic residential units of Israelite rural enclaves during the preexilic period.[9] That women continued to play this important role during Israel's postexilic period can be seen in Prov 31:10–31, where the "capable wife" is particularly associated with textile production (see vv 13, 19, 22, and 24).[10] See too the book of Tobit, from the fourth or third century BCE, where weaving is explicitly described as "women's work" (Tob 2:11–12; NRSV translation).[11] E. J. W. Barber has in addition written of Greek women that "spinning and weaving occupied most of women's time in Classical Greece . . . properly married Athenian women . . . spent their lives sequestered at home spinning and weaving for the family's needs."[12]

In fact, although the classical Greek evidence that Barber cites postdates by nearly two millennia the earliest Mesopotamian references to the ritual of bringing an infant girl into contact with a spindle, the Mesopotamian rite was nevertheless echoed in Greece, through the custom of placing a tuft of wool on the door of a house of a newborn girl in order to symbolize the critical role that spinning and weaving would play later in her life.[13] Mesopotamian traditions that associated girl infants with the left side of the body, which was less valued, as opposed to boy infants' association with the body's right and preferred side, were also echoed in later Greek and even Roman society; in all these cultures, for example, it was believed that a woman carried a female fetus on the left side of her womb and a male fetus on the right.[14] Somewhat similarly, a text from late antique Jewish tradition—the Talmudic tractate b. Niddah 31a—differentiates between female and male fetuses and judges the former negatively by claiming that a woman experiences greater labor pains during a girl infant's birth than during the birth of a boy. This is because, as the Talmud sees it, girl newborns come out of the womb in a more difficult position for delivery—face up (the position, according to the Talmud, that a female normatively assumed during sexual intercourse later in her life)—whereas boys are said to come from the womb in what the Talmud considers the normative intercourse position for men: face down.[15]

The Israelites of the biblical period, however, seem neither to have anticipated their Talmudic successors, nor to have followed their Mesopotamian and Hittite predecessors, in engaging in ritual acts or promulgating traditions that explicitly demarcated a baby's sex and gender at birth.[16] Certainly, no records have survived of ancient Israelite rituals analogous to the Mesopotamian, Hittite, and also Greek traditions catalogued above that used colored gemstones or objects such as spindles or tufts of wool to specify the sex and gender identity of a newborn girl.[17] The ritual that requires consecrating or dedicating Israel's boy children to the national god Yahweh (Exod 13:1–2, 11–16; 22:28 [22:29 in most English translations]; 34:20; Num 3:11–12, 40–51; 8:16–18; 18:15–16) likewise cannot be compared to the other Near Eastern and eastern Mediterranean traditions of sex and gender specification I have surveyed, given that this rite applies only to firstborn males. Also, according to Num 3:40 and 18:16, it applies only to male infants over a month old and not to the neonates who are the subjects of Mesopotamian, Hittite, and Greco-Roman tradition.

What's more, the Israelite ritual of circumcising a recently delivered boy on the eighth day of his life, although it is obviously a sex-specific birth rite, cannot be deemed comparable to Mesopotamian, Hittite, and Greco-Roman custom, as it does not have sex or gender demarcation of the male infant as its explicit aim.[18] Indeed, as we will see in Chapter 2, circumcision may originally have had nothing to do with birth, but instead was a rite performed to mark a young man's suitability for marriage. And even when the tradition shifted to the practice of infant circumcision, the rite's purpose was still not to denote the infant as male. Instead, at least in the P or Priestly source materials in which the institution of infant circumcision is espoused, the rite's primary focus—after the baby had lived for a week and the most acute dangers associated with childbirth had passed[19]—was to signal the boy's entry into the Israelite covenant community.[20] Or, as Francesca Stavrakopoulou has put it, circumcision does not *designate* a child as male, but renders a body *already identified* as male as "marked and manifested as a site of Yhwh-religion" and thereby "fit for the 'male' performativity of religious activity."[21] Dorothea Erbele has made much the same point: circumcision, she writes, is not "carried out on a gender-neutral body"; rather, flesh already classified as male "gets a special mark."[22] Thus, "manhood" is "made visible."[23]

Gendered Ritual Observances at Birth: Leviticus 12:1–8

Still, when Israelite tradition shifted from circumcision of young men to infant circumcision, this rite did come to serve indirectly to differentiate newborn males from females, and the sex and gender identity of both infant boys and girls seems also to have been indirectly marked by at least some ritual practitioners during at least some points in ancient Israelite history through observing the Lev 12:1–8 statutes that concern the impurity of a newborn's mother.[24] According to this passage from the Bible's P, or Priestly tradition, a newly delivered mother was considered impure (*ṭāmēʾ*), or as some translators would have it "polluted" or "unclean" for an initial seven-day period after giving birth to a boy. She then remained impure, although in a less serious state of impurity, for another thirty-three days thereafter (Lev 12:2,4). She was, however, considered impure for twice as long—an initial fourteen days, and then a subsequent sixty-six days—if her child was a girl (Lev 12:5).

The reason for this discrepancy is a matter of debate among scholars. Perhaps the most common explanation assumes that the end of the first stage of impurity of a mother newly delivered of a son was somehow coordinate with his circumcision on the eighth day after birth, possibly so that his circumcision might take "place in a state of purity" (a position articulated already in the Jewish Talmud).[25] Or possibly the boy's circumcision removed the mother's initial impurity.[26] But as Jacob Milgrom has pointed out in his magisterial three-volume commentary on Leviticus, a mother remained impure after the birth of a daughter longer than after the birth of a son in Hittite tradition (four months versus three months), even though circumcision was not a Hittite practice.[27] According to Milgrom, this datum renders arguments that link the duration of the Israelite mother's impurity to laws about circumcision "invalid."[28]

Milgrom, moreover, seems disinclined to embrace any of the alternate suggestions on offer: for example, the proposal that the ancient Israelites believed that the mother's postpartum discharge, which is the agent that renders the woman impure,[29] lasted longer in the case of a girl's birth than it did after the birth of a boy.[30] Rather, evidence suggests "a slightly longer period . . . but nowhere near to twice as long."[31] Milgrom likewise doubts that Lev 12:1–8 reflects the same conviction regarding the superior status and worth of a male as compared to a female that we saw manifest in the Mesopotamian, Greek, and Roman beliefs that associated female newborns with the body's left-hand and inferior side and that is suggested elsewhere in levitical tradition: for example, in Lev 27:2–7, where the monetary value assigned to females of various age groups is somewhere between 40 and 60 percent of the value assumed for males.[32] Rather, as Mayer I. Gruber points out, "greater defilement is not necessarily an indication of lesser worth": a human being, for example, is surely of superior status and worth as compared to a pig, even though biblical tradition maintains that a human corpse defiles more, rather than less, than does a pig's carcass.[33] "The reason for [the] disparity between the sexes is unknown," Milgrom concludes,[34] and most other commentators are equally stymied.[35] "No convincing explanation has been offered why the birth of a girl makes the mother unclean for twice as long as the birth of a boy," Gordon J. Wenham writes; "it is not clear why the birth of a girl doubles the time period of a mother's uncleanness and that of her purification," according to Saul M. Olyan; "I do not know," Jonathan Klawans admits, "why women are ritually defiled for a longer period after the birth of a daughter than after the birth of a son"; "we are unable," says Clarence J. Vos, "to give a satisfactory and conclusive answer to the question of why the period was longer for a girl than a boy."[36]

It seems to me, however, that the reason commentators are so stymied in their attempts to explain the dicta regarding impurity in Lev 12:1–8 is that they have looked for—and found unsatisfactory—answers that have their basis in ancient Israel's cultural customs or cultural milieu: positing a relationship between the duration of the mother's impurity and the ritual of infant circumcision, for example, or positing that the duration of the mother's impurity is related to Near Eastern and eastern Mediterranean traditions about girl infants' inferior status. I propose instead that we consider childbirth using the theoretical paradigms I explored in the Introduction concerning life-cycle rituals. In undertaking this evaluation, I also propose, as opposed to commentators' typical (though not exclusive) focus on the mother's time of postpartum defilement, that we attend to the concomitant period during which the newborn infant should be "at one," so to speak, with the impure mother. That is, the newborn infant should be, like its mother, subject to impurity, given that the recently delivered mother's impurity is said, in Lev 12:2, 5, to be like that of a menstruant's, and so, like a menstruant's, the mother's impurity should be contagious (see Lev 15:19–24).[37]

At a minimum, this means that anyone who touches the impure mother or touches anything on which she had sat or lain—a cohort that would surely have included her newborn child—is rendered impure for that day ("until the evening," in the words of Lev 15:19, 21–23). More maximally, we can posit that the newborn—who would doubtlessly be in contact with its mother day-in and day-out (I assume here the typical scenario within Israelite households, whereby a mother, and not a wetnurse, suckles a child)[38]—would repeatedly be rendered impure, on each of the seven or fourteen days that the mother's impurity was considered contagious.[39] We might thus imagine that after birth, both the mother and the newly delivered infant were kept isolated—at least to some degree—from all but those who must inevitably be contaminated by the mother's impurity (for example, the mother's midwife, as well as other women who may have attended a woman during childbirth).[40] Indeed, Olyan has noted, regarding parturients, that "some evidence from ... West Asian sources [other than the Bible] suggests that they were to be removed from the domicile or even the community during the time of their pollution."[41] Karel van der Toorn similarly imagines that Israelite women would withdraw to a separate shed on the outskirts of their village during the time of their menses, and so, one might wonder, during the menstrual-like period of postpartum impurity as well?[42] If this is the case (and I will catalog some of the relevant data in Chapter 6), then certainly the new mother's suckling child was removed with her.

Yet even if an Israelite infant and its mother were not wholly sequestered after birth, "impurity," to quote Olyan again, would still "severely limit opportunities for movement [and] social interactions."[43] Indeed, a major aspect of these limitations is spelled out in Lev 12:4, where it is specifically said of the postpartum woman that for the entire forty to eighty days of her impurity, she was not allowed to touch anything "holy" (*běkol-qōdeš lōʾ-tiggāʿ*), nor was she allowed to enter "holy" or sanctuary space (*ʾel-hammiqdāš lōʾ tābōʾ*). This is because Israelite concepts of purity were closely related (albeit not identical) to the Israelite concept of the "holy" (*qōdeš*), to the extent that, while "holiness had its *opposite* in the common or the profane (*ḥōl*), it encountered its *opposition* in the presence of impurity (*ṭāmēʾ*)."[44] Impurity, in other words, "is a threat to the holy."[45] Indeed, "biblical sources understand pollution [or impurity] to be the *ultimate threat* to what is holy" (emphasis mine).[46] As a result, that which was impure had, for the duration of the impurity, to be rigorously separated from that which was holy: "the essence of holiness is separation."[47]

To be sure, the newborn infant should not have been subject to the same forty to eighty days of separation as was the newly delivered mother, given that the newborn should be impure only as long as the mother's impurity was contagious: that is, for the initial seven or fourteen days after birth, when the mother's impurity is said to be like that of a menstruant's.[48] Nevertheless, I would identify the period of postpartum impurity, whether for infant or mother, as corresponding to a liminal phase within a rite of passage. Indeed, I noted in the Introduction that the seclusion, whether absolute or partial, to which an Israelite mother and child would seemingly have been subject for the seven to fourteen days after parturition is a characteristic feature of a rite of passage's liminal phase, including, notably, rites of passage related to childbirth. We saw regarding Hopi tradition, for example, that during what Arnold van Gennep described as the transitional or liminal period after a woman gave birth, the new mother remained confined in her home during daylight hours: for five days postpartum if she had previously borne children and for twenty days if the newborn child was her first.[49]

Van Gennep, moreover, characterized the moment of birth within Hopi tradition as corresponding to the first or "separation" phase of his rites-of-passage pattern. Van Gennep's focus in that discussion was the mother—who was separated at the moment of delivery from all attendants, including her own mother—but materials from Near Eastern tradition, including the Bible, suggest that the moment of birth can likewise be understood to separate the neonate (my particular concern in this discussion) from its previous identity and mode of existence as a fetus.[50] Indeed, in Near Eastern tradition, the period of "pre-birth was a well-defined and important stage" in a child's development.[51] In Mesopotamia, for example, the period of pre-birth can be traced, according to a mathematical text from the Seleucid era (ca. 312–63 BCE), from the time of conception, when the fetus is an entity of "a half grain . . . in the womb of its mother," through its growth to a size of "five grains" by the tenth day in utero, and onward to measure "three fingers" by the end of a month, and finally "a cubit" by the tenth month, at which point delivery takes place.[52] In fact, this pre-birth period in Mesopotamian thought was so significant that "Babylonian horoscopes take as their start-date the day of conception rather than the day of birth."[53] Similarly, Lynn Meskell reports that in ancient Egypt, "while already in the womb, the unborn child was considered a living being and as such required protection in the social realm."[54] Thus, a magical spell from the New Kingdom (ca. 1539–1075 BCE) describes Meskhenet, a goddess closely associated with childbirth, creating a child's *ka*, or its vital essence and life force, while the baby was still *in utero*.[55]

This sensibility is also manifest within the Israelite worldview. The two unborn children who strive to crush one another in Rebekah's womb in Gen 25:22–23, for example, are but preliminary (or we might even say preliminal) representations of her two sons, Jacob and Esau, who will contend with one another throughout much of their adult lives. Likewise, according to Jer 1:4–5, before Jeremiah was born, Yahweh had already ordained his fetus to be the prophet that Jeremiah would one day become, and in Isa 49:1, Yahweh is similarly said to decree, while the deity's anonymous servant was still in the womb, that this servant would eventually speak and act on God's behalf. Note too the episode in first-century CE New Testament tradition, when, according to Luke 1:39–45, the fetal John the Baptist, who will many years later announce the "good news" of Jesus's coming to his followers (Luke 3:18), adumbrates this proclamation by leaping for joy in the womb of his mother Elizabeth when Mary, pregnant with Jesus, comes to visit.

I thus propose, as I suggested already above, that we understand Israelite childbirth as the moment when a newborn child is separated from its preliminary (or preliminal) existence in the womb and enters into a period of liminal transition, as a rite-of-passage structure would predict, before being integrated or incorporated—when the liminal period of postpartum impurity ends—into a new stage in life: full-fledged membership within the family unit and larger household and village community.[56] Note, indeed, that elsewhere in the Mediterranean world, as I pointed out in the Prologue, this sort of "social birth"—that is, a child's integration into its family and community—need not be coordinate with the moment of physical birth: in Greek tradition, we will recall, it was only on the fifth day after birth (or even, according to some sources, the seventh or tenth day) that an infant was formally accepted (or rejected) by its father and incorporated into (or dismissed from) its family.[57] In ancient Rome, similarly, the "lustral day" (*dies lustricus*) at which a child's name was conferred—eight or nine days after birth—"marked the entry of the child into the family and society,"[58] so much so that in his *Roman Questions* (in Book IV of Plutarch's *Moralia*), the first-century CE Greek philosopher Plutarch opines that before this time, the child is "more like a plant than animal."[59] Or we might say, following Victor Turner's classic formulation, that during this time, the child is "betwixt and between" two modes of being.[60] More simply put, the child is liminal.

In the Introduction, moreover, I have suggested that women's liminal experiences during life-cycle events and their associated rituals can be intensified or exacerbated as compared to liminality as experienced by men. Consequently, in the case we are considering here—the liminal period of impurity that according to Lev 12:1–8 follows the birth of an Israelite child—I suggest liminality is intensified or exacerbated for newborn girls. More specifically, I propose that female infants, who, like females generally, are intrinsically liminal simply by virtue of their sex (again, see my discussion in the Introduction), need to experience, during the liminal postpartum period, some exaggerated version of normal liminality. Normal liminality in this case, I further propose, is defined by the infants of the sex that is normative in Israelite society: the males.[61] Childbirth's normal liminal experience can thus be described as the seven-day period in which newborn boys are contaminated by their mother's impurity.

Indeed, seven days is a quite standard liminal period—or at least the standard duration of a transitional period—within the priestly traditions of which the Levitcus 12 text that we are considering here is a part.[62] According to Exod 29:35 and Lev 8:33, for example, the process of priestly ordination lasts seven days; the period of corpse contamination for those who have come into contact with a deceased's person body is seven days (Num 19:11, 14, 16; 31:19); and the Sukkot (or Ingathering) festival that marks the end of the agricultural year and the beginning of the winter rains—a ritual event that van Gennep and Turner, not coincidentally, would define as a cyclical or calendrical rite of passage—lasts seven days (Lev 23:34, 42–43). But if a seven-day liminal period is the priestly norm, then the period of ritually demarcated liminality for a female infant should, under the terms of the analysis I presented in the Introduction, somehow exceed this, and so the already liminal baby girl becomes doubly liminal through the doubled (fourteen-day) period of her mother's ritual defilement. Likewise, the period of the mother's lesser defilement is doubled for the baby girl (sixty-six days, as opposed to thirty-three), as a result of the intensification of liminal markers that can define female life-cycle rituals.[63]

More on a Girl Child's Birth: Ezekiel 16:4–9

To be sure, not all commentators embrace a critical element of the argument I have just put forward: my presumption that a recently delivered child is, like its mother, impure during the initial seven-/fourteen-day period after childbirth.[64] According to Baruch A. Levine, for example, the "child is *born pure*" (emphasis mine),[65] which I agree is perfectly plausible, since it is not the act of delivery itself, but the postpartum discharges from a the newly delivered mother's uterus and vagina that are the cause of her childbirth-related impurities.[66] But what of the neonate after the delivery has been completed and during the ensuing seven/fourteen days? Levine writes only that the newly delivered mother's "impure condition would cause defilement through certain types of contact," but he offers no explicit comment about whether the mother's child would have been among those subject to that defilement.[67] Saul M. Olyan similarly notes that the mother's impurity was "probably" polluting "for others who have contact with her," but nevertheless cautions that the "text says nothing about the child's purity."[68] Jacob Milgrom also states, regarding the child's purity, that "the text [of Leviticus 12] is silent," although he seems inclined to think that, as in classical rabbinic exegesis,[69] the mother's impurity was not transmitted to her child.[70] But because there is not "even a hint" of a clarification elsewhere in biblical tradition, Milgrom concludes that "there is no clear answer."[71]

Yet is the tradition really as unhelpful as Milgrom suggests? Certainly, as I have intimated above and will discuss more thoroughly in Chapter 6, there is ample cross-cultural evidence, attested in Mesopotamian, Hittite, Egyptian, and Greek sources, that "the parturient and her newborn child both suffered ritual impurity."[72] Indeed, according to the Hittite text I previously cited that, like Lev 12:1–8, mandates differing lengths of impurity after the birth of a boy versus a girl child, it is explicitly indicated that it is the *newborn* who suffers from impurity during the three-/four-month postpartum period.[73] According, moreover, to some of Leviticus 12's earliest interpreters, whose witness can be found in first-century BCE and first-century CE Jewish and New Testament texts, the newborn of Lev 12:1–8 is considered to share in its mother's impurity—including even her thirty-three or sixty-six days of lesser impurity. For example: while the interpretation of Luke 2:22–24 is debated, Matthew Thiessen has persuasively argued that the author of Luke-Acts understands both Mary and her infant son Jesus to have been impure for forty days after childbirth, until they came to the Jerusalem temple, along with Joseph, to offer (as Lev 12:8 requires) "a pair of turtledoves or two young pigeons" when "the days of *their* purification were completed" (emphasis mine).[74]

Even more compellingly, Thiessen draws attention to a text from the roughly contemporaneous Dead Sea Scroll tradition, 4Q266 (part of the Qumran Cave 4 version of the so-called Damascus Document), which "forbids the new mother to nurse her child and requires the use of a wetnurse (4Q266 6 ii 10–11)."[75] This is because a wetnurse, the text indicates, is able to nurse the newborn "in purity" (*bṭwhrh*). Thiessen, following Martha Himmelfarb, suggests that the text's logic here is identical to the interpretation of Lev 12:1–8 that I have offered above: without a wetnurse, a newborn child, even if pure at delivery, could not remain in a state of purity after birth, given that the mother's impurity is said to be contagious, like that of a menstruant's, and so would inevitably communicate itself to her infant were she breastfeeding the child.[76] Lawrence H. Schiffman similarly observes that the related 4Q265, the so-called Miscellaneous Rules, which discusses Lev 12:1–8 in conjunction with the story of the Garden of Eden, "essentially treats Adam and Eve as newborn children and transfers to them the purificatory rites required for the mother in Leviticus . . . therefore, each entered the garden only after purification, requiring forty days for Adam and eighty for Eve."[77] This same understanding is found, moreover, in the book of Jubilees (Jub. 3:8–14).[78]

Finally, consider Ezek 16:4, which implies that a baby was standardly bathed on the day of its birth. Typically, commentators suggest that this was done to cleanse the child of blood and other fluids excreted during the birthing process, an interpretation that is supported by the description in v 6 of the unwashed newborn lying in its birth blood.[79] But could a natal-day bathing also remove at least the initial impurities that my reading of Lev 12:1–8 suggests a child would have contracted after delivery through contact with its ritually impure mother? At least two Hittite texts include notices that a newborn, in one case, or a lamb that stands in as a ritual substitute for the child, in the other, is to be bathed after parturition, and given that there is no need to remove birth fluids from the substitute lamb, and even more so given that in the "substitute lamb" text, the bath water is subsequently poured out before some deity, these postpartum baths are best interpreted as having a ritual purpose.[80] That purpose is most logically, I submit, the purification of the newly delivered infant.[81] Indeed, according to Lev 15:19–24, anyone who comes into contact with something on which a menstruant has sat or lain must bathe as part of the process that removes his or her impurity, a regulation that might plausibly apply to Israelite neonates made impure by contact with their menstruant-like mothers.

We will in addition recall that Lev 15:19–24 indicates that impurities generated by contact with a menstruant or something on which a menstruant sat or lay lasted throughout a day and "until the evening"; could this suggest that there might have been a bath each evening during an infant's first week or two of life (depending on whether the child was male or female), to cleanse it from the mother's impurities that the child had contracted that day? Or would there at least have been one final bath, to cleanse the infant at the end of its own and its newly delivered mother's initial seven- or fourteen-day period of impurity? Keith W. Carley may be suggesting as much when he states regarding the infant of Ezek 16:4 (with, unfortunately, no reference) that at the end of seven days, "the washing [of Day 1] . . . was repeated."[82] Milgrom similarly argues that a recently delivered mother bathed on Day 7 or Day 14 after parturition, as a means of removing her initial state of contagious impurity.[83] In fact, according to Milgrom, "all statements regarding the duration of impurity," such as the seven-/fourteen-day period of a newly delivered mother's impurity—and thus the concomitant period of impurity that I have argued affects her newborn child—"*automatically imply* that it [the impurity] is terminated by ablutions" (emphasis mine).[84]

Ezekiel 16:4, in addition to noting that an infant was normally bathed on the day of its birth, indicates that a newborn was rubbed with salt and wrapped in cloths. According to some interpreters, salt was rubbed on the neonate due to its hygienic and/or antiseptic properties,[85] while swaddling cloths were wrapped around the baby because of their ability to reduce a child's "energy requirement for temperature and physical maintenance."[86] Or, as Marten Stol proposes in his book *Birth in Babylonia and the Bible*, salt may have been thought to help harden the newborn's skin, and the cloth wrappings were similarly understood as giving form to a newly delivered child.[87] Carol Meyers, however, and also Marjorie D. Gursky in her New York University doctoral dissertation "Reproductive Rituals in Biblical Israel," consider the rubbing with salt to be primarily (or even exclusively) of ritual significance. Perhaps, Meyers suggests, rubbing salt on a newborn was an apotropaic ritual that warded off evils that might threaten the child.[88] But Gursky more convincingly proposes that a newborn was rubbed with salt for reasons of purification, just as salt was used in purificatory rites elsewhere in the Bible.[89] For example, Elisha uses a bowl of salt in 2 Kgs 2:20–21 to purify a spring of water that is otherwise foul. More specifically, the spring's unpurified waters are said to be causing the land roundabout to "miscarry" (*měšakkālet*; 2 Kgs 2:19, 21), suggesting, at least metaphorically, that the Israelites associated salt's purificatory properties with healthy childbearing. Even more noteworthy for our purposes is a text from elsewhere in the book of Ezekiel, Ezek 43:24, in which God commands that salt is to be thrown on two burnt offerings as part of the ritual that *purifies* the altar of the rebuilt Jerusalem temple that Ezekiel envisions.

In the Ezekiel 16 text we are examining, I propose that salt had the same purpose: that it was to be used, just as was bathing according to my arguments above, to purify the newborn child of at least the initial impurities it would have contracted through its postpartum contact with its contagiously impure mother. And what of the one other postpartum act referenced in Ezek 16:4, the cutting of the umbilical cord? We might note that in ancient Egypt, according to the *Book of the Dead* (Spell 17), "cutting the umbilical cord had religious significance and meant a freeing from evil and wicked things."[90] So too in Israel? Even if not, I still take Ezek 16:4 to be strong evidence in support of my claim that according, at least, to priestly traditions in the Bible (as represented both in Lev 12:1–8 and Ezekiel), a newborn child was considered impure, along with its mother, during the initial seven-/fourteen-day period after childbirth.[91]

Ezekiel 16:4, in conjunction with the five verses that immediately follow, also substantiates my claim that liminality during Israelite childbirth rituals is intensified or exacerbated if the newborn infant is female. To be sure, the birth described in Ezek 16:4 is metaphorical: the baby is the city of Jerusalem, imagined as a newborn girl in accord with the Bible's general sensibility that cities are gendered as female.[92] The text is also polemical: an attempt to describe how Jerusalem became so estranged from God that the city was doomed to be destroyed by the Babylonians in the early sixth century BCE. Thus, neither the prescribed bathing nor the rubbing with salt takes place, and other possible birth-related rituals (cutting the umbilical cord), as well as the swaddling of the child, are likewise ignored—because, Ezek 16:5 implies, Jerusalem was considered *gōʿal*, "loathsome" or "abhorrent," already on the day she was born, so much so that the infant is thrown out (*hišlîk*) after parturition.

Many interpreters of this verse have followed a proposal originally made by Mordechai Cogan that *hišlîk* here has a technical meaning that refers to the act of "leaving," "abandoning," or exposing": specifically, "the abandonment of an item with which one can or does not want to deal."[93] Moshe Greenberg, for example, references Cogan in discussing "the practice of exposing infants" and the putative "viciousness of the parents" that motivated it in Ezek 16:5, and Daniel L. Block likewise notes Cogan's work in stating, regarding Ezek 16:5, that "Jerusalem's parents flung her out... to die."[94] Block also cites Meir Malul, who has sought to build on Cogan's analysis by highlighting legal traditions that he sees underlying Ezek 16:5: specifically, materials suggesting that in Mesopotamia, "the washing, cleansing, and clothing of the newborn represented an act of legitimization" and that "parents who did not perform such an act upon their newborn child were understood to have relinquished all rights to it."[95] Stol cautions, however, that no Mesopotamian evidence explicitly indicates that the washing of a newborn child was "the token of recognition in Babylonia."[96]

Indeed, my reading of bathing in Ezek 16:4 as (at least in part) a purificatory act urges us to think of Ezek 16:5 not so much in legal terms but in terms of ritual, and more specifically in terms of the birth of the infant Jerusalem as a life-cycle ritual. In that case, we might suggest that what *hišlîk* intimates in Ezek 16:5 is that contrary to the rites-of-passage pattern that I have previously suggested characterizes ancient Israelite childbirth, at least according to Lev 12:1–8, the postpartum Jerusalem's liminal period of impurity was not followed by a stage of integration or incorporation. That is, not only is the newborn Jerusalem made to endure her liminal period of postpartum impurities without the mitigation that bathing and rubbing with salt can (I have argued) provide. In addition, because she is abandoned or exposed shortly after delivery, rather than being integrated into her family and community once the days of her postpartum impurity end, the rite-of-passage's liminal phase that began with her birth continues unabated. It continues unabated, moreover, with Jerusalem being forsaken in a *śādeh*, a word which means both cultivated fields and the lands of the outback or steppe.[97] It is also "a term which... in Ezek 16:5 and elsewhere," in the words of Malul, "denotes the idea of a domain outside another domain... a lawless place outside society."[98]

As his description of the *śādeh*—and also the "wilderness," *midbār*—as "lawless" indicates,[99] Malul's focus here is again on the legal allusions he understands to underlie Ezek 16:4–5. But of greater significance for my analysis is Malul's sense of the *śādeh* as "outside society" and even more so social anthropologist Edmund Leach's description of the biblical steppe or wilderness as a *liminal* place, what Leach describes (using Turner's language) as "a 'betwixt and between' locality... which is neither fully in This World nor in The Other."[100] We might say, then, that the intensified duration of the liminal period that I have suggested characterizes the life-cycle ritual of childbirth for a girl infant according to Lev 12:1–8 becomes so intensified in Ezek 16:5 through the motif of abandonment (*hišlîk*) in a paradigmatically liminal space (the *śādeh*) that the text intimates here a potentially endless liminality faced by the outcast Jerusalem.

Indeed, although the circumstances are significantly different, the experience of the girl-child Jerusalem in Ezek 16:5 is quite at odds from that of the two male children who are victims of abandonment in the Bible: Ishmael, who in Gen 21:14–15 is left or abandoned (*hišlîk*) under a bush in the wilderness (*midbār*) of Beersheba, when the food and water needed to nurture him has run out, and Moses, who is placed in the Nile in Exod 2:3 in accord with the pharaoh's command in Exod 1:22 that Hebrew boy children be abandoned or exposed (*hišlîk*) there. In both of those accounts, Ishmael and Moses are abandoned by their own mothers, yet in both instances, they, unlike the girl-child Jerusalem in Ezek 16:5, end up reintegrated or reincorporated (to use rites-of-passage language) with these mothers in short order.[101] The girl-child Jerusalem, conversely, stays "excluded," or "other," according to Julie Galambush's study of Ezekiel 16, "in terms of her family membership, her national identity, her community status, and her ritual purity," so much so that "she is entirely outside the boundaries of the ordered world and on the brink of the ultimate 'exclusion,' death."[102]

To be sure, one could argue that some form of integration or incorporation for the forsaken Jerusalem does immediately follow her abandonment in Ezek 16:5, in 16:6, when Yahweh passes by the forsaken newborn as she lies in the *śādeh*, kicking about in her blood, and decrees that, despite her predicament, she is in fact to live and grow.[103] And so she does, until, according to Ezek 16:7, she "grew up" (using the verb *g-d-l*, "to become great") and "developed the loveliest of adornments" (*'ădî 'ădāyîm*), which the verse goes on to gloss as "breasts" (*šādayim*) and "[pubic] hair" (*śē'ār*; for the meaning "pubic hair," see Isa 7:20, *śa'ar hāraglāyim*).[104] Catalogued here (albeit slightly out of order) are the bodily changes that mark the initial stages of biological puberty in females: first, breast tissue starts to develop; about six months later, pubic hair begins to appear; and then, roughly a year later, a young woman experiences a significant growth spurt.[105] In communities today in the industrialized world, this process typically commences somewhere between the ages of eight and thirteen,[106] especially in girls who are generally in good health and have access to high-quality nutrition.[107] For young women in ancient Israel and elsewhere in the ancient world, however, the onset of biological puberty—which is slowed by factors such as an abnormal amount of body fat (especially too little) and a significant amount of physical exercise and/or physical labor[108]—surely occurred significantly later, most likely during the middle or latter half of the teenage years.[109] Because, moreover, menarche typically occurs only two years or so into pubescence, as a girl's growth spurt wanes,[110] and because women in preindustrial societies are likely to remain infertile for a year or even longer following their initial menses,[111] we can estimate that women in the ancient world would have fully matured, biologically speaking, only as they approached age twenty.[112]

This estimate is confirmed in several ancient sources.[113] For example, Lev 27:2–7, a text I mentioned briefly above that categorizes human lives into various age groupings, differentiates between females (and males) who are between five and twenty years of age—or, in the reading adopted here, those who are biologically prepubescent and pubescent—and those between twenty and sixty years old—or, in the reading adopted here, those who have fully matured, biologically speaking, as adults. Wilma Ann Bailey in addition has catalogued materials from Plato (*Republic* V.460e.4–5) and Aristotle (*History of Animals* VII.1.582a.27–29) suggesting that women in classical Greece began to bear children at about age twenty,[114] and, somewhat similarly, Michael L. Satlow has collected data showing that despite the ideal articulated in several rabbinic texts that girls marry in their early teens,[115] Jewish women in the first centuries of the Common Era, at least in Palestine and the western Diaspora, actually wed in the middle or toward the end of their teenage years.[116] To be sure, Satlow does not correlate these data regarding marriage with a discussion of a bride's sexual maturation, but a logical inference is that the "average age of female marriage at 20" that he cites corresponds to the age at which Jewish women in the rabbinic era achieved full physical maturity.[117] The first-century CE Jewish historian Josephus may in fact bear witness to such a correlation when he reports that at least among the Essene community of his day, marriage took place after a woman had menstruated three times.[118]

But what sort of childhood does Ezekiel 16 envision for Jerusalem during what we can now suggest are the almost two decades between her birth and her sexual maturation? According to Ezek 16:8, it is only when Jerusalem reaches her 'ēt dōdîm, the "age of love,"[119] that Yahweh, having "passed by" the newborn Jerusalem in v 6 (*'-b-r*), again passes by (*'-b-r*) and resolves to marry her. We thus seem to be asked to imagine that this girl child had been left alone—and so at least symbolically abandoned—for twenty years or so in between. Ezekiel 16:7, by describing Jerusalem as naked at the time she comes into biological maturity, also asks us to imagine that Jerusalem has been left unclothed ever since she had been abandoned as an unswaddled foundling in v 5. Indeed, some commentators have suggested that the doubled description of Jerusalem as both "naked" (*'ērōm*) and "bare" (*'eryâ*) at the very end of v 7 is meant to emphasize the exceedingly long duration of Jerusalem's exposed state.[120] Then, as the preparations for marriage go forward in v 8, Yahweh spreads the edge or skirt of the deity's robe over Jerusalem. This act, the next phrase in v 8 implies, covers Jerusalem's nakedness, but more important, as a comparison with Ruth 3:9 suggests, Yahweh's spreading over Jerusalem the edge or skirt of God's garment indicates that the two have become formally betrothed.[121] Indeed, Yahweh signals this by saying of Jerusalem at the end of v 8, "you became mine."

Next, according to v 9, as Yahweh continues to speak, "I bathed you with water, and I rinsed your blood from upon you." But what blood is this? Perhaps the most obvious answer according to the chronology that Ezek 16:7–8 has suggested to us is that it is the blood of Jerusalem's recently begun menses.[122] That is, it seems chronologically reasonable to suggest that Jerusalem, having passed through the initial stages of female puberty in v 7 (the development of breast tissue; the appearance of pubic hair; and a significant growth spurt), is to be understood in v 8 as having begun to menstruate. Indeed, the fact that Jerusalem, according to v 8, has reached her *'ēt dōdîm*, or her "age of love," intimates strongly the onset of her menses, given the correlation we saw above regarding menarche and a young woman's readiness for marriage (and therefore for *dōdîm*, or the sexual relationship that comes with marriage).[123]

Nevertheless, it seems unthinkable that Ezekiel, a priest whose ideology is closely aligned with that of the Priestly writers, or P, and the Holiness source, or H,[124] could envision Yahweh rinsing off menstrual blood, which the P and especially H traditions unrelentingly categorize as impure.[125] Instead, just as we are pressed by the language of 16:5–8 to imagine that the foundling Jerusalem was left alone and unclothed for nigh on two decades from the time of her birth through the various stages of her pubescent development, Ezek 16:9 can be taken to imply that Jerusalem has been covered with the blood of childbirth throughout that same period of time, until she finally comes fully of age.[126] After all, the bath that is cited in 16:9 is the only bath that has been mentioned since Jerusalem was left unwashed on her natal day according to 16:4,[127] and Yahweh's twice-repeated dictum to the newborn Jerusalem in v 6, exhorting her to "in your blood, live," can be taken to parallel the twofold description of Jerusalem as both "naked" and "bare" at the end of v 7.[128] Thus, v 6's doubled exhortation can be taken to underscore the same point commentators have suggested is emphasized by the doubling in v 7: that Jerusalem has remained terribly neglected—unclothed and bloodied—from her natal day until some twenty or so years later, when she finally comes into her majority.

Under the terms of this reading, Yahweh, although acting to save the foundling Jerusalem from a sure death in Ezek 16:6, does nothing else, throughout the long years of Jerusalem's infancy, childhood, and pubescence, to resolve her indeterminate status. Rather, Yahweh might be counted among those who, in vv 4–5, are accused of failing to extend to the newborn Jerusalem acts of compassion: bathing, swaddling, salting, the cutting of the umbilical cord. But "why did Yhwh not pick up baby Jerusalem who was flailing around in her birth blood?" Carol J. Dempsey asks. "Why did Yhwh not bathe her, salt her, swaddle her, and hold her close to his cheek?"[129] Why not "take her to a home where she may be cared for?"[130] In response, we might say, to return again to the theoretical point regarding women's exaggerated liminal experiences that I have offered, that the exaggerated marginalization suffered by the outcast Jerusalem in v 5—a grotesque exacerbation, I have argued above, of the prolonged period of liminality that girl infants otherwise experienced, according to Lev 12:1–8, during the life-cycle ritual of childbirth—is exacerbated even further during the years upon years that Yahweh leaves the girl child in a liminal state.[131] Indeed, multiple marks of liminality are arguably present during these twenty or so years—isolation, nakedness, as well as life in the steppe-land and, presumably, suffering—until God undertakes rites of clothing, bathing, and also anointing (v 9) to integrate the newly matured Jerusalem into some semblance of community (even into covenant; v 8) when it serves Yahweh's purposes in securing a bride.[132]

These rites of clothing, bathing, and anointing that Yahweh performs in Ezek 16:8–9 are something, but as multiple students of trauma and abuse have suggested in their exegeses of Ezekiel 16, they are not much given the motifs of neglect and abandonment found in vv 4–6, and it is thus no wonder, given what we know about cycles of abuse, that Jerusalem fails to thrive in her marriage.¹³³ Nor is Ezekiel 16 a stand-alone text. God likewise leaves another young woman and, symbolically, all young women abandoned as they come into sexual maturity in Judg 11:29–40, as we will see in the next chapter when we turn to consider a young woman's coming of age and the life-cycle ritual that marks it.

2
Women's (and Men's) Coming of Age

Men's Coming of Age: Circumcision

The tradition that circumcisions were performed on males eight days old is found both in the Hebrew Bible and in later New Testament and extrabiblical accounts. In Gen 17:12, for example, God tells Abraham that "when eight days old, every male among you shall be circumcised," and then, in Gen 21:4, Abraham does just as God has commanded and circumcises his newborn son Isaac eight days after his birth. The same P or Priestly writers who authored these Genesis 17 and 21 accounts were also responsible for the Lev 12:1–8 text discussed in Chapter 1 and thus are responsible for the verse in Lev 12:3 that similarly states regarding a male child, "on the eighth day the flesh of his foreskin shall be circumcised."[1] Centuries later, in the apocryphal book of Jubilees, which dates from the second century BCE, circumcision of male infants on the eighth day of their lives is likewise mandated (Jub. 15:12, 14, 25–26). In addition, according to Luke 1:59 and 2:21, John the Baptist and Jesus were both circumcised eight days after they were born, and in Phil 3:5, Paul reports that he too was circumcised when he was eight days old.

Still, other (and sometimes arguably older) biblical materials associate circumcision with the institution of marriage.[2] For example, in Gen 34:13–17, Jacob's sons require the Shechemites to circumcise themselves before their sister Dinah can marry into their community. Circumcision is also associated with the maritally allusive phrase "bloody bridegroom" in Exod 4:24–26 (more on this passage presently), and in 1 Sam 18:25, King Saul demands that his prospective son-in-law David give him a marriage present of one hundred Philistine foreskins before he can wed Saul's daughter Michal (more on this passage also to follow, in Chapter 3).[3]

Elsewhere in the Near East, circumcision can likewise be linked with marriage or with a young man's sexual maturation, or both. For example, Robert K. Ritner, along with many others, has argued that in ancient Egypt, circumcision was a "puberty rite . . . connected with . . . sexual maturity."[4] Ritner also argues forcefully for circumcision as the second in a twofold

Maturity, Marriage, Motherhood, Mortality. Susan Ackerman, Oxford University Press.
© Oxford University Press 2025. DOI: 10.1093/9780197809686.003.0004

sequence of male puberty rites in Egypt. First came the "tying of the fillet" or the cutting of the childhood sidelock of hair. This "marked the entrance to adulthood for males," according to Ritner, transforming a "child" into a "youth." Subsequently, this "youth," when circumcised, became a sexually mature "man."[5] Ritner does not suggest, however, specific ages at which these fillet-tying and circumcision rituals might have been performed, and as I noted in the Prologue and discussed in more detail in my consideration of Ndembu circumcision rituals in the Introduction, social puberty—the age at which a boy is considered to have come into manhood—need not correspond to manhood as marked by biology.[6] After all, Ndembu boys who were circumcised and "made men" in the *Mukanda* ritual might be as young as seven.[7] Or—to take an example that is somewhat more kindred to biblical tradition—Jewish law in the first centuries of the Common Era dictated that a boy transitioned from being a minor and became an *'îš*, a "man" and "a legally responsible adult," at age thirteen and one day, even if the only biological markers of puberty were two hairs in the pubic region.[8]

Nevertheless, we can assume that the onset of biological puberty for males, like the initial stages of the female pubescent process that I described in Chapter 1, occurred at a later point in the ancient world than it does today. More specifically: today, "in the United States and most industrialized countries, pubertal changes usually begin ... between 9 and 14 years of age in boys,"[9] whereas Aristotle in his *History of Animals* (VII.1.581a.12–14) reports that in his day (the fourth century BCE), the onset of male puberty did not occur until a boy had reached age fourteen. According to the third-century CE Roman grammarian Censorinus, moreover, Aristotle may be too optimistic: while "puberty occurs after fourteen years in some," Censorinus writes, it is only experienced "by the seventeenth year in all youths."[10] Indeed, even though Aristotle assumes that the presence of pubic hair is one of the markers of puberty's onset at age fourteen (*History of Animals* VII.1.581a.16–17), the fourth- and fifth-century CE church father Augustine comments in his *Confessions* on his pubic hair appearing when he was sixteen years of age.[11]

As for the conclusion of the male pubescent process, ancient commentators also give varying information.[12] The sixth-century CE *Institutes of Justinian* (11.1.4) and related sources (the *Digesta* or *Pandects* I.7.40; XXXIV.1.14.1) indicate that a male was considered to have completed the full term of puberty at age eighteen, although this seems to be primarily a legal determination. According to Aristotle's more biologically based assessment, semen only became effective at age twenty-one, at which time a young man's pubescent growth spurt also ended and his initial facial hairs had developed into a full beard (*History of Animals* VII.1.582a.18, 33–34). Notably, the Ptolemaic-era Egyptian priest Ankhsheshonq, a rough contemporary of Aristotle's,[13] advised his youngest son to marry at twenty, the point at which, we might propose, the son had reached the age of full sexual maturity that Ritner takes the Egyptian ritual of circumcision to mark.[14]

Other Near Eastern evidence more explicitly associates circumcision and marriage. For example, Nicolas Wyatt has proposed that the pruning imagery that appears in lines 8–11 of the "Feast of the Goodly Gods" (*KTU* 1.23), a Late Bronze Age text from the city-state of Ugarit on the northern Levantine coast, symbolizes the circumcising of the god El "in preparation for his subsequent marriage."[15] Wyatt also follows Robert Allan's rendering of the first lines of another Ugaritic text, *KTU* 1.24, which tells of the marriage of the moon-god Yariḫ and the goddess Nikkal-Ib, as referring simultaneously to Nikkal-Ib's father Ḫarḫab as "king of circumcision" and "king of weddings."[16] William H. C. Propp has in addition catalogued evidence that pairs circumcision and marriage among pre-Islamic Arabs, and Propp likewise surveys ethnographic reports of circumcision rituals that are correlated with marriage among some twentieth-century Muslims.[17] In these accounts, from Egypt, Palestine, Turkey, the Arabian peninsula, and the North Arabian and Syrian desert, the age of circumcision can vary, but—as in Vincent Crapanzano's study of Moroccan circumcision rituals that I cited in the Prologue[18]—circumcision, if not practiced at the time of marriage, is conjoined with marital language and allusions in ways that at least "call to mind" a boy's "future marriage."[19]

Indeed, Shaye J. D. Cohen cites Crapanzano, among others, in commenting on Islamic communities where, "on the day of the circumcision, the boy, who is typically six to eight years old . . . dress[es] up as if for a *wedding* . . . is marched in procession as if he were a *bridegroom* . . . and a meal *rivaling a wedding feast* is served" (emphases mine).[20] Moreover, as both Cohen and Propp (among many others) point out, in Arabic the base form of the verb ḫātana, "to become related by marriage," and of the noun ḫatan, "male relation by marriage," is ḫatana, which means "to circumcise."[21] "In light of these traditions," Propp suggests, "it seems likely" that the cognate root in Hebrew, ḥ-t-n (reflected in lexemes such as ḥōtēn, "father-in-law"; ḥātān, which means both "son-in-law" and "bridegroom"; and ḥătunnâ, "marriage," "wedding"), "formerly connoted," as in Arabic, "both circumcision and marriage."[22] Thus the noted biblical scholar Roland de Vaux concludes: "originally, and as a general rule, circumcision seems to have been an initiation-rite before marriage."[23] Or, we might say, following Arnold van Gennep, that, originally, circumcision seems to have been a life-cycle ritual that signals a young man has reached sexual maturity and so renders him able to wed.[24]

David Flusser and Shmuel Safrai have furthermore described how, in the Bible and elsewhere in the Near East, the near death or death of a male offspring could be associated with circumcision.[25] From Near Eastern tradition comes the report of Philo of Byblos in *The Phoenician History*, of the Canaanite god El's both circumcising himself and sacrificing his only son when "war's gravest dangers gripped the land."[26] In the Bible, we read in the Passover saga of Exodus 12 that the deaths of the Israelites' firstborn sons are averted by each family's slaughtering a sacrificial lamb and then, with the exception of those who are uncircumcised (Exod 12:48), eating it together in a ritual meal. Also in Exodus, in the aforementioned Exod 4:24–26, Yahweh's stated intent—to kill Moses, or perhaps Moses's unnamed son[27]—is averted only when Zipporah, Moses's wife and the child's mother, circumcises her son and possibly her husband as well, by touching Moses's genitals [literally, his "feet"] with the circumcision flint.[28] Zipporah then addresses Moses with the maritally allusive language that I cited above: "You are surely a bridegroom of blood [or a "bloody bridegroom"] to me" (Exod 4:25).

All this might suggest that if circumcision in ancient Israel was originally a rite signaling that a young man had reached sexual maturity and thus was rendered suitable for marriage, a young man's marital fitness was also ritually affirmed by a near-death ordeal: perhaps to be understood as the circumcision itself (as, say, in the Ndembu circumcision rite of *Mukanda* that I described in the Introduction) or perhaps as a near death that had to be endured in association with circumcision. Consider in this regard the Bible's most famous account of a near-death ordeal, the Gen 22:1–19 story of the almost-sacrifice of Isaac by his father, Abraham. This story can certainly be taken to intimate that it is set at a point when Isaac had reached an age of physical and mental maturity, as Isaac is physically able to carry the wood for the sacrificial fire (Gen 22:6) and is mentally astute enough to question his father concerning deviations from normal sacrificial practice ("And Isaac spoke to Abraham . . . and said, 'Here is the fire and the wood, but where is the lamb for the burnt offering [*ōlâ*]?'"; Gen 22:7). Indeed, as Jon D. Levenson points out, the earliest "commentary" on Gen 22:1–19, the second-century BCE book of Jubilees, identifies Isaac as being fifteen years of age at the time of his near sacrifice (Jub. 17:15–16).²⁹ More notably for our purposes, Isaac's immediately prior appearance in Genesis, in Gen 21:1–7, includes an account of his being circumcised.

To be sure, this circumcision is said to have been performed when Isaac was only eight days old, and it is also the case that in the biblical text as it has come down to us, the stories of Hagar's expulsion from Abraham's home (Gen 21:8–21) and of Abraham's and Abimelech's covenant at Beersheba (Gen 21:22–34) intervene between the accounts of Isaac's circumcision and his near death. Nevertheless, the juxtaposition of texts describing Isaac's circumcision and near death within the narrative arc of Isaac's life story hints at a memory or tradition in which circumcision and near death were more closely associated. More important still: Isaac's next appearance in the Genesis narrative after the Genesis 22 sacrifice is averted can be understood to suggest that in Gen 22:1–19, he has successfully negotiated a near-death ordeal that has confirmed his suitability for marriage. Thus, in Gen 24:1–9, Abraham initiates endeavors to secure a bride for his son.

Granted, this juxtaposition of near death and marriage is again obscured in the Genesis narrative as it has come down to us, as the chronology proposed by the biblical text (or, more specifically, by the Bible's Priestly authors) indicates that Sarah was one hundred and twenty-seven years old (Gen 23:1), and so Isaac was thirty-seven at some point after Genesis 22's aborted sacrifice. Yet Isaac was forty when he married (Gen 25:20). This P chronology thus presumes at least a three-year gap in time (and seemingly longer) between Isaac's near-death ordeal and his marriage, much as the chronology recorded in Genesis 21 and 22 seems to presume a significant time gap between Isaac's circumcision as an infant and his near-death ordeal. Nevertheless, the juxtaposition of circumcision, near death, and marriage within the narrative arc of Isaac's life story again hints at a closer association. Once more, that is, we might say, following van Gennep, that circumcision in ancient Israel, coupled with (or perhaps itself understood as) a near-death ordeal, seems to have been a life-cycle ritual signaling that a young man had reached sexual maturity and so was rendered suitable for marriage.³⁰

We might also note, following now Victor Turner, the many liminal features we can locate in the Gen 22:1–19 account of Isaac's near death. The story, for example, takes place in a seemingly wilderness location, the otherwise unknown and faraway land of Moriah (Gen 22:2–4),³¹ and, as we saw in Chapter 1, this sort of wilderness setting is a paradigmatically liminal space within biblical tradition.³² Those who enter into or dwell within the biblical wilderness are thus often to be identified as liminal beings. Examples include, as I discussed in Chapter 1, the foundling Jerusalem as she lay abandoned, according to Ezek 16:5–8, in the wilderness-like śādeh from the day of her birth until she reached sexual maturity, and also the Israelites as they wandered for forty years in the wilderness during their exodus sojourn in the Sinai. There, like the foundling Jerusalem and in accord with Turner's classic description of liminal beings, these Israelites are "betwixt and between":³³ "betwixt and between" their former abode in Egypt and the land of Canaan that they are to possess, and likewise "betwixt and between" the status of slaves that defined their existence in Egypt and their ability to live constituted as their own social polity once they settle in Canaan. Somewhat similarly in Isaac's case, according to the interpretation of Gen 22:1–19 that I am pursuing here, he comes to the wilderness of Moriah "betwixt and between" his old status as a youth in his father's house and the new stage in life toward which he is moving: marriage. Note, moreover, that in the process of this transition, Abraham and Isaac come to a *mountain* in the land of Moriah (Gen 22:2), just as do the Israelites in their Sinai wanderings—and not coincidentally so, for in biblical tradition, mountains are one of the "main types of liminal spaces where people are transformed."³⁴

Other features of liminality intimated in the Gen 22:1–19 story include the motifs of traveling and provisional lodging versus sedentary life (Moriah is said in Gen 22:4 to have been a three-day journey from Abraham's home in Beersheba), and isolation and seclusion versus life in the heart of society (Abraham and Isaac are said to travel only with two attendants from Abraham's household, and even those are left behind in 22:5 when Abraham and Isaac draw near to the site of the proposed sacrifice).³⁵ Still another experience typically endured by liminal beings, as I noted in the Introduction, is that they can be required to submit to ordeals, and even, in Turner's words, "ordeals and tests . . . that amounted to tortures,"³⁶ which is surely an apt description of Isaac's experience as he lies bound atop a wooden pyre while his father approaches, knife in hand (Gen 22:9–10). Note also that such ordeals, as we again saw in the Introduction, are usually inflicted upon the subject of a life-cycle ritual by a community's elders, just as Isaac's father Abraham proposes to inflict upon his son a sacrificial ordeal in response to a command from the ultimate elder of biblical tradition, who is God.³⁷

Women's Coming of Age: The Story of Jephthah's Daughter

A life-cycle ritual for young women analogous to the young men's ritual about which the Isaac story hints may be alluded to in the Judg 11:29–40 story of Jephthah's daughter. Within biblical tradition, this narrative is set in "the days of the judges" (2 Kgs 23:22), when there was "no king in Israel" (Judg 17:6; 18:1; 19:1; 21:25). Rather, leadership was less formally determined, to the extent that, at least according to the claims of the text, it was at points charismatically delegated by "the spirit of Yahweh" coming upon a chosen individual. Often, this was so that he (in the text of Judges, it is always a "he" upon whom the spirit of Yahweh comes) might act militarily on the people's behalf to deliver them from enemy oppression. Certainly, this is the case for Jephthah, who is first introduced to us in Judg 11:1 as a member of the tribe of Gilead and a mighty warrior (and also, interestingly enough, as the son of a prostitute; *'iššâ zônâ*). Because of his prowess as a warrior, Jephthah (after some difficulties, having to do with his tenuous position in his father's house due to his mother's marginal social status) becomes the military leader of the Gileadites when they are attacked by the neighboring peoples of Ammon. Jephthah initially seeks peace with the Ammonites, but once his attempts at diplomacy fail, "the spirit of Yahweh came upon Jephthah" (Judg 11:29), and he prepared to wage war.

It is at this point that Jephthah makes a vow that, as Phyllis Trible has famously noted, is at best superfluous and in fact implies a lack of faith:[38] he vows that if he is successful in battle, he will sacrifice to the deity as a burnt offering (*'ōlâ*) whomever or whatever (the Hebrew *'ăšer* is ambiguous) comes out of his house to meet him when he returns home triumphant (Judg 11:30–31). The vow is superfluous and an act of unfaithfulness, according to Trible, because Jephthah has already been possessed by the spirit of Yahweh and as such has become assured of victory. Its compromised nature becomes even more obvious once its consequences become clear. While anyone hearing the Jephthah story would want to imagine that it will be some animal from his flocks that Jephthah will first encounter upon his homecoming, it turns out, in v 34 of the account, that when Jephthah returns victorious, it is not some sheep or goat that comes forth to meet him, but his only child, a daughter.[39] Jephthah is deeply distressed: the first word out of his mouth is a cry of woe, *'ăhāh* ("Alas!"; Judg 11:35), and he also engages in a typical Israelite mourning ritual, tearing his clothes.[40] Still, both he (in v 35) and his daughter (in v 36) realize that his vow, like almost all vows in the Bible, is irrevocable (for exceptions, see only Num 30:4–16 [30:3–15 in most English translations]), and thus the daughter must be sacrificed as Jephthah has promised.

It is within the context of this tragic realization that the story introduces information relevant for our current inquiry. The daughter, although she acknowledges the necessity of honoring her father's vow, asks for a short reprieve before the sacrifice takes place: two months to "wander" in the mountains with her female companions (*rēʿôtāy*, a feminine plural form),[41] "so that I might bewail *ʿal-bĕtûlay*," or, as it is usually translated "so that I might bewail my virginity" (better, as we will see momentarily, "so that I might bewail my coming into sexual maturity" or "so that I might bewail the onset of my menses"; Judg 11:37). This request Jephthah grants, the two-month period of bewailing is undertaken, and upon her return, her father "enacted against her his vow that he had vowed" (Judg 11:39). Then, after the daughter is killed, we are told that a custom arose in Israel that every year, for four days, the daughters of Israel would "go" (*h-l-k*)—where to is not necessarily clear—to *tannôt* Jephthah's daughter (Judg 11:39–40).[42]

In ancient translations of the Bible, as well as many modern versions, this verbal infinitive form *tannôt* is rendered as "to lament," which suggests that the young women of 11:39–40 gather annually to mourn Jephthah's daughter's tragic and untimely death. But *tannôt* is better translated as "to rehearse" or "recount."[43] Moreover, while it might seem that the daughters of Israel would gather every year to rehearse or recount the story of Jephthah's daughter,[44] Peggy L. Day has persuasively argued that the rehearsal in question is better described as a "repetition of the actions that tradition ascribed to her [the daughter]."[45] Which is to say, according to Day's interpretation: the daughters of Israel do not join together annually to retell the story of Jephthah's daughter's tragic death, but rather to reprise the original bewailing that the daughter undertook in 11:37–38 to mark "her [Jephthah's daughter's] transition to physical maturity." This annual reprise of the daughter's original mourning over her "transition to physical maturity" in fact functions, according to Day as well as other scholars, as "a women's life-cycle ritual" for the daughters of Israel, who, like Jephthah's daughter, go forth at the time of their own "transition to physical maturity" so that they, again like the daughter, can "bewail" the onset of their menses and the symbolic death of the childhood stage of life they leave behind.[46] In other words, Day suggests that Jephthah's daughter's story serves as an aetiological legend: a narrative, that is, that "project[s] . . . contemporary practices backwards in time to their imagined point of origin," thereby describing the putative foundation of and rationale for those practices.[47] Under the terms of this aetiological analysis, Jephthah's daughter's past actions serve as a model for a ritual of weeping and lamentation that all young Israelite women are compelled to enact to mark their movement into physical maturity and thus, according to the Israelite life-cycle calendar (see my discussion of Ezek 16:7–8 in Chapter 1), the age of marriageability.

To prove this hypothesis, Day first reviews evidence demonstrating that the usual translation of "my virginity" for Hebrew *bĕtûlay* in Judg 11:37 is mistaken, Nor does the related word *bĕtûlâ* generally mean "virgin."[48] This is because, while a woman could presumably be a virgin throughout her lifetime (although this would be practically unheard of in the highly maritally oriented culture of ancient Israel),[49] the term *bĕtûlâ* most typically refers only to a young woman of a particular age: one who has entered the stage during pubescence when she has begun to menstruate and so is potentially fertile (or is at least moving toward reproductive fertility),[50] but who has not yet borne a child. Day then goes on to suggest that the preposition *'al* that precedes the term *bĕtûlay* in Judg 11:37 does not imply that Jephthah's daughter laments *because of* the state of *bĕtûlay*, as commentators have more typically interpreted (that is, she grieves because she will die, according to the traditional translation of *bĕtûlay*, before—as in Judg 11:39—"ever knowing a man"). Rather, in Day's reading, the daughter laments *upon the occasion of entry* into the state of *bĕtûlay*, or "my physical maturity."

As Day would have it, moreover, it is this same entering into their own state of *bĕtûlîm*, or "physical maturity" (*bĕtûlîm* is the same word as *bĕtûlay*, but without the possessive suffix meaning "my"), that Jephthah's daughter's companions bewail when they accompany her on her two-month retreat into the mountains. More important, it is this entering into the state of *bĕtûlîm*, or "physical maturity," that the "daughters of Israel" who go forth for four days annually mourn as well.[51] Such mourning, as Day points out, is not uncommon in life-cycle rituals as one marks the loss of one stage of life while moving into another.[52] "What I would reconstruct," Day concludes, "is an annual ceremony at which young women were socially recognized as having left childhood behind and entered *bĕtûlîm*, physical maturity. This ceremony included a ritual lament which, in the vernacular of rites of passage, acknowledged the 'death' of one stage in life in preparation for entry into a new stage."[53]

Day in addition suggests that while the participants in this annual ceremony "most likely" would have understood the ritual "to be the repetition/commemoration of a first-time event," we, reading "from a scholarly point of view," should interpret the story of Jephthah's daughter as an aetiology (as noted above) and so "speak of Jephthah's daughter as a culture heroine."[54] This observation might in turn prompt us to return to Bruce Lincoln's work on young women's initiation rituals that I considered in the Introduction, in which he notes, in addition to the points I have previously discussed, that "rituals involving identification with a mythic heroine, whether goddess, culture heroine, primordial ancestress, or some other prototypical figure" are a feature in three of the five initiation ceremonies that he surveyed:[55] the Navajo ritual of the Kinaaldá; the Festa das Moças Novas, or the "Festival of the New Maiden," as practiced among the Tukuna of the northwest Amazon; and the Greek initiation rite that Lincoln believes "reenacted details of the Demeter-Persephone mythos."[56]

Indeed, Day appeals to Lincoln's study of the myth of Demeter and Persephone in her analysis, along with other Greek materials, in order to demonstrate the existence of an eastern Mediterranean cultural tradition that incorporates, like Jephthah's daughter's story, motifs both of sexual maturation and of a young maiden's near or actual death. Regarding Persephone's sexual maturity, for example, we can note that the very reason that the god Hades seizes Persephone while she is in a meadow, dancing and picking flowers, is that he intends to have sexual intercourse with her, now that she is, in the words of the late seventh-/early sixth-century BCE *Homeric Hymn to Demeter*, a "ripened" and "nubile" young woman.[57] Or, we could as easily say, Hades's goal is sexual intercourse with a maiden called Kore, an epithet by which Persephone is otherwise known. Yet Kore is also a term that, not insignificantly for our purposes, means more or less the same thing as does Hebrew *bĕtûlâ*: per Lincoln's definition, "a maiden who has reached physical maturity and is thus of marriageable age."[58] Persephone/Kore, that is, is to be understood just as is Jephthah's daughter: as a pubescent who has come into sexual maturity and is on the threshold of her married life.

Upon abducting Persephone/Kore, moreover, Hades takes her to his underworld domain, or the realm of death, and while this is often taken as a fertility motif in an interpretation of the story that focuses on seasonal allegory ("a mythopoeic description of winter, the time when crops are underground"),[59] both Day and Lincoln argue that Persephone/Kore's time in the underworld should be understood as a description of the young woman's "figurative death."[60] Thus, we can associate the underworld setting in the Persephone/Kore story with the imagery of death that, as noted in the Introduction, often characterizes the liminal phase of a rite of passage. Which is to say: as Persephone/Kore comes into physical maturity, she—like Jephthah's daughter, the daughter's companions, and the daughters of Israel who follow in the footsteps of these founder figures—"dies" to her old prepubescent identity during a liminal period, in order to be reborn into a new adult stage in life. Indeed, in the late seventh-/early sixth-century BCE *Homeric Hymn to Demeter* that I quoted above, which Lincoln describes as the "oldest, most complete, and most important version of the Persephone myth,"[61] the name Kore is used exclusively of its young woman subject up until the time Zeus decrees that she is to return temporarily to earth, to be reunited with her mother. At that point, she starts to be called Persephone. As Lincoln writes, "The girl's proper name is bestowed on her only after she has been initiated, become an adult, lost her maiden status," and he then goes on to say: "Such a change of name is a regular feature in the initiatory rites of innumerable peoples as a mark of the initiand's total transformation."[62]

To be sure, there is no analogous renaming of Jephthah's daughter, who remains anonymous throughout her story. Still, other features typical of the liminal phase of a rite of passage are present in Judg 11:29–40. Mieke Bal has noted, for example, that Jephthah's daughter specifically asks to go to the *mountains* (*hehārîm*) with her female companions to undertake her lamentation rite, and she argues that these "mountains" in Judg 11:37 seem to be portrayed as a wilderness locale in the conceit of the text (in contrast to the settlement of Gileadite Mizpah where Jephthah's home was located).[63] That is, as Jephthah's daughter leaves behind her old identity and stage in life, she simultaneously leaves home to go a paradigmatically liminal space—just as did Isaac in his Genesis 22 journey to a wilderness mountain.[64]

By describing the daughter as "wandering" the mountains with her companions (reading, with many commentators, the verb *rād*, "to wander," in v 37, for the Masoretic text *yārad*, "to go down"),[65] the Jephthah's daughter story further invites us to imagine that, like Isaac and other liminal beings, the daughter and her companions travel and make use of provisional lodging.[66] The act of wandering also implies a quality of aimlessness reminiscent of the "betwixt and between" ambiguity that characterizes the liminal phase of a rite of passage. I have already suggested, for example, that the Israelites' exodus journey from Egypt to Canaan that had them *wandering* for forty years in, as previously noted, the Sinai *wilderness* marks a liminal phase in a rite of passage that moved the Israelite community from its old status of slavery to its new identity as a politically and religiously united confederation.[67] Similarly, in the Mesopotamian Epic of Gilgamesh, the text stresses repeatedly how the arguably liminal hero Gilgamesh "wanders" (*rapādu*) the steppe after his beloved companion Enkidu dies and he separates himself from his fiefdom of Uruk.[68] His goal is to gain immortality and so protect himself from Enkidu's fate. Needless to say, this quest is a futile one. Thus, if Gilgamesh is successfully to move beyond his liminal phase of wilderness wandering (at least as I would interpret),[69] he must abandon his unrealistic dreams of eternal life to accept instead the fact of his own eventual death. More important, he must find some peace in this apprehension.

Notably for our purposes, in the Old Babylonian version of the Gilgamesh Epic (the Epic's later, Standard version is different), at least again as I would interpret, Gilgamesh is urged to find this measure of peace in human sociability as manifest in marriage and family. Thus, in one of the Old Babylonian text's most famous passages, the alewife Siduri, whom Gilgamesh encounters when his wanderings bring him to the very ends of the earth, says to him:[70]

> The life [that is, immortality] you seek, you shall not find . . .
> [Instead] look to the little one who holds your hand,
> May your spouse rejoice continuously in your lap.

Marriage and family life, however, are not aspects of human existence that seem previously to have been part of Gilgamesh's experience.[71] Rather, Gilgamesh, according to the Epic, has previously experienced sexual relations only outside of marriage, and he in fact shuns an offer of marriage that the goddess Ishtar extends to him just prior to Enkidu's death.[72] Therefore, when the alewife tells Gilgamesh that he should leave off wandering the steppe in order to reengage with his society (or, in the language of Arnold van Gennep, he should reintegrate or reincorporate with his community), she implies that he should reengage (or be reintegrated or reincorporated) in a way that marks the changes the transitional phase within a rite of passage should engender. He should, that is, reenter his community as one who now embraces rather than rejects marriage and family as two of the primary institutions of his society.

Unfortunately, the Old Babylonian text of the Gilgamesh Epic breaks off shortly after Siduri's speech, and unless more fragments are some day found, we will never know whether the Old Babylonian Gilgamesh was envisioned within Mesopotamian tradition as returning to Uruk and marrying and so completing his narrative movement through van Gennep's rites-of-passage model. And, of course, Jephthah's daughter never achieves the aggregation or incorporation into the married stage of her life that her coming into physical maturity should entail, as she is sacrificed as her father had vowed upon her return from her two-month wilderness wanderings, having never "known a man" (Judg 11:39). Still, the images of wilderness, wandering, and also trials (in the form of a sacrificial ordeal) seem vivid enough within Jephthah's daughter's story that we can follow Day in arguing that the Judg 11:29–40 account must have been for its ancient Israelite audience a meaningful representation of a life-cycle ritual for young women that describes their transition into physical maturity and becoming of marriageable age. We can, moreover, follow Bal in suggesting that the similarities between the imagery of Gen 22:1–19 and Judg 11:29–40—in particular, the imagery of wilderness mountains, of travel and provisional lodging, and of a sacrificial trial (with the ritual subject in both cases described as an *ʿōlâ*, or "burnt offering"; Gen 22:2 and Judg 11:31)—may indicate that this young women's ritual paralleled a ritual that rendered young men suitable for marriage.

Yet despite the similarities between the imagery of Gen 22:1–19 and Judg 11:29–40—especially their common image of a sacrificial trial—there is an obvious difference: Jephthah's daughter is actually killed by her father (Judg 11:39), whereas Isaac is spared when a divine messenger intervenes and stays Abraham's hand (Gen 22:11–12). As in Chapter 1, I would explain by suggesting that within women's life-cycle rituals, the liminal experience is somehow intensified or exacerbated. In Chapter 1, I argued that in the case of life-cycle rituals that concerned a newborn child, this intensification manifested itself in terms of *time*. Thus, in Lev 12:1–8, the postpartum period of liminality was doubled if a newborn infant was a girl as opposed to a boy, and in Ezek 16:4–9, the foundling Jerusalem's liminal stage is not resolved until her late teens or age twenty, when Yahweh resolves to marry her once she reaches sexual maturity. At that point, the deity finally provides the postpartum bath and clothing that Jerusalem had been denied at birth and throughout her childhood. There is some intimation of this intensified temporal motif in the story of Jephthah's daughter as well, in that Isaac and Abraham ascend Mount Moriah on the *third* day of their journey from Abraham's home (Gen 22:4). This suggests more generally that the story models a *three*-day life-cycle ritual for young Israelite men, whereas we are told explicitly that young Israelite women who, I have suggested, engage in a life-cycle ritual modeled after Jephthah's daughter's story do so for *four* days (Judg 11:40).[73]

More so, however, the intensification of liminality characteristic of women's rites of passage manifests itself in Jephthah's daughter's story in terms of *degree*, so that the kind of trial characteristic of the liminal experience is more dangerous and fraught for a woman subject than for a male. Thus, Jephthah's daughter dies as a result of her sacrificial ordeal, while Isaac does not. Of course, this is not to say that the actual life-cycle rituals that I (following Day and Bal) have suggested that these two aetiological legends model ended in the deaths of young women and the salvation of young men; that would be patently ridiculous. Rather, I propose that the excessiveness of liminal markers that I have argued we should look for in women's life-cycle rituals plays itself out narratively in the story of Jephthah's daughter's death. While the "daughters of Israel" who follow in her footsteps every year certainly are not meant to endure Jephthah's daughter's actual fate, their liminal ordeal is intensified by reliving a story where the premonition of death comes significantly nearer than does death in the story that models the ritual marking their male counterparts' readiness for marriage.

Jephthah's daughter's death comes, moreover, at the hands of the preeminent male authority in her life—her father. Thereby, the autonomy to which Jephthah's daughter and the daughters of Israel who follow in her footsteps might be said to claim as part of a young women's coming-of-age ritual (remember in this regard the daughter's request for a two-month reprieve in order that she might wander the mountains with her female companions) is ceded to male superiors. To be sure, one could argue that in the Isaac story, autonomy is likewise ceded to male superiors—Abraham and, ultimately, God—but the fact of the matter is that the sex of the initiatory agent vis-à-vis the sex of the initiand has, as Lincoln writes, "serious implications." If a male agent is positioned as the ritual supervisor of a woman's initiation (as is presumed in Jephthah's daughter's story and so in the female life-cycle rituals for which this story is the model), then "female initiation must be seen as an act imposed on women from the outside, an indoctrination, a subjugation, an assault," whereby "the initiands must be understood as ... passive objects who are remade according to the tastes and desires of people quite different from themselves." Conversely, when the initiator and the initiand are of the same sex, the ritual becomes "a rite of solidarity ... an act of unity, of resistance, of commiseration."[74]

Indeed, one is struck here by the fact that while both the Abraham and Isaac story and the story of Jephthah's daughter stress that each tale's sacrificial victim is the father's "only" (*yāḥîd*, *yĕḥîdâ*) child (Gen 22:2, 12, 16; Judg 11:34), the Abraham and Isaac story, in Gen 22:2, pairs the notice of "only" with an emphasis on Abraham's love for his son, whereas Jephthah never commiserates with his daughter.[75] "If words can kill" (as do the words of Jephthah's vow), J. Cheryl Exum observes, "they can also heal," but Jephthah says nothing to heal (or even comfort) his daughter.[76] Even when he first realizes the consequences of his vow and cries out in distress (*'ăhāh*), his concern seems to be about his own welfare, as can be seen in the accusing and even antagonistic remarks he makes to the girl immediately thereafter (Judg 11:35): "*you* have brought me to my knees," he says, and "*you* have caused me trouble" (emphases mine).[77] Contrast Abraham and Isaac, who, as they approach the site designated by God for the sacrifice in the land of Moriah, "walk together" (Gen 22:6, 8) or even, as Jon D. Levenson provocatively translates, "as one—the father and son undivided."[78]

Moreover, "you" and "daughter" are the only terms used to describe the otherwise anonymous *bĕtûlâ* of Judg 11:29–40, whereas Isaac is called by name five times in Gen 22:1–19—and typically in contexts that concern his relationship with his father. Thereby, the narrative stresses the father's and son's solidarity in terms of genealogy and likewise their joint solidarity with the "God of Abraham, the God of Isaac, and the God of Jacob." Even more telling, of course, is how the male authorities in Gen 22:1–19—Abraham and the preeminent male authority, God—ultimately act in accord with the solidarity fostered by their identification with the story's male initiate in order to spare Isaac, whereas Jephthah slaughters his own daughter as he had vowed to do, while God—to whom, of course, Jephthah's vow was directed—does nothing to intervene. For Jephthah's daughter, to quote again Exum, "there is no word from the deity," "no ram in the thicket."[79] Rather, God, despite beginning the Judg 11:29–40 episode that concerns the daughter by engaging decisively to ensure Jephthah's well-being (sending the divine spirit upon Jephthah in order to enable his success in battle), disappears from the story immediately thereafter, abandoning the daughter to her fate and thereby condoning, at least implicitly, Jephthah's sacrificial act.[80]

Yet again, then, we see how women's experience of liminality during female life-cycle rituals is exacerbated, as Isaac is reintegrated after his near-death ordeal into a harmonious relationship with his father and his God, whereas Jephthah's daughter—and, by extension, the "daughters of

Israel" who come after her—find themselves alienated both in the religious realm and in the domain of their natal families as they come into the age of marriageability. Indeed, Esther Fuchs titled her 1989 article on Judg 11:29–40 "Marginalization, Ambiguity, Silencing: The Story of Jephthah's Daughter," and while Fuchs's overall focus was different from mine, her title in many respects captures precisely the point I have been seeking to prove. This point is that excess liminal symbols of marginalization, ambiguity, and silencing—silencing even to the point of a symbolic death—arguably accrue in the life-cycle ritual that marks the readiness for marriage of Israelite young women as opposed to the rituals that mark the preparation for marriage for ancient Israel's young men.

PART II
MARRIAGE

3
Israelite Betrothal Rituals

In many modern societies, especially those within the Euro-American cultural orbit, the typical means for finding a marital partner might be described by the cliché "boy meets girl" or increasingly, in more contemporary contexts, "girl meets boy" (assuming here a paradigm of heterosexual marriage, which was normative in ancient Israel). Then, as this process plays itself out, "boy" and "girl" begin to date (or, in somewhat more old-fashioned terms, to court), and if all goes well, they may decide to marry. Sometimes, especially in somewhat more old-fashioned settings, the couple's parents might be involved in this decision; one still occasionally hears, for example, of the groom-to-be asking the prospective bride's father for permission to propose marriage to his daughter. More commonly, though, the couple's families get involved in the marital arrangements only after the future bride and groom are affianced and there is a wedding to be planned (and its bills to be paid!).

In ancient Israelite tradition, parts of this pattern, especially the motif of "boy meets girl," are not wholly unknown. In Gen 34:2–4, the Hivite Shechem sees Dinah, the daughter of Jacob and Leah, and, after acting sexually upon his desires, he wishes to marry her.[1] Similarly, in Judg 14:1–2, Samson, having "gone down" to the town of Timnah, sees a Philistine woman there whom he wants to marry. Somewhat kindred are stories where a man happens upon a woman who, it turns out, he will eventually marry, even though this intention is not immediately expressed. After Moses flees from Egypt to Midian, for example, he comes upon his eventual wife Zipporah and her six sisters at a well (a conventional place for meeting prospective wives in biblical narrative; see Gen 24:10–27 and Gen 29:1–12).[2] Subsequently, Moses is invited to lodge with Zipporah's family, and he and Zipporah are wed (Exod 2:15–21). The Bible also contains at least two narratives that speak to a scenario of "girl meets boy": in 1 Sam 18:20, King Saul's daughter Michal comes to love David after he has become resident in her father's court, and in the book of Ruth, Ruth begins to glean in the fields of a Bethlehemite named Boaz, and then,

Maturity, Marriage, Motherhood, Mortality. Susan Ackerman, Oxford University Press.
© Oxford University Press 2025. DOI: 10.1093/9780197809686.003.0005

after he responds kindly to her, she visits him in the night and prompts his interest in marrying her.

Yet even in these cases, where one or the other of a couple identifies the spouse-to-be, the biblical record indicates that the prospective groom's and bride's families soon become integrally involved in the marital arrangements—especially the parents of the prospective groom and the father, brothers, and/or other close male relatives of the prospective bride. In the story of Shechem and Dinah, for example, Shechem, after seeing Dinah and acting sexually upon his desires, goes to his father Hamor and asks that Hamor secure Dinah for him as a wife (literally, "take" her as a wife [*lāqaḥ*]; more on this idiom below). Hamor in turn goes to Dinah's father Jacob, and also to Jacob's twelve sons who are gathered with their father, to make this request (Gen 34:4, 8–12). Likewise Samson, having come to yearn for the woman he saw in Timnah, goes to his parents to ask that they get her for him as his wife (again, literally "take" her [*lāqaḥ*]; Judg 14:2). His parents initially demur, because the woman is Philistine, not Israelite, but eventually we are told that both Samson's father and mother (according to Judg 14:5) or his father alone (according to Judg 14:10) went to Timnah, presumably to negotiate a marriage agreement with the prospective bride's father. To be sure, the Timnite woman's father is not specifically mentioned at this juncture in the story, but he does subsequently appear in Judg 15:1–2 as the authority who oversees his daughter's marital affairs.

In the Moses story, while it is impossible for his family to be involved in his marital negotiations (since Moses has been separated from his birth parents since he was weaned and since he is a fugitive from the Egyptian pharaoh who heads his foster family), Zipporah's father Reuel (also called Jethro) plays exactly the role we would expect of a male in a bride-to-be's family, by "giving" his daughter to Moses in marriage in Exod 2:21 (the verb used is *nātan*; again, more on this idiom below).[3] Saul likewise takes responsibility for negotiating the conditions of his daughter Michal's marriage to David once Michal's interest in David becomes known to him (1 Sam 18:20–25), and even in the Ruth story, although Ruth, who is living in a foreign land after her husband has died, is bereft of male relatives, a surrogate for these men—her deceased husband's mother, Naomi—helps arrange the nuptials. Indeed, it is Naomi who, after Ruth has met Boaz in the fields, sends her daughter-in-law to engage in the nighttime liaison that culminates in her being wed (Ruth 3:1–4).

Other biblical accounts speak even more strongly of family members as the engineers of a prospective bride and groom's marriage. For example, Isaac, as urged by his wife Rebekah (Gen 27:46), instructs his younger son Jacob to go to the house of Rebekah's brother Laban in Paddan-aram and take one of Laban's daughters as a wife (Gen 28:1–5), in much the same way that, a generation previous, Abraham had secured Rebekah as a wife for Isaac (Gen 24:1–67) and Hagar had secured a wife for Isaac's half-brother Ishmael (Gen 21:21). Indeed, Abraham so takes on the responsibility for arranging Isaac's marriage to Rebekah that Isaac does not even go to Rebekah's homestead in the land of Aram-naharaim (also called Paddan-aram; Gen 24:10; 25:20) to identify or get to know his prospective bride. Instead, a servant is sent from Abraham's Canaanite abode to bring a wife home for Isaac (Gen 24:1–9). Moreover, although Rebekah's mother and, more importantly, Rebekah are consulted about the proposed marital arrangements, even to the extent that Rebekah is asked if she consents to go to Canaan to be wed to Isaac (Gen 24:57–58; yet again, more on this below), it is still Rebekah's father Bethuel and her brother Laban with whom Abraham's servant makes the principal dispositions that secure Rebekah as Isaac's betrothed (Gen 24:34–51).

In Gen 29:15–30, Laban similarly assumes responsibility for negotiating the key aspects of his two daughters' marriages to Jacob, so much so that he chooses the order in which his daughters are to wed and gives priority to the elder, Leah, despite Jacob's preference for the younger, Rachel. We are perhaps likewise to envision that Moses's father-in-law chose which of his seven daughters was to become Moses's bride (Exod 2:21).[4] Note too how King Saul, prior to arranging David's marriage to Michal, sought to give his older daughter Merab to David as what we might think of, quite literally, as a "trophy wife." That is, Saul promised that whoever defeated the great Philistine warrior Goliath would be given Merab as a wife (1 Sam 17:25). This same tradition of a father offering his daughter as a battlefield "trophy" is found in Josh 15:13–19 (paralleled almost exactly in Judg 1:11–15), in which, as the Israelites attempt to claim territory in the southern half of Canaan, the Judahite chieftain Caleb offers to wed his daughter Achsah to whomever takes the town of Kiriath-sepher.

To be sure, there are some exceptions to this pattern of familial superintendence. In Gen 11:29, Abraham (at this point in the text he is called Abram) and his brother Nahor are said to take wives without any indication that their father Terah was involved. Also later in Abraham's life, after his first wife Sarah had died and after Hagar, named in Gen 16:3 as his second wife, had been expelled from his household, he takes another wife, Keturah (Gen 25:1). While we could not expect Abraham's parents to be involved in his marriage at this point (as Terah and presumably Abraham's mother were long since dead; Gen 11:32), the text makes no mention of Keturah's family's involvement either. Jacob's brother Esau is in addition said to take wives on his own, even though his parents Isaac and Rebekah are still alive and much to their distress (Gen 26:35; 27:46): Judith, the daughter of Beeri the Hittite, and Basemath, the daughter of another Hittite, Elon (Gen 26:34; see also Gen 36:2, where it seems that these same wives are mentioned, although with somewhat different names). Eventually, Esau also takes a wife who is a close relative and thus presumably more to Isaac and Rebekah's liking: Mahalath, the daughter of Abraham's son Ishmael (Gen 28:9). Yet he still seems to act independently of his parents in making this marriage. Elsewhere in Genesis, Jacob's son Judah, although he takes on the responsibility we would expect for arranging his sons' nuptial affairs (Gen 38:6, 8, 11, 14, 26), seems to act independently in the matter of his own marital arrangements (Gen 38:2).

Of additional note is the story of the five daughters of Zelophehad, for, as their future marriages are being contemplated, Moses proclaims, "Let them marry as seems best to them."[5] It turns out, however, that there are some limitations, as Moses goes on to decree, on behalf of God, that the daughters must marry into one of the clans that comprise their father's tribe (Num 36:6). I will have more to say about this constraint in Chapter 4; for now, the crucial point is that Moses has only gotten involved in the discussion of these daughters' marital affairs because their father had died and they have no brothers (Num 27:3). That is, they have no father or other male authority to make marriage decisions on their behalf, and so extraordinary arrangements must be put into place.

A somewhat similar situation seems to pertain in the stories of two of David's marriages: first, his marriage to Abigail, which David's servants, acting on David's orders, arrange with her directly (1 Sam 25:40), and, second, his marriage to Bathsheba, which occurs when David "sent" (šālaḥ) and brought Bathsheba to his house (2 Sam 11:27). In both of these cases, no parent or other relative of either the prospective groom or prospective bride is involved. Yet it is probably significant that in each tale, the woman in question had a previous husband who has died. Neither woman, moreover, is reported to have borne a son to her deceased husband. Both are thus without any male figure who would otherwise have authority over her regarding marital and other matters: neither the father and brothers of their natal households, which they have left behind, nor men within their marital homes (or, seemingly, male in-laws from their extended marital families).[6] According to the Samuel narratives, David also had long since left his family home and therefore, perhaps his parents' jurisdiction. Biblical tradition intimates, moreover, that David's father Jesse had died prior to his son's marriages to Abigail and Bathsheba: after all, Jesse is said already in 1 Sam 17:12 to be elderly; David's brother seems to act as the family's paterfamilias in 1 Sam 20:29;[7] and the last we hear of Jesse is in 1 Sam 22:3–4. Furthermore, it may not hurt that David is depicted as the head of a local militia on the occasion of his marriage to Abigail, and when he marries Bathsheba, he holds a position that is probably best described as small-scale chieftain or petty king.[8] David may thus be envisioned at the time of these marriages as a figure powerful enough to exercise his own will regarding marital matters rather than having to be bound by his parents' dictates (see further 2 Sam 5:13; 1 Chr 14:3). Elsewhere in the Bible, kings are similarly described as arranging their own marriages (1 Kgs 3:1; 16:31; 2 Chr 11:18, 21; 13:21).

The Nature of Israelite Marriage

The reason a prospective groom's parents, along with the father, brothers, and/or other close male relatives of the prospective bride, were so integrally involved in negotiating their children's marital arrangements—the various exceptions I have listed just above notwithstanding—is that marriage in Israelite tradition was not primarily an institution grounded in two individuals' interest in or attraction to one another. Or, as Joseph Blenkinsopp puts it, "marriage in Israel of the biblical period was not, for the vast majority, a matter of individual decision and choice."[9] In part, reflected here is the fact that in the ancient world, individuals did not command the same position of priority they occupy in many modern societies, especially, again, modern societies within the Euro-American cultural orbit. Rather, as Karel van der Toorn writes, "in the ancient world . . . individuals were first and foremost members of *groups*" (emphasis mine).[10] Marriage, moreover, "was a commitment underwritten by two [of these] groups to make manifest the mutual obligation that each group acknowledged toward the other."[11] Marriage, in other words, was a matter whose disposition extended far beyond the prospective bride and groom to affect entire families and households. This was especially the case for women. Again, we can quote Blenkinsopp: "The choice of a partner for an unmarried woman was a matter of concern for the entire household to which she belonged, and for the one to which she was destined to be transferred." Indeed, he writes: "the exchange of women was the most important of the transactions between households."[12]

Notice Blenkinsopp's language here that speaks of women as the subjects of "exchange" and "transactions." This terminology is wholly consistent with other commentators' descriptions of ancient Israelite marital practice—for example, Victor H. Matthews and Don C. Benjamin's claim that "marriage was more a matter of business than of pleasure."[13] It is also consistent with the standard biblical idiom, which repeatedly speaks of a bride as "given" (*nātan*) by her natal family and "taken" (*lāqaḥ*) by the groom's.[14] According to Gen 29:28, for example, Laban "gave" Rachel to Jacob; Reuel/Jethro likewise "gave" Zipporah to Moses according to Exod 2:21; and the Israelites, in the midst of a civil war with the tribe of Benjamin, vowed not to "give" any of their daughters to the Benjaminites as wives (Judg 21:1, 7, and 18).[15] The description of a bride as "taken" by the groom's family likewise occurs regularly in texts concerning marriage, appearing ten times, for example, in the Genesis 24 story of Rebekah's betrothal alone (Gen 24:3, 4, 7, 37, 38, 40, 48, 51, 61, and 67). Most notable, perhaps, is the narrative's ultimate verse (Gen 24:67): "He [Isaac] took Rebekah."[16]

As in almost any situation of "give and take," moreover, some gesture of reciprocity within the context of the exchange is expected. Thus, according to Israelite tradition, the groom's family, in order that they be "given" a bride, must first give the woman's family—or more specifically, the woman's father—some form of indemnity when the marriage is arranged. This is what in biblical tradition is sometimes called the *mōhar* (Gen 34:12; Exod 22:15–16 [22:16–17 in most English translations]; 1 Sam 18:25), often translated as the "bride price," the "bridal price," or the "marriage price" (for example, in the New American Bible [Revised Edition], the New English Bible, the New Jerusalem Bible, the New Jewish Publication Society Version, the Revised English Bible, and in the NRSV at Exod 22:15–16 [English 22:16–17]). These translations can be misleading, however, for they suggest that the bride is understood as commanding a "price" that her in-laws-to-be must pay in order to "buy" or "purchase" her.[17] Yet as Millar Burrows pointed out some eighty-five years ago in an important monograph on Israelite marriage, were the bride thought of as this sort of object of commerce, then the groom and/or his family would have the right to sell her again if they so desired.[18]

But although biblical law certainly allowed for the selling of some family members by others who were considered to "own" them—fathers, for example, were allowed to sell their children, or at least their daughters, into debt slavery if need be (Exod 21:7; Neh 5:5)—the legal tradition makes no provision for husbands' selling off their wives.

The *mōhar* proffered by the prospective groom's family to the bride-to-be's natal household should thus be analyzed not as a purchase *price*, but as a *gift* that the prospective groom's family extends to the bride-to-be's father at the time of betrothal.[19] It follows that the Hebrew term *mōhar* is better translated as "marriage *present*" (as, for example, in the NRSV at Gen 34:12 and 1 Sam 18:25), in order to emphasize the ethos of compensatory gifting that is presumed as the prospective groom's family renders indemnification in order that a wife be "given" by the family of the future bride. This point is also emphasized in Gen 34:12, where *mōhar*, or "marriage present," stands in apposition to—and thus seems to be presented as a synonym of—the word *mattān*, which means "gift."[20] Moreover, anthropologists, drawing on the famous 1925 work of Marcel Mauss on gift-giving in what Mauss called "primitive" or "archaic" societies,[21] have noted that "the gift . . . although it operates under the *illusion* that it is free, voluntary, and disinterested . . . is in fact obligatory, constrained by social rules, and necessarily reciprocated."[22] Under the terms of Mauss's understanding, that is, it would be wholly expected that in order for a groom's family in Israel be "given" (or we might say "gifted") a bride, the groom's family must give a gift to the bride's household in exchange. Indeed, anthropologists, again following on the work of Mauss, regularly categorize the use of marriage presents in nuptial arrangements under the larger rubrics of "gift exchange" or "ceremonial exchange."[23]

Anthropologists, as students of social systems, often stress the *social* benefits of this sort of exchange. They speak, for example, of the new social relations that are established through the gifts offered by a groom's family when acquiring a bride and the ways in which social solidarity is enhanced, so much so that even though real wealth is typically transferred from the bridegroom's familial assets to the bride's father (more on this below), "the economic content of the exchange is suppressed" in favor of the language of social bonding.[24] Biblical scholars can describe the Israelite marriage present as an instrument of social bonding as well. Carol Meyers, for example, argues that marriage presents in Israelite tradition should be conceptualized "as exchanges or gifts that helped maintain connections between two family groups" and as "marriage customs . . . that increased the likelihood that families connected in this way would offer economic or other assistance" to one another, especially during times when one of the families experienced difficulty or hardship.[25] Likewise, Daniel I. Block writes that the purpose of the marriage present is "to strengthen the links between the families of those being married,"[26] just as the marriage present that Shechem and his father Hamor offer to give for Dinah in Gen 34:8–12 is depicted as an instrument that will facilitate group alliances between Hamor's and Shechem's Hivite community and Jacob's family. Thus, as Hamor negotiates with Jacob and his sons regarding the proposed marriage, he promises that "you shall live with us, and the land shall be open to you; dwell and trade in it, and establish holdings within it" (Gen 34:10).

Simultaneously, however, and more significantly given this study's interests, the proffering of the marriage present needs to be considered in *ritual* terms. As Katarzyna Grosz has written, "An important part of the socio-anthropological theory of bridewealth," which is anthropologists' preferred term for a marriage present given by the groom's family to the family of the bride, "concerns its *strongly ritual aspect*" (emphasis mine). Grosz then goes on to urge that bridewealth as practiced in the region of her special expertise, the northern Mesopotamian city of Nuzi during the fifteenth and fourteenth centuries BCE, should be analyzed "within the realm of ritual."[27] Parallels from elsewhere in Mesopotamia and the Near East even suggest that the gifting of the marriage present ritually seals the marriage contract, even though the wedding might be celebrated far in the future.[28] Indeed, with regard to marriage presents in southern Mesopotamia during the Old Babylonian period (ca. 1894–1595 BCE), Matthews goes so far as to state that "acceptance of the gift or payment [Akkadian *terḫatu*] . . . was *tantamount to marriage*" (emphasis mine), even if "physical consummation . . . was to be delayed for months or even years."[29] Thus, as soon as the future bride's family received the marriage present, the bride-to-be was known as an *aššatu*, "wife," and any man who presumed to have sexual intercourse with her other than her betrothed was considered to have committed an act of adultery against the bridegroom.[30] The same sensibility is found in the Bible in Deut 22:23–27 and 28:30. In the former text, for example, a man who takes a woman sexually when she is betrothed to another is condemned to death. It follows, as T. M. Lemos writes in her important study on marriage gifts in ancient Israel, that "the giving of the *mōhar* is one of the main rituals"—and perhaps even "*the* ritual"—"that actualizes marriage."[31]

It is my contention, moreover, that a closer examination of the gifting of the *mōhar*, or marriage present, as well as an analysis of the larger betrothal rite in which the gifting of the marriage present is embedded, has much to tell us regarding the objectives I have set for myself in this book: to describe and analyze the distinctive features that characterize Israelite women's life-cycle events and the rituals associated with them. Indeed, while Chapters 1 and 2 have considered only three of the six theoretical points for understanding women's life-cycle rituals that I presented in the Introduction—(1) the way women's life-cycle rituals can be understood, at least to some degree, according to the basic tripartite structure of separation–liminality–reintegration originally defined by Arnold van Gennep in his 1909 book *Les rites de passage*; (2) the way women's life-cycle rituals can manifest, at least to some degree, some of the basic features of liminality that Victor Turner identified in his foundational 1964 and 1966 essays as characteristic of van Gennep's second, or transitional/liminal phase; and (3) the way liminality can be exacerbated or intensified in women's life-cycle rituals as compared to liminality as manifest in comparable men's rites—it is my contention here that Israelite betrothal traditions manifest all six features of women's life-cycle rituals that I have previously outlined. I thus turn to consider these six features in sequence, although, to be clear, not with the same degree of attention given to each. Instead, the bulk of my discussion will concern what I identified above as the most important rite within betrothal traditions, the gifting of the marriage present, and the way this gifting facilitates the same sort of moment we saw manifest in some women's life-cycle rituals in the Introduction, when the ritual subject's typically abject status is temporarily elevated and enhanced.

Betrothal as a Women's Life-Cycle Ritual

To begin, let us consider how Israelite betrothal rituals might correspond to Arnold van Gennep's account of a rite of passage. Indeed, they correspond in the most fundamental of ways, as betrothals are, to quote van Gennep's definition of a rite of passage, "ceremonies whose essential purpose is to enable the individual to pass from one defined position to another which is equally well defined."[32] More specifically, Israelite betrothals can be said to separate their ritual subjects—both the prospective bride and prospective groom—from the state of being unmarried and then, after a transitional or liminal period, reintegrate them into a new position within their community: the state of affianced.

As is typical in a rite of passage, moreover—and as is suggested by the second point I proposed in the Introduction regarding women's life-cycle rituals—the transitional or liminal period that obtains between the subjects' old position as unmarried and their new state as affianced is marked by features of marginalization. In Israelite betrothal rituals, this can be most clearly seen in the decision-making processes that I have described above, whereby the parents of the prospective groom and the father, brothers, and/or other close male relatives of the prospective bride take on the responsibility for arranging all, or almost all aspects of a couple's marriage, while the prospective bride and groom are largely disenfranchised during the discussions leading up to their nuptials. Most notably, as we have seen, the prospective bride and groom can be disenfranchised in discussions regarding their choice of one another. The parade instance is perhaps the story of Isaac's betrothal to Rebekah in Genesis 24. As I have previously documented, Isaac and Rebekah are so disenfranchised during the negotiations that contract their marriage that, even though they have never met one another, Isaac does not journey to Aram-naharaim with Abraham's servant in order that he might assert some preference regarding his bride-to-be, or so that he and Rebekah might at least become acquainted as their nuptials are arranged.

I have also identified several like narratives in which the prospective bride and groom are sidelined while family members play the predominant role in arranging their marriage: the stories of Ishmael's marriage in Gen 21:21; Jacob's betrothals and marriages in Gen 28:1–5 and 29:15–30; Shechem and Dinah in Genesis 34; Moses's marriage to Zipporah in Exod 2:15–21; Samson's betrothal and marriage in Judg 14:1–10; David's marriage to Michal in 1 Sam 18:20–25; and Ruth and Boaz in Ruth 3:1–4. In all these accounts, I submit, and more generally in the Israelite marital traditions that they reflect, the way in which the parents of the prospective groom and the father, brothers, and/or other close male relatives of the prospective bride take on the responsibility for negotiating a couple's nuptials marks a liminal period of marginalization and disenfranchisement for the betrothal's ritual subjects.

I also submit that the marginalization and disenfranchisement of this liminal period are more exacerbated for the bride-to-be than for her prospective groom. Consider in this regard some of the ritual gestures that, in conjunction with the gifting of the marriage present, enact the betrothal.

For example, as we saw in Chapter 1, an Israelite bridegroom spreads the edge or skirt of his garment over his prospective bride as a ritual gesture that indicates the couple has become formally betrothed. Accordingly, in Ezek 16:8, Yahweh spreads the edge or skirt of the deity's robe over Jerusalem, and in Ruth 3:9, Ruth asks Boaz, whom she seeks to marry, to spread the edge or skirt of his garment over her.[33]

As we also saw in Chapter 1, after the edge or skirt of Yahweh's robe is spread over Jerusalem, Yahweh bathes her, rinsing off the blood that is said to cling to her body (Ezek 16:9). Some commentators interpret this blood, as noted in my previous discussion, as the discharge from Jerusalem's recently begun menses, but it is better understood, I suggested, as the blood of childbirth with which the foundling Jerusalem had been covered since she was abandoned postpartum.[34] The bath Yahweh gives Jerusalem in 16:9 should thus be regarded as a very belated version of the cleansing that, according to Ezek 16:4, was due at Jerusalem's birth. This might suggest that Yahweh's anointing Jerusalem with oil in 16:9, immediately after bathing her, is also to be understood as a long delayed childbirth rite, especially given that Hittite and Mesopotamian accounts of birth rituals mention anointing a newborn infant.[35] But since in Old Babylonian tradition (ca. 1894–1595 BCE), as well as in Assyria and among residents of Syria, betrothal was marked by anointing the bride-to-be with oil,[36] it is also possible that the anointing of Jerusalem in Ezek 16:9 was a standard element in Israelite betrothal rites.[37] The "pledging myself to you [Jerusalem]" that Yahweh is said to undertake in Ezek 16:8, along with the deity's making of a covenant with the city, may in addition be analogous to the entering into formal contractual arrangements typical of Mesopotamian betrothal ceremonies.[38] In Mesopotamia during the Old Babylonian period, the moment of betrothal was further signified by a drinking party, hosted by the future bride's father.[39] This custom is perhaps reflected in Gen 24:54, where Abraham's servant and his entourage eat and drink, presumably with Bethuel and others of Bethuel's household, after arranging Rebekah's betrothal to Isaac.

Most of these betrothal rituals require the engagement of both the prospective bride and groom (the exception may be the drinking parties of Old Babylonian tradition, which the bride probably did not attend).[40] Still, the prospective bride's and groom's experience of these rites should not be taken to be equivalent. Rather, the bride-to-be arguably experiences the intensified or exacerbated liminality that I suggested in the Introduction was a third feature that characterizes women's life-cycle rituals, especially when compared to men's. In particular, the liminal experiences of submission and subordination that Victor Turner identified as characteristics of a rite of passage's middle or liminal phase are exacerbated for the bride-to-be during Israelite betrothal rituals.[41] Note regarding the anointing described in Ezek 16:9, for example (if is to be understood as an element within Israelite betrothal rites): the prospective groom is cast as the actor, whereas the bride-to-be is acted upon. Likewise in Ezek 16:8 and Ruth 3:9, even though both members of an affianced couple participate in the ritual spreading of the garment that, according to my understanding, secures the betrothal, the bride-to-be is the object of this gesture, whereas her prospective husband assumes responsibility for performing the rite (this is especially clear in Ruth 3:9, where Ruth petitions Boaz to act). As for the associated pledge and covenant utterances that we find in Ezek 16:8: it is the prospective husband who speaks to the bride-to-be, whereas it is her place only to listen.

Note, moreover, what is professed when the prospective husband speaks: claims of authority that the groom-to-be asserts over his future bride ("you became mine," Yahweh tells Jerusalem). Here we see a particularly dramatic demonstration of the woman's subordinated position: what Aldina Da Silva describes as "the husband's right of ownership."[42] Or, as Daniel I. Block puts it, referring to the text from Deut 22:23–27 that I discussed earlier, "From the bride's perspective, with engagement the commitment to marriage was deemed so firm that a betrothed woman who willingly engaged in sexual intercourse with a man other than her husband was treated as an adulteress and stoned to death." Yet, "from the vantage point of the groom, during the period of engagement he was exempted from military service (Deut 20:7)."[43] Analogously, we might say, "from the bride's perspective," she becomes subject, with betrothal, to what Mary Douglas, as we saw in the Introduction, described as the dangers that can be incurred by "the person who must pass from one [state] to another,"[44] whereas "from the vantage point of the groom," the dangers (or at least the potential dangers) of the battlefield are averted during the period of betrothal because his engagement excuses him from military endeavors.

Note also that whatever role family and household members typically play in arranging a prospective couple's marriage, the Bible, as we have seen, contains a fair number of accounts in which a groom-to-be apparently makes his own marital arrangements (Abraham and Keturah, Esau and his two Hittite wives, Judah and Shua's daughter, David and Abigail, David and Bathsheba). I have also catalogued biblical narratives in which a groom-to-be either initiates a prospective union before his parents get involved (Shechem and Dinah, Samson and his Timnite bride) or identifies a prospective bride based on the guidelines his parents have set forward (Jacob). Yet the brides-to-be in these and related texts are most typically without agency (the only significant exception in biblical lore is the story of the daughters of Zelophehad, and even their marriages are restricted according to certain kinship precepts decreed by male authorities: Moses and God). In short, and to use the biblical idiom, a bride-to-be is standardly the object of her natal and marital families' give-and-take, whereas the groom is never "given" (*nātan*) or "taken" (*lāqaḥ*) in marriage.[45] Again, then, I suggest that the third general principle I articulated in the Introduction regarding women's life-cycle rituals holds: the liminal experience is exacerbated or intensified during women's life-cycle rituals when compared to liminality as experienced by men, so that if a male goes down one rung of a hypothetical ladder in terms of, say, submission and subordination during the liminal phase of a betrothal ritual, a female goes down at least two.

Consider also the fourth point regarding women's life-cycle rituals that I proposed in the Introduction: that men's life-cycle rituals are more likely to be marked by dramatic ruptures than are women's life-cycle rituals, which are more marked by continuity. At first, it may seem as if this condition does not apply in analyzing Israelite betrothal rituals, for even though we can describe betrothal as a life-cycle ritual that moves its ritual subjects through a liminal phase in order to bestow on them a new social position, the new position as "affianced" that the ritual effects for both the future bride and groom turns out to be just another intermediate or liminal stage, with both members of the betrothed couple left in a "betwixt and between" state that exists between their previous identities as single and their future married state. Or, as T. M. Lemos more succinctly states, "Seemingly, betrothal was a liminal period in marriage rites between the giving of bridewealth and the actual marriage."[46] Marriage in ancient Israel, moreover, seems to have followed hard on the heels of betrothal (more on this just below): the only notable exception is found in the story of Jacob's marriages to Leah and Rachel, each of which requires seven years of Jacob's labor in order to secure the bride (more on this below as well). Typically, though, the rituals of betrothal and marriage flow in an unbroken sequence for both bride and groom; both bride and groom, that is, experience these occasions as a ritual continuum of interconnected and enmeshed events.

Still, it seems that for ancient Israelite women, a greater continuum is defined, as betrothal and marriage apparently followed shortly after a woman came of age physically, whereas for a man, there seems to be a break between physical maturation, on the one hand, and betrothal and marriage, on the other. More specifically, regarding women: we have seen in Ezekiel 16 that, according to the interpretation I put forward in Chapter 1, Yahweh, immediately after noting that Jerusalem's menses had begun in Ezek 16:8, becomes betrothed to her by enacting various ritual gestures (the spreading of the robe and the contractual declaration at the end of 16:8; maybe also the anointing in 16:9). Promptly thereafter, in 16:10–12 (as I will discuss in Chapter 4), they wed. Somewhat similarly, as we saw in discussing the story of Jephthah's daughter in Chapter 2, the daughter is sacrificed at the end of what is presented as a relatively brief interim (a little more than two months) between her having entered into the state of *bĕtûlîm* according to Judg 11:37—meaning her entering into the stage during the pubescent process when she has begun to menstruate and so is potentially fertile—and marriage, or what is described in Judg 11:39 as her "knowing a man."

Like Jephthah's daughter, Rebekah is identified as a *bĕtûlâ*, or one who has come to the stage during the pubescent process when she had begun to menstruate. More specifically, Rebekah's identity as a *bĕtûlâ* is noted in Gen 24:16, within the same pericope in which Abraham's servant determines that she is the woman whom he should seek to secure as Isaac's betrothed (Gen 24:15–21). Then, that very day, before Abraham's servant even eats the food offered to him upon his arrival at Bethuel and Laban's house (Gen 24:32–33), the betrothal is agreed to (Gen 24:50–51), and Rebekah leaves almost immediately thereafter to go with the servant to Canaan (Gen 24:59–61). To be sure, the wedding—which is intimated by the notice that Isaac "took" Rebekah in Gen 24:67, at which point she became his "wife"—cannot happen forthwith, given that we must imagine a long-ish journey to get Rebekah from her natal home to Canaan (depending on where, exactly, we envision Aram-naharaim to be). Nevertheless, biblical tradition suggests that Rebekah moves from the position of *bĕtûlâ*, to betrothed, to bride within a matter of months, much as is implied regarding Jephthah's daughter in Judg 11:29–40 and Jerusalem in Ezek 16:8–12 and much as I have also previously quoted the first-century CE historian Josephus as reporting regarding the Essenes, about whom it is said that a woman marries after she has menstruated only three times.[47] Note as well texts from the Bible's prophetic corpus such as Isa 62:5 and Jer 2:32, where the term *bĕtûlâ* is used in parallel with the word *kallâ*, "bride."

This evidence, like the other data I have cited, suggests a close connection between a young woman's sexual maturation and her marriage—or an extended complex of interrelated and enmeshed events, with a young Israelite woman's becoming a *bětûlâ,* and then her betrothal, and then her marriage following quickly upon one another in ritualized progression.

The situation for men is somewhat different. More specifically, and as my discussion in Chapter 2 has suggested, young men in the ancient world came fully into biological maturity at roughly the same age as did young women: in their late teens or by age twenty or so. Yet while an Israelite woman's physical maturation seems to have been followed almost immediately by betrothal and marriage, biblical tradition is not as clear that this was true for Israelite men. To be sure, in one of the prophetic texts I just mentioned, Isa 62:5, the *bāḥûr,* which is the term used to describe the male counterpart of the *bětûlâ,* is said, like the *bětûlâ,* to be on the verge of marriage. If we take the term *bāḥûr* to refer, as many do, to a male who is "young but fully grown," or to the period in male development "spanning late puberty to young adulthood,"[48] then we might take Isa 62:5 to indicate that Israelite young men, like Israelite young women, married shortly after they had come sexually of age. Judges 14:10, in which Samson seems to be one among the *baḥûrîm* (the plural form of *bāḥûr*) at the time of his marriage, might indicate this as well.

However, in Ruth 3:10, Boaz praises Ruth for seeking an offer of betrothal from him, rather than going after the *baḥûrîm,* which implies that he is a better marriage partner for Ruth because he is not a *bāḥûr,* but (presumably) older.[49] Other evidence similarly suggests that Israelite men did not marry until they were older: perhaps in their late twenties or early thirties. For example, as Milton Eng has noted, Abraham is said in Gen 17:17 to be ten years older than Sarah, so, say, thirty at the time of their marriage, while she would have been twenty. Genesis 41:45–46 also seems to suppose (although the text is not totally clear) that Joseph was thirty when he married, and Gen 25:20 and 26:34 indicate that both Isaac and Esau married at age forty[50]—and notably, in Isaac's case, to a woman cast in Genesis 24 as Abraham's great-niece and so a generation younger than he.[51] To be sure, the marital age of "forty" given for Isaac and Esau in Gen 25:20 and 26:34 must be taken as symbolic, the proverbial number of fullness (here, fullness of years) used by the P or Priestly writers responsible for these texts.[52] I also acknowledge that, in general, numbers in Genesis (and elsewhere in the Bible) should not be taken as reliable. Still, I maintain that the basic descriptions of marital ages presented in Genesis must have generally made sense and so have fundamentally "rung true" to their ancient Israelite audience. That is, I assume that the paradigm of "high age for man, low for woman"[53] corresponded to Israelites' experience of the society in which they actually lived.

In his book *Jewish Marriage in Antiquity*, Michael L. Satlow reports that a similar situation pertained in Jewish communities in Palestine and the western diaspora during the late Second Temple Period and into the early centuries of the Common Era, with thirty being a "usual age for men to marry." Satlow cites, for example, evidence suggesting that Josephus "married for the first time when he was around 30"; the assessment of the Jewish philosopher Philo of Alexandria (ca. 15 BCE–50 CE) that "the proper age of marriage is between 28 and 35" (*De Opificio Mundi* 103); "scattered rabbinic dicta" that "locate marriage around the age of thirty"; and texts from the Testament of Levi (11:1 and 12:5) and the Testament of Issachar (3:5) that indicate Levi and Issachar married at ages twenty-eight and thirty, respectively.[54] Yet Satlow has also shown, as we will remember from Chapter 1, that Jewish women from this same period married in the middle or toward the end of their teenage years.[55] Satlow notes, moreover, that the data from Greek and Roman tradition are similar ("Greek and Roman men . . . tended to marry when they were in their late twenties or early thirties," whereas "Greek and Roman women . . . appeared to have married in their mid or late teens").[56] While this might suggest the Second Temple and rabbinic-era materials that Satlow cites should be discounted in this study of biblical Israel because they are compromised by Hellenistic and Roman influences from the last third of the first millennium BCE and the early years of the first millennium CE,[57] the pattern that Satlow describes—"high age for man, low for woman"—is in fact well represented elsewhere in the ancient world centuries earlier. For example, in Mesopotamia during the Neo-Assyrian and Neo-Babylonian periods (ca. 911–612 BCE and ca. 626–539 BCE), females typically married in their "mid to late teens" and males "in their late twenties or early thirties."[58]

All of which is to say: a significant body of evidence suggests that, like many of their Near Eastern and eastern Mediterranean counterparts, men in biblical Israel married only a decade or so after fully maturing biologically, meaning that while both Israelite men and women seem to experience the life-cycle events of betrothal and marriage as a continuum that comprises interconnected rituals, there is a break in the life cycle of the Israelite male between his biological coming of age and the betrothal–marriage ritual complex, whereas Israelite females move rapidly through the life stages of coming of age, betrothal, and marriage. We thus can propose that in the case of Israelite betrothal rituals, the fourth general principle regarding women's life-cycle rituals that I articulated in the Introduction holds: that woman's life-cycle events, more so than men's, need to be understood in terms of a continuum, or as interrelated parts of an extended ritual complex, which for a young Israelite woman of marriageable age extends from sexual maturation through betrothal to marriage.

For a woman, moreover, the ritual of betrothal arguably looks beyond marriage, to motherhood—although this connection may not be immediately obvious. It is my contention, though, that the prospective position of the betrothed young woman as a childbearer, along with the special value Israelite tradition assigned to that role, is the primary (though not exclusive) focus of what I identified above as the most significant ritual gesture of Israelite betrothal rites: the gifting of the marriage present. As I also indicated above, it is my contention that the gifting of the marriage present makes manifest the fifth feature that I identified in the Introduction as a characteristic of some women's life-cycle rituals: the temporary enhancement of the ritual subject's typically subordinated status. Indeed, as I have just intimated, the status of the ritual subject—the bride-to-be—is enhanced according to what I described in the Introduction as the sixth feature that can distinguish women's life-cycle rituals: the esteem in which many cultures hold women's sexual and reproductive capacities.

In order to prove these points, I turn to consider the marriage present in more detail.

The Marriage Present

Biblical tradition suggests that the marriage present that the prospective groom's family gives to the bride-to-be's father and/or others among her close kin can take many different forms:[59] Shechem, for example, offers any marriage present (*mōhar*) or gift (*mattān*) that Jacob and his sons might ask for Dinah (Gen 34:12). Elsewhere in Genesis, Abraham's servant gives silver and gold ornaments and garments to Rebekah, Isaac's bride-to-be, but he also gives her mother and her brother "choice items" (*migdānōt*) that presumably served as a marriage present (Gen 24:53). Jacob, offering "brideservice" in lieu of "bridewealth," is said to labor on Laban's behalf for seven years and then seven years over in order that he might marry Laban's two daughters

Leah and Rachel (Gen 29:20, 28),[60] and Moses, who takes on keeping the flocks of his father-in-law Reuel/Jethro (Exod 3:1), may also use his own labor as "brideservice" in order to claim Zipporah as his wife. In 1 Sam 18:25, Saul, as I noted in my earlier discussion of coming-of-age rituals (Chapter 2), asks of David the rather macabre marriage present (*mōhar*) of one hundred Philistine foreskins in order that David might marry Michal, even as, according to Hos 3:2, the prophet Hosea confers more conventional gifts in order to acquire (*kārâ*) the wife of the symbolically laden marriage described in Hos 3:1–5: fifteen pieces of silver, a homer of barley (about 220 liters), and, perhaps, a measure of wine (the Hebrew here is confused).[61] However, the seemingly kindred legal traditions of Deuteronomy (Deut 22:28–29) make no mention of any payment in foodstuffs and instead require a marriage present of fifty silver pieces.[62] To be sure, the term *mōhar* is not used in this Deuteronomy text, but the closely related passage in Exod 22:15–16 (English 22:16–17) makes reference to the *mōhar habbĕtûlōt*.

The Bible also occasionally mentions dowries—that is, assets of her natal family that a bride brings with her to her husband's home—but this notion of the bride bringing resources to the marriage does not seem to have been a typical feature of Israelite marital ritual, especially during the preexilic period.[63] Rather, dowries, especially, again, during the preexilic period, most often appear in biblical accounts of elite marriages.[64] For example, Achsah, the daughter of the Judahite chieftain Caleb (Josh 15:13–19; Judg 1:11–15), asks that her father give her what we can take to be a dowry of land upon the occasion of her marriage. What's more, this land—the basins of Gullothmayim, which are two pools of water or, perhaps, two wells—was arguably quite valuable, given that Achsah's story is set in the relatively arid region of the Negev. Another elite marriage that includes a dowry (*šilluḥîm*) is Solomon's marriage to Pharaoh's daughter in 1 Kgs 9:16; note in addition that this marriage is to a foreigner. Laban's giving of the maidservants Zilpah and Bilhah to Leah and Rachel immediately after their marriages to Jacob might also be considered an occasion where a foreigner—a man of Paddan-Aram—gives a dowry to his daughters (Gen 29:23–24, 28–29).[65] Genesis 31:14–16 may further suggest that the giving of a dowry was an expected custom within Laban's Paddan-Aram household.

Foreign imagery dominates as well in Ezek 16:26–34. There Jerusalem, still rendered metaphorically as female, is said to "play the harlot" within her marriage to Yahweh that was contracted in 16:8 by entering into treaty agreements with alien "lovers"—Egypt, Assyria, Babylon—to whom she gives her dowry (*nātatt 'et-nĕdānayik lĕkol-mĕ'ahăbayik*; Ezek 16:33).[66] In fact, the very word used for "dowry" in this Ezekiel passage (*nādān*, or possibly *neden* or *nōden*) is itself "foreign," a loanword into Hebrew from Akkadian *nudunnû*, "dowry."[67] This association of dowries and foreignness may be of significance, as traditions of giving bridal dowries are much better attested elsewhere in the Near East than in Israel. For example, the giving of dowries, as well as (sometimes) the giving of marriage presents, was a part of marriage practice among the Sumerian inhabitants of southern Mesopotamia during the third millennium BCE.[68] Subsequently, in southern Mesopotamia during the Old Babylonian period (ca. 1894–1595 BCE), a bride standardly received from her father a dowry that was equal or even larger in value to the marriage present that the groom's family had given for her.[69] Further north, in Nuzi, the institutions of both marriage present and dowry are likewise attested in texts from ca. 1450–1350 BCE,[70] and the same situation pertains in Hittite Anatolia and in the northern Levant, at the Late Bronze Age city-state of Ugarit.[71] First-millennium BCE Babylonian texts, however, speak almost exclusively of dowries and not of marriage presents.[72]

What explains these differing Near Eastern traditions regarding marriage presents and dowries? In *Marriage Gifts and Social Change in Ancient Palestine*, T. M. Lemos's important study of marriage present traditions that I cited above, Lemos follows the anthropologist Jack Goody in arguing that a society's preference for a marital economics of dowry, on the one hand, or marriage presents (what Lemos, following standard anthropological terminology, calls bridewealth), on the other, depends on the nature of the society, with kinship-based societies in which there is little social stratification or class differentiation preferring a system of marriage presents or bridewealth, whereas highly stratified and complex societies prefer an economics of dowry.[73] Accordingly, a kinship-based and relatively unstratified society like Israel—especially nascent Israel in the late second millennium BCE and in the first centuries of the first millennium BCE according to Lemos, and also, in my opinion, Israel, especially rural Israel, until the time of the Babylonian destruction in 586 BCE[74]—would be expected to favor a marital economics of bridewealth. This corresponds exactly to the "marriage present" texts surveyed above, all of which I take to date from this preexilic period of Israelite history.[75]

Conversely, more urbanized and socially stratified societies—or perhaps a small enclave of elites ensconced within an otherwise minimally stratified society—would be expected to make dowries the basis of their marital economic system. This sort of differentiation could explain, as I already intimated, the biblical references to dowries in elite marriages such as those of Caleb's daughter Achsah (Josh 15:13–19, = Judg 1:11–15) and the marriage of Solomon to the pharaoh's daughter (1 Kgs 9:16).[76] It also explains why a system of dowry is much more robustly attested in the more socially stratified world of early second-millennium BCE Babylon than it is in preexilic Israel. Such an account explains, moreover, why dowry comes to dominate in first-millennium BCE Mesopotamia, as the great Neo-Assyrian and then Neo-Babylonian empires came into existence and the society became more and more complex and increasingly divided along class lines. This is, in fact, precisely what Lemos argues in her discussion of changes over time in Babylonian marriage economics.[77] She presents the same argument with respect to Israel in the Persian era (ca. 539–332 BCE) and even more so concerning the Israel of the Hellenistic and Roman periods (ca. 332–63 BCE and ca. 63 BCE–135 CE): that during this half millennium or so, Jewish communities, both in Judea and in the diaspora, became not only more economically stratified, but also came, in terms of the economics of marriage, increasingly to orient themselves around a dowry system rather than the older system of marriage presents.[78] According, for example, to fifth-century BCE marriage contracts from the Jewish colony of Elephantine, in southern Egypt, a marriage present is conveyed by the prospective groom to the bride-to-be's father, or whomever in the future bride's family has authority over her, but it is then returned to the bride as part of the dowry she brings with her into her marital home. Moreover, by the first century BCE (according, at least, to rabbinic tradition), the groom paid the marriage present only in the case of divorce.[79]

Yet as helpful as Lemos's analysis is for explaining changes in Mesopotamian and Israelite marital economics over time, and also for explaining the occasional presence of dowry marriages in preexilic Israel even as a marital economics of bridewealth dominates, Lemos's focus on stratification or the lack thereof in a social *system* means that the actual subject around whom a marriage's financial arrangements revolve—the prospective bride—becomes curiously absent. To be sure, a major goal of Lemos's project is to direct biblical scholars' attention toward anthropological theories about bridewealth and dowry and so to focus, as any anthropologist would, on models of social organization. More specifically, Lemos aims to demonstrate that the view of the marriage present that is generally expressed in biblical scholarship—which considers this present in terms "of compensation for productive and economic loss" and does not take into account how marriage presents operate within larger social systems—is, to use her language, "oversimplified."[80]

Even so, Lemos admits that "a review of anthropological scholarship would not necessarily contradict" an understanding that sees the marriage present as compensating for material loss.[81] Rather, in her survey of anthropological studies of bridewealth, Lemos indicates that some societies do use marriage presents to compensate the bride-to-be's natal lineage for the loss of her labor that marriage in patrilocal communities engenders.[82] As indicated just above, several biblical scholars have similarly suggested that in Israel, the marriage present is used to compensate a bride-to-be's father for the loss to his household's material productivity once his daughter has wed and moved to her husband's home.[83] It is easy, moreover, to marshal evidence in support of this thesis, for in a number of studies, Carol Meyers has shown that ancient Israelite women's contributions to their households' labor force were prodigious, especially during the preexilic period and particularly within the so-called four-room, or pillared, or pillar-courtyard houses that were the typical dwelling places of preexilic Israelite families, preeminently in the countryside, where an estimated 80–90 percent of the preexilic population lived.[84] More specifically, women in these kinship-based and relatively unstratified rural enclaves (to use the anthropological terminology that is central to Lemos's analysis) were crucially involved in the processing and allocation of their households' foodstuffs, in the spinning and weaving of their households' textiles, and in the production of their households' domestic pottery: all critical enterprises in insuring the well-being of their homes, which are best described as self-sufficient and self-sustaining agrarian-pastoralist compounds.[85]

The overseer of these various female enterprises was surely the wife of her household's paterfamilias, but all of a household's women must have been substantially involved in executing a household's chores. Meyers has noted, for example, that archaeological excavations within a domestic enclave at the Canaanite/Phoenician site of Tel Dor, on the Mediterranean coast, have revealed what seems to be a late twelfth- or early eleventh-century BCE communal trough for kneading dough.[86] In addition, in the Israelite highlands, at the late eleventh- to early tenth-century BCE village site of 'Izbet Ṣarṭah, three grinding stones for processing grain were found within one room of a single household.[87] Likewise, at the Israelite sites of Khirbet Qeiyafa and Beth-Shean, multiple grinding sets (grinding slabs and handstones) were discovered within the same building.[88] According to Meyers, these data suggest that the women of southern Levantine households (including Israelite households) labored together at the bread-making tasks that comprised the most substantial part of their domestic work.[89] This required an investment of approximately two, three, or four hours per woman per day according to Meyers[90]—or, according to other scholars, up to five hours daily![91]

To lose a woman from this labor pool was surely an economic blow to a preexilic Israelite family. It could especially have been a blow to lose, at the time of her marriage, a young and presumably healthy woman who was unencumbered by the fairly significant obligations of motherhood (breastfeeding, the supervision and care of small children, etc.; more on this in Chapter 7). Nehemiah 5:5, which notes that both sons and daughters could be sold into debt slavery by an impoverished father, in addition suggests that continuing into the Persian period, a family's daughters were considered to be of economic value. In his study of social and economic life in Israel in the second half of the first millennium BCE, Samuel L. Adams specifically argues that these daughters were of value because they performed "work to make households function."[92] Thus, as I noted when I began this discussion of women's household labor, several biblical scholars have argued that the particular commodity for which the marriage present is meant to compensate a bride-to-be's father is the loss to his household's material productivity that the daughter's marriage engenders.

But this explanation is not without problems, for it does not adequately explain at least one of the Bible's "marriage present" texts, Exod 22:15–16 (English 22:16–17).[93] This text and the related Deut 22:28–29 concern a physically mature and unbetrothed daughter (a *bĕtûlâ*) who has been taken sexually by a man. This compromises the daughter's marital prospects, so much so that biblical tradition can consider such a woman to be unmarriageable (see 2 Sam 13:1–20; note also the similar sentiment articulated in 2 Sam 16:21–22 and 20:3).[94] The reasons why this must be so are debated.[95] Tikva Frymer-Kensky suggests that because the daughter has been shown to come from a dishonorable family whose male members have proven themselves unable to safeguard the sexual chastity of their household's women, the daughter is considered to be of diminished social worth and so less desirable as a marital partner.[96] Others argue that in ancient Israel's system of patrilineal descent and patrimonial inheritance, paternity claims are insured by insisting that a woman has sex with only one man. Thus, prospective husbands would eschew marriage with a nonvirgin daughter in favor of a marriage in which they could be assured that offspring were truly their own.[97]

To be sure, a prospective husband's paternity claims could presumably be guaranteed in the cases presented in Exod 22:15–16 (English 22:16–17) and Deut 22:28–29 were he to wait to marry for ten months after the illicit sexual congress took place; at that point, there would be no risk that the nonvirgin daughter was carrying another man's child.[98] But Eve Levavi Feinstein has demonstrated that according to biblical tradition, "a woman who has sex outside marriage has been contaminated in a lasting way," as she is considered to be "'marked' by the essence of another man."[99] This contamination compromises her marital prospects (Feinstein goes so far as to say she is ruined for other men),[100] so much so that according to Lev 21:13–14 and (less emphatically) Ezek 44:22, a priest's marriage to *any* nonvirgin woman is forbidden, even if the woman's previous sexual activity took place in the distant past and only within the context of marriage (a marriage that ended, say, in divorce or a husband's death). This is because, in the words of Lev 21:15, a priestly husband's progeny—and so Israel's priestly lineage—could be "profaned" in ways the tradition deems unacceptable through introducing another man's enduring essence into the priestly husband's patriline.[101]

Yet whatever the logic underlying their unease, both Exod 22:15–16 (English 22:16–17) and Deut 22:28–29 seek to ensure that the father of the now-nonvirgin daughter receives the entire marriage present that his daughter, had she remained a virgin, would have commanded (what Exod 22:16 [English 22:17] calls "the marriage present of the *bĕtûlōt*"). The two texts also seek to ensure that the less-than-desirable daughter still has some marital prospect. Thus, these texts require that the woman's seducer (this is more the sense of the passage in Exodus) or rapist (this is more the sense of the Deuteronomy text) remit the standard marriage present for her and make her his wife.[102] However, the Exodus version of the law states that the father can refuse to give his daughter to her seducer, although the seducer is still required to give the father the marriage present. That is, a father who intends to retain his daughter in his household—and who will thus presumably continue to benefit from her presence among his household's labor force and her contributions to his household's economic well-being—is nevertheless to be compensated as if his daughter had been given in marriage.[103] Exodus 22:15–16 (English 22:16–17) thereby suggests that the marriage present given for the daughter and more generally for a woman at the time of her betrothal must compensate for something more than her contributions to a household's sustenance and material needs.

Anthropological evidence—for example, from modern-day Africa—argues for this conclusion as well. As we will see in more detail below, bridewealth is a common cultural practice throughout much of the continent's sub-Saharan expanse, even among peoples where the relative value ascribed to women's labor is not necessarily high—and so, presumably, not worthy of compensation.[104] Pierre Bourdieu's more theoretical analysis of the role of *time* within customs of gifting, or compensatory gift exchange, is also of note.[105] As Bourdieu maintains, what distinguishes gifting customs like the Israelite marriage present from ordinary economic exchanges, or barter, is the time lag between gift and recompense: it is this gap in time that allows "the subjective experience of pure generosity" (gifting as altruism) "to coexist with the objective truth of exchange" (gifting as a process of reciprocity and also of calculated self-interest).[106] Which is to say: what makes a gift—in the case of our inquiry, the Israelite marriage present—function as a gift and not a purchase price is that no immediate *quid pro quo* is realized in the exchange. Again, this suggests that an understanding that sees the Israelite marriage present as recompense given to a bride's father for his daughter's contributions to the material productivity of his household is flawed, for, as discussed above, a young woman in ancient Israel, after she came of age, was typically and in short order betrothed and wed, as indicated in the stories of Rebekah, Jephthah's daughter, and Jerusalem in Ezek 16:8–12. Indeed, according, at least, to the chronology assumed in Genesis 24, the gifting of the marriage present and the loss of the bride-to-be's contributions to the material well-being of her natal household could happen in the same twenty-four hour period, as Rebekah goes forth from Aram-naharaim just one day after Abraham's servant arrives and undertakes the negotiations (including the gifting of marriage presents) that secure her betrothal to Isaac. Within such a compressed timeframe, it becomes impossible to realize what Bourdieu's analysis requires: a meaningful interval between the gifting of the marriage present at betrothal and the loss of a daughter's labor within her natal home when she leaves it to be wed.

There is a kind of productivity whose realization is, however, necessarily delayed when a woman joins the household of her new husband. This is the woman's reproductive ability (or, at least, her potential reproductive ability), for it is not until ten months, at the earliest, after a marriage has begun and been consummated that a child can be born.[107] Hence, my understanding that what ancient Israelite marriage presents sought preeminently to acknowledge was a bride-to-be's reproductive potential—and, ideally, her potential to reproduce abundantly (in the words of the biblical idiom, to "be fruitful and multiply"). Important to note here is how vital successful reproduction was in ancient Israel, "because of the dominant, labor-intensive agrarian regimes" and the resulting need that self-sustaining farm families had for children who could provide "an adequate labor supply."[108] To quote Meyers, "successful reproduction was essential to household life," and Frymer-Kensky likewise observes that "the encouragement of childbirth was vital to Israel's survival needs."[109] Note as well Exod 23:25–26, where Yahweh promises that a woman's reproductive ability will be safeguarded if the Israelites are faithful to their covenant obligations: "You shall serve Yahweh your God . . . and the miscarrying and barren female will not be present in your land." The same promise—that Yahweh will ensure against a woman's barrenness (as well as male infertility) in response to the Israelites' covenant fidelity—is found in Deut 7:14. In both passages, moreover, Yahweh couples the guarantee of reproductive fertility with a promise of agricultural bounty, good health, and long life if the Israelites keep their obligations to the deity. Suggested here is the degree to which a woman's reproductive ability is understood as one of the preeminent necessities of survival within the Israelite worldview, equivalent to the basic needs of "food, clothing, and shelter" that are often evoked in contemporary discourse.

The importance of a woman's reproductive ability is also intimated in the Bible's various "marriage present" texts. We might suggest, for example, that the reason Shechem made such an extravagant offer for Dinah—any marriage present that Jacob and his sons might ask (Gen 34:12)—was because he perceived Dinah to have the same extraordinary potential as a childbearer as had been manifest by Leah, her prolifically fertile mother. Likewise, it could be that Saul's demand that David deliver a marriage present of one hundred Philistine foreskins in order to wed Michal obliquely indicates, through its evocation of genital imagery, that the Israelites associated the marriage present with sexual activity and reproduction. Exodus 22:15–16 (English 22:16–17) and Deut 22:28–29 too, in considering sexual trespasses that necessitated the gifting of marriage presents, may hint that it is a sexually related matter—the daughter's role as a potential childbearer—for which the marriage present must compensate. The designation of the marriage present in Exod 22:16 (English 22:17) as the *mōhar habbětûlōt*, or "the marriage present of the *bětûlōt*," signals even more that the marriage present's focus is the woman's reproductive potential, given that *bĕtûlōt* refers to young women who have come into the age of sexual maturity that renders them able to bear a child.

In fact, it is Exod 22:15–16 (English 22:16–17) that Ronald A. Simkins explicitly cites when speaking of "biblical laws . . . [that] treat women as . . . *commodities for reproduction*" (emphasis mine).[110] Jack Goody also, though referring not to the Bible but to the West African communities that were the subject of his anthropological fieldwork, writes of "the passage of bridewealth [as] allocat[ing] reproductive powers over women," to the extent that "the child belongs to the man who paid the bridewealth."[111] More simply put, to quote Goody again, bridewealth is "a kind of prospective childwealth."[112] Goody's second wife, Esther N. Goody, writing in 1982 with her then-husband, similarly describes bridewealth in West Africa as "a form of childwealth,"[113] as is vividly illustrated by the fact that among the LoWiili people of Northern Ghana, bridewealth, which is typically paid out in installments, is not disbursed past the initial payment if the woman turns out to be barren.[114] Likewise, an older woman among the LoWiili people who is divorced commands lesser bridewealth when she remarries, presumably because her childbearing potential has been reduced with age.[115] The anthropologist Parker Shipton, writing about the Luo population in western Kenya, also observes that if a Luo marriage ends in divorce, the woman's family will return some or all of the bridewealth, depending on how many children the woman has borne to her husband's lineage and also on whether those children are male or female.[116] More generally, Shipton observes that "*bridewealth* and *childwealth* . . . are usually understood in Luoland to be one and the same." Thus, he notes that while the "goods and services passing from the groom and his natal kin to the bride's natal kin" could serve a number of purposes, "not least important" was "compensating for a woman's . . . childbearing in the past, present, or future."[117]

Scholars of the Near East have made similar observations. JoAnn Scurlock has argued, for example, that in various legal codes from second-millennium BCE Mesopotamia, the brideprice, or *terḥatu*, should be understood as a payment that gives a prospective groom claim over any children produced by the betrothed couple, whereas "if a *terḥatu* was not paid, any children produced by the couple would belong to their mother (and her family)." Scurlock also reports that in Mesopotamian law, a woman who remarries after her previous husband had died commands a reduced brideprice because she is "less likely to produce lots (more) children," much as the family of a LoWiili groom gives less bridewealth if his marriage is to an older woman.[118] As among the

LoWiili, moreover, bridewealth at fifteenth- and fourteenth-century BCE Nuzi could be paid in installments, with payments tied to a woman's success as a childbearer, so that the final payment was delivered to the wife's family only after she bore the couple's first child.[119]

Also significant are the noted Finnish ethnographer Hilma Granqvist's reports regarding the bridewealth customs of the mid-twentieth century Palestinian village of Arṭās, just southwest of Bethlehem, where she conducted fieldwork for a little under three years between 1925 and 1927 and during 1930–1931 and then again for four months in 1959. There, as Granqvist writes, bridewealth, although it "can be thought of as compensation" for the loss of the "valuable labour power" that the bride-to-be provided "in her father's home" before marriage, is better understood, "at least, in the first place," as pertaining to reproduction. Granqvist's informants, for example, told her accounts that were similar to the evidence from second-millennium BCE Mesopotamia that I discussed above, regarding women whose previous husbands had died and who commanded a lesser brideprice upon remarriage than would a "maiden"—although, to be clear, Granqvist indicates that this is not something she herself witnessed.[120] Still, she concludes, based on her own research, that the marriage presents given in Arṭās by a groom's family "imply acknowledgement of" and compensate the bride's family for the fact that their daughter, upon leaving her natal home, "'ruins her father's house, and builds up a stranger's house,'" by "means of bearing sons to a stranger instead of for her own family."[121] Moreover, and significantly for our purposes, Granqvist illustrates this point by citing Ruth 4:11, in which the hope is expressed that Ruth—having left her homeland of Moab far behind—will build up the house of her new husband Boaz, just as Rachel and Leah, who left their homeland in Paddan-Aram, built up the house of their husband Jacob, or Israel.[122]

I conclude, therefore, that in ancient Israel, the gifting of the marriage present marked a moment within the life-cycle ritual of betrothal that preeminently signaled the bride-to-be's value as a potential childbearer within her impending marriage and celebrated her for her reproductive potential. Thereby, her status was elevated and enhanced, in much the same way, as we saw in the Introduction, that other women's status could occasionally be elevated and enhanced during certain life-cycle rituals and events. In particular, as we saw in the Introduction, a woman's status can be elevated and enhanced when the womanly attributes that a society holds in highest regard—here, a woman's reproductive capacities—are most fully on display. Indeed, Genesis

24 includes several markers that suggest Rebekah's status has been enhanced in conjunction with the gifting of the marriage present to Rebekah's mother and brother. For example, in Gen 24:53, Abraham's servant gives Rebekah silver and gold ornaments and new garments at the same time that he gives the "choice items" that comprise the marriage present to her mother and brother. Similarly, as we saw in the Introduction, the Tiyyar, Navajo, Tiv, and Tukuna young women studied by Bruce Lincoln were specially adorned at key junctures during the course of their initiation rituals, most typically to mark the elevated and enhanced status that accrued to them due to their newly realized sexuality and reproductive potential.[123] Thus, at precisely the moment when the *tāli*, the golden ornament that symbolizes male creative power, is hung around her neck, the Tiyyar initiate is transformed into a woman and is marked as eligible for marriage. In addition, the elaborate sash and special turquoise and white shell jewelry with which the girl initiate is clothed at a central point during the Navajo Kinaaldá ritual "makes her over in the image of Changing Woman," a powerful Navajo goddess of life, fertility, and creation.[124]

The bride-to-be in the Ndembu rite of *Nkang'a* is also elaborately adorned with, among other things, strings of beads and a special skirt and girdle to wear as she dances before her community on that ritual's culminating day.[125] Again these adornments mark, I have argued, the elevated and enhanced status conferred on the girl at the moment when she publicly presents and is extolled on account of her newly sexualized body. We will also remember that the *Nkang'a* initiate was able to assert claims of authority at key points while she danced: first, when she "is given the eland-tail switch of authority belonging to the village headman" and next when she seized a huntsman's gun.[126] Then, later that night, after her first marital intercourse, she had the opportunity to give her instructress an evaluation of her husband's sexual performance.[127] Once more, I have contended that these expressions of authority take place at the moments during *Nkang'a* when the young woman's nascent sexuality and potential reproductive fertility are most prominently on display, with the result that status enhancement and elevation accrue to her. So too is Rebekah able to assert agency and even authority when she is asked in Gen 24:58 if she is willing to go to Canaan to be married to Isaac. Which is to say: although Rebekah is in almost all respects the passive object of negotiations in which her father, brother, and Abraham's servant engage regarding her nuptials, she is able to give voice in Gen 24:58 to her own preferences in the matter of her marriage, and this just a scant five verses after

Abraham's servant gives the "choice items" to Rebekah's brother and mother that seemingly constitute the marriage present. Again, I suggest, this juxtaposition is not coincidental: Rebekah is able to speak for herself at precisely the point when her reproductive potential, as symbolized by the gifting of the marriage present, is highlighted and her status is as a result enhanced.

Note, moreover, that after Rebekah agrees to travel to Canaan to marry, her reproductive potential is further lauded in Gen 24:60, as she is made the subject of a benediction that blesses her with a plethora of descendants. More typically in the Bible, especially in the ancestral narratives of Genesis, this sort of valedictory is delivered to a male. In Gen 17:20, for example, God says of Abraham's son Ishmael that "I will bless him, and I will cause him to be fruitful and multiply greatly. . . . I will make him a great nation," and in Gen 12:2 and 22:17, God says even more fulsomely to Abraham, "I will make of you a great nation," and "I will cause your descendants to become as many as the stars in the heavens and as the sands on the shore of the sea." Similar divine pronouncements are extended to Isaac in Gen 26:4 and 24 and to Jacob according to Gen 48:4. Yet in Gen 24:60, it is Rebekah, shortly after the gifting of the marriage present, to whom future progeny are promised, and the benediction pronounced over her anticipates that she will become "thousands of ten thousands," so many will her offspring be. Thereby her status, already enhanced through the special adornments given to her in Gen 24:53 and the authority extended to her in Gen 24:58, is further elevated.

To be sure, within Ndembu culture, the bride's status elevation is temporary, as she has experienced three months of seclusion, submission, and suffering prior to her wedding day, and within two weeks after her marriage takes place, she is taken from her natal village and transferred to her bridegroom's home. And even on her wedding night, remember, she is to say, upon achieving orgasm, "'*Nafwi*,' 'I am dying,'"[128] for in Victor Turner's words, "she 'dies' as an active member of her own family group, and is 'born' into membership of her husband's village and the adult tribe."[129] Thus dies too her brief experience of status enhancement, and likewise Lincoln argues, as we will recall from the Introduction, that the initiation rituals he has surveyed ultimately serve to "assert . . . control over women's sexual and reproductive capacities, while also asserting that women's primary sphere of activity is to be located within domestic space."[130] The status enhancement that is conveyed to an Israelite bride-to-be through the gifting of the marriage present is temporary as well. After all, the "present" remains with an Israelite bride-to-be's father, even though she, like a Ndembu young woman at the end of the *Nkang'a* ritual or Rebekah in Genesis 24, is typically expected to leave her natal family and her natal home in order to join her husband's household. The children for whom the marriage present has made indemnification are assigned, moreover, to the husband's patriline.

Still, much as Ndembu brides and Tiyyar and Kinaaldá initiates temporarily experience status enhancement and elevation at the points during their cultures' rituals that focus on sexuality and reproductive fertility as these women's most important and most admired characteristics, so too, I conclude, does an Israelite bride-to-be temporarily experience status enhancement and elevation at the moment in the betrothal ritual when the marriage present is gifted and her reproductive potential is highlighted as her most important and admired attribute. As such, betrothal as a rite of passage adds new insights that supplement our previous analyses of Israelite women's life-cycle rituals. These insights will further illuminate the associated wedding rites that I now turn to examine.

4
A Young Woman's Wedding

Marriage, according to many interpreters, is an institution grounded in the earliest days of human existence, when the man (*hā'ādām*) with whom creation begins recognizes the woman that Yahweh has formed from his side as "bone of my bone, and flesh of my flesh" (Gen 2:23).[1] Genesis 2:24 also seems to ground a model of marriage in the earliest days of creation that is called uxorilocal, meaning that a groom leaves his home to reside with his bride in the house of her natal family: "therefore a man leaves his father and mother and clings to his wife." Still, it is hard to think of many instances in biblical tradition where uxorilocality—as opposed to patrilocality (whereby a bride leaves her natal home to reside with her husband in his family's household)—actually pertained.[2] The possibility is perhaps allowed in Genesis 24, where Rebekah, as I noted in the last chapter, is asked whether she is willing to leave her home to marry Isaac (Gen 24:58), the alternative being, as Gen 24:5 implies, that Isaac could relocate to her family's homestead. This option, however, is vetoed by Abraham before his servant even leaves Canaan (Gen 24:6–8), although in the story of Isaac and Rebekah's son Jacob, Jacob does relocate to his father-in-law Laban's abode for an extended period (twenty years according to Gen 31:38 and 41). Eventually, however, as traditions of patrilocal marriage require, Jacob returns to his own home with his wives Leah and Rachel (Gen 31:17–18). Moses's marriage likewise seems eventually to conform to a pattern of patrilocality, even though his status as a fugitive required that he live with his wife's family in Midian for many years before he returned with her to Egypt (Exod 4:20).

The only possible instances of true uxorilocal marriages in the Bible are David's first marriage, to Saul's daughter Michal (1 Sam 18:20–27), and the marriage of Samson, who, as Judg 14:10–18 and 15:1–2 perhaps imply, may be meant to live out his married life in the home of his Philistine wife's family in Timnah. But the setting the Bible envisions for David's marriage is a household and family context that is wholly atypical within Israelite society—David at the time he is wed to Michal is bound to the service of King Saul and resident within the royal court—and thus the marriage can hardly

Maturity, Marriage, Motherhood, Mortality. Susan Ackerman, Oxford University Press.
© Oxford University Press 2025. DOI: 10.1093/9780197809686.003.0006

be taken as illuminative of usual Israelite marital practices. Likewise, because the story of Samson's marriage has him leaving his new in-laws' house in a huff toward the end of his seven-day wedding feast (Judg 14:19; more on this below), it is difficult to say whether the Samson story means for us to understand that Samson would otherwise have remained in Timnah for the long term. Karel van der Toorn has suggested that the Samson story may instead presume a model of marriage known from Mesopotamia, whereby the bride continued to live with her natal family for some time after her marriage while her husband either visited regularly or temporarily joined her as a resident in his in-laws' home.[3] Some interpreters suggest this period was used to judge the compatibility of the new marriage partners, so that as the bride and groom got to know each other and as her family got to know him, the affinities of these various actors could be assessed, and, if found wanting, the marriage might be dissolved on grounds of enmity.[4] Van der Toorn hypothesizes, however, that this intermediate period had a more pragmatic purpose: to determine whether the woman was able to conceive or was barren.[5] If the latter, the marriage could be brought to an end (that the man might be barren is a possibility that Near Eastern tradition considered only as a last resort).[6] But whether the focus was compatibility or fertility, a custom of temporary uxorilocality would, for van der Toorn, explain well the opening verses of Judges 15, where at some point after his wedding has taken place, Samson comes from elsewhere to his father-in-law's house—presumably while the marriage's "trial period" was still underway—to spend the night with his Timnite wife. The father-in-law, though, had assumed Samson had abandoned the marriage for good when he left abruptly toward the end of his wedding feast, and so he had given Samson's wife away to another man.

In addition to uxorilocality, Gen 2:24 seems to prescribe a marriage ideal of monogamy: "therefore a man leaves his father and mother and clings to his wife, *and they become one flesh*" (emphasis mine). Yet, much as one is hard-pressed to think of biblical examples where an uxorilocal marital arrangement actually pertained, one must also admit that monogamy, though certainly well attested in the Bible, was hardly an absolute norm according to biblical tradition. Rather, multiple examples of polygamy are reported. Or, more technically speaking, multiple examples of polygyny (a marriage where a man has more than one wife) are reported. For a woman, ancient Israel's systems of patrilineal descent and patrimonial inheritance precluded her from marrying multiple husbands (the technical term is polyandry), who might make competing claims regarding her children's paternity.

The most famous biblical instances of polygynous marriages are, perhaps, royal marriages. And perhaps the best known of these are the traditions that claim King Solomon was married to seven hundred princesses (*śārôt*) and to another three hundred *pīlagšîm,* or lesser wives (1 Kgs 11:3).[7] To be sure, these numbers must be grossly exaggerated, as numbers in the Bible are wont to be. Still, it is clear that this account was meant to signal Solomon's international stature, especially given that the "princesses" to whom he was married are to be understood as royal women from other nations (including, we are told, the daughter of the Egyptian pharaoh; 1 Kgs 3:1; 9:16; 11:1). These women were wed to Solomon to secure alliances between those domains and Solomon's kingdom. The tradition of Solomon's multiple wives in addition serves to indicate his elite status, given that considerable wealth would have been required to support such a sizeable household. No surprise, then, that the Bible most frequently describes kings as polygynous (in addition to 1 Kgs 11:3, see 2 Sam 3:2–5; 5:13; 15:16; 16:21–22; 1 Kgs 20:3; 2 Chr 11:21; 13:21; and 24:3).

Yet, biblical tradition does record accounts of nonroyal polygynists. One character in the Genesis primordial history, Lamech, is said to have had two wives (Gen 4:19–24), and Abraham's wife Sarah attempts to address her barrenness by giving Abraham her maidservant Hagar as a second wife (Gen 16:3). Abraham, moreover, is said in Gen 25:6 to have had concubines or lesser wives (*pīlagšîm*) at some point in his life (after Sarah's death?). Isaac and Rebekah's son Esau has three wives (Gen 26:34; 28:9), and their other son Jacob is married to both Rachel and Leah. In addition, Rachel and Leah give Jacob their maidservants—Bilhah and Zilpah, respectively—as wives (Gen 30:4, 9). Gideon, one of the heroes of the book of Judges, is said to have many wives and also a concubine or lesser wife (*pîlegeš*; Judg 8:30–31), and a *pîlegeš* features significantly as well in the Judg 19:1–30 story of "a certain Levite," which I discuss in more detail below. The Ephraimite Elkanah's two wives, Hannah and Peninnah, likewise feature significantly in the story of Samuel's birth recounted in 1 Sam 1:1–28. Furthermore, in a list of the descendants of Jacob's fourth-born son, Judah, 1 Chr 2:46 and 48 report that Caleb had at least two concubines, or lesser wives, and 1 Chr 4:5 describes "Ashhur father of Tekoa" as having two wives, Helah and Naarah. Similarly, in a list of the descendants of Manasseh, 1 Chr 7:14 includes a son born to Manasseh by his Aramaean *pîlegeš*, and 1 Chr 8:8–9, in a list of the descendants of Jacob's twelfth and youngest son Benjamin, speaks of the sons born to Shaharaim by a woman who seems to be his third wife, Hodesh, "after he had sent away his wives Hushim and Baara."

All these texts describe marriages that purport to date either from the ancestral period that, in the Bible's conceit, preceded the formation of an actual Israelite polity, or, in three cases (the stories of Gideon's many wives; the Levite's *pîlegeš*; and Elkanah's two wives, Hannah and Peninnah), from the premonarchic period of the Israelite history (ca. 1200–1000 BCE). We might conclude, therefore, that the Israelites of the first millennium BCE imagined nonroyal polygyny to be a feature only of their past. Polygyny is presented, however, as a possible marriage arrangement in preexilic legal texts—for example, Exod 21:10 and Deut 21:15–17—suggesting it may have been practiced, albeit occasionally, throughout preexilic times and into the Persian era (ca. 539–332 BCE).[8] Indeed, even though evidence for polygynous marriages lessens in the Hellenistic and Roman periods (ca. 332–63 BCE and ca. 63 BCE–135 CE),[9] archival texts from the first quarter of the second century CE attest to a polygynous marriage in which a Jewish man named Judah, who lives on the southwestern shores of the Dead Sea, is married to two women, Miriam and Babatha.[10] Moreover, in 537 CE, the Emperor Justinian granted the Jews of Tyre an exemption from the imperial prohibition against polygynous marriages that he had issued two years prior, which demonstrates that "as late as the early sixth century [CE] . . . at least some Jewish communities in Byzantium continued to practice polygyny."[11]

At least three of the Bible's polygynous relationships involve barren women (Sarah, Rachel, and Hannah), and we might speculate that like many Israelite marriage practices, whatever nonroyal polygyny took place (i.e., polygyny not driven primarily by diplomatic agendas and/or by an attempt to demonstrate status and wealth) stemmed, at least to some degree, from the typical household's urgent need for child labor that I discussed in the previous chapter. Thus, it was imperative that heads of households be married to reproductively able females. Still, according to many interpreters, the legal text found in Exod 21:10, though ambiguously phrased, forbids a man who has taken an enslaved woman as a wife from denying her access to certain entitlements allotted to her (food, clothing, and the right of sexual relations?) if he takes another woman.[12] We might extrapolate that custom would likewise have forbidden a man from withdrawing support from a barren wife in favor of a fertile one. Elkanah's continued support of the barren Hannah, even as Hannah is tormented by Elkanah's other wife Peninnah, suggests this as well (1 Sam 1:4–8). Custom might also be presumed to have protected a wife who was less desirable for other reasons from being materially slighted in favor of a more favored spouse. Indeed, Deut 21:15–17 protects, at least in part, the material well-being of a disliked wife (or, as Bruce Wells has argued, a wife demoted to secondary status) by safeguarding the inheritance rights of her son if he was her husband's firstborn.[13]

In addition to being typically patrilocal and occasionally polygynous, Israelite marriages were ideally endogamous, meaning one's spouse should be a fellow Israelite and, better yet, come from one's own kin group. Within narrative sources, this is particularly stressed in the book of Genesis, as Abraham quite emphatically tells the servant who is commissioned to secure a wife for his son Isaac that the woman must come from among his relations (*môledet*) still resident in his homeland and not from the Canaanites in whose land Abraham sojourns (Gen 24:3–4). Isaac in turn, along with his wife Rebekah, is said to have been embittered by his son Esau's marriages to two Hittite women (Gen 26:35; 27:46). He thus orders his other son Jacob that he, too, is to go to the family's ancestral homeland in order that he might marry one of Rebekah's brother's daughters (Gen 28:1–2).

Within legal texts, a similar antipathy regarding Canaanite and Hittite wives, among others, is found in Exod 34:11–16: Moses, speaking for God, commands the Israelites that they are not to take wives for their sons from the peoples who inhabit the so-called promised land to which the Israelites who have escaped from bondage in Egypt, according to the conceit of the text, will eventually lay claim. These inhabitants are "the Amorites, the Canaanites, the Hittites, the Perizzites, the Hivites, and the Jebusites." In Deut 7:1–4, Moses, again speaking on behalf of God, is more forceful still, forbidding the Israelites to take wives from and also to give wives to the inhabitants of the "promised land" they are soon to enter. This text identifies these inhabitants as "the Hittites, the Girgashites, the Amorites, the Canaanites, the Perizzites, the Hivites, and the Jebusites."

Judges 3:5–6, however, castigates the Israelites for doing precisely what Moses, in Exod 34:11–16 and Deut 7:1–4, had outlawed, by intermarrying with the Canaanites, Hittites, Amorites, Perizzites, Hivites, and Jebusites. In 1 Kgs 11:1–8, King Solomon is similarly criticized for marrying Hittite wives, as well as the daughter of the Egyptian pharaoh and wives from the nations of Moab, Ammon, Edom, and the Phoenician city-state of Sidon. Some decades later, according to biblical chronology, King Ahab of Israel's Northern Kingdom is likewise castigated for marrying a Sidonian princess, Jezebel (1 Kgs 16:31). The phenomenon of intermarriage—specifically, Israelite men marrying foreign wives—is then condemned again, according to biblical tradition, in the early postexilic era.[14] In this period, intermarriages with an amalgam of the peoples listed in Exod 34:11–16; Deut 7:1–4; and 1 Kgs 11:1–8 (Canaanites, Hittites, Perizzites, Jebusites, Ammonites, Moabites, Egyptians, and Amorites), along with intermarriages with the daughters of Ashdod, are harshly criticized by the community leaders Ezra and Nehemiah (Ezra 9:1–4; Neh 13:23–27).[15]

Exodus 34:11–16; Deut 7:1–4; Judg 3:5–6; and 1 Kgs 11:1–8; 16:31 clearly articulate why certain intermarriages are forbidden: it is feared that non-Israelite spouses, and especially non-Israelite wives, will lead their Israelite marital partners to worship their spouses' non-Israelite gods. Exodus 34:16, for example, warns that were the Israelites to take wives from among other peoples' daughters for their sons, these "daughters who are prostitutes to their gods will make your sons prostitutes to their gods." Deuteronomy 7:3–4 similarly cautions the Israelites not to "marry them [the inhabitants of Canaan at the time of the Israelites' purported entry into the land]," and so the people should not "give a daughter of yours to one of their sons or take a daughter of theirs for one of your sons, for your sons would turn away from me and serve other gods." Then, in 1 Kgs 11:4–5, Solomon's marriages to non-Israelite women are presented as proof that the fear articulated in Exodus and Deuteronomy is valid: "When Solomon was old, his wives turned his heart toward other gods . . . [and] Solomon followed Astarte the goddess of the Sidonians, and Milcom the abomination of the Ammonites." Nehemiah 13:26–27 in turn evokes Solomon's marriages to argue that intermarriage is an act of unfaithfulness against God that leads to sin, presumably the sin of religious assimilation. But Ezra 9:1–4 and 10:10–14 suggest that something different is at stake: the mixing of what Ezra 9:2 calls the *zeraʿ haqqōdeš*, or the "holy seed" of the Israelites with the "peoples of the lands." According to Ezra, that is, the "peoples of the lands" are inherently "polluted" (*niddâ*) and "unclean" (*ṭāmēʾ*; see Ezra 9:11), and so intermarriage, "by intermingling of the holy and the profane,"[16] threatens the "sanctity" of Israel's "bloodlines."[17]

Yet while apprehensions regarding apostasy and what we might think of as ethnic purity may justify an Israelite animus toward marriages with non-Israelites, such concerns do not explain the Israelite preference for marriages contracted only within one's own kin group. During the purported ancestral era described in Genesis, as I noted above, Abraham is said to define this "kin group" somewhat generically as one's relations (*môledet*). For the Israelite polity of the first millennium BCE, however, the meaning was more specific: to marry within one's "kin group" meant to marry within one's clan (*mišpāḥâ* or *ʾelep*) or at least to marry within the several clans, or *mišpāḥôt*, that comprised one's *šēbeṭ* or *maṭṭeh*, or tribe. As we saw Chapter 3, for example, Moses, speaking for God, decrees in Num 36:6 that the five daughters of Zelophehad must marry men from within the clans of their father's tribe.

In Num 36:7, Moses then explains that these intratribal marriages are required to guarantee that Zelophehad's *naḥălâ* (meaning his patrimonial or familial landholdings of which the daughters are the custodians since Zelophehad had died without male heirs) will stay within Zelophehad's kinship group.[18] Moreover, since Israelite tribes were constituted not just by kinship ties among their various clans but by each tribe's claims to, and its residence within, a particular region in the land of Israel, keeping Zelophehad's landholdings within Zelophehad's kinship group sustained the integrity of their tribe's territorial domain. Were Zelophehad's daughters to marry outside of their father's tribe, however, Zelophehad's *naḥălâ* would become the property of their husbands' clans and part of the territorial holdings of their husbands' tribes. No wonder, then, that in Num 38:8–9, Moses declares that his decree is binding not just on Zelophehad's daughters, but also on any daughter who finds herself in the same situation: "Any daughter from among the Israelite tribes who inherits a *naḥălâ* will marry someone from the clan of her father's tribe, so that all Israelites will inherit their patrimonial *naḥălâ*. No *naḥălâ* will go round from one tribe to another tribe; each of the Israelite tribes will keep its own *naḥălâ*."

Issues of property transfer could also have driven an Israelite preference for intraclan and intratribal endogamy in cases other than those involving landholdings. I discussed in Chapter 3, for example, how, in the preexilic period, a prospective groom's family typically gave a marriage present to the father of the bride-to-be. If we assume that this marriage present involved material wealth—the fifty silver pieces mandated by Deut 22:29, say, as opposed to payment in the form of indentured labor, as in the Jacob story (Gen 29:18–20, 27–28)—a norm of intraclan or intratribal endogamy would insure that this bridewealth stayed within the couple's kin group rather than be disbursed across clan or tribal boundaries. Intraclan or intratribal endogamy also kept resources within a kin group during the latter half of the first millennium BCE and into the first centuries CE, when an economy of dowry dominated. Thus, the Jewish philosopher Philo (ca. 15 BCE–50 CE) writes of husbands that "these should be, if possible, of the same family as the girls, or if that cannot be, at any rate of the same ward and tribe, in order that the portions assigned as dowry should not be alienated by inter-marriage with other tribes, but should retain the place given to them in the allotments originally made on the basis of tribes."[19]

Carol Meyers has in addition proposed that in preexilic Israel, intraclan and intratribal endogamy would have been of significant pragmatic value, given the challenges subsistence agriculture posed in the hill country, the heartland of Israelite settlement. Again, I have noted some of those challenges in Chapter 3, but here, quoting Meyers, we can add that the highlands of Palestine "represent perhaps the most fractured, complex combination of ecosystems in the world." Thus, knowing "household practices suitable to the local ecology," as would a woman who came from a prospective groom's tribe or (even better) from his clan within any given tribe (which would mean, typically, that the woman came from a family resident within the groom's village or the villages nearby), provided "a strong functional advantage."[20] Van der Toorn suggests, however, that "hardly less important" than the economic "considerations in favour of endogamy" was the "social motive": that the "woman should not be too far removed from the family of the man," lest their different backgrounds promote frictions within the marriage that could affect not only the couple themselves but the larger patrilineal household of which they were a part.[21] Joseph Blenkinsopp similarly argues that endogamy helped facilitate the social well-being of family and household. "Since the woman introduced into her husband's household always remained, in a certain sense, an outsider," he writes, "there was some pressure to seek an alliance with a household as close in terms of consanguinity as possible."[22]

Blenkinsopp, moreover, is not the only scholar to describe "the woman introduced into her husband's household" as, at least to some degree, a permanent "outsider." Phyllis A. Bird also writes that as a consequence of patrilocality, "married women are *outsiders* in the household of their husband and sons," to the extent that married women are "*aliens* . . . within their family of residence" (emphases mine).[23] Gale A. Yee likewise describes ancient Israelite women as "marginalized" and "disenfranchised" with respect to (among other things) their "marriage residence."[24] Similarly, in her 1993 book *Fragmented Women: Feminist (Sub)versions of Biblical Narrative*, J. Cheryl Exum includes a chapter whose title, "The (M)other's Place," and especially the parentheses within it, tries to capture the ambiguously "othered" position that the matriarchs Sarah, Rebekah, Rachel, and Leah, respectively, occupy in the households of Abraham, Isaac, and Jacob.

More specifically, Exum argues that, on the one hand, the matriarchs are central to moving the Genesis narrative forward, since the generational progression on which Genesis relies cannot be accomplished without the patriarchs Abraham, Isaac, and Jacob begetting a son or sons with a "right" or proper wife. What makes a wife "right," moreover, is her endogamous or "insider" status, meaning first, as I noted above, that she is neither of the Canaanites nor of some other people (for example, Hagar, whose son by Abraham is unprivileged in his father's genealogy because his mother is an Egyptian). Instead, and as I have again noted above, the "right" wife is of the patriarchs' own ethnos and indeed, according to the endogamous ideal as articulated in Genesis, from the patriarchs' near family: Sarah is Abraham's half-sister according to Gen 20:12; Rebekah and Isaac are patrilateral parallel cousins once removed; Rachel and Leah are Jacob's matrilateral cross-cousins. On the other hand, the matriarchs stand as "outsiders" within the narrative. Rebekah, Leah, and Rachel, for example, are residents of faraway lands they must leave to dwell with their husbands in Canaan, and once there, as Exum writes, "they are 'other.'"[25]

Or we might say that these matriarchs, along with other Israelite wives, are liminal, as the state of being an outsider and alien, who is marginalized, disenfranchised, and other, corresponds in multiple respects to the features that characterize liminality. Moreover, the notion that within the house of her husband, an ancient Israelite wife is both "insider" (of her husband's kin group) and yet "outsider" (a woman introduced into the household from elsewhere) evokes profoundly Victor Turner's notion of liminal persons as "betwixt and between," those who are "neither one thing nor another; or may be both," who are "neither this nor that, and yet [are] both."[26] In a careful study of women's status in ancient Israel, T. M. Lemos also suggests that "married women were in many ways subordinate to their husbands," especially "in cases where sexuality is discussed" and "a husband's . . . exclusive control" over the body of his wife is presumed.[27] Indeed, the term *ba'al*, "master," can be used interchangeably with the term used for husband, *'îš*, and a husband can be referred to as a woman's "lord," or *'ādôn* as well.[28] These data are again evocative of Turner's descriptions of liminal persons and how, as part of the liminal experience, they are placed in positions of submission, where they must acquiesce to whatever authorities have jurisdiction over them.

Furthermore, according to Turner's account, liminal persons are required to divest themselves of property (they are without "status, property, insignia, secular clothing, rank, kinship position"),[29] just as the daughters of Zelophehad, as I intimated above, will be required to divest themselves of the property they have inherited from their father when they marry, at which point their father's *naḥălâ* will pass into their husbands' care and then onward to their sons. Somewhat similarly, the account of Micah's mother in Judg 17:1–5 suggests—at least as I would interpret—that the mother is able to lay claim to her cache of eleven hundred silver pieces only after her husband, who typically would have controlled the couple's wealth, had died and she is no longer bound by the restrictions regarding property ownership that were placed on her during her marriage. Micah's theft of his mother's silver cache may be meant to indicate, however, that he views the matter differently and assumes that the property his father held during his parents' marriage should have passed directly to him.[30]

Othered, subordinate, without property, and disenfranchised as well "with respect to descent . . . and other social customs":[31] we can conclude that in ancient Israel, married women were liminal. More specifically, we can conclude, following Bruce Lincoln's and Caroline Walker Bynum's assessments of Turner's theory of liminality detailed in the Introduction, that married women in Israel were liminal as part of the *normal* course of their existence. But what does this conclusion mean regarding Israelite weddings, the life-cycle rituals that arguably propel women into their liminal identity within marriage? Weddings, moreover, are arguably the life-cycle rituals that move women out of the period of "betwixt and between" liminality that, as I suggested in Chapter 3, begins with betrothal. During this "betwixt and between" period, a woman can no longer be described as single but cannot be said to be married either. An Israelite wedding, in short, is arguably positioned between two periods of female liminality, betrothal and married life. Given this positioning, we might wonder whether Israelite weddings functioned for women as something of a respite from the liminal experience. That is, we might ask whether ancient Israelite weddings functioned for women as what Turner, as we saw in the Introduction, categorized as "rituals of status reversal." In these rituals, hierarchical inversions and reversals temporarily elevate or enhance the status of "the permanently structural inferior," meaning in this particular case the Israelite woman who is liminal *both* during her betrothal *and* during the course of her marriage. Or do Israelite weddings function as Turner's more typical rites of passage, which in moving women from one state (betrothed) to another (married) require a movement *into* liminality, and so the typical liminal experience of "a putting down or humbling" as a central and constitutive part?[32]

As we will see in what follows, the latter is the case. More specifically, for an ancient Israelite woman, the only signals of temporarily elevated or enhanced status associated with her marriage are expressed prior to the wedding proper, through, as I have argued in Chapter 3, the future groom's family's gifting of the marriage present to the bride-to-be's father. Conversely, during the wedding itself, the bride—which is to say, the liminal wife-to-be who is already liminal on account of both her betrothal and more generally her sex—simply becomes more liminal. Moreover, during the wedding, as we have come to expect, the bride's experience of liminality is more exaggerated or exacerbated than the aspects of liminality experienced by the groom, her male counterpart in this life-cycle event.

Ancient Israelite Weddings

To be sure, some scholars have raised doubts as to whether there was in fact an actual wedding ritual that marked a marriage's beginning in ancient Israel.[33] In part, these doubts have arisen because certain other cultures of the Near East had no formal marriage ceremony: for example, ancient Egypt.[34] In addition, the biblical record includes precious few indications of a wedding ceremony. But though few, the Bible contains enough references to suggest that ritually marking the occasion of a wedding in Israel was the norm. According to two texts in the latter half of the book of Isaiah, for example, the bride was specially adorned with some sort of ornaments (*ădî*, *kĕlî*) on her wedding day (Isa 49:18; 61:10). Although these passages are both metaphorical in nature (their subject is God's symbolic marriage to Jerusalem) and surely also hyperbolic (since the Israelites would have imagined a divine marriage to be celebrated on a scale well beyond the standard mere mortals might expect), each of these Isaiah texts must nevertheless have alluded to actual marriage practices in order for the metaphor of an ornamented Jerusalem to have made sense to its ancient audience.

Jeremiah 2:32 similarly suggests that a bride wore special "ribbons" or "sashes" (*qiššurîm*) for her wedding. If we follow the interpreters who take the text of Ezek 16:10–12 to be a description of the metaphorical wedding of God and Jerusalem (as opposed to those who contend that vv 10–12 describe the gifts God lavishes on the city after they are wed),[35] then we can infer that at least at the marriage ceremonies of elites (a status that, as in Isa 49:18 and 61:10, God can surely claim!), the bride's wedding-day adornments could have included rich robes made of embroidered cloth and linen, sandals made of fine leather, and jewelry in the form of bracelets, a necklace, earrings, a nose ring, and a crown. Psalm 45:14–15 (45:13–14 in most English translations) speaks similarly of multicolored robes worn by an elite bride (in this case, a king's daughter) when she married.[36] Canticles 3:11 further indicates that a king wore a crown for his wedding, and while this may seem unexceptional—for would we not expect a king to wear a crown upon the occasion of a royal wedding?—Isa 61:10 suggests that wearing some sort of garland was standard for all grooms.[37]

A related passage in Isa 62:2 hints that a bride may have adopted a new name (presumably, by adding her husband's name to her own) when she married. Isaiah 4:1 implies this as well.[38] Our textual evidence further seems to indicate that at some point during the wedding event, the bride put on a veil,[39] as Rebekah does immediately before meeting Isaac in Gen 24:65 and as Leah may well have worn on the night of her wedding, facilitating Jacob's mistaken sense that it was Leah's sister Rachel with whom he lay (Gen 29:23–25).[40] Near Eastern parallels and a few biblical passages may also intimate that the marriage was formalized by the groom's uttering some version of the statement that "She will be my wife, and I will be your husband" (cf. Hos 2:4 [2:2 in most English translations]).[41] Whether the bride uttered the reciprocal form of this pledge is not known.[42] Nor is it known whether a formal marriage contract was part of marital ritual in Israel either in preexilic tradition or during the early postexilic period, although such contracts—which became standard within Judaism by the rabbinic period—are attested at the fifth-century BCE Jewish colony of Elephantine, in southern Egypt. Their use is in addition documented in the fourth- or third-century BCE book of Tobit (Tob 7:13).[43]

It is also unclear whether all brides were accompanied by female attendants, as was the royal bride of Ps 45:15 (English 45:14). Some commentators have likewise wondered whether a groom was typically attended at his wedding by a "best man," given the reference in Judg 14:20 to the companion to whom Samson's wife is given after Samson abandons his father-in-law's house and so also his bride who was resident there.[44] However, the verb that commentators interpret to mean "to be a special friend," that is, "a best man" (*rēʿâ*), occurs in the Bible only at this point, rendering its translation uncertain. Nor can the passage in 1 Macc 9:37–39 that describes a procession in which a large entourage conducts a bride to her wedding, and that the bridegroom and a host of male companions eventually join, be used to suggest that both Israelite grooms and brides were normally escorted by, respectively, male and female attendants, since this passage postdates the heart of the ancient Israelite period by centuries and also concerns an elite wedding.[45] It seems more definite, though, that Israelite weddings involved feasting, as did Samson's wedding and as his story also reports to be cultural custom (Judg 14:10). Laban likewise "made a feast" (Gen 29:22) at the time of Jacob's first marriage, which, as noted above, Jacob expected to be to Rachel but was actually to Leah. The postexilic account of Esther's being taken into the harem of King Ahasuerus of Persia similarly describes this event as celebrated by a feast (Esth 2:18).

In all these cases, the Hebrew term for the "feast" in question is *mišteh*, a noun derived from the verb *šātâ*, "to drink." This suggests (not surprisingly, if cross-cultural analogies, including modern parallels, are of significance) that Israelite wedding feasts involved abundant consumption of alcohol. The New Testament story of the wedding at Cana (John 2:1–11), at which the wine runs out, suggests this as well. Indeed, C. F. Burney goes so far as to translate *mišteh* in Judg 14:10 as "a drinking bout."[46] The guests at these marital "drinking bouts," however, may have been only men (the presence of Jesus's mother at the wedding feast at Cana notwithstanding).[47] Thus, Gen 29:22 specifies that it was all the *'anšê hammāqôm*, literally "the *men* of the place," whom Laban invites to feast upon the occasion of Jacob's first marriage, and Samson's wedding feast is said to be a custom among "young men" (*baḥûrîm*). The featured guests at Samson's feast are, it follows, his thirty *male* companions who have been assembled from among the Philistines. The banquet marking Esther's entry into Ahasuerus's harem in Esth 2:18 is also arguably an all-male affair, as is the case for at least two of the other five banquets that take place in Esther's opening chapters: Ahasuerus's banquet for all his (male) courtiers and officials in Esth 1:3 and his banquet with his senior adviser Haman in Esth 3:15. In fact, as Elias Bickerman proposed some fifty years ago, it may have been the norm in Persian culture (with which Esther's author seems to have had a basic familiarity)[48] for men and women—or, more specifically, husbands and wives—to keep separate during banquets, especially when drinking was taking place.[49] Somewhat similarly, in classical Greek tradition, men sat "on one side of the room" during a wedding feast and "the women on the other."[50]

Samson at his wedding feast also poses a riddle to his thirty Philistine companions who are in attendance; does this indicate that Israelite wedding feasts generally involved not only drinking, but also gaming and even more specifically riddling contests? Does the fact that Samson's feast lasts seven days likewise indicate that wedding feasts generally lasted this long? That certain other biblical festivals were seven days in length might argue for this possibility, as might the prevailing interpretation of Gen 29:27, which sees an allusion to a seven-day wedding feast in the account of Jacob's marriage to Leah.[51] Also, one of the two wedding feasts of Tobias described in the deuterocanonical book of Tobit is of seven days' duration (Tob 11:18). Tobias's other wedding feast, however, is said to last fourteen days (Tob 8:20; 10:7). Because, moreover, Tobit, as noted above, is a fourth- or third-century BCE text, its witness cannot be taken as a solid parallel to the much earlier Genesis and Judges accounts of Jacob's and Samson's weddings. The reference to a seven-day wedding feast in the text of Joseph and Aseneth (21:8),[52] which seems to date "from the second century BCE to the first century CE,"[53] offers an even less compelling comparison. Indeed, the chronologies of both the Tobit and Joseph and Aseneth accounts of wedding feasts may have been shaped to correspond to older biblical tradition.[54]

When working with only the Samson account and the account of Jacob's wedding feast, it is also impossible to say definitively whether, as both texts suggest, it was the norm to hold the feast at the bride's natal home.[55] However, a third text—Deut 22:13–21—may help clarify this matter somewhat. This passage concerns a legal issue: a husband who accuses a newly married wife of not being a virgin at the time of their wedding. According to Deuteronomy's dictates, the charge is to be addressed by the bride's father and mother presenting evidence of her virginity to a body of adjudicating elders. The evidence in question, we are told more specifically, is some sort of cloth. Most logically, this cloth would have come from the couple's wedding bed and should have on it blood that would attest to the fact that, on the wedding night, the woman's hymen had been pierced: it is hard to imagine any other cloth that could conclusively prove that the bride was a virgin.[56] But how would the bride's father and mother come to have this cloth had the marriage not been consummated at their home? And if the marriage was consummated at the bride's family's home, then would we not expect that the wedding celebration took place there as well, just as Gen 29:22; Judg 14:10–18; and also Tobit 7–8, from the later deuterocanonical tradition, indicate?

Yet even though her wedding and the subsequent consummation of her marriage took place (apparently) at the bride's natal home, it is not clear that the marital rite was a "homey" occasion—that is, easy and/or comfortable—for the woman. We have already seen, for example, that it is not necessarily clear that she (or any women) attended the wedding's celebratory feast. Furthermore, Judg 14:10–18 indicates that even from her position on the periphery, Samson's wedding feast quickly became a miserable affair for his Timnite bride, as she was sucked into the agon of the riddling contest on the feast's fourth day in ways that put her in an impossible position.[57] On the one hand, Samson's thirty companions-cum-opponents threaten to immolate her and also to set fire to her father's house if she does not coax Samson to reveal the answer to his utterly enigmatic riddle (whose solution requires knowing that without telling anyone, Samson had taken honey from a hive of bees that had settled in a lion's carcass). On the other hand, Samson repeatedly refuses to give into her entreaties. Only on the seventh day, after she weeps and "nags at" or "presses upon" (*hĕṣîqathû*) Samson for, presumably, half the festal period (throughout the feast's fourth, fifth, and sixth days), does he explain the riddle to her.[58] She in turn reveals the riddle's answer to "her people" (Judg 14:17)—meaning, presumably, Samson's thirty Philistine companions, who then claim victory in the riddling contest. At that point, Samson leaves and soon thereafter returns to his natal home in anger and, at least as his bride's father sees it, for good (Judg 15:2). Thus, the father gives his newlywed daughter to another man (Judg 14:20).

Obviously, this rather unhappy experience for Samson's Timnite bride is the result of a very idiosyncratic set of circumstances and can hardly be taken as evidence of what an Israelite bride's experience at her wedding routinely would have been. Still, Jean Bottéro has written regarding a Mesopotamian account of a wedding feast that although it "*appeared* to be a light-heated and festive meal," "in reality, in the mentality and habits of the time . . . it was what one might call, in quotation marks, a 'sacrament': a ritual both symbolic and effective, which, taken as a whole, *symbolized* a state of affairs."[59] The fate of Samson's wife might thus lead us to ask: does Samson's wedding feast "symbolize a state of affairs" whereby Israelite weddings were, at least to some degree, sorrowful occasions for all women? A certain amount of evidence suggests this may have been the case.

The Tragic Wedding

There are at least three evocations of the Samson story's motif of a bride's sorrowful wedding elsewhere in the book of Judges: in Judg 19:1–21:25. As these chapters begin, the *pîlegeš*, or lesser wife, of a Levite from Ephraim spurns her husband and returns to her father's home in Bethlehem, in the tribal territory of Judah (Judg 19:1–2).[60] After an unexplained interval of four months, the Levite determines to reclaim this woman and travels to Bethlehem to do so. Once there, the wife's father greets him warmly, and the Levite and father (but not, according to any indication in the story, the *pîlegeš*) then engage in a multiday feast before, finally, at the end of the fifth day, the Levite takes his *pîlegeš* and heads for his home in Ephraim (Judg 19:4–10). The journey is a disastrous one, as the *pîlegeš* ends up raped and murdered by the Benjaminites of the town of Gibeah, in which the Levite and his traveling party have stopped for the night (Judg 19:25–28).[61] This offense eventually leads to the tribe of Benjamin being declared outcast by the rest of Israel's tribes (Judg 20:12–17), a state that persists until the Benjaminites are defeated by their compatriots in civil war (Judg 20:35–48).

A project of rebuilding and repeopling the formerly ostracized tribe of Benjamin is then undertaken, which involves, first, taking from the town of Jabesh-Gilead four hundred maidens (*nĕʿārôt*), who are further designated as *bĕtûlôt*, young women of marriageable age.[62] They are given to Benjamin's surviving males as wives, while the rest of the inhabitants of Jabesh-Gilead—men, women, and children—are killed as punishment for Jabesh-Gilead's failure to join the Israelite militia in its war against Benjamin (Judg 21:8–14). But these four hundred maidens are not sufficient for the Benjaminites' needs, and so a second plan is hatched: the two hundred men from among the Benjaminites who remain unwed are to emerge from hiding places in the vineyards of Shiloh, and—as in the Greek tale of Hades abducting the dancing Persephone (see Chapter 2) and as in the Roman tale of the rape of the Sabine women—they seize wives for themselves from a company of Shilonite maidens who have come out to dance during the celebration of the autumn harvest festival of Ingathering or Sukkot (Judg 21:19–21).[63]

These two episodes in Judg 21:8–14 and 19–21 surely must be classified, as was the Timnite woman's marriage in Judg 14:10–18, as sorrowful occasions for the six hundred "brides" of Jabesh-Gilead and Shiloh. For example, in her monograph on the incidents of "marriage by capture" in Judges 21, Katherine Southwood quotes anthropologists Ayse Kudat and Brian Stross in order to suggest that, from the point of view of an ancient Israelite audience, the four hundred women of Jabesh-Gilead would have had little choice but to marry the Benjaminites to whom they were given after being taken from their town, since "once these women have been captured, they are 'presumed to have been' violated sexually." This means that even if the town of Jabesh-Gilead and its other inhabitants had not been destroyed according to the conceit of Judg 21:8–14, the captured women could not have returned to their homes, for within the Israelite worldview, where the preservation of an unmarried woman's virginity can be, as we saw in Chapter 3, a matter of great honor, the result of the captured women's return would be "social shame and stigmatisation" for both them and their families. Moreover, even if the women were to be envisioned as defying these perceptions and fleeing from the Benjaminites, the chances of these supposedly nonvirgin women "attracting another suitor drop significantly."[64] Southwood similarly writes of the lack of options that an ancient Israelite audience would have thought available to the abducted women of Shiloh, as the fact that they are captured would suggest to an ancient audience that their "virginity had been taken" and thus their "reputation is ruined from that point onwards." It would thereby be thought "unlikely" that any of the abducted maidens could "find another partner let alone a bride-price," and so their "best option" was to "marry the Benjaminite captors."[65]

Note as well how the motif of a bride's sorrowful wedding is subtly evoked in our passage's initial episode in Judg 19:1–10 regarding the *pîlegeš*. In this account, as in the Samson account in Judg 14:10–18, a man comes to the house of his father-in-law (or, in Judg 14:10–18, his father-in-law-to-be) to claim (or, in Judg 14:10–18, to wed) a wife. Once that is accomplished, he joins with the father-in-law (and/or, in Judg 14:10–18, with other men) in a multiday feast at which the woman is (apparently) not present. Yet, when the woman does appear during the course of the feasting, on the fourth or fifth day (Judg 14:15; 19:10),[66] the result for her is calamitous. Samson's bride becomes caught between the threats of her fellow Philistines and the recalcitrance of her husband until Samson, after being bested in the riddling contest, seemingly abandons her, at least from the point of view of her father (Judg 14:20; 15:2). The Levite likewise abandons his *pîlegeš*, as it is *he*, in Judg 19:25, who shoves her out the door of the Gibeahite house in which they lodge after having left her father's house in Bethlehem. The result for the *pîlegeš*, as noted above, is that she ends up dead on that house's doorstep after a night of being sexually abused by Gibeah's Benjaminite residents. Samson's bride likewise seems to end up dead after Samson abandoned her, burned (presumably to death) by her Philistine countrymen in response to Samson's vengeful burning of their wheatfields, vineyards, and olive groves (Judg 15:4–6). Just as the occasion of Samson's wedding becomes the occasion of his bride's death, that is, and at the hands of her Philistine compatriots, so too does a scene cast as a "second wedding," so to speak—the Levite's coming to his father-in-law's house to retake his *pîlegeš*—result in the murder of the "bride" by her fellow Israelites.[67]

Might the repeated evocation of this literary trope furthermore indicate, we can again ask, that Israelite weddings were to some degree sorrowful occasions for all brides? Consider in this regard Ps 78:63 which is part of a catalog that describes God's punishments of rebellious Israelites during the premonarchic period. In this passage we read, most literally, "Their young women of marriageable age [*bĕtûlôt*] were not praised/celebrated [*hullal*]." Some commentators have interpreted this to mean something like "Their maidens had no nuptial song." This is the translation, for example, advanced by the NRSV. Such an interpretation quite plausibly posits that music would have been made upon the occasion of a wedding, as is also suggested by the most plausible interpretation of an important piece of comparative evidence, a text from the Late Bronze Age city-state of Ugarit, on the northern Levantine coast. According to several scholars, this poem (*KTU* 1.24), in which a singer recounts the story of the marriage of the moon-god Yariḫ and the goddess Nikkal-Ib, was performed commonly "at marriage ceremonies to ensure for the bride the same blessing and protection by the *katharat* [the divine patronesses of wedlock and conception] as was accorded the goddess Nikkal at her wedding."[68]

Further comparative evidence specifically associates the performance of at least some of a wedding's nuptial songs with women, as in Greek tradition, where marriage hymns were sung by a bride or by a young women's chorus that performed on her behalf. Yet while our contemporary understanding of a wedding as an occasion of celebration for both bride and groom might lead us to expect these Greek nuptial hymns to be songs of joy, these women's songs in fact express profound ambivalence about the bride's experience of matrimony: what commentators David and Sharon Hoffman have called "the passion, joy, and *sacrifice* of women as they enter marriage" (emphasis mine).[69] On the one hand, the bride or the young woman's chorus that speaks for her acknowledges the wedding as marking her entry into maturity and adulthood.[70] On the other hand, sentiments of dread are expressed, regarding especially the bride's losing the security of her childhood home (Greek marriage, like Israelite marriage, was patrilocal) and life in the alien world of a new husband's abode, as well as fears regarding the unfamiliar experiences of sexual intimacy, pregnancy, and childbirth.[71]

A fragment from a marriage hymn of the sixth-century BCE poet Sappho speaks evocatively to the young woman's misgivings:[72]

(The bride speaks): Maidenhood, maidenhood, whither have you gone and left me?
(Maidenhood responds): Never will I return to you, never return.

Another Sappho fragment describes in even more biting terms maidenhood's loss, as the end of the bride's maiden days is compared to the destruction of a delicate flower:[73]

Just as in the mountains the shepherd men trample a hyacinth
With their feet, and the purple flower lies on the ground.

Moreover, often in the Greek marriage hymns sung as the bride departs from her birth family and her childhood companions, "the bride's friends oppose the unnatural wrestling of a child from her mother."[74] In her study of Greek weddings, Rebecca Hague reports that even "in parts of Greece today, the bride's mother sings laments" when the bride leaves her natal home, "grieving for the daughter she is losing."[75]

More poignant still within classical Greek tradition are the *epithalamia*, the songs that are sung by a bride's female attendants throughout the night once the bride, after she has come to her new husband's house, first lies with the bridegroom. These performances, according to one fairly disconcerting explanation, provide for the bride "the comfort of her friend's [sic] voices throughout the first night she spent with the stranger who had become her husband."[76] The scholia (marginal notes penned by later commentators) to an *epithalamium* (the singular form of *epithalamia*) written by the third-century BCE Sicilian poet Theocritus (Idyll 18) suggest an even more foreboding purpose: "Maidens sing the *epithalamium* before the bridal chamber so that the voice of the virgin might not be heard as she is violated by her husband."[77] In her book *Women's Songs in Ancient Greece*, Anne L. Klinck notes somewhat similarly the ominous undertones of Sappho Fragment 110a, which otherwise seems an outlandish and humorous song about a wedding ceremony's giant doorkeeper (his feet are so large that it took five ox-hides to make his sandals). The role this oaf performs at the wedding, though, is hardly a laughing matter: it "was to prevent the bride's friends from coming *to her rescue* in the bridal chamber" (emphasis mine).[78]

Equally ominous for the bride are "the basic similarities between Greek ... wedding and funerary ritual."[79] Both include, for example, the "taking away" of a loved young woman from her family and that family's experience of grieving and loss.[80] More specifically, as Rush Rehm writes in his revealingly titled study *Marriage to Death: The Conflation of Wedding and Funeral Rituals in Greek Tragedy*:[81]

> A bride will offer a lock of hair before her marriage; mourners will offer the same when visiting a grave. Like the bride and groom, the dead are ritually bathed, dressed, adorned, and crowned. ... The corpse is covered, the bride is veiled, the dead are laid out on a bed or couch, the wedding leads to the nuptial bed. Both events involve a journey at night to a new "home," often taken by horse- or mule-cart, in a procession that includes torchbearers, family, and friends, and where song and dance mark the occasion. A *makarismos* [a pronouncement of blessing] ... is used for the "happy" couple and the "blessed" dead. The bride receives gifts in her new home, corpses receive gifts in theirs, and both rites include a final banquet.

Rehm elsewhere adds that a particular type of Greek pottery, the *lebes gamikos*, or "wedding bowl," which was used in the nuptial ritual and was then "given as a wedding gift afterwards," may also be given as a grave gift,[82] and that the so-called *xeira epi karpōi*, a scene that is often depicted on Greek vase painting whereby a groom takes his bride by the wrist to lead her to her new home, may also appear on vase paintings that represent the messenger god Hermes taking a deceased woman by the wrist to lead her to the boat that takes the dead across the River Styx and into the underworld.[83]

With all of this in mind, let us look again at the potential reference to wedding songs found in Ps 78:63, along with the succeeding verse in 78:64. Here, "nuptial songs" (if that is how we should translate) in v 63 and weeping in lamentation in v 64 are paired in a way that is highly reminiscent of the Greek materials wherein marriage hymns and funerary laments are paralleled. Somewhat similarly, in Jer 16:1–9, Jeremiah is forbidden both to marry and to engage in funerary rites, which are therefore possibly to be taken, as in Greece, as kindred institutions of Israelite ritual life.

It may be, then, that in Israelite tradition, as in the Greek world, young men, including the groom, engaged in raucous drinking, gaming, and joyous music-making at a wedding (as is suggested in Judg 14:10–18 and attested in various Greek materials),[84] while the bride and perhaps her women companions marked the occasion by making music of a more somber nature. Indeed, the paralleled evocations of wedding songs and lamentation that may be found in Ps 78:63–64 could lead us to imagine that, as in the coming-of-age rite of Jephthah's daughter that I described in Chapter 2, a young woman engaged during her wedding in "a ritual *lament* which . . . acknowledged the 'death' of one stage in life in preparation for entry into a new stage" (emphasis mine).[85]

I also described in Chapter 2 how the "death" that must be confronted in young women's coming-of-age rituals is, according to our biblical sources, more symbolically fraught than the death imagery encountered by young men in their coming-of-age rites, and in wedding rituals similarly, "brides were particularly vulnerable."[86] This is because marriage "represents a rite of passage for young girls more so than it does for young men,"[87] given that brides, in leaving behind their childhood home, are *separated*, to use the language of Arnold van Gennep's rites-of-passage paradigm, from far more, due to the conventions of patrilocal marriage, than are grooms. A wedding is in addition the occasion of a bride's sexual initiation, and so it marks her transformation from virgin to wife, whereas "virginity was not emphasized for young men in the same way it was for young women."[88] Furthermore, because—as we saw in Chapter 3—an Israelite bride, unlike an Israelite groom, is married very shortly after she becomes sexually mature, the bride, unlike the groom, is physically transformed from "a child to an adult."[89]

With respect to the marriage traditions of the Israelite and eastern Mediterranean world that we have surveyed, van Gennep's language describing marriage rites is thus profoundly ironic. As he writes, "To marry is to pass from the group of children or adolescents into the adult group, from a given clan to another, from one family to another, and often from one village to another." He then continues: "An individual's separation from these [former] groups weakens them but strengthens those he joins."[90] In ancient Israel, though, as elsewhere in the eastern Mediterranean, it is much more so the bride, as opposed to the groom, who passes "from the society of children or adolescents into the adult group," and it is emphatically only the bride who passes "from one family to another, and often from one village to another." Thus, it is *her* integration into her husband's household and village that strengthens these groups that *she* joins. In particular, as I have argued in Chapter 3, she strengthens her husband's household and village through her reproductive ability and thus her potential to add children to her husband's family's labor force, in order better to sustain his family's well-being as self-sufficient agrarian-pastoralists. While it may be, moreover, that an Israelite bride's "separation" from her natal family and village "weakens them," this effect is mitigated, I have suggested, by the gifting of the marriage present. Instead, it is the bride herself who is weakened, as, by entering into matrimony, she assumes the permanently liminal existence that, as detailed earlier, defines married women in ancient Israel.

In sum: by incorporating liminal features such as disenfranchisement, suffering, and evocations of death into the bride's experience (but not the groom's), the wedding is a life-cycle ritual that adumbrates the liminal nature of the woman's marriage that will follow. In this respect, the description that I proposed above of Israelite weddings as a women's life-cycle event seems confirmed: it is an occasion during which the bride—that is, the liminal wife-to-be who is already liminal both through her betrothal and her gender—simply becomes more liminal. Moreover, and as I again proposed above, the typically liminal experiences of marginalization, vulnerability, risk, and danger that both male and female participants in any rite of passage endure are intensified during the course of an ancient Israelite wedding for the woman, as she is pushed, like Samson's bride, to the periphery of the wedding's celebratory festivities, where she is left to face with dread her new identity as wife and her new responsibilities of childbearing and childrearing in a home that is not her own.

PART III
MOTHERHOOD

5
Pregnancy and Childbirth

In Chapter 3, I described an Israelite woman's coming of age, betrothal, and marriage as a continuum of interconnected and enmeshed ritual events that looked forward, moreover, to motherhood—which we might think of as the culmination of an extended "pubescence through maternity" ritual complex. But for Israelite women, motherhood is itself an extended ritual complex that progresses through the interconnected and enmeshed ritual events of pregnancy and parturition and then incorporates rituals that surround a neonate's first days of life. These postpartum rituals include some of the practices discussed in Chapter 1, such as marking a period of ritual impurity for both a newly delivered mother and her newborn child, with the child's impurity perhaps mitigated, as Ezek 16:4 might suggest, through the postpartum rituals of bathing the infant and rubbing its body with salt. Postpartum rituals also include the circumcision of male children on the eighth day after their births—once, that is, infant circumcision became the Israelite norm (see Chapter 2). More important for our purposes, though, given this study's focus on women and my focus in what follows on motherhood, is a mother's bestowing a name on her newborn shortly after birth, the ritual significance of which I will consider in Chapter 6. Then, in Chapter 7, I will argue that the ritual continuum of motherhood stretched significantly beyond name-giving and the other events that occurred immediately after a baby was born, lasting until a woman's offspring was fully weaned—which happened only when a child was about three years of age.

But in this chapter, before examining the rituals associated with naming and weaning, I discuss the beginnings of the motherhood ritual complex: an Israelite woman's ritual observances during pregnancy and childbirth. Unfortunately, though, we have only spotty evidence for rituals that address an Israelite mother-to-be's experiences from conception through parturition.[1] Yet ancient Near Eastern data can help illuminate rituals that were deployed during an Israelite mother-to-be's pregnancy, labor, and delivery. More specifically, I begin this chapter by surveying select childbirth rituals from the ancient Near East—and especially from Hatti, Mesopotamia,

Maturity, Marriage, Motherhood, Mortality. Susan Ackerman, Oxford University Press.
© Oxford University Press 2025. DOI: 10.1093/9780197809686.003.0007

and Egypt, where our evidence is the richest—in order to highlight traditions that arguably have relevance for students of ancient Israel and the Bible.² Then, in the second half of this chapter, I look at the Israelite and biblical materials illuminated by my survey of the Near Eastern evidence.

Childbirth Rituals from the Ancient Near East

I begin my account of ancient Near Eastern childbirth rituals with a Hittite Empire text from ca. 1450–1350 BCE that indicates that a special festival in honor of the Hittite "Mother-goddesses of the body" or "Great goddesses of the body" might be observed when a woman became pregnant and that many other propitiatory rites were performed in honor of these same goddesses throughout the time the woman carried her baby.³ This text also indicates that prior to delivery, oracles could be sought, presumably to discern whether the mother-to-be would be able to carry and give birth to her child successfully and in order that corrective measures could be undertaken to address any problems that were revealed.⁴ In addition, the text describes dietary restrictions and constraints on sexual relations with her husband that were imposed on a pregnant woman.

Conversely in Hittite tradition, there was "an apparent lack of reliance on amulets" in general and on childbirth amulets in particular,⁵ whereas in Egypt and in Mesopotamia, mothers-to-be standardly wore amulets to ensure the period of gestation would be successful. Indeed, according to the second of the two stories of Setne Khamwas, an Egyptian text that dates from the Roman era (ca. 63 BCE–135 CE), the first thing Setne does when he learns that his wife Mehusekhe is pregnant is hang an amulet on her.⁶ The use of amulets to protect pregnant women is also well known from much earlier periods in Egyptian history, especially amulets representing Taweret, the hippopotamus goddess of pregnancy, and Bes, the dwarf demigod who safeguarded pregnant women and their newborn children (see Fig. 5.1 and 5.2 and also Fig. 5.6).⁷ Similarly, in Mesopotamia, Lamaštu plaques—small tablets that depict the child-snatching demon Lamaštu on one side and that typically have a protective incantation inscribed on the other—were used as amulets from the second millennium BCE onward to ward off this fearsome female monster who otherwise could mercilessly attack infants: in the womb, during childbirth, or postpartum.⁸ In first-millennium BCE Mesopotamia, amulets representing the head of the ferocious yet benevolent Assyro-Babylonian

PREGNANCY AND CHILDBIRTH   145

Fig. 5.1   Lapis Lazuli Taweret Amulet. Egyptian, Eighteenth Dynasty (ca. 1539–1292 BCE). 3.5 cm high, 1.5 cm wide. From the collection of the Metropolitan Museum of Art, New York. Accession no. 17.194.2477.

Fig. 5.2 Single-Strand Necklace with Taweret Amulets. Egyptian, ca. 1332–1292 BCE. Faience, 1.9 x 20.5 x 0.4 cm. Brooklyn Museum, Gift of Mrs. Lawrence Coolidge and Mrs. Robert Woods Bliss, and the Charles Edwin Wilbour Fund, 48.66.42. Creative Commons-BY. Photo: Brooklyn Museum, 48.66.42_PS2.jpg.

demon Pazazu, who was able to force Lamaštu to abandon her human prey and return to her underworld domain, could likewise be hung around the necks of pregnant women.[9]

Mesopotamian texts also refer to amulets such as the *išqillatu*, "the stone of pregnancy,"[10] and the *aban erê*, the "stone of staying/remaining pregnant."[11] The name of this latter stone points to one of a pregnant women's greatest fears, miscarriage,[12] and Mesopotamian tradition indicates that in order to prevent this misfortune, special amulet stones could be tied to a mother-to-be's body if she was experiencing difficulties. For example, a text from the Neo-Assyrian period (ca. 911–612 BCE) describes how nine special stones—the *ḫaltu*-stone, the right-handed *šubû*-stone, the left-handed *šubû*-stone, the masculine and feminine *šû*-stones, blood-red carnelian, the *kapāṣu*-shell, the *ianibu*-stone, and the *zibtu*-stone—could be tied around the waist of a pregnant women who suffered from excessive vaginal bleeding.[13] The knots that secured these stones onto a string and were then used to tie that string onto the woman's body also were significant. Thus, after the nine amulet stones and other protective objects (for example, seeds from the "it purifies" plant) were threaded onto an elaborately entwined cord made of red- and blue-colored wool, combed wool, rushes, and sinews from a dead cow and a male and a female gazelle, this cord was specially knotted fourteen times. Next, after an incantation was recited three times, the cord was tied around the woman's waist. Through this act of sympathetic magic, the knots that bound the amulets on their special cord and the knots that bound the cord to the woman's waist also bound and thereby closed her uterus and so caused her vaginal bleeding to cease.

A similar use of an amuletic object in conjunction with knot magic to forestall vaginal bleeding is documented in an earlier text from the Old Babylonian period (ca. 1894–1595 BCE), where a *kapāṣu*-shell (perhaps representing female genitalia?)[14] is threaded onto a piece of red-colored wool smeared with cow's fat, which is then tied (sequentially?) around a woman's head, throat, and limbs to stop the abnormal bleeding coming from her birth canal.[15] Knot magic could even be deployed independent of amulets, as can be seen in this Neo-Assyrian spell meant to stop excessive uterine bleeding:[16]

> You twine together white wool (and) red wool. You tie seven knots. You dribble *ḫūratu* (on the knots). Whenever you tie one of the knots, you recite the recitation seven times. If you tie it on her hip region, she should recover.

Yet another Mesopotamian text, dating to the Late Babylonian period (sixth century BCE), describes how a cloth band made from red-colored wool could be tied on a mother-to-be to prevent miscarriage.[17]

Note likewise Egyptian spells from the New Kingdom (ca. 1539–1075 BCE), which direct that a piece of knotted material should be placed in a hemorrhaging woman's vagina to keep her from miscarrying.[18] Kindred traditions are attested in a Hittite Empire text from ca. 1450–1350 BCE, which, in an extensive account of purificatory rites "carried out soon before ... the actual birth," details how a *patili*-priest binds red wool to the expectant mother's hand.[19] According to Hittitologist and classicist Mary Bachvarova, the goal, as in Mesopotamia and in Egypt, is "to magically ensure that the womb remains closed until the proper term of the pregnancy has been reached."[20]

Bachravova somewhat similarly suggests that a Hittite woman's girdle must be untied when it is time for her to deliver,[21] and Mesopotamian and Egyptian sources in addition document the removal of bands or the untying of knots at the time of the actual birth. In her detailed study of Mesopotamian rituals meant to protect pregnant and parturient women, JoAnn Scurlock explains the reasoning that underlies this widespread Near Eastern custom: because knots were otherwise "designed to keep the foetus from emerging, it was necessary to remove them before the actual birth could take place."[22] Indeed, in Egypt, knots were so much thought to "constrain birth" that all knots in a pregnant woman's household had to be loosened at the time of delivery. For example, according to the miraculous tale recorded on the early second millennium BCE Westcar Papyrus that describes the extraordinary births of three Fifth Dynasty kings,[23] the knot that secured the kilt of Rawoser, the parturient's husband, had to be untied during her delivery.[24] Egyptian artistic representations likewise suggest that a parturient woman's hair was intentionally unbraided (or unknotted) and left to hang unbound during delivery and immediately postpartum.[25] Classical Greek depictions of women giving birth similarly show them "ungirdled and with hair flowing loose."[26] Note too the following remark from the first-century CE Roman author Pliny the Elder in *Natural History* 28.9.42: "the man by whom the woman has conceived hastens delivery if he unties his belt and ties it around her waist and then unties it."[27]

Other rituals enacted at the time of parturition include, in Mesopotamia, a midwife making "a pattern of meal" during a pregnant woman's delivery (often interpreted as a ring of flour on the floor) and an exorcist making offerings of bread.[28] According to Scurlock, the midwife's ring of flour created a "magic circle" in which birth could safely take place and in which the afterbirth—which could attract demonic agents—could be safely deposited, while the exorcist's bread offerings were seemingly meant to sate the hunger of demons that might otherwise snatch newborn infants.[29] During delivery, Mesopotamian women might also wear the same sorts of amulets that had protected them during their pregnancy in order to counteract the dangers of childbirth.[30] A Neo-Assyrian text, for example, lists a set of twelve amulet stones that could be tied to the hands, feet, and hips of a woman who struggles during labor and "does not give birth easily."[31] In Late Babylonian tradition, we find similar references to the *turminû*, a stone for "a woman having difficulty in childbirth."[32]

In Egypt, laboring women likewise sought to ward off the dangers of childbirth by wearing amulets to save them from "death in the House of Birth,"[33] including, according to spells from Papyrus Leiden I 348 (Nineteenth Dynasty; thirteenth century BCE), "a dwarf of clay" placed on the brow of a woman suffering during labor. This is almost undoubtedly a reference to a clay amulet representing Bes, the dwarf demigod who, as I noted above, safeguarded pregnant women and their newborn children (see also Fig. 5.6).[34] A drawing on a roughly contemporaneous limestone chip from the late thirteenth-/early twelfth-century BCE workman's village of Deir el-Medina, which shows a woman sitting with a male child atop a bed whose legs are in the form of Bes, has been similarly interpreted as a charm used by Egyptian mothers-to-be to depict "the desired, happy outcome of successful childbirth."[35]

Egyptian mothers-to-be also made use of "pregnancy vases"—alabaster jars in the shape of a pregnant woman—which held oil that may have been used to anoint the delivering woman (see Fig. 5.3).[36] Evidence from elsewhere in Egyptian tradition and from Mesopotamia and Hatti more definitively indicates that women were anointed with oil during labor.[37] An Egyptian incantation, for example, describes anointing the top of the parturient's head with oil, and a Mesopotamian text similarly describes anointing the delivering woman's brow. Yet another Mesopotamian text speaks of anointing the woman's shoulder and sides.[38] Arguably, the point in each of these cases is similar to the aim of the knot-magic rituals I discussed previously: to enact a ritual of sympathetic magic, whereby the anointing oil that lubricated various parts of a mother's body caused lubricating fluids to coat the body of her fetus, allowing the baby to slip from its mother's womb more readily.

In addition, Egyptian, Mesopotamian, and Hittite sources all suggest that the mother-to-be was required to separate herself from at least certain members of her household as the time of delivery approached, so much so that childbirth sometimes took place in a special structure designated for the parturient's use. For example, one Hittite Empire text intimates that a delivering mother gave birth in a separate house or hut, although in his careful study of Hittite birth rituals, Gary Beckman cautions that these separate houses or huts were not necessarily a feature of all Hittite births.[39] Rather, several Hittite sources suggest that the mother gave birth in her home, perhaps in the "bedroom of the expectant parents."[40] Still, even if

Fig. 5.3 Calcite ointment jar, for holding anointing oil used by pregnant and parturient women. From Abydos, Egypt, ca. 1479–1352 BCE. 19 cm high. From the collection of the British Museum, London. BM no. EA65275. © Trustees of the British Museum.

parturition took place in the expectant parents' bedroom, it seems clear that during delivery, this space—as well as any other space used by a Hittite parturient—would have been off-limits to the infant's father. Thus, a Hittite text that describes ceremonies "carried out soon before . . . the actual birth" details how a male *patili*-priest performs purificatory rituals on behalf of the expectant mother, but as she seats herself on the birthing stool, "her husband [and] the *patili*-priests . . . go," and, furthermore, the priest "makes a sealing of" (meaning, presumably, that he seals shut) the birth chamber, so that the husband cannot reenter.[41] Indeed, no Hittite text attests to "the participation of the husband during the actual delivery of his child."[42]

Mesopotamian evidence similarly indicates that a woman should be separated from certain men—especially male family members?—during parturition. More specifically, JoAnn Scurlock and Burton R. Anderson, in their 2005 study of Assyrian and Babylonian medicine, quote a Sumerian hymn that describes how the birth goddess Nintu is assigned "the [functions of] the *qadištu*," a title given to a female attendant who, along with a woman's midwife, seems to assist during childbirth. The hymn then notably defines the *qadištu*'s functions as "everything pertaining to women that *no man* must see" (emphasis mine).[43] In addition, Marten Stol, referring to the work of Karel van der Toorn and Claus Wilcke, draws attention to materials from the Instructions of Šuruppak from mid-third millennium BCE Sumer and from an incantation against the demonic Lamaštu's evil eye from the Old Babylonian period (ca. 1894–1595 BCE). Stol notes as well a reference in the Epic of Atraḫasis to the "house" or "room" of the *qadištu* (I.290). These three texts, he suggests, indicate that at least during the eras and in the locales in which they were generated (and perhaps in Mesopotamia more generally), Mesopotamian women were expected to bear their children in a location that was sequestered from their family domicile. For example, birth may have taken place in a room situated on the outskirts of the family's house that was entered from the outside through a door other than the portal used by the rest of the household's inhabitants.[44]

In ancient Egypt, at least one letter from the late Ramesside period (twelfth century BCE) suggests that a baby's father was present for his child's delivery—"it was when I [the father] was in the house that you were born"—although whether this text indicates that the father was actually in his wife's birth chamber or just present in the family's greater domicile cannot be determined.[45] The Westcar Papyrus's early second-millennium BCE birth story of the three Fifth Dynasty pharaohs mentioned above suggests, however, that the latter interpretation is more likely. In this text, "the first act" of the four goddesses who are sent by the god Ra to serve as midwives to the parturient, who is named Ruddedet, "is to close or seal the room in which the birth is to take place." Ruddedet's husband, who seems previously to have been in his wife's company, is thereby restricted to spaces elsewhere in their home.[46] Likewise, in the Egyptian tale of "The Two Brothers," from the Nineteenth Dynasty (thirteenth century BCE), word must be brought to Pharaoh that his wife has given birth to a son. This is a clear indication that, even if he were in the residence where the birth took place, he was not present in the birth chamber.[47]

Egyptian iconographical materials from the second and first millennia BCE that depict childbirth scenes (for example, Fig. 5.5 below) somewhat similarly suggest that a delivering mother was attended only by female servitors and aides.[48] Indeed, certain iconographical evidence—from Pharaoh Akhenaton's fourteenth-century BCE capital city of el-Amarna and some seventy-three painted ostraca from the thirteenth- and twelfth-century BCE workman's village at Deir el-Medina—intimates that, at least at el-Amarna and Deir el-Medina, parturients were so separated, both from their husbands and their households writ large, that childbirth took place outside the usual confines of the home: "in an upper chamber like those found on the roof of some houses" (at el-Amarna) or (at Deir el-Medina) "in a specially built arbor or hut outside the house."[49] A roughly contemporaneous childbirth spell from Papyrus Leiden I 348 (Nineteenth Dynasty; thirteenth century BCE) in addition mentions the specially designated "fine pavilion" or birth arbor in which a pregnant woman awaits delivery (see Fig. 5.4).[50]

Delivering mothers in the Late Bronze Age city-state of Ugarit may also have been isolated during birth, or at least isolated from their children's fathers, given that in a Ugaritic mythological text, the "Feast of the Goodly Gods" (*KTU* 1.23), word must be brought to the god El that his two wives had successfully delivered the divine offspring Šaḥar and Šalim, or "Dawn" and "Dusk" (*KTU* 1.23.52–53). In the same text a few lines later (*KTU* 1.23.59–60), word is again brought to El concerning his two wives' delivery of the "goodly gods" or the "gracious gods," who—depending on how one interprets—may or may not be identical to Šaḥar and Šalim.[51] In another Ugaritic mythological text, word must likewise be brought to the god Baal that a theriomorphic son (a bull) has been born to him (*KTU* 1.10.3.32–36).

In the preceding lines of this text, as Baal's bull-son is being delivered, the goddess Anat seems to serve as a midwife to the son's cow-mother (*KTU* 1.10.3.19–26). Indeed, evidence from throughout the Near East indicates that midwives were critical actors throughout the parturition process and in the period immediately postpartum. According to a Hittite Empire text, two midwives could attend at a birth,[52] and, as noted above, four goddess midwives attend to the parturient Ruddedet in the Egyptian Westcar Papyrus tale describing the births of three Fifth Dynasty pharaohs. Two or more midwives also appear in various second- and first-millennium BCE representations of Egyptian childbirth (see Fig. 5.5).[53] However, these representations, much like the description of parturition found in the

Fig. 5.4 Limestone ostracon depicting an Egyptian woman in a birth arbor after delivery, as a maid offers a mirror and kohl. From Deir el-Medina, Ramesside period (ca. 1292–1075 BCE). 14.5 cm high, 11.2 cm wide. From the collection of the Musée du Louvre, Paris. Inv. no. E 25333. Photo: Christian Decamps. © RMN-Grand Palais/Art Resource, New York.

Westcar Papyrus, tend to depict the births of extraordinary children (gods or kings), and so they cannot necessarily be taken to document typical birthing practices. Rather, the Egyptian norm may have been for the delivering woman to be attended by only one midwife. This may have been the norm in Hatti as well,[54] just as the Ugaritic mythological text describing the birth of

154 MOTHERHOOD

Fig. 5.5 Queen Mutemwiya giving birth to Amenhotep III after his divine conception by Amun-Re, with Isis and Nephthys serving as midwives. Birth room of Amenhotep III, Luxor Temple, Egypt, first half of the fourteenth century BCE. Photograph by the author.

Baal's theriomorphic son seems to presume Anat was the sole midwife who attended to the laboring cow-mother.

In addition to the obvious role midwives played in tending to the physical well-being of delivering mothers during labor and postpartum, Near Eastern midwives enacted many childbirth and postpartum rituals on behalf of parturients and their newborns. Indeed, even though Hittite, Mesopotamian, and Egyptian male magicians could be called on to make offerings and recite certain spells and prayers at the time of parturition, especially if a woman was struggling to deliver,[55] midwives took responsibility for many of the magical performances that took place during a woman's labor and after she gave birth. I have previously noted, for example, that a Mesopotamian midwife might sprinkle meal on the floor of a laboring woman's birth chamber to create a "magic circle" in which the delivery could safely take place. Hittite, Mesopotamian, and Egyptian midwives may also have been responsible for the anointing rituals that were arguably used in those cultures to magically lubricate the fetus's body. It is equally plausible that midwives enacted at least some of the amuletic and knot-magic rituals that, according to Hittite, Egyptian, and Mesopotamian lore, took place while a woman was giving birth.

We have clear evidence, moreover, that Near Eastern midwives recited incantations to keep harm away from delivering mothers and their newly delivered children. Among the Hittites, the midwife could recite incantations on behalf of a newborn, "beseeching the gods to remove evil influences,"[56] and ancient Egyptian and Greek sources, as well as one Hittite text, also describe the midwife reciting incantations before the birth on behalf of a laboring mother-to-be.[57] For example, in the Hittite text, the midwife is said to conjure repeatedly "The Incantation of Crying Out" as the woman is in the throes of delivery, and the midwife in addition is said to recite an incantation over an ewe that was brought into the birth chamber as part of a ritual that was seemingly meant to transfer whatever evils might be afflicting the parturient onto the animal. Another Hittite text indicates that "The Incantation of Blood" and "The Incantation of the Wind" are to be recited over a woman who is experiencing difficulty while giving birth, although this text does not specify that it was a midwife who performed these recitations.[58] Likewise in Mesopotamia, it is not necessarily clear who we should identify as reciting the several spells found in the incantation text known as "The Cow of Sîn" that were conjured on behalf of mothers experiencing difficult births.[59] According to at least one Mesopotamian text, an incantation recited during a problematic delivery was articulated by the mother herself.[60] Nevertheless, "The Cow of Sîn" includes one short spell uttered in the name of Asalluḫi, who, although he is a *male* god of magic (he is the son of Enki/Ea and is sometimes identified with Marduk), describes himself as "the midwife" who urges the child about to be born to slip swiftly and easily out of the womb.[61]

Near Eastern midwives, along with others who attended a parturient woman, could also assume responsibility for decreeing a child's fate after a successful delivery, as in this Sumerian text that quotes the midwife deity Manungal:[62]

> I assist Nintur [the mother goddess] at the place of delivery (lit. "extraction of the child")
> I know the propitious words pertaining to cutting the umbilical cord and determining fate.

Likewise in Egypt, according to the Westcar Papyrus, Meskhenet, who is one of the four goddess-midwives present as Ruddedet gives birth, proclaims the destiny of Ruddedet's three sons after they are delivered.[63] Thus, as each of these future kings of the Fifth Dynasty comes out of the womb, Meskhenet says, "A king who will assume the kingship in this whole land."[64] Similarly, in the New Kingdom tale of the "The Doomed Prince," the Hathor deities—Hathor being a goddess who is closely associated with pregnancy and parturition in Egyptian tradition[65]—appear in order to "determine a fate" for a king's newborn son.[66] According to Beckman, moreover, "an incantation to secure a favorable fate for a child" is among "the most widely attested of the rites directly following birth" in Hittite tradition.[67] Sometimes, this incantation is uttered by an "Old Woman" who is differentiated from the parturient's midwife,[68] but on other occasions the incantation is recited by the midwife herself.[69]

Childbirth Rituals in Ancient Israel

Not all of these ritual observances necessarily pertained in Israel; for example, in a survey article on life-cycle rituals in the Near Eastern and Mediterranean world, Jan N. Bremmer suggests that the special Hittite festival that took place at the onset of a woman's pregnancy may not have been enacted anywhere else in the ancient Near East.[70] Still, the Hittite tradition that has mothers-to-be seeking oracles about their condition and the outcome of their deliveries seems well paralleled by the Gen 25:19–26 story of the pregnant Rebekah, who, not knowing she was carrying twin sons (Esau and Jacob), inquires of Yahweh regarding the strivings and struggles she feels in her womb. That Rebekah's inquiry should be understood as seeking an oracle is clearly indicated by the Hebrew text's use of the verb *dāraš* to describe her petition (Gen 25:22); *dāraš* is a technical term that refers to the soliciting of an oracular response.[71] It is also of note that Rebekah "went" (*wattēlek*) somewhere to solicit Yahweh's oracle, and while that "somewhere" is unfortunately unspecified in the Genesis text, it is reasonable to surmise that she went to some sort of shrine or sanctuary where Yahweh was thought to be present. In addition, we may reasonably presume that Rebekah's oracular entreaty at this sacred space was in some way facilitated or mediated by a priest, diviner, or a similar sort of oracular specialist, as is usual in other biblical texts that describe the seeking (*dāraš*) of a divine oracle.[72]

The well-attested use of amulets during pregnancy and at the time of parturition in both Egypt and Mesopotamia also seems to be part of Israelite women's pregnancy and parturition rituals, including even the use of amulets that have their origin in Egyptian and Mesopotamian tradition. We have some evidence, for example, that by the Assyrian period (the eighth and seventh centuries BCE), the ancient Israelites were aware of the Mesopotamian demon Lamaštu and the dangers she posed to a childbearing mother and her infant,[73] given that a fragmentary Lamaštu plaque was discovered in the 1960s near Tel Burna (biblical Libnah?).[74] However, Mordechai Cogan has suggested that this plaque (which has a cuneiform inscription evoking the Mesopotamian gods Enlil and Marduk) may not have belonged to (or been used by) an ancient Israelite, but rather was the property of an Assyrian soldier in King Sennacherib's army, who dropped it while campaigning in the area.[75] More suggestive, though, are three seventh-century BCE representations of the Assyro-Babylonian demon Pazuzu found at Megiddo, Beth-Shean, and Ḥorvat Qitmit in ancient Edom.[76] These Pazuzu images may have been used by women in ancient Israel and among their Edomite neighbors, just as Pazuzu images were used in Mesopotamian tradition: to ward off Lamaštu and thus protect childbearing and newly delivered mothers and their infants from the various threats Lamaštu posed. Indeed, the representation of Pazuzu found at Beth-Shean—which is small (3.08 centimeters tall and 2 centimeters wide), has a hole at the top, and depicts only the demon's head—was clearly meant to be worn as an amulet, much as pregnant women in Mesopotamia wore amulets representing Pazuzu's head around their necks.[77]

More widely attested is the ancient Israelites' use of amulets depicting the demigod Bes, the dwarf deity who, as noted above, was believed to safeguard pregnant and delivering women in Egypt, as well as their newborn infants. Indeed, in the most recent installment of his multivolume study *Ägyptische Amulette aus Palästina/Israel*, Christian Herrmann has catalogued some 225 Bes amulets that have been recovered from archaeological sites that today are located in Israel and the Palestinian territories (see Fig. 5.6).[78] To be clear, not all these Bes amulets date from the Iron Age and the early Persian period that are my interest in this study (some are from the Late Bronze Age and the Hellenistic period).[79] In addition, not all come from the territories of preexilic and early postexilic Israel (some come, for example, from Philistine sites). What's more, many of the Israelite amulets come from contexts that are not related to matters of childbirth (for example, tombs).[80] Nevertheless,

158   MOTHERHOOD

at least some of the Bes amulets that come from preexilic and early postexilic Israel could have been used by Israelite women to safeguard their well-being during pregnancy, labor, and also post-parturition, just as Bes amulets were used by pregnant and delivering women in Egypt, as well as by new mothers postpartum.

Israelite images of Bes also show up elsewhere than on amulets: most famously at the late ninth-/early eighth-century BCE site of Kuntillet 'Ajrûd in the eastern Sinai, 50 kilometers south of Kadesh Barnea. There, a drawing of two animal-faced figures who stand side-by-side and face frontally, each with legs akimbo, is best interpreted as depicting either two renditions of Bes or (less likely) Bes and his female counterpart Beset.[81] Granted, this drawing—found within a building complex identified as a caravanserai—cannot be said to speak to Bes's role as a protector of pregnant women and their newborn children (its referent, rather, is Bes's generally apotropaic character). Nevertheless, the Kuntillet 'Ajrûd images do attest to a place for Bes within

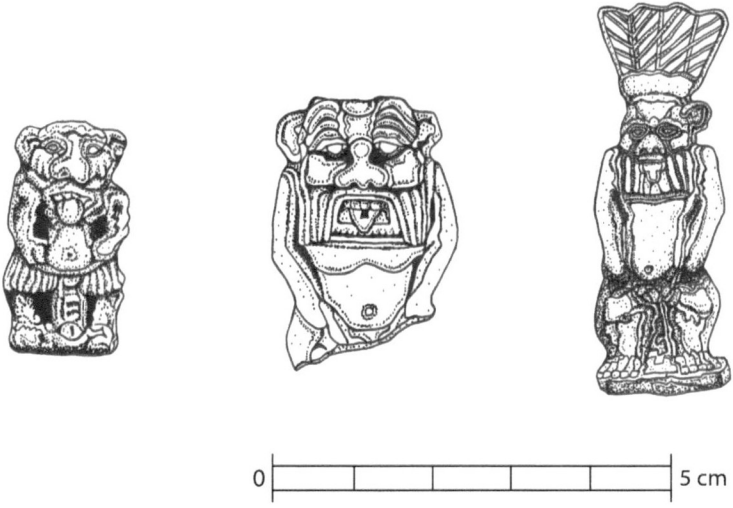

Fig. 5.6 Bes amulets, from (left to right) Iron IA Azekah, Iron IIB Megiddo, and Iron IIB Lachish. After Herrmann, *Ägyptische Amulette aus Palästina/Israel* IV, 345 (Azekah: 0214.2006) and 347 (Megiddo: 0409: 1994; Lachish: 0393: 1994). Drawing by Dorothea Ulrich.

Israelite religious thought, as do the representations of Bes occasionally found on Iron Age stamp seals.[82]

Bes's name can also appear as a theophoric element within Hebrew names: five times within Rainer Albertz's catalog of 2922 Hebrew names that come from the epigraphic corpus of preexilic Israel and Judah. The name Besai (*bēsāy*, or "the one who belongs to Bes") is in addition found in the postexilic book of Ezra (2:49).[83] Although rare, these Bes names attest yet again to the presence of Bes traditions in preexilic and early postexilic Israel. Moreover, Albertz has argued that one of the Bes names, from the eighth-century BCE Samaria ostraca (Sam 1:5), *Qdbś*, which Albertz vocalizes as *Qadbeś* and describes as an Egyptian loan-name meaning "Bes has formed" (that is, "Bes has formed the child in the womb"), speaks explicitly to the role Bes was understood to play in childbearing and childbirth within an Israelite context.[84]

Nancy R. Bowen has furthermore made a strong case for the use of pregnancy rites in Israel that are akin to the knot-magic rituals known from Egyptian, Hittite, and, especially, Mesopotamian tradition.[85] To be sure, the biblical text on which Bowen depends to make this argument—Ezek 13:17–23, in which Ezekiel condemns a cadre of "daughters of your people who prophesy" for, among other things, their use of wrist bands (*kĕsātôt*), some kind of head drapes (*mispāḥôt*), "handfuls of barley," and "morsels of bread"—is enigmatic in many respects, and thus interpreters' understanding of it can vary considerably.[86] According to many commentators, the "daughters . . . who prophesy" are necromancers. Jonathan Stökl, for example, focuses on the Hebrew word *mitnabbĕʾôt* that is used to describe the passage's female subjects (as opposed to the more expected term for female prophets, *nĕbîʾôt*).[87] He then compares the feminine plural form *munabbiātu* that appears in four texts from twelfth-century BCE Emar, a Syrian site on the mid-Euphrates. Unfortunately, these four Emar texts divulge little about the *munabbiātu*, but Stökl suggests that we look at them in conjunction with eight other Emar texts in which the related verb *nubbû* appears, each time in the idiom "to *nubbû* my gods and my dead."[88] He proposes that in each case, "the context makes it likely that the verb refers to some form of interaction with the dead, be it invoking them, caring for them, or talking to them."[89] This leads him to conclude that the *mitnabbĕʾôt* of Ezek 13:17–23 are also to be understood as women who somehow engage in interactions with the dead, or, more specifically, as necromancers.[90]

Others who come to this conclusion cite the description in Ezek 13:18 and 20 of the "daughters ... who prophesy" as "hunting for *něpāšôt*." This phrase is often translated as "hunting for souls," a reference, under the terms of these scholars' interpretation, to the daughters' seeking to communicate with spirits of the dead through necromancy.[91] Evidence for necromancy in Ezek 13:17–23 also includes, according to at least some commentators, the fact that in Ezek 13:20, the "daughters" are said to hunt for *něpāšôt* "like birds," given that, according to these commentators, "the dead can manifest themselves in the shape of birds."[92] However, the proposition that the dead can assume the shape of birds according to West Semitic thought has been challenged by such noted experts as Marvin H. Pope, Mark S. Smith, and Elizabeth Bloch-Smith.[93] Moreover, while those who interpret the daughters' acts as necromantic rituals that summon bird-like spirits of the dead can offer an interpretation of the text's allusions to barley and bread (this food is "meant to allure the bird-like souls," according to Marjo C. A. Korpel),[94] these scholars are less able to explain the references to wrist bindings and head drapes. Korpel, for example, can only suggest that the daughters "sew bird-nets which they spread out over their arms" in order to snare the bird-like dead spirits.[95]

But this reading defies the (admittedly difficult) syntax of the passage, which is best understood as distinguishing between those who sew the wrist and head bands and those upon whom these fabrics are bound.[96] Richard C. Steiner's interpretation, that the "daughters ... who prophesy" attach "pillow casings" to their arms in order to hold captive "dream souls" (that is, souls that have left people's bodies while they sleep), suffers from the same problem.[97] Moreover, Steiner's translation of *kěsātôt* as "pillow casings," based on the meaning of the term *keset* in Mishnaic Hebrew, problematically rejects the Akkadian cognate of *kěsātôt* that is ready to hand (more on this below), even though an Akkadian cognate is a more probable referent for Ezekiel, whose oracles were written, after all, while Ezekiel lived in an Akkadian-speaking milieu (sixth-century BCE Babylonia).[98] Indeed, we saw in Chapter 3 an important example of Ezekiel's use of an Akkadian loanword: *nudunnû* for "dowry" in Ezek 16:33.[99]

I have thus been more compelled, as I suggested above, by Bowen's suggestion that the daughters' sewing bands of cloth onto others' wrists and putting headbands (Bowen's preferred translation of the more usual "veils"; Hebrew *mispāḥôt*)[100] on others' heads are acts reminiscent of the Mesopotamian rituals of tying bands and knotted strings around the heads, necks, torsos, and limbs of childbearing women to address the difficulties these women were facing during their pregnancies. To be sure, Ezek 13:20–21, where the cloth bands are said to be sewn onto "your [masculine plural] arms" and where the headbands are likewise described using a second-person masculine plural suffix, might seem to disallow any suggestion that the cloth bands of Ezek 13:18 were sewn or bound onto the wrists and heads of Israelite *women*, whether childbearing or not. But as Walther Zimmerli points out, these masculine plural suffixes and other masculine forms used in Ezek 13:20 and 21 are extremely problematic (note preeminently the wholly illogical use of a *masculine* plural pronoun toward the end of v 20, *'attem*, to denounce the *women* prophets). The masculine forms of 13:20–21, Zimmerli thus concludes, may be the result of textual corruption, or they may come from material that was secondarily added to Ezekiel's original oracle.[101] Alternatively, "the changes in grammatical gender" may be, as in Ezekiel 1, "the result of the redactional processes that shaped the entire prophetic book."[102]

At any rate, the grammatical oddities of Ezek 13:20–21 need not contradict Bowen's proposal regarding parallels between Mesopotamian and Israelite pregnancy rituals. Indeed, Bowen's analysis is strengthened by her observation (following others) that the specific term used for the "wrist bands" that the women prophets apply according to Ezek 13:18, *kĕsātôt*, is arguably related to the Akkadian verb *kasû*, "to bind."[103] It is also important to note that while deploying knot-magic rituals to stem vaginal bleeding, prevent miscarriages, and otherwise tend to the well-being of pregnant women may not strike some biblical readers as a typical prophetic role, one way in which the biblical prophets did in fact enact their basic task of mediating between the divine and human worlds was by ministering to those who were ill and effecting their recovery.[104] Indeed, because health care was understood in the ancient world as a divine prerogative,[105] those needing medical assistance would often solicit a prophet in order to secure the divine intervention for which the petitioner hoped. For example, in 1 Kgs 14:1–18, the wife of King Jeroboam solicits the prophet Ahijah on behalf of her ailing son, and in 2 Kgs 4:8–37, the so-called Shunammite woman solicits the help of the prophet Elisha when her son is unexpectedly stricken and dies. Other prophetic healing stories can be found in 1 Kgs 17:17–24 and 2 Kgs 5:1–14; 20:1–11 (= Isa 38:1–8). In these stories, prophets can effect healing by apparently magical means, just as the women prophets of Ezek 13:17–23 might be understood as using knot magic to provide medical assistance to pregnant women.[106]

Furthermore, while the prophets solicited for medico-magical help in 1 Kgs 14:1–18; 17:17–24; 2 Kgs 4:8–37; 5:1–14; and 20:1–11 (= Isa 38:1–8) are all men, it may be more typical for Israelite women who need medical help during a pregnancy to seek the aid of women prophets, as Ezek 13:17–23 might suggest.[107] Certainly, this should be the case at the time of parturition, when, as I will discuss more thoroughly below, Israelite women appear to have been served exclusively by female attendants. Indeed, Bowen suggests that Ezek 13:19, in which Ezekiel's women prophets are associated with "handfuls of barley" and "morsels of bread," might parallel Mesopotamian parturition rituals in which a delivering woman's midwife makes a pattern of meal (to be interpreted, as suggested above, as sprinkling a "magic circle" of flour on the floor?) and an exorcist makes offerings of bread.[108] It thereby can be proposed—although, as discussed just above, not all commentators agree[109]—that "the activities that Ezekiel ascribes to the female prophets... share some of the same imagery as these various Mesopotamian incantations associated with childbirth. In particular, they share the imagery of the binding and removal of knots or bands of cloth (13:18, 20, 21) and the use of grain and bread for ritual use (13:19)."[110]

Archaeologists excavating at ancient Israelite sites have also found evidence suggesting that childbirth rituals may have been enacted within the small shrine corners or shrine niches that were an architectural feature in many Israelite homes. At ninth- and eighth-century BCE Beersheba, for example, about 45 percent of the houses had artifacts that arguably came from the shrine nooks of these homes.[111] Among these remains were small terracotta models of furniture, including what is often described as a model couch.[112] Such couches, according to some interpreters, might represent a birth stool or a birthing bed (a standard apparatus used during labor in the Near East and eastern Mediterranean).[113] They therefore might be ritual objects used "to insure ... a woman's ability to give birth."[114] If so, we could consider them to be analogous to the limestone ostracon from Deir el-Medina that I described above, which depicts a woman sitting with a male child atop a bed and which Geraldine Pinch has interpreted as an amuletic object used by Egyptian mothers-to-be to represent "the desired, happy outcome of successful childbirth."[115] Even more so, we might compare the Israelite model couches to the so-called woman-on-bed figurines and the related model beds that come from the Egyptian New Kingdom (ca. 1539–1075 BCE), the Third Intermediate Period (ca. 1075–715 BCE), and the Late and Greco-Roman Periods (ca. 715 BCE–395 CE).[116] These are often interpreted as being somehow related to birth, with the bed representing the "birth couch."[117] Most have been found in domestic contexts (especially in houses at Deir el-Medina and el-Amarna),[118] and it is theorized that Egyptian women "desiring or expecting a child would have . . . kept them in household shrines, with the hope of successful procreation or birth"[119]—the same function that has been posited for the model couches found in Israelite household shrines.

Excavations from sites that today are located in Israel and the Palestinian territories have also produced exemplars of the sorts of "pregnancy vases" designed to resemble a childbearing woman that are known from ancient Egypt (see Fig. 5.3 above), and while some of these southern Levantine "pregnancy vases" date from the Late Bronze Age period, which is prior to my interests in this study, others are from the preexilic or Iron Age period of Israelite history.[120] These vases, as I have previously noted, held anointing oil, which Israelite parturients may have used ritually during the delivery process, as did parturients in Mesopotamia, Egypt, and the Hittite world. The Hittite, Mesopotamian, Egyptian, and Ugaritic tradition of isolating pregnant women from certain men, especially male family members, at the time of delivery seems in addition to have been paralleled in Israel. Or at least it seems that Israelite women were separated from their *husbands* at birth, given that word must be brought after delivery to the father of Jeremiah (Jer 20:15) that a son has been born to him.[121]

Yet even though an Israelite woman was separated from her husband and perhaps other male family members during labor and delivery, she was joined by certain female attendants. I have already suggested, for example, that the "handfuls of barley" and the "morsels of bread" with which the women prophets of Ezek 13:17–23 are associated may have been part of a protective ritual these women enacted on behalf of a mother-to-be during parturition. Other female attendants who assisted Israelite parturients include the unspecified number of women (*hanniṣṣābôt*) said to be with the wife of Phinehas when she gives birth in 1 Sam 4:20 and the women who speak to Naomi after her daughter-in-law Ruth delivers (Ruth 4:14–15). To be sure, it is not clear where, precisely, these women are when they address Naomi, but the fact that Naomi is said to take Ruth's newborn son Obed to her breast after the women speak arguably indicates that she and the other women were in Ruth's birth chamber at the time of their interaction and even earlier: at the time of Obed's birth and even throughout the course of Ruth's labor. This may in turn indicate that Israelite mothers could be attended during birth by women from their family, like, say, Naomi, as well as by "women of the neighborhood" (*haššĕkēnôt*)—which is the language used to identify the women who speak to Naomi in Ruth 4:17.

Still, in Israel, as elsewhere in the Near East, midwives were surely the most crucial of the female attendants who ministered to delivering mothers. It seems, moreover, that just as it may have been the norm for most parturients in Egypt, the Hittite Empire, and Late Bronze Age Ugarit to have been ministered to by a single midwife,[122] only one midwife attended Israelite women during their deliveries. Note, indeed, that even in the Exod 1:15–19 passage that speaks of the two midwives (*mĕyallĕdōt*) who served Israelite mothers during the Hebrews' sojourn in Egypt, these midwives, Shiphrah and Puah, explain to Pharaoh that they have not been able to carry out his command to kill the Hebrews' newborn males because the Hebrew women are so vigorous that they routinely deliver before the *midwife* (singular; *mĕyalledet*) arrives (Exod 1:19). A single midwife likewise attends Rachel during her tragic death in childbirth according to Gen 35:17. Tamar too is assisted by only one midwife when giving birth to her twin sons (Gen 38:28).

As elsewhere in the Near East, the range of duties undertaken by Israelite midwives and by other women who attended a delivering mother was surely manifold and extended far beyond seeing to the parturient's physical well-being during labor and facilitating her child's birth, in order to include ritual acts. We can once again note, for example, the ritual of protection that the women prophets of Ezek 13:17–23 may have enacted on behalf of a delivering woman by deploying "handfuls of barley" and "morsels of bread." It is also easily imaginable that Israelite midwives and/or a parturient's other female attendants performed the ritual anointing of the delivering mother that I have associated with the "pregnancy vases" found by archaeologists at some Iron Age Israelite sites. Midwives and/or a parturient's other female attendants may likewise have enacted the purificatory rituals that, according to the interpretation of Ezek 16:4 I put forward in Chapter 1, followed an infant's birth:[123] bathing the baby and rubbing it with salt. To be sure, in the "Ritual of Papanikri," one of the Hittite texts that I compared to Ezek 16:4 in Chapter 1, which describes how a lamb that stands in as a ritual substitute for the newborn is to be bathed after birth in order to purify the child, the bath is performed by the *patili*-priest who oversees the substitution rite. Moreover, in the other Hittite bathing text that I cited in Chapter 1, the newborn infant is given its purificatory bath by an "Old Woman" who is differentiated from the parturient's midwife.[124] Gary Beckman identifies this "Old Woman" as the child's nurse, who "takes charge of the infant immediately after the midwife has brought him to birth."[125] But in Israelite tradition, where nurses for newborns are generally described as being present only in foreign or royal households (the household in which Rebekah was raised in Paddan-aram [Gen 24:59; 35:8]; the Egyptian household of the pharaoh's daughter who raised Moses [Exod 2:7–9]; the household of Saul and his son Jonathan [2 Sam 4:4]; and the household of King Joram/Jehoram of Judah [2 Kgs 11:2; 2 Chr 22:11]), it may have been more typical for midwives to administer the postpartum ritual bath.

Certainly, it was the midwife who attended Tamar in Genesis 38 who tied a red thread around the hand of the baby Zeraḥ during the course of Tamar's delivery. While the reason given for the thread's use in Gen 38:28 is idiosyncratic to the Tamar account (it is used to mark which of Tamar's twin sons first breached the womb), Carol Meyers has suggested that the tying of a red thread around one of a newborn's limbs was a ritual act performed routinely in ancient Israel in order to protect an infant from the many sorts of evil he or she might face.[126] We can again compare the Hittite "Ritual of Papanikri," where, before he washes the lamb that substitutes for a newborn child, the *patili*-priest ties red wool around the lamb's feet.[127] Just as the lamb's bath "must be understood" (as Beckman writes) "as reflecting a normal purificatory rite carried out on a human infant,"[128] the red thread tied to the lamb's foot should be understood as a ritual act that was somehow meant to ensure the infant's well-being. As in Hatti, so too in Israel: should we see the red thread in Genesis 38 as a ritual object the midwife ties to Zeraḥ's wrist in order to offer supernatural protection to Tamar's newborn son?

And should we further envision that, like their Near Eastern counterparts, Israelite midwives and/or other women who attended a parturient woman recited incantations in order to keep harm away from laboring mothers and their newly delivered children and subsequently to determine the newborn child's fate? Jack M. Sasson has argued that through their proclamation "A son has been born to Naomi" in Ruth 4:17, the neighborhood women who seem to have been in attendance when Ruth gave birth "established his [the newborn son's] reputation" and "defin[ed] the child's future."[129] One might also suggest that underlying Job 3:1–26, in which the suffering and miserable Job utters imprecations denouncing the day he was born, is evidence of a more typical Israelite custom of midwives and/or other women who attended at birth uttering incantations meant to bring good fortune to the newborn on its natal day.[130]

166   MOTHERHOOD

Indeed, at least one of Job's specific denunciations, Job 3:10, might be taken as the antithesis of a more hopeful Israelite birth incantation, analogous to a Mesopotamian birth incantation from the Old Babylonian period (ca. 1894–1595 BCE). In this Mesopotamian text, the magician god Asalluḫi, the son of Enki who can nevertheless, as we saw earlier, be identified as a "midwife," utters a spell that opens "the doors . . . wide" to free a baby whose mother is struggling to bring it forth from her womb:[131]

> In the fluids of intercourse
> Bone was formed.
> In the tissue of sinews
> Baby was formed.
> In the ocean waters, fearsome, raging,
> In the distant waters of the sea,
> Where the little one's arms are bound.
> . . .
> Asalluḫi, Enki's son, saw him,
> He loosened his tight-tied bonds
> He set him on the way
> He opened him the path.
> . . .
> "The lock is [fre]ed,
> The doors thrown wide,
> Let him strike [. . .],
> Bring yourself out!"

Contrast Job's wish in Job 3:10 that the doors of his mother's womb had remained closed. This is an allusion, we might theorize, to Job's wish that a midwife had not uttered the incantation that otherwise opened the doors of his mother's womb and brought forth the newborn Job.

Note likewise another Mesopotamian birth incantation from the eleventh century BCE, which concludes with lines spoken both by the paturient's midwife, according to Benjamin R. Foster, and the unborn child. Both call to the god Marduk for help, asking, in the midwife's case, that Marduk help the child "come out and see the light."[132] Contrast again Job, who wishes that the day of his birth had been shrouded in darkness of the most foreboding sort (ḥōšek, ṣalmāwet, and 'ōpel; vv 4–6), which once more we might take as an allusion to Job's wish that no midwife—much less his fetal self—had uttered the incantation that brought him out to "see the light."

Childbirth as a Women's Life-Cycle Ritual

Even if midwives' incantations were not a part of Israelite childbirth rites, it seems clear that pregnancy and parturition in Israel were, as elsewhere in the ancient Near East, highly ritualized events. During pregnancy, multiple measures could be brought to bear to safeguard a mother-to-be: soliciting oracles, using amulets, and tying protective strings and bands onto the expectant woman's body. Likewise, during labor and delivery, rituals such as sprinkling grain, anointing the parturient, and perhaps reciting incantations protected a woman from the manifold dangers that childbirth entailed, just as rituals such as bathing, salting, and tying a red thread onto the arm of the neonate protected the newly delivered baby.

Indeed, while all of the women's life-cycle rituals I have examined so far in this book have manifest motifs of danger, as life-cycle rituals characteristically do, it is the processes associated with pregnancy and childbirth that were truly the most dangerous within an Israelite woman's life course. Physical dangers such as abnormal vaginal bleeding that could harm a woman's fetus were manifold and could even bring about the end of a pregnancy through miscarriage or stillbirth. The health of the pregnant woman could also be threatened by excessive vaginal discharge, as well as by conditions we know today as ectopic pregnancy and pre-eclampsia. And, of course, like Rachel in Gen 35:18 and Phinehas's wife in 1 Sam 4:20, every pregnant woman had to face the very real threat of death during delivery, the result of conditions such as "hemorrhage, pelvic deformity, disproportion between the size of the child's head and the pelvis, severe abnormal presentations such as transverse lies, eclampsia and uterine inertia early in labour."[133] In fact, according to Scurlock, "the greatest single cause of death among [Mesopotamian] women was complications attending childbirth."[134] Meyers likewise estimates that in ancient Israel, the mortality rate for women during their childbearing years was so great that women's average life expectancy would have been about thirty years of age, as opposed to forty years of age for men.[135] John H. Oakley somewhat similarly postulates that in classical Greece, while the life expectancy rate was about 45 years of age for men, it was only 36.2 years women,[136] just as "skeletal remains in caves in the Judean wilderness from the Hellenistic period give a mean age at death of 44.2 years for males, 34.7 for females."[137] Egyptian evidence too—albeit from a somewhat later period (ca. 50–360 CE)—suggests that a large number of women "died due to complications during pregnancy and childbirth," given that half the adult females buried in a cemetery in the Dakhleh Oasis were of childbearing age.[138] In fact, "a study of maternal mortality" that postdates these Near Eastern materials by as much as three millennia (it comes from Renaissance Italy) still estimates that "one out of every five women died as a result of childbirth."[139]

In the ancient world, superimposed atop the biological dangers a mother faced when giving birth was the conviction that the parturient herself was a *source* of danger because of all the preternatural hazards that accrued to her. These hazards include the dangerous presence of evil spirits during a woman's pregnancy, as well as those spirits who appear in association with birth to threaten the life of the newborn child: for example, the hungry demons that, according to Mesopotamian lore, might snatch a newborn infant unless they were sated with bread offerings and likewise, as Bowen's analysis of Ezek 13:19 suggests, the childbirth demons that the Israelites sought to ward off with "morsels of bread."[140] Parturition's preternatural hazards also include the perilous childbirth pollution that the mother's community perceives her to embody. I will have more to say about this latter issue in the next chapter as I consider the ways in which childbirth pollutions can linger during the period after parturition. For now, however, it is enough to recollect the Lev 12:1–8 materials we encountered in Chapter 1 and that text's propositions regarding the forty- to eighty-day period of postpartum pollution that affected newly delivered Israelite mothers.

For our present purposes, that is, it is enough to reiterate how truly dangerous pregnancy and parturition were in ancient Israel, both for the childbearing woman and for her community and in both a physical and a preternatural sense. As I noted above, all of this danger is a characteristic feature of life-cycle rituals, and more specifically of the liminal phase of such rituals. Indeed, I understand the entire period from conception through parturition to comprise the liminal phase of childbirth as an ancient Israelite life-cycle event, during which the pregnant woman, especially a woman pregnant for the first time, can be said to be "betwixt and between" her old identity of "not mother" and the new identity of "mother" that is to come.[141] I also understand the excess dangers that a woman faces during pregnancy and parturition, and the accretion of so many dangers around her, both biological and preternatural, to illustrate one of the key propositions that has guided my analysis elsewhere in this book. This is the proposition that liminality as experienced during women's life-cycle rituals can be intensified or exacerbated when compared to the way men experience liminality. Thus, although a baby's birth can entail, at least to some degree, a rite of passage for a newborn's father (especially if he is becoming a parent for the first time), the liminal dramas and traumas of childbirth as a transformative life-cycle event are overwhelmingly the province of the mother-to-be. In addition to childbirth's biological and preternatural traumas, we should recall the culturally decreed challenges imposed on pregnant and parturient women: the culturally decreed birthing customs, say, that during delivery, require a mother-to-be's separation and isolation from at least her husband and seemingly from certain other members of her family and community as well.

Furthermore, and as my comment above about Lev 12:1–8 suggests, an Israelite woman's experience of the biological, preternatural, and culturally determined dramas and traumas of pregnancy and parturition can continue into the postpartum period. Thus, as I proposed in my introductory comments to this chapter, pregnancy and parturition need to be understood as components within an extended ritual complex that continues into the early days and even early years of motherhood. I now turn to explore those early days and early years, considering first, in Chapter 6, the ritual significance of the mother's bestowing a name upon her newborn child.

6

Naming a Child

In the Bible, fathers sometimes take responsibility for bestowing names upon their children. According to Gen 16:15 and 21:3, for example, Abraham bestows the names Ishmael and Isaac upon the sons he fathered with, respectively, Hagar and Sarah. Occasionally also, both a mother and father can be said to confer a child's name, as in Gen 25:25, where Isaac and Rebekah might logically be understood as the "they" who give Esau his name. Somewhat similarly, at least in the biblical text as it has come down to us, Eve confers the name Seth upon her thirdborn son according to Gen 4:25, while Adam bestows Seth's name according to Gen 5:3.[1]

Nevertheless, somewhat more often than not, children's names are bestowed on them by their mothers or by a mother's female surrogate or surrogates—who include Leah and Rachel, who in Gen 30:6, 8, 11, and 13 confer names on the sons borne by their maidservants Zilpah and Bilhah; Tamar's midwife, who implicitly gives Tamar's son Perez his name in Gen 38:29; Pharaoh's daughter, who in Exod 2:10 bestows the name Moses on the foundling she had earlier rescued from the Nile; and the women associates of Naomi, who confer the name Obed on Ruth's son and Naomi's grandson in Ruth 4:17.[2] More specifically, a child's name is bestowed by the infant's mother or her female surrogate(s) in about 63 percent of the naming episodes in the Hebrew Bible where a name-giver is identified.[3] More specifically still, there are, by my count, forty-six instances in the biblical text where a child's name-giver is explicitly identified, and in twenty-nine of these episodes, the child's mother or her female surrogate(s) gives the baby its name.[4]

Many of these maternal naming accounts, as can be seen in Table 6.1, come from Genesis. For example, in Gen 4:1, Eve implicitly bestows the name Cain (*qayin*) on her eldest son through her statement *qānîtî ʾîš*, "I have created a man" (or, less plausibly in my opinion, "I have acquired a man").[5] In addition, as just noted, Eve bestows the name Seth on her thirdborn son in Gen 4:25. Lot's daughters likewise confer names on their sons Moab and Ben-ammi according to Gen 19:37–38. Then, in the accounts of Rachel's and Leah's pregnancies and childbirths and those of their maidservants Bilhah

Maturity, Marriage, Motherhood, Mortality. Susan Ackerman, Oxford University Press.
© Oxford University Press 2025. DOI: 10.1093/9780197809686.003.0008

Table 6.1 Name-Giving in the Hebrew Bible

Mothers or Female Surrogates as Name-Givers (episodes marked with an asterisk include a "name-giving" speech)	Fathers as Name-Givers (episodes marked with an asterisk include a "name-giving" speech)
Gen 4:1 – Eve (implicitly) names Cain*	
Gen 4:25 – Eve names Seth (J)*	
	Gen 4:26 – Seth names Enosh (J)
	Gen 5:3 – Adam names Seth (P)
	Gen 5:29 – Lamech names Noah*
	Gen 16:15 – Abram names Ishmael (P), but cf. Gen 16:11 (J), where Hagar is told she will be the one to name her son
Gen 19:37 – Lot's older daughter names Moab	
Gen 19:38 – Lot's younger daughter names Ben-ammi	
	Gen 21:3 – Abraham names Isaac (P), but cf. Gen 21:6 (E),* where Sarah gives the "name-giving" speech
Gen 29:32 – Leah names Reuben*	
Gen 29:33 – Leah names Simeon*	
Gen 29:34 – Leah (implicitly) names Levi (although note the end of 29:34, ʿal-kēn qārāʾ-šĕmô lēwî, "therefore *he* called his name Levi") *	
Gen 29:35 – Leah names Judah*	
Gen 30:6 – Rachel names Dan*	
Gen 30:8 – Rachel names Naphtali*	
Gen 30:11 – Leah names Gad*	
Gen 30:13 – Leah names Asher*	
Gen 30:18 – Leah names Issachar*	
Gen 30:20 – Leah names Zebulon*	
Gen 30:21 – Leah names Dinah	
Gen 30:24 – Rachel names Joseph*	
Gen 35:18 – Rachel names Ben-oni (E)*	Gen 35:18 – Jacob renames Ben-oni as Benjamin (E)
	Gen 38:3 – Judah names Er (J), but cf. the LXX, where the grammar most logically suggests that Shua's daughter names Er. Note also Gen 38:4, 5.

(continued)

172 MOTHERHOOD

Table 6.1 Continued

Gen 38:4 – Shua's daughter names Onan (J)	
Gen 38:5 – Shua's daughter names Shelah (J)	
Gen 38:29 – Tamar's midwife (implicitly) names Perez (although note the end of Gen 38:29, *wayyiqrā' šěmô pāreṣ*; literally, "and *he* called his name Perez")*	
	Gen 41:51 – Joseph names Manasseh*
	Gen 41:52 – Joseph names Ephraim*
Exod 2:10 – Pharaoh's daughter names Moses*	
	Exod 2:22 (= 18:3) – Moses names Gershom*
	Exod 18:4 – Moses names Eliezer*
	Judg 8:31 – Gideon names Abimelech
Judg 13:24 – Manoah's wife names Samson	
1 Sam 1:20 – Hannah names Samuel*	
1 Sam 4:21 – Phinehas's wife names Ichabod*	
2 Sam 12:24 – Bathsheba names Solomon (reading with the *Qěrē'*)	
	2 Sam 12:25 – David (presumably) names Jedidiah (although the "he" that bestows the name is not clearly specified)
Isa 7:14 – the *'almâ* is to name her sign-child Immanu-El (reading the form *qārā't* as a third-person feminine singular perfect; see similarly Lev 25:21; Deut 31:29; Jer 44:23)	
	Isa 8:3 – Isaiah is to name his sign-child Maher-Shalal-Hash-Baz
	Job 42:14 – Job names Jemimah
	Job 42:14 – Job names Keziah
	Job 42:14 – Job names Keren-happuch
Ruth 4:17 – the women friends of Naomi name Obed	
1 Chr 4:9 – Jabez's mother names Jabez*	
1 Chr 7:16 – Maacah names Peresh	
	1 Chr 7:23 – Ephraim names Beriah*, but cf. the LXX. There the grammar most logically suggests that Ephraim's wife names Beriah.

and Zilpah, multiple episodes of maternal name-giving and name-giving by maternal surrogates appear. In Gen 29:32–35 and 30:18, 20, Leah bestows names on her sons Reuben, Simeon, Judah, Issachar, and Zebulun, and she implicitly confers the name Levi (*lēwî*) on her sixth son through a wordplay based on the root *l-w-h*, "to join," that she pronounces after his birth (*'attâ . . . yillāweh 'îšî 'ēlay*, "now . . . my husband will be joined to me").⁶ In Gen 30:21, Leah also confers the name Dinah on her daughter, and in 30:11, 13, she bestows names on the two sons Gad and Asher who were borne on her behalf by her maidservant Zilpah.

Jacob's other wife Rachel similarly bestows names on the two sons that her maidservant Bilhah bore on her behalf, Dan and Naphtali. Rachel in addition bestows the name Joseph on her own firstborn son (Gen 30:6, 8, 24). She furthermore confers the name Ben-oni on her second son, during whose delivery she died, but Jacob subsequently renames this child Benjamin (Gen 35:18). In Gen 38:4–5, Judah's wife, the daughter of Shua, bestows names on the couple's second and third sons Onan and Shelah, although in Gen 38:3, at least according to the Masoretic text, Judah bestows the name Er on their firstborn (more on this below). Later, in Genesis 38 (v 29), as already noted, Tamar's midwife implicitly confers the name Perez (*pereṣ*) on one of the twin sons whom Tamar bore to Judah, by virtue of the midwife's description of the "breach" (*pereṣ*) the child made when exiting the womb.⁷

Beyond Genesis, naming accounts are not as richly represented in the biblical text, but the basic pattern established in Genesis still holds, as mothers or their female surrogates bestow names on their children somewhat more often than not: in nine instances out of seventeen in texts where the name-giver can be identified. Notably, moreover, and as in Genesis, it is hard to discern any clear preferences regarding naming traditions among different biblical sources. Which is to say: in Genesis, one might suggest that the Priestly authors, or P, show a preference for fathers as name-givers,⁸ but it is hard to demonstrate even this definitively, for while fathers bestow their children's names in all of the Genesis naming episodes that can be attributed to P, there are only three such accounts (and no P naming accounts elsewhere in the Pentateuch).⁹ Conversely, Genesis accounts ascribed to both the Yahwistic (J) and Elohistic (E) traditions sometimes designate fathers and sometimes mothers as conferring names on their children. These include accounts such as the J story of the naming of Er, Onan, and Shelah, where father-naming and mother-naming traditions are juxtaposed cheek by jowl: Judah bestows Er's name in Gen 38:3 while his wife, Shua's daughter, bestows the names Onan and Shelah in 38:4–5. Or at least father-naming and mother-naming traditions are juxtaposed cheek by jowl in the Masoretic text of Gen 38:3–5: in the Septuagint, the grammar of v 3 most logically suggests that Shua's daughter bestows the name Er on her firstborn son, just as she bestows names on Onan and Shelah in vv 4–5.[10] Still, J unequivocally juxtaposes father-naming and mother-naming traditions in Gen 4:25–26, where Eve gives her son Seth his name in v 25, yet Seth bestows the name Enosh on his own son in v 26. Also in E, father-naming and mother-naming are juxtaposed in the account of Rachel's death in childbirth and the naming of her son as, first, Ben-oni and then Benjamin.

Somewhat similarly, in the Deuteronomistic History, the account of Gideon conferring the name Abimelech on his son in Judg 8:31 occurs reasonably proximate to the account of Manoah's wife bestowing the name Samson on her son in Judg 13:24. Also in 2 Sam 12:25, some male (presumably David, following instructions conveyed to him by the prophet Nathan) bestows the name Jedidiah on the son born to David and Bathsheba after the couple's firstborn had died, yet the *Qĕrē'* of the preceding v 24, as well as the most logical interpretation of the grammar of the Septuagint, credits Bathsheba with giving this child the name Solomon.[11] In the genealogies of 1 Chronicles, too, children's names can sometimes be conferred on them by their mothers (Jabez in 1 Chr 4:9; Peresh in 7:16) and sometimes by their fathers (Beriah in 1 Chr 7:23).[12] In addition, although we should perhaps not make too much of prophetic texts that describe the bestowing of symbolic names upon children, it is worth noting that according to most modern interpreters of Isa 7:14, Isaiah indicates that the *'almâ* ("young woman") of this verse will be bestowing the name Immanu-El upon her soon-to-be-delivered sign-child, whereas God decrees that the name of the next sign-child who appears in this oracle, Maher-Shalal-Hash-Baz, is to be conferred by Isaiah, who is this child's father (Isa 8:3).[13]

What to make of this catalogue? As I signaled in the Introduction, I am more of an optimist than not regarding the historical usefulness of the biblical text, and I am particularly an optimist regarding the biblical text's "unintended evidence," or what I take to be incidental data that can be embedded in biblical texts and that can unwittingly or unintentionally reveal, in my opinion, valuable information about ancient Israelite cultural practices and the Israelite cultural milieu. The point of the stories of the suggestively named children in Isa 7:14 and 8:3, for example, is the symbolically laden meanings of the names and the oracular advice these names are meant to convey to

King Ahaz of Judah regarding the Syro-Ephraimite war (for example, the message that "God is with us," or Immanu-El, as long as Ahaz resists making an alliance with the Assyrians to protect himself from the Syro-Ephraimite coalition). Conversely, there is no particular significance (as far as I can tell) regarding the incidental information that identifies the *'almâ* and Isaiah as name-givers in 7:14 and 8:3, respectively.

This means (in my opinion) that Isaiah 7–8's incidental information about name-giving—precisely because it is not necessary for the text's communicating its larger point of view—is less likely to have been shaped by the text's author(s) and/or redactor(s) to conform to a particular outlook or ideological perspective and thus is more likely to provide an accurate reflection of ancient Israel's historical reality: in this case, a historical reality regarding Israelite naming practices and the role Israelite mothers or their female surrogates could sometimes assume in bestowing children's names. Likewise, because other biblical sources make no apparent attempt to skew the data one way or another regarding which parent bestows a child's name (the only exception here may be P), I am inclined to take seriously the biblical tradition that suggests that Israelite mothers or their female surrogates assumed the responsibility for bestowing names on children somewhat more often than not: at least 63 percent of the time.[14] Indeed, I suspect mothers or their female surrogates bestowed names on newborn children more frequently still, with supporting evidence obscured by the Bible's characteristically male focus and its (presumed) privileging of men's name-giving accounts.

I am also inclined to accept as authoritative the Bible's childbirth narratives that indicate that in ancient Israel, an infant typically received its name at birth,[15] as well as the Bible's intimation that delivering women were separated during birth from everyone except their midwives and/or from other women who attended them. Or at least, as I noted in the last chapter, biblical tradition intimates that Israelite women were separated from their *husbands* during birth, given that word must be brought to Jeremiah's father after his wife's delivery that a son had been born to him (Jer 20:15).[16] These two points, regarding, first, the timing of name-giving (at birth) and, second, the newly delivered mother's seclusion, could in turn be said to have had a pragmatic effect on the role Israelite mothers or their female surrogates could assume in bestowing an infant's name. After all, if only a child's mother, her midwife, and/or other women attending the mother were present at the time of delivery, and if children were named at birth, then it follows that only a child's mother, her midwife, or other women in attendance would have been available to confer a name upon a newborn child.

But in point of fact, the matter is not so straightforward. As we saw in Chapter 5, women throughout the ancient Near East, like Israelite women, were separated from most men, including their husbands, during birth.[17] Yet Near Eastern cultures handle the logistics of naming a newborn child very differently. Sometimes—in Egypt, for example—we find traditions of name-giving that are very like those found in biblical tradition. Thus, according to the birth story recounted in the early second millennium BCE Westcar Papyrus, as the four goddess-midwives who serve the parturient Ruddedet work in tandem to deliver her three miracle children (who, according to the conceit of the story, are the great pharaohs of the Egyptian Fifth Dynasty), one of the goddesses, Isis, bestows a name on each child as he is born, just as a midwife or other women attending an Israelite parturient can be said to bestow an infant's name in Hebrew Bible childbirth accounts.[18] Indeed, in conferring names on Ruddedet's children, Isis uses the same sort of naming wordplays we have already seen in Hebrew Bible naming episodes: for example, in Eve's naming of Cain, in Leah's naming of Levi, and in Tamar's naming of Perez. More specifically, Isis declares to each fetus, as she seeks to expedite Ruddedet's labor and hasten the delivery of her three sons: "Don't be so mighty in her womb, you whose name is 'Mighty' [Pharaoh Userkaf] ... don't tread in her womb, you whose name is 'Tread-of-Re' [Pharaoh Sahure] ... [and] don't be so dark in her womb, you whose name is 'Dark' [Pharaoh Neferirkare]."[19]

Similar customs regarding name-giving also seem to have pertained in Egypt several centuries later, at the time of the New Kingdom (ca. 1539–1075 BCE). During that period, as we saw in the last chapter, evidence from Pharaoh Akhenaton's fourteenth-century BCE capital city of el-Amarna and from the thirteenth- and twelfth-century BCE workmen's village of Deir el-Medina suggests that Egyptian parturients were separated from their households in order to give birth "in an upper chamber ... on the roof" (at el-Amarna) or (at Deir el-Medina) "in a specially built arbor or hut outside the house" (see Fig. 5.4).[20] Here we can add that a New Kingdom hymn to the god Amun, which refers to "his mother who made his name," indicates that an Egyptian child's name was typically, or at least sometimes, conferred by the newborn's mother,[21] seemingly immediately after birth and so (presumably) within the same set-off space in which the delivery took place.[22] A like naming practice may have prevailed at the Late Bronze Age city-state of Ugarit, where it is clear, according to the mythological "Feast of the Goodly Gods" that I again had occasion to mention in the last chapter, that the god El's divine offspring Šaḥar and Šalim ("Dawn" and "Dusk") had already been named when word was brought to El of their birth (*KTU* 1.23.52–53). And named by whom? The text does not explicitly say, but since the two wives of El who bore Šaḥar and Šalim and the unidentified messenger who brings the news that the pair has been delivered are the only characters other than El who appear in this childbirth account, it most logically follows that the wives—much less likely, in my opinion, the messenger—conferred upon Šaḥar and Šalim their names.[23]

According to two Hittite myths, however, a baby was taken from the birth chamber after delivery in order to be presented to and given a name by its father. In the second-millennium BCE Hittite text of the Hurrian myth known as "The Song of Ullikummi," the god Kumarbi bestows the name Ullikummi on his son after the child has been brought to Kumarbi and set on the father's knees subsequent to parturition,[24] and in the roughly contemporary tale of "Appu and His Two Sons," a "nurse" brings Appu's firstborn son to Appu after his wife has delivered the child. This nurse then sets the baby on Appu's knees, at which point Appu "put a fitting name upon him." Appu likewise "put the right name" upon his second son once the nurse brought the boy to him after the child had been born.[25] In a study of Hittite birth and name-giving traditions, Harry A. Hoffner hypothesizes that this all happened "only a few minutes after birth," although Hoffner appropriately cautions that we cannot automatically assume that "the ceremonies described in connection with birth and name-giving in these myths" (and, we can add, in the Egyptian and Ugaritic mythological traditions that I previously cited) "have any similarity with the procedures followed by historical parents."[26] Nonetheless, it is my conviction, as noted in the Introduction and referred to above, that ancient texts' descriptions of—or, somewhat more typically, their allusions to— women's life-cycle events and rituals, including descriptions and allusions found in myths, must generally have "rung true" to their ancient audiences. Thus, they should correspond to those audiences' experiences of life-cycle events and rituals that took place in the cultural milieu in which the audience members actually lived.

Indeed, the description found in "The Song of Ullikummi" and "Appu and His Two Sons" of placing a newborn "on the knees" is also found in a

Hittite ritual text that "is concerned with post-parturition activities on behalf of a mother and child within the royal family."[27] While this royal text, like Hittite mythological texts, is still separated by considerable measure from the experiences of an everyday Hittite, the ritual's account does suggest that there are notable continuities between mythological and nonmythological accounts of Hittite birth and name-giving—including, perhaps, the Hittite father's role in bestowing a name on his child.[28] There are also certain parallels between the Hittite materials I have catalogued and ritual traditions found a millennium or so later, in classical and Hellenistic Greece. In those cultures, it was also the father who played a central role in postpartum rituals, first, by formally accepting (or rejecting) a newborn child and thereby marking (or dismissing) the neonate as a member of the family. This paternal decision took place at a ceremony called the Amphidromia that was observed on the fifth day after a child's birth (or, according to some sources, the seventh or tenth day).[29] At the same time—or perhaps at a separate though roughly concurrent "naming ceremony" known as the Dekatē—a name was bestowed on the child, again (apparently) by the father.[30] Roman children were similarly named several days after birth: on the eighth day postpartum if the newborn was a female or on the ninth day if male.[31] According to Christian Laes, in his book *Children in the Roman Empire*, the maternal uncle bestowed the praenomen, or the personal name, upon a boy child (girl children were not given a praenomen).[32] A child's nomen, or clan name (Latin *gens*), was, conversely, predetermined, as it was the same as or (for a girl child) a feminized form of the father's nomen. Originally, the cognomen (the third name for boys, the second name for girls) was also inherited, although over time, individuating cognomena came into existence.[33]

Parturients in both Greek and Roman tradition, we can add, while served and supported by "an experienced woman [for example, a midwife] and female helpers—relatives, friends, slaves, or neighbors," were separated from their husbands and other men during birth.[34] I therefore conclude that even though a shared sensibility existed across the Near East and wider Mediterranean regarding the logistics of birth—with husbands and men generally absent from the birth chamber—this shared sensibility does not drive shared convictions regarding name-giving, whereby the mother or other women who attend at the birth often confer the newborn's name. Rather, in Hatti (apparently) and in Greece and Rome, different conventions prevailed.

Moreover, the materials I have surveyed from, especially, Hatti, Greece, and Rome urge us to treat name-giving as a highly ritualized event, and ritually significant, I intend to argue, not just for the male name-givers of Hittite, Greek, and Roman tradition, but also for the female name-givers of other Near Eastern cultures. These include, I contend, the name-giving mothers of ancient Israel who are my focus in this chapter.[35] Indeed, in what follows, I propose that for Israelite mothers who assumed responsibility for bestowing their children's names, the conferring of those names was a singularly important moment within the extended ritual complex that comprised motherhood—that is, the ritual complex that, as I suggested at the beginning of Chapter 5, extended through a woman's pregnancy, parturition, and her infant's neonatal period, until culminating, finally, in weaning (which, as I again noted in my introductory remarks in Chapter 5, typically took place only when a child was three or so years of age).[36]

More specifically, I argue below that just as the gifting of the marriage present, according to my analysis in Chapter 3, enhanced and elevated the status of a bride-to-be at the point at which it was conferred during her betrothal ritual, so too did a woman's bestowing of a name on her infant shortly after the birth took place enhance and elevate the status of this new mother during the immediate ritual period postpartum. In addition, I will argue that just as a bride-to-be is accorded a certain degree of agency and autonomy in conjunction with the enhanced status that accrues to her when the marriage present is gifted (for example, Rebekah is able to say whether she will go to Canaan to wed Isaac or not; Gen 24:58), so too is a newly delivered mother, when bestowing a name of her child, able to act in ways that signal her recently elevated status. For example, I propose that due to her elevated and enhanced status, the maternal name-giver is able to convey to her newborn infant certain intimations of its future station in life: in particular, the first intimations of this child's social identity. Thereby the new mother initiated her child's entry into key institutions of Israelite culture: the family, the household, and the family's and household's larger community. I also will suggest that a maternal name-giver's elevated and enhanced status allowed a newly delivered woman to articulate important aspects of her engagement with God during her pregnancy and at parturition and thus to give voice to her religious experience and convictions. Elsewhere in the Bible, however, it is relatively rare to find accounts of women able to engage in religious discourse as a mode of self-expression.

Maternal Name-Giving and Status Enhancement

I begin my discussion by considering in more detail a point that I raised briefly at the end of the previous chapter: the ancients' conviction that the reason a woman must be secluded, at least to some degree, during delivery and also for a period thereafter is because she is a source of danger to others in her household and community, due both to the various malevolent spirits that childbirth attracts and to the perilous childbirth impurities that accrue to her. According to Geraldine Pinch, for example, the reason the four goddess-midwives described in the Egyptian Westcar Papyrus immediately seal the door of the birth chamber when they arrive to deliver Ruddedet's three babies is to create "a protective zone around the mother," which not only "insulated the rest of the household from the . . . danger and pollution of childbirth," but also from the "demons and ghosts who might be attracted" by childbirth's dangerous and polluting environment.[37] Pinch writes similarly of the rooftop chambers and outside arbors used for giving birth a few centuries later at the New Kingdom sites of el-Amarna and Deir el-Medina (see again Fig. 5.4): their purpose was "to maximize magical protection and to save the rest of the household from ritual pollution."[38] This period of pollution persists, according to the Westcar Papyrus, for fourteen days,[39] and an inscription from Deir el-Medina seems likewise to suggest that mothers there, along with their newborns, remained secluded in their birth arbors for a fourteen-day period so that childbirth's dangerous impurities could pass.[40]

In Mesopotamia, too, "delivery caused serious impurity,"[41] and so, Karel van der Toorn writes: "both the mothers and their babies were kept separate from the other inhabitants of the house," perhaps until the tenth day after birth during the Old Babylonian period (ca. 1894–1595 BCE),[42] or, according to a Seleucid-era text (ca. 312–63 BCE), for a period of thirty days.[43] Also, as I noted briefly in Chapter 1, second-millennium BCE Hittite tradition mandated a prolonged period of childbirth impurity to be observed postpartum—three months for a boy and four months for a girl—although the Hittite text that includes this dictum does not explicitly state that a newly delivered mother is considered to be impure alongside her newborn child.[44] Nor does this text explicitly indicate that those in a state of postpartum impurity should be separated or isolated from others in their social orbit. Nevertheless, commentators generally assume that a Hittite infant's mother was held to be impure along with her child and that both were therefore sequestered, at least to some degree, from their extended family and/or their community. In his book *Hittite Birth Rituals*, for example, Gary M. Beckman suggests that after the three- or four-month period of impurity, "*mother and child* would (re-)enter into normal relations with the *rest of their community*," and another noted Hittitologist, Billie Jean Collins, likewise writes of the "*reentry into the community*" that took place "for *mother and child* after three months for a boy and four months for a girl" (emphases in both quotes are mine).[45]

We know, of course, again from Chapter 1, of the similar tradition that is put forward in first-millennium BCE Israel by the Priestly source, or P, where, in Lev 12:1–8, a newly delivered mother is said to be impure for seven days and then enters into a less serious state of impurity for another thirty-three days if her child is a boy, but is considered impure for twice as long—an initial fourteen days and then a subsequent sixty-six days—if her child is a girl. More specifically, as noted yet again in Chapter 1, a newly delivered mother is said in Lev 12:2, 5 to manifest the same sort of ritual uncleanliness as does a menstruant for an initial seven days after the birth of a son and for fourteen days after the birth of a daughter. Like a menstruant, therefore, the new mother could transmit her impurity to anyone who touched her or touched a piece of furniture on which she had sat or lain. Those affected would have included, I argued in Chapter 1, her newborn infant. I also argued in Chapter 1 that the new mother's communicable impurity would have constrained, at least to some degree, her interactions with certain members of her family, her household, and/or others in her community.

Yet while these Leviticus 12 restrictions that constrained an Israelite woman's contact with certain family, household, and community members would have eased after one or two weeks, once the recently delivered mother was no longer likened to a menstruant, she was still prohibited, according to Lev 12:4, from touching anything classified as *qōdeš*, or holy, and from entering holy or sanctified space (*hammiqdāš*) for another thirty-three or sixty-six days. In classical Greece as well, different stages of a newly delivered mother's ritual impurity were registered after birth. Initially, as in Israel, a Greek mother's childbirth impurities were considered to be communicable: to her child; to all those who had assisted her during the child's birth; to the inhabitants of the mother's domicile, or *oikos*; and to all those from without the *oikos* who might come into her household domain. This "general household pollution" seems to have lasted until the time of the Amphidromia, which, as noted above, took place (at least according to most ancient sources' reckoning) five days after the delivery and was the event at which the newborn was presented to its father and formally accepted (or rejected) as a member of the family.[46] According to Robert Garland, in his book-length study of the Greek life cycle, this was "very likely... the first occasion that the new arrival left the *gunaikeion*," the part of the household's living quarters that was "reserved exclusively for women" and where the birth most probably took place.[47] Garland and other scholars therefore conclude that for the infant, the impurity that childbirth occasioned was deemed to have run its course by the time the Amphidromia occurred. This seems also to be the case for those who attended the mother at delivery and for almost everyone else who had been affected by childbirth's impurities. Indeed, this appears to have been the case for everyone except for the mother herself. She—most probably—remained impure, although she was no longer polluting to others, until the fortieth day after delivery.[48]

This fortieth day after delivery, and so, it seems, the end of the mother's period of impurity, was likely marked by a "joyous celebration" called the Tesserakostaion. Unfortunately, the source that most clearly attests to this celebration is late (third century CE), but Garland suggests that the rite was an ancient one, coordinated with the point identified in other texts as the end of a woman's lochial discharge.[49] In Egypt, a purification ceremony and a celebration seem similarly to have taken place after a newly delivered mother's fourteen-day period of isolation had ended. Both inscriptional and iconographic evidence suggest that the purification ceremony included some form of washing.[50] Furthermore, iconographic materials from late thirteenth-/early twelfth-century BCE Deir el-Medina indicate that female attendants offered various cosmetic items (a mirror and a kohl case) for newly delivered mothers to use as their postpartum seclusion came to an end (see once more Fig. 5.4).[51] According to some scholars, these cosmetic items were used as part of the purification process; according to others, they were meant to adorn the newly delivered mother in advance of her return to her community.[52]

In addition, if reliefs of the divine births of pharaohs found at the fifteenth-century BCE site of Deir el-Bahri and in the fourteenth-century BCE "Birth Room" of the Luxor Temple are any indication, the newly delivered mother's hair—which needed to hang loose and unbound during delivery (see Chapter 5)—was also restyled during the period of postpartum isolation and then, in accord with Egyptian social norms, covered with an elaborate wig.[53] Drawings from Deir el-Medina similarly intimate that in accord with Egyptian social norms, the mother's restyled hair was coated with perfumed oil.⁵⁴ In addition, Pinch, citing a kindred drawing from Deir el-Medina, suggests that at "the celebration that marked the end of both a mother's and a newborn baby's period of isolation," the mother wore festal clothes and received offerings of flowers and perfume, while a protective dance was performed (Fig. 6.1).⁵⁵ Barry J. Kemp has interpreted a fourteenth-century BCE wall painting from el-Amarna as likewise depicting dancing at a celebration that marked the "termination to childbirth and its ensuing period of uncleanliness."⁵⁶ In one text from Deir el-Medina, this celebration is described as "a big drinking party," whose rations include six jugs of beer as well as various foodstuffs (bread, vegetables),⁵⁷ and another two to three Deir el-Medina texts have also been taken to refer to a feast held during a postpartum celebration.⁵⁸ In the Westcar Papyrus too, a "day of feasting" at which jugs of beer seem to be a crucial component takes place at some point after Ruddedet's fourteen days of confinement come to an end.⁵⁹

Fig. 6.1 Limestone ostracon that may depict the celebration after an Egyptian woman's period of postpartum impurity ends, with female attendants offering flowers and perfume while a figure above the new mother's left shoulder (the demigod Bes?) dances. From Deir el-Medina, Ramesside period (ca. 1292–1075 BCE). 8.5 cm high, 12 cm. wide. From the collection of the Musée du Louvre, Paris. Inv. no. E 25318. Photo Christian Decamps. © RMN-Grand Palais/Art Resource, New York.

Third-millennium BCE Mesopotamian texts somewhat similarly suggest that among the upper classes, a feast could be held after a birth at which the newly delivered mother received presents. The tradition of giving presents to a new mother is also attested in Mesopotamian materials from the Old Babylonian period, where texts list oil and garments as gifts received by women who had recently given birth.[60] In the Hittite world of the mid-second millennium BCE, there can similarly be festivals at the time of birth, although not necessarily in honor of the mother. Rather, the "Festival of Birth" is held on the day of delivery in honor of the "Mother-goddesses of the body" or "Great goddesses of the body," and the "Festival of the Womb," the "Festival of Crying Out," and the "Festival of Pigeons" are held in honor of the Hurrian goddess Šaušga, who is kindred to the Mesopotamian goddess of love and fertility Ishtar.[61] Still, at least one Hittite source indicates that a ceremony could also be held after birth to ensure the continued fertility of the mother.[62] More important for our purposes: both Beckman and Collins specifically refer to the occasion of a woman's reentry into her community after the three to four months of postpartum impurity has passed as a "ceremony" or as "ceremonial"—what we can take, that is, as a "rite" (Collins's word) that celebrates the Hittite mother's coming forth into her body politic in the company of her newborn child.[63]

Indeed, I take all these events—the Greek Tesserakostaion, along with the third- and second-millennium BCE Egyptian, Mesopotamian, and Hittite ceremonies, feasts, and/or gift-giving celebrations that focus on the newly delivered mother—to exemplify the sort of reincorporation or reintegration into society that, according to Arnold van Gennep's and Victor Turner's work on rites of passage, characterizes the experience of a ritual subject at the conclusion of any life-cycle event, including childbirth. In fact, as I documented in the Introduction, van Gennep explicitly described the twenty days of restrictions imposed on a Hopi woman after she gave birth—including the prohibition that forbade a first-time mother from leaving her house during daylight hours—as a post-parturition liminal period and then identified the twentieth day, when a special ritual meal was served to the entire community, as marking the new mother's reincorporation or reaggregation into her household and pueblo.[64] Egyptologist Marie-Lys Arnette, along with her sometimes co-author Anne Austin, also uses van Gennep's language of aggregation and integration to describe the process that brings a newly delivered mother back into her community in New Kingdom Egypt once her fourteen-day period of postpartum seclusion comes to an end, and rightly so:[65] because the New Kingdom feasts associated with the new mother's reentry into her society are by definition so communal, as are the Mesopotamian, Hittite, and Greek traditions of ceremonies, feasting, and gift-giving celebrations in honor of a new mother, they seem to me perfectly to mark a reincorporation of the previously segregated woman into her community. Consequently, it is at this point, just as van Gennep and Turner indicate should occur within a rite of passage's reintegration phase, that the new mother fully assumes her new maternal identity, or what Turner has referred to as her "new station in life."[66]

As we move, however, from Egypt, Mesopotamia, Hatti, and Greece to consider the Bible, we find no indications that a newly delivered mother in ancient Israel was feasted, or given gifts, or was otherwise the focus of the sorts of postpartum ceremonies or celebrations that we find attested in Egyptian, Mesopotamian, Hittite, and Greek texts. To be sure, in situations like these, one must always remember the adage that "absence of evidence is not evidence of absence." That is, there might well have been some feasting, gift-giving, or other postpartum ceremony or celebration focused on the newly delivered Israelite mother of which no record has been preserved.[67] Still, the scant evidence we can adduce—from Priestly or P texts in Gen 17:11–12; Gen 21:4; and Lev 12:3 and from later biblical and apocryphal texts (Jub. 15:12, 14, 25–26; Luke 1:59 and 2:21; Phil 3:5)—is not promising, as it suggests that any postpartum ceremonies held in Israel, at least in the late preexilic and the Persian, Hellenistic, and Roman periods, focused on a male infant's circumcision eight days after childbirth. The subject of these postpartum rituals, that is, was not the newly delivered *mother* but her newborn *son*.

Could, however, the *ḥaṭṭā't* or purification offering that, according to Lev 12:6–8, a recently delivered mother is mandated to bring to Yahweh's sanctuary forty or eighty days after parturition signify her postpartum reintegration?[68] Intuitively, it seems that this could be the case, but in point of fact, the woman's postpartum sacrifice does not reincorporate her into her community. Instead, it is really a reintegration with the *qādōš*, or holy, and not with any social group, that this offering effects. After all, it is only from the *qādōš*, or holy, and not from her family, her household, or her larger community, that the new mother has been separated for the thirty-three or sixty-six days that comprise the second stage of her postpartum period of impurity. And even this reading of a woman's reincorporation or reintegration is called into question if we take into account Jacob Milgrom's argument that the focus of the *ḥaṭṭā't* or purification offering required of a recently delivered mother is not in fact the woman but the sanctuary to which her offering is delivered, which must be purged of *its* impurity.[69] As Milgrom explains, this is because the sanctuary (or, in Lev 12:6–8, the tent of meeting that, according to the predominant strain in biblical tradition, was Israel's central place of worship during the people's exodus sojourn in the Sinai wilderness) is stationed among the Israelites, and so, in the words of Lev 16:16, "in the midst of their impurities" (*bĕtôk ṭum'ōtām*). The sanctuary can therefore be polluted by these impurities and so requires purification in order that it remain suitable for the presence of Yahweh, who is understood to dwell within—for "a polluted sanctuary," as Saul M. Olyan writes, "is not fit for a deity's continuing residence and cult."[70] The *ḥaṭṭā't* or purification offering that the postpartum mother offers forty to eighty days after childbirth effects the needed cleansing. Thus, while the mother's postpartum sacrifice might be said to reincorporate the previously impure and compromised *sanctuary* back into the Israelites' midst, so that God can continue to dwell among Israel's people, it does not bring about the *woman's* postpartum reincorporation or reintegration into her community.

Yet without some sort of ceremony, feast, or gift-giving celebration at the end of the postpartum period, how do the ancient Israelites mark what is perhaps the most crucial component of childbirth as a life-cycle event: the registering of a recently delivered woman's new maternal identity? I suggest this is accomplished through the mother bestowing on her infant a name. More specifically, I suggest that by bestowing her child's name, and bestowing the name, as we have seen, immediately after birth, the new Israelite mother indicates that at that moment, she has, in the words of cultural studies specialist Della Pollock, brought her newborn "over the last threshold of nothingness into being" and has thereby successfully accomplished the task of childbearing that, as I discussed in Chapter 3, is so critical to a woman's standing in Israelite society.[71] Consequently, the new mother, especially a mother who has given birth for the first time, assumes a new role within her community or, to quote again Turner, a "new station in life."[72] Indeed, Naomi Steinberg has proposed that it is only with childbearing that an Israelite women comes fully into adulthood.[73]

To be sure, Steinberg's assessment may overreach;[74] yet whether a recently delivered woman is only a new mother or also a new adult, I still suggest that this mother's pronouncement of her child's name asserts that within her family, her household, and her community, she has assumed a new role.

Name-giving, in other words, is the means by which a new mother claims her new life station. Moreover, the Israelite mother can be said to *proclaim* her new life station, for in striking contrast to the Egyptian, Mesopotamian, Hittite, and Greek ceremonies, feasts, and/or gift-giving celebrations I described above, at which these cultures' mothers are the *objects* of ritual activities that mark their new position within their communities, an Israelite mother is the *subject* of the name-giving act that asserts her new social role. More simply put: an Israelite mother is not a woman for whom the ritual marking her new maternal identity is enacted, but the one who enacts the ritual that marks her newly achieved maternal status,

Indeed, status is a key word here, for as I indicated already above, what we are seeing in the Egyptian, Mesopotamian, Hittite, and Greek postpartum events that mark a new mother's reincorporation or reintegration into her community is the culmination of the typical rite-of-passage pattern as described by van Gennep and Turner, whereby the ritual subject assumes, at the time the rite ends, a new position within her community. In particular, as we saw in the Introduction and in subsequent discussions, Turner described these rites of passage as a process in which "the ritual subject" moves through a liminal period involving "putting down or humbling . . . as its principal cultural constituent," in order to be "conveyed irreversibly from a lower to a higher position in an institutionalized system of such positions."[75] Examples include, as I suggested above in my discussion of Egyptian, Mesopotamian, Hittite, and Greek postpartum ceremonies, feasts, and/or gift-giving celebrations, a move from the position of "not mother" to "mother" after a liminal period of impurity, or, as I argued in my consideration of the *Nkang'a* initiate in the Introduction, a move from the position of girl within Ndembu social structure to the position of woman and wife.

Nevertheless, in my consideration of the *Nkang'a* initiate, I concluded that van Gennep's and Turner's rites-of-passage paradigm cannot be applied indiscriminately to her, or to women generally, given that Turner, especially, assumes that liminality, the phase within a rite of passage during which the ritual subject, according to Turner's account, is subordinated, *ends* when a new station in life is assumed in the rite's reincorporation or reintegration phase. Yet in many societies, according to the analyses of Caroline Walker Bynum and Bruce Lincoln, women are *permanently liminal*, or liminal as part of the *normal course* of their existence.[76] I take these societies to include ancient Egypt, Mesopotamia, Hatti, and Greece. I therefore suggest that while Egyptian, Mesopotamian, Hittite, and Greek women—especially women who have given birth for the first time—take on a new maternal identity at the postpartum events that reincorporate or reintegrate them into their communities, their ritual position as *objects* at these events signals (albeit subtly) motifs of liminal disenfranchisement. That is: while reincorporation does bring to an end a heightened phase of liminality (the period of postpartum seclusion), it does so only to move these new mothers back into their permanently liminal mode of existence, where they are subordinate to others who have authority over them: for example, the (male?) authorities who oversee their reintegration ceremonies, feasts, and gift-giving rituals.

No ritual authorities, however, oversee the Israelite woman's bestowing of her new baby's name. In fact, because the baby's name is bestowed immediately after birth, at a time when our evidence suggests the parturient is in the company of only her midwife and/or other female attendants, name-giving takes place independent not only of ritual authorities, but also of men, who are otherwise women's superiors within Israel's social order. This is not coincidental: rather, the fact that name-giving takes place immediately after birth, when no men are present, liberates the recently delivered mother to be the subject of the ritual moment that defines her new maternal identity. Consequently, maternal name-giving can be identified as an example of the fifth feature cited in the Introduction as a characteristic of some women's life-cycle rituals, as it marks a moment in the life-cycle rite (here, a moment in the midst of the forty- to eighty-day postpartum ritual period) during which the "liminality of the permanently structural inferior"[77] (here, Israelite women) expresses itself in terms of a hierarchical reversal. This reversal temporarily elevates or enhances the status of the female subject (here, the newly delivered mother)—just as the gifting of the marriage present, I argued in Chapter 3, signaled a moment of elevated or enhanced status for a young woman at the moment it was bestowed during her betrothal ritual. Likewise, the bodily adornment of Guinea Fowl, and her dances wielding the village headman's eland-tail switch and a hunter's gun, signaled a period, I argued in the Introduction, where her status was elevated or enhanced during the Ndembu ritual of *Nkang'a*.

We might recall, moreover, that Guinea Fowl was accorded an elevated or enhanced status as she danced and then again later that night, when she was allowed to pass judgment on the quality of her bridegroom's sexual performance, because it was at precisely these moments that the attributes the Ndembu most value in a woman—her sexuality and reproductive fertility—were most on display: in Guinea Fowl's bare-breasted dance that showed off her newly sexualized body and in her initial experience of penetrative sexual intercourse. Likewise, the gifting of the marriage present, I argued in Chapter 3, elevated and enhanced the Israelite bride-to-be's status because it anticipated the betrothed woman's future childbearing role that was of such overwhelming importance in Israelite society. So too, according to the analysis presented above, did an Israelite mother's bestowing a name on her newborn elevate and enhance a newly delivered woman's status at precisely the moment when her reproductive abilities were most vividly on display: immediately after she had successfully given birth. We might say, in fact, that maternal name-giving conjoins with the moment of elevated and enhanced status that was previously signaled by the marriage present, as a new mother's bestowing on her child a name confirms that she has fulfilled the role of childbearer that the gifting of the marriage present had adumbrated.

In short: name-giving establishes that an Israelite mother has successfully brought to term the child anticipated through the gifting of the marriage present. As such, maternal name-giving marks a moment within the postpartum ritual period that is not only analogous to, but the culmination of, the moment within the betrothal ritual at which the marriage present is gifted. Once more, therefore, I propose that just as the gifting of the marriage present signified a stage within the betrothal ritual during which the status of the bride-to-be was elevated and enhanced, name-giving marks a point within the postpartum ritual period during which a status reversal of an otherwise structural inferior (the female) manifests itself so that the newly delivered mother's social position is elevated and enhanced. Again, then: while Steinberg may overstate when she suggests that it is only in bearing a child that an Israelite woman becomes truly an adult,[78] her basic impulse—that a newly delivered woman experiences a moment of elevated and enhanced status precisely because she has realized the critical achievement that has been anticipated since betrothal and even her coming of age—is right on the mark.

Maternal Name-Giving and a Child's Social Identity

Bestowing a name on her newly delivered child allows a woman not only to experience a moment of elevated and enhanced status as she claims and proclaims her new maternal identity; it also allows her to assert agency and authority in ways consistent with her enhanced status position. For example: much as a recently delivered woman defines her new maternal station in life by bestowing on her infant a name, she also defines the child's new life station by inaugurating the newborn into his or her social identity within the family and household and the family's and household's larger community. This is because, as anthropologist Carol McClain argues, naming for a child marks a beginning, for it is through naming that "the new child becomes a separate person and a member of a social group."[79] Or, as biblical scholar Søren Lorenzen writes in his aptly titled book *Spoken into Being*, on names and selfhood in the Hebrew Bible, "naming is the symbolic birth that accompanies a physical birth," establishing what Lorenzen calls a "semantic" and (quoting Pierre Bourdieu) a "social essence."[80] The analyses produced by McClain, Lorenzen, and Bourdieu were anticipated, moreover, by Arnold van Gennep, who writes: "when a child is named, he is both individualized and incorporated into society."[81]

In the Near East and wider Mediterranean, naming as an act—even (to quote again van Gennep) a "rite"—of incorporation is perhaps most clearly a feature of Greek and Roman tradition.[82] In both cultures, as I have previously noted, the child is not given a name until several days after birth, at which point other significant aspects of the child's identity are registered as well. In Rome, for example, the "lustral day" (*dies lustricus*) at which a child's name was conferred—eight or nine days after birth—also "marked the entry of the child into the family and society,"[83] or what I have described in this book's Prologue as the child's "social birth." Regarding this social birth's importance, we can again quote Christian Laes, *Children in the Roman Empire*, who writes that prior to the *dies lustricus,* "if a father wanted to abandon a nameless infant," he more or less could do so, "as the child did not 'exist' yet."[84] A legal text from Flavian-era Spain (69–96 CE) likewise numbers a man's children, living and dead, by counting only those who lived past their naming day and not those who died before.[85] As I noted in Chapter 1, Plutarch, in his *Roman Questions* (in Book IV of Plutarch's *Moralia*), opines that this was because a child, before its naming day, was "more like a plant than animal."[86]

As we have seen, the Greek Amphidromia, too, marked a child's "formal acceptance into the family" and, we can now add, "the creation of a legal social identity,"[87] with the father publicly acknowledging, once a name had been conferred upon the child (either at the Amphidromia or at the roughly concurrent Dekatē), that the newborn was his legitimate offspring.[88] The noted Egyptologist Erik Hornung has likewise suggested that in Egypt, even though the timing of name-giving was very different from that found in Greece and Rome, bestowing a child's name actualized the child's identity as a being within the world. "At the time of birth," Hornung writes, "a child receives a name immediately, for without a name the individual does not exist."[89]

Karel van der Toorn argues that ancient Israel was also a culture where this understanding of naming pertained; thus he writes, speaking of a girl child, "Once a girl has her own name, she can be addressed and is acknowledged as a person."[90] Isaiah 40:26, which places cola describing God's creating and bestowing names on the heavenly host in parallel, similarly intimates that in the Israelite worldview, name-giving was synonymous with existence. This idea is also reflected in Eccl 6:10 ("whatever exists has already been named") and Gen 2:19–20 (where Yahweh follows on the creation of all the animals and birds by bringing them to the man, or *hā'ādām*, in order that each be given a name).[91] The need to invoke the dead by name—as in 2 Sam 18:18— further suggests a link between a (male) person's name and that person's identity and place in Israelite society: in this case, the society of Israel's deceased kin (more on this in Chapter 9).[92] If there is no name to invoke, however (because, say, some ancestor has been forgotten), the deceased (presumably) ceases to exist: "the loss of a name was regarded as complete annihilation."[93] As in death, I suggest, so too at birth; I suggest, that is, that for Israelite mothers who took on the responsibility of bestowing children's names, the conferring of a child's name brings the newborn truly into existence and thereby inaugurates the infant into membership within his or her social collective. Furthermore, through bestowing children's names and thus introducing infants into their families', households', and communities' structures, mothers build up and accordingly reconstitute their families, households, and community. The conferring of names on their recently delivered children therefore denotes Israelite mothers as important agents of community formation.

To be sure, as indicated in Chapter 1, naming cannot be said to be the end-all-and-be-all of what we might again refer to as an Israelite infant's social birth. Rather, as I suggested in that previous discussion, we also need to attend to the end of the seven-/fourteen-day period during which, according to Lev 12:1–8 and also (as I have interpreted) Ezek 16:4, the child is rendered impure due to its contact with its contagiously impure mother. Moreover, Kristine Henriksen Garroway has proposed that Israelite infants "were not considered full members of the community" until weaning, which did not take place until the child was about three years old.[94] Yet these intimations of a multistage social birth need not disturb us; instead, as Laes points out in a study of social birth that spans Mediterranean traditions from the early Greek period to the early Middle Ages, the "gradual" admission of "children into family-based social groups" was the norm.[95] In classical Athens, for example, male infants were introduced into hereditary associations, or "brotherhoods" known as the *genê* and the *phratriai* at some point after the Amphidromia. Male children's initiation as *choïkoi*, which allowed them to participate in the Choës festival associated with Dionysus (and to taste their first wine!), came later still (between age three and four).[96] Likewise in Rome, the observation of the *dies lustricus* on the eighth or ninth day after birth was followed by other events that marked the "gradual admission of Roman infants into various social groups": an official registering of newborns, for example, within "thirty days after receiving their name or after their birth."[97]

Consider also the Egyptian materials I have surveyed, where, as Hornung's comment above suggests, name-giving immediately at birth established the new child's existence, even though Egyptian evidence suggests that this existence was not publicly acknowledged until a mother and her newborn child emerged from their postpartum period of seclusion fourteen days after delivery. Israelite tradition, at least according to the interpretation I have proposed, is remarkably parallel. While we cannot therefore claim that an Israelite mother, in naming her child, fully establishes that child's social identity, the name-giving mother, having physically delivered her newborn into the world, subsequently gives social birth to the infant in the sense that she inaugurates or initiates her child's multistaged journey into personhood. Having shepherded a newborn's previous transition from "nothingness into being," to quote again Della Pollock (that is, the newborn's movement from conception to delivery),[98] so too does a mother who bestows an infant's name initiate the development of her child as a social entity. As such, Israel's name-giving mothers, as an expression of their enhanced position and status, convey the first intimations of their newborns' position and place in the world.

Name-Giving as an Act of Women's Religious Discourse

The Bible's descriptions of maternal name-givers closely tie together the two births I have discussed above—the physical delivery and the child's birth into social identity—through the content of the names that mothers or their female surrogates bestow. We see this is the way in which a woman's experiences during pregnancy and parturition or other circumstances that pertain to a child's physical birth can frequently be evoked in the name bestowed on the infant at its social birth.[99] Even more so is this the case in the "naming speeches" that are often found within maternal name-giving accounts. More simply put: when bestowing a name, and especially when supplementing the name-giving with a speech that explains the name's meaning, a mother or her female surrogate(s) often tells us something about the mother's perceptions of and reactions to the childbirth process and/or other matters related to her experience of becoming a mother. Indeed, as Ilana Pardes writes in her study of Israelite mothers as name-givers, "biblical naming (especially when accompanied by a speech) usually reveals more about the character of the name-giver than the recipient."[100]

For example: according to what I, at least, take to be the most plausible translation of Gen 4:1, Adam and Eve's firstborn Cain is so named because "I created" him, Eve puns, playing on the assonance of the name *qayin*, Cain, and the verb *qānîtî*, "I created." "I created a man," she continues, "with Yahweh."[101] At one level, we may be inclined to hear mythological resonances here, as the language of creation as applied to Eve, the "mother of all the living," evokes thoughts of the great mother goddess of the Canaanite world, Asherah, called at Ugarit "the creatress of the gods" (*qnyt ilm*). It follows that Eve's statement that she created Cain "with Yahweh" can call to mind Asherah's position as the consort of and creator alongside the god El, Yahweh's Canaanite precursor.[102] More mundanely, we can take Eve's paronomastic account of "creating" Cain "with Yahweh" as an acknowledgment of Yahweh's oft-attested role in biblical tradition as a giver of children.[103] Whether mythological, though, or mundane, of note in either case is that Eve stresses, through the name she bestows on Cain, her own experience of becoming pregnant and delivering a child: "*I* created" him, she says of Cain (emphasis mine). Similarly, Rachel stresses in Gen 35:18 her experience during delivery—an impending death in childbirth—through the name she bestows on her second-born son: Ben-oni (*ben-'ônî*), "Son of *my* sorrow" (emphasis again mine).

Each of the names that Leah and Rachel confer on Jacob's other eleven sons likewise evokes or is explained by some aspect of the two women's experiences in childbearing or, in Leah's case, the relation between childbearing and her rather unhappy marriage to Jacob. For example, in Gen

29:32, Leah confers on her firstborn the name Reuben (*rĕ'ûbēn*, meaning "Look! A son!") because, she says, his birth shows that Yahweh has "seen" (*rā'â*) that she is unloved by Jacob and is compensating her with a baby boy (*bēn*). Likewise, in Gen 29:33, she confers the name Simeon (*šim'ôn*) on her second son, whom Yahweh has given her because, she says, the deity "heard" (*šāma'*) that she was hated and wished to offer redress. Rachel similarly bestows the name Joseph (*yôsēp*) on her firstborn in the hopes that Yahweh will "add" (*hôsîp*) another son to her progeny after her prolonged stint of barrenness, during which Leah gave birth seven times over. Rachel also bestows the name because God has "gathered," presumably in the sense of "gathered up and taken away" (*'āsap*), "my humiliation" (that is, the humiliation of childlessness; Gen 30:23–24). Etymologically, this second explanation is much less convincing, as it relies on the root *'-s-p* rather than the root *y-s-p* that actually appears in Joseph's name. However, as Rainer Albertz points out in a detailed study of all Hebrew names known from the epigraphic corpus of the preexilic period, several examples of *'-s-p* names are attested (see also Exod 6:24). This serves as evidence, Albertz suggests, that, like Rachel, "the mother who bestowed one of these names on her child constructed a reminder of her former distress and confessed that god had reversed her social humiliation."[104]

Beyond Genesis, accounts of a mother bestowing on her child a name and explaining it with a speech that evokes her experiences during pregnancy and parturition or circumstances that otherwise pertain to childbirth can be found in 1 Sam 1:20 (Hannah's bestowing on her son the name Samuel); 1 Sam 4:21 (Phinehas's wife's bestowing the name Ichabod on her son); and 1 Chr 4:9 (the name bestowed by Jabez's mother).[105] Overall, by my count (see again Table 6.1), nineteen out of the Bible's twenty-nine accounts of a mother or her female surrogate(s) bestowing a name on a child include (obliquely, in the case of Rachel in Gen 35:18) a naming speech that describes aspects of the woman's pregnancy and delivery that the child's name commemorates or related circumstances that pertain to the child's birth. The tally of women's naming speeches increases, moreover, if we consider Gen 21:1–7, at least in the redacted form in which this text has come down to us.[106] There, even though it is Abraham who confers the name Isaac (*yiṣḥāq*) upon his son by Sarah in Gen 21:3, it is *Sarah* who reflects in Gen 21:6 on the relationship of the name to *her* miraculous pregnancy after her prolonged ordeal of barrenness. Thus, she pronounces that "God has made laughter [*ṣĕḥōq*] *for me*; anyone who hears will laugh [*yiṣḥaq*] *for me*" (emphasis mine). A very similar trope occurs in Genesis 16, at least (again) in the redacted form in which we have received this text.[107] In that passage, even though the divine messenger who decrees that Hagar's son by Abram (Abraham) is to be named Ishmael (*yišmāʿēl*) is presented in the text as male (v 11), and even though it is Abram (Abraham) who is subsequently said to give Ishmael his name (v 15), the messenger addresses Hagar when decreeing "you [feminine singular] will name him Ishmael [*yišmāʿēl*]," in commemoration of her misery during pregnancy, of which God (*ʾēl*) has heard (*šāmaʿ*) and seeks to address.

Overall, then, nineteen out of the twenty-nine instances where mothers or their female surrogates bestow on a newborn child its name include a naming speech that ties the child's name to the mother's experiences during pregnancy and parturition or to circumstances that otherwise pertain to the child's birth. In addition, both Hagar and Sarah are implicitly associated with a naming speech related to their childbirth experiences, even though neither actually bestows a name on her son. Conversely, only six out of the seventeen instances where a father bestows a name on his child include a naming speech (see again Table 6.1). Moreover, the content of women's and men's naming speeches differs. As we have seen, the naming speeches delivered by a mother or her female surrogate(s) address, again and again, the mother's experiences during pregnancy and parturition, or circumstances otherwise related to the child's birth.[108] But fathers' naming speeches tend to reflect more on the father's life in general. Moses, for example, names his son Gershom (*gēršōm*) because the name expresses Moses's experience as a "stranger" (*gēr*) in a foreign land (Exod 2:22).[109] Similarly, Joseph names his firstborn Manasseh (*měnaššeh*) because God has made him forget (*niššâ*) all of his troubles, by which Joseph seems especially to mean his fraught relations with his ten half-brothers (Gen 41:51).[110]

There is another difference between paternal and maternal naming speeches: unlike fathers' naming speeches, those of mothers and their surrogates often reference the role of the deity in describing the experiences evoked by the newborn's name. I have cited several examples already—Eve's speech naming Cain; Leah's speeches naming Reuben and Simeon; and Rachel's double evocation of the deity in Gen 30:23–24, when she bestows the name Joseph on her firstborn son—but we could cite still more: for instance, Eve's speech bestowing the name Seth (*šēt*) on her thirdborn son because God had "appointed" (*šāt*) this son for her to take the place of her murdered son Abel (Gen 4:25), and Rachel's speech conferring the name Dan (*dān*) on the son that her maid Bilhah bore on her behalf because with the baby's birth, Rachel says, "God has judged me" (*dānannî 'ĕlōhîm*) and presumably found, after her prolonged barrenness, that she is deserving of a child (Gen 30:6). Overall, the deity is evoked in eleven of the nineteen instances where mothers or their surrogates bestow a name upon a newborn child and give a related naming speech. God is evoked as well on the two occasions where the mothers Hagar and Sarah are implicitly attributed a naming speech concerning their sons Ishmael and Isaac.[111]

The reason for not evoking the deity in the eight other naming speeches ascribed to women, moreover, is often easily understood. The naming speeches that evoke God typically do so in order to offer praise or express thanks.[112] (The only exception is Rachel's naming of Naphtali in Gen 30:8, whose name is based on her description of the "mighty wrestlings" or, literally, the "wrestlings of God" [*naptûlê 'ĕlōhîm*] that characterize her contentious relationship with her sister Leah.) Thus, occasions of name-giving where praise or thanksgiving is not warranted appropriately omit referring to the deity in the name and the associated naming speech. For example, Rachel bestows the name Ben-oni (*ben-'ônî*), "Son of my sorrow," on her second son as she dies in childbirth (Gen 35:18), and Jabez's mother evokes in his name (according to the etymology proposed in 1 Chr 4:9) the "pain" (*'ōṣeb*) she experienced during delivery. Pharaoh's daughter also omits any reference to the divine when she names Moses, which we should perhaps take as appropriate for a devotee of gods other than the God of Israel. Somewhat similarly, in bestowing the name Ichabod, or *î-kābôd*, "Where is the glory?," on the son during whose delivery she dies in 1 Sam 4:21–22, Phinehas's wife (obliquely) evokes the deity only to lament God's absence because, with the capture of God's divine palladium, the ark of the covenant, and the death of the ark's priestly attendants, her father-in-law Eli, her brother-in-law Hophni, and her husband Phinehas, the glory (*kābôd*)—more specifically, God's glory—had departed from Israel.

The women who do evoke the deity in naming speeches speak in a language that Pardes describes as "ceremonial discourse" and that might be more explicitly characterized as religious.[113] Seldom, however, do women in the Bible get to give voice to religious discourse. I have noted elsewhere, for example, that, rather astonishingly, Hannah is the only woman in the Hebrew Bible who is the subject of the verb *hitpallēl*, which is the verb in the Bible most commonly used to describe the act of praying.[114] Moreover, the other verb most commonly associated with prayer in the Bible—*'ātar*, "to make an entreaty, plead, supplicate"—is never used of a woman.[115]

For all we know, that is, Hannah is the only woman in all of Israelite history who prayed.[116] Hannah is likewise one of only three individual women identified in the Hebrew Bible as making a vow (*neder*) to Yahweh (the other two are found in Prov 7:14 and 31:2),[117] although certain issues regarding women's vows are the subject of legal materials found in Num 6:2; 30:4–16 (30:3–15 in most English translations); and Deut 23:19 (23:18 in most English translations).[118] Vows made by a cohort of women (along with their husbands) are also described in Jer 44:15–19, 25.

My own sense is that these fairly sparse data regarding women's religious speech do not necessarily reveal a historical situation where ancient Israelite women were barred from, or constrained regarding opportunities to pray, make vows, or otherwise engage in acts of religious expression. Rather, evidenced here is the characteristically male focus of the biblical text and consequently the text's frequent failure to document or otherwise attend to women's religious experiences. It is thus at a minimum interesting, and I suspect significant, that this omission does not happen in conjunction with maternal naming speeches. Indeed, I have indicated that just the opposite is the case: maternal naming speeches are a well-documented and a seemingly well-accepted form of women's religious expression. One reason for this, I might suggest, is that the birth and (as I have argued) the immediately subsequent naming of a child were matters of importance for these children's fathers as well as their mothers in ancient Israel, as Israelite men were deeply invested in their wives' childbearing success. I noted in Chapter 3, for example, that children were an important source of labor on the self-sufficient family farms that were the means of livelihood for most Israelites, so much so that modern population studies show that even in locales that might seem to nonagriculturalists to be vastly overpeopled, farm families seek to bear and raise as many children as possible, to the extent that they will eschew an increased standard of living in favor of an increased family size.[119] Sons were also important for maintaining a father's lineage within ancient Israel's social system of patrilineal descent. In addition, a son played a critical role in caring for his aging father and in performing proper death-cult rites for him.[120]

Given the importance of sons, it may not be a coincidence that amid the long string of Leah's and Rachel's naming speeches found in Gen 29:32–30:24, there is no naming speech for Jacob's one daughter, Dinah (Gen 30:21). Nor is there a naming speech for any girl child in the Bible.[121] This tells us again that the interests of the Bible's male authors and/or redactors may impose themselves in the recording of name-giving accounts and naming speeches by reflecting fathers' interest in the birth and subsequent naming of their *sons*. In Pardes's words, "the power of naming [ascribed to women] is limited by patriarchal exigencies."[122] The fact remains, however, that in the nineteen speeches by women name-givers that I have identified and also in the implied naming speeches of Sarah and Hagar, the voices of mothers and their surrogates are preserved, and in thirteen of these twenty-one cases, as noted above, the women evoke God. When mothers or their surrogates evoke God, moreover, they give voice to what the deity has done *for them*, not for their child's father or even for their family at large. While it may be "patriarchal exigencies," therefore, that led the biblical writers to preserve accounts of women's name-giving and the associated naming speeches, something more must have facilitated the ability of newly delivered women to speak so evocatively and powerfully about their religious experiences and their engagement with Yahweh during pregnancy and parturition.[123]

Once again, I suggest that the key is to recognize the elevated and enhanced status that accrues to women when they confer names on their newborn children and their ability to exercise the agency and authority created by this elevated and enhanced status. The result is an opportunity for women's religious self-expression that is virtually unparalleled in biblical tradition. Much as Rebekah can "speak her mind," we might say, regarding a domestic matter—her proposed marriage to Isaac—because of the enhanced status she assumes with the gifting of the marriage present (Gen 24:58), so too can newly delivered mothers "speak their minds" religiously at the moment of name-giving, when their status has been elevated in recognition of their reproductive capacities.

Overall, then: because the names that mothers or their female surrogates bestow on newborn infants are explained by speeches that evoke mothers' reproductive experiences or circumstances that otherwise pertain to the child's birth, the names and the naming speeches become an important means through which the events of childbirth are marked and remembered. Because, moreover, women's naming speeches somewhat more often than not evoke God, and indeed evoke God in almost every case when it is appropriate to do so (that is, when the intent is to offer praise or give thanks), Israelite mothers' and their surrogates' acts as name-givers, along with the speeches that explain a child's name, should be seen as an important instance of these women's religious self-expression. Naming and naming speeches thus conjoin with the important role name-giving mothers play as agents of community formation, as the mother's ability to inaugurate her newborn's social birth, together with her ability to speak powerfully as a religious agent during the naming process, attest to the enhanced and elevated status that accrues to a newly delivered mother when she confers a name on her infant. The conclusion that follows is that, for ancient Israelite women, the responsibility of name-giving that they somewhat more often than not assumed within their communities should be understood as an exceptionally meaningful and multidimensional ritual act.

7
Nursing and Weaning a Child

In the Introduction, I used the word "temporary" to describe the elevated or enhanced status that accrued to Guinea Fowl at the points during the *Nkang'a* ritual when she danced wielding a hunter's gun and the eland-tail switch of her village's headman and when she was subsequently able to pass judgment on the quality of her bridegroom's sexual performance. These status-enhanced junctures were "temporary," I argued, because by the end of *Nkang'a*, and even in the moments immediately following her status-elevating dances and during the subsequent intercourse with her husband, the *Nkang'a* initiate was returned to the submissive or liminal state that had otherwise characterized the three-plus months of the *Nkang'a* ritual and that Caroline Walker Bynum and Bruce Lincoln have identified as normative for women's lives in many preindustrial (and arguably many industrial) cultures.[1] Likewise in Chapter 3, I suggested that the elevated or enhanced status that an Israelite woman experienced when the marriage present was gifted during the course of her betrothal ritual was "temporary," given that the marriage present stays with the bride-to-be's father while she leaves her natal family and natal home in order to join her husband's household, where, at least to some degree, she lives out her married life as an "outsider" and "alien," who is "marginalized," "disenfranchised," and "othered."[2] During her marriage, that is, she lives in the liminal state that Bynum and Lincoln define as normative for women in many cultures.

As with *Nkang'a* and Israelite betrothal rites, our analysis of women's life-cycle rituals might lead us to suggest that the elevated or enhanced status that accrues to a newly delivered Israelite mother when naming her child should only be temporary. But if so, when does the mother's status enhancement cease? It is difficult, if not impossible, to say, given that we have virtually no evidence regarding Israelite mothers or their mothering activities that illuminates the long period between the days immediately postpartum and weaning, which as I have now indicated several times, did not take place until a child was about three years of age. Nevertheless, I will argue in what follows that it is with weaning that the extended ritual complex of motherhood that began with conception and pregnancy comes to an end, and so too ends any position of status enhancement that the mother attained when she bestowed a name on her infant.

Suckling and Weaning Children in the Ancient World

That children in the ancient world were typically not weaned until three years of age is well attested in both biblical and other ancient Near Eastern sources. For example, Mesopotamian legal texts from the Old Babylonian period (ca. 1894–1595 BCE) suggest that wetnurses in that era were employed for three years, presumably because children entrusted to their care were intended to suckle throughout that three-year timespan. These Old Babylonian texts include the Laws of Eshnunna, from ca. 1770 BCE, which specify that food, oil, and clothing rations were legally owed to a wetnurse for three years,[3] and several contracts between parents and wetnurses, which indicate that the nurse was hired for a three-year period.[4] Somewhat similarly, in "The Instruction of Ani," a text from Eighteenth Dynasty Egypt (ca. 1539–1292 BCE), the scribe Ani urges his son to take good care of the boy's (seemingly) aging mother, whose "breast [was] in your mouth for three years."[5] A papyrus from the Egyptian Late Period (ca. 715–332 BCE) likewise states, "Your mother carried you for ten months, she nourished you for three years."[6] Scientific studies from Roman-era Egypt corroborate these older textual accounts. Stable isotope analyses of infant skeletal remains and teeth from juvenile and adult bodies interred in the Kellis 2 cemetery in the Dakhleh Oasis, which dates from ca. 250 CE, suggest that "infants at Kellis were breastfed and weaned slowly until 3 years of age."[7]

From biblical tradition, we can cite first the Hellenistic-era book of 2 Maccabees, where the "mother of seven," speaking to her youngest son, recounts that she carried him in her womb for nine months and nursed him for three years (2 Macc 7:27).[8] The presumption that a child nursed for three years also seems to underlie earlier biblical texts. Some scholars have proposed, for example, that instead of the usual sacrificial animal that is a year in age, Hannah is atypically said to bring "a three-year old bull" to the sanctuary at Shiloh when she comes to dedicate her son Samuel to God's service in 1 Sam 1:24,[9] because this animal is the same age as the newly weaned boy.[10] Certainly, the newly weaned Samuel, who is represented in 1 Sam 2:11 as beginning to attend to Yahweh immediately after Hannah's dedicatory sacrifice, cannot be taken to be many months under the age of three, as a child any younger would have been unable to take on even the most rudimentary of cultic duties.[11]

Isaiah 28:9–10 is difficult to interpret, but many interpreters presume it likewise indicates that a child who has been "weaned from milk" and "removed from the breast" is of an age—once more, about age three—when he (or far less probably, she) can begin to learn religious teachings or, at least, begin to learn the letters of the alphabet (if it is to a mnemonic alphabetic chant that the enigmatic phrase in these verses, *ṣaw lāṣāw, ṣaw lāṣāw, qaw lāqāw, qaw lāqāw*, refers).[12] Also of significance is our modern cliché that speaks of wisdom coming from the "mouths of babes," whose roots are found in Ps 8:3 (8:2 in most English translations; see also Matt 21:16). This text actually reads "from the mouths of nurslings and sucklings [*ʿôlĕlîm wĕyônĕqîm*]." As in the other examples I have catalogued, it is implied here that ancient Israelite children continued to nurse well past their infancy and into their second and third years of life, at which point they had learned to speak and had even begun to make noteworthy remarks.[13]

As the Mesopotamian texts I cited above suggest, it was not uncommon during the Old Babylonian period for mothers to use wetnurses to suckle children during the three-year period before a child was weaned. Indeed, according to Marten Stol, in his extensive study of childbirth in Mesopotamia, "in the Old Babylonian period there is plenty of evidence that the nursing was done by professional 'wet nurses' (*mušēniqtu*)," who were paid with "'the suckling fee' (*tēnīqu*)" or "'the rearing' (*tarbītu*)," which consisted of "rations of barley, oil, and wool; sometimes silver." Stol also seems to suggest—citing a text dated to 551 BCE that contracts a wetnurse's services—that professional wetnurses were frequently used in Mesopotamia in the Neo-Babylonian period (ca. 626–539 BCE).[14] Mesopotamian customs regarding the use of wetnurses may also be reflected in texts such as Gen 24:59 and 35:8, where Rebekah, Isaac's wife, who, according to biblical tradition hails from northwestern Mesopotamia, is described as having a wetnurse, Deborah, whom she brings with her when she moves to the southern Levant to marry Isaac.

In Egypt, engaging a wetnurse was less typical, as "normally ... the baby was nursed by its mother,"[15] as, for example, in both the Eighteenth Dynasty and Late Period Egyptian texts that I cited above. Note also that Egyptian "birth arbor" images from the thirteenth-/twelfth-century BCE workman's village of Deir el-Medina depict the newly delivered mother nursing her child (see Fig. 5.4).[16] Nevertheless, the use of wetnurses is attested in records from Deir el-Medina.[17] In addition, wetnurses were often employed by elite Egyptian families.[18] "Royal children," for example, "had many nurses ... who were highly esteemed."[19] Indeed, even in the modest Egyptological collection of my own university's museum, there is an impressively decorated and inscribed fragment from a linen shroud from ca. 1430 BCE that was used in the funerary rites of the "chief nurse Mahu," who was clearly appreciated enough for her work by her patrons (sucklings?) that she was accorded a highly formal and elaborate burial.[20]

In Israel, the use of a wetnurse was possible, especially in elite families (2 Sam 4:4; 2 Kgs 11:2 [// 2 Chr 22:11]).[21] A wetnurse would also have been required in cases where an infant's mother, like Rachel, died in childbirth. But ancient Israelite mothers generally assumed the responsibility for suckling their children.[22] Yet to nurse a child for three years is a demanding obligation for a mother, especially given that she continued to undertake the obligations routinely demanded of women in ancient Israelite households: preeminently food preparation, textile production, and possibly the manufacture of other small-scale handicrafts (for example, pottery).[23] A recently delivered mother must take on some new responsibilities as well: during the first months of life, for example, she must assume the tasks of carrying her newborn around with her as she moves from place to place and of accommodating the onerous schedule of nighttime feedings that a neonate requires.

A nursing mother must also assume, at least to some degree, the obligation of producing increased foodstuffs for her family during the course of the day. Nutritional data strongly suggest, for instance, that by the time an infant is six months of age, breastfeeding needs to be supplemented with other foods,[24] which the child's mother, along with other women in the typical Israelite household, would have needed to prepare. More important, the mother, even before giving birth and then continuing after her delivery, would have needed to prepare additional food for herself, as pregnant and nursing women should consume, at a minimum, an extra five hundred calories daily to sustain their nutritional status through gestation and lactation, and this is if a woman's physical exertion is minimal.[25] In the labor-intensive agrarian economy of the ancient Israelite countryside, where it is estimated 80 to 90 percent of the Israelite population lived,[26] a woman might require—and thus might be required to prepare for herself—a thousand additional calories a day.[27] In this regard, we might note an Egyptian painting from the Eighteenth Dynasty tomb of Menna (TT 69; ca. 1400–1352 BCE), where "a woman is shown in an agricultural setting cradling a young child," a scene that "is reiterated in a relief fragment from the Twenty-Sixth Dynasty tomb [ca. 670–650 BCE] of Mentuemhat" (Fig. 7.1). "One assumes," writes Catherine H. Roehrig of these images, "that at the height of the harvest, when every able-bodied person was needed, even nursing mothers probably participated"—and so they had to keep both themselves and their sucklings fed while in the fields.[28]

Fortunately for us *homo sapiens* and for our survival as a species (although not necessarily so fortunate for a nursing mother), a lactating woman's milk production is not significantly compromised if her increased caloric needs are not met.[29] A study of marginally nourished mothers in Gambia has shown, for example, that the quantity of milk produced among these Islamic women was largely unaffected by their fasting during the month of Ramadan, even as the women lost an average of 7 percent of their body weight. More strikingly, the data concerning these Gambian mothers indicate that "in the

Fig. 7.1 Egyptian tomb relief depicting an agricultural scene, including a woman with a baby stacking fruit, ca. 670–650 BCE. Limestone, 9 7/16 x 11 5/16 in. (23.9 x 28.7 cm). Brooklyn Museum, Charles Edwin Wilbour Fund, 48.74. Creative Commons-BY. Photo: Brooklyn Museum, 48.74_SL1.jpg.

annual hungry season, during which the mothers are working extremely hard in the fields [and] are in negative energy balance," "milk output declines by only 10%."[30] Moreover, not only the *quantity*, but also the nutritional *quality* of breast milk "appears to be surprisingly insensitive to differences in maternal nutrition,"[31] so much so that it is only at "quite an extreme level of malnutrition" that "the maternal system can no longer sustain lactation and its own survival."[32] Biblically, such a situation might be intimated in Lam 4:4, which describes the futile attempts of the *yōnēq*, or suckling, to nurse during the horrific famine caused by the Babylonians' siege and then destruction of Jerusalem in 586 BCE. Overall, though, even when their mothers are severely undernourished, breastfed babies remain well fed, at least for the six months before supplemental foodstuffs are required.

Nevertheless, even for an adequately nourished mother, "the total cost" of lactation, "at least in terms of energy, is high."[33] As Susan Scott and Christopher J. Duncan write in their book *Demography and Nutrition: Evidence from Historical and Contemporary Populations*, "the mother has to supply the maintenance needs, in addition to the growth needs, of the infant over a long period," and this after "the mother has already invested heavily [in terms of her increased caloric needs] through gestation."[34] Even more important for our consideration, though, are the enormously high stakes associated with the mother's lactation success in a culture like ancient Israel's, for (to quote again Scott and Duncan) "up to the early part of the twentieth century, the infants of mothers who were unable to provide adequate supplies of breast milk had a high probability of dying."[35] By way of example, they cite "a study of infant mortality in Derby, England, shortly after 1900," which shows that "breast-fed infants were *three times* as likely to survive as 'hand-fed' infants" (emphasis mine).[36] The cause of death for the "hand-fed" according to this and related studies is most typically diarrheal infection resulting from the consumption of "foods other than breast milk," especially milk that "originated from animals and was nutritionally inappropriate for human neonates."[37] A 1989 study of nine hundred and ten Pakistani infants, for example, "revealed that although all mothers started breast-feeding, 50% of mothers introduced a breast-milk substitute [typically, buffalo milk] from one month of age." The result was that "75% of children had at least one episode of diarrhea and 60% had at least two."[38] A 2003 Brazilian study likewise revealed "non-breastfed infants were 82 percent more likely to experience diarrhea than infants who were exclusively breastfed for the first 6 months of life."[39]

Equally a problem, historically, that neonates and young infants faced if they were forced to consume "foods other than breast milk" is that these children were typically weaned onto a diet that caused them to "become deficient in a variety of nutrients."[40] This is because certain nutritional deficiencies to which infants are particularly susceptible are characteristic of the "largely vegetarian diet based on grains" on which "the bulk of pre-industrial communities" survived.[41] Certainly, such a "vegetarian diet based on grains" seems to have been the norm in ancient Israel. Indeed, in his paired monographs, *What Did the Ancient Israelites Eat?* and *Not Bread Alone*, both published in 2008, Nathan MacDonald reports that "for the typical Israelite, bread or other grain-based foods such as porridge probably provided over half their caloric intake, with estimates varying between 53 and 75 percent."[42] Biblical texts such as Josh 5:11 and Ruth 2:14 support this claim: Josh 5:11 describes the Israelites as eating unleavened cakes (*maṣṣôt*) and parched grain on the day after their celebration of Passover at Gilgal, and in Ruth 2:14, Ruth's meal in the fields with Boaz during the barley harvest is said to consist only of bread dipped in vinegar and parched grain.

To be sure, Oded Borowski, in his book *Daily Life in Biblical Times,* suggests that the evening meals of the ancient Israelites were perhaps more substantial than those that, like the daytime meal of Ruth 2:14, were eaten during a break while working or otherwise "on the run." These evening repasts, Borowski proposes, consisted of soup, gruel, or a stew of lentils or the like.[43] MacDonald also indicates that lentils and other pulses (broad beans, field peas, chickpeas, etc.) were an important component of the Israelite diet, perhaps comprising—if data from the Mishnaic era are any indication—15 to 20 percent of an ancient Israelite's daily caloric intake. "For the majority of Israelites," MacDonald adds, these "pulses would have been the principal source of protein."[44] Still, the ancient Israelite diet lacked the more substantial access to protein that comes from eating meat, assuming that outside of elite contexts, most Israelites ate meat primarily (or perhaps only) on sacrificial and similarly festive occasions. (I estimate that feasts of this sort occurred maybe fifteen to eighteen times per year: at the monthly celebration of the new moon; at a clan's annual sacrifice; during the three annual pilgrimage festivals of Maṣṣôt, Shavuot, and Ingathering/Sukkot; and on a few other festive occasions, such as a wedding.)[45] Breast milk, conversely, is a significant source of the proteins that growing infants need and also of the "fat and essential fatty acids" for which "infants have a specific requirement," "to provide energy" and "to facilitate the absorption of fat-soluble vitamins

A, E, and D." These would have otherwise been found in only "low amounts" in the Israelite diet.[46]

To sum up, we can again quote Scott and Duncan: "in pre-industrial populations" that, like ancient Israel's, "did not enjoy . . . a varied diet," and in which food, moreover, may have been "in short supply at times," "weaning nutrition was often suboptimal."[47] Indeed, weaning nutrition was so suboptimal in these preindustrial populations that even for infants who only started consuming foodstuffs supplemental to breast milk at the appropriate age of six months, "the continuation of breast-feeding for 1–2 years after the introduction of other foods appears to have several major benefits. These include the supply of nutrients, the delivery of protective, digestive and trophic agents . . . [and] a reduced severity of infectious diseases."[48] Thus, as already noted, Scott and Duncan conclude that "infants who are not breast-fed, or who are weaned early, generally have higher mortality."[49] Katherine A. Dettwyler and Claudia Fishman in a study of infant feeding practices state even more forcefully that the "evidence overwhelmingly indicates that . . . breastfeeding is positively correlated with lower morbidity and mortality rates . . . breastfed infants have fewer and less serious infections and lower morality [sic] rates."[50]

To be sure, the ancient Israelites could not have known as much as we do about the benefits of prolonged breastfeeding and, especially, about the reasons that underlie these benefits (breast milk's capacity for delivering essential fatty acids, for example). Still, they must have perceived through observation and based on anecdotal evidence that prolonged breastfeeding conferred significant and, for them, highly desirable advantages in terms of a child's survival and well-being.[51] Certainly, elsewhere in the ancient Near East, there was an awareness that successful lactation was required in order to stave off infant mortality. This can be seen in one of the threats put in the mouth of the god Erra in the Mesopotamian myth of "Erra and Ishum," where Erra is imagined to say, "I shall dry out the breast so that the baby cannot live."[52] Moreover, as Arthur Niehoff and Natalie Meister report in a broadly cross-cultural study of breastfeeding,[53] "the importance of nourishment from human milk . . . appears to have been common knowledge around the world . . . the importance of breastfeeding seems to have been universally recognized."[54]

Yet even as Israelite women responded to the imperative to breastfeed by suckling children for up to three years, mothers could suffer, as can women today, from various forms of lactation failure, which Hos 9:14 describes as "dry breasts" (šādayim ṣōmĕqîm).[55] Indeed, ancient Israelite mothers may have been more susceptible to various lactation failures than are contemporary women. For example, while breastfeeding problems that stem from inverted or nonprotractile nipples (reported to occur in 7 to 10 percent of pregnant women)[56] are addressed today by using various suction devices that work to draw out the nipple,[57] these technologies would not have been available to Israelite women. Mastitis as a cause of lactation failure may have also affected ancient women more than their contemporary peers.[58] This is in part because today's standard treatment for acute mastitis, which is experienced by perhaps 10–20 percent of lactating women (or, according to some data, up to 33 percent),[59] is a course of antibiotics, to which, obviously, Israelite women had no access. Chronic mastitis, moreover, is usually "a secondary effect of systemic diseases such as tuberculosis, fungal infections, yeast infections,"[60] by which ancient Israelite women—again without our modern recourse to antibiotics—may have been significantly affected.

Rituals to Promote Lactation

Given the risks of lactation failure, yet the pressing need to ensure successful lactation in order to avoid a significantly increased risk of infant disease and death, and given also the generally high rate of infant mortality in the ancient world,[61] we might ask whether the ancient Israelites deployed ritual strategies to ensure that nursing women produced an adequate supply of breast milk, much as rituals to safeguard a mother's breast milk were enacted by their Near Eastern neighbors. A Mesopotamian incantation from the Old Babylonian period (ca. 1894–1595 BCE), for example, describes the measures to be undertaken to drive away the baby-snatching demon Lamaštu, because otherwise, among Lamaštu's manifold evils, she "slew the fat" and "slew the milk" of lactating mothers and thereby endangered the lives of these mothers' sucklings.[62] A first-millennium BCE Mesopotamian incantation similarly seeks magical recourse if a wetnurse's breast is "too sweet," "too bitter," or has become infected.[63] An Eighteenth Dynasty papyrus from New Kingdom Egypt (Papyrus Berlin 3027; ca. 1500 BCE), which scholars have named the "Book for Mother and Child" or "Magical Spells for Mother and Child," also contains an incantation for safeguarding a lactating mother. It mandates, among other things, the use of "magical knots . . . to protect the mother's breasts from any being who would make them sore or halt the flow of milk."[64]

The so-called Ebers Papyrus, an ancient Egyptian medical text from c. 1500 BCE, documents how Egyptians determined good breast milk (it smelled like "pounded *w'ḥ*-legume" or "crushed earth almonds") as opposed to bad (it smelled like fish).[65] This papyrus in addition describes how Egyptian mothers used special ointments and potions to ensure adequate lactation: a concoction of fishbones and oil could be spread on a nursing woman's backbone, for example, or a lactating woman could eat a specially prepared bread while sitting in the *njnj* position.[66] Breastfeeding women who suffered from the opposite problem—breasts overflowing because of excessive milk production—were also advised in the Ebers Papyrus to have various body parts (their breasts, bellies, thighs, and all of the limbs) rubbed with special substances: the "blood of one whose menstruation has come for the first time" or a decoction of "dried swallow liver and fermented herbs."[67] The Ebers Papyrus furthermore describes a specially prepared ointment of bull bile, fly droppings, ochre, and a mineral called *hetem* that could be spread on an Egyptian woman's breasts for four days to address "a breast that aches," meaning, perhaps, breast pain that a woman experienced due to nursing.[68] Some Egyptian mothers, however, might prefer the ointment for breast pain prescribed in the Papyrus Berlin 3038 (Nineteenth Dynasty; thirteenth century BCE), whose somewhat more appealing ingredients (at least according to today's sensibilities) include honey and thyme.[69]

The mid-eighth-century BCE Aramaic treaty text between Bir Ga'yah and Mati'ilu from the Syrian site of Sefire may suggest that special ointments were also used in first-millennium BCE Aram to address problems associated with lactation. There, in the list of curses to be inflicted upon Mati'ilu and his people if he violated the treaty, we read that "should seven nurses anoint [their breasts and] nurse a young boy, may he not have his fill."[70] This "anointing" (*mšḥ*), André Dupont-Sommer theorizes, was "without doubt" ("sans doute") thought by the nurses to facilitate the production of richly abundant breast milk.[71]

No record exists showing that similar strategies were deployed in ancient Israel. However, because the comparative evidence from Mesopotamia, Egypt, and (possibly) Aram suggests that rituals to facilitate lactation were a common enough aspect of the Near Eastern medico-magical repertoire, it seems reasonable to propose that some sorts of lactation-enhancing rituals would have been known and used in Israelite tradition. Such rituals might have been as straightforward as asking God for "blessings of the breasts," as in Gen 49:25, but perhaps Israelite ritual practices could, as in Mesopotamia and Egypt, have made use of incantations, or, as in Egypt and at Sefire, could have involved using special ointments or eating special foods. And might Israelites hoping to promote successful lactation have made use of ritual objects? Perhaps the seventh-century BCE representations of the ferocious yet benevolent Assyro-Babylonian demon Pazazu from Beth-Shean and Megiddo (discussed in Chapter 5) served Israelite women in this way. According to Mesopotamian tradition, Pazazu was able to ward off Lamaštu and thereby protect childbearing and newly delivered mothers from the various threats (such as the threats to a mother's breast milk) that Lamaštu posed.[72] Remember, in fact, that the Beth-Shean Pazazu image was designed to be worn as an amulet[73]—perhaps by a nursing mother who used this talisman to ensure successful lactation. In my opinion, moreover, there is much to be said in favor of the oft-voiced proposal that the Judean pillar figurines (JPFs) may have been used ritually to promote milk production, at least in the period and place where they are abundantly represented: eighth- and seventh-century BCE Judah, from which about 1000 exemplars are known (see Fig. 7.2).[74]

To be sure, one raises the topic of the extensively debated JPFs at one's own (great) peril; still, as I have just intimated, I am hardly alone in suggesting that the JPFs could be associated with matters of lactation. Already in 1912, R. A. S. Macalister, in reports from his excavations at Gezer, characterized various head and body terracotta fragments that he found there, along with a kindred and complete figurine—which had a "body of a pillar shape, with a slight expansion like the bell of a trumpet at the lower end, and with breasts, generally very prominent, at the top"—as a "form of the *dea nutrix*."[75] This same terminology ("the figurine ... as the *dea nutrix*, the protector of nursing mothers") was employed by William F. Albright in his 1932 monograph *The Archaeology of Palestine and the Bible*, as well as in a brief note on the pillar figurines that appeared in his 1939 article "Astarte Plaques and Figurines from Tell Beit Mirsim."[76] Also, as pointed out by both Judith Hadley, in her 2000 monograph *The Cult of Asherah in Ancient Israel and Judah*, and Elizabeth Bloch-Smith, in a 2014 article that discusses (among other topics) the JPFs, Adolphe Lods makes a similar proposition in his 1932 book *Israel: From Its Beginnings to the Middle of the Eighth Century*. (Lods describes the figurines as representing a goddess who "presses her breasts to make the milk start from them.")[77]

Fig. 7.2 Terracotta Judean Pillar Figurine, from Lachish, ca. eighth-seventh century BCE. 18.4 cm high. From the collection of the Metropolitan Museum of Art, New York, gift of Harris D. and H. Dunscombe Colt, 1934. Accession no. 34.126.53.

More recent proponents of this view include Bloch-Smith herself, who, drawing attention to the way the JPFs' encircling arms "accentuate visually the breasts,"[78] has written (less definitively) that the JPFs represent a "concern for adequate lactation to nourish newborns and infants"[79] and (more emphatically) that the JPFs' "symbolic function was to beseech adequate lactation to sustain newborns and infants" and that they "served to promote lactation."[80] Somewhat similarly, in a 2007 study of the JPFs, Carol Meyers suggested that "perhaps the cupped breasts so prominent in the JPFs represent lactation and thus the survival of newborns," although Meyers went on to propose that the "images of women holding their breasts" represent only "the final stage in the conception-birth-lactation sequence" (or what I have called here the extended ritual complex of motherhood). Thereby, Meyers argued, the pillar figurines represent the entire reproductive sequence "in *pars pro toto* fashion."[81] Elsewhere, in her 2005 book *Households and Holiness: The Religious Culture of Israelite Women*, Meyers advances the same position: "It is likely," she writes, "that they [the pillar figurines] have some relation to female nurturance of infants" (which I take to be a reference to lactation), yet a few pages later, she remarks that "they [the pillar figurines] were meant to secure fertility, safe childbirth, and/or adequate lactation."[82]

Othmar Keel and Christoph Uehlinger, too, have offered this sort of "both lactation and more" interpretation of the JPFs,[83] as have William G. Dever and Ziony Zevit. In his 2005 book *Did God Have a Wife?*, Dever writes, for example, that while "the female function of lactation is somehow part of the 'psychology' of these figurines . . . the figure of a woman with full breasts would have suggested the overall notion of 'plenty,' the gods' ability to nourish the human family." Zevit similarly states: "[JPFs] may have been used in rituals addressing goddesses or aspects of a goddess concerned with promoting pregnancy, lactation, and the general health of a woman's body."[84]

That said, in her 2013 book *Rediscovering Eve: Ancient Israelite Women in Context*, Meyers repudiates her earlier "lactation and more" interpretation, writing that "it now seems unlikely that they [the JPFs] were used for pregnancy or lactation problems." Rather, an "exhaustive archaeological and phenomenological study suggests they had general apotropaic or healing purposes."[85] The "exhaustive" study (773 pages!) is the 2011 PhD thesis of Meyers's student Erin Darby, subsequently published in a revised (though not significantly shorter) form in 2014 under the title *Interpreting Judean Pillar Figurines: Gender and Empire in Judean Apotropaic Ritual*.[86] Darby has also discussed her findings in several articles.[87]

In her book and articles, Darby advances several arguments in support of her thesis. She notes, for example, that in accounts of figurine rituals found in Neo-Assyrian texts that are roughly contemporaneous with the JPFs, "clay figurines are . . . mentioned in connection with . . . with sympathetic, exorcistic, and protective rituals."[88] Also, Darby compares the JPFs to other representations of women holding their breasts that appear in Iron Age Levantine tradition.[89] These images appear, for example, (1) on ninth-, eighth-, or seventh-century BCE metal horse frontlets from northern Syria; (2) on two Ammonite seals; and (3) on the façades of cult stands from the late ninth-/early eighth-century BCE Philistine site of Yavneh and a reconstructed model shrine from the late seventh-/early sixth-century BCE site of Ḥorvat Qitmit, in ancient Edom (Fig. 7.3).[90] In her discussion, Darby embraces the common and eminently plausible interpretation that these breast-holding female figures perform an apotropaic role.[91] The horse-frontlets' breast-holding females, for example, should be understood as going protectively before war horses and their associated personnel to keep them safe as they go into battle.[92] Likewise, Pirhiya Beck, who reconstructed the Qitmit model shrine, specifically identifies the breast-holding females who flank its entryway as offering protection to the deity who is to be imagined as resident within.[93] So too, Darby urges, should the breast-holding JPFs be understood as apotropaic.[94]

Darby in addition notes Egyptian magical spells that indicate breasts and breast milk could be associated with healing in the ancient world, suggesting that the apotropaic function that the breast-holding JPFs perform could be medicinal.[95] According to spells in the Ebers Papyrus, for example, assorted eye ailments could be treated by applying concoctions containing ingredients such as various eye paints and the milk of a woman who has borne a male child.[96] The Ebers Papyrus also contains a spell for healing burns using the milk of a boy baby's mother.[97] Further in relation to healing, Darby draws attention to the healing role of clay in Mesopotamian ritual texts.[98] More notably, she cites, from the Levantine realm, an episode from the Kirta Epic, part of a fourteenth-/thirteenth-century BCE textual archive from the city-state of Ugarit. In this text, the god El forms a female healer called Shaʻtiqatu from clay in order to cure King Kirta of the mortal illness that afflicts him (*KTU* 1.16.5.23–1.16.6.2).[99] This could suggest that the terracotta JPFs represent a similar entity who could be called upon during eighth- and seventh-century BCE Judean healing rituals, especially if one were to follow the suggestion floated (though not necessarily embraced) by

Fig. 7.3 Late seventh-/early sixth-century BCE model shrine from the Edomite site of Ḥorvat Qitmit, as reconstructed by Pirhiya Beck. From Beck, "Catalogue of Cult Objects," 103. Drawing by Yoseph Kapelyan. Courtesy of the Institute of Archaeology of Tel Aviv University.

Theodore J. Lewis that Shaʿtiqatu should be understood as an apotropaic figurine that El creates out of clay and then magically animates.[100]

It must be noted, however, that the breast-holding female figures who appear on horse frontlets, many of the Yavneh cult stands, and the Qitmit model shrine have some significant differences from the JPFs: most notably, these breast-holding female figures are depicted as full-bodied, with legs and often with their pudenda prominently featured.[101] The JPFs, however, have no features delineated below their breasts: there is only the eponymous pillar. P. R. S. Moorey, in his 2003 collection *Idols of the People*, has thus suggested that the better Levantine parallel to the JPFs are the "free-standing, handmodelled, solid pillar-shaped figurines" that come from Syria: for example (among those that can be securely dated), "those found at Tell Rifaʿat ... in the seventh century BC."[102] To be sure, as Darby notes, the parallel is not perfect, for most of these Syrian figurines "have hands covering where breasts should be, though the breasts are not depicted."[103] Nevertheless, Moorey uses the epithet "nurturing" to describe these Syrian figurines, noting in particular that some of them show a child pressed against one side of the female figure's chest.[104]

A small number of the JPFs also show the female holding a child.[105] For example, a JPF that comes from Albright's excavations at Tell Beit Mirsim has a small handmade figure of a child applied to its body, although this child figure is applied to the figurine's back rather than the chest (Fig 7.4).[106] Other JPF fragments that might depict the female figure holding a child come from Jerusalem: for example, five pillar figurine fragments from Yigal Shiloh's City of David excavations. More specifically, in her catalog of the ceramic figurines found during Shiloh's excavations, Diana Gilbert-Peretz identifies two pillar figurine fragments that depict a "female torso with baby in arms" (E1/15547 and E3/15634); a third fragment of a "female torso holding baby horizontally in arms, close to body" (G 11152); a fourth of a "female torso" with "one hand supporting baby (?)" (E1/9284); and a fifth pillar figurine fragment of a "human body holding baby vertically in arms, close to body" (G 11059).[107] Thomas A. Holland's 1975 catalog of Iron Age Israelite clay figurines somewhat similarly includes a pillar-figurine bust "with shoulder and arm, holding unidentified object" from Jerusalem Cave 1,[108] and, also from Jerusalem, a pillar figurine with a "hand-made head" and "a small part of the chest preserved," holding an object (identified by Holland as a sack) "that is placed on the figure's back."[109] In addition, Yohanan Aharoni identified two pillar figurine fragments that hold objects in his excavations at nearby Ramat Raḥel.[110]

In considering these object-bearing—and seemingly child-bearing—pillar figurines, I take seriously one of Darby's key arguments about the JPFs: that form need not follow function.[111] Yet this does not mean that form *cannot* follow function, and the presence of child figures on some JPFs seems to me most obviously to evoke the enterprise of motherhood. While

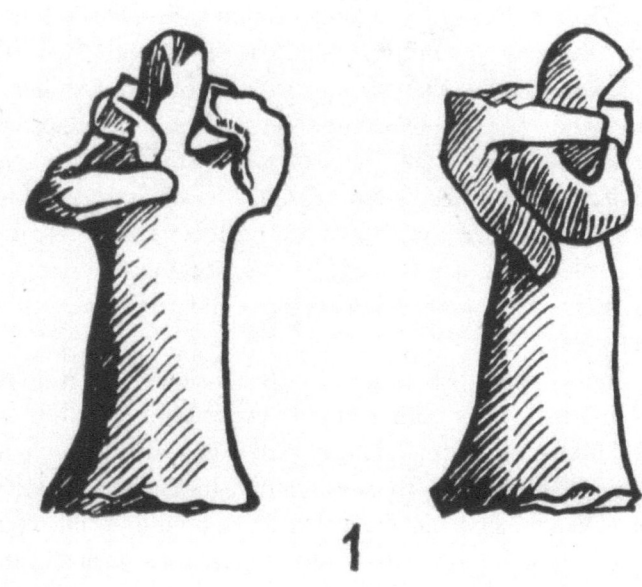

Fig 7.4 Judean Pillar Figurine, with a figure of a child applied to the figurine's back, from Tell Beit Mirsim, Iron Age II. From Albright, *Excavation of Tell Beit Mirsim III*, Pl. 32:1. Courtesy of the American Society of Overseas Research.

it is possible, moreover, to imagine that the child figures—as per Meyers's 2007 suggestion—are supposed to evoke the entire mothering sequence of conception-birth-lactation "in *pars pro toto*,"[112] I think it more likely that we are to take the child figure that can appear on pillar figurines as recently or relatively recently born and that the figurines' referent is thus a stage postpartum in that child's life. When coupled with the emphasis on the breasts found on other pillar figurines, and breasts that are often depicted as exceedingly full, it further seems to me that these child-bearing pillar figurines most obviously evoke the postpartum enterprise of nursing. By extension, I deem it most reasonable to argue that pillar figurines generally are related to lactation. More maximally, based on the materials that I previously surveyed regarding, first, the pressing need in preindustrial societies to ensure successful lactation in order to avoid an increased risk of infant illness and mortality and, second, the ritual responses to this need that are found in Mesopotamian, Egyptian, and (possibly) Aramaean tradition, I suggest, to quote again Bloch-Smith, that the JPFs "served to promote lactation."[113]

To this extent, I agree with Darby that the JPFs perform a medico-magical function. But I propose that we can specify the health care need that the JPFs address: the well-being of sucklings, for which a mother's successful lactation is essential.

Rituals at the End of the Breastfeeding Period

At the beginning of this chapter, I listed several verses in the Bible that suggest that a child nursed for at least three years, and two other biblical texts likewise intimate that the Israelites formally marked the end of this suckling period, at least for a boy child. The first, 2 Chr 31:16, implies that priests' sons became enrolled in their families' genealogy at age three, which is perhaps to be understood as a moment that ritually demarcated the end of the nursing period, at least for these sons of priestly fathers and at least during the postexilic era from which 2 Chronicles dates.[114] A second biblical text suggests that the end of the nursing period could be formally and even ritually demarcated during the preexilic period, and within nonpriestly families: this is Gen 21:8, which indicates that a feast was held to mark Isaac's weaning.[115]

For the weaned child, these formal demarcations of weaning must denote some sort of transition from one stage of life to another: at a minimum, the transition from "nutritional biological dependency on another human being . . . to a stage of nutritional autonomy that results in a stage of semi-independence."[116] Indeed, according to Kristine Henriksen Garroway, in her book *Children in the Ancient Near Eastern Household,* Babylonian and Assyrian census lists explicitly distinguish between the life stages of "child at the breast, weaned child, and then child."[117] Several scholars have made equivalent claims regarding ancient Israel. Joseph Blenkinsopp, for example, writes: "For the period from birth to weaning, generally about three years, there are three terms (*ʿōlēl, ʿōlāl, yônēq*), all derived from two verbal stems with the meaning 'suck' or 'suckle.' Once past this stage . . . the child is a *gāmûl* (fem. *gĕmûlâ*), 'a weaned child' (Isa 11:8) or simply a *yeled* or *naʿar.*"[118] Milton Eng similarly defines the stages of a child's life as "infancy" (ending with weaning), "childhood" (lasting until puberty), and then "young adulthood" (culminating in marriage), and in his study of the life cycles of ancient Babylonian and Israelite women, Karel van der Toorn likewise identifies three stages of a girl child's life: "the nursing period," "youth," and "puberty."[119]

In ritual terms, or at least in the terms describing life-cycle rituals that were originally proposed by Arnold van Gennep and then refined by Victor Turner, weaning, as the occasion that moved children from the stage of "the nursing period" to the position of "weaned child," can be understood as the point in a rite of passage at which the child was "separated" from a previous identity as a suckling, and then, after a ceremonial observance such as, say, a feast or being enrolled in a family's genealogy, "reintegrated" or "reaggregated" into its community with a new identity. Garroway writes regarding Mesopotamia, for example, that once children were weaned, "they were considered members of society who, with age, became increasingly more contributing members."[120] Somewhat similarly in Egypt, the autobiography of an early thirteenth-century BCE official named Bakenkhonsu describes how, after "four years as an excellent youngster" (meaning, presumably, after a four-year period during which Bakenkhonsu was breastfed and that culminated with his being weaned), he "spent eleven years as a youth, as a trainee stable-master, for King Men[maat]re (Sety I)."[121] Biblical scholars will readily think of the similar story of Samuel that I have already mentioned, who was left at the temple in Shiloh to render cultic service shortly after he had been weaned (1 Sam 1:28). We should also consider Exod 2:10, which suggests that it is only after he is weaned that Moses is integrated into the Egyptian identity that defines his youth. It is only at this point, after all, that he is brought to the house of Pharaoh's daughter, where she gives him his name and he becomes "her son."

Yet this "reintegration" of a weaned child—and especially, one presumes, a male child—into the community with a new identity necessarily means at least some degree of "disintegration," so to speak, of the bond that breastfeeding had formed between the child and the mother. The just-mentioned stories of Moses and Samuel provide particularly dramatic examples. In the latter story, Hannah—although she had insisted on keeping her son with her during the time (presumably three years) that he suckled (1 Sam 1:22–24)—gives him over completely to the temple at Shiloh once he is weaned, and she is thereafter described as seeing him only once a year during her family's annual pilgrimages to the Shiloh sanctuary (1 Sam 2:19). And Moses's mother, of course, surrenders her newly weaned son to the pharaoh's daughter for good. But even in less sensational contexts, disintegration of the bond between mother and her theretofore nursing child can be marked: Garroway notes, for example, that in Mesopotamian legal texts, at least in the case of enslaved children, "once the child has been weaned, it is no longer listed in conjunction with its mother, as if the break in the physical bond between the two is symbolized by a separation in their names."[122] Somewhat similarly in biblical tradition, to be enrolled in a genealogy, as are the presumably just-weaned sons in 2 Chr 31:16, is to be enrolled in a *patri*line, and while women are not wholly absent in the texts that record these lineages, they are also not standardly present. Or, if they are present, they are not independently presented. For example, although women are said to be part of the enrolled list of priestly families mentioned in 2 Chr 31:16, they—"wives," "daughters," and the girl toddlers I take to be among the "little children," or *ṭap*—are subsumed in their families' genealogies, according to 2 Chr 31:18, under the priestly male who is their head of household.

How subsumed? Did the mothers of the priestly children mentioned in 2 Chronicles participate in any formal ceremony that might be associated with their sons' enrollment in the genealogical record? Was Sarah anything more than a bystander at Isaac's weaning feast? To be sure, Sarah is witness to the festivities: according to Gen 21:9, she sees Ishmael there (suggesting, incidentally, that like his father Abraham and his half-brother Isaac, Ishmael is a full-fledged participant at the feast). But does Sarah engage in any more substantial way? Note that she is said only to watch from the sidelines at the other festive meal that Genesis describes Abraham as hosting, in Gen 18:1–15. In that text, she stands or sits in the entryway of the family tent while Abraham's guests—Yahweh and the deity's two divine attendants—eat outside under the oak at Mamre. From our discussion in Chapter 4, we might also recall that although ancient Israelite weddings seem clearly to have involved feasting (Gen 29:22; Judg 14:10; see also Esth 2:18), it is not at all clear that the bride (or any women) attended these nuptial banquets.[123]

Overall, then, our data might lead us to suggest that the mothers of the priestly children mentioned in 2 Chronicles did not participate in their sons' genealogical recording; that Sarah was only an onlooker at Isaac's weaning feast; and that all mothers analogously might have been disassociated from their children's weaning celebrations. Speaking in ritual terms, we might thus say that at weaning, as the mother's bond with her suckling child disintegrates, she, like the child, is reintegrated or reaggregated into her community with a new identity. Yet as we have seen, the child—and especially, one again presumes, a male child—is reintegrated into the community with a new identity that reflects a newly elevated status: at a minimum, a status of "nutritional autonomy that results in a stage of semi-independence."[124] More important, the newly weaned child can assume an elevated status in terms of social role: a newly established role as his father's sole heir, as in the linked stories of Isaac's weaning and Ishmael's expulsion in Gen 21:8–21;[125] or a new position as a temple apprentice, as in 1 Sam 1:28; or newly designated membership in a priestly lineage, as in 2 Chr 31:16. Conversely, the new identity of the weaned child's mother is one of "not." She is no longer the agent on which the child is, to at least some degree, biologically dependent, nor is she the agent who might enact rituals to stimulate and sustain successful lactation and so facilitate the child's well-being.[126]

Or, we might say: during the three or so years during which her child has been breastfed, the mother—as a source of nutrition and as a ritual agent—may well have been able to claim, to at least some degree, the same sort of elevated status position that I argued in Chapter 6 could be claimed by mothers who served as their children's name-givers. This nursing mother may thus have been recognized as an important and even powerful actor within her family, her household, and her larger community. But this sort of powerful and important status position, I have also repeatedly argued (following upon the work of Caroline Walker Bynum and Bruce Lincoln), was the inverse of an ancient Israelite woman's normal experience and something women, if they experienced it at all, experienced only temporarily. This means that at weaning, as the mother's role as her child's nurse comes to an end, she returns to the marginal and disenfranchised state typical for women in ancient Israel. Indeed, in Sarah's case, she is so disenfranchised and marginalized that, after Isaac's weaning and the related events concerning Hagar's and Ishmael's expulsion, she appears in the Genesis narrative only once more, to die (Gen 23:1–2). Abraham instead, at least in the Genesis narrative as it has come down to us, takes over all the "parenting" decisions having to do with his son, including the rather momentous decision to offer Isaac as a sacrifice in obedience to God's command (Gen 22:1–19).

Overall, a new mother can be seen as a powerful figure. Yet once her child is weaned, she is equally the object of acts of disempowerment that relegate her to a peripheral and diminished position.

INTERLUDE

8
Menopause

The information available to us suggests that menopause was not a life-cycle event for ancient Israelite women that was ritually marked (in contrast, say, to a young woman's coming of age, betrothal, and subsequent wedding, or a mother's giving birth and then naming her child). Nor, for many Israelite women, would menopause have been a life phase they could expect to experience, given that menopause in the ancient world probably occurred at about age forty, whereas ancient women's life expectancy, as we saw in Chapter 5, was about thirty-five years of age.[1] Nevertheless, for some women, menopause or its equivalent (what I will define in this chapter as social menopause) seems to have been an important life stage. This is the case, for example, for the nineteen women identified in the Bible as queen mothers: that is, the mother (or, in one case, the grandmother) of the reigning king.

Ancient Israelite Queen Mothers

At the end of the last chapter, I noted the way in which Sarah virtually disappears from the biblical narrative immediately after her son Isaac is weaned. Many other biblical mothers do not fare much better. While we might imagine, for example, that Moses's mother is among those who believe that Moses, after his long exile in the wilderness of Midian, has brought back a message of divine salvation to the Israelites enslaved in Egypt (Exod 4:31), the fact that Moses's message is specifically said to have been delivered to Israel's (presumably male) "elders" (*zĕqēnîm*; Exod 4:29) does not inspire confidence that Moses's mother was present during her son's redemptive pronouncement. Instead, Moses's mother, after handing over her newly weaned son to the pharaoh's daughter to raise in Exod 2:10, appears subsequently in the Bible only in genealogical accounts (Exod 6:20; Num 26:59). Conversely, Samuel's mother Hannah is described as able to interact with her son after he is weaned, but even so, she is said to see him just once a year, during her family's annual pilgrimage to Shiloh (1 Sam 2:19). Beyond this, the biblical authors, aside from offering a brief note that Hannah bore three more sons and two daughters (1 Sam 2:21), express no interest in her.[2]

Other mothers can remain part of the biblical accounts of their families' stories somewhat longer, through, say, a child's betrothal and marriage. As we saw in Chapter 3, for example, Samson approaches both his mother and father to ask that they secure the Philistine woman of Timnah for him as a bride (Judg 14:2), and in Gen 27:46, Rebekah sets in motion the process that sends her son Jacob to her brother Laban in Paddan-Aram, in order that he marry one (ultimately both!) of Laban's daughters. Still, when Jacob returns to his homeland in Canaan, some twenty years later (Gen 31:38, 41), he is said to reunite only with his brother Esau and his father Isaac (Gen 33:4; 35:27); there is no mention of his mother Rebekah until Jacob is on his deathbed and, in his last words, tells us that Rebekah had been interred in the family burial cave at Machpelah (Gen 49:31). But when did she die? Who buried her? Neither Jacob nor the biblical writers elsewhere address these questions. Somewhat similarly, although we are told that Leah and her children came to Canaan with Jacob and were present during Jacob's initial encounter with Esau (Gen 33:1–7), Leah subsequently disappears from the biblical text until we learn, again in Jacob's last words, that Jacob buried her in the cave at Machpelah alongside Abraham, Sarah, Isaac, and Rebekah (Gen 49:31). But at what point during her life course did Leah die? Are we to envision her to be alive at the time when the Hivite Shechem lay with her daughter Dinah (Gen 34:2), when negotiations for a subsequent marriage were then engaged (Gen 34:6–17), and when her two sons Simeon and Levi undermined those arrangements with a ruthless attack on Shechem, his family, and the Hivite city (Gen 34:25–26)? And if so, should we imagine that she shared Jacob's reaction to this calamitous chain of events (Gen 34:30)? Likewise, was she imagined to be alive, and what did she think, when her husband favored her sister Rachel's firstborn, Joseph, over her six sons and his other five brothers (Gen 37:3)? Again, the biblical writers offer no comment.

Yet there is one group of mothers whom biblical texts depict as engaged in their children's affairs much later on in their lives—after these women's husbands have died and their sons (on whom these narratives focus) have assumed the role of paterfamilias within the deceased father's household. These women are queen mothers: that is, each is the mother (or, in one case, the grandmother) of a son who has become king after the death of his father, the previous king. Seventeen of these queen mothers are known from archival records found in 1–2 Kings that concern the Judahite kings of the

Divided Monarchy.³ Judah, although Judah in the time of the so-called United Monarchy, is also the setting for the story of an eighteenth queen mother: Bathsheba, the queen mother of Solomon (1 Kgs 1:5–40; 2:13–25). In accounts regarding Israel's Northern Kingdom, one other woman is identified as a queen mother: Jezebel, after the death of her husband King Ahab, when relatives of King Ahaziah of Judah refer to her using the title *gĕbîrâ* that queen mothers can be accorded (2 Kgs 10:13).⁴

Two points regarding these biblical queen mothers initially attract our attention. First, these queen mothers, if not actually menopausal, are what we might describe as socially menopausal, a term I derive from studies I have previously cited that describe life stages such as "social birth" (for infants) and "social puberty" (for somewhat older children). For example, we will recall from Chapter 6 that in classical and Hellenistic Greece, it was only on the fifth day after an infant's physical birth (or even, according to some sources, the seventh or tenth day) that the child was formally accepted (or rejected) by its father and marked (or dismissed) as a new member of the family.⁵ Thus, it was only at this point that the infant was socially born, even though, obviously, the physical birth had occurred several days prior. So too in ancient Rome, as I also noted in Chapter 6, the "lustral day" (*dies lustricus*) on which a newborn's name was conferred, eight or nine days after the baby's physical birth, "marked the entry of the child into the family and society," or the infant's social birth.⁶ Prior to that, the child was more or less a nonentity, or, as I have quoted in Plutarch as opining, "more like a plant than animal."⁷

Similarly, regarding "social puberty," we will recall from the Prologue Vincent Crapanzano's analysis of circumcision traditions in Moroccan villages during the late 1960s.⁸ There, circumcisions were typically performed as soon as a boy was deemed old enough to remember the event (usually between three and six years of age). Likewise, as we saw in the Introduction, Ndembu boys could be as young as seven when they were circumcised.⁹ Yet despite the young age of these Moroccan and Ndembu boys, their circumcisions were understood to declare, at least at some level, that these boys had been "made men."¹⁰ Thus, the boys had at least at some level achieved social puberty, even though the markers of biological puberty—"the development of facial hair, the deepening of the voice or the first nocturnal emission"¹¹—would only manifest many years later. I have also noted in the Prologue and Introduction that in many parts of the world, adulthood, at least for females, seems to be a social rather than a biological category. Females in ancient Greece and among the Gisu people of eastern

Uganda, the Manam islanders of Papua New Guinea, and the Malay people of Sumatra, for example, only became fully-fledged adult women when they bore a child, regardless of how many years past her biological coming of age the woman might have been.[12]

Analogously, I suggest that we understand ancient Israel's queen mothers to be socially menopausal. After all, a woman, by definition, cannot become queen mother to a son who is the reigning king until the previous king—the son's father and the woman's husband—has died. It follows that upon becoming a queen mother, a woman can no longer fulfill the typical female role of childbearer, for she no longer has a husband with whom to procreate. Queen mothers are thus positioned as functionally equivalent to biologically menopausal women, for whatever a queen mother's age and whatever her status as a menstruant when her son ascends to the throne, she, like a biologically menopausal woman, is at the end of her childbearing years. Hence my identification of ancient Israel's queen mothers as socially menopausal.

The second point to note about these ancient Israelite queen mothers is the considerable political and religious power they are able to wield, comparable in many respects to the political and religious power exercised by queen mothers elsewhere in the Near East. I have discussed in previous publications, for example, the powerful political role that queen mothers in the Late Bronze Age city-state of Ugarit could play within the royal court. For instance, Ugaritic queen mothers could serve as regents on their sons' behalf, if a son, say, came to the throne while still a minor and was too young to rule, or if an adult son, for whatever reason (war, a diplomatic mission), was away from the palace.[13] Indeed, even before a son assumed his kingly office, a Ugaritic queen-mother-to-be might exert political power on his behalf, in order to ensure that her son, instead of some rival claimant, ascended to the throne.[14] No wonder, then, that in a collection of eight "queen mother" letters from Ugarit (letters sent to Ugaritic queen mothers from their kingly sons), the king can describe himself as paying homage to the authority of his queen mother by bowing at her feet (in one case, "seven and seven" times), or by addressing her as *adt*, a feminine form of *adn*, "lord."[15]

We find further evidence of the kind of political power that a Near Eastern queen mother could wield in a text from a site on the Levantine coast about 230 kilometers south of Ugarit, which is almost a millennium later in date: this is the Phoenician inscription of King Eshmunazor II of Sidon, which dates from the mid-fifth century BCE.[16] This text begins by describing Eshmunazor as "an orphan, the son of a widow" (*ytm bn 'lmt*; line 3 and also line 13). It thereby implies that Eshmunazor's father Tabnit had died before Eshmunazor was born.[17] The inscription also states that Eshmunazor was "the son of a few days" (*bn msk ymm*; lines 3, 12–13) who died "before my time" (*bl 'ty*; lines 3, 12), in the fourteenth year of his reign (*bšnt 'sr w'rb'14 lmlky*; line 1). This suggests that Eshmunazor was still a minor when he died, or, at a minimum, that he had been a minor during most of his tenure upon Sidon's throne. The text also indicates that the regent who guided the reign of this boy king was his father Tabnit's wife and Eshmunazor's queen mother, who is named Ummiʻashtart or Amoʻashtart.[18] In lines 18–20 of the inscription, for example, Eshmunazor (who, in the conceit of the text, speaks from the grave) describes how the "lord of kings" (that is, the Persian emperor who was overlord of the Sidonians) gave "us" (that is, Eshmunazor and his mother Ummiʻashtart/Amoʻashtart) two cities in the Plain of Sharon, Dor and Joppa, which "we" (again, that is, Eshmunazor and his mother Ummiʻashtart/Amoʻashtart) added to Sidon's territorial holdings "forever."[19] In other words, King Eshmunazor describes himself as acting in tandem with his queen mother, first in their engagements with their Persian sovereign and then in facilitating Sidon's actions following the emperor's largesse.

In the Eshmunazor inscription, Ummiʻashtart/Amoʻashtart is further said to have joined with her son in several temple-building projects (lines 15–18): (1) a temple to Astarte, in a region of Sidon called "Sidon-Land-of-the-Sea"; (2) a temple to Eshmun, who was Sidon's chief god, as Astarte was the city's chief goddess, at the "spring of YDLL," somewhere in Sidon's environs; (3) a temple for Baal of Sidon, the "lord," that is, of the city and, in the words of P. Kyle McCarter, a "divine embodiment of Sidon itself"; and (4) a temple for Astarte-Name-of-Baal, who was the Baal of Sidon's consort and, to quote again McCarter, "a personification of his cultically available presence."[20] Ummiʻashtart/Amoʻashtart can thereby be understood to have acted as a religious functionary during her tenure as Eshmunazor's queen mother, alongside her exercise of political authority as her son's regent.

Certain biblical materials are strikingly similar to these Ugaritic and Phoenician data. In 1 Kgs 1:5–40, for example, Bathsheba, the queen-mother-to-be, exerts herself to secure the throne for her son Solomon at the time of her husband David's death, just as a Ugaritic queen-mother-to-be might work to ensure her son's claim to the throne. Indeed, just as a Ugaritic queen-mother-to-be might work to ensure the throne for her son in the face of some rival claimant, so too does Bathsheba. Thus, urged on by the prophet Nathan, Bathsheba persuades the dying David to name Solomon as his heir rather than Adonijah, who is David's oldest surviving son. To be sure, the final decree is David's. Nevertheless, it is Bathsheba who, practically speaking, determines the royal succession. Then, in 1 Kgs 2:13–25, Bathsheba, who is now, after David's death, Solomon's queen mother, approaches her son as would a royal official or courtier, bearing a petition on behalf of the recently deposed Adonijah. And while Solomon hardly receives this particular petition with favor, as it asks for David's concubine (tantamount to asking for David's kingdom; see 2 Sam 3:6–11), this does not affect the respect the king accords Bathsheba as queen mother. He rises and, as in the Ugaritic "queen mother" letters, bows down to her (*wayyištaḥû*) and then has a seat placed for her at his right hand (1 Kgs 2:19). A comparison with Ps 80:18 (80:17 in most English translations) and Ps 110:1, where the king is described as sitting at the right hand of God, suggests that after the throne of the monarch himself, the chair assigned to Bathsheba is the place of highest honor on the royal dais.[21]

These texts in 1 Kings 1–2 thus attest to the considerable political power to which Bathsheba lays claim, similar to the political power wielded by queen mothers in Ugarit and by Ummiʿashtart/Amoʿashtart in Sidon. First Kings 15:1–15 likewise suggests ways in which Israelite queen mothers can exercise political power and also the sort of religious power that the Eshmunazor inscription ascribes to Ummiʿashtart/Amoʿashtart.

The queen mother who appears in this 1 Kings 15 text is Maʿacah, the queen mother of a son who is alternatively called Abijam (in 1 Kgs 15:1–2) and Abijah (in the parallel texts in 2 Chr 11:20–22; 13:1–2).[22] Abijam/Abijah ruled Judah for three years (ca. 914–911 BCE). Subsequently, Maʿacah served as queen mother for Abijam's/Abijah's son Asa (1 Kgs 15:9–10; 2 Chr 15:16), who had a forty-one-year reign (ca. 911–870 BCE). Already, these data imply that Maʿacah as queen mother was able to exercise the kind of political power ascribed to Bathsheba and to her Ugaritic and Phoenician counterparts. For example, the fact that Asa reigned for forty-one years suggests that he assumed the throne at an early age, and it is quite possible that Maʿacah, as queen mother, served as regent before Asa reached maturity.

That Maʿacah continued to act as Asa's queen mother after her son Abijam/Abijah had died also indicates that she commanded a significant degree of power within the Judean royal court. Maʿacah must have been powerful enough, for example, to have somehow supplanted Asa's actual mother, who is mentioned nowhere in the biblical text. To be sure, Maʿacah may have been aided in this quest by natural causes (Asa's mother's death in childbirth perhaps?). Nevertheless, Ma'acah's ability to remain queen mother after Abijam/Abijah had died indicates that she can claim a noteworthy measure of authority independent of the authority she derived through her relationship to her son. Indeed, the Bible's description of her as Asa's "mother," biology notwithstanding, as well as the way the term "mother" is used almost as a title in the archival records of 1–2 Kings,[23] suggests that the queen mother played an official role within the Judahite monarchy. This is also indicated in 1 Kgs 15:13 (paralleled in 2 Chr 15:16), which describes how Asa became angry at Ma'acah and removed her (*sûr*) from the queen mother's designated post as *gĕbîrâ*.[24] In this text, even though it is clear that power within the palace ultimately lay with the king, we find evidence that Ma'acah held an authoritative position as a court functionary from which she had to be formally deposed.[25]

The act that so angers Asa is that Ma'acah has made what is called in 1 Kgs 15:13 a *mipleṣet lā'ăšērâ*,[26] to be translated either as "an abominable image for Asherah," the great mother goddess of the Canaanite world, or as "an abominable image of the asherah," the stylized tree used in Israelite religious settings to symbolize Asherah's cultic presence.[27] Ma'acah, that is, acts as a religious functionary by making a cult statue or cult image dedicated to the goddess Asherah.[28] It is probable, moreover, that Ma'acah had this statue or image erected at some location within the Jerusalem temple precinct, perhaps even within the temple itself. I propose this for several reasons. First, in 2 Kgs 23:6, we are told that in the seventh century BCE, during the reign of King Josiah (ca. 640–609 BCE), an Asherah image stood within the Jerusalem temple compound and perhaps within the temple proper, seemingly because the seventh century BCE was a point during Israelite history when Asherah worship was prevalent in the practice of Israelite religion, even to the extent that Asherah was worshipped as the consort of the Israelite god Yahweh.[29] The fact that Ma'acah commissioned an Asherah icon in the late tenth/early ninth century BCE suggests that this era, too, was a time in Israelite history when the conviction pertained that Asherah and Yahweh should be worshipped in conjunction. If, moreover, this conviction manifested itself physically in the seventh century BCE by erecting an Asherah image in the temple compound and perhaps within the temple itself, then we might well expect it to manifest itself similarly during the time of Ma'acah.

We can also note that the palace in Jerusalem stood essentially next door to the Jerusalem temple: indeed, in the words of Ezek 43:8, "[there was just] a wall between." Given this proximity, a temple location seems the most logical place for a member of the royal family, including Ma'acah, to place her

Asherah image. Indeed, state temples such as the Jerusalem temple complex really functioned as "kings' sanctuaries" in ancient Israel (paraphrasing here the words of Bethel's high priest Amaziah from Amos 7:13). Therefore, Israelite and Judean kings—and, by extension, I would argue, members of the Israelite and Judean royal families—typically assumed for themselves the right to appoint their state temples' personnel and determine appropriate furnishings for these temple complexes.[30] It follows that Maʿacah, as a member of the Judean royal family, would have assumed the right to erect the cult image she had made in Asherah's honor somewhere within the Jerusalem temple compound. In doing so, moreover, she demonstrates the means by which queen mothers can exercise their religious authority, analogous to the way Ummiʿashtart/Amoʿashtart exercised religious authority in erecting temples in Sidon in honor of Astarte, Eshmun, Baal of Sidon, and Astarte-Name-of-Baal.

I propose, moreover, that two aspects of Ummiʿashtart/Amoʿashtart's and Maʿacah's identities as queen mothers that I have stressed here—(1) their status as socially menopausal and (2) the authority they are able to wield as religious functionaries—are not unrelated. More specifically, I propose that these women are freer to act as religious functionaries, even establishing and furnishing sanctuary spaces, than women in their societies otherwise might have been because Ummiʿashtart/Amoʿashtart and Maʿacah are understood to be past the point of childbearing. There is thus no risk that they will pollute sacred spaces with the childbirth impurities that, as we saw in Chapter 6, were standardly regarded as a pernicious threat among the cultures of the Near East and eastern Mediterranean. Indeed, we will remember from Chapter 6 that according to Lev 12:4, it is especially sacred spaces and their accoutrements that are threatened by an Israelite woman's postpartum impurities, and thus the primary restriction placed on a recently delivered mother in ancient Israel was that for forty to eighty days after giving birth, she could not touch anything classified as $qōdeš$, or holy, and/or enter holy or sanctified space ($hammiqdāš$). Restrictions imposed on postpartum women elsewhere in the Near East, we can suggest, would have been analogous. Note, for example, that Near Eastern dictates regarding priestesses frequently require that to be eligible for sanctuary service, these women, like Ummiʿashtart/Amoʿashtart, must be celibate or otherwise forego procreation—in order, presumably, that they not introduce childbirth impurities into the sanctified spaces where they render cultic service.[31]

In Israel, moreover, even after the forty to eighty days of a woman's childbirth impurity had ended, a lingering fear regarding her potential to pollute seemed to persist. This can be seen in Lev 12:6, which mandates of a recently delivered woman, when her postpartum period of impurity is over, that she is to "bring" (*tābî*) a burnt offering (*'ôlâ*) and purification offering (*ḥaṭṭā't*) to the entrance of the tent of meeting, the sanctuary space construed as Israel's central place of worship during the period of the Sinai wanderings in which Leviticus is set. Yet according to Lev 15:14, a man who is at the end of a period of impurity brought on by some sort of genital excretion (generally thought to be "an inordinate secretion of mucus" due to his having contracted gonorrhea)[32] is to "give" (*nātan*) the *'ôlâ* and *ḥaṭṭā't* required of him to the priest. As Judith Romney Wegner, who has studied these passages with utmost care, writes, he "hand[s] the birds [the two turtledoves or two pigeons required] over directly, thereby making a meaningful physical contact with the priest as his intermediary to God." The woman, conversely, does not place her offerings "directly into the hands of the priest." Rather, she "presumably sets her offering down somewhere outside" the entrance of the tent of meeting for the priest to pick up.[33]

Wegner proposes that this discrepancy is driven by a concern to protect the priest from contact with women's dangerous impurities, which—despite the end of her forty-/eighty-day period of impurity—were perhaps conceived to be unrelentingly omnipresent. Or perhaps a woman's impurity—or at least the potential of impurity—was thought to linger after the requisite forty- to eighty-day period after parturition has passed, as Saul M. Olyan suggests: "Even when ... women are not ... giving birth," he writes, "their potential to pollute ... is presumably never forgotten."[34] Regardless, the point is the threat that childbearing women can pose to the holy, even after their period of postpartum impurity has ended. This leads me to suggest, again, that it is their status as socially menopausal, or as nonchildbearing, that allows women like Ummi'ashtart/Amo'ashtart and Ma'acah to act as religious functionaries in ways that women who still have the potential to bear children cannot.

Other Socially Menopausal Women

The biblical record in addition suggests that there are parallels between Israelite queen mothers' exercise of political and religious power and the political and religious power that can be wielded by certain nonelite Israelite women who, like queen mothers, are socially menopausal. Consider, for example, the story of Micah's mother, who, as I briefly suggested in Chapter 4, is best understood as having been predeceased by her husband in the Judg 17:1–5 text in which she appears.[35] Note in this regard that while Judg 17:1–5 mentions several of Micah's kin (Micah himself, Micah's mother, and Micah's son whom Micah is said to appoint to serve his household as a priest at the end of 17:5), nowhere in this text, or in the larger Judges 17–18 narrative of which Judg 17:1–5 is a part, is any reference made to Micah's father. Rather, the Judges 17–18 narrative consistently and repeatedly (some eleven times; Judg 17:4, 8, 12; 18:2, 3, 13, 15, 18, 22, 25, and 26) refers to Micah, and not his father, as his household's head. Most logically, this is because we are to understand that the father has died, leaving his wife to reside (and be cared for) in a household that is now headed by her son, who has succeeded his father as the family's paterfamilias.

That Micah's father is dead and the mother now resides in a household headed by her son is further suggested by the fact that the mother, as our story opens, lays claim to ownership of eleven hundred pieces of silver. Unfortunately, because our story begins *in medias res*, we are not told how the mother came into possession of her silver cache. We can be sure, however, of some ways in which she did not. For example, based on our discussion in Chapter 3, where I documented the preexilic Israelites' overwhelming preference for the gifting of marriage presents as opposed to dowries at the time of betrothal, we can be sure that the eleven hundred pieces of silver belonging to Micah's mother were not a dowry payment that she brought into her marriage. Nor does it make sense to suppose that Micah's mother came to possess her eleven hundred pieces of silver during the course of her married life, given that typically within an Israelite household, property would have been held by a woman's spouse.[36] Yet if Micah's mother could not have come into possession of her cache of silver during her marriage, and if the norms of Israelite marital practice dictate that she did not bring this silver with her to her nuptials, then it necessarily follows that the mother could have only acquired the silver after her marriage to Micah's father had come to an end. That is, as I suggested in Chapter 4: after her husband's death, the silver that the father had previously held on their household's behalf came to his wife, who had survived him.[37]

I also suggested in Chapter 4 that Micah, as his father's heir, may not have agreed that the silver properly belonged to his mother, which would plausibly explain why, according to Judg 17:2, he stole it. The mother, unaware that her son was the thief, swore an oath cursing whoever had purloined her silver, but she subsequently blesses her son in the name of Yahweh when he confesses that he is the culprit and returns her cache (Judg 17:2–3).[38] At this point, the event in the story most significant for our purposes takes place: the mother takes two hundred pieces of the silver, gives them to a craftsman (more specifically, a metallurgist or a refiner; *ṣōrēp*), and commissions him to make a cast-metal figurine (*pesel ûmassēkâ;* Judg 17:4)[39]—arguably some sort of image representing the god Yahweh, whom she had evoked in her blessing.[40] Arguably, moreover, this Yahweh image was then housed in the *bêt 'ĕlōhîm*, or shrine, that is mentioned in the next verse of our text and that seems to have been a dedicated sanctuary building within Micah's household compound.[41] To be sure, Judg 17:5 does not definitively indicate that the mother's figurine was housed in Micah's household shrine, but the juxtaposition of the phrase "and the man Micah had a shrine" (*wĕhā'îš mîkâ lô bêt 'ĕlōhîm*) in the first half of Judg 17:5 with the notice regarding the fabrication of the mother's figurine in 17:4 strongly suggests that the image and the shrine are to be associated with one another.

We therefore have in Judg 17:1–5 the story of a woman (1) whose husband has died, or, to use the language I have adopted here, a woman who is socially menopausal because she is no longer in a position to bear children; (2) who commissions the fabrication of some sort of cult image; and (3) who then sees this image placed within sanctuary space affiliated with her household. That is, in Judg 17:1–5 we have an account of a nonelite counterpart of Maʿacah, (1) a socially menopausal queen mother, (2) who had made a cult statue or cult image of the goddess Asherah, and then arguably (3) had that image housed in the Jerusalem temple precinct adjacent to her home in the royal palace. I suggest, moreover, as I suggested above, that the amalgam of these motifs is not a coincidence: rather, in Micah's mother story, as in Maʿacah's, a socially menopausal woman is able to exert herself as a religious agent in a way that is otherwise not readily available to women in Israelite tradition because she is understood to have left behind the typical female role of childbearer and has concomitantly left behind the potential to pollute holy objects or holy spaces with even a lingering miasma of childbirth impurities. Indeed, the mother of Micah and Maʿacah are the only two women described in the Hebrew Bible as commissioning a cult statue or a cult image. Given the geographic, temporal, and status differences that otherwise divide them—Micah's mother is said to live in the Ephraimite countryside during Israel's premonarchic period, in the sort of household compound seemingly typical of agrarian-pastoralist peasants,[42] whereas Maʿacah is represented as living in the royal palace in Jerusalem during the early decades of Israel's divided monarchy—I propose again that what unites them in their endeavors as religious functionaries is the ability to engage the holy and to access sacred space that stems from their socially menopausal status.

Worth noting, finally, is the way socially menopausal nonelite women can exert the sort of political power that queen mothers can wield, as is illustrated by the biblical story of the wise woman of Tekoa (2 Sam 14:1–20). As the story goes, this woman presents herself as one whose husband has died when she comes before King David with a petition. Her request is that he act to save the life of her son, who has murdered his brother and is therefore, according to the decree of her extended family, to be killed, even though this would extinguish the patriline of the Tekoan woman's husband and leave her without immediate kin. David responds to her request favorably, swearing to the woman that her surviving son's life will be spared. It turns out, however, that the wise woman's petition is fictitious and is not really offered on behalf of her murderous son. Rather, it is offered on behalf of David's son Absalom, who is in exile because he had arranged for his servants to kill his half-brother Amnon in retaliation for Amnon's rape of Absalom's sister Tamar. David is persuaded, therefore, to extend to Absalom the same mercy he had offered to the wise woman in response to her petition, and in 2 Sam 14:23, Absalom is described as returning safely to Jerusalem. The fictional son's story, that is, redeems a real son's life. My point, though, is that a woman presenting herself as predeceased by her husband—or, to use the language I have adopted here, a woman we can categorize as socially menopausal—is able to petition Israel's king, much as the queen mother Bathsheba, say, was able to petition King Solomon in 1 Kgs 2:13–25. Furthermore, unlike Bathsheba, the wise woman of Tekoa succeeds in getting the king to follow her counsel.

Granted, we cannot definitively say that the wise woman's husband has died; we only know that she describes her circumstances in this way. The text of 2 Sam 14:1–20 makes clear, moreover, that she is coached by David's general Joab regarding her appearance before the king and the argument she is to present (see especially vv 3 and 19). The political adroitness the Tekoan woman manifests might thus be said only to reflect Joab's acumen.[43]

Nevertheless, we can still suggest that the respect David accords her, and his willingness to hear her request, stem from the socially menopausal status she assumes. Like the socially menopausal queen mothers, that is, the wise woman of Tekoa may be able to act as a counselor in the royal court because of the life stage she is perceived to embody.

PART IV
MORTALITY

9
Ritually Marking a Woman's Death

As is so often the case when investigating ancient Israelite traditions, most of our information concerning both the funerary rituals enacted at the time of an individual's demise and the mortuary practices performed on an ongoing basis on a deceased person's behalf comes from biblical texts that pertain exclusively to men.[1] Indeed, the Hebrew Bible contains only a dozen or so accounts of women's deaths and/or related funerary rites such as burial and mourning, and even fewer allusions to subsequent mortuary rituals.[2] Most of these narratives, moreover, provide a bare minimum of detail. For example, we are told in Gen 49:31 that Jacob interred his first wife Leah in his family's burial cave at Machpelah, but, as I noted in Chapter 8, we are otherwise offered no comment, either in this verse or anywhere else, about the circumstances of Leah's death or about any formalities that might have been enacted in conjunction with her inhumation. Moreover, biblical texts that recount women's deaths with greater specificity often describe events that can hardly be taken to reflect usual custom: for instance, the Levite's cutting the body of his secondary wife, or *pîlegeš*, into twelve pieces in Judg 19:29 after she had been raped and murdered by the Benjaminites of Gibeah,[3] or dogs devouring almost all of Queen Jezebel's body after she had been thrown to her death from one of the palace windows in Jezreel (2 Kgs 9:35–37).[4]

Women and Ancient Israelite Funerary Traditions: What Can We Know?

With only this sort of evidence at hand, it is difficult to identify funerary rites the ancient Israelites might have performed at the time of a woman's demise.[5] We can note that Abraham is said to weep (*bākâ*) and engage in some sort of lamentation (*sāpad*) when Sarah died (Gen 23:2), and Ezek 24:16 seems to presume that such weeping and lamentation—described, as in Genesis, using the verbs *bākâ* and *sāpad*—were the norm upon a woman's death (in this case, Ezekiel's wife). Deuteronomy 21:13 speaks similarly of

Maturity, Marriage, Motherhood, Mortality. Susan Ackerman, Oxford University Press.
© Oxford University Press 2025. DOI: 10.1093/9780197809686.003.0011

daughters weeping (*bākâ*) over their deceased mothers (as well as their deceased fathers), and in Gen 35:8, Rebekah's nurse, Deborah, is interred under a tree designated as the "Oak of Weeping" (*'allôn bākût*)—perhaps because weeping was part of the funerary ritual practiced there. But did the weeping and lamentation enacted at the time of a woman's demise involve a formally sung dirge (a *qînâ*), such as was performed in conjunction with weeping and lamentation according to the most fulsome description of a burial rite found in the Bible: the account of the army commander Abner's funeral in 2 Sam 3:31–37?[6] We do not know. Similarly, we do not know whether a woman's body would have been placed atop a bier that was carried to the grave followed by a procession of mourners, as was the body of Abner and the body of the man from Nain who appears in much later New Testament tradition (Luke 7:12–15).[7]

And in what other mourning behaviors might those who buried a woman have engaged? Ezekiel 24:17, 22–23 suggests that abandoning a normal headdress (and then, as is perhaps indicated in texts such as Ezek 27:30, rubbing dust into one's skull?), going barefoot, covering one's face, and eating mourner's food would have been part of the mourning rituals that were to be undertaken after Ezekiel's wife died.[8] But what about mourning rites the Bible mentions elsewhere: sitting or lying upon the ground;[9] tearing one's clothes;[10] donning sackcloth or other special mourning garb;[11] cutting incisions in one's skin;[12] making one's self bald, and, for male mourners, pulling out one's beard?[13] Would these acts have been performed upon a woman's demise? Was an Israelite woman mourned for a day, as was, say, Abner (2 Sam 3:35), or for a longer period: for example, seven days, as was Judith according to later deuterocanonical tradition (Jdt 16:24)? Was there a memorial bonfire at the end of a woman's funeral, as there was at the end of the funeral of King Asa (2 Chr 16:14; see also Jer 34:5 and 2 Chr 21:19) and as seems alluded to in the reference in Amos 6:10 to "a burning for the dead"? Were these rites even normative for all men? Each of these questions is unanswerable based on our available data.

Nevertheless, some things seem clear. First, in the same way that biblical tradition seems to consider that a proper burial was essential for men upon their demise, it also seems generally to have been assumed that a proper burial was essential for women. Indeed, a proper burial is deemed to be essential enough that it is mandated in the Bible even for men and women for whom the Israelites had little respect. Regarding men, for example: it is decreed in Deut 21:22–23 that the corpse of a criminal who has been hung that day cannot be left exposed for the night but must be buried on the day of the execution. Joshua 8:29 and 10:26–27 likewise indicate that while the bodies of enemy kings who have been killed in battle can hang exposed throughout the day of their death (a standard Near Eastern military tactic, meant to strike fear in the hearts of these kings' surviving allies), the corpses must be taken down at sunset for burial. Indeed, in 1 Sam 31:11–13, the men of Jabesh-Gilead do as much for an Israelite king, as they "traveled through the night" to recover the bodies of Saul and his three sons from the walls of Beth-Shan, where the Philistines had hung them, exposed, after these men had died in battle at Mount Gilboa. The bodies were then brought to Jabesh-Gilead, where the corpses were cremated and the bones formally buried under a tamarisk tree.

Likewise, regarding women: the army commander Jehu, who overthrew Israel's King Ahab, instructs the men in his entourage to perform the proper burial rites on behalf of Ahab's queen, Jezebel, after she died when she was thrown out of a palace window at Jezreel during Jehu's coup and trampled by horses in the courtyard below.[14] Indeed, Jehu issues this order even though it was at Jehu's urging that Jezebel's attendants threw her out of her palace's window in the first place and even though Jehu calls her, in the same breath in which he orders her burial, "that cursed woman" (*hāʾărûrâ hazzōʾt*; 2 Kgs 9:34). Theodore J. Lewis has argued, moreover, that Jehu's command to care for Jezebel's body calls upon his officers not only to bury Jezebel properly, but to ensure the performance of rituals that Near Eastern tradition suggests should subsequently be undertaken on a dead person's behalf: periodic offerings of food and drink, for example.[15] Lewis makes this proposal because "elsewhere in the ancient Near East, particularly Mesopotamia," the terminology used in Jehu's order concerning Jezebel's corpse—Hebrew *piqdû-nāʾ*, usually translated as something like "attend to" or "see to" the body—"has a cultic sense when tied to the funerary ritual." More specifically, the Mesopotamian *pāqidu* serves as the "caretaker" who "fulfill[s] customary rites" for the deceased:[16] as above, burying the body and providing regular food and drink offerings after death and also regularly commemorating the deceased by, for example, invoking a dead person's name.[17]

The proper burial and subsequent care of Jezebel's corpse cannot, however, take place because, as I mentioned above, almost all of her remains had been devoured by dogs by the time Jehu ordered her inhumation: only her skull, feet, and the palms of her hands remained (2 Kgs 9:35). In the biblical account, this "horrifyingly graphic description" of Jezebel's ravaged body both fulfills the prophet Elijah's excoriating oracle that cursed her corrupt actions during life (1 Kgs 21:23; see also 2 Kgs 9:10, 36) and symbolizes more generally the "complete annihilation" of the corrupt dynasty of her husband Ahab.[18] Somewhat similarly, the biblical authors understood the lack of a proper burial, and the dismembering of a corpse instead, to be an appropriate response to the corrupt actions of the brothers Rechab and Ba'anah. According to 2 Sam 4:2–12, these two men, thinking to please David as he attempts to secure the Israelite throne previously held by Saul, betray their former commander, Saul's son Ishba'al, by killing him as he lay in his bedchamber and then beheading him. Triumphantly, they bring the head to David, but rather than respond with the joy they expect, David berates them for their wickedness. More important for our purposes, he commands that they be killed and their bodies hung up for public display, with their hands and feet cut off. The proper retort to Rechab and Ba'anah's untoward dismembering of Ishba'al's body, that is, is to disgrace them by dismembering and exposing their corpses. For any but these most heinous members of the Israelite community, however, biblical tradition presumes that proper burial of an intact corpse was the norm.

Biblical tradition also seems to presume that in the case of normative burials for both women and men, family members—or, in certain cases, readily identifiable surrogates—take on the primary responsibility for funeral rites.[19] For example, Jer 16:7 suggests, as did the text from Deut 21:13 that I cited above, that children should assume the obligation for mourning their deceased parents,[20] much as Gen 23:2 and Ezek 24:16–17 presume that husbands—Abraham and Ezekiel—should mourn their deceased wives. Abraham is also said to have buried his wife Sarah (Gen 23:19), and Jacob likewise is reported to have buried his two wives Rachel and Leah (Gen 48:7; 49:31; see also Gen 35:19–20). We are also probably to envision Jacob as having buried Deborah, his mother Rebekah's nurse, in Gen 35:8. After all, the biblical text imagines Deborah to have left behind any family she might have had in her homeland of Aram-naharaim when, at the time of Rebekah's marriage, she traveled to Canaan with Rebekah to join Abraham's household (Gen 24:59). It is therefore appropriate that a member of Abraham's family assumes responsibility for burying her.

Jacob also indicates, in a speech that concerns his own burial, that women were customarily interred alongside men in the sort of multigenerational family tomb that seems typical of Israelite burial practice. Thus he instructs his sons, who are gathered around him on his deathbed, that even though he is about to die at least three hundred kilometers to the south and west, in Egypt, they are to inter his body in Canaan, "in the cave in the field at Machpelah, which is near Mamre," as it was in that cave that Jacob's paternal grandparents, Abraham and Sarah, and his parents, Isaac and Rebekah, had been buried, and in which Jacob had buried his first wife, Leah (Gen 49:29–32). Barzillai of Gilead, who helped escort King David across the Jordan when the monarch returned to Jerusalem after the suppression of his son Absalom's revolt, also refers to a multigenerational tomb in which both male and female family members—his father and his mother—were buried (2 Sam 19:38 [19:37 in most English translations]).

Archaeological evidence likewise indicates that it was the norm, at least in the Southern Kingdom of Judah, for men and women to be buried alongside one another in communal tombs.[21] Our data are limited, however, since "only a very small number of the individuals interred have been analyzed for sex" despite the "large number of Iron Age burials excavated."[22] Still, in the interments surveyed by Elizabeth Bloch-Smith in her important monograph *Judahite Burial Practices and Beliefs about the Dead*, "there was no example of an adult female buried alone." Rather, in the Iron Age Judean tombs Bloch-Smith studied, "the greatest number of women were buried with children, adolescents and other adults in cave and bench tombs." (A cave tomb, as its name implies, uses natural fissures that extend back into a rock outcrop as a burial space; a bench tomb is, essentially, a human-made cave tomb in which several waist-high benches—usually three, used for the placement of bodies—are carved into the side and back walls that form the perimeter of a chamber that has been hewn into a hillside or dug into the earth; see Fig. 9.1.)[23] Indeed, in Judean cave tombs, as Bloch-Smith notes, "females to males exhibited a 1:1 ratio,"[24] although in the overall corpus of cave tombs from Iron Age Israel and Judah (ca. 1200–586 BCE), the ratio of male burials to female is 2:1.[25] Similarly, in Judean bench tombs, which become "the signature burial form of Iron II Judah from the eighth to the sixth centuries BCE,"[26] "adults and adolescents displayed a 3:2 ratio of men to women."[27]

In short: texts such as Gen 49:29–32 and 2 Sam 19:38 (English 19:37), as well as our archaeological evidence, appear to indicate that typically in ancient Israel, and especially in Judah, men and women were buried together in multigenerational family tombs. (This seems the most logical way to interpret the archaeological record I just described, although whether the multiple burials found by archaeologists in Israelite and Judean cave and bench tombs in fact belong to the same *family* cannot necessarily be determined

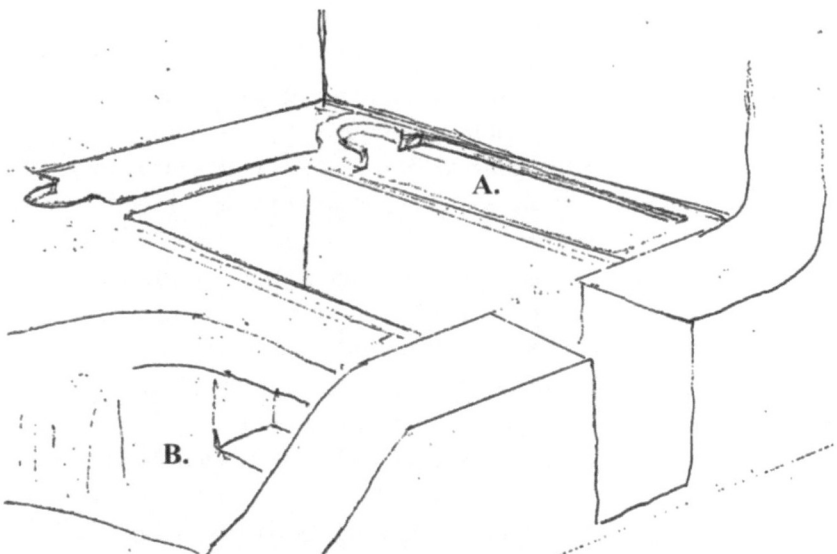

Fig. 9.1 Judahite Rock-Cut Bench Tomb. A. Bench; B. Repository. From Suriano, *History of Death*, 41. Courtesy of Matthew J. Suriano.

from the remains as we have them.)[28] Yet even though Israelite tombs were apparently used for the burials of both a family's male and female members, the data catalogued by Bloch-Smith cited just above suggest that Israelite tombs were male-dominated spaces. The biblical data suggest this as well. For example, biblical texts typically identify a tomb by reference to a family's patriarch. Thus, we read in Judg 8:32 that Gideon was buried in "the tomb of his father Joash," and likewise in Judg 16:31 we learn that Samson was buried in "the tomb of his father Manoah." So too, according to 2 Sam 2:32, was David's nephew Asahel buried in "the tomb of his father" in Bethlehem, just as elsewhere in the David story, it is reported that the royal counselor Ahithophel was buried "in the tomb of his father" (2 Sam 17:23). Moreover, at some point after the deaths of his predecessor Saul and Saul's son Jonathan, David recovered their bones from their burial place in Jabesh-Gilead and had them reinterred in the tomb of Saul's father Kish (2 Sam 21:12–14). Somewhat similarly, in 1 Kgs 13:22; 2 Kgs 9:28, 14:20; and Neh 2:3, 5, we find references to burials in the tombs of one's "fathers" (*'ābôt*), which are in turn echoed centuries later in 1 Macc 2:70 and 9:19, in accounts of the tombs of their fathers in which the Maccabean patriarch Matthias and his son Judas were interred.

Tombs are typically identified by reference to family *patri*archs because ancient Israelite tombs, it turns out, are closely linked to a family's *patri*mony—or what is often referred to in the Bible using the term *naḥălâ* that I introduced in Chapter 4. There, I defined *naḥălâ* as a kinship group's patrimonial or familial landholdings, although this term has a much more multivalent and complex meaning than translations such as "patrimony" or the commonly found rendering "inheritance" might suggest. Indeed, so multivalent and complex is the term *naḥălâ* and the concepts associated with it that no one definition can adequately gloss its every occurrence in the Bible, much less the use of the cognates of *naḥălâ* found elsewhere in Near Eastern literature. Still, it is clear that in several instances in the Bible, *naḥălâ* does refer to the land each Israelite family claimed perpetually to hold as an inalienable patrimonial estate, passed down through the generations from father to son.[29]

The biblical witness speaks clearly, moreover, of the need to bury the primary members of a family's lineage in a tomb located within this *naḥălâ*, even if this required extraordinary measures. For example, as I noted above, David, according to 2 Sam 21:12–14, exhumed the bones of Saul and Jonathan from their burial site in Jabesh-Gilead and had them reburied in the tomb of Saul's father Kish, which was in Zela, a town that we can take, based on Josh 18:28, to be the *naḥălâ* held by Saul's family within the territory of Benjamin, which was the Saulides' tribe. Likewise, the Israelites of the Exodus generation are said to have moved the body of the long-dead Joseph out of Egypt during the course of the Exodus event (Exod 13:19), so that it might be interred "in the portion of the field that Jacob had acquired from the sons of Hamor, the father of Shechem," which we are explicitly told "belonged to the descendants of Joseph as a *naḥălâ*" (Josh 24:32). Somewhat similarly in 2 Sam 2:32, David's followers, even though they are in the midst of a demanding military engagement, take the time to move the body of the recently deceased Asahel, David's nephew, about twenty kilometers—almost a full day's journey—from Gibeon, where he had fallen in battle, to his father's tomb in the Davidic ancestral homestead, or *naḥălâ*, in Bethlehem.[30] We are probably also meant to imagine that Samson's family expended considerable effort to recover his body from Philistine territory and move it some sixty to seventy kilometers—at least a two-day journey—from the place of his death in Gaza to his family's *naḥălâ* in the southwest of Israel (Judg 16:31).[31]

Joshua, according to Josh 24:30 and Judg 2:9, is also buried in his family's *naḥălâ*, and the notice that Aaron's son Eleazar was buried "in the town of his [Eleazar's] son Phinehas, which had been given to him in the hill country of Ephraim" (Josh 24:33), although it does not specifically deploy the term *naḥălâ*, clearly has in mind the same notion of burial in the land that a family claims as its patrimonial estate. So too is the description of Jephthah's burial in his "town in Gilead" (Judg 12:7) meant to evoke this ideological conviction,[32] as are the accounts of Tola's burial in his hometown of Shamir (Judg 10:1–2); Ibzan's burial in his hometown of Bethlehem (Judg 12:8–10); Abdon's burial in his hometown of Pirathon (Judg 12:13–15); and Samuel's burial in his ancestral homestead at Ramah (1 Sam 25:1).[33] This conviction is evoked as well, albeit by way of counterexample, in 1 Kgs 13:22, where Yahweh has the prophet from Bethel curse his rival, the man of God from Judah, by decreeing that the Judahite's corpse will not be buried in the tomb of his ancestors, which we are to presume lay within his family's *naḥălâ*.[34]

But why is burial in a tomb within a family's *naḥălâ* so important? As Francesca Stavrakopoulou notes, there are several reasons: "interment in the family tomb on ancestral land facilitated the transition of the dead into the underworld and manifested the integration into the realm of the ancestors," and "it also transformed the corpse from its liminal state into a once-living-now-dead member of the social group, thereby reincorporating the individual into the community." Yet "most significantly," Stavrakopoulou goes on to say: "interment in a family tomb . . . embodied and reinforced the territorial claims of the deceased's living descendants and their socioeconomic well-being."[35] More simply put, as Bloch-Smith states, "ancestral tombs served to reinforce the family claim to the . . . *naḥălâ*." The existence of the tomb," that is, "constituted a physical, perpetual witness to ownership of the land," which is to say, again: "the tomb . . . constituted a physical claim to the patrimony."[36] "The land represented the family," Karel van der Toorn writes, "joining the ancestors with their progeny," and he adds, "an important reason why the family land was inalienable was the fact that the ancestors were buried there."[37] In short, a family's tomb inexorably tied a family to its *naḥălâ*, commingling the ancestors' remains with the very earth of the family homestead.[38] Indeed, so tied were the ancestors' remains to a family's land that, according to Lewis, in a brilliant reading of 2 Sam 14:16, the *naḥălâ* can more expansively be described as the *naḥălat ʾĕlōhîm*, which (interpreting *ʾĕlōhîm* here as deceased spirits in general and the spirits of a family's deceased ancestors in particular) means "the patrimony of the ancestors" or "the ancestral estate."[39]

More precisely speaking, though, as I have already indicated, we need to take the phrase "*patri*mony of the ancestors" quite literally and understand a family's *naḥălâ* as the "the *male* ancestral estate," for within ancient Israel's system of patrilineal descent and patrilocal marriage, it is the presence of *male* forebears within a family's tomb that secures the family's claim to their *naḥălâ*. Indeed, not only can a family's *naḥălâ* be described as the *naḥălat 'ĕlōhîm*, or "the ancestral estate"; it can quite specifically be called the *naḥălat 'ābôt*, the "patrimony" or "estate of the *fathers*" (Num 36:3, 8; 1 Kgs 21:3; emphasis mine). Hence the imperative for the "fathers," or the primary males within a patriline, to be buried in a family's tomb, even if considerable efforts are needed to relocate their bodies.[40] Even today, in fact, English speakers refer to such relocations as re*patri*ations, and in doing so they bear witness to a heritage that prioritizes the exhumation, transportation, and reburial of men's remains: Joseph's body according to Exod 13:19 and Josh 24:32; the bones of Saul and Jonathan according to 2 Sam 21:12–14: and also Jacob's body, as Joseph, according to Gen 50:4–14, secures permission from the Egyptian pharaoh to transport Jacob's corpse out of Egypt and take it to Canaan, in order that his father—as Jacob had requested on his deathbed—be buried in his familial homestead, "in the cave in the field at Machpelah ... which Abraham had acquired as a burial site from Ephron the Hittite" (Gen 49:30; 50:13).

Yet the same imperative to repatriate a corpse to a family tomb does not seem to have been as urgently felt for women. Rather, three of the dozen or so accounts found in the Bible regarding women's deaths and/or burials—the interment of Rebekah's nurse Deborah; of Jacob's second wife Rachel; and of Moses's sister Miriam—report that each was buried at the spot where she died. Moreover, each was interred in an individual grave (the Hebrew term for this seems to be *qĕbûrâ*, as opposed to the more usual *qeber*).[41] Thus, Deborah was buried under an oak tree near Bethel (Gen 35:8); Rachel somewhere along the road that ran south from Bethel to Ephrath (Gen 35:16–20); and Miriam at Kadesh, in the wilderness of Zin (Num 20:1).[42] As Bloch-Smith notes, only two other interments of this type are catalogued in the Bible—the burials of Aaron on Mt. Hor (Num 20:28–29; 33:38–39) and of Moses in Moab, near Baal-Peor (Deut 34:5–6),[43] although somewhat analogous are the large eighth-century BCE tomb edifices that various royal affiliates built in Jerusalem's Silwan Valley. Each of these was meant for "the burial of a single person or for a couple, and in one or two cases for three individuals at most."[44] Still, these Silwan tomb edifices are not—as the very name "edifice" implies—extemporized graves that, like those of Deborah, Rachel, Miriam, Aaron, and Moses, were dug expeditiously at the site (and time) of their occupant's death. Rather, the carefully designed and meticulously constructed Silwan tombs are best understood (in my opinion) as a specialized reconceptualization, promulgated within elite circles, of the standard Israelite family tomb.[45] They are thus not to be taken as the sort of aberration in Israelite burial custom reflected in the Bible's accounts of Deborah's, Rachel's, Miriam's, Aaron's, and Moses's impromptu and individual interments.

Indeed, the biblical writers seem to perceive Aaron's and Moses's interments to be so aberrant that they go to great lengths to explain them. In Num 20:2–13, for example, the Bible's Priestly authors (P) describe these burials as the just punishment that God inflicted on Aaron and Moses because Moses, with Aaron at his side, sought to provide drink for the thirsting Israelites by drawing water from a rock through some means (not necessarily clear) that incurred God's wrath. As a result, God decreed that neither Moses nor Aaron would be permitted to enter into the so-called promised land with the rest of the Israelites. Hence, the only option was to bury first Aaron and then Moses in isolated graves outside the land of Canaan. Alternatively, in Deut 1:37, 3:26, and 4:21, Deuteronomic tradition (D) proposes that Moses is condemned to die and be buried in Moab not for any misdeed on his or Aaron's part, but because of Yahweh's general frustrations with the Israelites' wrongdoings, especially the Israelites' refusal to invade Canaan from the south after the spies who were sent forth to investigate that possibility reported the Canaanites to be a gigantic people with cities fortified "up to heaven" (Deut 1:28). The deity seemingly has no patience with such trepidation, so much so that Moses reports in Deut 1:37 that "Even with me, Yahweh was angry on account of you." Thus, Yahweh decrees to Moses regarding the promised land, "You ... shall not enter there," and so Moses must die and be buried on the east bank of the Jordan, at a site overlooking, but not within, Israel's domain.[46]

But these Priestly and Deuteronomic explanations cannot, of course, account for Deborah's, Rachel's, and Miriam's anomalous burials. Moreover, and more important, the biblical authors seem to feel no need to offer some other justification. Is this because according to Israelite tradition, even though men and women were typically buried together in multigenerational family tombs, not all women's burials needed to adhere to this norm? Indeed, in certain cases, it may be that a woman's burial in a multigenerational family tomb was proscribed. In many parts of the world, for example, women who die in childbirth, as did Rachel, are interred, just as was Rachel, in burial sites that isolate the deceased's body from the community's other dead.[47] We might recall, moreover, from Chapter 5, how common childbirth deaths were in ancient times: "the greatest single cause of death among [Mesopotamian] women," according to JoAnn Scurlock,[48] and, according to Carol Meyers, the cause of an average life expectancy for Israelite women of thirty years of age, as opposed to forty years of age for men.[49] Recall as well the 2:1 ratio of males to females that Bloch-Smith reports for Iron Age Israelite cave tombs and the 3:2 ratio of men to women that she reports for Judean bench tomb burials of adults and adolescents.[50] Might women's deaths in childbirth and a subsequent individual interment in an isolated site account for these numbers? Regardless, we might generally conclude that while it seems that the Israelites felt an urgent need to inter the bodies of a family's *patri*line in their ancestral tomb in order to preserve the family's *patri*mony, even if considerable efforts were required to relocate these men's remains, the presence of a family's deceased women in the ancestral tomb was not as critical, and in certain instances, it might be eschewed.[51] Israel's male-dominated social order, to put the matter somewhat more bluntly, persisted even in death.

The Ongoing Existence of the Deceased: Women and Ancient Israelite Mortuary Practices

As I have observed earlier in this chapter, the ancient Israelites understood that deceased persons had an ongoing existence after death. More specifically, ancestral spirits who were properly attended to (through mortuary practices such as regular food and drink offerings, along with other regular actions directed toward or undertaken on behalf of the dead) could remain engaged in the affairs of the living and benefit their descendants from beyond the grave. Yet the male-dominated Israelite social order that I have argued persisted at the time of death also persisted, I argue below, in rituals pertaining to the dead's ongoing life.

Consider in this regard the *tĕrāpîm*/teraphim, which are mentioned in eight texts in the Hebrew Bible (Gen 31:19–35; Judges 17–18; 1 Sam 15:23; 19:11–17; 2 Kgs 23:24; Ezek 21:26 [21:21 in most English translations]; Hos 3:4; and Zech 10:2). To be sure, the proper interpretation of the term *tĕrāpîm* is a matter of some debate, but careful studies by Karel van der

Toorn and Theodore J. Lewis have convincingly demonstrated, in my opinion, that the tĕrāpîm are best understood as representations of a family's deceased ancestors.[52] Accordingly, in a 2012 article, I, along with my co-author, Benjamin D. Cox, proposed that the reason Micah made a tĕrāpîm in Judg 17:5 was because his father had recently died, and Micah appropriately responds by manufacturing a representation of this newly deceased member of his family's progenitors.[53] Micah's newly manufactured tĕrāpîm, Cox and I further argued, then became part of a larger collection of Micah's family's tĕrāpîm. Bolstering this interpretation is the fact that the Hebrew term tĕrāpîm, though formally marked as a plural through use of the masculine collective ending -îm, can in fact have both a singular and plural meaning. Rachel sits atop multiple tĕrāpîm according to Gen 31:34, for example, whereas David's wife Michal puts a lone tĕrāpîm in David's bed in 1 Sam 19:13 to serve as a doppelgänger for her fugitive husband.[54] Similarly Cox and I suggested that Micah is to be understood as manufacturing a lone tĕrāpîm in Judg 17:5, representing his recently deceased father, which he then housed among the collection of multiple tĕrāpîm, or ancestor figurines, that his family had amassed over the years.[55]

But would this larger collection of Micah's family's tĕrāpîm have included tĕrāpîm of, say, Micah's dead grandmother, or great aunt, or other deceased *women* among his ancestors? (Micah's mother, according to the conceit of the Judges 17–18 story, is still very much alive; see Chapter 8.) Some scholars—most recently, Manfred Görg and Karel J. H. Vriezen—have argued that tĕrāpîm figurines would have included female images. Indeed, Görg maintains that *all* tĕrāpîm figurines were female. But this is because Görg interprets the term tĕrāpîm to refer to an Egyptian goddess Repit, who was worshipped in Egypt as a mother goddess in the same sorts of private and family cults that texts such as Gen 31:19–35; Judges 17–18; and 1 Sam 19:11–17 presume as the locus for Israelite tĕrāpîm.[56] Vriezen somewhat similarly suggests that the so-called Judean pillar figurines (JPFs) that I discussed in Chapter 7 and that are found frequently in Israelite archaeological excavations (especially at sites from eighth- and seventh-century BCE Judah) are to be taken as "a symbol of the goddess who cares, nourishes, and brings prosperity" and that "it is likely these objects may be related to the teraphim."[57] In making this claim, Vriezen echoes older theories of William F. Albright (the "biblical writers seem to have included" various goddess figurines known from the archaeological record "under the general head of *teraphîm*"); John Gray ("possibly the many figurines with the features of Ashera and Astarte found at Palestinian sites . . . rank as *tᵉrāpīm*"); and Herbert G. May ("it is extremely probable that sometimes the term *tᵉrāphîm*" was used to designate "mother-goddesses and other fertility figurines").⁵⁸

But how to interpret the JPFs, as I noted in Chapter 7, is not necessarily clear. Moreover, I suggested they have a function that is rather different from Vriezen's understanding. More important, neither Görg nor Vriezen engages with the research I cited above that sees the *tĕrāpîm* as ancestor figurines. Thus, neither Görg nor Vriezen claims that the female figurines he associates with the *tĕrāpîm* are representations of female *ancestors*. My suspicion, however, is that once we embrace the identification of the *tĕrāpîm* as representations of a family's deceased ancestors, we should set aside any conviction that these ancestor figurines could have included females. Rather, I propose that just as Israelite burial tradition asserted that a family's male ancestors should be buried in a family's tomb, whereas normal burial practices could be suspended when necessary for women, so too did customs concerning a family's *tĕrāpîm* pertain exclusively (or at least primarily) to the male ancestral line.⁵⁹ In a recent study of family and household religion, Rüdiger Schmitt reaches a similar conclusion: the "*tĕrāpîm* are perhaps best understood as (male) figurines used in the context of domestic and familial religion."⁶⁰

In addition, if biblical genealogies are any guide, women are normally absent from the genealogical lists that, according to Abraham Malamat, were used during the periodic mortuary rites performed to "invoke the names of dead ancestors."⁶¹ In her 2020 monograph *Caring for the Dead in Ancient Israel*, Kerry M. Sonia adds that the institution of levirate marriage as described in Deut 25:5–6 is similarly concerned only with commemorating a deceased male's name. More specifically, Deut 25:5–6 requires that a woman whose husband has died without fathering a son marry the dead man's brother, in the hopes that she will bear a son who will be named for her deceased husband. Thus the husband's name need not be "wiped out in Israel."⁶²

To be sure, 2 Kgs 9:37 presumes that had Jezebel been given a proper burial and been the subject of the mortuary rituals that Jehu (fruitlessly) commanded she was owed, her name—through the utterance "This is Jezebel"—would have been appropriately invoked and remembered after her death. Likewise, according to Gen 35:20, Jacob erects a memorial or commemorative stele—a *maṣṣēbâ*—at Rachel's grave that can be understood as functioning perpetually to evoke her name, just as the etymologically kindred *maṣṣebet* erected in 2 Sam 18:18 by Absalom was to be the means by which his name would be remembered perpetually after his death. Nevertheless, the fact that two of the other Hebrew terms used to describe the stele that seemingly invoked a dead ancestor's name—*zikkārôn* and *yād* (1 Sam 15:12; 2 Sam 18:18; Isa 56:5; 57:8)—are tied etymologically to the terms for male (*zākār*) and (euphemistically) phallus (*yād*) may suggest that, much like the Bible's prevailing tendency to evoke men's names in genealogical lists and like the Deut 25:5–6 dictum that perpetuates men's names through the institution of levirate marriage, the memorial stele that were erected as part of Israelite mortuary practice functioned primarily to commemorate the names of deceased *males*.[63]

Indeed, as Karel van der Toorn states, all the rites enacted as part of ancient Israelite mortuary practice—by which he means, among other things, the periodic provisioning of the deceased with food and drink offerings; the manufacture and use of *tĕrāpîm*; and the commemoration and regular invocation of the deceased through pronouncing their names—were "addressed predominantly to male ancestors."[64] Van der Toorn supports this conclusion by taking a careful look at both Israelite and comparative evidence. With regard to comparative evidence, he cites Old Babylonian materials (ca. 1894–1595 BCE): for example, a prayer to the moon god that "enumerates the names of the dead addressed by the living."[65] Women are included in this list of ancestors and are invited alongside their male counterparts to partake of the food and drink offerings that, according to mortuary ritual, should be provided to the deceased. Some women, moreover, are explicitly cited by name.[66] These include two of the male ancestors' wives and five *nadītu* women (women from elite families who were dedicated to some god and who, as part of their service to the god, practiced sexual chastity).[67] Still, these women "are mentioned only as 'wife of' one of the [male] ancestors, or . . . as 'daughter' of an ancestor." In fact, in both this prayer to the moon god that van der Toorn examines and in kindred incantations, women are often *only* the "wife of"; they are not given a name.[68] Somewhat similarly, in the so-called Genealogy of the Hammurapi Dynasty, while deceased women from Hammurapi's lineage are included in the list of those who are invited to share in the food and drink offerings made to the dead, these women are identified only as "the daughters of kings" (as opposed to the twenty-eight male ancestors that this text carefully lists by name).[69] Within Old

Babylonian tradition, van der Toorn concludes that "women were apparently not regarded as ancestors themselves."⁷⁰

In considering Israelite evidence, van der Toorn also turns to names, more specifically, to the so-called theophoric names from ancient Israelite tradition. These include names that have within them terms such as *'āb*, "father," *'āḥ*, "brother," and *'am*, meaning something like "paternal uncle." Most typically, these names' kinship terms have been taken as references to a god (Greek *theos*; hence the names' common designation as "theophoric") that their bearer and/or the name's bestower were thought to have worshipped. For example, an Israelite such as Abiel, a name that means "My father [*'ābî*] is *'ēl*," is understood to have come from a family that worshipped Israel's god, or *'ēl* (Yahweh), as a divine *'āb*, or father. Van der Toorn suggests, however, that these names' kinship terms should be taken not as references to some metaphorical familiarity with a deity, but much more literally: as references to deceased ancestors who have been deified upon their demise. Abiel thus refers to "my [ancestral] father" who is (or, more specifically, has become upon his death) a deified spirit known as an *'ēl* or an *'ĕlōhîm*.⁷¹

As van der Toorn explains, his hypothesis—that "the gods referred to in these theophoric names are not gods in the usual sense of the term, but deified ancestors"—accounts well for the fact that the names in question can use kinship terms such as *'āḥ*, "brother," and *'am*, "paternal uncle," which otherwise are not epithets used of known divinities. More important for my purposes, however: "the interpretation of the theophoric kinship names" as evidence of a mortuary cult of the ancestors reveals that "the cult was addressed to male ancestors only."⁷² This is because all the kinship terms used in the names in question are *male* in their referent (such as the previously cited terms *'āb*, "father," *'āḥ*, "brother," and *'am*, "paternal uncle," and also terms such as *dôd*, "father's senior brother"). Conversely, van der Toorn writes, "in Hebrew anthroponymics there is not one feminine kinship term used as a theophoric element." Once more, van der Toorn concludes, "The ancestor cult was apparently concerned primarily with patrilineal ancestors."⁷³

Above, I reached this same conclusion by looking at men's burials in relation to women's; at traditions concerning the manufacture of male, but not female, ancestral figurines (*tĕrāpîm*); and at mortuary practices that commemorate deceased males' but not females' names. Again, that is, our evidence suggests that Israel's male-dominated social order persisted not only in death but afterwards, in the ongoing life of the deceased.

Death as a Women's Life-Cycle Ritual

Death is, of course, the last life-cycle event in the human life course; death has, moreover, been considered by some to be the life-cycle ritual *par excellence*, as it is suggested that all other life-cycles rites are ultimately derived from funerary and mortuary customs.[74] Yet even if such a claim overstates, it nevertheless can be argued that ancient Israelite funerary rites and mortuary practices correspond particularly well to the definition of life-cycle rituals, or rites of passage, originally advanced by Arnold van Gennep. For example, as Matthew J. Suriano points out in his book *A History of Death in the Hebrew Bible*, death in ancient Israel—in contrast to, say, later Christian concepts of heaven and hell— did not involve "the migration of an immortal soul to some otherworldly destination." Rather, "the transition of the dead . . . was not a question of place . . . but of status . . . the status of *ancestor*."[75] Likewise, Karel van der Toorn writes. "In the eyes of the ancients, death was not the end but a transition to another state of being."[76] So too did van Gennep define rites of passage to be about transitions in state or status: "ceremonies whose essential purpose is to enable the individual to pass from one defined position to another which is equally well defined."[77]

Previously, moreover, I quoted Francesca Stavrakopoulou's observation that an ancient Israelite's transition to the status of ancestor is enabled by proper burial in a family's ancestral tomb: in her words, "interment in the family tomb on ancestral land facilitated the transition of the dead . . . and manifested the integration of the individual into the realm of the ancestors."[78] Note, however, the sense of process implied by Stavrakopoulou's term "facilitate," for as Suriano, among others, has convincingly argued, the initial act of interment is not enough to effect ancestor status in and of itself. Rather, the deceased's full transition to the ancestral state is coordinate with, and dependent on, the gradual transition of the corpse inside the tomb, as can especially be seen in examining the standard Judean bench tomb of the eighth-sixth centuries BCE (see again Fig. 9.1). More specifically, the architecture of a Judean bench tomb is designed so that the body of a newly deceased individual is first laid out on one of the waist-high benches that lined the side and back walls of the tomb. Indeed, these benches can feature stone headrests, often shaped like a horseshoe for cradling the deceased's head. In conjunction with remains from a few tombs where a body still rests atop a bench, this architectural feature allows us to determine that newly interred corpses were placed on a tomb's benches in a supine position.[79] Then, as the corpse lies on a bench after being interred, it, obviously, begins to decompose, until only the skeleton remains. Yet if the tomb is to fulfill its function as a family's multigenerational burial place, this excarnated skeleton cannot rest on a bench forever (notwithstanding the few exceptions referred to just above of skeletons that archaeologists have found *in situ*). Rather, the bench will sooner or later need to be cleared so that it can accommodate the body of some more recently deceased family member.

Bench tombs thus typically included, in addition to their burial benches, a repository: "a separate area for the secondary disposal of the dead . . . a pit, a unit carved under a bench like a crawl space, or a specific place on the floor."[80] At some point, a skeleton's bones were gathered up from the bench on which the corpse had originally been laid and were placed in this repository in an act of a secondary burial, which can be defined as "the regular and socially sanctioned removal of the relics of some or all deceased persons from a place of temporary storage to a permanent resting place."[81] Within the repository, the skeleton's disarticulated bones are intermingled with the disarticulated bones of older skeletons. The number of skeletons represented in any given tomb generally ranges from fifteen to one hundred, although in a study of secondary mortuary practice in Israel, James F. Osborne reports that some repositories (for example, Tomb 4012 at Akhzib) have remains from as many as three hundred and fifty skeletons.[82] Osborne also notes that while repositories are not necessarily found in all bench tombs, especially in these tombs' earlier manifestations, secondary burial was nevertheless practiced: disarticulated skeletons can be deliberately piled on the floor, for example.[83]

Osborne in addition points out that secondary burial is hardly a phenomenon unique to Israel.[84] Rather, secondary burial is well attested cross-culturally, as famously documented in a foundational study by the French sociologist of religion Robert Hertz, "Contribution à une etude sur la representation collective de la mort" ("A Contribution to the Study of the Collective Representation of Death"), published in 1907.[85] Hertz, moreover, sought not only to document but to offer a theoretical model concerning secondary burials, which he described as the culmination of a process that moved an individual from being a living member within a society to the status of deceased ancestor by way of an intermediate phase. This intermediate phase corresponded, Hertz further argued, to the period in which a newly buried corpse decomposed, or in which, we might say, the body was "betwixt and between" its original position as a living being and its final position as a fully excarnated skeleton. In other words, as my evocation of Victor Turner's catchphrase regarding liminality might suggest,[86] we can follow the lead of multiple scholars in understanding Hertz to have anticipated—or even to have inspired—his French contemporary Arnold van Gennep. According to Hertz, that is, mortuary traditions that depend on secondary burials follow a tripartite pattern analogous to the tripartite model that van Gennep suggested in 1909 characterized all rites of passage.[87]

More specifically, we might understand the sequence of primary and then secondary burial in Israelite tradition to reflect (1) separation, at the moment of an individual's biological death, from "an earlier fixed point in the social structure or from an earlier set of social conditions" (that is, separation from the subject's earlier social state as a living being); (2) a transition, or threshold, or liminal period, corresponding to the time of the corpse's decomposition after it has been interred, "when the state of the ritual subject is ambiguous: he is no longer in the old state and has not yet reached the new one"; and (3) the stage of (re)incorporation, (re)integration, or (re)aggregation, "when the ritual subject enters a new, stable state with its own rights and obligations."[88] This would be the deceased's assumption of the state or status of ancestor that is achieved once the skeleton is fully free of decaying flesh. It is at that point, as Suriano observes, that the individual identity of the interred has been "almost literally" broken down (into a disarticulated skeleton) in order that a new "group identity" can be adopted: membership in the family's multigenerational ancestral community.[89] In the typical bench tomb, the deceased's incorporation, integration, or aggregation into this ancestral collective is realized when the excarnated skeleton's bones are deposited among the bones of the deceased's forebears in the tomb's repository.[90]

Indeed, Hertz writes that because every skeleton "is similar to those of its ancestors,"[91] a family's skeletons are easily able to be amalgamated into what Suriano calls "an aggregate of ancestors."[92] Under the terms of such an analysis, we might imagine that the transition of Israelite women to the status of ancestor—or at least the status transition of women who (unlike, say, Deborah, Rachel, and Miriam) are accorded a normative Israelite burial in a multigenerational family tomb—would be no different from that of men's. Indeed, the fact that, excepting the bones of the pelvic cavity, bones from male and female skeletons cannot easily be distinguished could suggest that, as Israelite women's bones were gathered into a bench tomb's repository alongside Israelite men's, deceased Israelite women were conjoined with a family's deceased forebears and so were assimilated—just as were deceased Israelite men—into the family's ancestral collective.

Nevertheless, as we have seen earlier in this chapter, there is much that should give us pause about this proposition. We should also be given pause by certain biblical turns of phrase that describe burial within a family tomb. For example, although biblical tradition understands Abraham to have been buried alongside Sarah when he died and ultimately alongside other women from his family (Rebekah and Leah) in a multigenerational family tomb (Gen 23:19; 25:9–10; 49:31), God, when speaking to Abraham (then Abram) about his death in Gen 15:15, tells him that at the time of his demise, he will go to his "fathers" (*'ābôt*). Likewise, in Gen 47:30 and 49:29, Jacob—even though he is, like Abraham, to be buried alongside Sarah, Rebekah, and Leah—speaks of his wish to be buried with his "fathers" (*'ābôt*).

Note as well that the standard idiom regarding death, "to be gathered to one's people," is used only of men (Abraham, Ishmael, Isaac, Jacob, Aaron, and Moses).[93] Moreover, the term "people" (*'ām*), even though it might suggest to English speakers that Abraham, Ishmael, Isaac, et al., are to be gathered into a gender-inclusive ancestral community, often refers in Hebrew to all-male cohorts. In Exod 19:15, for example, Moses commands "the people" (*hā'ām*) not to "go near a woman"; in Jer 44:24, Jeremiah speaks to "all the people [*kol-hā'ām*] and all the women"; and in Gen 14:16, Abram (Abraham), upon defeating the kings who have taken his nephew Lot captive, returns Lot to his home in Sodom along with Sodom's "women and people" (*hā'ām*). Similarly, Gen 26:10 and Num 25:1 refer to the "people" (*'ām*) engaging with various women in what is surely to be understood as heterosexual intercourse. Further, in Josh 5:5, it is explained that the mass circumcision that takes place in 5:8 is necessary because, while all the "people" (*'ām*) who came out of Egypt were circumcised, the "people" (*'ām*) born in the Sinai wilderness had never undergone this procedure.[94] That the phrase "to be gathered one's fathers" (*'ābôt*), though less common (Judg 2:10; 2 Kgs 22:20; 2 Chr 34:28), is used as an analog to the idiom "to be gathered to one's people" further implies an Israelite presumption that, in death, it is *men* among the deceased who are gathered into a community of their deceased *male* ancestors. Indeed, if these two idioms, as some have suggested, are "a direct reference to the gathering of disarticulated bones and their placement in the repositories,"[95] each implies that even though the bones of women's skeletons are gathered up and deposited alongside men's within a family tomb's assembly of ancestral remains, it is really only the male bones within that collection that constitute the family's ancestral community.

Similarly, if we follow the suggestion of Abraham Malamat that I noted above—that the Bible's genealogical lists are in effect a roster of a family's ancestral community, used when the ancestors' names are invoked as part of Israelite mortuary practice—then we also see, due to the near absence of women's names in these genealogies, that women are not really considered members of their family's ancestral collective.[96] Moreover, consider yet again ancient Israel's traditions concerning the *tĕrāpîm*/teraphim. Earlier in this chapter, I suggested that the Israelites felt no need to fabricate *tĕrāpîm* images representing deceased women, even as I argued that this undertaking does seem incumbent for deceased men. Here, we can add that the related component of this mortuary practice—housing the *tĕrāpîm* of a newly deceased male together with the other *tĕrāpîm* images of his family's deceased ancestors (see, for example, Judg 17:5; 18:14, 17, 18, 20)—brings the deceased man that the recently manufactured *tĕrāpîm* represents into his community of dead forebears just as profoundly as does a man's being "gathered to one's people" or "one's fathers" in a family tomb. Indeed, the integration of *tĕrāpîm* images of newly deceased males into their family's larger *tĕrāpîm* collection may especially have served to herald men's entry into their family's ancestral community. This is because we have no sense that there was a formal ritual enacted at or in a family tomb to mark a skeleton's secondary burial. Rather, the archaeological evidence suggests that the depositing of skeletal remains in a tomb's repository was performed in a perfunctory and sometimes even careless fashion.[97] Conversely, it seems possible (even probable) that the enshrining of a new *tĕrāpîm* amid a family's larger *tĕrāpîm* collection entailed some sort of ceremony within, at least, the family's home, thereby formally commemorating the entry of the recently deceased male that the new *tĕrāpîm* represents into the company of his forebears. For a deceased woman, though, to be unrepresented within her family's *tĕrāpîm* collection is to emphasize once more that she will not readily be admitted into the corporate community of deceased *male* ancestors.

As Suriano notes, "not every dead person qualifies as an ancestor,"[98] and while he is not speaking here explicitly about women, women are the subject of Karel van der Toorn's quote about women in Old Babylonian tradition that I cited above: "women were apparently not regarded as ancestors themselves."[99] As in Babylon, our analysis over and over suggests, so too in Israel. Indeed, note in this regard that in the two biblical accounts in which a woman seems to come closest to ancestor status, in each case there is a glitch. Although Jacob erects a *maṣṣēbâ* for Rachel that can be understood as functioning perpetually to evoke her name, she is not buried in the sort of multigenerational family tomb designed to facilitate the transition to ancestor status. Jezebel, though designated by Jehu to receive the proper burial and mortuary rites that would bring her into an ancestral collective and sustain her therein, is subject beforehand to the devouring of her corpse that consigns her to postmortem limbo.

Or, we might say, Jezebel is consigned to postmortem liminality, unable to realize (re)incorporation, (re)integration, or (re)aggregation as an ancestor in the afterlife. More generally, the observations I have made above—about the privileging of a male ancestral community in certain biblical idioms and about women's seeming absence, or near absence, within the symbolic community of ancestors catalogued in biblical genealogies and represented by the *tĕrāpîm*—suggests that while Israelite men experienced, through secondary burial and associated mortuary rituals, important moments of (re)incorporation, (re)integration, or (re)aggregation that propelled them into a new identity within the larger community of a family's deceased ancestors, Israelite women did not. Thus while, the deceased males of ancient Israel can enter into "a new stable state with its own rights and obligations,"[100] Israel's deceased women remain, at least to some degree, unincorporated, unintegrated, and unaggregated into their family's ancestral collective—which is to say: they remain, at least to some degree, liminal, and liminal into eternity.[101] This is a particularly excessive form of the exaggerated and exacerbated experience of liminality that I have suggested in earlier chapters of this book typically characterizes women's life-cycle rituals.

In this regard, I am moved to consider Jer 31:15, in which the dead Rachel sings a dirge from her tomb, lamenting the fate of the Israelites who, in the early sixth century BCE, are being taken away into captivity by their Babylonian conquerors. As my co-author Benjamin D. Cox and I have noted in discussing this passage, there is no other biblical text of which we can think where a dead spirit similarly speaks from the grave unbidden.[102] Rather, although biblical tradition admits the possibility that the dead might speak to the living (as in Isa 8:19–20, for example), it indicates that this communication can only be brought about with difficulty, requiring elaborate necromantic rituals. Saul, for example, requires the aid of a medium to summon the ghost of the dead Samuel in order to ask for his advice (1 Sam 28:3–25), and even though Samuel's ghost does appear when summoned by the medium's magic, Samuel responds with reluctance and seems to perceive that his rest has been unduly disturbed. Why, then, might Rachel speak forth from her grave voluntarily, and even after she has been dead, according to the predominant strain within biblical chronology, for at least a thousand years? Is it because she has been left restless and unsettled, unaggregated and unincorporated into the ancestral community of her male peers? Therefore, she lingers among the living to speak in ways that the men who have been (re)incorporated, (re)integrated, and (re)aggregated into their families' ancestral communities do not.

Epilogue

Of Fragments and (W)holes

I am hardly the first biblical scholar who has sought to describe an ancient Israelite woman's life cycle. Indeed, it has been almost four decades since Karel van der Toorn published his groundbreaking monograph on the topic, initially in Dutch in 1987 and then in 1994 in English: *From Her Cradle to Her Grave: The Role of Religion in the Life of the Israelite and the Babylonian Woman*.[1] Those who have followed suit include Jennie R. Ebeling, who in 2010 produced a similar book-length study, *Women's Lives in Biblical Times*, in which she aimed to "reconstruct women's activities and lifecycle events in the Iron Age."[2] Briefer treatments, often concerning both women and men, include the chapter "The Circle of Life" in Erhard S. Gerstenberger and Wolfgang Schrage's 1981 book *Woman and Man*, originally published in German in 1980; Oded Borowski's examination of the Israelite life cycle in his 2003 book *Daily Life in Biblical Times*; Rüdiger Schmitt's 2012 essay, "Rites and Rituals Associated with the Cycle of Human Life"; and Carol Meyers's 2013 remarks in her book *Rediscovering Eve*.[3]

These scholars' works have also anticipated several aspects of my methodological approach. For example, as the subtitle of van der Toorn's study suggests, he makes extensive use of comparative data from the ancient world, as have I, although van der Toorn particularly (albeit not exclusively) focuses on Mesopotamian materials, whereas I have tended to range more broadly across the Near East and eastern Mediterranean. In addition, Ebeling, Borowski, Schmitt, and Meyers make use, as have I, of archaeological data. In fact, since, unlike me, they are all trained archaeologists, they make much more expert use, so much so that Ebeling describes archaeology as being her "primary source."[4] All the scholars I have cited also organize their studies, as have I, by examining life-cycle events one by one in a chronological fashion. Thus, each starts with birth and then moves through various life stages, albeit not necessarily the same life stages I have considered in this book. Van der Toorn, Ebeling, and Gerstenberger and Schrage include accounts of

Maturity, Marriage, Motherhood, Mortality. Susan Ackerman, Oxford University Press.
© Oxford University Press 2025. DOI: 10.1093/9780197809686.003.0012

youth as a life stage, for example, while I do not. Yet while I devote a chapter to death, Schmitt does not address this topic at all, and van der Toorn's and Gerstenberger and Schrage's discussions each comprise little more than a page. These differences are largely due, I submit, to my particular focus: not just the stages of an ancient Israelite woman's life, but specific rituals associated with life-cycle events. For example, while youth, at least as far as I can tell, was a life stage in ancient Israel, it was not marked as a life-cycle event with attendant rituals. Thus, while it is present in van der Toorn's, Ebeling's, and Gerstenberger and Schrage's studies, it is absent in mine. Conversely, I have understood death to be a highly ritualized life-cycle event and so to mandate my thorough consideration.

I have also sought to add to previous scholars' inventories ritual moments in a woman's life cycle that have previously been neglected or have only occasionally been highlighted: for example, the point after giving birth when a mother names her child, and, for some women who live long enough, the chance, come menopause, to exercise a degree of religious and political agency that might not have been previously possible for them. Moreover, and most important: unlike all previous studies, I have sought to put forward an analytical model that explains the distinctive features manifest within women's life-cycle events and their attendant rituals and that accounts for the differences between ancient Israelite women's life-cycle rituals and the way these rituals are experienced by Israelite men. What has resulted are conclusions that in some of my other works on Israelite women, I have characterized as "on the one hand"/"on the other hand."[5] "On the one hand," for example, I have documented occasional moments when women's status seems to be temporarily elevated or enhanced within the course of a life-cycle ritual: at the time when the marriage present is gifted during betrothal rites and at the moment shortly after giving birth when a woman bestows a name on her newborn child. Yet, and "on the other hand," I have drawn attention to several instances where the experiences a woman goes through during a life-cycle ritual have a negative valence: the way women, for example, can be subject to a more exaggerated and exacerbated experience of liminality than is experienced by their male counterparts within a life-cycle ritual's intermediate phase.

In addition, and again "on the one hand": my attempt to chart the events and attendant rituals of an Israelite woman's life cycle has revealed a fuller and richer life course narrative than we find for men. More specifically, we can identify five ritualized events that are part of an Israelite man's life cycle: birth, circumcision/coming of age, betrothal, marriage, and death. But while these life-cycle moments also are part of, or have analogs in, the life cycles of Israelite women, there are, in women's lives, several additional life-cycle events and associated rituals that happen between marriage and death: pregnancy, parturition, and motherhood rituals (I have argued) such as naming and weaning a child. I have also documented life-course changes that, though not ritualized, come for some Israelite women with menopause. Indicated here is the degree to which adult women's bodies have a much more complex biological life than do adult men's bodies: women get pregnant, give birth, lactate, nurse and wean children, and then, those women who live long enough lose, with menopause, the ability to do all these things. Conversely, adult men obviously age, but they retain basically the same bodies that they have had since puberty.

Still (and here begins the "on the other hand" part of this argument): even though the stages we can identify within a woman's life course are more numerous and varied than the life stages we can identify for men, the Bible at several points charts a man's entire life journey from birth to death, whereas we do not have even one "whole life" narrative for women. The parade example for men is perhaps Isaac. The book of Genesis includes an elaborate story of his birth, and especially the events that lead up to it: Sarah's barrenness; her attempt to secure a son for Abraham through Hagar; and God's announcement during the deity's visit to Abraham's tent that Sarah will bear a son after all (Gen 16:1–2; 18:10). Genesis in addition contains an account of Isaac's circumcision, on the eighth day after his birth as per the biblical norm (21:4), but also, I have argued, a tale of a near-death experience that should be associated with older traditions that understand circumcision as a ritual associated with a young man's sexual maturation and readiness for marriage (22:1–19). Shortly thereafter, a long narrative in Genesis 24 describes the events that culminate in Isaac's betrothal and subsequently his wedding (taking Gen 24:67 to be an elliptical statement that documents the moment of Isaac and Rebekah's nuptials). In Gen 35:29, moreover, we read of Isaac's death and burial, including the notice that he was "gathered to his people"—perhaps, as I have noted in Chapter 9, an allusion to the secondary burial that would have taken place at some point significantly after Isaac's original interment.[6]

Although not necessarily recounted in such fulsome form, we can trace the same narrative arc for Isaac's half-brother Ishmael—from conception and birth, through circumcision, to his mother's Hagar securing an Egyptian wife for him, and then death and being gathered to his people (Gen 16:4, 15; 17:25; 21:21; 25:17). This narrative arc more or less repeats itself (minus circumcision) in the biblical account of Isaac's younger son Jacob: conception and birth (Gen 25:21, 26); betrothal (Gen 29:18–20, 27); marriage (Gen 29:22–23, 28, 30); death, burial, and being gathered to his people (Gen 49:33; 50:4–14). The life-cycle events that comprise a man's life story are also fundamentally present, though in an abbreviated form, in the life story of Jacob's eldest son Joseph: conception and birth (Gen 30:23–24), marriage (Gen 41:45), and death and burial (Gen 50:26; Josh 24:32). So too are all these events, plus a seeming reference to circumcision and three renditions of the refrain about being gathered to one's people, marked in the story of Moses (Exod 2:2; 2:21; 4:24–26; Num 27:13; 31:2; Deut 32:50; 34:5–6). We also have accounts of, or at least allusions to, the life-cycle events of conception, birth, marriage, death, and burial in the stories of Samson (Judg 13:5, 7, 24; 14:10–18; 16:30–31), Samuel (1 Sam 1:19–20; 8:2; 25:1), and Solomon (2 Sam 12:24; 1 Kgs 3:1; 11:1–3, 43).

Conversely, in my survey of women's life-cycle events, I have had to jump between multiple biblical texts to capture van der Toorn's "cradle to grave" picture of a woman's life course. For example: while the story of Jephthah's daughter in Judg 11:29–40 illustrated for us traditions regarding an Israelite woman's coming of age, I had to turn to the story of Rebekah in Gen 24:1–67 to illuminate an Israelite woman's experiences at betrothal, and for an account of weddings as a life-cycle event, I was dependent on the story of the Timnite bride in Judg 14:10–18. Sometimes, moreover, I had to make recourse to texts that are not about a woman the Bible takes to be "real": recall in this regard my use of Ezek 16:4, the metaphorical description of baby Jerusalem, personified as female, to describe rituals that were arguably enacted at the time of a girl child's birth. My discussions of the extended ritual complex of motherhood, moreover, as well as my discussion of rituals enacted in association with a woman's death, might best be described as relying on snippets of biblical tradition from here and there: for example, the one-or-two-verse accounts that are scattered through the biblical tradition that describe a mother conferring a name on her child.

In effect, what I have sketched is what J. Cheryl Exum has described as "fragmented women," whereby the stories we find in the Bible regarding women appear only as occasional "fragments" interspersed within the larger biblical story of men.[7] While "on the one hand," that is, women's life stories are richer and fuller than men's in terms of the life-cycle events and attendant rituals that comprise a woman's life course, the biblical record, "on the other hand," marginalizes those stories, so that we see ancient Israelite women's life cycles only in pieces.

Nevertheless, it is my hope that in this book, by pulling together some of these pieces, I have provided a larger picture of Israelite women's life-cycle events and the rituals associated with them than the biblical text might initially seem to present. It is also my hope that I have provided a theoretical model that explains the distinctive features of these life-cycle events and rituals.

Notes

Prologue

1. Austen, *Pride and Prejudice*, 1.
2. Austen, *Pride and Prejudice*, 1.
3. Schorer, "Pride Unprejudiced," 82.
4. Deresiewicz, "Community and Cognition in *Pride and Prejudice*," 503.
5. Austen, *Pride and Prejudice*, 18.
6. Austen, *Pride and Prejudice*, 141.
7. Knuth, "Sisterhood and Friendship in *Pride and Prejudice*," 99.
8. Austen, *Pride and Prejudice*, 105.
9. Austen, *Pride and Prejudice*, 95.
10. Gilchrist, "Archaeological Biographies," 326.
11. C. Bell, *Ritual*, 94.
12. Carsten, "The Process of Childbirth," 29, as cited in Kamionkowski, *Gender Reversal and Cosmic Chaos*, 98.
13. This has been documented by multiple scholars, including, recently, Dasen, "Childbirth and Infancy," 303; Garland, "Children in Athenian Religion," 209; Laes, "Infants between Biological and Social Birth," 366–68; and Liston and Rotroff, "Babies in the Well," 77.
14. Tappy, "Did the Dead Ever Die in Biblical Judah?," 59–68.
15. Van Gennep, *Rites of Passage*, 65; Gilchrist, *Gender and Archaeology*, 96.
16. La Fontaine, "Ritualization of Women's Life-Crises in Bugisu," 159, 173.
17. Lutkehaus, "Gender Metaphors," 197; Swift, *Malay Peasant Society in Jelebu*, 124.
18. I have not been able to identify the precise dates of Crapanzano's fieldwork in Morocco. In his memoir *Recapitulations*, 124, he reports being present for a boy's circumcision in a "forlorn Moroccan village in the fall of 1968." In "Rite of Return," 15–16, n. 1, he reports that he first presented the results of his research on Moroccan circumcision rituals at the American Anthropological Association meetings in 1975.
19. Crapanzano, "Rite of Return," 32; this quote was drawn to my attention by C. Bell, *Ritual*, 57.
20. C. Bell, *Ritual*, 57; Crapanzano, "Rite of Return," 32; Grimes, *Deeply into the Bone*, 99.
21. A good summary within biblical scholarship of the ways marriage can vary widely across cultures, even as every society has some system of marriage, can be found in Southwood, *Marriage by Capture*, 55–61.

Introduction

1. Van Gennep, *Rites of Passage*, as paraphrased in V. Turner, "Betwixt and Between," 94.
2. Kertzer, "Introduction," xvii; Thomassen, *Liminality and the Modern*, 2.
3. Van Gennep, *Rites of Passage*, 2–3.
4. Van Gennep, *Rites of Passage*, 3.
5. Deflem, "Ritual, Anti-Structure, and Religion," 7–8, paraphrasing V. Turner, "Betwixt and Between," 94.
6. Van Gennep, *Rites of Passage*, 43–44.
7. Van Gennep, *Rites of Passage*, 44.

8. Van Gennep has been badly misunderstood on this point: originally, shortly after the publication of *Les rites de passgae* by the noted French sociologist Marcel Mauss, who accused van Gennep of forcing his "law" of rites of passage "into a principle that governs all religious representations" (Mauss, "Review of A. Van Gennep," 200–202, as discussed by Thomassen, *Liminality and the Modern*, 60); more recently, by ritual theorist Ronald L. Grimes, who, like Mauss (albeit without acknowledgment), criticizes van Gennep for applying his tripartite rites-of-passage structure as if it were a "law," "imposed rather than discovered in the texts" (Grimes, *Deeply into the Bone*, 107). For rebuttals, see Belmont, *Arnold Van Gennep*, 62; Kertzer, "Introduction," xxii; and Thomassen, *Liminality and the Modern*, 60–62.
9. Van Gennep, *Rites of Passage*, 11, with commentary in Belmont, *Arnold Van Gennep*, 60; Kertzer, "Introduction," xviii–xix; and Kimball, "Introduction," viii.
10. Kertzer, "Introduction," xviii, drawing on van Gennep's comments in *Rites of Passage*, 11–12.
11. C. Bell, *Ritual*, 36.
12. Van Gennep, *Rites of Passage*, 3, 191.
13. V. Turner, "Betwixt and Between," originally published in 1964 in *Symposium on New Approaches to the Study of Religion*, 4–20; republished with minor revisions in 1967 in V. Turner, *Forest of Symbols*, 93–111. All citations herein come from the 1967 publication.
14. V. Turner, "Betwixt and Between," 96–97.
15. V. Turner, "Betwixt and Between," 95, 98.
16. V. Turner, "Betwixt and Between," 99–100.
17. V. Turner, "Betwixt and Between," 96–97.
18. V. Turner, "Betwixt and Between," 96, 99.
19. V. Turner, "Betwixt and Between," 101–2.
20. V. Turner, "Betwixt and Between," 99–100.
21. Above, n. 13.
22. V. Turner, "Liminality and Communitas," 94–130.
23. These descriptions come from, respectively, Leach, "Anthropological Approaches to the Study of the Bible," 24, and Bynum, "Women's Stories, Women's Symbols," at p. 107 in the original 1984 publication in *Anthropology and the Study of Religion*, and at p. 30 in the 1991 republication of this essay in Bynum, *Fragmentation and Redemption*. All citations to Bynum's essay that follow are from the 1991 printing.
24. V. Turner, "Liminality and Communitas," 96.
25. V. Turner, "Liminality and Communitas," 107.
26. V. Turner, "Liminality and Communitas," 107.
27. V. Turner, "Liminality and Communitas," 110.
28. V. Turner, "Liminality and Communitas," 112.
29. Above, n. 23.
30. V. Turner, "Liminality and Communitas," 95.
31. Lincoln, *Emerging from the Chrysalis*, 102.
32. I have suggested other ways in which ancient Israelite women manifest many of the features of liminality identified by Turner in Ackerman, *Women and the Religion of Ancient Israel*, 270–72.
33. Bynum, "Women's Stories, Women's Symbols," 33, citing V. Turner, "Liminality and Communitas," 99–105, and idem, "Frame, Flow, and Reflection," 104–5.
34. Deflem, "Ritual, Anti-Structure, and Religion," 2, reports that Turner's fieldwork was conducted from December 1950 to February 1952 and from May 1953 to June 1954.
35. V. Turner, "Liminality and Communitas," 101–2.
36. V. Turner, "Liminality and Communitas," 101.
37. V. Turner, "Liminality and Communitas," 99.
38. V. Turner, "Liminality and Communitas," 99–100.
39. Davis, "Reasons of Misrule," 97–123, and eadem, "Women on Top," 124–51.
40. V. Turner, "Frame, Flow, and Reflection," 104–5. On Turner's notion of liminality as a time associated with the "subjunctive mood" of a culture, see V. Turner, "Are There Universals of Performance?," 295.
41. Bynum, "Women's Stories, Women's Symbols," 33.
42. Douglas, "Victor Turner, 1920–1983."
43. https://sha.americananthro.org/victor-turner-prize-in-ethnographic-writing.
44. Bynum, "Women's Stories, Women's Symbols," 33.
45. V. Turner, *Drums of Affliction*, 55–56.

46. V. Turner, "Nkang'a: Part One," 198–239, and idem, "Nkang'a: Part Two," 240–68.
47. V. Turner, *Schism and Continuity*, 292. The two other life-cycle rituals that, according to Turner, are of greatest import among the Ndembu are the circumcisions of young boys and funeral rituals.
48. V. Turner, "Nkang'a: Part One," 199–200.
49. E. Turner, "Prologue: From the Ndembu to Broadway," 1.
50. E. Turner, "Girl into Woman," 27–32; eadem, "Zambia's Kankanga Dances," 57–71; eadem, *Spirit and the Drum*, 58–87.
51. V. Turner, "Nkang'a: Part One," 201.
52. V. Turner, "Nkang'a: Part One," 200.
53. V. Turner, *Schism and Continuity*, 53.
54. V. Turner, "Nkang'a: Part One," 200.
55. V. Turner, "Nkang'a: Part One," 201; idem, "Nkang'a: Part Two," 260.
56. E. Turner, "Girl into Woman," 27; eadem, *Spirit and the Drum*, 59.
57. V. Turner, "Nkang'a: Part One," 212; see similarly E. Turner, "Girl into Woman," 29; eadem, *Spirit and the Drum*, 70.
58. E. Turner, "Girl into Woman," 27.
59. V. Turner, "Nkang'a: Part One," 212–13, 216–21; E. Turner, "Girl into Woman," 27–28; eadem, "Zambia's Kankanga Dances," 58–59; eadem, *Spirit and the Drum*, 59–63, 65–69.
60. V. Turner, "Nkang'a: Part One," 222.
61. V. Turner, "Nkang'a: Part One," 222; E. Turner, "Girl into Woman," 28; eadem, *Spirit and the Drum*, 65.
62. E. Turner, "Girl into Woman," 29–30; see similarly eadem, "Zambia's Kankanga Dances," 60; eadem, *Spirit and the Drum*, 70, 75.
63. E. Turner, "Girl into Woman," 27; eadem, *Spirit and the Drum*, 60; V. Turner, "Nkang'a: Part One," 213; see similarly idem, *Drums of Affliction*, 17.
64. V. Turner, "Nkang'a: Part One," 211; idem, "Nkang'a: Part Two," 240–41.
65. V. Turner, "Nkang'a: Part Two," 242.
66. E. Turner, "Girl into Woman," passim; eadem, "Zambia's Kankanga Dances," passim; eadem, *Spirit and the Drum*, passim.
67. V. Turner, "Nkang'a: Part Two," 240.
68. V. Turner, "Nkang'a: Part Two," 243–45.
69. According to Deflem, "Ritual, Anti-Structure, and Religion," 7, Turner read van Gennep's *Rites of Passage* and then wrote his foundational "Betwixt and Between" essay in 1963, when he was back in the United Kingdom after his 1961–62 residency at the Center for Advanced Studies in the Behavioral Sciences had ended and before he was able—because of delays caused by visa problems—to return the United States to take up the professorship he had been offered at Cornell. Nevertheless, Turner registers familiarity with van Gennep's work somewhat earlier: e.g., in his 1962 essay "Three Symbols of *Passage*," 124–25, that, not insignificantly, appeared in a volume dedicated "To the Memory of Arnold Van Gennep" and that began with an essay titled "Les Rites de Passage" by Turner's graduate school mentor Max Gluckman.
70. Above, n. 5.
71. V. Turner, "Nkang'a: Part One," 201, 222; idem, "Nkang'a: Part Two," 249. On seclusion as a feature of liminality, see, as above, van Gennep's description of the multiday seclusion imposed on a newly delivered mother in Hopi tradition (*Rites of Passage*, 43–44) and V. Turner, "Betwixt and Between," 98, as cited in n. 15.
72. E. Turner, "Girl into Woman," 28.
73. V. Turner, "Betwixt and Between," 98.
74. V. Turner, "Liminality and Communitas," 106.
75. V. Turner, "Nkang'a: Part One," 222.
76. E. Turner, "Girl into Woman," 28; eadem, *Spirit and the Drum*, 65.
77. V. Turner, "Betwixt and Between," 96–97.
78. E. Turner, "Girl into Woman," 29; eadem, *Spirit and the Drum*, 70.
79. V. Turner, "Nkang'a: Part Two," 244.
80. V. Turner, "Betwixt and Between," 99.
81. V. Turner, "Nkang'a: Part Two," 248–49.
82. V. Turner, "Betwixt and Between," 102.

83. V. Turner, "Nkang'a: Part Two," 246–48; E. Turner, "Girl into Woman," 30; eadem, *Spirit and the Drum*, 75.
84. E. Turner, "Girl into Woman," 27; eadem, *Spirit and the Drum*, 59.
85. V. Turner, "Liminality and Communitas," 106.
86. Van Gennep, *Rites of Passage*, 3.
87. Cheung, *Women's Ritual in China: Jiezhu*, 257.
88. Northup, "Pass-Aging Women," 4.
89. Northup, "Pass-Aging Women," 5.
90. Northup, "Pass-Aging Women," 3.
91. Northup, "Pass-Aging Women," 9.
92. Meskell, "Cycles of Life and Death," 425.
93. Gilchrist, "Archaeology and the Life Course," 144. Note that this article appeared in a volume that Meskell co-edited; note also that Gilchrist authored the introductory essay in the special issue of *World Archaeology* in which Meskell's 2000 article, "Cycles of Life and Death" (above, n. 92), was published. These data suggest, as I have here, Meskell's and Gilchrist's intellectual concord regarding the concept of the "lifecycle" or the "life course."
94. See, e.g., Gilchrist, *Medieval Life*, 91–97, 181–89.
95. Gilchrist, *Medieval Life*, 91–92, 94, and 96.
96. Gilchrist, *Medieval Life*, 91–92.
97. See Meskell, "Cycles of Life and Death," 438, regarding eadem, *Private Life in New Kingdom Egypt*.
98. Meskell, *Private Life in New Kingdom Egypt*, 87–88.
99. Meskell, *Private Life in New Kingdom Egypt*, 182.
100. Meskell, *Private Life in New Kingdom Egypt*, 182–83.
101. Meskell, *Private Life in New Kingdom Egypt*, 188.
102. Meskell, "Cycles of Life and Death," 425, 434, 438.
103. Lincoln, *Emerging from the Chrysalis*, 101.
104. V. Turner, "Nkang'a: Part One," 204, 209, 211–12, 221, 230; idem, "Nkang'a: Part Two," 240–41, 243, 248, 252, 254, 257, 259.
105. V. Turner, "Three Symbols of *Passage*," 124; see also idem, "*Mukanda*: The Rite of Circumcision," 151.
106. V. Turner, "*Mukanda*: The Rite of Circumcision," 151–279.
107. V. Turner, "*Mukanda*: The Rite of Circumcision," 152, quoting White, "Notes on the Circumcision Rites of the Balovale Tribes," 42.
108. V. Turner, *Forest of Symbols*, 68, quoting Vergiat, *Les Rites Secrets des Primatifs de l'Oubangui*, 92.
109. V. Turner, "Nkang'a: Part One," 212; idem, *Forest of Symbols*, 52, 72.
110. V. Turner, "*Mukanda*: The Rite of Circumcision," 187.
111. V. Turner, "*Mukanda*: The Rite of Circumcision," 223; note also ibid., 152, quoting White, "Notes on the Circumcision Rites of the Balovale Tribes," 42.
112. V. Turner, "Nkang'a: Part One," 201; idem, "*Mukanda*: The Rite of Circumcision," 187.
113. V. Turner, "Nkang'a: Part One," 204.
114. Douglas, *Purity and Danger*, 96.
115. Turner does register this difference, in *The Forest of Symbols*, 7–8, but, quoting a Ndembu woman, he offers an economic reason to account for it: "If many girls and their instructress were away for a long time, who would work in the gardens, fetch water and cook for the men?" Conversely, since men "spent most of their time in irregular hunting and shooting, their withdrawal in large numbers from economic activities would not produce such a marked effect." Turner goes on, however, to express some reservations about this economic account, since the two rituals of *Nkang'a* and *Mukanda* do not have a similar economic focus. In Turner's words, "the main theme of *Mukanda*" is "productive activity" (e.g., hunting), while that of *Nkang'a* is "reproductive activity." Indeed, he remarks that "women's economic activity," although "essential to the existence of the community, is hardly ritualized at all." This suggests (to me) that using an economic explanation to account for differences in the *Nkang'a* and *Mukanda* rituals misses the mark.
116. V. Turner, "Nkang'a: Part Two," 245–49; E. Turner, "Girl into Woman," 30; eadem, *Spirit and the Drum*, 75.
117. V. Turner, *Drums of Affliction*, 12.

118. E. Turner, *Spirit and the Drum*, 33. Because *Mukanda* happens only infrequently, Victor Turner reports that he "observed only one complete performance" of the rite during his time among the Ndembu (V. Turner, "*Mukanda*: The Rite of Circumcision," 154), whereas he writes, in *The Ritual Process*, 7, that "from the beginning of my stay among the Ndembu, I ... attended ... frequent performances of the girls' puberty rites (*Nkang'a*)."
119. V. Turner, "*Mukanda*: The Rite of Circumcision," 188; idem, *Drums of Affliction*, 12.
120. V. Turner, "Betwixt and Between," 100.
121. V. Turner, "*Mukanda*: The Rite of Circumcision," 233; there, Turner calls those who supervise the circumcision lodge "guardians." In idem, *Drums of Affliction*, 12, he refers to them as "shepherds."
122. V. Turner, "*Mukanda*: The Rite of Circumcision," 208.
123. V. Turner, "*Mukanda*: The Rite of Circumcision," 217.
124. V. Turner, *Forest of Symbols*, 24; idem, "Nkang'a: Part Two," 210, 218–19, 248.
125. V. Turner, "Nkang'a: Part One," 208–9.
126. V. Turner, "*Mukanda*: The Rite of Circumcision," 226, 236.
127. Above, n. 33.
128. The Ndembu situation, moreover, is hardly unique: the anthropologist Paul B. Roscoe, writing of initiation, notes that "about three times as many societies practice group rites for males as practice them for females" ("'Initiation' in Cross-Cultural Perspective," 227). Gilchrist, *Gender and Archaeology*, 95, makes a similar observation.
129. V. Turner, "*Mukanda*: The Rite of Circumcision," 192, 268; idem, "Three Symbols of *Passage*," 160.
130. C. Bell, *Ritual*, 54, citing V. Turner, "*Mukanda*: The Rite of Circumcision," 192; see also ibid., 153–54, and idem, "Three Symbols of *Passage*," 161.
131. V. Turner, "*Mukanda*: The Rite of Circumcision," 193, 216; see also ibid., 188, on the *Kajika*.
132. V. Turner, "*Mukanda*: The Rite of Circumcision," 153–54, 268.
133. V. Turner, "Three Symbols of *Passage*," 160.
134. V. Turner, "Nkang'a: Part Two," 257.
135. V. Turner, "Nkang'a: Part One," 200.
136. V. Turner, *Drums of Affliction*, 83.
137. P. B. Roscoe, "'Initiation' in Cross-Cultural Perspective," 232–33.
138. La Fontaine, "Ritualization of Women's Life-Crises in Bugisu," 159, 173.
139. Lutkehaus, "Gender Metaphors," 197; Swift, *Malay Peasant Society in Jelebu*, 124.
140. Thompson, "Bloody Women: Rites of Passage, Blood and Artemis," 22.
141. Meskell, "Cycles of Life and Death," 425.
142. Meskell, "Cycles of Life and Death," 434.
143. Turner suggests only that women, because they have "more to do with children throughout their lives than adult males," may have a less marked transition than do males between their own childhood and their adult lives: V. Turner, "Nkang'a: Part Two," 257.
144. Bynum, "Women's Stories, Women's Symbols," 32.
145. Bynum, "Women's Stories, Women's Symbols," 41.
146. Bynum, "Women's Stories, Women's Symbols," 43, citing Weinstein and R. M. Bell, *Saints and Society*, Part I, especially 34, 48, 71, 97, 108, 121, and 135.
147. De Vitry, "Life of Marie d'Oignies," 53–54.
148. Bonaventure, "Life of Saint Francis," 193–94.
149. De Vitry, "Life of Marie d'Oignies," 55–56.
150. Bynum, "Women's Stories, Women's Symbols," 47.
151. Note, e.g., the subtitle of Turner's 1969 book *The Ritual Process: Structure and Anti-Structure*.
152. Bynum, "Women's Stories, Women's Symbols," 30–31.
153. V. Turner, "Betwixt and Between," 98.
154. Bynum, "Women's Stories, Women's Symbols," 33.
155. Bynum, "Women's Stories, Women's Symbols," 34.
156. Bynum, "Women's Stories, Women's Symbols," 49.
157. Bynum, "Women's Stories, Women's Symbols," 43.
158. Bynum, "Women's Stories, Women's Symbols," 30–31.
159. Bynum, "Women's Stories, Women's Symbols," 32–33.
160. Bynum, "Women's Stories, Women's Symbols," 47.
161. Lincoln, *Emerging from the Chrysalis*, 5–6.
162. Lincoln, *Emerging from the Chrysalis*, 17.

163. Lincoln, *Emerging from the Chrysalis*, 72.
164. Lincoln, *Emerging from the Chrysalis*, 100.
165. Van Gennep, *Rites of Passage*, 15, 22.
166. Thomassen, *Liminality and the Modern*, 91.
167. Van Gennep, *Rites of Passage*, 15.
168. Belmont, *Arnold Van Gennep*, 65.
169. Van Gennep, *Rites of Passage*, 192.
170. Lincoln, *Emerging from the Chrysalis*, 100.
171. Lincoln, *Emerging from the Chrysalis*, 100.
172. Lincoln, *Emerging from the Chrysalis*, 9, 21, 51, and 53.
173. Turner was told that the circimcision lodge in which Ndembu boys are secluded during *Mukanda* was, at least at some point "in the past," "far from the village"—perhaps "over a mile" away: V. Turner, "*Mukanda*: The Rite of Circumcision," 223.
174. Lincoln, *Emerging from the Chrysalis*, 100-101.
175. Lincoln, *Emerging from the Chrysalis*, 102.
176. Lincoln, *Emerging from the Chrysalis*, 101.
177. Lincoln, *Emerging from the Chrysalis*, 102.
178. Above, n. 168.
179. Lincoln, *Emerging from the Chrysalis*, 102.
180. Lincoln, *Emerging from the Chrysalis*, 102.
181. V. Turner, "Betwixt and Between," 98.
182. Lincoln, *Emerging from the Chrysalis*, 103.
183. Bynum, "Women's Stories, Women's Symbols," 33.
184. Lincoln, *Emerging from the Chrysalis*, 103.
185. Lincoln, *Emerging from the Chrysalis*, 7, 11, 19, 45-49, 61-63. Note also in this regard my discussion above of Gilchrist's catalog of the special articles of clothing that marked crucial moments of transition in a medieval woman's life course (Gilchrist, *Medieval Life*, 91-92, 94, and 96).
186. But as in n. 112 above, see V. Turner, "*Mukanda*: The Rite of Circumcision," 187, regarding Turner's somewhat different translation of this term in describing the third phase of *Mukanda*.
187. V. Turner, "Nkang'a: Part Two," 252-54.
188. E. Turner, "Girl into Woman," 32; eadem, *Spirit and the Drum*, 79.
189. V. Turner, "Nkang'a: Part Two," 258; see similarly E. Turner, "Girl into Woman," 32; eadem, *Spirit and the Drum*, 79.
190. V. Turner, *Schism and Continuity*, 27.
191. V. Turner, "Nkang'a: Part Two," 260.
192. V. Turner, "Nkang'a: Part Two," 266.
193. V. Turner, "Humility and Hierarchy," 166-203.
194. V. Turner, "Humility and Hierarchy," 167-68.
195. V. Turner, "Liminality and Communitas," 95.
196. V. Turner, "Humility and Hierarchy," 167.
197. Van Gennep titled Chapter 9 of *Les rites de passage* "Autres groupes de rites de passage," or in the English translation, "Other Types of Rites of Passage." In the English translation, his discussion of "rites which accompany and bring about the change of the year, the season, or the month" is found on pp. 178-81.
198. V. Turner, "Humility and Hierarchy," 168.
199. V. Turner, "Humility and Hierarchy," 167.
200. V. Turner, "Humility and Hierarchy," 172.
201. Marriott, "Feast of Love," 201-12, discussed in V. Turner, "Humility and Hierarchy," on pp. 185-88.
202. V. Turner, "Humility and Hierarchy," 168.
203. Bynum, "Women's Stories, Women's Symbols," 45.
204. Bynum, "Women's Stories, Women's Symbols," 45-46.
205. Lincoln, *Emerging from the Chrysalis*, 104.
206. Lincoln, *Emerging from the Chrysalis*, 116-17.
207. Lincoln, "Initiatory Paradigm," 250.
208. E. Turner, "Zambia's Kankanga Dances," 61-62.
209. V. Turner, "Nkang'a: Part Two," 264-65.
210. V. Turner, "Nkang'a: Part Two," 249.

211. Lincoln, *Emerging from the Chrysalis*, 101.
212. Lincoln, *Emerging from the Chrysalis*, 102.
213. V. Turner, *Forest of Symbols*, 8.
214. V. Turner, *Schism and Continuity*, 27.
215. V. Turner, "Humility and Hierarchy," 168.
216. For a formative discussion of the Native American evidence, see W. Roscoe, *Changing Ones: Third and Fourth Genders in Native North America*.
217. This text comes from the Late Assyrian fragments K 3399 + 3934, corresponding to and augmenting the Old Babylonian Tablet I, lines 254–290: see Lambert and Millard, *Atraḫasīs*, 61–63.
218. See Asher-Greve, "From La Femme to Multiple Sex/Gender," 30; Helle, "Weapons and Weaving Instruments," 107; and my discussion in Chapter 1 of gendering a Mesopotamian newborn, with references in nn. 4–6 there.
219. Stavrakopoulou, "Materiality of Life," 4, with multiple references.
220. Brettler, "Gender in the Bible," 2184.
221. Garroway, *Growing Up in Ancient Israel*, 86; see also eadem, "Gendering a Child."
222. See (among others) Garroway, *Children in the Ancient Near Eastern Household*, 16–19; eadem, *Growing Up in Ancient Israel*, 6–8; and Steinberg, *World of the Child*, 3–8, 11–25.
223. At birth: Garroway, *Children in the Ancient Near Eastern Household*, 10, 18; eadem, "Children and Religion," 118. Shortly thereafter: Steinberg, *World of the Child*, 68–70, 124.
224. Garroway, *Growing Up in Ancient Israel*, 8.
225. See similarly Blenkinsopp, "Family in First Temple Israel," 68; idem, "Life Expectancy in Ancient Palestine," 45–46; Eng, *Days of Our Years*, 57; Steinberg, *World of the Child*, 74, n. 37; and van der Toorn, *From Her Cradle to Her Grave*, 18.
226. See similarly, regarding infants, Valk, "'They Enjoy Syrup and Ghee at Tables of Silver and Gold,'" 696 and n. 3 on that page.
227. Garroway, "Methodology," 69.
228. See my discussion on menarche and reproductive capacity in Chapter 1 and n. 111 there.
229. Further on the definition of *bĕtûlâ*, see Chapter 2 and n. 48 there.
230. See Chapter 1 and nn. 105 and 110 there.
231. See likewise, for ancient Israel, Garroway, *Children in the Ancient Near Eastern Household*, 10, 18; for ancient Egypt, Toivari-Viitala, "Marriage and Divorce," 5, and eadem, *Women at Deir el-Medina*, 53, 71; for ancient Mesopotamia, Matthews, "Marriage and Family," 10; and for Roman-Byzantine Palestine, Tropper, "Economics of Jewish Childhood in Late Antiquity," 227, as brought to my attention by Garroway, "Gendered or Ungendered?," 95, n. 2. But cf., for ancient Israel, Steinberg, *World of the Child*, 71, who suggests that as in Greece and among the Gisu of eastern Uganda, the Manam islanders of Papua New Guinea, and the Malay people of Sumatra (above nn. 138–40), a female's movement into full adulthood was realized only with childbirth—or, in Steinberg's words, for an Israelite woman, "menstruation was the antepenult . . . marriage the penultimate . . . and childbearing the ultimate stage of female adulthood."
232. E.g., van der Toorn, *From Her Cradle to Her Grave*, 18, posits a four-year gap between puberty and marriage.
233. For those who hold this view, see Chapter 1, n. 112.
234. Above, n. 53.
235. Eyben, *Restless Youth in Ancient Rome*, 5, citing Musgrove, *Youth and the Social Order*, 13.
236. Crapanzano, "Rite of Return," 32.
237. Miller, *Religion of Ancient Israel*, 71, writing of ancient Israelite practices associated with death. Likewise marriage in ancient Israel, and elsewhere in the Near East, was not a religious institution of "divine order/nature/sanction" (Jackson, "'Institutions' of Marriage and Divorce," 222). For discussion, see, in addition to ibid., 222, 244–52, de Vaux, *Ancient Israel*, 33, who writes "in Israel . . . marriage was a purely civil contract, not sanctioned by any religious rite"; also, Block, "Marriage and Family," 44 ("weddings [in ancient Israel] were civil rather than religious affairs"); Pressler, "'Biblical View' of Marriage," 204; and Shectman, "What Do We Know about Marriage?," 172–73. Note too, regarding the civil nature of marriage, as well as some other life-cycle rituals, the comments of Zevit, *Religions of Ancient Israel*, 665.
238. See the sources cited in the Prologue, n. 13, and also Chapter 6, n. 29.
239. King and Stager, *Life in Biblical Israel*, 7.
240. I have recently discussed my position on this matter at greater length in Ackerman, *Women and the Religion of Ancient Israel*, 21–24.

241. See Jenks, *The Elohist*, and R. M. Wright, *Linguistic Evidence*.
242. See similarly Gertz, Berlejung, Schmid, and Witte, *T&T Clark Handbook of the Old Testament*, 301; B. A. Levine, *Numbers 1–20*, 104; Nicholson, *The Pentateuch*, 220–21; and Propp, *Exodus 19–40*, 732.
243. Knohl, "Priestly Torah," 65–177; idem, *Sanctuary of Silence*. This position has been further articulated, refined, and (in some cases) modified by Milgrom, *Leviticus 1–16*, 13–35; idem, *Leviticus 17–22*, 1349–52; Nihan, *From Priestly Torah to Pentateuch*; idem, "Israel's Festival Calendars," 177–231; and Stackert, *Rewriting the Torah*.
244. See Chapter 1, n. 124.
245. A theory positing two editions of the Deuteronomistic corpus, one preexilic and one exilic, was advanced already in the nineteenth century by both Abraham Kuenen and Julius Wellhausen (as pointed out by Cross, in *Canaanite Myth*, 275, n. 6, and Lohfink, "Cult Reform of Josiah," 462). For modern proponents, see the bibliographies assembled in Knoppers, "Aaron's Calf and Jeroboam's Calves," 93–94, n. 5, and Miano, *Shadow on the Steps*, 5, n. 10, to which add, more recently, Leuchter, *Samuel and the Shaping of Tradition*, 13–21. I have identified what I take to be the most crucial works of the countervailing European position in Ackerman, *When Heroes Love*, 282, n. 6. See also, for a position that combines the American and European views, Römer, *So-Called Deuteronomistic History*.
246. This thesis was first articulated by the German scholar W. M. L. de Wette in his 1805 doctoral dissertation; for a more recent affirmation, see (among others) Rofé, *Deuteronomy*, 4–9. O'Brien, "Book of Deuteronomy," 103–5, surveys other scholarly positions.
247. Morris, "Use and Abuse of Homer," 88.
248. Morris, *Burial and Ancient Society*, 45.
249. Morris, "Use and Abuse of Homer," 90; idem, *Burial and Ancient Society*, 44–45.
250. Morris, *Burial and Ancient Society*, 44.

Chapter 1

1. See further my discussion of the demographic data regarding women's deaths in childbirth in Chapter 5 and nn. 134–39 there.
2. J. Lawrence Angel, "Ecology and Population," 94–95, 97, estimates, based on Greek data, that in the early Iron Age, there was an average of 4.1 births per female, with 1.9 survivors, and Carol Meyers, *Rediscovering Eve*, 98–99, likewise cites data that put infant mortality rates in the ancient world at somewhere between 50 and 70 percent. Gay Robins, "Women and Children in Peril," 28, notes that in Egypt, at three New Kingdom and Third Intermediate Period cemeteries (ca. 1539–1075 BCE and ca. 1075–715 BCE), infant graves comprised, respectively, 50 percent, 48 percent, and 42 percent of total burials, and writing about early first-millennium CE Jewish burials from sites in modern-day Israel and the Palestinian territories, Tal Ilan, in *Integrating Women*, 201, estimates a rate of child mortality between 39 and 44 percent. Parkin, "Demography of Infancy and Early Childhood," 47, 50, and Dasen, "Probaskania," 178, offer similar figures for the Roman era. Brien Garnand, Lawrence E. Stager, and Joseph A. Greene, in "Infants as Offerings," 207, more generally propose that "before the demographic transition of the 18th–19th century in the industrialized West, one would expect the mortality rate during infancy (< 12 months) to exceed 50% and the rate before reproductive age (< 15 years) to exceeded [sic] 60%."
3. See Bachvarova, "Hurro-Hittite Stories," 296, §10′–§11′, and Beckman, *Hittite Birth Rituals*, 251, citing that volume's Text B, §11″–§12″ (pp. 34–35), with commentary on p. 40. This ritual is also briefly discussed by Imparati, "Private Life among the Hittites," 575, and Pringle, "Hittite Birth Rituals," 132.
4. For discussion, see Bachvarova, "Successful Birth, Unsuccessful Marriage," 77; Bergmann, *Childbirth as a Metaphor*, 44; Scurlock, "Baby-Snatching Demons," 144 and 169, n. 97; Stol, *Birth in Babylonia and the Bible*, 62, with additional references in n. 87 on that page; and Whitekettle, "Human Reproduction," 244.

5. See, especially, Stol, *Birth in Babylonia and the Bible*, 60–61, 63, with several additional references at p. 63, n. 93, and see also van der Toorn, *From Her Cradle to Her Grave*, 20, and idem, *Family Religion*, 97. Stol, in "Private Life in Ancient Mesopotamia," 490, explains that the "pin" or "clasp" (which is how he interprets the *kirid/kirissu*) was the toggle pin worn on a woman's breast to hold her garment together.
6. Asher-Greve, "Decisive Sex, Essential Gender," 13–14.
7. Hoffner, "Symbols for Masculinity and Femininity," 329–33; also Bird, "Women (OT)," 954, and Holloway, "Distaff, Crutch or Chain Gang," 370–71.
8. Frymer-Kensky, *In the Wake of the Goddesses*, 23.
9. C. Meyers, "Material Remains and Social Relations," 432–34.
10. Note, however, that the date of Prov 31:10–31 is debated: Yoder, *Wisdom as a Woman of Substance*, 15–39, has argued for a Persian-era date, but Fox, *Proverbs 10–31*, 899–902, has raised significant doubts (without offering an alternative).
11. Pointed out by Adams, *Social and Economic Life in Second Temple Judea*, 48–49, who also draws attention to evidence of women's textile production from the New Testament: Dorcas makes tunics (Acts 9:39) and Lydia deals in "purple cloth" (Acts 16:14).
12. Barber, "The Peplos of Athena," 104; see similarly, for Greek tradition, Redfield, "Notes on the Greek Wedding," 194–95.
13. Garland, *Greek Way of Life*, 75; Neils, "Children and Greek Religion," 143.
14. Stol, "Women in Mesopotamia," 124; idem, *Birth in Babylonia and the Bible*, 12, 207; see similarly idem, "Private Life in Ancient Mesopotamia," 490, and, regarding Greek tradition, Garland, *Greek Way of Life*, 32.
15. Stol, *Birth in Babylonia and the Bible*, 128.
16. Indeed, birth generally does not seem to have been ritually observed to the same degree in biblical Israel as it was elsewhere in the Near East and eastern Mediterranean. See Bremmer, "Rites of Passage," 438, who writes: "Birth . . . seems not to have been ritualized everywhere [in the ancient world] to the same degree. We hear little about it in Israelite . . . rituals"; likewise, J. F. Parker, *Valuable and Vulnerable*, 43: "more often the birth of a child does not occasion a formal ritual or celebration."
17. Van der Toorn, *From Her Cradle to Her Grave*, 22.
18. Some scholars disagree. E.g., Steinberg, *World of the Child*, 69, argues that "circumcision . . . conferred gender on the male infant." Garroway, *Children in the Ancient Near Eastern Household*, 175, counters that Steinberg's "link between circumcision and assignment of male gender seems too rigid," given that a woman postpartum must have known "whether she birthed a male or a female baby," as "the length of her ritual impurity [which I discuss just below] depends on this knowledge." Note similarly that Exod 1:15–17 presumes that the midwives who attend Hebrew women when they give birth in Egypt can determine immediately whether a child is male or female and so whether the child should be killed according to the pharaoh's decree or "let live." Still, cf. Garroway in ibid., 176, where she writes that Israelite "children with a penis are understood as males *in potentia*, until their circumcision," and that one might likewise surmise that "children with a vagina" had the "potential to become female," but whether at the end of the two-week period that corresponds to the seven days prior to circumcision in Lev 12:5, or at menarche, "is difficult to say." Also, in "Gendered or Ungendered?," 105, Garroway suggests, based on burials from the Second Temple period from ca. 50 BCE–50 CE, that babies of that era were not considered "gendered" at birth nor, based on Greek and Roman customs, until at least the eighth- to tenth-day postpartum (see the Prologue, n. 13, nn. 57–58 below, and nn. 29–31, 83–86 in Chapter 6 for references). In ibid., 112, Garroway makes a similar argument regarding Middle Bronze Age II Canaanite burials (ca. 1950–1559 BCE), and then, in ibid., 112–14, she suggests her conclusions have implications for understanding the nongendered identity of infants in ancient Israel.
19. On the physical dangers infants face immediately after childbirth, see n. 2 above. Léonie J. Archer, in *Her Price Is Beyond Rubies*, 30–31, proposes that the dangers a neonate faces were more supernatural in character, as during the first week of life, the newborn infant "was believed to be especially threatened by evil spirits," a point I also discuss in Chapter 5.
20. This has been argued by multiple commentators, preeminently Isaac, "Circumcision as a Covenant Rite," 444–56. See also Flusser and Safrai, "Who Sanctified the Beloved in the Womb?," 47; Fox, "Sign of the Covenant," 557–96, especially 588, 594–96 (concerning the understanding of circumcision in the P, or Priestly source); Gursky, "Reproductive Rituals," 147–48, 156–63

(with additional references at p. 148, n. 2); King, "Circumcision," 50; and Propp, "Origins of Infant Circumcision," 357.
21. Stavrakopoulou, "Making Bodies," 535.
22. Erbele, "Gender Trouble," 134.
23. C. Bell, *Ritual*, 54, citing V. Turner, "*Mukanda*: The Rite of Circumcision," 192; see also ibid., 153–54.
24. See Ackerman, *Women and the Religion of Ancient Israel*, 173–74, for evidence that the dictates regarding female impurity articulated in Lev 12:1–8 and related biblical texts were actually operative within some circles of Israelite society at some points in Israelite history.
25. Milgrom, *Leviticus 1–16*, 744, summarizing the position of Rabbi Simeon ben Yohai, in b. Niddah 31b, that "originally the mother of a male was impure for fourteen days, just as in the case of a female, but the term was reduced" in the case of a newborn male to accommodate the boy's circumcision. Rhonda Burnette-Bletsch, "Women after Childbirth (Lev 12:1–8)," 204, similarly considers that the longer period of impurity associated with a female child's birth was originally the norm for all infants but that it was shortened for males to coordinate with the boy's circumcision, thus allowing the mother to "comfort her son during this ritual procedure." But Burnette-Bletsch does not necessarily endorse this position; see below, n. 35.
26. Milgrom, *Leviticus 1–16*, 744, summarizing the position of Hoffmann, *Sefer Va-Yiqra'*; see also B. A. Levine (citing Hoffmann), in *Leviticus*, 73. Yet cf., on Levine's interpretation of Lev 12:1–8, ibid., 249–50, and n. 35 below.
27. As I discuss in Chapter 6, the text in question—Bachvarova, "Hurro-Hittite Stories," 291, §10–11; Beckman, *Hittite Birth Rituals*, Text K, §10–§11 (pp. 134–37) and §28–§29 (pp. 142–43)—in fact addresses only the boy child's and girl child's three- and four-month periods of impurity. Commentators generally assume, however, that an infant's mother was held to be impure along with her child.
28. Milgrom, *Leviticus 1–16*, 744.
29. Burnette-Bletsch, "Women after Childbirth (Lev 12:1–8)," 204; Wenham, *Book of Leviticus*, 188; Whitekettle, "Leviticus 12," 397, 405–8; and D. P. Wright and Jones, "Discharge," 205.
30. Older interpreters who hold this view include Dillmann, *Die Bücher Exodus und Leviticus*, and certain medieval Jewish commentators: see Z. Farber, "Biological Explanation 2." For an up-to-date presentation of this argument, grounded in Greco-Roman medical theory, see Thiessen, "Legislation of Leviticus 12," 297–319.
31. Magonet, "'But if it is a Girl,'" 144. Other objections to this thesis are put forward by Hartley, *Leviticus*, 168; Milgrom, *Leviticus 1–16*, 750; Vos, *Woman in Old Testament Worship*, 68–69; and Wenham, *Book of Leviticus*, 188.
32. Those who hold this view include the medieval Jewish commentator Isaac Abravanel (see his *Commentary on the Torah* on Leviticus 27 [p. 176b], as cited by Milgrom, *Leviticus 1–16*, 750); Bird, "Images of Women," 54; Stol, *Birth in Babylonia and the Bible*, 207; and D. P. Wright and Jones, "Discharge," 205.
33. Gruber, "Women in the Cult," 56, n. 13. Other objections to this thesis are put forward by Hess, "Review: A Reassessment of the Priestly Cultic and Legal Texts," 382; Magonet, "'But if it is a Girl,'" 145; and Milgrom, *Leviticus 1–16*, 750.
34. Milgrom, *Leviticus 1–16*, 750. But cf. idem, *Leviticus*, 126, where Milgrom writes that "the biblical distinction . . . is probably based on physiology, that is, early medical science."
35. Exceptions include, in addition to the scholars whose views are catalogued in nn. 25–26, 30, and 32 above, B. A. Levine, *Leviticus*, 249–50, who proposes that impurity in ancient Israel corresponded to what "modern health care" would refer to as "susceptible" or "vulnerable." The new mother, he goes on to say, although "a source of joy to the community . . . was particularly vulnerable." Therefore, the mother "generated anxiety—as did all aspects of fertility and reproduction," including "the infant daughter's potential fertility." Hence, according to Levine, the longer period of impurity associated with her birth (but cf., regarding Levine's position, n. 26 above). See also Burnette-Bletsch, "Women after Childbirth (Lev 12:1–8)," 204, and Magonet, "'But if it is a Girl,'" 145, who suggest, like Levine in *Leviticus*, 249–50, that "the infant daughter's potential fertility" might account for the longer period of impurity associated with her birth. Unlike Levine, however, Burnette-Bletsch sees this as an affirmation of "a female's greater potential role in reproduction," rather than a commentary on the anxieties engendered by women's reproductive capabilities. Gruber, "Breast-Feeding Practices," 79, and Nakhai, "Female Infanticide in Iron II Israel and Judah," 261, also offer more woman-affirming

interpretations of the difference between impurity's duration after the birth of a female versus a male child.

Yet whether Burnette-Bletsch ultimately subscribes to the woman-affirming theory she puts forward is unclear; see n. 25. Magonet likewise, after proposing a theory focused on the newborn girl's potential fertility, eventually rejects it ("'But if it is a Girl,'" 152), in favor of a proposal that a baby girl can sometimes suffer from vaginal bleeding "following the withdrawal of maternal hormones." He suggests that this is a ritual uncleanness that the mother must deal with (since the baby cannot) through the doubling of the mother's period of ritual impurity.

For other theories still, see the succinct yet thorough lists of possibilities that have been assembled by Hartley, *Leviticus*, 167–68; Philip, *Menstruation and Childbirth*, 116–18; Sprinkle, "Rationale of the Laws of Clean and Unclean," 644, with references in nn. 17–23 on that page; and Thiessen, "Legislation of Leviticus 12," 298–99.

36. Wenham, *Book of Leviticus*, 188; Olyan, *Rites and Rank*, 44; Klawans, *Impurity and Sin*, 39; Vos, *Woman in Old Testament Worship*, 70.
37. See Milgrom, *Leviticus 1–16*, 244, regarding Lev 12:2: "the quality of the impurity and not just its length is equivalent to that of the menstruant"; similarly, Klee, "Menstruation in the Hebrew Bible," 45, n. 7.
38. See Flynn, *Children in Ancient Israel*, 90, citing Gruber, "Breast-Feeding Practices," 79–80; see also my comments in Chapter 7.
39. Matthew Thiessen, "Luke 2:22, Leviticus 12, and Parturient Impurity," 23, offers a more maximal interpretation still: that the newborn might be considered analogous to a man who lies with a menstruating woman and so comes directly into contact with the source of her impurity, i.e., menstrual blood. Just like the menstruating woman, this man, according to Lev 15:24, is rendered impure for a full seven days; so too, Thiessen theorizes, a mother's newborn, having come into direct contact with the fluids that are the source of her impurity, would suffer "the same impurity as that which the parturient endures—a seven- or fourteen-day period of impurity, followed by a lessened state of impurity lasting thirty-three or sixty-six days."
40. Van der Toorn, *From Her Cradle to Her Grave*, 92. In "Menstruation in the Hebrew Bible," 5, Klee, citing S. J. D. Cohen, "Menstruants and the Sacred," 284–85, notes that in rabbinic tradition, a midwife was taken to have the impurity of a menstruant, presumably because the impurity of the mother she has attended in childbirth has communicated itself to her, just as the impurity of a menstruant is communicable.
41. Olyan, *Disability in the Hebrew Bible*, 57, and 150–51, n. 31.
42. Van der Toorn, "Nine Months among the Peasants," 395; see also idem, *From Her Cradle to Her Grave*, 53, where van der Toorn notes that in the first chapter of Lamentations, Jerusalem, which has been "plundered and devastated by the Babylonians," is presented as a menstruant who "sits 'alone' or 'in seclusion.'" In certain texts from later Jewish tradition (more specifically, "one vocalization of the Mishnah and the *Temple Scroll*"), impure menstruants were likewise exiled to a special house: see Schiffman, "Purification after Childbirth," 177, and idem, "Laws Pertaining to Women and Sexuality," 559.
43. Olyan, *Disability in the Hebrew Bible*, 57.
44. Miller, *Religion of Ancient Israel*, 150.
45. D. P. Wright, "Spectrum of Priestly Impurity," 158.
46. Olyan, *Rites and Rank*, 39.
47. Maccoby, "Holiness and Purity," 152.
48. But see above, n. 39, regarding Thiessen's interpretation of Lev 12:1–8; see also my discussion below regarding the impurities of Lev 12:1–8 as understood in Second Temple textual traditions.
49. Van Gennep, *Rites of Passage*, 43–44.
50. In Chapter 6, I will return to the matter of the mother and the way van Gennep's rite-of-passage pattern does, and does not, correspond to her postpartum ritual experiences.
51. Flynn, *Children in Ancient Israel*, 24. In addition to the data that follow, see, for Mesopotamia, Valk, "'They Enjoy Syrup and Ghee at Tables of Silver and Gold,'" 725–26.
52. For this text, see Flynn, *Children in Ancient Israel*, 26–27, who cites as his source Scurlock and B. R. Anderson, *Diagnoses in Assyrian and Babylonian Medicine*, 264; see also Stol, *Birth in Babylonia and the Bible*, 12. As the text suggests, ancient sources typically count a gestation period of ten months between conception and birth: see Stol, *Birth in Babylonia and the Bible*, 23–25.
53. Flynn, "Birthing New Life," 78, citing Sachs, "Babylonian Horoscopes," 59. See also Stol, *Birth in Babylonia and the Bible*, 97–98.

54. Meskell, "Cycles of Life and Death," 425, citing Feucht, *Das Kind im Alten Ägypten*, 94; see also Meskell, "Dying Young," 38.
55. Marshall, *Motherhood and Early Childhood*, 42–43, citing Berlin Papyrus 3027, Chapter F (5, 8–6, 8).
56. The sense that the period immediately following birth marks a "transitional" (which is to say, liminal) state for an Israelite neonate is similarly evoked in Archer, *Her Price Is Beyond Rubies*, 31; Erbele-Küster, "'She Shall Remain (in Accordance to) Her Blood-of-Purification,'" 69; and Steinberg, *World of the Child*, 68–72, although Steinberg, on p. 69, identifies circumcision, and not the end of the period of ritual impurity, as the ritual gesture that marks "the start of community identity [and also gender identity; above, n. 18] for a male infant." Yet by her own admission (on p. 70), Steinberg is thus pressed (as the analysis I have put forward is not) to offer a comparable act that "initiate[d] a newborn female into full personhood," so much so that she suggests this initiation can be long delayed, until "possibly it was the blood of menstruation [parallel to the blood of circumcision] that marked the stage when social personhood was attributed to a girl" (p. 71).

    Kristine Henriksen Garroway, in *Children in the Ancient Near Eastern Household*, has somewhat similarly argued that in ancient Israel, full-fledged family membership took longer than my analysis suggests and was not completely realized until the child was weaned and no longer dependent on its mother (a period that may have lasted as long as three years (see 2 Macc 7:27 and my discussion in Chapter 7, with references in nn. 3–8, 10–13). This proposal depends primarily on evidence Garroway assembles regarding child burials in Bronze and Iron Age Canaan, and, specifically, the predominant use of jar burials for infants up to two years of age. Then, "once a child grew older, s/he was no longer buried in a jar but in a manner similar to adults," which suggests to Garroway that "Canaanite infants were not considered full members of the community, because they were not buried like other members of the community" (ibid., 216, 242). However, as Garroway acknowledges (ibid., 219, Table 2, note c), discussion of Israelite infant burials is compromised by the fact that 75 percent of infant jar burials come from one site (Tel Zeror). Garroway in addition admits (ibid., 239–40) that factors other than an infant's social status may have dictated the use of jar burials (e.g., the size of the deceased). Given all this, I think it unlikely that an Israelite infant was only "a member of the household or society *in potentia*" until weaning (ibid., 245). See also Erbele-Küster, "'She Shall Remain (in Accordance to) Her Blood-of-Purification,'" 69, who perceptively notes that infants in Lev 12:1–8 go from being identified only "by biological terms [that] refer to the newborn's gender" (vv 2, 5) to being a "son" or a "daughter," "words that express social and family relationships," by the time the mother's impurity ends (v 6).
57. For references, see the Prologue, n. 13, and also Chapter 6, n. 29.
58. Corbier, "Child Exposure," 55.
59. Plutarch, *Quaestiones Romanae* §102 (*Moralia* 288C), as cited in Dasen, "Childbirth and Infancy," 293, and Laes, *Children in the Roman Empire*, 66.
60. V. Turner, "Betwixt and Between," 93–111.
61. See similarly, regarding "the normative time period [being] that of the male," Philip, *Menstruation and Childbirth*, 114.
62. This has been particularly well argued by Segal, *Hebrew Passover*, 139–40, 177. Whitekettle, "Levitical Thought," 381, 390, similarly makes a case for the number seven symbolizing "wholeness" and "completeness" in the priestly worldview.
63. As in n. 62 above, Whitekettle, "Levitical Thought," 381, 390, makes a case for the number "forty"—the total duration of the impurity associated with the birth of a male infant—being, in the priestly worldview, a number symbolizing "wholeness" and "completeness."
64. Among those who do agree with my presumption, see, e.g., S. J. D. Cohen, *Why Aren't Jewish Women Circumcised?*, 19; Eilberg-Schwartz, *Savage in Judaism*, 174; Klee, "Menstruation in the Hebrew Bible," 78; Thiessen, "Luke 2:22, Leviticus 12, and Parturient Impurity," 20–24; van der Toorn, *From Her Cradle to Her Grave*, 91–92; and Vos, *Woman in Old Testament Worship*, 67.
65. B. A. Levine, *Leviticus*, 72.
66. Above, n. 29.
67. B. A. Levine, *Leviticus*, 72.
68. Olyan, *Rites and Rank*, 44, and 146, n. 35.
69. According to Tzvi Novick, "Mother and Child," the earliest rabbinic commentary on Leviticus, the Sifra, holds that "the newborn is not defiled." See also S. J. D. Cohen, *Why Aren't Jewish Women Circumcised?*, 19.

70. Milgrom, *Leviticus 1–16*, 746, 764. See also ibid., 744, 750; idem, *Leviticus*, 123; Burnette-Bletsch, "Women after Childbirth (Lev 12:1–8)," 204; and D. P. Wright and Jones, "Discharge," 205.
71. Milgrom, *Leviticus 1–16*, 746.
72. Thiessen, "Luke 2:22, Leviticus 12, and Parturient Impurity," 21, with references regarding Hittite, Egyptian, and Greek evidence at ibid., nn. 18 and 19. For Mesopotamia, see van der Toorn, *From Her Cradle to Her Grave*, 84, 92; idem *Family Religion*, 123; and idem, "Magic at the Cradle," 142.
73. Above, n. 27.
74. Thiessen, "Luke 2:22, Leviticus 12, and Parturient Impurity": see p. 16 for Thiessen's translation as quoted here, and pp. 16–29, especially 23–29, for his argument. But cf. Milgrom, *Leviticus 1–16*, 762, who suggests (following to some degree Fitzmyer, *Gospel According to Luke*, 424), that Luke, based on his Hellenistic background and thorough immersion in "Hellenistic atmosphere and culture" (Fitzmyer, *Gospel According to Luke*, 42), reads Greek religious custom, where both the mother and child were considered impure, into Palestinian Jewish tradition.
75. Thiessen, "Luke 2:22, Leviticus 12, and Parturient Impurity," 26.
76. Himmelfarb, "Impurity and Sin," 25; see similarly Schearing, "Double Time . . . Double Trouble?," 433.
77. Schiffman, "Purification after Childbirth," 173; see also Thiessen, "Luke 2:22, Leviticus 12, and Parturient Impurity," 25, and, with somewhat less certainty, Baumgarten, "Purification after Childbirth," 5.
78. Schiffman, "Purification after Childbirth," 175; Novick, "Mother and Child"; Thiessen, "Luke 2:22, Leviticus 12, and Parturient Impurity," 24–25; and, with somewhat less certainty, Baumgarten, "Purification after Childbirth," 5.
79. See, e.g., Garroway, *Growing Up in Ancient Israel*, 60; Scurlock, "Baby-Snatching Demons," 147.
80. See Beckman, *Hittite Birth Rituals*, Text C, §5, line 20 (pp. 42–43), and the commentary on pp. 46, 49, and ibid., "The Ritual of Papanikri," IV, lines 12–16 (pp. 118–19), and the commentary on p. 123. See similarly Pringle, "Hittite Birth Rituals," 133 and 140.
81. Note, indeed, that in Beckman, *Hittite Birth Rituals*, Text C, purification of the newborn child is the subject of §5, line 18 (pp. 42–43), just two lines prior to the notice that the newborn was bathed.
82. Carley, *Book of the Prophet Ezekiel*, 96; Carley is perhaps drawing here on Cooke, *Critical and Exegetical Commentary on the Book of Ezekiel* 1, 161–62, who quotes Masterman, "Hygiene and Disease," 118–19, as writing, regarding early twentieth-century CE Palestine: "As soon as the navel is cut the midwife rubs the child all over with salt, water, and oil, and tightly swathes it in clothes for seven days; at the end of that time she removes the dirty clothes, washes the child and anoints it."
83. Milgrom, *Leviticus 1–16*, 756.
84. Milgrom, *Leviticus 1–16*, 934. But cf. Philip, *Menstruation and Childbirth*, 50–51.
85. E.g., Archer, *Her Price Is Beyond Rubies*, 39, citing Canaan, "Child in Palestinian Arab Superstition," 163; Brownlee, *Ezekiel 1–19*, 223, citing Masterman, "Hygiene and Disease," 118–19; and Coleson, "Israel's Life Cycle," 250, n. 7, citing Taylor, *Ezekiel*, 134.
86. Rogers, Emmett, and Golding, "Growth and Nutritional Status of the Breast-Fed Infant," S158; see similarly Garroway, *Growing Up in Ancient Israel*, 62; Kamionkowski, *Gender Reversal and Cosmic Chaos*, 100; and Philip, *Menstruation and Childbirth*, 95.
87. Stol, *Birth in Babylonia and the Bible*, 177; this same thesis is advanced by Greenberg, *Ezekiel 1–20*, 274, citing the reports of Granqvist, *Birth and Childhood*, 74, 93–101, 243; Grant, *People of Palestine*, 66; and Morgenstern, *Rites of Birth, Marriage, Death*, 8–9, regarding twentieth-century CE customs among Palestinian Arabs. See also, regarding salt, de Vaux, *Ancient Israel*, 43.
88. C. Meyers, "From Household to House of Yahweh," 290, 296; eadem, *Households and Holiness*, 39–41, 53; see similarly Carley, *Ezekiel*, 96; Fuhs, *Ezechiel 1–24*, 81; Honeyman, "The Salting of Shechem," 195; and Zimmerli, *Ezekiel 1*, 338–39.
89. Gursky, "Reproductive Rituals," 85–91, but cf. ibid., 92, where Gursky speaks of rubbing the newborn with salt as apotropaic. Archer, *Her Price Is Beyond Rubies*, 39–40, somewhat similarly discusses salt as a substance used to "strengthen the child" (above, n. 87) but also as able to "repel evil spirits" and as "a means of purification"; likewise, Kamionkowski, *Gender Reversal and Cosmic Chaos*, 99, suggests the salt "may have had both pragmatic and apotropaic

functions," while also noting that in Exod 30:35, incense with salt is referred to as *"pure* and *holy"* (emphasis mine).
90. Vymazalová and Strouhal. "Mother and Child Care," 170, citing Goelet, *The Egyptian Book of the Dead*, 34.
91. On the relation of Ezekiel to the P writers responsible for Lev 12:1-8, see, among others, Haran, "Ezekiel, P, and the Priestly School," 211-18; Hurvitz, *Linguistic Study*; Milgrom, *Leviticus 1-16*, 451-53; and Zimmerli, *Ezekiel 1*, 46-52.
92. For recent discussions, see Maier, *Daughter Zion, Mother Zion*, especially Chapters 3-7.
93. Cogan, "A Technical Term for Exposure," 133-35.
94. Greenberg, *Ezekiel 1-20*, 275; Block, *Book of Ezekiel*, 476.
95. Malul, "Adoption of Foundlings," 109, following Wilcke, "Noch einmal," 94.
96. Stol, *Birth in Babylonia and the Bible*, 178.
97. Lewis, *Origin and Character of God*, 681-82.
98. Malul, "Adoption of Foundlings," 102; see also Maier, *Daughter Zion, Mother Zion*, 114: "the open field constitutes the reverse of a secured settlement . . . a chaotic space, a marginal space."
99. Malul, "Adoption of Foundlings," 103.
100. Leach, "Anthropological Approaches to the Study of the Bible," 16. See likewise idem, "Fishing for Men," 585-89.
101. To be sure, Ishmael and Moses are not neonates when abandoned and so are not directly comparable to the female neonate whose abandonment I have interpreted according to a rites-of-pattern paradigm in Ezek 16:4-5. Nevertheless, it is striking that these male children are ultimately reunited with their birth mothers and even, in Moses's case, with his natal family, whereas the girl-child Jerusalem is depicted as suffering an exaggerated or exacerbated experience of abandonment that is not resolved by reintegration with her parents. Moreover, while the baby Jerusalem—like Ishmael—is ultimately spared from death because of divine intervention, God's subsequent engagement with these two foundlings does not go as well for the girl child as it does for the boy (see the discussion that follows just below).
102. Galambush, *Jerusalem in the Book of Ezekiel*, 91-92; see likewise, Kamionkowski, *Gender Reversal and Cosmic Chaos*, 98, n. 28, and 101-2.
103. This is precisely the point that Malul, "Adoption of Foundlings," 111, seeks to prove: that Ezek 16:6 is to be read as a "formal declaration of adoption" of Jerusalem by God. Malul is followed by Block, *Book of Ezekiel*, 481; for counterarguments, see Fleishman, "Did a Child's Legal Status in Biblical Israel Depend upon his being Acknowledged?," 363-65; Kamionkowski, "Gender Ambiguity," 130-34; eadem, *Gender Reversal and Cosmic Chaos*, 103; and Koller, "Pornography or Theology?," 409-11.
104. Many commentators—e.g., BDB 725b, s.v. *'ădî*; BHS; Coleson, "Israel's Life Cycle," 240; Cooke, *Critical and Exegetical Commentary on the Book of Ezekiel* 1; 163; Eichrodt, *Ezekiel*, 199, n. k; and van der Toorn, *From Her Cradle to Her Grave*, 48—emend *ba'ădî 'ădāyim* here to *bĕ'ēt 'iddîm*, as Zimmerli, *Ezekiel 1*, 324, notes was originally proposed by Alfred Bertholet, or, similarly, emend to *bā'iddîm* (Brownlee, *Ezekiel 1-19*, 218; Zimmerli, *Ezekiel 1*, 324) or to *'ad 'iddîm* (a possibility noted by Greenberg, *Ezekiel 1-20*, 277, although note that Greenberg prefers the MT reading of *'ădî 'ădāyim*). This emended text is then taken to refer to the onset of menstruation, based on Isa 64:5 (64:6 in most English translations), where *'iddîm* describes a cloth or garment stained with menstrual blood.

But as suggested in the exegesis that follows, for which I am indebted to my student Sophia Gawel, Ezek 16:7-8 invites us to read female pubescence as an extended process that takes place over about eighteen months or two years, beginning with the development of the *'ădî 'ădāyim*, "the loveliest of adornments" (translation Greenberg, *Ezekiel 1-20*, 276), or breasts and pubic hair in v 7, and culminating with the onset of menstruation in v 8. One might recall, regarding this process, my description of *Nkang'a* in the Introduction, a ritual that marks a young Ndembu woman's breast development but that takes place before the onset of her menses: see V. Turner, "Nkang'a: Part One," 200.
105. McVeigh, Guillebaud, and Homburg, *Oxford Handbook of Reproductive Medicine*, 36. As in n. 104 above, I am indebted to my student Sophia Gawel for bringing this reference to my attention and demonstrating its significance in interpreting Ezek 16:7.
106. Kakarla and Bradshaw, "Disorders of Pubertal Development," 339.
107. Bolin, Whelehan, Vernon, and Antoine, "Sexuality through the Life Stages," 233.
108. Frisch, "Fatness, Puberty, and Fertility," 29-30, and Warren, "Physical and Biological Aspects of Puberty," 19.

109. One might recall in this regard that even in the 1950s among the Ndembu, as I noted in the Introduction, the ritual of *Nkang'a*, which marked a girl's breast development but which took place before menarche, was enacted when a Ndembu girl was about fifteen or sixteen: see V. Turner, *Schism and Continuity*, 53. See similarly, for data from the ancient Mediterranean, Avery, "Coming of Age in the Roman Empire," 54, who reports, based on osteological evidence from the first- to fourth-century CE necropolis of Isola Sacra, 23 km south of Rome, that females buried there had begun to menstruate, on average, at 15.8 years of age, more than three years later than the mean age of menarche in the United States in 2013–2017 (12.5 years), as determined by a large body of survey data presented in Martinez, "Trends and Patterns in Menarche," 8 (Table 1). Indeed, even in mid-nineteenth-century Britain, according to Frisch, "Fatness, Puberty, and Fertility," 45, the average age at menarche was similar to what Avery reports for Isola Sacra: 15.5 to 16.5 years; see similarly Sperling and Beyene, "Pound of Biology," 144. At ibid, Sperling and Beyene also note that in 1940, the age of menarche in rural China was 17.1 years. Only in late nineteenth- and twentieth-century CE Euro-American/industrialized contexts do we begin to see a marked drop in the age when menstruation begins: "3 or 4 months per decade in Europe in the last 100 years," according to Frisch, "Fatness, Puberty, and Fertility," 31. See further W. A. Bailey, "Baby Becky, Menarche and Prepubescent Marriage," 115, and Bolin, Whelehan, Vernon, and Antoine, "Sexuality through the Life Stages," 232–33, in both cases with additional references.

110. Bradshaw, "Diagnosing and Treating Precocious Puberty," 40; in Kakarla and Bradshaw, "Disorders of Pubertal Development," 339, the authors suggest that in the United States at the time their article was published (2003), breast development began at a mean age of 10.9 years, whereas the average age for menarche was 12.8 years.

111. W. A. Bailey, "Baby Becky, Menarche and Prepubescent Marriage," 119, citing Paige, "A Bargaining Theory of Menarcheal Responses," 305; see also Bolin, Whelehan, Vernon, and Antoine, "Sexuality through the Life Stages," 232, 265–66. According to ibid., 266 (with additional documentation), this time lag between menarche and reproductive fertility is due to the fact that "ovulation occurs only when certain relative levels of body fat have been reached," something that is delayed in preindustrial communities whereas "in contemporary societies … 'sedentism combined with high levels of caloric intake lead to early deposition of body fat in young girls,'" which "'fools the body into early biological maturation.'"

112. Many commentators fail to reckon with the different timeline we should assume for female pubescence in the ancient world. See, e.g., Block, "Marriage and Family," 57, n. 113; J. R. Ebeling, *Women's Lives in Biblical Times*, 61–64; Garroway, *Children in the Ancient Near Eastern Household*, 18; Gerstenberger and Schrage, *Woman and Man*, 30, 32, 40; Steinberg, *World of the Child*, 77–78, and van der Toorn, *From Her Cradle to Her Grave*, 18, 48, all of whom suggest that the onset of female puberty in the ancient world comes at about age twelve. See also Garroway, "Methodology," 70, who suggests the onset of puberty for girls, whether the "individual is a twenty-first century Westerner, a first-century CE Roman, or an eighth-century BCE Israelite," is age ten; see similarly Koller, "Pornography or Theology?," 411, who posits there was "more than a decade" (but not much more?) between the infant Jerusalem's birth in Ezek 16:4 and the onset of her menses that he presumes is intimated by the reference to her blood in 16:9.

113. Concerning the analysis that follows, I am yet again indebted, as in nn. 104–5, to my student Sophia Gawel.

114. W. A. Bailey, "Baby Becky, Menarche, and Prepubescent Marriage," 117–18.

115. Satlow, *Jewish Marriage in Antiquity*, 104–5; this is the sort of data upon which D. W. Chapman, "Marriage and Family," 186, seems to depend when he writes, citing m. Niddah 5:6–8, that a girl in the Second Temple Period was considered of age "typically in her twelfth year."

116. Satlow, *Jewish Marriage in Antiquity*, 107–8. Satlow reports, e.g., that "a survey of the epitaphs of Jewish women from late antiquity" reveals that most women married in their mid-teens or later, and he quotes an inscription from Egypt that describes a twenty-year-old Jewish woman as "ripe for marriage," although at the time she was only betrothed. Satlow also notes that his evidence correlates well with Mesopotamian evidence assembled by Martha T. Roth from the Neo-Assyrian and Neo-Babylonian periods (ca. 911–612 BCE and ca. 626–539 BCE). These data suggest that females typically married in their "mid to late teens": see Roth, "Age at Marriage," 747, and similarly, though less precisely, eadem, "Marriage and Matrimonial Prestations," 248–49. Satlow's evidence in addition correlates well with that reported by

Avery, "Coming of Age in the Roman Empire," 4 (with multiple references): that "studies of Roman epitaphs demonstrate that middle-class women often married in their late teen or early twenties."
117. Satlow, *Jewish Marriage in Antiquity*, 110.
118. Josephus, *Jewish War* 2.161.
119. On 'ēt dōdîm as referring specifically to the age of sexual maturation appropriate for lovemaking, see Block, *Book of Ezekiel*, 482, n. 117; Greenberg, *Ezekiel 1–20*, 277; and Maier, *Daughter Zion, Mother Zion*, 115 and 249, n. 104; also Sasson, *Judges 13–21*, 749, who comments more generally on translating dōdîm as "(sensual) lovemaking." See in addition my discussion below that suggests we should correlate this moment of sexual maturation with the onset of Jerusalem's menses.
120. Galambush, *Jerusalem in the Book of Ezekiel*, 93–94; Shields, "Multiple Exposures," 9–10.
121. For discussion, see, most recently, Quick, "Spread the Hem of Your Cloak over Me," 39–41; also Greenberg, *Ezekiel 1–20*, 277; Kruger, "The Hem of the Garment in Marriage," 79–86, and especially 83–85; idem, "Rites of Passage Relating to Marriage and Divorce," 77; Propp, *Exodus 19–40*, 721 (on parallels to this tradition in Luke 1:35); and Viberg, *Symbols of Law*, 136–44, and the references listed there. Cf., however, the scholars cited in Chapter 3, n. 33, who view Yahweh's spreading of the robe's edge over Jerusalem in Ezek 16:8 to be a gesture that enacts the couple's marriage instead of their betrothal and likewise those who take the gesture to be a euphemism for sexual intercourse. Yet in considering the former of these arguments, note that in Ruth, Boaz does not "take" Ruth as his wife until Ruth 4:13, which suggests the spreading of the cloak in Ruth 3:9—and, mutatis mutandis, in Ezek 16:8—must be a gesture only of betrothal.
122. See, e.g., Eichrodt, *Ezekiel*, 199, n. o; Klee, "Menstruation in the Hebrew Bible," 103; and Wevers, *Ezekiel*, 96. Others, who take the reference to the spreading of the robe in 16:8 to refer to marriage or sexual intercourse, as opposed to betrothal (above, n. 121, and Chapter 3, n. 33), suggest that the blood of 16:9 is the blood of the young Jerusalem's first coitus: see Block, *Book of Ezekiel*, 484; C. R. Chapman, *Gendered Language of Warfare*, 119–20; Dempsey, "The 'Whore' of Ezekiel 16," 67, who in turn cites Brownlee, *Ezekiel 1–19*, 225; also, Kamionkowski, "Savage Made Civilized," 130; eadem, *Gender Reversal and Cosmic Chaos*, 108; and Pope, "Mixed Marriage Metaphor," 394. For still other interpretations, see below, n. 126.
123. On 'ēt dōdîm as referring specifically to the age of sexual maturation appropriate for lovemaking, see above, n. 119. Interpreters who correlate Jerusalem's readiness for sexual lovemaking with the onset of her menses, as I do here, include Bowen, *Ezekiel*, 85; Joyce, *Ezekiel*, 131; Shields, "Multiple Exposures," 9; and Wevers, *Ezekiel*, 96.
124. On the relation of Ezekiel to P, see above, n. 91. Exactly how Ezekiel and H are related is a matter of considerable scholarly debate, with some arguing for H's literary dependence on Ezekiel; others arguing for Ezekiel's literary dependence on H; others still arguing for a common heritage but not direct dependence; and yet other scholars arguing for a complex scribal process of back-and-forth cross-fertilization over the prolonged period that it took for these corpora to come into their final form. For recent discussions, with abundant references to the history of the debate, see Ganzel and Levitt Kohn, "Ezekiel's Prophetic Message," 1075–84; Kopilovitz, "What Kind of Priestly Writings Did Ezekiel Know?," 1041–54; Lyons, *From Law to Prophecy*; idem, "How Have We Changed?," 1055–74; and Nihan, "Ezekiel and the Holiness Legislation," 1015–39.
125. See, in P, the texts in Lev 12:1–8 and 15:19–24 that I have previously cited; in H, see Lev 18:19 and 20:18. P's and H's related, yet distinct attitudes toward menstruation are reflected in Ezekiel in 18:6; 22:10; and 36:17–18.
126. So Greenberg, *Ezekiel 1–20*, 278, and D. J. Halperin, *Seeking Ezekiel*, 173. Other commentators adopt a "fused" reading of the "blood" of 16:9 as referring not only to the blood of childbirth, but also menstrual blood and the blood of first coitus associated with Jerusalem's marriage (on which see above, n. 122): see Galambush, *Jerusalem in the Book of Ezekiel*, 94–95, n. 16 (albeit with reservations); Koller, "Pornography or Theology?," 411; and Shields, "Multiple Exposures," 9. But cf. L. Day, "Rhetoric and Domestic Violence in Ezekiel 16," 209, n. 9: "discussions about whether this is uterine, menstrual, or hymenal blood are really not necessary to resolve."
127. See, on this point, Shields, "Multiple Exposures," 9; also (although without Shields's negative judgment of Yahweh's negligence) Greenberg, *Ezekiel 1–20*, 278.

128. This exhortation presents several text-critical and interpretive problems. Many commentators, as well as multiple ancient versions, delete the second bĕdāmayik ḥăyî in v 6: see, e.g., Brownlee, *Ezekiel 1–19*, 218; Eichrodt, *Ezekiel*, 199, n. h; and Zimmerli, *Ezekiel 1*, 323. Commentators also differ on whether the phrase "in your blood" belongs with Yahweh's command to "live" (the translation I have adopted here) or is to be taken as part of what Yahweh sees in passing by the infant Jerusalem: so., e.g., the NRSV, "As you lay in your blood, I said to you, "Live!" Greenberg, *Ezekiel 1–20*, 275–76, offers a particularly good discussion of the doublet (and also of the fact that the reference to Jerusalem's "blood" is in the plural [dāmîm], on which see as well C. R. Chapman, *Gendered Language of Warfare*, 119). Koller, "Pornography or Theology?," 408, n. 15, offers a good discussion of the text's translation and its history.
129. Dempsey, "The 'Whore' of Ezekiel 16," 65.
130. Brownlee, *Ezekiel 1–19*, 224.
131. See similarly Galambush, *Jerusalem in the Book of Ezekiel*, 93, who explicitly describes Jerusalem in Ezek 16:6–7 as liminal. See also Maier, *Daughter Zion, Mother Zion*, 115, regarding Yahweh's command to Jerusalem to grow like a plant in v 7: the "terminology of creation and vegetation signifies her liminal state between the open field and the human realm."
132. Yahweh's anointing Jerusalem with oil, immediately after bathing her, might be understood— parallel to the interpretation I have offered of the bathing with which v 9 begins—as a long delayed childbirth rite, given that Hittite and Assyrian accounts of birth rituals mention anointing a newborn infant. E.g., a lamb is rubbed with oil as part of a Hittite birth ritual in which the animal stands in for a newborn child: see Beckman, *Hittite Birth Rituals*, "The Ritual of Papanikri," IV, lines 5–6 (pp. 118–19); Gursky, "Reproductive Rituals," 74, 88; and Pringle, "Hittite Birth Rituals," 140. An Assyrian incantation similarly describes a newborn's chest being massaged with oil: see Scurlock, "Baby-Snatching Demons," 149, and Stol, *Birth in Babylonia and the Bible*, 177. However, it is also possible, given Old Babylonian, Assyrian, and Syrian traditions about anointing a bride-to-be, that the anointing of Jerusalem in Ezek 16:9 was part of the standard Israelite betrothal ritual. See Chapter 3, n. 36.
133. Preeminent expressions of this interpretive direction can be found in L. Day, "Rhetoric and Domestic Violence," 212–24, and Koller, "Pornography or Theology?," 414–15.

Chapter 2

1. As I suggested in the Introduction, I take the P materials, including these materials regarding infant circumcision, to have roots in the late preexilic period, a point that may be supported by the appearance of the name *mlyhw* in the seventh-century BCE onomastic corpus. This name, which means "Yahweh has circumcised," was presumably given to its bearer at birth or shortly thereafter (see Chapter 6), seemingly because he was circumcised at that time. See Albertz, "Personal Names and Family Religion," 291–92, and Schmitt, "Rites of Family and Household Religion," 392, 394.
2. Among the examples listed below, it is Exod 4:24–26 and 1 Sam 18:25–27 that have especially struck commentators as archaic: on the date of the former, see already S. R. Driver's 1911 volume, *Exodus*, 32, where Driver writes that the text is an "evidently antique narrative." On the date of 1 Sam 18:25–27, and more generally the so-called History of David's Rise of which it is a part, see McCarter, *1 Samuel*, 27–31.
3. These examples have been assembled by (among others) S. J. D. Cohen, *Why Aren't Jewish Women Circumcised?*, 11–12; Fox, "Sign of the Covenant," 592–93; Houtman, "Exodus 4:24–26," 93; King, "Circumcision," 51; Propp, "Origins of Infant Circumcision," 358–61; idem, "That Bloody Bridegroom," 508; idem, *Exodus 1–18*, 237; van der Toorn, *From Her Cradle to Her Grave*, 71–72; and de Vaux, *Ancient Israel*, 47. On the number of foreskins reported in 1 Sam 18:27, see McCarter, *I Samuel*, 316.
4. Ritner, "Household Religion in Ancient Egypt," 178; see also E. Bailey, "Circumcision in Ancient Egypt," 15–28; Sasson, "Circumcision in the Ancient Near East," 473–74; and Willems, "Note on Circumcision in Ancient Egypt," 553–58. It may be, however, that by the time of the New Kingdom (ca. 1539–1075 BCE), circumcision was not commonly practiced in Egypt: see R. M. Janssen and J. J. Janssen, *Growing Up and Getting Old*, 76–80, and Meskell, *Private Life*

in New Kingdom Egypt, 88; less completely, eadem, "Cycles of Life and Death," 431, citing the cautions raised by Robins, "Review of Rosalind M. Janssen and Jac J. Janssen, *Growing Up in Ancient Egypt*," 233-34. Rosalie David, *Religion and Magic in Ancient Egypt*, stakes out a middle ground: "Not all Egyptian males were circumcised" (p. 201), although, "at puberty, many boys were" (p. 271). For priests, moreover, circumcision was "seemingly obligatory" through the Ptolemaic and Roman periods (ca. 332 BCE-395 CE): see Ritner, "Household Religion in Ancient Egypt," 178.

5. Ritner, "Household Religion in Ancient Egypt," 178.
6. E. Bailey, "Circumcision in Ancient Egypt," 20-21, suggests, contrary to Ritner, that in the New Kingdom (ca. 1539-1075 BCE), circumcision of prepubescent boys is attested, and Megahed and Vymazalová, "Ancient Egyptian Royal Circumcision," 161, argue that generally in Egypt, from the Old Kingdom period (ca. 2575-2150 BCE) forward, "circumcision ... seems to have been performed on young children." But cf. Robins, "Hair and the Construction of Identity," 57, who writes that images of male children from the one-hundred-and-thirty-year period that she studies (ca. 1480-1350 BCE) "show them to be uncircumcised."
7. On Ndembu boys' age at circumcision, see V. Turner, *Drums of Affliction*, 12; the phrase "made men" is from idem, "Betwixt and Between," 102.
8. See Eng, *Days of Our Years*, 56, with references.
9. Kakarla and Bradshaw, "Disorders of Pubertal Development," 339.
10. Cited in Eyben, "Antiquity's View of Puberty," 696.
11. Cited in Eyben, "Antiquity's View of Puberty," 696.
12. Surveyed in Eyben, "Antiquity's View of Puberty," 696-97.
13. "No firm dating" of "The Instruction of Ankhsheshonq" has "yet been achieved," as the handwriting is late Ptolemaic, but "the composition itself may be earlier": so Lichtheim, *Ancient Egyptian Literature* 3: 159.
14. "The Instruction of Ankhsheshonq," 11.1.7; translation Lichtheim, *Ancient Egyptian Literature* 3: 168.
15. Wyatt, "Pruning of the Vine," 426; see also idem, "Circumcision and Circumstance," 422-26; Dijkstra, "Astral Myth," 286-87; and the careful discussion of Pardee, "Dawn and Dusk," 277, n. 13. Cf., however, Smith, *Rituals and Myths of the Feast of the Goodly Gods*, 46-47.
16. Wyatt, "Circumcision and Circumstance," 423-34, following Allan, "Now That Summer's Gone," 19-25; see likewise Becking, "Then Zipporah Took a Flint," 9.
17. Propp, "That Bloody Bridegroom," 507, 515-18; see also idem, "Origins of Infant Circumcision," 355, n. 1; idem, *Exodus 1-18*, 237; and Patai, *Family, Love and the Bible*, 181-83.
18. Crapanzano, "Rite of Return," 15-36.
19. Propp, "That Bloody Bridegroom," 516.
20. S. J. D. Cohen, *Why Aren't Jewish Women Circumcised?*, 12; see also ibid., 58.
21. S. J. D. Cohen, *Why Aren't Jewish Women Circumcised?*, 12; Propp, "Origins of Infant Circumcision," 358; idem, "That Bloody Bridegroom," 507; idem, *Exodus 1-18*, 237; see similarly, Fox, "Sign of the Covenant," 592; Houtman, "Exodus 4:24-26," 93; Isaac, "Circumcision," 451; Kosmala, "'Bloody Husband,'" 27; van der Toorn, *From Her Cradle to Her Grave*, 72; and de Vaux, *Ancient Israel*, 47.
22. Propp, "That Bloody Bridegroom," 508.
23. De Vaux, *Ancient Israel*, 47.
24. All of this contra Daniel I. Block, "Marriage and Family," 79, who claims regarding Israelite tradition that other than "circumcision ... on the eighth day ... passages in a child's life were not clearly marked," and Jan N. Bremmer, "Rites of Passage," 439, who writes that in Israel, "male initiation seems to have disappeared without a trace."
25. Flusser and Safrai, "Who Sanctified the Beloved in the Womb?," 46-48; note, however, that the significance that Flusser and Safrai assign to this association is somewhat different than I will propose. Likewise, while T. Desmond Alexander, "Genesis 22 and the Covenant of Circumcision," 17-22, proposes, as will I, that there is a relationship between Isaac's circumcision and his near death in Gen 22:1-19, his interpretation of this relationship is different from mine.
26. Philo of Byblos, *Phoenician History*, as quoted in Eusebius, *Praeparatio evangelica* 1.10.33, 44, and translated by Attridge and Oden, *Philo of Byblos*, 63.
27. As many commentators have pointed out, the "him" to which Exod 4:24 refers is unclear. Some thus see Yahweh's intended victim as Moses's son (either his firstborn, Gershom or his second, Eliazer): so, e.g., Greenberg, *Understanding Exodus*, 113-14, 116; Kosmala, "'Bloody

Husband,'" 20–23; and Morgenstern, "'Bloody Husband,'" 45. Most commentators maintain, however, that Yahweh's target is Moses: for discussion, see Becking, "Then Zipporah Took a Flint," 5; Hays, "'Lest Ye Perish in the Way,'" 41–42; Houtman, "Exodus 4:24–26," 98; Kaplan, "'And the Lord Sought to Kill Him,'" 65–74; Propp, "That Bloody Bridegroom," 499; idem, *Exodus 1–18*, 233; and Robinson, "Zipporah to the Rescue," 455–57. I have also commented on this issue in Ackerman, "Why Is Miriam Also among the Prophets?," 73, revised and republished in *Gods, Goddesses, and the Women Who Serve Them*, 102.

28. After Zipporah, Moses's wife, moves in Exod 4:25 to avert Yahweh's attack by circumcising her son, the "feet" she is next said to touch are to be interpreted, in the opinion of the majority of commentators (myself included), as Moses's (although the text uses a pronoun referent that does not make this totally clear). I further agree with the majority of commentators that the reference to Moses's "feet" is to be taken as a euphemism for his genitalia and that what Zipporah is doing is either actually or symbolically circumcising Moses. As in n. 27 above, see further Ackerman, "Why Is Miriam Also among the Prophets?," 73–74, revised and republished in *Gods, Goddesses and the Women Who Serve Them*, 102.

29. Levenson, *Death and Resurrection*, 133.

30. On the story of Isaac's near sacrifice in Gen 22:1–19 as a rite of passage, see also Bal, *Death and Dissymmetry*, 110–12, and Propp, "Symbolic Wounds," 20.

31. As pointed out by Bal, *Death and Dissymmetry*, 110. However, in 2 Chr 3:1, Mount Moriah is identified not with an unknown wilderness location, but with the temple mount in Jerusalem. On the relationship of this identification in 2 Chronicles to "Moriah" in Gen 22:1–19, see Levenson, *Death and Resurrection*, 115–23.

32. See Chapter 1, n. 100.

33. V. Turner, "Betwixt and Between," 93–111.

34. Kunin, "Bridegroom of Blood," 6. On Mount Sinai as the specific locus where the Israelites are transformed from their old slave identity to their new identity as a social and religious polity, see Ackerman, "Why Is Miriam Also among the Prophets?," 76–78, revised and republished in *Gods, Goddesses and the Women Who Serve Them*, 106–7.

35. On traveling and provisional lodging as liminal motifs, see Droogers, "Symbols of Marginality," 105–6; on isolation and seclusion, see ibid.; van Gennep, *Rites of Passage*, 43–44; V. Turner, "Betwixt and Between," 98; and my discussion in the Introduction of the seclusion hut and the seclusion lodge used, respectively, in the Ndembu rituals of *Nkang'a* and *Mukanda* and the "seclusion chamber" used in the initiation of Tukuna girls (Lincoln, *Emerging from the Chrysalis*, 53). See also my discussion in Chapter 1 of Lev 12:1–8 and that text's intimations regarding the postpartum seclusion of a newly delivered woman and her neonate.

36. V. Turner, "Betwixt and Between," 100.

37. Propp, *Exodus 19–40*, 683, 695; see also King and Stager, *Life in Biblical Israel*, 4–5, who describe God as Israel's "supreme patrinomial lord" and "ultimate patrinomial authority."

38. Trible, "Daughter of Jephthah," 96–97. As well documented by DeMaris and Leeb, "Judges," 179, and by Logan, "Rehabilitating Jephthah," 666, n. 4, many others have offered similar assessments. However, DeMaris and Leeb, "Judges," 184–85, and Logan, "Rehabilitating Jephthah," 675–78, put forward spirited alternatives to this line of interpretation.

39. Some scholars argue that the language of Judg 11:31 indicates that Jephthah always had a human victim in mind; see, e.g., Monroe, "Disembodied Women," 35–36, and also ibid., 35, n. 11, where Monroe lists other adherents of this position. As Susan Niditch, *Judges*, 130, n. w, observes, some ancient translations likewise indicate that Jephthah's language specifies that he will sacrifice the first person to emerge from his house. Conversely, Robert G. Boling, *Judges*, 208–9, makes the case, based on the design of ancient Israelite homes, which had incorporated stables, that the story's original audience would have anticipated an animal coming forth from Jephthah's house. David Marcus, *Jephthah and His Vow*, 13–18, lists evidence for both lines of interpretation, although Marcus concludes that "the weight of the evidence seems to be that Jephthah intended an individual, not an animal" (ibid., 13).

40. See Gen 37:34; Lev 10:6; 2 Sam 1:2, 11; 3:31; 13:31; Job 1:20; 2:12; and Esth 4:1; see also the Epic of Gilgamesh, Tablet VIII, line 64 (following the enumeration of George, *Babylonian Gilgamesh Epic* 1), where King Gilgamesh of Uruk "tears off his finery" upon the death of his bosom companion Enkidu.

41. I read here the verb *rād*, "to wander," for MT *yārad*, "to go down," and with the *Qěrē' rě'ōtāy*, for the *Kětîb rě'yōtāy*.

42. According to some commentators—preeminently Marcus, *Jephthah and His Vow*, passim, but see especially 10–11, 38–52—the daughter is not killed but is consecrated to a celibate life.
43. The Hebrew verb *tinnâ* used here is found elsewhere in the Bible only in Judg 5:11, where it means "to recount," with the more specific sense of recounting to commemorate. See P. L. Day, "From the Child Is Born the Woman," 67, n. 4, and the references there; also see van Dijk-Hemmes, "Traces of Women's Texts," 90.
44. The best case for this reading has been made by Logan, "Rehabilitating Jephthah," 675, 682–83. See also the interpretations of Bal, Beavis, and Gerstein catalogued in n. 46 below.
45. P. L. Day, "From the Child Is Born the Woman," 67, n. 4.
46. P. L. Day, "From the Child Is Born the Woman," 58. For others who hold this view, see van Dijk-Hemmes, "Traces of Women's Texts," 88–90; Kamrada, "Sacrifice of Jephthah's Daughter," 81–82; Keuken, "Richter 11.37f.," 41–42; Niditch, *Judges*, 134; and Steinberg, "Problem of Human Sacrifice," 127. This interpretation is also mentioned in Exum, *Fragmented Women*, 39, and in Garroway, "Failure to Marry," 66–67, although neither necessarily endorses it. See in addition DeMaris and Leeb, "Judges," 187–88, 190, who, while they agree with Day and others that "Jephthah's daughter and her companions were away on the mountains undergoing their passage from childhood to adulthood," differ by suggesting that the occasion for the "passage" was "the annual ritual in which the daughters who are ready for marriage are displayed as available." Note in addition Mieke Bal, who, writing independently yet at roughly the same time as Day (P. L. Day, "Jephthah's Daughter," 465), proposed an understanding of vv 37–38 kindred to Day's and yet differed from Day regarding vv 39–40, which Bal reads as a ritual enacted annually by the daughters of Israel that memorialized the daughter and thus ensured her survival despite "the life that she has been denied" (Bal, *Death and Dissymmetry*, 48–49, 66–67). Somewhat similarly, Beth Gerstein, in "A Ritual Processed," 186–87, and Mary Ann Beavis, "Daughter in Israel," 21–22, while agreeing with Bal's and Day's reading of vv 37–38, suggest that the ritual taken up by the "daughters of Israel" in vv 39–40 celebrated Jephthah's daughter as a "heroine," who, in Beavis's words, is "honoured as . . . a saviour" because, as in various stories of Greek sacrificial virgins, she willingly gave herself up to be sacrificed to secure a military victory.
47. This definition of aetiology is taken from D. M. Halperin, *One Hundred Years of Homosexuality*, 21.
48. This has been preeminently demonstrated by Wenham, "*Bᵉtûlāh*," 326–48; see also, for similar understandings of the cognates of *bětûlâ* in Mesopotamia and at Ugarit, Landsberger, "Jungfräulichkeit," 41–105; Roth, "Age at Marriage," 742–46; and Walls, *The Goddess Anat*, 78–79. Wenham goes too far, however, in insisting that in the Bible, *bětûlâ* and *bětûlîm* never refer to a virgin or virginity; rather, in some legal and related texts (Lev 21:13–14; Deut 22:14; Ezek 44:22), "virgin" and "virginity" seem the appropriate translation. For discussion, see Feinstein, *Sexual Pollution*, 89–90; Frymer-Kensky, "Virginity," 79–80; and Pressler, *View of Women*, 25–28, with multiple references.
49. As King and Stager, *Life in Biblical Israel*, 56, point out, "In biblical history, Jeremiah alone [in Jer 16:2] was enjoined by Yahweh not to take a wife and have a family . . . to symbolize the impending death and destruction confronting parents and children before the fall of Judah and the exile."
50. See my discussion in Chapter 1 and n. 111 there.
51. P. L. Day, "From the Child Is Born the Woman," 59–60.
52. P. L. Day, "From the Child Is Born the Woman," 70, n. 17.
53. P. L. Day, "From the Child Is Born the Woman," 60.
54. P. L. Day, "From the Child Is Born the Woman," 58–59.
55. Lincoln, "Initiation," 4487; idem, *Emerging from the Chrysalis*, 95.
56. Lincoln, *Emerging from the Chrysalis*, 72.
57. Lincoln, *Emerging from the Chrysalis*, 74, quoting the *Homeric Hymn to Demeter*, lines 5 and 79.
58. Lincoln, *Emerging from the Chrysalis*, 74.
59. Lincoln, *Emerging from the Chrysalis*, 77.
60. Lincoln, *Emerging from the Chrysalis*, 78.
61. Lincoln, *Emerging from the Chrysalis*, 74.
62. Lincoln, *Emerging from the Chrysalis*, 79.
63. Bal, *Death and Dissymmetry*, 49.
64. As in n. 34 above, see again Kunin, "Bridegroom of Blood," 6, on mountains as one of the major types of liminal space in Hebrew tradition.

65. Above, n. 41.
66. Although it is difficult to imagine how the male-dominated society of ancient Israel, in which female sexuality and so women's mobility were tightly controlled, could have envisioned a scenario whereby a pubescent woman and her female counterparts roamed the mountains without escort for two months.
67. I have argued for this reading and have cited many others who make the same case, in "Why Is Miriam Also among the Prophets?," 66–71, 76–80, with references at 66, n. 57; revised and republished in *Gods, Goddesses and the Women Who Serve Them*, 94–100, 105–9, with references at 94, n. 58.
68. The verb *rapādu* is used of Gilgamesh's wandering in the Epic of Gilgamesh at Tablet VII, line 147; Tablet VIII, line 91; Tablet IX, lines 2, 5; and Tablet X, lines 45, 52, 62, 64, 66, 77, 118, 125, 139, 141, 143, 154, 218, 225, 239, 241, 243 (following here the enumeration of George, *Babylonian Gilgamesh Epic* 1).
69. I have argued for Gilgamesh's liminal nature in *When Heroes Love*, 88–138.
70. Old Babylonian Meissner Fragment, col. iii, lines 2, 12–13, now held in the Vorderasiatisches Museum, Berlin (Vorderasiatische Abteilung Tontafel [VAT] 4105). For the text, see George, *Babylonian Gilgamesh Epic* 1: 278–79.
71. Two enigmatic lines in Tablet III of the Standard version (lines 10 and 225, according to the enumeration of George, *Babylonian Gilgamesh Epic* 1) apparently connect Gilgamesh with "wives" (*ḫirāti*), but it is not at all clear if these are "wives" already in his harem or "brides" he is to wed on his anticipated return, triumphant, from his expedition to kill Ḫuwawa/Ḫumbaba, the fearsome guardian of the Cedar Forest. Possibly, as Stephanie Dalley suggests (*Myths from Mesopotamia*, 127, n. 26), the Epic's intent in these passages, in which Gilgamesh is warned about his proposed expedition's dangers, is a pun between *ḫirāti*, "wives," and *ḫirāti*, "graves." Benjamin R. Foster seems to capture this potential wordplay by translating "let him [Gilgamesh] return, to be a grave husband" (*Epic of Gilgamesh*, 23, 28). George offers further commentary in *Babylonian Gilgamesh Epic* 2: 810.
72. Tablet I, line 76 (although how to interpret this line is debated; see George, *Babylonian Gilgamesh Epic* 1: 449), and Tablet VI, lines 6–79, in the Epic's Standard version; col. iv, lines 147–63, in the Old Babylonian Pennsylvania Tablet (all according to the enumeration of ibid.)
73. This point was brought to my attention by my colleagues in the Colloquium for Biblical Research, who heard a version of this chapter when it was in process. I am grateful to them for their insight and, indeed, for all the help and support they have given me throughout the process of writing this book.
74. Lincoln, *Emerging from the Chrysalis*, 92. One might recall in this regard one of the points I made regarding Ndembu circumcision in the Introduction: that the "guardians" or "shepherds" of the lodge where *Mukanda* initiates are housed after their circumcisions are "often their own fathers, their circumcised older brothers, or 'just special friends'" (V. Turner, "*Mukanda*: The Rite of Circumcision," 233). These "guardians" or "shepherds," that is, are close intimates of the boys who might therefore be expected to offer them special comfort and care as they heal. Recall also Turner's remarks on the special comfort and care a boy's father offers his son during the circumcision proper: see the Introduction and nn. 122–23 there.
75. Cf., however, Levenson, *Death and Resurrection*, 26–31, who argues that in both biblical and extrabiblical stories of a father sacrificing a child, *yāḥîd* does not mean "only" or "sole," but "beloved." Marcus, *Jephthah and His Vow*, 28, makes the opposite case: that, at least in Judg 11:34, *yĕḥîdâ* means "only." As Niditch, *Judges*, 130, n. x, observes, some ancient translations explicitly add "his beloved" to the description of Jephthah's daughter in Judg 11:34.
76. Exum, *Fragmented Women*, 19, 28. In ibid., 28, Exum goes on to point out that it is the daughter who must ask for the *dābār* (which means, among other things, "word") that might bring her some measure of consolation: the two-month sojourn in the mountains with her companions. But cf. Logan, "Rehabilitating Jephthah," 678–80.
77. Exum, *Fragmented Women*, 19, describes this as "a classic case of blaming the victim"; as Shemesh, "Sacrifice of Jephthah's Daughter," 9, n. 23, points out, this interpretation goes back to Trible, "Daughter of Jephthah," 102.
78. Levenson, *Death and Resurrection*, 134.
79. Exum, *Fragmented Women*, 20.
80. Exum, *Fragmented Women*, 20.

Chapter 3

1. The bibliography on Shechem's intercourse with Dinah in Gen 34:2, and whether he takes Dinah by rape, is extensive. Multiple perspectives (with extensive references) have been catalogued by Blyth, *Narrative of Rape*, 38–92; the most recent studies of this passage of which I am aware are Feder, "Defilement of Dina," 281–309, and Joseph, "'Is Dinah Raped?' Isn't the Right Question," 27–37.
2. For studies of this so-called betrothal type-scene, where a bride-to-be is encountered at a well, see Alter, *Art of Biblical Narrative*, 51–62; Fuchs, "Structure and Patriarchal Functions in the Biblical Betrothal Type-Scene," 7–13; and M. W. Martin, "Betrothal Journey Narratives," 505–23.
3. The name of Moses's father-in-law is a matter of some confusion in the biblical text. Exodus 3:1; 4:18; and 18:1–27 identify the father-in-law as Jethro. But in Exod 2:15–21, the father-in-law is assigned the name Reuel, and, although the Hebrew is ambiguous, Num 10:29–32 seems to take the father-in-law's name to be Reuel as well. That text further mentions Hobab, identified there as Reuel's son but described in Judg 1:16 and 4:11 as Moses's father-in-law.
4. Suggested by V. P. Hamilton, "Marriage (OT and ANE)," 563.
5. Literally, they are to marry as is "good in their eyes," although with a masculine singular suffix affixed to the term "eyes" (*'ênêhem*). Commentators overwhelmingly assume, however, that the suffix refers to the daughters and what seems good to them. See B. A. Levine, *Numbers 21–36*, 576, 578.
6. The position of an Israelite woman whose husband has died depends greatly on whether she has a father-in-law, brothers-in-law, and/or sons to see to her well-being. See Adams, *Social and Economic Life in Second Temple Judea*, 51–58; Hiebert, "'Whence Shall Help Come to Me?,'" 125–41; and Steinberg, "Romancing the Widow," 327–46, but cf., on the specific meaning of the term *'almānâ*, "widow," van der Toorn, "Torn between Vice and Virtue," 5–6. Regarding parallels from elsewhere in the Near East, especially Mesopotamia, see Harris, *Gender and Aging*, 108–12; Roth, "Neo-Babylonian Widow," 1–26; Stol, *Women in the Ancient Near East*, 275–95.
7. Alternatively, one could follow 4QSam[b] and LXX[B] to read that David's "brothers" commanded him to attend their clan's yearly sacrifice in 1 Sam 20:29.
8. See my recent comments in Ackerman, *Women and the Religion of Ancient Israel*, 129–30, with additional references.
9. Blenkinsopp, "Family in First Temple Israel," 59.
10. Van der Toorn, "Introduction," 423; see similarly idem, *Family Religion*, 3, and idem, "Recent Trends," 228. See also Albertz, *History of Israelite Religion* 1: 19 ("in ancient Israel . . . there was no such thing as the individual detached from the family"); Gerstenberger, *Theologies*, 25–26, 75–78; Matthews and Benjamin, *Social World of Ancient Israel*, xviii ("the world of the Bible was dyadic, or group-oriented . . . an individual without a household, a village, or a tribe was a convict sentenced to death"); and C. Meyers, "Household Religion," 129 ("Israelites . . . were not really viable as individuals and would not have understood the pronounced individualism of today").
11. Glassner, "Rites of Passage," 441.
12. Blenkinsopp, "Family in First Temple Israel," 59.
13. Matthews and Benjamin, *Social World of Ancient Israel*, 13.
14. Blenkinsopp's observation is also wholly consistent with commentators' descriptions of marriage practice elsewhere in the Near East. See, e.g., regarding marriage in Mesopotamia, Cooper, "Virginity," 101: "the choice of a mate for a daughter was a social and economic decision reserved for her parents," and Stol, "Women in Mesopotamia," 125: "The future wife is the passive object of this [the marriage] transaction."
15. Other texts that use this language of a bride as "given" by her natal family or by others who assert control over the bride include Gen 16:3; 30:4, 9; 34:8, 12; 38:14; 41:45; Exod 21:4; Deut 22:16; Josh 15:16, 17; Judg 1:12, 13; 1 Sam 18:17, 19, 27; 1 Kgs 2:17, 21; 11:19; 2 Kgs 14:9; 1 Chr 2:35; and 2 Chr 25:18. Many of these examples were gathered by da Silva, "Condition of Women," 56, n. 16.
16. Other texts that use this language of a bride as "taken" by a husband include Gen 4:19; 6:2; 11:29; 12:15, 19; 20:2; 21:21; 25:1, 20; 26:34; 27:46; 28:1, 2, 6, 9; 31:50; 34:4, 21; 36:2; 38:6; Exod 6:20, 23, 25; Lev 21:14; Num 12:1; Deut 21:11; 22:13; 24:1, 3–5; 25:5; Judg 3:6; 14:2, 3, 8; 19:1; 1 Sam 25:39–40, 43; 2 Sam 5:13; 12:9–10; 1 Kgs 4:15; 16:31; Jer 16:2; 29:6; Ezek 44:22; Hos 1:2; Ruth 4:13; Ezr 2:61; Neh 7:63; 1 Chr 7:15; 14:3; and 2 Chr 11:18. Many of these

examples were gathered by da Silva, "Condition of Women," 56, n. 15, and Shectman, "What Do We Know about Marriage?," 167, n. 6.
17. Many biblical scholars have also understood the *mōhar* as a form of "marriage by purchase": see the catalog assembled by Lemos, *Marriage Gifts and Social Change*, 4–7.
18. Burrows, *Basis of Israelite Marriage*, 3–52; see the similar position articulated by de Vaux, *Ancient Israel*, 27, and the discussion of Lemos, *Marriage Gifts and Social Change*, 7–8.
19. As Katarzyna Grosz makes clear (in "Some Aspects of the Position of Women," 171), this point is true cross-culturally: "the transfer of bridewealth [anthropologists' preferred term for the so-called bride price] is not considered a purchase . . . and a suggestion that a woman is being transferred as chattel is considered offensive in societies where bridewealth is being practiced." She further points out that "sale/purchase terminology is conspicuously absent" in the bridewealth contracts from fifteenth- and fourteenth-century BCE Nuzi on which her analysis focuses.
20. Lemos, *Marriage Gifts and Social Change*, 44.
21. Mauss, "Essai sur le don," 30–186; English translation: *The Gift*.
22. Ohnuma, "Gift," 105.
23. E.g., Mauss himself, in *The Gift*, 17.
24. "Exchange." See also, on bridewealth as facilitating social bonding, S. Anderson, "Economics of Dowry and Brideprice," 159; Chae, Agadjanian, and Hayford, "Bridewealth Marriage in the 21st Century," 411; and the additional references cited in both articles.
25. C. Meyers, "Guilds and Gatherings," 172.
26. Block, "Marriage and Family," 63.
27. Grosz, "Some Aspects of the Position of Women," 171.
28. Imparati, "Private Life Among the Hittites," 573; Marsman, *Women in Ugarit and Israel*, 87; Stol, *Women in the Ancient Near East*, 75; van der Toorn, *From Her Cradle to Her Grave*, 64; Wenham, "Marriage and Divorce," 7; and Yamauchi, "Cultural Aspects of Marriage," 243.
29. Matthews, "Marriage and Family," 9.
30. Malul, *Studies in Mesopotamian Legal Symbolism*, 168; Matthews, "Marriage and Family," 10, 12; Stol, "Women in Mesopotamia," 125; idem, *Women in the Ancient Near East*, 74, 114; and Westbrook, *Old Babylonian Marriage Law*, 29.
31. Lemos, *Marriage Gifts and Social Change*, 40.
32. Van Gennep, *Rites of Passage*, 3.
33. For further discussion, see the references catalogued in Chapter 1, n. 121. Note, however, that as mentioned there, some commentators take Yahweh's spreading of the robe's edge or skirt over Jerusalem in Ezek 16:8 to be a gesture that enacts the couple's *marriage* instead of their *betrothal*. See, e.g., van der Toorn, *Family Religion*, 43–45, who discusses the rite found in Old Babylonian marriage custom of a husband veiling his new wife on the occasion of their wedding, which is how van der Toorn, in ibid, 309, n. 96, interprets the act of spreading the robe's edge in Ezek 16:8 ("a symbolic gesture belonging to the wedding rites"); see similarly idem, "Significance of the Veil," 334–35; also Block, "Marriage and Family," 44, and C. R. Chapman, *Gendered Language of Warfare*, 119. Alternatively, Kamionkowski, "Savage Made Civilized," 128, and eadem, *Gender Reversal and Cosmic Chaos*, 107, takes the spreading of the cloak as a "euphemism for sexual intercourse," following Brownlee, *Ezekiel 1–19*, 225, and L. Day, "Rhetoric and Domestic Violence in Ezekiel 16," 208, among others.
34. For other interpretations, with references, see Chapter 1, nn. 122 and 126.
35. For references, see Chapter 1, n. 132.
36. For the Old Babylonian materials, see Stol, *Women in the Ancient Near East*, 513 (but cf. ibid, 79), and van der Toorn, *Family Religion*, 43. For Assyrian and Syrian tradition, see Malul, *Studies in Mesopotamian Legal Symbolism*, 161; Stol, *Women in the Ancient Near East*, 79–82; idem, "Women in Mesopotamia," 128; and idem, "Private Life in Ancient Mesopotamia," 488. Note, though, that there is some debate whether the anointing took place at betrothal or at the actual wedding in Mesopotamia. For arguments that associate anointing with *betrothal*, see Malul, *Studies in Mesopotamian Legal Symbolism*, 168–70, as well as the list of proponents who hold this view in ibid., 169, n. 43. For those who see anointing as a symbolic act performed at *marriage*, see Matthews, "Marriage and Family," 11, citing Greengus, "Old Babylonian Marriage Ceremonies," 65–66 (see also the Sumerian text analyzed in ibid., 61–62); Westbrook, "Dowry," 149, n. 1; and Yamauchi, "Cultural Aspects of Marriage," 246, who states—with, unfortunately, no reference—that "the *wedding* was celebrated in Sumer and Assyria by the act of

anointing" (emphasis mine). Other proponents of this view are catalogued by Malul, *Studies in Mesopotamian Legal Symbolism*, 168–69, n. 42.
37. Further on anointing in Ezek 16:9, see Zimmerli, *Ezekiel 1*, 340, and also Westbrook, "Dowry," 149, who, based on his understanding of anointing as a Mesopotamian marriage (versus a betrothal) ritual (above, n. 36), takes Ezek 16:9 to refer to a wedding ceremony, as opposed to a betrothal rite (although Westbrook does seem to see an allusion to betrothal in 16:8). Block, "Marriage and Family," 45, also sees anointing in Ezek 16:9 and generally in Israel and the Near East as a wedding ritual.
38. For contractual arrangements in Mesopotamia, both oral and written, see Greengus, "Old Babylonian Marriage Contract," 505–32; Matthews, "Marriage and Family," 7–10; Stol, "Women in Mesopotamia," 125; and idem, *Women in the Ancient Near East*, 74–76. Note, however, regarding Ezek 16:8, that Greenberg, *Ezekiel 1–20*, 278, takes the pledge and covenant language there to refer not to a betrothal contract, but to the oath God made to the patriarchs in Genesis, promising them the land of Canaan, as well as referring to the covenant traditions of Exodus. For other scholars who hold this view, see the catalogue in Hugenberger, *Marriage as a Covenant*, 306, n. 104, and for Hugenberger's own view, see ibid, 302–9, especially 305–9.
39. Greengus, "Redefining 'Inchoate Marriage,'" 130–32; Stol, "Women in Mesopotamia," 128; idem, "Private Life in Ancient Mesopotamia," 488; and idem, *Women in the Ancient Near East*, 75–76.
40. See my kindred discussion in Chapter 4 about women's seeming absence from weddings' drinking feasts.
41. Also on this point, and on my larger point here regarding the greater ritual impositions to which betrothal and marriage subjected women, see Kruger, "Rites of Passage Relating to Marriage and Divorce," 71.
42. Da Silva, "Condition of Women," 55.
43. Block, "Marriage and Family," 58; this quote was brought to my attention by Lemos, *Marriage Gifts and Social Change*, 41.
44. Douglas, *Purity and Danger*, 96, as previously cited in the Introduction, at n. 114.
45. Da Silva, "Condition of Women," 56–57; Shectman, "What Do We Know about Marriage?," 168.
46. Lemos, *Marriage Gifts and Social Change*, 40.
47. Josephus, *Jewish War*, 2.161, as previously cited in Chapter 1, n. 118.
48. Eng, *Days of Our Years*, 46, 52; J. F. Parker, *Valuable and Vulnerable*, 58. See also, on the definition of *bāḥûr*, S. M. Wilson, *Making Men*, 65–68.
49. Although it must be granted Ruth is envisioned to be older too, having been married to one of Naomi's sons in Moab for ten years (Ruth 1:4) before being widowed and coming with her mother-in-law to Israel.
50. Eng, *Days of Our Years*, 55.
51. J. R. Parker, *Valuable and Vulnerable*, 57.
52. As in Chapter 1, n. 63, see Whitekettle, "Levitical Thought," 381, 390.
53. I take this phrase from Satlow, *Jewish Marriage in Antiquity*, 109.
54. Satlow, *Jewish Marriage in Antiquity*, 106.
55. See Chapter 1 and the data from Satlow, *Jewish Marriage in Antiquity*, 107–8, cited in n. 116 there.
56. Satlow, *Jewish Marriage in Antiquity*, 108–9. See further, for Greek women's age at marriage, the references cited in Chapter 4, n. 70; for Roman women's age at marriage, see, as in Chapter 1, n. 116, Avery, "Coming of Age in the Roman Empire," 4.
57. In the "Introduction and Annotations to Luke," 99 (note on 1:27), Amy-Jill Levine suggests just this: that Josephus followed "Roman norms" in marrying at age thirty.
58. Roth, "Age at Marriage," 747, estimates that during the Neo-Assyrian and Neo-Babylonian periods, the bride was age fourteen to twenty at the time of her marriage, whereas the groom was twenty-six to thirty-two. See similarly, although less precisely, eadem, "Marriage and Matrimonial Prestations," 248–49.
59. Note that the catalog that follows differs in certain ways from that found in Lemos's important study, *Marriage Gifts and Social Change*, 36–50: e.g., Lemos does not consider Exod 3:1, and she raises several concerns about the interpretation of Hos 3:2.
60. For discussion of "brideservice" in Genesis 29, see Lemos, *Marriage Gifts and Social Change*, 45–46.

61. According to Ezek 45:11, a homer is equal to 10 ephahs. Borowski, in *Daily Life in Biblical Times*, 134, n. 31, gives the measure of an ephah as 5.8 gallons (22 liters). A homer, therefore, is about 220 liters.
62. Hosea is well known for his theological affinities with Deuteronomic thought: see preeminently Weinfeld, "Hosea and Deuteronomy," in idem, *Deuteronomy and the Deuteronomic School*, 366–70.
63. While the preeminent presentation of this thesis is now Lemos, *Marriage Gifts and Social Change*, 50–61, this point had previously been noted by others: e.g., de Vaux, *Ancient Israel*, 28. Cf., however, Westbrook, "Dowry," 142–64, especially 142, where Westbrook, although he acknowledges that "the dowry receives little mention in the Bible," argues that this is due to "the very centrality of the institution"; "for the biblical authors," he suggests, "the dowry was a common, everyday thing." See similarly Fleishman, "A Daughter's Demand," 358, who writes, "despite the fact that biblical law does not discuss the dowry institution, it may be assumed that the laws [concerning dowry] current in the ancient Near East . . . were prevalent also in biblical Israel"; Wenham, "Marriage and Divorce," 15, who states, "in the light of extra-biblical evidence," it "seems most unlikely" that "the Hebrews did not give dowries"; and Westbrook and Wells, *Everyday Law*, 99: "the dowry . . . virtually universal in the ancient world . . . must have been equally central to the law of biblical Israel."
64. As noted in the Introduction, I assign a preexilic date to the so-called J and E authors within the Pentateuch, and a late preexilic/early exilic date to the Deuteronomistic History, and it is to these authors that I would attribute the smattering of "dowry" texts I discuss just below: Gen 29:23–24, 28–29; 31:14–16; Josh 15:13–19; Judg 1:11–15; and 1 Kgs 9:16. Ezekiel's oracles, and so Ezek 16:26–34 (also discussed just below), date from the last decade of the preexilic period and first decade of the exile.
65. Westbrook, "Dowry," 145.
66. As the passage makes clear, this giving away of her dowry on Jerusalem's part is paradoxical, as a harlot should collect a fee, rather than extend payment to those who use her services.
67. See, most recently, Boyd, *Language Contact*, 255. Note, moreover, that Akkadian *nudunnû* can mean both "dowry" in its most formal sense—resources given to a bride by her natal family upon the occasion of her marriage—and also resources given to a wife by her husband once the marriage has been made. This dual sense of *nudunnû* may likewise be alluded to in Ezekiel 16, where Yahweh, who has bestowed upon Jerusalem the *nādān/neden/nōden* that she squanders, is depicted in the passage both as the city's foster father who offers her some measure of protection after she is abandoned at birth and as the husband who takes her in marriage once she has reached maturity.
68. Greengus, "Bridewealth in Sumerian Sources," 28, 75–77.
69. Greengus, "Legal and Social Institutions of Ancient Mesopotamia," 480; idem, "Redefining 'Inchoate Marriage,'" 127; Matthews, "Marriage and Family," 13; Stol, "Private Life in Ancient Mesopotamia," 489; and Yoffee, "Rites of Marriage, Divorce, and Adoption," 63. See further on marriage presents and dowries during the Old Babylonian period, Dalley, "Old Babylonian Dowries," 53–74, and Greengus, "Old Babylonian Marriage Ceremonies," 59–61.
70. Grosz, "Some Aspects of the Position of Women," 169, and eadem, "Bridewealth and Dowry," 197, 199–205. See n. 76 below, however, regarding the specific way the institutions of bridewealth and dowry are exercised in Nuzi.
71. Hoffner, "Legal and Social Institutions," 558; Rowe, "Ugarit," 725–26.
72. Roth, "Marriage and Matrimonial Prestations," 248 and 252, reports that she "know[s] of dowries . . . provided by the families of one hundred and sixty-one Neo-Babylonian women," whereas "bridewealth . . . given by the husband to the wife's kin is attested for only three marriages." See similarly (and more fully) eadem, *Babylonian Marriage Agreements*, 8, 11–12, 26–28, and also Abraham, "Dowry Clause," 311–20. See in addition, albeit much less completely, the comments of Greengus, "Legal and Social Institutions of Ancient Mesopotamia," 480, and Stol, "Payment of the Old Babylonian Brideprice," 132.
73. Lemos, *Marriage Gifts and Social Change*, passim, but especially 17–19 and Chapters 4–5, citing J. Goody, "Bridewealth and Dowry," 1–58; idem, *Production and Reproduction*; and idem, *The Oriental, the Ancient, and the Primitive*.
74. Lemos sees greater evidence of increasing social stratification in Israel in the last century or two before the exile (ca. 800–586 BCE) than I believe the evidence—especially the archaeological evidence from the Israelite countryside—allows. See further below, n. 84, on the essentially rural character of Israel throughout the preexilic era,

75. As noted in the Introduction, I assign a preexilic date to the so-called J and E authors within the Pentateuch, as well as to the author of Deuteronomy, and it is to these authors that I would attribute the "marriage present" texts of Gen 24:1–67; 29:15–30; 34:1–31; Exod 3:1; 22:15–16 (English 22:16–17); and Deut 22:28–29. I also assign a late preexilic/early exilic date to the Deuteronomistic Historian, to whom I would attribute 1 Sam 18:25 (at least in its final redaction); see McCarter, *1 Samuel*, 27–31, regarding the date of the pre-redacted text). The prophet Hosea is dated to the eighth century BCE.
76. To be clear, this is not the argument that Lemos advances; as Daniel Fisher puts it in "Review of *Marriage Gifts and Social Change in Ancient Palestine*," 90: "Her [Lemos's] discussion of the biblical evidence focuses on diachronic socioeconomic changes and does not consider synchronic socioeconomic differences," whereas Fisher suggests, as do I, that "synchronic socioeconomic differentiation might account at least partially for the occurrence of dowry . . . in pre-exilic literature." Grosz, "Bridewealth and Dowry," 205, makes much the same argument about the fifteenth- and fourteenth-century BCE Nuzi materials she has studied: "Bridewealth is practiced by the poor, while . . . Nuzian princesses and rich women married with huge dowries."
77. Lemos, *Marriage Gifts and Social Change*, 137–52.
78. Lemos, *Marriage Gifts and Social Change*, 200–29.
79. D. W. Chapman, "Marriage and Family," 193–97, following J. J. Collins, "Marriage, Divorce, and Family," 108, 114. As Chapman points out, however, on p. 197, one should note the cautions raised by Satlow, "Reconsidering the Rabbinic *Ketubah* Payment," 133–51, and idem, *Jewish Marriage in Antiquity*, 213–16, who suggests that the rabbinic tradition that had the groom paying the marriage present solely in cases of divorce comes into being only in the late first century CE.
80. Lemos, *Marriage Gifts and Social Change*, 13.
81. Lemos, *Marriage Gifts and Social Change*, 13.
82. Lemos, *Marriage Gifts and Social Change*, 232; see also Grosz, "Bridewealth and Dowry," 198, and Chae, Agadjanian, and Hayford, "Bridewealth Marriage in the 21st Century," 411.
83. E.g., Emmerson, "Women in Ancient Israel," 383; Lipiński, "*mōhar*," 143–44; Neufeld, *Ancient Hebrew Marriage Laws*, 94–110 (as brought to my attention by Lemos, *Marriage Gifts and Social Change*, 6, n. 20); and Pressler, "'Biblical View' of Marriage," 202. See also Keefe, *Women's Body and the Social Body*, 164–65, n. 3, and Patrick, *Old Testament Law*, 83, who consider the marriage present in relation to economics yet also in relation to the creation of alliances between kinship groups, as discussed above.
84. For this estimate, see Dever, *Did God Have a Wife?*, 18, and King and Stager, *Life in Biblical Israel*, 21. Cf., however, Borowski, *Daily Life in Biblical Times*, 9, 13, who estimates that only 66 percent of the Israelite population, at least during the Iron II period (ca. 1000–586 BCE), lived in rural locations.
85. Meyers has argued this in numerous publications: perhaps first in C. Meyers, *Discovering Eve*, 145–49, and in eadem, "Family in Early Israel," 25–26, and then far more thoroughly in eadem, "Having Their Space and Eating There Too," 14–44; eadem, "Material Remains and Social Relations," 425–44; eadem, "From Field Crops to Food," 67–84; eadem, *Rediscovering Eve*, 128–35; and eadem, "Women's Daily Life," 489–92.
86. C. Meyers, "Guilds and Gatherings," 176. On the Dor bread trough, see, preeminently, Zorn, "Daily Grind at Tel Dor," 267*–80*.
87. C. Meyers, "From Field Crops to Food," 71. On the ʿIzbet Ṣarṭah materials, see also eadem, "Material Remains and Social Relations," 430–31; eadem, "Having their Space and Eating There Too," 22; and J. R. Ebeling and Rowan, "Archaeology of the Daily Grind," 114.
88. C. Meyers, "Food and Gender," 388.
89. Van der Toorn similarly imagines that Israelite women "from the same [household] compound would often team up to distract themselves from the monotony of grinding": see his "Nine Months among the Peasants," 198.
90. Meyers has argued this in numerous places: perhaps first in C. Meyers, "Family in Early Israel," 25 and 45, n. 67; most recently, in eadem, *Rediscovering Eve*, 130; eadem, "Women's Daily Life," 490; and eadem, "Food and Gender," 387.
91. Dever, *Lives of Ordinary People*, 170; J. R. Ebeling, *Women's Lives in Biblical Times*, 48.
92. Adams, *Social and Economic Life in Second Temple Judea*, 66.
93. It is also hard to see how David's marriage present of one hundred Philistine foreskins (1 Sam 18:25, 27; 2 Sam 3:14) might compensate Saul for the loss of Michal's contributions to the

material productivity of Saul's household (Westbook and B. Wells, *Everyday Law*, 60), but since Saul's household is a royal one, the biblical writers surely do not mean us to envision it as one in which royal daughters performed onerous domestic chores. Which is to say: while Saul's royal house, if it even existed, is surely to be imagined as an extremely modest residence (Ackerman, *Women and the Religion of Ancient Israel*, 193–94), biblical tradition nevertheless understands royal households to be staffed by servitors from among the king's subjects who perform domestic chores (1 Sam 8:10–18).

94. Pressler, "Sexual Violence and Deuteronomic Law," 105.
95. Frymer-Kensky, "Virginity," 81–85.
96. On the importance of a woman's virginity as a marker of her family's honor in biblical tradition, see Frymer-Kensky, "Virginity," 84–85; Matthews, "Honor and Shame," 108; idem, "Marriage and Family," 9, and nn. 46 and 47 there; and Southwood, *Marriage by Capture*, 104–14.
97. Feinstein, *Sexual Pollution*, 234, n. 323, cites Keefe, *Woman's Body and the Social Body*, 164; Niditch, "Wronged Woman Righted,"146; Phillips, *Ancient Israel's Criminal Law*, 117; and Pressler, *View of Women*, 42, as among the scholars who put forward this view.
98. Cooper, "Virginity," 104–5; Feinstein, *Sexual Pollution*, 99; and Frymer-Kensky, "Virginity," 81. On ten months as the presumed period of gestation in ancient Israel, see Chapter 1, n. 52.
99. Feinstein, *Sexual Pollution*, 94–95.
100. Feinstein, *Sexual Pollution*, 88.
101. Shectman, "Priestly Marriage Restrictions," 181.
102. On these two passages' sense of seduction versus rape, see Feinstein, *Sexual Pollution*, 78–79 and 227, n. 225; Greengus, *Laws in the Bible*, 63–68; Jackson, *Wisdom-Laws*, 368–70 and nn. 7–9. 20–21 there; Lipka, *Sexual Transgression*, 170, n. 3, and 174–76; Pressler, *View of Women*, 37–38; and Southwood, *Marriage by Capture*, 114–21. But other scholars read differently: see Fleishman, "Exodus 22:15–26 and Deuteronomy 22:28–29," 59–73; idem, "Biblical Laws of Marriage vis-à-vis Seduction and Rape," 87–129; Frymer-Kensky, "Virginity," 92; Lemos, *Marriage Gifts and Social Change*, 37–38, nn. 95, 98; and Weinfeld, *Deuteronomy and the Deuteronomic School*, 286–87.
103. But cf. Jackson, *Wisdom-Laws*, 378–79, who argues that in Exod 22:15–16 (English 22:16–17), a "full marriage" (just as in Deut 22:28–29) is implied.
104. Shipton, *Nature of Entrustment*, 122.
105. Bourdieu, "Work of Time," 135–47.
106. Ohnuma, "Gift," 118.
107. As in n. 98 above, see Chapter 1, n. 52, on ten months as the presumed period of gestation in ancient Israel.
108. C. Meyers, "From Household to House of Yahweh," 298; eadem, *Households and Holiness*, 59; eadem, *Discovering Eve*, 62.
109. C. Meyers, "From Household to House of Yahweh," 298, and eadem, *Households and Holiness*, 59; Frymer-Kensky, *In the Wake of the Goddesses*, 97.
110. Simkins, "Class and Gender in Early Israel," 81.
111. J. Goody, *Production and Reproduction*, 8; idem, *Social Organization of the LoWiili*, 64.
112. J. Goody, *Production and Reproduction*, 8.
113. E. N. Goody, with J. Goody, "Circulation of Women and Children in Northern Ghana," 107.
114. E. N. Goody, with J. Goody, "Circulation of Women and Children in Northern Ghana," 101.
115. E. N. Goody, with J. Goody, "Circulation of Women and Children in Northern Ghana," 97. See also S. Anderson, "Economics of Dowry and Brideprice," 158–59, who more generally observes (with additional references) that in some African societies, "a divorced woman who already has children will receive a lower brideprice, whereas women who reach puberty earlier receive a higher price."
116. Shipton, *Nature of Entrustment*, 136.
117. Shipton, *Nature of Entrustment*, 123. Other purposes of bridewealth can include, as discussed above, the creation of alliances between kinship groups and compensating the bride's family for the productive and economic losses that can ensue once her labor is no longer available within her natal family.
118. Scurlock, "'Not Even Her Own Jewelry,'" 245–46.
119. Grosz, "Dowry and Brideprice," 171; see also Stol, "Payment of the Old Babylonian Brideprice," 132–35.
120. Granqvist also suggests that reasons other than reproductive potential may explain these alleged differences in brideprice: see Granqvist, *Marriage Conditions*, 120–21. Nevertheless,

"there is a very close connection between the brideprice given and the value ascribed to a woman": ibid., 132.
121. Granqvist, *Marriage Conditions*, 133.
122. Granqvist, *Marriage Conditions*, 133, n. 2.
123. Lincoln, *Emerging from the Chrysalis*, 7, 11, 19, 47.
124. Lincoln, *Emerging from the Chrysalis*, 7, 11, 19.
125. V. Turner, "Nkang'a: Part Two," 252–54.
126. V. Turner, "Nkang'a: Part Two," 258–59; see similarly E. Turner, "Girl into Woman," 32; eadem, *Spirit and the Drum*, 79.
127. V. Turner, "Nkang'a: Part Two," 260.
128. E. Turner, "Zambia's Kankanga Dances," 62.
129. V. Turner, "Nkang'a: Part Two," 264–65.
130. Lincoln, *Emerging from the Chrysalis*, 116–17.

Chapter 4

1. For the promulgation of this interpretation in Hellenistic- and Roman-era Jewish sources (ca. 63 BCE–135 CE), see J. J. Collins, "Marriage, Divorce, and Family," 127–30, and Satlow, *Jewish Marriage in Antiquity*, 58–66.
2. Cf., however, van der Toorn, *From Her Cradle to Her Grave*, 61, who takes Gen 2:24 to indicate that a groom went to the bride's house only for his wedding and perhaps some period afterward (see further below). Others who comment on the uxorilocal–patrilocal disjunction in Gen 2:24 include Gunkel, *Genesis*, 13; Hendel, *Genesis 1–11*, 176; von Rad, *Genesis*, 83; and Skinner, *Critical and Exegetical Commentary on Genesis*, 70.
3. Van der Toorn, *From Her Cradle to Her Grave*, 66, 73–74; also idem, *Family Religion*, 199. The Mesopotamian materials—particularly a text from the Old Babylonian period (ca. 1894–1595 BCE) that describes the groom taking up residence with his new wife's family for four months—are discussed in Greengus, "Old Babylonian Marriage Ceremonies," 66–68, and Yoffee, "Rites of Marriage, Divorce, and Adoption," 64.
4. Yoffee, "Rites of Marriage, Divorce, and Adoption," 64.
5. Van der Toorn, *From Her Cradle to Her Grave*, 73.
6. In the Bible, see only Gen 20:17, which might be read to indicate that Abimelech is among the victims of the barrenness that God had inflicted upon Abimelech's house; Deut 7:14, where the Israelites are assured that if they are obedient to God's covenant, there will be neither male nor female barrenness (*'āqār wa'ăqārâ*) among them; and 2 Kgs 4:14, where the Shunammite women's childlessness is attributed to her husband's old age. Elsewhere in the Near East, traditions of male barrenness are equally rare: I know of one Egyptian text that speaks of male infertility (see Galpaz-Feller, "Pregnancy and Birth," 52), and likewise of one Hittite text that addresses male impotence (see Hoffner, "Paskuwatti's Ritual," 271–87), although Whitekettle, "Human Reproduction," 98–108, discusses the somewhat more fulsome corpus of Mesopotamian magico-medical texts that concern male impotency. Also, King Dan'il is identified as barren in the Epic of Aqhat, from the Late Bronze Age city-state of Ugarit (*KTU* 1.17.1.36–42). Yet, as I have argued in Ackerman, *Warrior, Dancer*, 193–94, the motif of Dan'il's barrenness is driven by a special concern within the Epic's plot: that although King Dan'il, like any king, needs a royal heir, he is without a son. Because, moreover, a king typically would have had many wives, able to bear him many sons (see, e.g., 2 Sam 3:2–5; 5:13–16), the crisis of Dan'il's childlessness could have been easily addressed were it his primary wife, Danataya, who was barren. Thus, to sustain the narrative tension regarding Dan'il's heir, the Epic takes the unusual step of depicting the man as infertile. That said, I should be clear that royal status is never explicitly claimed for Dan'il. Still, the assumption that Dan'il is a king is implicit throughout the text: see again my discussion in ibid., 211, n. 27.
7. The term *pîlegeš* can refer to a woman who is married to a man as a secondary wife or to a concubine who is part of a king's harem but not one of his actual wives. In 2 Sam 5:13; 15:16; 19:6 (19:5 in most English translations); 1 Chr 3:9; 2 Chr 11:21; Cant 6:8, 9; and Esth 2:14, the latter

meaning seems intended. First Kings 11:3, however, lists Solomon's *pīlagšîm* as being among his "wives" (*nāšîm*).
8. As noted in the Introduction, I assign a preexilic date to the so-called E author within the Pentateuch, to whom I would ascribe Exod 21:10, and also to the book of Deuteronomy.
9. Satlow, *Jewish Marriage in Antiquity*, 190–91.
10. J. J. Collins, "Marriage, Divorce, and Family," 122; Satlow, *Jewish Marriage in Antiquity*, 97–98, 189, 191–92.
11. Satlow, *Jewish Marriage in Antiquity*, 190.
12. On the complexities of this text and the passage in which it is embedded, see Propp, *Exodus 19–40*, 196–204.
13. B. Wells, "First Wives Club," 105–15.
14. The date of Ezra's mission to postexilic Jerusalem and even the question of whether there was an Ezra have been much debated among scholars: for a recent summary of various positions, see Eskenazi, *Ezra*, 6, 30–31, with multiple references. If we agree, with Eskenazi, that there was an actual Ezra (ibid., 6), then the two viable dates for his mission are during the reign of Artaxerxes I in ca. 458 BCE or of Artaxerxes II in ca. 398 BCE. Conversely, almost all scholars agree that Nehemiah's initial mission should be dated to ca. 445–433 BCE and his second mission somewhat later.
15. This list is an anachronistic description of the postexilic population—"only the Ammonites, Moabites, and Egyptians were still in existence"—and is thus best taken as a symbolic catalogue of those "peoples of the land" taken to be "other" by "those returning from the Babylonian exile"; see Southwood, "An Ethnic Affair?," 52, with additional references. Elsewhere, Southwood ("Holy Seed," 198, 206) suggests these "others" were a remnant group of "Yahwists" who survived the Babylonian destruction "and stayed in the land"; see also Dor, "Rite of Separation," 173–74, and the additional references cited by both.
16. Southwood, "Holy Seed," 201.
17. Lemos, "Where There Is Dirt, Is There System?," 284.
18. On *naḥălâ*, see my much fuller discussion in Chapter 9.
19. Philo, *De Specialibus Legibus*. 2.126; translation Colson, *Philo VII*, 381, 383: this quote was brought to my attention by Archer, *Her Price Is Beyond Rubies*, 148. In ibid., 146, Archer notes texts from Tob 1:9 and Jdt 8:2 that also extol intratribal marriages.
20. C. Meyers, *Discovering Eve*, 185–86.
21. Van der Toorn, *Family Religion*, 200–201; see similarly Block, "Marriage and Family," 37.
22. Blenkinsopp, "Family in First Temple Israel," 59; see somewhat similarly Patai, *Family, Love and the Bible*, 26.
23. Bird, "Women (OT)," 952.
24. Yee, "Recovering Marginalized Groups," 12.
25. Exum, *Fragmented Women*, 110.
26. V. Turner, "Betwixt and Between," 97, 99.
27. Lemos, "Were Israelite Women Chattel?," 238.
28. King and Stager, *Life in Biblical Israel*, 54.
29. V. Turner, "Betwixt and Between," 98.
30. Cox and Ackerman, "Micah's Teraphim," 12–13.
31. Yee, "Recovering Marginalized Groups," 12.
32. V. Turner, "Humility and Hierarchy," 167–68.
33. See, e.g., the questions Patai raises in *Family, Love and the Bible*, 56–57.
34. According to Dominic Montserrat, "Rites of Passage," 439, "a marital union" in ancient Egypt was determined only "by the partners agreeing to cohabit" and not by any formal ceremony. Likewise, Betsy M. Bryan, "In Women Good and Bad Fortune," 31, writes that "in ancient Egypt . . . there was no marriage ceremony," and Gay Robins, *Women in Ancient Egypt*, 56, similarly states of ancient Egypt that "there is no mention in our sources of any legal or religious ceremony to formalize a marriage." Cf., however, Toivari-Viitala, "Case Study of Ancient Egyptian Marriage Practices," 613–19, especially 615–17, regarding New Kingdom tradition (ca. 1539–1075 BCE), and eadem, "Marriage and Divorce," 4, regarding "standardized . . . marriage contracts" from the Late Period (ca. 715–332 BCE).
35. Moshe Greenberg, e.g., takes vv 10–12 to describe "the clothing with which the royal husband dowers his wife for life"; see *Ezekiel 1–20*, 279.
36. On Psalm 45 as a wedding song of the northern court, see, among recent commentators, Smith, *Poetic Heroes*, 302 and 556, n. 134.

37. Except for Isa 49:18, all the references I have just cited were brought to my attention by Yamauchi, "Cultural Aspects of Marriage," 247.
38. Andersen, "Renaming and Wedding Imagery," 75–80.
39. See, preeminently, van der Toorn, "Significance of the Veil," 330–34; also, on veiling in Mesopotamian marriage ritual, see Matthews, "Marriage and Family," 11–12; Stol, "Women in Mesopotamia," 124; and idem, *Women in the Ancient Near East*, 22–24, 27. On veiling in conjunction with marriage at Mari, see Sasson, "Servant's Tale," 245, and on veiling as part of Greek marriage ritual, see Garland, *Greek Way of Life*, 220–22.
40. This interpretation of Gen 29:23–25 has been suggested by a plethora of commentators, but cf. Gibson, *Genesis* 2: 178.
41. Block, "Marriage and Family," 45; Geller, "Elephantine Papyri and Hosea 2, 3," 139–48; Greengus, "Old Babylonian Marriage Contract," 515–17, 520; Westbrook and B. Wells, *Everyday Law*, 59 (regarding Elephantine); Yaron, *Introduction to the Law of the Aramaic Papyri*, 46–47; and Yoffee, "Rites of Marriage, Divorce, and Adoption," 63. But cf. Westbrook, *Old Babylonian Marriage Law*, 48–50 (regarding Mesopotamia).
42. But regarding Mesopotamia during the Old Babylonian period (ca. 1894–1595 BCE), see Greengus, "Old Babylonian Marriage Contract," 520–22.
43. J. J. Collins, "Marriage, Divorce, and Family," 109–10.
44. This suggestion seems originally to go back to G. F. Moore, *Critical and Exegetical Commentary on Judges*, 339 (so BDB, 946a, s.v. *rāʿâ*); see also van Selms, "The Best Man and Bride," 71–74.
45. Cf., however, Sasson, *Judges 1–12*, 146, regarding the marriage of Achsah as described in Judg 1:14.
46. Burney, *Book of Judges*, 344.
47. Note in this regard the comments of Ritva H. Williams, "The Mother of Jesus at Cana," 681, who writes of "first-century East Mediterranean weddings": "although women were present throughout the festivities, they dined and celebrated apart, segregated from the men."
48. Well documented by C. A. Moore, *Esther*, xxxiv–xliv, especially xli.
49. Bickerman, *Four Strange Books of the Bible*, 185.
50. "Tying the Knot: Marriage in Ancient Greece," 56. See similarly n. 47 above; Garland, *Greek Way of Life*, 220; and Rebecca Hague, "Marriage Athenian Style," 34: "the usual ritual separation of the sexes prevailed . . . and the women reclined on banquet couches apart from the men."
51. But cf. Sasson, *Judges 13–21*, 909, n. 8, and Yamauchi, "Cultural Aspects of Marriage," 247, who argue for a one-day feast.
52. Following here the reconstruction of the text in Ahearne-Kroll, "Joseph and Aseneth," 2525–80, which in turn depends on Burchard, *Joseph und Aseneth*.
53. Wills, *Ancient Jewish Novels*, 123.
54. Satlow, *Jewish Marriage in Antiquity*, 178.
55. Cf., therefore, Block, "Marriage and Family," 45: "He [the groom] would prepare his finest meal for her [the bride], and they would feast together in *his* house" (emphasis mine); similarly, de Vaux, *Ancient Israel*, 34: "as a general rule it [the feast] was certainly given at the bridegroom's house."
56. Extensive discussions of this passage can be found in Lafont, *Femmes, droit et justice*, 249–52; Locher, *Die Ehre Frau in Israel*; and Pressler, *View of Women*, 22–30.
57. Reading "fourth" with the LXX and Syriac in Judg 14:15 rather than following the MT, which reads "on the seventh day."
58. If we read "fourth" with the LXX and Syriac in Judg 14:15 (above, n. 57), then the companions are said to come to Samson's bride on the fourth day of the seven-day wedding feast and set her on her task of enticement. Yet, according to 14:17, Samson does not reveal the answer to his riddle until the seventh day of the banqueting, implying that the wife tried to persuade him to speak on days four, five, and six but was rebuffed.
59. Bottéro, *Oldest Cuisine in the World*, 101.
60. Here, *pîlegeš* must mean "secondary" or "lesser" wife, given that we are told in 19:3 that the Levite is the woman's husband (*ʾîšāh*) and in 19:4, 7, and 9 that the woman's father is the Levite's father-in-law (*ḥōtnô*): see further Ackerman, *Warrior, Dancer*, 235–37. The reading *wattiznaḥ*, "she spurned him," is derived from the LXX and Vulgate, as opposed to the MT *wattizneh*, "she prostituted herself against him." Alternatively, one could read *wattizneh* and, following Lipka, *Sexual Transgression*, 249, understand it to mean that the *pîlegeš*, while not literally prostituting herself, violated the Levite's right to exclusive sexual control over her body by leaving him to return to the man (her father) who, before her marriage, exercised sexual control over her.

61. Although Judg 19:28 does not say so explicitly, the text clearly presumes that the woman has died: see Lasine, "Guest and Host in Judges 19," 45–46. In fact, a notice of the woman's death was probably originally included in the Hebrew text and is missing only because of scribal error. Both of the major Greek witnesses (LXX^A and LXX^B) state unambiguously that when the Levite found the woman on the Ephraimite's doorstoop in the morning, she was dead, which suggests a Hebrew original of ky mth, probably lost because of haplography induced by homeoteleuton from the preceding 'nh: I am grateful to the late David Noel Freedman, of the University of California, San Diego, for this observation. See also Boling, Judges, 38–42 (on the textual traditions of Judges) and 276 (on Judg 19:28).
62. On the translation of bĕtûlâ (singular) and bĕtûlôt (plural), see Chapter 2, n. 48.
63. Although Judg 21:19–21 does not state explicitly that the festival being celebrated is Ingathering/Sukkot, I have catalogued multiple indications that suggest this interpretation in Ackerman, *Women and the Religion of Ancient Israel*, 231–33.
64. Southwood, *Marriage by Capture*, 158–59, citing Kudat, "Institutional Rigidity and Individual Initiative in Marriages," 291, and Stross, "Tzeltal Marriage by Capture," 328–46.
65. Southwood, *Marriage by Capture*, 158, 160, and 167.
66. On Judg 14:15, see above, n. 57.
67. In this regard, consider also the degree to which the vocabulary of the story of the Levite's pîlegeš casts her as a "bride" during the "wedding" scene that takes place (as I have interpreted) in her father's house. Six times during this episode, she is described as a na'ărâ (in Judg 19:3, 4, 5, 6, 8, and 9), a term that is usually translated simply as "girl" but often refers specifically to a "girl" as bride-to-be. See, as above, Judg 21:12, regarding the young women of Jabesh-Gilead, as well as the discussion of S. M. Wilson, *Making Men*, 52–53. Conversely, between the time that the woman leaves her Levite husband in 19:2 and the time that he departs from her father's house with her in tow in 19:10, the term pîlegeš is not used. Therefore, it is as if the pîlegeš leaves her position as a "secondary" or "lesser" wife behind in 19:2 to revert to the state of na'ărâ until her second "wedding" is completed, at which point (in 19:10) she becomes a pîlegeš again.
68. Marcus, "Betrothal of Yarikh and Nikkal-Ib," 215; see also Lewis, "Family, Household, and Local Religion," 65; de Moor, *Anthology of Religious Texts*, 141; Wyatt, *Religious Texts*, 336; and, on the katharat, Pardee, "Kosharoth," 491–92.
69. D. and S. Hoffman, "Sappho and the Songs of Marriage," 36; see similarly ibid., 40.
70. As I noted in Chapter 3 (with preliminary documentation at n. 56), Greek women married shortly after reaching sexual maturity, while their husbands were often significantly older. See, e.g., Robert Garland, *Greek Way of Life*, 26 (with further discussion at ibid., 210–13). He reports that "in Classical Athens . . . the majority of well-to-do girls seem to have been married around the age of thirteen or fourteen to men who were about thirty." Also see Jenifer Neils, *Women in the Ancient World*, 62, who writes that a Greek woman was a teenager at marriage and the groom a man of about thirty, and John H. Oakley and Rebecca H. Sims, *Wedding in Ancient Athens*, 10 and 14, who estimate that Greek brides were about fourteen years of age, whereas the groom "was sometimes considerably older," between the ages of thirty and thirty-seven. Anne L. Klinck, *Women's Songs in Ancient Greece*, 23, similarly notes that in classical Athens, women married in their mid-teens or even earlier, although in Sparta, girls married somewhat later, at perhaps age eighteen to twenty.
71. Seaford, "Tragic Wedding," 113–14. See also the discussion of the "uneasy compromise" and "ambiguous good" that marriage represented for Greek women in Redfield, "Notes on the Greek Wedding," 181 and 190, respectively.
72. Sappho Fragment 114, as translated by Klinck, *Women's Songs in Ancient Greece*, 123.
73. Sappho Fragment 105b, as translated by Klinck, *Women's Songs in Ancient Greece*, 121.
74. Hague, "Marriage Athenian Style," 34; see similarly D. and S. Hoffman, "Sappho and the Songs of Marriage," 38.
75. Hague, "Marriage Athenian Style," 34. See, similarly, the discussion of parallels between ancient and modern (as well as medieval) Greek wedding songs in Seaford, "Tragic Wedding," 111 and 113, with references at 113, n. 82.
76. Oakley and Sims, *Wedding in Ancient Athens*, 37.
77. As quoted in Oakley and Sims, *Wedding in Ancient Athens*, 37.
78. Klinck, *Women's Songs in Ancient Greece*, 146.
79. Lonsdale, *Dance and Ritual Play in Greek Religion*, 234.
80. Lonsdale, *Dance and Ritual Play in Greek Religion*, 234; see similarly ibid., 239; Jenkins, "Is There Life after Marriage?," 138–39, 141–42; Redfield, "Notes on the Greek Wedding," 188–91;

Seaford, "Tragic Wedding," 106–7, 113–14, and the references found in nn. 4, 12–21, and 82–92 on those pages. Robert Garland, *Greek Way of Life*, 222, more generally speaks of Greek "marriage [as] a potentially traumatic experience for the bride."
81. Rehm, *Marriage to Death*, 27.
82. Rehm, *Marriage to Death*, 32–33.
83. Rehm, *Marriage to Death*, 14 and 35. As we saw in Chapter 2, parallels between Greek marriage and funerary ritual manifest themselves as well in Greek mythology, as Persephone's union with the god of the underworld, Hades, "even if expressed in terms of a wedding, means at least symbolic death," to which Persephone's mother Demeter reacts by mourning (DeBloois, "Rape, Marriage, or Death?," 246, 254).
84. Lonsdale, *Dance and Ritual Play*, 213.
85. P. L. Day, "From the Child Is Born the Woman," 60. See, similarly, on laments sung on an Israelite bride's behalf at the time of her wedding, J. R. Ebeling, *Women's Lives in Biblical Times*, 80, 86, 89.
86. Hague, "Marriage Athenian Style," 33.
87. Lonsdale, *Dance and Ritual Play*, 218; see similarly Oakley and Sims, *Wedding in Ancient Athens*, 10.
88. Fleming, "Children," 27. See similarly, regarding Israelite tradition, King and Stager, *Life in Biblical Israel*, 54, and Matthews and Benjamin, *Social World of Ancient Israel*, 13. See also, concerning Mesopotamia, Cooper, "Virginity," 103, and for like data from ancient Greece, Jenkins, "Is There Life after Marriage?," 138, 141; Oakley and Sims, *Wedding in Ancient Athens*, 12; and Redfield, "Notes on the Greek Wedding," 189, 191.
89. Matthews, "Marriage and Family," 10.
90. Van Gennep, *Rites of Passage*, 124.

Chapter 5

1. As Rainer Albertz points out, in "Personal Names and Family Religion," 269, the Bible pays only "scant attention" to childbirth rites, and perhaps as a result, scholars of the Bible and ancient Israel often "deal only very broadly with Israelite rituals surrounding pregnancy, labor, and birth"; otherwise "they deemphasize or even overlook the ritual and religious significance of childbirth in ancient Israel." Yet Albertz goes on to say, as I will also argue here, that "the undoubted importance of childbirth to the economic and biological survival of families in ancient agrarian societies ... and its dramatic and often very dangerous character for women ... strongly imply that it would be improper to deny its ritual and religious significance."
2. Do note that my intent is to survey only Near Eastern childbirth rituals that I deem to have analogs in biblical and Israelite tradition, as there is a large corpus of Near Eastern childbirth rites that I will not discuss: e.g., the well-documented use of birthing "wands" in Middle Kingdom and early New Kingdom Egypt (Altenmüller, *Apotropaia*; Quirke, *Birth Tusks*; and Rose, "Change and Continuity," 469–99).
3. For references to and discussion of the various Hittite customs discussed in the text in question, see Beckman, *Hittite Birth Rituals*, Text K, §2; §6; §14; §15; §18; §21–§22 (pp. 132–41), and p. 250; also, for §2; §6; §14; and §15, see Bachvarova, "Hurro-Hittite Stories," 290–92. See too ibid., 303, n. 83, on how to translate the reference to the Hittite "Great" or "Mother" goddesses.
4. Beckman, *Hittite Birth Rituals*, 250, writes that the oracles were meant to determine whether the mother-to-be "was in the proper moral condition to give birth successfully," but I am unable to discern concerns regarding the mother's moral well-being in the materials Beckman cites (Text K, §21–§22, on pp. 140–41 of *Hittite Birth Rituals*).
5. McMahon, "Comparative Observations on Hittite Rituals," 129.
6. Lichtheim, *Ancient Egyptian Literature* 3: 125 (for the date), 3: 138 (for the text).
7. For a recent and thorough study of Taweret and Bes, see Rose, "Change and Continuity," 24–45 and 69–94. Further on Bes, see, in addition to the standard dictionaries and handbooks, Backhouse, "'Scènes de gynécées' Figured Ostraca," 233–44; Dasen, *Dwarfs*, 55–83; and the extensive study by Romano, "Bes Image."

8. See, preeminently, W. Farber, *Lamaštu*, and Wiggerman, "Lamashtu," 217–52; also Scurlock, "Baby-Snatching Demons," 153–58, and eadem, "Medicine and Healing Magic," 114–19, 126–28.
9. Black and Green, *Gods, Demons, and Symbols of Ancient Mesopotamia*, 148, and Maiden, "Counterintuitive Demons: Pazazu and Lamaštu," 99–100, with further references. In ibid, 88, n. 1, Maiden also provides a good bibliography of recent Pazazu scholarship.
10. As cited in Stol, *Birth in Babylonia and the Bible*, 52, with reference to Civil, "Medical Commentaries from Nippur," 332, lines 38–39.
11. As cited in Stol, *Birth in Babylonia and the Bible*, 49, with reference to Landsberger, Reiner, and Civil, *Materialien zum sumerischen Lexikon* 10, 31, Lexical Series ḪAR.gud = *imrû* = *ballu* Recension B, Tablet IV, 72–73; see also van der Toorn, *From Her Cradle to Her Grave*, 83.
12. Gonzalez and Marti, "Miscarriage," 360, report that, according to Marshall, *L'enfant et la mort*, 23, one-third of children in ancient Egypt died at birth or in the weeks leading up to it.
13. BAM 237 i 1'–16', with translation and comment in Scurlock, "Baby-Snatching Demons," 136, and additional comments in Finkel, "Crescent Fertile," 49–51; Steinert, "K. 263+10934," 69; and Stol, *Birth in Babylonia and the Bible*, 203.
14. In *CAD* K, s.v. the noun *kapāṣu*, it is suggested that the *kapāṣu*-shell is to be associated with the verb *kapāṣu*, "to bend, curl," and so to be understood as curled in shape.
15. Collections of the University Museum, University of Pennsylvania, 1509 ii 9–19, with translation and comment in Finkel, "Crescent Fertile," 48, and Scurlock, "Baby-Snatching Demons," 137–38.
16. BAM 235 10–16 // BAM 236 r. 1'–9', with translation and comment in Scurlock, "Medicine and Healing Magic," 110. It is not necessarily clear, however, whether the abnormal flow of blood referred to in this text is related to excessive uterine bleeding during *pregnancy*: see Steinert, "K. 263+10934," 69–70.
17. Scurlock, "Baby-Snatching Demons," 138, citing W. Farber, *Schlaf, Kindchen, Schlaf!*, 110 (§39:14); also ibid., 112–14 (§40:7–9).
18. Audouit, "Women's Intimacy," 383, and Marshall, *Motherhood and Early Childhood*, 41, both citing Leitz, *Magical and Medical Papyri*, 69 (Papyrus London No. 29, IX,14–X,1); also Robins, "Women and Children in Peril," 27, citing Borghouts, *Ancient Egyptian Magical Texts: Volume Nine*, Text 31. See in addition Rose, "Change and Continuity," 321–24, 341, on Papyrus London No. 28–30, and Vymazalová and Strouhal. "Mother and Child Care," 123–24, 167, on Papyrus London No. 40–42, 45. More generally on the use of knot-magic in Egyptian gynecological tradition, see Wendrich, "Entangled, Connected or Protected?," 249–50.
19. Beckman, *Hittite Birth Rituals*, Text H, §16', lines 26–27 (pp. 90–91); for this text's date and Beckman's commentary as quoted here, see ibid., 98. For the text, see also Bachvarova, "Hurro-Hittite Stories," 293, §16'.
20. Bachvarova, "Hurro-Hittite Stories," 292.
21. Bachvarova, "Hurro-Hittite Stories," 292.
22. Scurlock, "Baby-Snatching Demons," 139; also ibid., 141, and Foster, *Before the Muses*, 171–72 (II.20.b).
23. Although the text as we have it comes from the Second Intermediate Period (ca. 1782–1570 BCE), it is generally agreed that the Westcar Papyrus contains traditions from the Middle Kingdom (ca. 2040–1782 BCE). See Lichtheim, *Ancient Egyptian Literature* 1: 215.
24. According to Lichtheim, *Ancient Egyptian Literature* 1: 220, Westcar Papyrus §10.2 describes the husband's "loincloth upside down," but see Ritner, "Household Religion in Ancient Egypt," 174, citing Staehelin, "Bindung und Entbindung," 125–39, for the reading "a kilt untied." Wendrich, however ("Entangled, Connected or Protected?," 258), raises cautions.
25. Arnette, "Purification du post-partum," 30, n. 99; Brunner-Traut, "Wochenlaube," 26–27; and Ritner, "Household Religion in Ancient Egypt," 174. But for different understandings of women's hairstyles that appear in Brunner-Traut's "Wochenlaube" imagery (e.g., Fig. 5.4), see Backhouse, "'Scènes de gynécées' Figured Ostraca," 169, 320–21, 545, and Pinch, *Votive Offerings to Hathor*, 219–20.
26. Garland, *Greek Way of Life*, 73. Kindred references from Greek texts are cited by Bachvarova, "Hurro-Hittite Stories," 302, n. 87.
27. As cited in Garland, *Greek Way of Life*, 71.
28. Scurlock, "Baby-Snatching Demons," 140, 150–51, 157.
29. Scurlock, "Baby-Snatching Demons," 150–51, 157.
30. In addition to the examples listed just below, note the *ittamir*, "the stone of giving birth," as cited in Stol, *Birth in Babylonia and the Bible*, 50, with reference to Landsberger, Reiner, and Civil,

Materialien zum sumerischen Lexikon 10, 31, Lexical Series ḪAR.gud = *imrû* = *ballu* Recension B, Tablet IV, 72–77; see also van der Toorn, *From Her Cradle to Her Grave*, 83.
31. Stol, *Birth in Babylonia and the Bible*, 132–33, with reference to E. Ebeling, *Keilschrifttexte aus Assur* 2, 223:5, and Gurney and Hulin, *Sultantepe Tablets* 2, 241:5.
32. Stol, *Birth in Babylonia and the Bible,* 133, with reference to von Weiher, *Spätbabylonische Texte aus Uruk* II, 113 no. 22, and idem, Uruk: *Spätbabylonische Texte aus dem Planquadrat U 18* IV, 24.
33. Pinch, "Private Life in Ancient Egypt," 376.
34. For these Papyrus Leiden I 348 spells (Spells #30 and #31), see Borghouts, *Magical Texts,* 29, with commentary in ibid., 13, 154–55; in Marshall, *Motherhood and Early Childhood,* 51–52; in Pinch, "Childbirth and Female Figurines," 412; in eadem, *Magic in Ancient Egypt,* 129; in Rose, "Change and Continuity," 330–31; and in Toivari-Viitala, *Women at Deir el-Medina,* 175.
35. Pinch, "Private Life in Ancient Egypt," 377; the drawing in question is Fig. B on that page.
36. For the Egyptian pregnancy vases, see Brunner-Traut, "Gravidenflasche," 35–48, and, most recently, Rose, "Change and Continuity," 221–26; for these vases' use for anointing pregnant women, see R. M. and J. J. Janssen, *Growing Up and Getting Old*, 3.
37. In addition to the references in n. 38 below, see, for Egypt, Vymazalová and Strouhal. "Mother and Child Care," 119 (Ebers 803 and 807) and 174–76; for Mesopotamia, Glassner, "Rites of Passage," 440, and Stol, *Birth in Babylonia and the Bible,* 124; and, for Hittite tradition, Bachvarova, "Hurro-Hittite Stories," 293, §16′; likewise, Beckman, *Hittite Birth Rituals,* Text H, §16′, lines 25–26 (pp. 90–91), with commentary in ibid., 106, and in Pringle, "Hittite Birth Rituals," 131.
38. Anointing the top of the head (Egypt): Papyrus Ramesseum IV.C, lines 28–30, as translated by Vymazalová and Strouhal. "Mother and Child Care," 115, with commentary on p. 174. Anointing the brow (Mesopotamia): Lambert, "Middle Assyrian Medical Text," 32, lines 59–61, as translated by Whitekettle, "Human Reproduction," 241; see also ibid., 240, for a description of oil used to anoint the forehead of the laboring cow Geme-Sîn in the Mesopotamian mythological text "The Cow of Sîn." Anointing the shoulder and sides (Mesopotamia): *Vorderasiatische Schriftdenkmäler* 17: 33, lines 28–30, as translated in Stol, *Birth in Babylonia and the Bible,* 124, following van Dijk, "Incantations accompagnant la naissance," 63.
39. The text in question can be found in Beckman, *Hittite Birth Rituals,* Text K, §5 (pp. 132–33), but cf. Bachvarova, "Hurro-Hittite Stories," 291, §5. For Beckman's commentary on these lines, see *Hittite Birth Rituals,* 154; for his cautions about Hittite tradition more generally, see ibid.; also Pringle, "Hittite Birth Rituals," 132.
40. Beckman, *Hittite Birth Rituals,* 154.
41. Beckman, *Hittite Birth Rituals,* 98, and Text H, §18′, lines 34–36, 38, and §19′, line 39 (pp. 92–93), but cf. Bachvarova's rendering, "Hurro-Hittite Stories," 293, §18′–§19′. Elsewhere ("Birth and Motherhood," 324), Beckman notes that *patili*-priests might remain in the birth chamber, although not to assist in gynecological matters but for the "performance of offerings and recitations and general housekeeping"; see also Beckman, *Hittite Birth Rituals,* 236, 238.
42. Beckman, "Birth and Motherhood," 324.
43. Scurlock and B. R. Andersen, *Diagnoses in Assyrian and Babylonian Medicine*, 729, n. 14, citing Civil, "Enlil and Ninlil," 57 (lines 152, 154), with translation on pp. 60–61. See also (as cited by Scurlock and Andersen) W. G. Lambert's comments in an "Appendix" to Civil's article, on p. 65, where Lambert writes that if Civil's translation and interpretation are correct, the hymn indicates that "men were not welcome at childbirth in Sumer and Babylon." That said, Scurlock elsewhere has suggested that if a woman experienced complications during labor, a male magical expert, as in Hatti (above, n. 41), "had to be called in." By way of example, she points to a prayer uttered by a male exorcist on behalf of a woman struggling to deliver, asking the sun god Utu/Shamash to loosen the "knot" that seems to be impeding the woman's womb. See Scurlock, "Baby-Snatching Demons,"140–41; also Seux, *Hymnes et prières aux dieux,* 216–17, and Stol, *Birth in Babylonia and the Bible,* 133–34.
44. Stol, *Birth in Babylonia and the Bible,* 206, citing van der Toorn, *Family Religion,* 122–23; idem, "Magic at the Cradle," 142; and Wilcke, "Philologische Bemerkungen," 230. See also Scurlock, "Baby-Snatching Demons," 140.
45. Quoted and discussed in Rose, "Change and Continuity," 392; Teeter, "Earthly and Divine Mothers," 151; and Toivari-Viitala, *Women at Deir el-Medina,* 173–74.
46. Pinch, *Magic in Ancient Egypt,* 128. Note, however, that as discussed in nn. 41 and 43 above regarding Hatti and Mesopotamia, male magicians in Egypt might attend at birth to offer aid

to a laboring mother. E.g., according to Robert K. Ritner, "Magic," spells such as those found in the early New Kingdom "Magical Spells for Mother and Child" (also called the "Book for Mother and Child"; Papyrus Berlin 3027), including spells performed at the time of parturition, were recited on a pregnant woman's behalf by male lector-priests or "magicians of the nursery"; see also idem, "Household Religion in Ancient Egypt," 176; Marshall, *Motherhood and Early Childhood*, 54; and Rose, "Change and Continuity," 304–5.

47. Lichtheim, *Ancient Egyptian Literature* 2: 210.
48. See the images reproduced in Töpfer, "Physical Activity of Parturition," 320–24, and J. Wegner, "Decorated Birth Brick," 449–51 (Figs. 1–4), with discussion on pp. 452, 455–63; also idem, "Tradition and Innovation," 128–30.
49. Pinch, "Private Life in Ancient Egypt," 376; see also eadem, "Childbirth and Female Figurines," 405, 414. Pinch's analysis is particularly dependent on Emma Brunner-Traut's study of the Deir el-Medina ostraca's depictions of the so-called *Wochenlaube*, or birth arbor scene: see Brunner-Traut, "Wochenlaube," 11–30, and, for a complete inventory of the ostraca, Backhouse, "'Scènes de gynécées' Figured Ostraca," 78–188. For further discussion, see ibid., 220–350; Friedman, "Aspects of Domestic Life," 99–106; Goudsouzian, "Becoming Isis," 95–98; Kemp, "Wall Paintings," 51–53; Rose, "Change and Continuity," 552–64; and Toivari-Viitala, *Women at Deir el-Medina*, 175–79. Cf. however, the cautions raised by Arnette regarding the function of the *Wochenlaube* ("Purification du post-partum," 25–26), with reference to the change of opinion Erika Feucht registers in "Der Weg ins Leben," 51, as opposed to her earlier assessment in "Birth," 192. See also the reservations of Lesko, "Household and Domestic Religion in Ancient Egypt," 205, and Marshall, *Motherhood and Early Childhood*, 67–68.
50. Borghouts, *Magical Texts*, Spell #33. For commentary, see, most recently, Marshall, *Motherhood and Early Childhood*, 66, and Rose, "Change and Continuity," 332.
51. See further Smith, *Rituals and Myths of the Feast of the Goodly Gods*, 105–9.
52. Beckman, *Hittite Birth Rituals*, Text B, §2', line 8' (pp. 32–33), with commentary on p. 36. See also Bachvarova, "Hurro-Hittite Stories," 295, §2, and Pringle, "Hittite Birth Rituals," 132.
53. For representative images, see Rose, "Change and Continuity," 548; Töpfer, "Physical Activity of Parturition," 320–24; J. Wegner, "Decorated Birth Brick," 449–51 (Figs. 1–4), with discussion on pp. 452, 455–63; idem, "Tradition and Innovation," 128–30; and the plaque of a woman giving birth held in the collection of the Egyptian Museum, Cairo: https://egypt-museum.com/plaque-of-a-woman-giving-birth.
54. See Beckman, *Hittite Birth Rituals*, Text A, §1–§2 (pp. 22–23).
55. Above, nn. 41 (regarding Hittite tradition), 43 (concerning Mesopotamia), and 46 (concerning Egypt).
56. Beckman, *Hittite Birth Rituals*, 234, with reference to ibid., Text B, §10" (pp. 34–35); see also Pringle, "Hittite Birth Rituals," 132, 135.
57. For Egypt, see Capel, "8a Statuette of Woman Dressing Hair" and "8b Relief of Woman and Child," 59, citing Pinch, *Magic in Ancient Egypt*, 128–30. For Greek tradition, see Garland, *Greek Way of Life,* 63. The Hittite text in question can be found in Bachvarova, "Hurro-Hittite Stories," 296, §3 and §6, and in Beckman, *Hittite Birth Rituals*, Text B, §3', line 10', and §6', lines 25'–27' (pp. 32–33).
58. Beckman, *Hittite Birth Rituals*, Text G, §1–§2 (p. 85) and p. 250. See also Pringle, "Hittite Birth Rituals," 137.
59. Stol, *Birth in Babylonia and the Bible*, 66–70; idem, "Private Life in Ancient Mesopotamia," 491; Whitekettle, "Human Reproduction," 239–40.
60. Stol, *Birth in Babylonia and the Bible*, 133; Whitekettle, "Human Reproduction," 237.
61. Stol, *Birth in Babylonia and the Bible*, 69.
62. Jacobsen, "Notes on Nintur," 292, as pointed out by Whitekettle, "Human Reproduction," 224.
63. As pointed out by Goudsouzian, "Becoming Isis," 160, and by Sasson, *Ruth*, 234.
64. Translation Lichtheim, *Ancient Egyptian Literature* 1: 220–21.
65. Rose, "Change and Continuity," 45–58.
66. Lichtheim, *Ancient Egyptian Literature* 2: 200. Further on what Josef Wegner describes as "the 'Seven Hathors' who visit the birth of a child and are involved in the determination of human character and destiny" (Wegner, "Decorated Birth Brick," 457), see the references assembled in ibid., 457, n. 17.
67. Beckman, *Hittite Birth Rituals*, 251.
68. Beckman, *Hittite Birth Rituals*, Text C, §9' (pp. 44–45).

69. Bachvarova, "Hurro-Hittite Stories," 296, §9; Beckman, *Hittite Birth Rituals*, Text B, §10″ (pp. 34–35).
70. Bremmer, "Rites of Passage," 438.
71. Wagner, "*dāraš*," 302–4.
72. I have discussed this conclusion elsewhere, regarding both a shrine setting for Gen 25:22 and the presence of an oracular specialist: see Ackerman, "The Blind, the Lame, and the Barren," 30–32. On the implied presence of an oracular specialist in Gen 25:22, see also Bowen, "Daughters of Your People," 425–26; Gursky, "Reproductive Rituals," 46; van der Toorn, *From Her Cradle to Her Grave*, 82; and Wagner, "*dāraš*," 302.
73. Kristine Henriksen Garroway. "Rattle and Hum," 189, more generally reports (citing Wiggerman, "Lamashtu," 228–29) that "texts about Lamashtu are found from the Iron Age in the west from Phoenician, Aramaic, Syrian, Hellenistic, and Greek sources dating to the seventh century BCE and beyond."
74. McKinny et al., "Tel Burna after a Decade," 14, n. 4.
75. Cogan, "Lamashtu Plaque," 161.
76. Ornan, "Chapter 14C: An Amulet of the Demon Pazazu," 517–19.
77. Ornan, "Chapter 14C: An Amulet of the Demon Pazazu," 517–18.
78. Herrmann, *Ägyptische Amulette aus Palästina/Israel IV*, 451. Herrmann's catalogue of Bes amulets in ibid., 123, 342–55, 452–85, includes examples from Achzib, Ashdod, Ashkelon, Azekah, Beth Shean, Beth Shemesh, Deir el-Balah, Dor, Ekron, Gezer, Jericho, Jerusalem, Jezreel, Khirbet el-Qôm, Lachish, Megiddo, Samaria, Tell el-Ajjul, Tell el-Far'ah South, Tell el-Hesi, Tell en-Naṣbeh, Tell eṣ-Ṣafi, Tell Jemme, and Tel Reḥov.
79. According to V. Wilson, "Iconography of Bes," 84, Bes images first appear in Canaan on Late Bronze Age ivories from Megiddo.
80. See, e.g., Dever, "Iron Age Epigraphic Material," 188, and idem, *Lives of Ordinary People*, 286, as pointed out by Schmidt, *Materiality of Power*, 148; more generally, on Bes amulets in tombs, see Schmitt, "Ongoing Relations," 316.
81. Two images of Bes: Beck, "Drawings and Decorative Designs," 165–69. Bes and Beset: Schmidt, *Materiality of Power*, 59–67. Note, however, that images identified as representing Beset become much rarer in New Kingdom Egypt than they are in earlier Egyptian history (Rose, "Change and Continuity," 36, 44), and in *Materiality of Power*, 201, Schmidt admits that "at present, the name Beset is only attested from the Greco-Roman period onward."
82. Schmitt, "Iconographic Evidence from Iconic Stamp Seals," 381–82.
83. See Albertz, "Personal Names and Family Religion," 322, and the associated table on p. 568, and Schmitt, "Rites of Family and Household Religion," 392.
84. See Albertz, "Personal Names and Family Religion," 279, and the associated table on p. 589, and Schmitt, "Rites of Family and Household Religion," 392.
85. Bowen, "Daughters of Your People," 417–33.
86. For interpretations of Ezek 13:17–23 other than those discussed or cited below, see Evans, "Death-Dealing Witchcraft," 57–84; Jost, "Die Töchter deines Volkes prophezeien," 59–65; eadem and Seifert. "Ezekiel," 351; Schmitt, *Magie*, 283–87, 360–62; idem, "Problem of Magic and Monotheism," 5–6; idem, "Theories Regarding Witchcraft Accusations," 190–92; Southwood, "Social Dynamics"; and Zevit, *Religions of Ancient Israel*, 561–62.
87. Stökl, "The *mtnb'wt* in Ezekiel 13," 61–76. Also regarding the odditiy of the form *mitnabbĕ'ôt* in Ezek 13:17–23, see Steiner, *Disembodied Souls*, 24, who points out that the typical term for male prophets (*nĕbî'îm*) is used in Ezek 13:2, the opening verse of an oracle condemning male prophets (Ezek 13:2–16) that parallels 13:17–23.
88. Stökl, "The *mtnb'wt* in Ezekiel 13," 70–72.
89. Stökl, "The *mtnb'wt* in Ezekiel 13," 71.
90. Stökl, "The *mtnb'wt* in Ezekiel 13," 73–74. Note, however, that at Ebla, albeit a millennium earlier, *munabbitum* in a funerary text means "a wailing woman" who led a chorus of mourners: see Archi, "Jewels for the Ladies of Ebla," 185–86.
91. E.g., Dumermuth, "Zu Ez. XIII 18–21," 228–29; Hamori, *Women's Divination*, 167–83; Kim, "*kstwt, msphwt*, and *npšwt*," 301–5; Korpel, "Avian Spirits," 102–9; Mowinckel, *Psalmenstudien* 1: 65; van der Toorn, *From Her Cradle to Her Grave*, 123; and idem, *Family Religion*, 232. The Dumermuth and Mowinckel references were brought to my attention by Fritschel, "Women and Magic," 133–34 and nn. 28 and 29 on those pages.

92. Van der Toorn, *From Her Cradle to Her Grave*, 123, quoting Spronk, *Beatific Afterlife*, 100, n. 3, 167, and 255. See similarly, with more extensive discussion, Korpel, "Avian Spirits," 99–102, and also Hamori, *Women's Divination*, 172–76.
93. Pope, "Review of Klaas Spronk, *Beatific Afterlife*," 458, and Smith and Bloch-Smith, "Death and Afterlife in Ugarit and Israel," 279. (These references were brought to my attention by Fritschel, "Women and Magic," 136, n. 38, and Korpel, "Avian Spirits," 99.)
94. Korpel, "Avian Spirits," 103–4. For further discussion of the references to barley and bread, see Liebermann, "For-Profit Prophets?," 213–14, 218–19, and 229.
95. Korpel, "Avian Spirits," 103.
96. Reading *yādayim*, "hands, wrists," in v 18, for the MT's nonsensical *yāday*, "my hands."
97. Steiner, *Disembodied Souls*, 28–54.
98. Hamori, *Women's Divination*, 171.
99. See more generally Boyd's recent discussion of Akkadian loanwords in Ezekiel, in *Language Contact*, 241–58, to which cf. Steiner, *Disembodied Souls*, 29–31.
100. Bowen, "Daughters of Your People," 424, n. 31.
101. Zimmerli, *Ezekiel 1*, 289.
102. Stökl, "The *mtnb'wt* in Ezekiel 13," 63
103. Bowen, "Daughters of Your People," 424. See also Boyd, *Language Contact*, 254; Davies, "Archaeological Commentary on Ezekiel 13," 121; Fritschel, "Women and Magic," 127, n. 4, and 130; and Stökl, "The *mtnb'wt* in Ezekiel 13," 64.
104. See especially Avalos, *Illness and Health Care*, 260–77, and Schmitt, *Magie*, 219–54.
105. Ackerman, "Illnesses and Other Crises: Syria-Canaan," 459–60, and Avalos, "Illnesses and Other Crises: Israel," 460–61; see also Avalos, *Illness and Health Care*, 238–46.
106. E.g., in 1 Kgs 17:17–24 and 2 Kgs 4:8–37, the prophets Elijah and Elisha bring dead children back to life by stretching themselves out over the body of the child, thereby "transferring [their] life force to the deceased" (Cogan, *I Kings*, 429); on 2 Kgs 5:1–14, see Cranz, "Naaman's Healing and Gehazi's Affliction," 540–55. I have more thoroughly discussed the relation of the medical to the magical, and the women prophets of Ezek 13:17–23 as medico-magical agents, in Ackerman, *Women and the Religion of Ancient Israel*, 260–64, 282–85.
107. I have discussed this point more thoroughly in Ackerman, *Women and the Religion of Ancient Israel*, 262–64, 290–91.
108. Bowen, "Daughters of Your People," 424.
109. Those who disagree include, curiously enough, Bowen herself, who after carefully documenting how "the language of tying and binding is found in incantations concerning pregnancy and childbearing," notes that this language is "also found generally in . . . incantations to cure various illnesses or maladies that are attributed to witches, sorcerers, sorceresses, and demons." "This means," Bowen goes on to say, "that it is nearly impossible to . . . decide with any certainty whether these female prophets were conducting childbirth rituals": see Bowen, "Daughters of Your People," 428–29.
110. Bowen, "Daughters of Your People," 424.
111. Holladay, "Religion in Israel and Judah," 277, with discussion on p. 276; see also Dever, *Lives of Ordinary People*, 269.
112. E.g., in a paved room within Building (or House) 25 at Beersheba (eighth century BCE), and in the entrance area of Building (House) 430 (also eighth century BCE): see Beit-Arieh, "The Western Quarter," 422, and Herzog, "The Southern Quarter," 264, 267.
113. See Exod 1:16. Birthing stools are also mentioned in a Late Bronze Age Ugaritic text (*KTU* 1.12.1.17–18) and are well attested among the Hittites: see Beckman, *Hittite Birth Rituals*, 250. The birth stool seems to be the norm in Greek and Roman culture as well: see Stol, *Birth in Babylonia and the Bible*, 121–22. On the possible use of birth stools in Egypt, see Marshall, *Motherhood and Early Childhood*, 60 (with additional references on p. 172, n. 30); Rose, "Change and Continuity," 538–40; and Toivari-Viitala, *Women at Deir el-Medina*, 174.
114. Zevit, *Religions of Ancient Israel*, 175–76.
115. Pinch, "Private Life in Ancient Egypt," 377.
116. Rose, "Change and Continuity," 9, 171–72; eadem, "Childbirth Magic," 40. For a catalog of the New Kingdom woman-on-bed figurines, see Backhouse, "'Scènes de gynécées' Figured Ostraca," 353–98. For some Third Intermediate Period and Late Period examples, see Teeter, *Baked Clay Figurines and Votive Beds*, 157–97.

117. Pinch, *Votive Offerings to Hathor*, 219, and Rose, "Change and Continuity," 191, both citing Bruyère, *Rapport sur les fouilles de Deir el Médineh* 16, 137–39. 142–43. See also Backhouse, "'Scènes de gynécées' Figured Ostraca," Fig. 7.1–7.3 on pp. 399–401, with accompanying discussion; also, on the evidence from Deir el-Medina and el-Amarna, ibid., 405–8.
118. Pinch, *Votive Offerings to Hathor*, 207–9.
119. Rose, "Childbirth Magic," 45; see similarly Backhouse, "'Scènes de gynécées' Figured Ostraca," 469; Del Vesco, "Votive Bed Fragment," 36; and Pinch, *Votive Offerings to Hathor*, 219.
120. See Keel and Uehlinger, *Gods, Goddesses, and Images of God*, 106; also R. M. Janssen and J. J. Janssen, *Growing Up and Getting Old*, 3, although the Janssens unfortunately do not indicate the specific find spots or dates of the Syro-Palestinian "pregnancy vases" that they mention.
121. Van der Toorn, *From Her Cradle to Her Grave*, 85.
122. See my discussion above of *KTU* 1.10.3.19–26, regarding Late Bronze Age Ugarit, and n. 54 regarding Hittite tradition.
123. See similarly, regarding a midwife's potential role in Ezek 16:4, Dempsey, "The 'Whore' of Ezekiel 16," 63. Manfred Görg, "Ein verkanntes Wort für die 'Hebamme' in Ez 16, 4," 13–16, has even suggested that the otherwise unattested term *miš'î* found in Ezek 16:4 refers to a midwife and her responsibility to wash the newborn baby. Most other commentators, however, see *lĕmiš'î* as an addition that is to be deleted from the text: see, e.g., Cooke, *Critical and Exegetical Commentary on the Book of Ezekiel* 1, 162; Eichrodt, *Ezekiel*, 199, n. d; and Zimmerli, *Ezekiel 1*, 323, note c on Ezek 16:4.
124. See Beckman, *Hittite Birth Rituals*, Text C, §5, line 20 (pp. 42–43), with commentary on pp. 46, 49, and "The Ritual of Papanikri," IV, lines 12–16 (pp. 118–19), with commentary on p. 123; see similarly Pringle, "Hittite Birth Rituals," 133 and 140.
125. Beckman, *Hittite Birth Rituals*, 49.
126. C. Meyers, "From Household to House of Yahweh," 290; eadem, *Households and Holiness*, 38–39. See similarly Bowen, "Daughters of Your People," 426.
127. Beckman, *Hittite Birth Rituals*, "Ritual of Papanikri," IV, lines 6–7 (pp. 118–19).
128. Beckman, *Hittite Birth Rituals*, 123.
129. Sasson, *Ruth*, 158, 233–34.
130. My thanks to Theodore J. Lewis for suggesting this interpretation of Job 3 to me. In general, according to Schmitt, "Rites of Family and Household Religion," 391, "It is likely that Israelite midwives recited ... incantations that served to activate Yhwh's creative power," but cf. Bergmann, "Turning Birth into Theology," 18: "In the Hebrew Bible, childbirth incantations similar to the ancient Near Eastern texts do not exist."
131. Van Dijk, Goetze, and Hussey, *Early Mesopotamian Incantations*, 49 (Text 86a), lines 1–28, as translated by Foster, *Before the Muses*, 171 (II.20.b).
132. Lambert, "Middle Assyrian Medical Text," 28–39, as translated and interpreted by Foster, *Before the Muses*, 1006 (IV.53a, lines 15–18).
133. Schofield, "Did the Mothers Really Die?," 235, as cited in Demand, *Birth, Death, and Motherhood*. 71.
134. Scurlock, "Baby-Snatching Demons," 135.
135. C. Meyers, *Discovering Eve*, 112–13; eadem, "Family in Early Israel," 28. See likewise Nakhai, "Female Infanticide in Iron II Israel and Judah," 258 (with additional documentation); see also Willett, "Infant Mortality," 80.
136. Oakley, "Death and the Child," 163; see similarly Angel, "Ecology and Population," 94, who, based on a sample of 126 adult individuals from Hellenistic Greece, estimates a life expectancy of 42.6 years for males and 36.6 years for females.
137. Blenkinsopp, "Life Expectancy," 52.
138. Dupras, Wheeler, L. Williams, and Sheldrick, "Birth in Ancient Egypt," 58–59. For the date of the cemetery, see ibid., 57. See also Goudsouzian, "Becoming Isis," 133–37; Toivari-Viitala, *Women at Deir el-Medina*, 171; and Vymazalová and Strouhal, "Mother and Child Care," 172–73, on the evidence from female skeletal remains from earlier in Egyptian history, as well as the analysis put forward by Onstine, et al., "Women's Health Issues," 397–98, regarding two female mummies found among the first-millennium BCE secondary burials from Theban Tomb 16, both of which have features that suggest a childbirth-related death.
139. Rieder, *On the Purification of Women*, 107, citing Herlihy and Klapish-Zuber, *Tuscans and Their Families*, 277.

140. Van der Toorn addresses Israelite beliefs concerning demonic threats to newborn infants in *From Her Cradle to Her Grave*, 26. Regarding the manifestation of such beliefs in later Jewish tradition, see Archer, *Her Price Is Beyond Rubies*, 30–32.
141. Such a reading of the period of pregnancy was already articulated in 1909 by van Gennep, in *Rites of Passage*, 41.

Chapter 6

1. This is not to deny, as a standard source critical analysis would posit, that Gen 4:25–26 and 5:1–5 stem from two different authors or authorial strands, typically identified as the Yahwistic, or J source (Gen 4:25–26) and the Priestly, or P source (Gen 5:1–5). My suggestion here is only that the tradition's final editors may have meant us to read the redacted text of Gen 4:25–26 and 5:1–5 sequentially, with both Adam and Eve giving Seth his name.
2. According to Rainer Albertz, "Introduction," 8, women's role in bestowing children's names was first pointed out by Bird, "Place of Women," 409–10.
3. The exact percentage that commentators cite can differ, depending on how, exactly, one counts: for various attempts at calculation, see Albertz, "Personal Names and Family Religion," 247 and n. 9 on that page; Block, "Marriage and Family," 67, n. 153; Bohmbach, "Names and Naming," 37; Bridge, "A Mother's Influence," 392–93; van Dijk-Hemmes, "Traces of Women's Texts," 97; Kessler, "Benennung des Kindes," 25–26; Marsman, *Women in Ugarit and Israel*, 235 and n. 231 on that page; C. Meyers, *Households and Holiness*, 42–43; eadem, "From Household to House of Yahweh," 291; eadem, *Rediscovering Eve*, 158; Pardes, *Countertraditions*, 163, n. 2; and Vos, *Woman in Old Testament Worship*, 161, n. 83. See also, on the Bible's naming accounts, Gursky, "Reproductive Rituals," 102–47.
4. Albertz, "Personal Names and Family Religion," 272–73, also notes other instances of biblical names that were arguably bestowed by the name-bearers' mothers: e.g., the names Ananiah in Neh 3:23 and Anani in 1 Chr 3:24. These names mean "[Yahweh] answered me"—that is, as Albertz interprets, Yahweh responded to the mother's petition for a child. The names Shealtiel (the father of Zerubbabel) and Saul can be similarly interpreted. Indeed, many commentators suggest that the birth story of Samuel in 1 Sam 1:1–28—or at least significant parts of it—must have originally been told about Saul, for only by substituting Saul's name for Samuel's do the wordplays of v 20 and v 28 make sense ("She [Hannah] called his name Samuel [*šĕmû'ēl*], for [she said], 'It was from Yahweh that I asked him [*šĕ'iltîw*]"; "I have dedicated him [*hiš'iltīhû*] to Yahweh ... he is dedicated [*šā'ûl*] to Yahweh" [literally, "he is Yahweh's Saul"]). For an extensive review of the literature, see Na'aman, "Samuel's Birth Legend," 51–57.
5. On the translation of this text, see below and n. 101 there.
6. Leah's wordplay, though, is followed by an enigmatic statement that *'al-kēn qārā'-šĕmô lēwî*; "therefore *he* called his name Levi," as if some heretofore unmentioned male has suddenly appeared to bestow on the child his name. See similarly below, n. 7.
7. Although note that the end of Gen 38:29 reads *wayyiqrā' šĕmô pāreṣ*, which means, literally, "and *he* called his name Perez," as if some heretofore unmentioned male has suddenly appeared to bestow on the child his name. See similarly above, n. 6.
8. So Ljung, *Silence or Suppression*, 17; Pardes, *Countertraditions*, 57.
9. These P texts are Gen 5:3 (Adam names Seth); Gen 16:15 (Abram [Abraham] names Ishmael, but cf. Gen 16:11 [J]); and Gen 21:3 (Abraham names Isaac).
10. In the LXX, Shua's daughter is the subject of the first two verbs of Gen 38:3, "to conceive" and "to bear"; therefore, she is most logically to be taken as the subject of the next verb in the verse, "to name." The Hebrew text, however, which (unlike Greek) differentiates gender in verbal forms, indicates that a feminine subject, Shua's daughter, is said to conceive and bear Er, whereas a masculine subject (presumably Judah) bestows the name Er on the couple's son.
11. The *Qĕrē'* reads, "she [Bathsheba] called his name ...," versus the *Kĕtîb*, which reads "he [David] called his name ..." In the LXX, as in the LXX of Gen 38:3 (above, n. 10), Bathsheba is the subject of the first two verbs of 2 Sam 12:24, "to conceive" and "to bear," and therefore she is most logically to be taken as the subject of the next verb in the verse, "to name."

12. Although note that, as in nn. 10 and 11 above, the grammar of the LXX can be interpreted to suggest that Ephraim's wife bestowed the name Beriah on her son in 1 Chr 7:23, given that the wife, as the third-person subject of the verse's first two verbs, "to conceive" and "to bear," continues to stand as the third-person subject of the next verb in the verse, "to name." The logic of the verse, however, where the name Beriah (bĕrî'â) is explained by reference to the rā'â, "evil," that is said to have befallen "*his* house" (bêtô), suggests that "he" (his father) conferred the name Beriah on his son, as in the Hebrew text, which differentiates between Ephriam's wife, who is said to conceive and bear Beriah, and Ephraim, who bestows this name on his son.
13. Under the terms of the interpretation followed here, the form qārā't in Isa 7:14, although it appears to be a second-person feminine singular perfect, is taken to be a third-person feminine singular perfect, with a final *t* rather than the expected final *h* (qārĕ'āh) as in some analogous third feminine singular perfect III-*hē*/III-*'alep* forms ('āśāt in Lev 25:21 for the expected 'āśĕtāh; qārā't in Deut 31:29 and Jer 44:23 for the expected qārĕ'āh). The ancient versions are wildly mixed and basically of no help: generally, the LXX reads a second-person singular form "you [presumably Isaiah] will name him Emmanuel," although LXX^S renders a second-person plural. 1QIsa^a reads *wqr'*, which can be read as either an indefinite third-person masculine singular Qal form, "one will name him," or a Pual third-person masculine singular, "he will be named." The Vulgate and Peshitta both reflect passive forms, *vocabitur* and *wntqr'*, respectively, although the Old Latin, like the LXX, renders the verb as a second-person masculine singular. The Targumic form *wtqr'* can be read as either a second-person masculine singular or a third-person feminine singular. Among commentators, the most thorough discussions are provided by Roberts, *First Isaiah*, 117; Wildberger, *Isaiah 1–12*, 286; and Williamson, *Critical and Exegetical Commentary on Isaiah 1–27*, 2: 140–42.
14. See similarly Bridge, "A Mother's Influence," 395, 397, 400, and Kessler, "Benennung des Kindes," 27–34.
15. Patai, *Family, Love and the Bible*, 172. But cf. van der Toorn, *From Her Cradle to Her Grave*, 23, who suggests that "the time at which the name giving occurred was not fixed," so that "it is possible the baby first received a temporary name and a permanent one only a few years later when a child had proven sufficiently strong and healthy." Cf. also Albertz, "Personal Names and Family Religion," 247, 287, who argues, based on Lev 12:1–5, that rather than a name being bestowed at birth, there would have been a "naming feast" on the eighth or fifteenth day after delivery, once the seven-/fourteen-day period of postpartum impurity prescribed by Lev 12:1–5 had ended. This position is reiterated by Albertz's co-author Schmitt, in "Rites of Family and Household Religion," 392. Léonie J. Archer, *Her Price Is Beyond Rubies*, 40–43, somewhat similarly posits that in the Greco-Roman period, a Jewish boy's name was given only on the eighth day after birth, in conjunction with his circumcision, and that this day was also the occasion of some sort of community celebration. Archer bases her arguments on, preeminently, Luke 1:59 and 2:21 (also cited by Albertz, "Personal Names and Family Religion"), where John the Baptist and Jesus, respectively, were named on the eighth day after their births. However, as far as I have been able to determine, the earliest Jewish (as opposed to Christian) source to specify that a baby boy should be named at his circumcision on the eighth day is the medieval-era Pirkei d'Rabbi Eliezer (Chapter 48), although this tradition is implied to some degree in the Talmud, in b. Šabbat 134b. Regardless, it seems unlikely that Luke's accounts of John and Jesus being named at their circumcisions—although a prevailing practice in Judaism today (references in Albertz, "Personal Names and Family Religion," 247)—reflect actual first-century CE Jewish custom. Rather, what we may be seeing is the Gentile author of Luke shaping his naming accounts according to the Roman cultural norms with which he would have been familiar. After all, in Roman tradition, as we will see below, name-giving was delayed until eight or nine days after birth. In the account of the naming of John the Baptist, and more specifically the initial proposal of the unspecified "they" to name the baby after John's father Zechariah, Luke may also be influenced by Roman name-giving custom, whereby the *nomen*, which was the second of a Roman male's three names, was passed down unchanged from father to son. More on this also to follow.
16. As in Chapter 5, see van der Toorn, *From Her Cradle to Her Grave*, 85.
17. As I noted in Chapter 5, there is some evidence that male magicians could attend delivering women in Mesopotamia, Egypt, and the Hittite Empire, especially if a parturient was experiencing problems during labor and delivery: see nn. 41, 43, and 46 there.
18. On the date of the Westcar Papyrus, see Chapter 5, n. 23.

19. Westcar Papyrus §10.9, 16, 23–24; translation Lichtheim, *Ancient Egyptian Literature* 1: 220, with commentary at p. 222, n. 7.
20. Pinch, "Private Life in Ancient Egypt," 376; see also the references regarding these birth chambers catalogued in Chapter 5, nn. 49–50.
21. R. M. Janssen and J. J. Janssen, *Growing Up and Getting Old*, 13; Posener, "Sur l'attribution d'un nom," 204–5; see also the less detailed remarks of Ritner, "Household Religion in Ancient Egypt," 175, and the somewhat contradictory comments offered in various publications by Feucht: "Birth," 193; eadem, "Childhood," 262; and eadem, "Motherhood in Pharaonic Egypt," 206.
22. Meskell, "Cycles of Life and Death," 425, citing Hornung, *Idea into Image*, 178; see also Feucht, "Childhood," 262.
23. See further Smith, *Rituals and Myths of the Feast of the Goodly Gods*, 99. Note, however, KTU 1.12.1.25–29, where, in a description of the birth of two tauromorphic devourers, we might read "May El pronounce their names" or "El pronounced their names": see S. B. Parker, "Wilderness," 191, n. 6, and Wyatt, *Religious Texts*, 163. Nevertheless, Parker, "Wilderness," 189, prefers to read "May the gods name them."
24. For the text, see Bachvarova, "Hurro-Hittite Stories," 280, §11–§12, and Hoffner, *Hittite Myths*, 57–58, §11–§12.
25. Hoffner, *Hittite Myths*, 84, §14–§15.
26. Hoffner, "Birth and Name-Giving in Hittite Texts," 203.
27. Beckman, *Hittite Birth Rituals*, 46, regarding Text C (pp. 42–59); see specifically §6, line 22.
28. Marten Stol, in *Birth in Babylonia and the Bible*, 178, suggests that in Mesopotamia, as in Hittite tradition, a baby received a name shortly after birth ("The child received a name. This happened quite soon, but for Mesopotamia we do not know when exactly"), and in "Private Life in Ancient Mesopotamia," 491, Stol adds that names in Mesopotamia were "given by the father." But Stol does not cite any supporting evidence. Indeed, there is not much to be had. The only Mesopotamian "father-naming" episodes I can cite are from (1) the so-called Will of Sennacherib, where Sennacherib changes the name of his son Esarhaddon, or Aššur-aḫa-iddina, "Assur has given a brother," to Aššur-etel-ilāni-mukīn-apli, "Assur, prince of the gods, is establishing an heir," seemingly in order to convey greater legitimacy on his younger son and his unorthodox claim to the throne (see Porter, *Images, Power, and Politics*, 17), and (2) the Ennigaldi-Nanna Stele I: 20–25, where Nabonidus reports that he renamed his daughter when he made her an *entu*-priestess at the Egipar temple of Ur ("I raised the daughter, my offspring, to high priestess-ship; and I called her name Ennigaldi-Nanna"; for the text, see Schaudig, *Die Inschriften Nabonidus*, Text 2.7; the translation is from Yun, "Mother of Her Son," 288). Conversely, in an "unusual note" found among the Mari archives (Sasson, *From the Mari Archives*, 320–21), whatever right the father has to determine a child's name was usurped by Princess Šimatum, who, based on the guidance she received from "a man" who appeared to her in a dream, urges that "my lord" (either her father or her husband) should bestow the name Tagid-nawu on the infant girl of the palace musician Tepaḫum.
29. See, the Prologue, n. 13, for references, as well as Boedeker, "Family Matters," 241; Garland, *Greek Way of Life*, 93–96; and Golden, "Names and Naming at Athens," 252–56. According to Laes, "Infants between Biological and Social Birth," 366, n. 11, "the fundamental study" of the Amphidromia "remains" R. Hamilton, "Sources for the Athenian Amphidromia," 243–51.
30. On the father as most likely bestowing the child's name, see R. Hamilton, "Sources for the Athenian Amphidromia," 246, n. 21, and Laes, "Infants between Biological and Social Birth," 367, especially n. 19; see also Stowers, "Greeks Who Sacrifice," 315.
31. Parkin, "Demography of Infancy and Early Childhood," 45. Parkin also cites Plutarch's explanation for the difference: that men had three names, and nine is three squared, whereas women only had two names, and two cubed is eight.
32. Laes, *Children in the Roman Empire*, 67. On women's lack of a praenomen, see Kajanto, "Women's praenomina Reconsidered," 13–30; Laes, "Infants between Biological and Social Birth," 370; and Salway, "What's in a Name?," 125.
33. Laes, "Infants between Biological and Social Birth," 370; Salway, "What's in a Name?," 125–28.
34. Dasen, "Childbirth and Infancy," 296; see similarly Garland, *Greek Way of Life*, 61–64, and Stowers, "Greeks Who Sacrifice," 315.
35. So too Gursky, "Reproductive Rituals," 102–33, 139–47, although note that Gursky only focuses on one aspect of the maternal name-giving rites that I consider here: the newly delivered woman's ability, through the name she bestows on her child, to articulate important aspects of

her engagement with God during pregnancy and parturition and thus give voice to her religious experiences and convictions. See also, on the ritualized aspects of name-giving, n. 15 above, regarding Albertz's discussion of Israelite name-giving as a ritual occasion, although ritualized according to a very different temporal schedule than I have argued for here. Cf., though, Miller, *Religion of Ancient Israel*, 71: "naming was less a religious activity in the strict sense."

36. Modern medicine typically defines the neonatal period as corresponding to the first month, or twenty-eight days, of the baby's life, while the ancients seemed to understand the neonatal period to last forty days: see Dasen, "Childbirth and Infancy," 293.
37. Pinch, *Magic in Ancient Egypt*, 128; the text is Westcar Papyrus §10.7 (Lichtheim, *Ancient Egyptian Literature* 1: 220).
38. Pinch, "Private Life in Ancient Egypt," 376.
39. Westcar Papyrus §11.18 (Lichtheim, *Ancient Egyptian Literature* 1: 221), with discussion in—among other places—Arnette, "Purification du post-partum," 24–25; Feucht, "Birth," 192; R. M. Janssen and J. J. Janssen, *Growing Up and Getting Old*, 7, 9–10; Marsman, *Women in Ugarit and Israel*, 201; Montserrat, "Rites of Passage," 439; and Pinch, "Private Life in Ancient Egypt," 376.
40. Arnette, "Purification du post-partum," 25, 27–29, regarding O. IFAO 1069/O. Dem 952; see also J. J. Janssen, "Absence from Work," 141–43, and Jauhiainen, "'Do Not Celebrate Your Feast without Your Neighbours,'" 250, n. 9, and 255. Throughout the Near East and wider Mediterranean, the passing of time is a standard means for bringing periods of impurity to an end: see regarding the Bible, D. P. Wright, "Unclean and Clean (OT)," 737.
41. Van der Toorn, *From Her Cradle to Her Grave*, 84.
42. This is how William L. Moran, "Atrahasis," 58–59, n. 3, interprets the Epic of Atraḫasis, Tablet I, lines 299–300, where the newly delivered woman and her husband seem to resume sexual relations on the tenth day after she gives birth, having first purified themselves, she from the ritual pollution she incurred in the process of delivery and he from any pollution he incurred through contact with her.
43. Van der Toorn, *Family Religion*, 123; idem, "Magic at the Cradle," 142; also idem, *From Her Cradle to Her Grave*, 84, 92 (with a reference there to the original publication of this text, by Thureau-Dangin, "Rituel et Amulettes Contre Labartu," 161–71).
44. For the text, see Bachvarova, "Hurro-Hittite Stories," 291, §10–§11, and Beckman, *Hittite Birth Rituals*, Text K, §10–§11 (pp. 134–37), §28–§29 (pp. 142–43).
45. Beckman, *Hittite Birth Rituals*, 160; B. J. Collins, "Rites of Passage," 444.
46. See above, n. 29, for variant traditions regarding the timing of the Amphidromia. The phrase "general household pollution" is from Boedeker, "Family Matters," 241.
47. Garland, *Greek Way of Life*, 61, 93.
48. This information on Greek childbirth impurity is derived from Boedeker, "Family Matters," 241; Dasen, "Childbirth and Infancy," 303; Garland, *Greek Way of Life*, 96–97; idem, "Children in Athenian Religion," 209; and R. Parker, *Miasma*, 49–51. Note, however, as both Boedeker's and Garland's accounts make clear, the information available from our ancient sources is not as exact as one might like. Hence, any description of the effects of childbirth impurities postpartum must be hedged with caveats such as "perhaps," "possibly," "apparently," and the like.
49. Garland, *Greek Way of Life*, 97.
50. Robins, *Women in Ancient Egypt*, 83; Romano, "18 Vessel in the form of Bes-image," 68. But cf. Arnette, "Purification du post-partum," 34, who understands the "washing of the feet" to take place in the beginning days of a newly delivered mother's fourteen-day seclusion, not during a purification ceremony at its end.
51. As in n. 50 above, cf. Arnette, "Purification du post-partum," 33, who understands the presentation of the mirror and kohl case to take place in the beginning days of a newly delivered mother's fourteen-day seclusion.
52. For purification, see Kemp, "Wall Paintings," 53; Pinch, "Private Life in Ancient Egypt," 377; and Robins, *Women in Ancient Egypt*, 83–84. For adornment, see R. M. Janssen and J. J. Janssen, *Growing Up and Getting Old*, 7; Romano, "18 Vessel in the form of Bes-image," 70.
53. Arnette, "Purification du post-partum," 36–37, with reference to the birth scene of Hatshepsut found at Deir el-Bahri (Arnette's Fig. 7a) and of Amenhotep III found at Luxor (Arnette's Fig. 7b).
54. Arnette, "Purification du post-partum," 37–38.
55. Pinch, "Private Life in Ancient Egypt," 377. But as in nn. 50 and 51 above, cf. Arnette, "Purification du post-partum," 34–35 and 38–39, who implies that the dancing takes place in the

beginning days of a newly delivered mother's fourteen-day seclusion and who also raises doubts that the image Pinch cites depicts a musical performance.
56. Kemp, "Wall Paintings," 53; see also ibid., 49–50, 52, for more on Kemp's analysis of this wall painting.
57. Arnette, "Purification du post-partum," 28; on pp. 39–40, Annette also considers two figured ostraca that might represent this drinking feast. For further discussion of the text (O. IFAO 1069/O. Dem 952), see J. J. Janssen, "Gift-Giving in Ancient Egypt," 255–56; Jauhiainen, "'Do Not Celebrate Your Feast without Your Neighbours,'" 255; and Toivari-Viitala, *Women at Deir el-Medina*, 180–81.
58. J. J. Janssen, "Gift-Giving in Ancient Egypt," 255–56 (O. Michaelides 48 rt.); Jauhiainen, "'Do Not Celebrate Your Feast without Your Neighbours,'" 255 (O. Cairo CG 25597; O. Cairo CG 25521); and Toivari-Viitala, *Women at Deir el-Medina*, 181 (O. Cairo CG 25521).
59. Westcar Papyrus §11.18 and §12.8: after "Ruddedet cleansed herself in a cleansing of fourteen days . . . they [Ruddedet and her husband Rawoser] sat down to a day of feasting." Translation Lichtheim, *Ancient Egyptian Literature* 1: 221.
60. Stol, *Birth in Babylonia and the Bible*, 180.
61. Beckman, *Hittite Birth Rituals*, 251, citing, on the "Festival of the Birth," that volume's Text K, §16 (pp. 138–39), and Text T, §3 (pp. 216–17); on the "Festival of the Womb," Text K, §12 (pp. 136–37) and §30 (pp. 144–45), and Text Y (pp. 222–23); and on the "Festival of Crying Out" and the "Festival of the Pigeons," Text Y (pp, 222–23). On how to translate the reference to the Hittite "Great" or "Mother" goddesses in Text K, see Chapter 5, n. 3.
62. Beckman, *Hittite Birth Rituals*, 251, citing that volume's Text B, §11″–§12″ (pp. 34–35); see also Bachvarova, "Hurro-Hittite Stories," 296, §10′–§11′, and Imparati, "Private Life Among the Hittites," 575.
63. Beckman, *Hittite Birth Rituals*, 251; B. J. Collins, "Rites of Passage," 444.
64. Van Gennep, *Rites of Passage*, 43–44.
65. Arnette, "Purification du post-partum," passim; Austin and Arnette, "Of Ink and Clay," 17.
66. V. Turner, "Liminality and Communitas," 95.
67. See in this regard Albertz, "Personal Names and Family Religion," 247, who hypothesizes that a woman's "first meeting with her husband and entire family" after the seven or fourteen days of a mother's seclusion prescribed in Lev 12:1–5 "would likely have been celebrated with a family feast." As noted above (n. 15), Albertz also hypothesizes that it is at this feast that a name would have been conferred upon a child.
68. Suggested, e.g., by Arnette, "Purification du post-partum," 19–22.
69. Milgrom, "Israel's Sanctuary," 390–99; see also idem, *Leviticus 1–16*, 253–92, especially 254–58.
70. Olyan, "Sin, Pollution, and Purity," 502.
71. Pollock, *Telling Bodies, Performing Birth*, 137; this quote was brought to my attention by Hammons, "Before Joan of Arc," 66.
72. V. Turner, "Liminality and Communitas," 95.
73. Steinberg, *World of the Child*, 71.
74. See my comments in the Introduction, n. 231.
75. V. Turner, "Humility and Hierarchy," 167–68.
76. Bynum, "Women's Stories, Women's Symbols," 33; Lincoln, *Emerging from the Chrysalis*, 103.
77. V. Turner, "Humility and Hierarchy," 168.
78. Above, n. 73.
79. McClain, "Toward a Comparative Framework for the Study of Childbirth," 47, citing Newman, "The Anthropology of Birth," 56. As in n. 71 above, this quote was brought to my attention by Hammons, "Before Joan of Arc," 66.
80. Lorenzen, *Spoken into Being*, 108 and 111, citing Bourdieu, *Language and Symbolic Power*, 120.
81. Van Gennep, *Rites of Passage*, 62.
82. Van Gennep, *Rites of Passage*, 63.
83. Corbier, "Child Exposure," 55.
84. Laes, *Children in the Roman Empire*, 66, citing Corbier, "Child Exposure," 58–60. See similarly Dasen, "Childbirth and Infancy," 297.
85. Corbier, "Child Exposure," 55–56.
86. Plutarch, *Quaestiones Romanae* §102 (*Moralia* 288C), as cited in Dasen, "Childbirth and Infancy," 293, and Laes, *Children in the Roman Empire*, 66.
87. Liston and Rotroff, "Babies in the Well," 77.

88. Garland, "Children in Athenian Religion," 209.
89. Hornung, *Idea into Image*, 178.
90. Van der Toorn, *From Her Cradle to Her Grave*, 23.
91. These examples were all brought to my attention by Cherry, "Paronomasia and Proper Names," 35-36.
92. On the differing use of men's names and women's names within, at least, the Old Babylonian ancestor tradition, see van der Toorn, "Family Religion in Second Millennium West Asia," 28-29, and my discussion of van der Toorn's analysis in Chapter 9.
93. Ross, "Paronomasia and Popular Etymology," 8.
94. Garroway, *Children in the Ancient Near Eastern Household*, 242; for more detail regarding Garroway's argument, and my reservations about it, see Chapter 1, n. 56; for modifications, which extend the child's "trial membership" even beyond weaning (about which I also have reservations), see Garroway, "Enculturating Children," 418.
95. Laes, "Infants between Biological and Social Birth," 368.
96. Garland, *Greek Way of Life*, 121-22.
97. Laes, "Infants between Biological and Social Birth," 371.
98. Above, n. 71.
99. See Patai, *Family, Love and the Bible*, 172; van der Toorn, *From Her Cradle to Her Grave*, 23; and especially Albertz, "Personal Names and Family Religion," at multiple points, first, 246-48 for Albertz's general convictions, and then 252-53, 255-57, 269-97, and 345-47, regarding the "birth names" Albertz considers to be so revelatory regarding the experience of childbirth; see also the associated Appendix B.5, on pp. 582-601, for Albertz's catalogue of "birth names."
100. Pardes, *Countertraditions*, 41.
101. As Gerhard von Rad writes, "every word of this little sentence is difficult" (von Rad, *Genesis*, 103). A baby boy should not be called an 'îš, "man," and *qānâ* elsewhere in the Bible more commonly means "to acquire" and much less often "to create" (Westermann, *Genesis 1-11*, 290). Yet to "acquire" *'et-YHWH* is hard to make sense of, and the standard rendition—"acquire . . . with the help of Yahweh"—is nothing more than a fudge, as "'et never means 'with the help of'" (von Rad, *Genesis*, 103). Given these complications, and given that Gen 4:1 follows hard on Gen 2:4b-3:24 and its story of creation, and of an 'îš no less, it seems most plausible to translate "I have created a man with Yahweh." Particularly helpful discussions can be found in U. Cassuto, *Commentary on the Book of Genesis* 2: 198-202; Pardes *Countertraditions*, 44-46; Wenham, *Genesis 1-15*, 101-2; Westermann, *Genesis 1-11*, 289-92; and *HALOT*, s.v. *qnh*.
102. Wallace, *Eden Narrative*, 111-14, 152-59, remains a paradigmatic statement regarding resonances of Asherah traditions in Genesis 2-3.
103. I have described this role further in Ackerman, *Under Every Green Tree*, 155-59, and eadem, *Warrior, Dancer*, 192.
104. Albertz, "Personal Names and Family Religion," 270-71.
105. I fully acknowledge the oddities of the naming accounts in 1 Sam 1:20 and 1 Chr 4:9 and, as they have come down to us, their imperfect etymologies regarding Samuel's and Jabez's names. On the former, see above, n. 4.
106. A standard source critical analysis would designate Abraham's naming his son in Gen 21:3 as a text from the P or Priestly source, while ascribing Sarah's speech reflecting on the name in 21:6 to the Elohistic source, or E.
107. A standard source critical analysis would designate Abraham's naming his son in Gen 16:15 as a text from the P or Priestly source, while ascribing 16:11, in which a divine messenger instructs Hagar to name her son, to the Yahwistic source, or J.
108. In only one possible case does a mother's or a female surrogate's or surrogates' naming speech address events beyond the mother's experiences in childbearing: this is 1 Sam 4:21-22, where Phinehas's wife names her son Ichabod (*î-kābôd*) in response to the news she hears just as she is about to deliver, that the "ark of God" that symbolized the deity's presence among the Israelites had been captured by the Philistines. Thus, she says in 4:22: "the glory [*kābôd*] has departed from Israel." Yet just prior, in v 21, she is said to give her son the name Ichabod in response *both* to the news about the ark's capture and to the much more personal news she also received as she was about to give birth, regarding the death of Phinehas, her husband (as well the deaths of her father-in-law, Eli, and brother-in-law, Hophni). See further my discussion below.
109. Although note that, as in nn. 10-12 above, the LXX takes Zipporah to have named Gershom in Exod 2:22, but this is due to the particulars of Greek grammar, whereby Zipporah, as the subject of the verb "to bear," continues to stand as the subject of the next verb in the verse, "to

name." The content of the naming speech only makes sense, however, if we understand Moses to have bestowed Gershom's name, just as reported in Exod 18:3 in both the MT and the LXX.
110. Note, however, Albertz's argument (in "Personal Names and Family Religion," 295), that in the two times the name Manasseh appears in the epigraphic record, it should be understood as a reference to a son "who makes [the parents] forget" the death of a previous offspring.
111. Genesis 4:1, 25; 16:11; 21:6; 29:32–33, 35; 30:6, 8, 18, 20, 23–24; 1 Sam 1:20.
112. See further Gursky, "Reproductive Rituals," 108–33, 139–47.
113. Pardes, *Countertraditions*, 43.
114. Ackerman, *Women and the Religion of Ancient Israel*, 111–13.
115. Although as Marc Zvi Brettler has pointed out (in "Women and Psalms," 31, n. 27), some midrashic traditions interpret the odd phrase *nōkaḥ 'ištô* in Gen 25:21 to mean that Rebekah joined together with Isaac during his entreaty (*'ātar*) to God regarding Rebekah's barrenness.
116. To be sure, some scholars have sought to identify women other than Hannah who pray. Patrick D. Miller, in "Things Too Wonderful," 237, identifies what he describes as ten or eleven instances of women praying in the Hebrew Bible (although he then lists thirteen— Gen 21:16–17; 25:22; 29:35; 30:24; Exod 15:21; Judg 5:1–31; 1 Sam 1:10, 12–15; 2:1–10; 1 Kgs 10:9; Psalm 131; Ruth 1:8–9, 4:14). Marc Zvi Brettler has also argued that Ps 113:4–9 so closely parallels the text of Hannah's prayer in 1 Sam 2:1–10 that it must be understood, like Hannah's utterance, as a newly delivered mother's "prayer of thanksgiving" (see Brettler, "A Woman's Voice in the Psalter," 155–70, especially 162–63). Blank, "Curse, Blasphemy," 95, and Scharbert, "'ālâ," 265, have in addition interpreted Micah's mother's curse in Judg 17:2 as a prayer. In none of these instances, though, is the woman explicitly identified as praying.
117. Men's vows: Jacob in Gen 28:20; Jephthah in Judg 11:30; Elkanah, according to 1 Sam 1:21; Absalom in 2 Sam 15:7–8; David, according to Ps 132:2; the sailors of Jon 1:16; and Jonah, according to the psalm that is put in his mouth in Jon 2:10 (2:9 in most English translations); also, Judas Maccabeaus in 1 Macc 5:5; Heliodorus in 2 Macc 3:35; Antiochus in 2 Macc 9:13; unnamed "heads of families" in 1 Esdras 5:44; and Artaxerxes in 1 Esdras 8:13.
118. Karel van der Toorn ("Female Prostitution," 193–205) has suggested that Deut 23:19 (23:18 in most English translations), which forbids using a female prostitute's wages to pay a vow, speaks more generally to ordinary women, who made frequent vows according to van der Toorn's understanding, but did not necessarily have the resources to fulfill their commitments. Hence, they resorted to prostitution to raise the required funds.
119. Hopkins, "Life on the Land," 189.
120. These rituals are detailed in the fourteenth-/thirteenth-century BCE Epic of Aqhat, from the Late Bronze Age city-state of Ugarit: see *KTU* 1.17.1.25–33. Within Israelite tradition, "the erection of a commemorative stele by Absalom because he had no son to do so (2 Sam 18:18) may ... be a reflection of the practice of a son honoring his father by setting up a funerary stele to the ancestral spirit of his father" (Miller, *Religion of Ancient Israel*, 55). Indeed, as van der Toorn writes, "to die without a son was feared as a major misfortune" (*Family Religion*, 208).
121. The exception—if it can be called that, given the speaker—is the naming speech God gives when directing Hosea to give the name Lo-Ruhamah to his daughter by Gomer (Hos 1:6).
122. Pardes, *Countertraditions*, 41.
123. It is hard to find parallels to this. In Mesopotamia, according to Stol, "Private Life in Ancient Mesopotamia," 491, names can sometimes speak to the *newborn's* engagement with the divine, as the name expresses a short prayer on behalf of the infant: "My god has had mercy on me" or "Sin, accept my supplication." In Egypt, according to R. M. Janssen and J. J. Janssen, *Growing Up and Getting Old*, 13, names can sometimes express the mother's hopes for the newborn, such as the boy's name Mersure, "May Re love him," or sometimes a mother's claim on her child, such as the girl's name Aneksi, "She belongs to me [the mother]." But Janssen and Janssen cite only one name that even comes close to the biblical accounts of a name reflecting a mother's experiences in pregnancy and childbirth, which is the name Gemnihiamente that, according to a New Kingdom legal text, was given to an enslaved Syrian girl. This name means "I found her on the West Bank [of Thebes]," and it apparently details the way the enslaved girl's mistress obtained her. Clearly, though, there is no mention here of the divine or of a religious experience on the part of the girl's adoptive mother. Somewhat more evocative, though, is the Egyptian name Nehy, meaning "(He who was) requested," cited by Marshall, *Motherhood and Early Childhood*, 99, and even more so the theophoric name Tadebastet, meaning "She who Bastet gave me" (ibid., 100).

Chapter 7

1. Bynum, "Women's Stories, Women's Symbols," 33; Lincoln, *Emerging from the Chrysalis*, 103.
2. See Joseph Blenkinsopp, Phyllis Bird, Gale A. Yee, and J. Cheryl Exum, as cited in Chapter 4, nn. 22–25.
3. Roth, *Law Collections from Mesopotamia*, 57 (for the date) and 64 (for the text).
4. Biggs, "Conception, Contraception, and Abortion," 6, and n. 40 on that page, and preeminently Gruber, "Breast-Feeding Practices," 92, 94, 102–3, n. 129.
5. Lichtheim, *Ancient Egyptian Literature* 2: 141.
6. Jonckheere, "Un chapitre de pédiatrie égyptienne," 215; this reference was brought to my attention by Marshall, "Nurture of Children," 51.
7. Dupras and Tocheri, "Reconstructing Infant Weaning Histories," 71; see also Dupras, Schwarcz, and Fairgrieve, "Infant Feeding and Weaning Practices," 204–11.
8. Note also that the first-century CE Jewish historian Josephus, in *Antiquities* 2.230, reports that God greatly increased Moses's stature when he was three years old, which might reflect Exod 2:10, where Moses is said to have been nursed by his mother until he "grew up" (*wayigdal*). Taken together, that is, these two texts may suggest an understanding that by the time he was three, Moses had grown big enough that he could be weaned. This Josephus reference was brought to my attention by Haran, "Ezekiel, P, and the Priestly School," 214; further on the association of weaning and the Hebrew verb *g-d-l*, see C. R. Chapman, *House of the Mother*, 277, n. 68.
9. Reading "a three-year-old bull," versus the MT "three bulls." As Driver, *Notes on the Hebrew Text and the Topography of the Books of Samuel*, 20, and McCarter, *I Samuel*, 56–57, among others, point out, the *m* of the original *bpr mšlš*, a "three-year old bull," has been mistakenly repositioned to yield *bprym šlšh*, "three bulls."
10. See, e.g., Blenkinsopp, "Family in First Temple Israel," n. 42 on p. 97; Fokkelman, *Narrative Art and Poetry in the Books of Samuel* 4: 67; and Pfeifer, "Entwöhnung und Entwöhnungsfest," 342.
11. Patai, *Family, Love and the Bible*, 175. According to Véronique Dasen, "Childbirth and Infancy," 292, "in classical Athens, the three-year-old was involved for the first time in the religious life of the community." See also ibid., 312.
12. For discussion, see Blenkinsopp, "Family in First Temple Israel," 68; Gruber, "Women in the Cult," 67–68, n. 40; idem, "Breast-Feeding Practices," 79–80; Hallo, "Isaiah 28:9–13," 337–38; Patai, *Family, Love and the Bible*, 174; and Pfeifer, "Entwöhnung und Entwöhnungsfest," 344–47.
13. Gruber, "Breast-Feeding Practices," 80; Patai, *Family, Love and the Bible*, 174.
14. Stol, *Birth in Babylonia and the Bible*, 181–82.
15. R. M. Janssen and J. J. Janssen, *Growing Up and Getting Old*, 15.
16. Other iconographic representations of Egyptian mothers giving suck are found in the Fifth Dynasty tomb of Niankhkhnum and Khnumhotep at Saqqara (ca. 2400 BCE), as cited by Graves-Brown, *Dancing for Hathor*, 66, and in the Eighteenth Dynasty tomb of Menna at Thebes (ca. 1400–1352 BCE) and the Twenty-Sixth Dynasty tomb of Mentuemhat (ca. 660 BCE) that are discussed below.
17. R. M. Janssen and J. J. Janssen, *Growing Up and Getting Old*, 15; Robins, *Women in Ancient Egypt*, 89.
18. Robins, *Women in Ancient Egypt*, 89; Vymazalová and Strouhal, "Mother and Child Care," 191.
19. Feucht, "Childhood," 262.
20. Dartmouth College Hood Museum of Art, object number 39.64.6623; image available online at https://hoodmuseum.dartmouth.edu/objects/39.64.6623.
21. There is some debate about the term *ōmenet* used in 2 Sam 4:4. Mayer I. Gruber, "Nursing Mothers," 322, argues that *ōmenet* means "a female deliverer of child care (in general)," and not specifically a wetnurse. (This reference was brought to my attention by Yee, "'Take This Child and Suckle It for Me,'" 181.) For counterarguments, see Bergmann, "Infant Israel Growing Up," 163–64, and C. R. Chapman, *House of the Mother*, 145–47.
22. See Chapter 1, n. 38.
23. See Chapter 3, n. 85.
24. Dettwyler and Fishman, "Infant Feeding Practices," 8, 10–11; Rogers, Emmett, and Golding, "Growth and Nutritional Status of the Breast-fed Infant," S161, S164–65, S166, S170; and S. Scott and Duncan, *Demography and Nutrition*, 145, 153, with additional documentation.

25. S. Scott and Duncan, *Demography and Nutrition*, 14.
26. See Chapter 3, n. 84.
27. S. Scott and Duncan, *Demography and Nutrition*, 14, 99–100.
28. Roehrig, "Women's Work," 16 and Fig. 7 (image from the Tomb of Menna).
29. American Academy of Pediatrics, Committee on Nutrition, *Pediatric Nutrition Handbook*, 73 (with additional references); Dettwyler and Fishman, "Infant Feeding Practices," 177 and 183 (with additional references); Rogers, Emmett, and Golding, "Growth and Nutritional Status of the Breast-fed Infant," S162; and S. Scott and Duncan, *Demography and Nutrition*, 50 (with additional references).
30. S. Scott and Duncan, *Demography and Nutrition*, 151, with additional references.
31. S. Scott and Duncan, *Demography and Nutrition*, 152; see similarly Stini, Weber, Kemberling, and Vaughan, "Lean Tissue Growth and Disease Susceptibility," 63, with additional references.
32. S. Scott and Duncan, *Demography and Nutrition*, 149, with additional documentation.
33. S. Scott and Duncan, *Demography and Nutrition*, 144.
34. S. Scott and Duncan, *Demography and Nutrition*, 144, with additional documentation.
35. S. Scott and Duncan, *Demography and Nutrition*, 153.
36. S. Scott and Duncan, *Demography and Nutrition*, 153, citing Howarth, "Influence of Feeding on the Mortality of Infants," 210–13.
37. S. Scott and Duncan, *Demography and Nutrition*, 153–54.
38. Rogers, Emmett, and Golding, "Growth and Nutritional Status of the Breast-fed Infant," S168, with additional documentation.
39. Lauwers and Swisher, *Counseling the Nursing Mother*, 170, with additional documentation.
40. S. Scott and Duncan, *Demography and Nutrition*, 155; see similarly Rogers, Emmett, and Golding, "Growth and Nutritional Status of the Breast-fed Infant," S162.
41. S. Scott and Duncan, *Demography and Nutrition*, 155; see similarly, on the nutritional problems incurred by infants fed vegetarian diets, Dewey, *Guiding Principles for Complementary Feeding*, 22–23, 25.
42. MacDonald, *What Did the Ancient Israelites Eat?*, 19; idem, *Not Bread Alone*, 60. See similarly M. Cohen, "Diet and Nutrition," 337–38, 342, and C. Meyers, "Food and Gender," 386. Today, by contrast, it is estimated that only about 20 percent of the world's calories come from our planet's major grain crop, wheat: see Shiferaw, Smale, Braun, et al., "Crops that Feed the World," 291, 294–95.
43. Borowski, *Daily Life in Biblical Times*, 65, 74.
44. MacDonald, *What Did the Ancient Israelites Eat?*, 27.
45. But cf. Mayer I. Gruber, "Private Life in Canaan and Ancient Israel," 638, who, writing of typical rural families in Late Bronze Age Ugarit, estimates that flock sizes and ewes' rates of reproduction were such that these families could only have slaughtered a sheep every six weeks (or about 8–9 times per year) without reducing the size of their herd. See similarly, regarding ancient Israel, Welton, "Ritual and the Agency of Food," 614–15.
46. S. Scott and Duncan, *Demography and Nutrition*, 145–47 (with additional documentation); see similarly, on an infant's need for fat and certain fatty acids, Dewey, *Guiding Principles for Complementary Feeding*, 12, 23–24.
47. S. Scott and Duncan, *Demography and Nutrition*, 156.
48. S. Scott and Duncan, *Demography and Nutrition*, 156 (with additional documentation). See similarly Dettwyler and Fishman, "Infant Feeding Practices," 176; Dewey, *Guiding Principles for Complementary Feeding*, 12; and Rogers, Emmett, and Golding, "Growth and Nutritional Status of the Breast-fed Infant," S170.
49. S. Scott and Duncan, *Demography and Nutrition*, 185.
50. Dettwyler and Fishman, "Infant Feeding Practices," 184.
51. Prolonged breastfeeding also confers significant advantages in terms of the mother's health, as well as the health of a child she might subsequently bear, as breastfeeding delays the return of ovulation (as in Hos 1:8, where Gomer conceives her third child only after she has weaned her second). This delay allows a mother "a longer period to rebuild some of her nutritional stores depleted through pregnancy and lactation" (Dettwyler and Fishman, "Infant Feeding Practices," 176 [with additional documentation]; see also ibid., 183). This in turn allows a mother to bear a healthier child during her next pregnancy, as "published results are remarkably consistent in showing that short inter-pregnancy intervals are associated with an increased risk of adverse perinatal outcomes": e.g., "low birthweight, preterm birth, or small size for gestational age" (S. Scott and Duncan, *Demography and Nutrition*, 187; see also ibid., 113, and Stini, Weber,

Kemberling, and Vaughan, "Lean Tissue Growth and Disease Susceptibility," 65). See also Gruber, "Breast-Feeding Practices," 72–73 (with additional references).
52. Translation Dalley, "Erra and Ishum," 414; this text was brought to my attention by Hillers, *Treaty Curses*, 62.
53. Fifty-three different cultures from the 185 surveyed in the Human Relations Area Files (HRAF), as developed and reported by Murdock and Provost, "Factors in the Division of Labor by Sex," 203–25.
54. Niehoff and Meister, "Cultural Characteristics of Breastfeeding," 182–83.
55. Lawrence, "Maternal Factors in Lactation Failure," 283–91, and Neifert and J. M. Scott, "Mammary Gland Anomalies and Lactation Failure," 293–99.
56. Walker, *Breastfeeding Management*, 266, with additional references.
57. Lauwers and Swisher, *Counseling the Nursing Mother*, 126; Walker, *Breastfeeding Management*, 367–68.
58. While a woman with mastitis can (and, in fact, according to practitioners, should) nurse, "any mother ... with symptoms of mastitis is at risk for weaning": Lauwers and Swisher, *Counseling the Nursing Mother*, 326.
59. Hansen, Hubbard, and Niebyl, "Mastitis," 376.
60. "Mastitis."
61. See Chapter 1, n. 2.
62. Quoted in Willett, "Infant Mortality," 82, who in turn cites van Dijk, Goetze, and Hussey, *Early Mesopotamian Incantations*, 49 (Text 86b). Further on Lamaštu, see Chapter 5 and the references cited in n. 8 there.
63. Foster, *Before the Muses*, 986 (IV.43); this text was brought to my attention by Stol, *Birth in Babylonia and the Bible*, 184, n. 81.
64. For this text and translation, see Vymazalová and Strouhal, "Mother and Child Care," 132. For comment, see, as quoted here, Pinch, *Magic in Ancient Egypt*, 130, and also Ritner, "Household Religion in Ancient Egypt," 176.
65. For the relevant texts and translation, see Ghalioungui, *Ebers Papyrus*, 201 (No. 788) and 203 (No. 796), and Vymazalová and Strouhal, "Mother and Child Care," 117–18, with further comment on p. 193.
66. For the relevant texts and translation, see Ghalioungui, *The Ebers Papyrus*, 212–13 (Nos. 836 and 837), and Vymazalová and Strouhal, "Mother and Child Care," 123, with further comment on p. 193. See also Robins, "Women and Children in Peril," 28–29.
67. For the relevant texts and translation, see Ghalioungui, *Ebers Papyrus*, 205–6 (Nos. 808 and 809), and Vymazalová and Strouhal, "Mother and Child Care," 119, with further comment on p. 184. For a somewhat different interpretation of the problem Papyrus Ebers 808 seeks to address (not overflowing breasts, but breasts lacking in vigor), see Audouit, "Women's Intimacy," 388.
68. For the text and translation, see Ghalioungui, *Ebers Papyrus*, 206 (No. 810), and Vymazalová and Strouhal, "Mother and Child Care," 120, with further comment on p. 185.
69. For the text and translation, see Vymazalová and Strouhal, "Mother and Child Care," 125, with further comment on p. 185.
70. Fitzmyer, *Aramaic Inscriptions of Sefire*, 14 (lines 21–22); this text was brought to my attention by Stol, *Birth in Babylonia and the Bible*, 184, n. 83.
71. Dupont-Sommer and Starcky, "Les inscriptions araméennes de Sfiré," as cited in Fitzmyer, *Aramaic Inscriptions of Sefire*, 42, where Fitzmyer notes that Hillers, *Treaty Curses*, 61, n. 52, questions Dupont-Sommer's hypothesis in favor of a more prosaic interpretation: that anointing would help prevent soreness and cracking.
72. See, as in Chapter 5, Ornan, "Chapter 14C: An Amulet of the Demon Pazazu," 517–19; also, for more on Pazazu, see Chapter 5, n. 9.
73. Ornan, "Chapter 14C: An Amulet of the Demon Pazazu," 518.
74. Bloch-Smith, "Judean Pillar Figurines."
75. Macalister, *Excavation of Gezer* 2: 417.
76. Albright, *Archaeology of Palestine*, 121; idem, "Astarte Plaques and Figurines," 120.
77. Hadley, *Cult of Asherah*, 196, and Bloch-Smith, "Acculturating Gender Roles," 12, citing Lods, *Israel*, 136.
78. Bloch-Smith, "Acculturating Gender Roles," 12.
79. Bloch-Smith, *Judahite Burial Practices*, 100.

80. Bloch-Smith, *Judahite Burial Practices*, 98; eadem, "Acculturating Gender Roles," 13. See similarly Cynthia R. Chapman, "'Oh that you were like a brother to me,'" 16, who writes, "I would argue that at least one of the functions of the JPFs was to insure an adequate milk supply for a nursing mother"; Jennie R. Ebeling, *Women's Lives in Biblical Times*, 118, who suggests "the Judean pillar figurines ... may have been used by women to protect themselves and their children ... and a woman's ability to nurse"; Richard S. Hess, *Israelite Religions*, 310, who posits that "the pillar-based figurines are connected with the priority and prestige that was given to motherhood ... and also with the concern to nurse ... the large breasts might suggest lactation after birth"; and Francesca Stavrakopoulou, "Religion at Home," 356, who opines that "the large size of the breasts on the figurines, as well as the position of the figurines' arms, supporting or presenting the breasts, suggests that the breasts are the most significant aspect of the objects," rendering it "more probable that it is ... specifically lactation which is in view here."
81. C. Meyers, "Terracottas Without Texts," 124.
82. C. Meyers, *Households and Holiness*, 27–28, 30.
83. Keel and Uehlinger, *Gods, Goddesses, and Images of God*, 333. There they write, "the figurines are supposed to show the goddess as a nursing *mother*," while stating more generally that their "overall purpose is apparently to mediate blessings, such as motherly closeness, peaceful rest, light and warmth."
84. Dever, *Did God Have a Wife?*, 187; Zevit, *Religions of Ancient Israel*, 273.
85. C. Meyers, *Rediscovering Eve*, 156.
86. Darby, *Interpreting Judean Pillar Figurines*. Darby's conclusions were anticipated in an article by Shawna Dolansky completed in 2008, although this article was not published until 2016: see Dolansky, "Re-Figuring Judean 'Fertility' Figurines," 16–20; see also ibid., 9, n. 17, for the original date of Dolansky's work. For a more recent and somewhat different exposition of Dolansky's views, see eadem, "Interpreting Iconography," 150–66.
87. Darby, "Seeing Double," 13–26; eadem, "Judean Pillar Figurines and the Making of Female Piety," 193–214; eadem, "Judean Pillar Figurines (JPFs)," 401–14; and eadem, "Sex in the City?," 178–214.
88. Darby, *Interpreting Judean Pillar Figurines*, 96.
89. See, e.g., Darby, *Interpreting Judean Pillar Figurines*, 319–20, 325–28, 330–31; eadem, "Seeing Double," 17–18; and eadem, "Judean Pillar Figurines and the Making of Female Piety," 199.
90. For the horse frontlets, Darby cites Burkert, *Orientalizing Revolution*, 16, 20, and Fig. 2 on p. 18, and Winter, "North Syria as a Bronzeworking Centre," 340, 374, Fig. 2; in ibid., 358, Winter indicates that the date of various bronze finds from North Syria, including the horse frontlets, is "uncertain" and cites various arguments that have been advanced for ninth-, eighth-, and seventh-century BCE dates. For the Ammonite seals, Darby cites Avigad, "Two Ammonite Seals," 63–66. For the Yavneh cult stands, Darby cites Kletter, "Typology of the Cult Stands," 40, 42–43; idem, "Functions of Cult Stands," 186–88; and idem and Ziffer, "Catalogues," with references to Stands 28–29, 37, 44, 49, 57, 59, 84–86, 90, 92, 113, and Detached Female Figure 123. For the model shrine from Ḥorvat Qitmit, see Beck, "Catalogue of Cult Objects," 99–103.
91. Darby, *Interpreting Judean Pillar Figurines*, 329–31.
92. Dolansky, "Re-Figuring Judean 'Fertility' Figurines," 16–17; eadem, "Interpreting Iconography," 152, 159; and Gubel, "Phoenician and Aramaean Bridle-Harness Decoration," 99–100, on the nude females on ivory frontlets from Nimrud.
93. Beck, "Catalogue of Cult Objects," 122–23, citing Dornemann, *Archaeology of the Transjordan*, 143–45. I have also advocated this interpretation of the Qitmit model shrine—see Ackerman, *Women and the Religion of Ancient Israel*, 330–31—and I and other scholars have advanced it as well about kindred shrine models whose entryways are flanked by various female figures: see ibid., 314–30, with additional references at 442, nn. 72, 79–80.
94. Darby, *Interpreting Judean Pillar Figurines*, 319–21, 326–27, 330–33; eadem, "Seeing Double," 17; eadem, "Judean Pillar Figurines (JPFs)," 409.
95. Darby, *Interpreting Judean Pillar Figurines*, 336, and eadem, "Judean Pillar Figurines (JPFs)," 409, citing Allen, *Art of Medicine in Ancient Egypt*, 34, and Robins, *Women in Ancient Egypt*, 90. The spell Robins cites can be found in Vymazalová and Strouhal, "Mother and Child Care," 131 (Papyrus Berlin 3037, Text I), who add on p. 192 that "the breast milk of a woman who had given birth to a boy ... was used to treat a cough in infants, and intestinal problems and eye diseases in children and adults." Allen writes similarly that "breast milk was ... included in medical prescriptions for head colds, burns, rashes, and fever in adults as well as infants."

96. For the relevant texts and translation, see Ghalioungui, *Ebers Papyrus*, 205–6 (Nos. 808 and 809),
97. For the text and translation, see Ghalioungui, *Ebers Papyrus*, 137 (No. 500).
98. Darby, *Interpreting Judean Pillar Figurines*, 307–8; eadem, "Seeing Double," 15.
99. Darby, *Interpreting Judean Pillar Figurines*, 337–38, and eadem, "Judean Pillar Figurines (JPFs)," 407, citing Lewis, "Shaʿtiqatu Narrative," 188–211, and idem, "Identity and Function of Ugaritic Shaʿtiqatu," 1–28.
100. Lewis, "Identity and Function of Ugaritic Shaʿtiqatu," 24, 26.
101. Darby does address this problem: see Darby, *Interpreting Judean Pillar Figurines*, 328–30.
102. Moorey, *Idols of the People*, 58 and Plate 12.
103. Darby, *Interpreting Judean Pillar Figurines*, 352; Darby also mentions these Syrian figurines in ibid., 343.
104. Moorey, *Idols of the People*, 60, with reference again (as in n. 102 above) to Plate 12, second figure from the left (Ashmolean Museum Collection 1913.634, from a seventh-century BCE cemetery at Deve Hüyük, about 25 miles west of Carchemish; see Moorey, *Ancient Near Eastern Terracottas*, 228–29, Item #358).
105. Darby mentions these only in passing, with key discussion relegated to a footnote: see Darby, *Interpreting Judean Pillar Figurines*, 310 and n. 23 on that page.
106. See Albright, *Excavation of Tell Beit Mirsim III*, Pl. 32:1; also Keel and Uehlinger, *Gods, Goddesses, and Images of God*, 333 and Illus. 326, and Kletter, *Judean Pillar-Figurines*, 36 and 195 (Catalog #232).
107. Gilbert-Peretz, "Ceramic Figurines," 47.
108. Holland, "Study of Palestinian Iron Age Baked Clay Figurines," 139; see also idem, "Typological and Archaeological Study" 2: 100, A.XI.37 and Fig. 12.3.
109. Kletter, *Judean Pillar-Figurines*, 247, 5.I.4.17; see also Holland, "Typological and Archaeological Study" 2: 94, A.I.h.1, and Fig 4.4, Pl. 1.10.
110. Aharoni, *Excavations at Ramat Raḥel: Seasons 1959 and 1960*, Pl. 5; idem, *Excavations at Ramat Raḥel: Seasons 1961 and 1962*, Pl. 36.1.
111. See, e.g., Darby, *Interpreting Judean Pillar Figurines*, 56–58, 60, 65, 404–5; eadem, "Judean Pillar Figurines and the Making of Female Piety," 196.
112. Above, n. 81.
113. Above, n. 80.
114. Pfeifer, "Entwöhnung und Entwöhnungsfest," 342.
115. Karel van der Toorn, "Nine Months among the Peasants in the Palestinian Highlands," 406, similarly imagines a weaning feast taking place among nonelites in a preexilic Israelite village, and some scholars have interpreted Hannah's sacrifice in 1 Sam 1:24 as comprising food offerings that, after the sacrificial rites were performed, were to be consumed in a weaning feast. See Miller, *Religion of Ancient Israel*, 71; Gerstenberger and Schrage, *Woman and Man*, 34; and Zevit, *Religions of Ancient Israel*, 665. However, I would take weaning feasts to be home-based, as in Gen 21:8, as opposed to sanctuary-based rituals.
116. Steinberg, *World of the Child*, 66. More generally on weaning as a life-cycle event for children in ancient Israel, see ibid., 65–67; Bergmann, "Infant Israel Growing Up," 164–70; and Carey Ellen Walsh. *Fruit of the Vine*, 233, who writes of weaning as "a rite of passage for [especially] the Israelite male child ... an obvious shift toward independence from his mother."
117. Garroway, *Children in the Ancient Near Eastern Household*, 67, n. 81, citing multiple references to "the distribution lists from Kish and the census lists from Haran, as well as food ration lists from Sumerian archives."
118. Blenkinsopp, "Family in First Temple Israel," 68; see similarly idem, "Life Expectancy," 45–46.
119. Eng, *Days of Our Years*, 57; van der Toorn, *From Her Cradle to Her Grave*, 18. As I have noted in Chapter 1, n. 112, however, van der Toorn mistakenly understands the age at puberty for a girl child to be about twelve.
120. Garroway, "Construction of 'Child,'" 334.
121. E. R. Wells, "Display and Devotion," 293.
122. Garroway, *Children in the Ancient Near Eastern Household*, 148.
123. See further the references cited in Chapter 4, at nn. 47 and 50.
124. Above, n. 116.
125. C. R. Chapman, *House of the Mother*, 138–41.
126. See somewhat similarly Claudia D. Bergmann, "Infant Israel Growing Up," 165, 169, who writes of Isaac's weaning feast as a rite of passage for Sarah but also states more generally

about breastfeeding narratives in the Hebrew Bible that "one quickly realizes that it is not the breastfeeding mothers ... but the breastfed children who are the actual focus of the text."

Chapter 8

1. Greek and Roman sources suggest the age of menopause in those cultures was typically around forty, although some instances of women bearing children up to age fifty are known. See Aristotle, *History of Animals* VII.5.585a: "The menses cease in most women around the fortieth year, and in those in whom it goes on longer, the menses continue until the fiftieth year, and at this time some women of that age have borne children." Also see Pliny the Elder, *Natural History* 7.14.61: "A woman does not bear children after the age of fifty, and with the majority menstruation ceases at forty," both as cited in Amundsen and Diers, "Age of Menopause," 80–81. Roberta Gilchrist, *Gender and Archaeology*, 106 (citing Sperling and Beyene, "Pound of Biology," 145), reports that even in modern populations, the average age at menopause for women in nonindustrial societies is forty-two to forty-three.
2. Following here LXX^B, LXX^L, and 4QSam^a, all of which read: "she [Hannah] bore *again*" (emphasis mine), in order to make clear that the three sons Hannah is said to bear in 1 Sam 2:21 are in addition to Samuel, Hannah's firstborn. See McCarter, *I Samuel*, 80.
3. First Kings 14:21; 15:1–2, 9–10; 22:41–42; 2 Kgs 8:25–26; 12:2 (12:1 in most English translations); 14:1–2; 15:1–2, 32–33; 18:1–2; 21:1, 19; 22:1; 23:31, 36; 24:8, 18.
4. The term *gĕbîrâ* is used six times in the Hebrew Bible. In 1 Kgs 11:19, it should be translated "queen," referring to the wife of the Egyptian pharaoh. Elsewhere in Kings, and also in Jeremiah and Chronicles (1 Kgs 15:13; 2 Kgs 10:13; Jer 13:18; 29:2; 2 Chr 15:16), it is used as a title for the queen mother. The related term *gĕberet* means "mistress" (e.g., in Gen 16:4, 8, and 9, describing Sarah's relationship with Hagar); see also 2 Kgs 5:3; Isa 24:2; 47:5, 7; Ps 123:2; and Prov 30:23.
5. See the Prologue, n. 13, and Chapter 6, n. 29.
6. Corbier, "Child Exposure," 55. See also the references cited in Chapter 6, n. 84.
7. Plutarch, *Quaestiones Romanae* §102 (*Moralia* 288C), as cited in Dasen, "Childbirth and Infancy," 293, and Laes, *Children in the Roman Empire*, 66.
8. Crapanzano, "Rite of Return," 24–32.
9. V. Turner, *Drums of Affliction*, 12.
10. The phrase is V. Turner's, from "Betwixt and Between," 102.
11. Gilchrist, *Gender and Archaeology*, 96.
12. See the references cited in the Prologue, nn. 16–17, and the Introduction, n. 140.
13. Ackerman, *Warrior, Dancer*, 135, citing Heltzer, *Internal Organization of the Kingdom of Ugarit*, 182.
14. The text that describes this is RS 17.352 (= Nougayrol, *Le palais royal d'Ugarit IV*, 121–22), discussed by Lipiński, "Aḫat-milki," 79–115.
15. The pertinent texts are *KTU* 2.11; 2.12; 2.13; 2.16; 2.24; 2.30; 2.33; and 2.34. I have discussed these thoroughly in Ackerman, "Queen Mother and the Cult in the Ancient Near East," 182–83, revised and republished in *Gods, Goddesses, and the Women Who Serve Them*, 173–75.
16. The text is *KAI* 14. For the date, see McCarter, "Sarcophagus Inscription of 'Eshmun'azor," 182.
17. Gibson, *Textbook of Syrian Semitic Inscriptions* 3: 110; McCarter, "Sarcophagus Inscription of 'Eshmun'azor," 182, n. 6.
18. On the name, see Gibson, *Textbook of Syrian Semitic Inscriptions* 3: 112; McCarter, "Sarcophagus Inscription of 'Eshmun'azor," 182, n. 9.
19. Translation McCarter, "Sarcophagus Inscription of 'Eshmun'azor," 183, with commentary in nn. 9 and 19.
20. McCarter, "Sarcophagus Inscription of 'Eshmun'azor," 183, nn. 17–18.
21. Gray, *I and II Kings*, 104.
22. The variant names are most probably the result of textual confusion; see Noth, *Die israelitischen Personennamen*, 234, #117. In 2 Chr 13:2, moreover, the name given to Abijah's mother, Micaiah, seems to be a variant of the name Ma'acah. The textual tradition also presents variant accounts of Ma'acah's ancestry: in 1 Kgs 15:1–2 and 2 Chr 11:20–22, she is identified as the daughter of

Abishalom (Kings) or Absalom (Chronicles), although in 2 Chr 13:1-2, Micaiah is said to be the daughter of Uriel of Gibeah.
23. Above, n. 3.
24. Above, n. 4.
25. Note also in this regard Jer 29:2, where the queen mother of King Jehoiachin/Jeconiah of Judah (identified as Nehushta in 2 Kgs 24:8) is listed among the court officials who were deposed by the Babylonians and taken into exile in 586 BCE.
26. The noun *mipleṣet*, which occurs only in 1 Kgs 15:13 and in the Chronicles parallel (2 Chr 15:16), derives from the verb *p-l-ṣ*, "to shudder." Presumably it means "a thing to be shuddered at," "a horrid thing," or, as here, "an abominable image."
27. I take the biblical tradition to be emphatic in its understanding of the *'ăšērâ* as a stylized wooden tree. Deuteronomy 16:21 speaks of "planting" (*nāṭaʿ*) the *'ăšērâ*; elsewhere in the Bible (e.g., 1 Kgs 14:15, 23; 16:33; 2 Kgs 17:10, 16; 21:3; 2 Chr 33:3), the *'ăšērâ* cult object is "made" (*'āśâ*), "built" (*bānâ*), "stood up" (*'āmad*), or "erected" (*hiṣṣîb*). If destroyed, the *'ăšērâ* is "burned" (*bīʿēr* or *śārap*), "cut down" (*kārat*), "hewn down" (*gādaʿ*), "uprooted" (*nātaš*), or "broken" (*šibbēr*). I also, along with most commentators, presume that the *'ăšērâ* cult object represented the goddess Asherah and so was called by her name, although cf. Smith, *Early History of God* (1st ed.), 80–94, and also the more nuanced position Smith puts forward in this volume's 2nd ed., xxx–xxxvi.
28. I have discussed Maʿacah's role as a religious functionary, and, more generally, the religious role of queen mothers, in multiple publications. See Ackerman, "Queen Mother and the Cult in Ancient Israel," 385–401; eadem, "Queen Mother and the Cult in the Ancient Near East," 179–209; and eadem, "At Home with the Goddess," 459–61, all revised and republished in *Gods, Goddesses, and the Women Who Serve Them*, at 151–69, 170–88, and 198–201, respectively. See also Ackerman, *Warrior, Dancer,* 138–54, and eadem, *Women and the Religion of Ancient Israel,* 134–37, 345–46.
29. I have discussed the evidence for Asherah worship in ancient Israel in multiple publications. See Ackerman, "Asherah, the West Semitic Goddess of Spinning and Weaving?," 9–29; eadem, "Queen Mother and the Cult in Ancient Israel," 390–95; eadem, "At Home with the Goddess," 455–63; and eadem, "Women and the Worship of Yahweh in Ancient Israel," 189–91, all revised and republished in *Gods, Goddesses, and the Women Who Serve Them*, at 30–49; 158–64, 192–204, and 210–14, respectively. See also Ackerman, *Under Every Green Tree,* 60–66, and eadem, *Women and the Religion of Ancient Israel,* 135–37, 339–43, 345–46.
30. I have argued this elsewhere: see Ackerman, "Queen Mother and the Cult in the Ancient Near East," 194–95, revised and republished in *Gods, Goddesses, and the Women Who Serve Them*, 183–84; eadem, *Women and the Religion of Ancient Israel,* 128–33.
31. I have detailed some of the Near Eastern traditions that suggest this in Ackerman, "Women and the Religious Culture of the State Temples of the Ancient Levant," 271–72, 279, revised and republished as "Priestesses, Purity, and Parturition" in *Gods, Goddesses, and the Women Who Serve Them*, 133–35, 145–46. On similar traditions from classical Greece, see Demand, *Birth, Death, and Motherhood*, 27, citing J. A. Turner, "Hiereiai," 198–99.
32. Milgrom, *Leviticus 1–16,* 907.
33. J. R. Wegner, "'Coming Before the Lord,'" 457.
34. Olyan, *Disability in the Hebrew Bible,* 59.
35. Several scholars—especially Boling, *Judges,* 258–59, and van der Toorn, *Family Religion,* 247—have proposed that Judg 17:1-4 was originally a separate tale from the episode that follows in Judg 17:7–13; this is particularly indicated by the fact that Micah's name is rendered differently in the two passages (*mîkāyěhû* in Judg 17:1, 4 versus *mîkâ* in Judg 17:8, 9, 10, 12, 13). Judges 17:5-6, according to this reconstruction, was added by a redactor to bring 17:1-4 and 7–13 together. Leuchter, "'Now There Was a [Certain] Man,'" 436–38, argues similarly, but takes 17:5 to be part of the account found in 17:1-4, as I have here. A thorough discussion can be found in Mueller, *Micah Story,* 7–15.
36. See my discussion in Chapter 4, and also B. A. Levine, *Numbers 21–36,* 435.
37. This interpretation is also urged by Emmerson, "Women in Ancient Israel," 381.
38. As pointed out by Josef Scharbert ("*ʾālâ*," 262), the mother's curse in Judg 17:2 should be understood as analogous to the "audible curse oath" referred to in Lev 5:1, which is by definition conditional. This means that once Micah came forward and confessed as Lev 5:1 requires, the mother acted to nullify her curse by uttering a blessing.

39. Grammatically, the phrase *pesel ûmassēkâ*, which is referred to in Judg 17:4 using a singular verb, is best understood as a hendiadys, whereby two nouns (*pesel*, "image," and *massēkâ*, "molten image") are connected by *û*, "and," to indicate a single concept: a "cast-metal figurine"; so, e.g., Boling, *Judges*, 256; J. D. Martin, *Book of Judges*, 185; and Soggin, *Judges*, 265. But cf. (among the standard commentaries) Gunn, *Judges*, 231; Niditch, *Judges*, 172, 177, n. g, and 181; and Schneider, *Judges*, 233, who, based on the wording of Judg 18:17, 18, and perhaps of 18:20, 30, 31, understand the phrase *pesel ûmassēkâ* to refer to two separate objects.
40. I have presented the evidence that supports this claim in Ackerman, *Women and the Religion of Ancient Israel*, 35. On the religious custom that underlies the mother's consecration of only a portion of her eleven hundred pieces of silver, see Faraone, Garnand, and López-Ruiz. "Micah's Mother," 161–86.
41. I have presented the evidence that supports this claim in Ackerman, *Women and the Religion of Ancient Israel*, 44–46, 50–53.
42. Ackerman, *Women and the Religion of Ancient Israel*, 43–50; King and Stager, *Life in Biblical Israel*, 9–12.
43. This point has been particularly stressed by Nicol, "Wisdom of Joab," 97–104, who argues (at p. 97) that "the woman functions purely and simply as an agent who does no more than deliver the words of Joab to the king."

Chapter 9

1. A distinction between funerary rituals—rites performed at the time of a person's death—and mortuary practices—ongoing actions directed toward or undertaken on behalf of the dead—is championed by many scholars. See, e.g., Pardee, "Marzihu, Kispu, and the Ugaritic Funerary Cult," 273–74; Schmidt, *Israel's Beneficent Dead*, 4–12; and Suriano, *History of Death*, 12.
2. These texts include accounts regarding the deaths and/or burials of Sarah (Gen 23:2–4, 19; 25:10; 49:31); Rebekah (Gen 49:31); Deborah, Rebekah's nurse (Gen 35:8); Rachel (Gen 35:16–20; 48:7); Leah (Gen 49:31); Shua's daughter (Gen 38:12); Miriam (Num 20:1); the Levite's concubine (Judg 19:25–28); Jezebel (2 Kgs 9:33–37); Athaliah (2 Kgs 11:15–16); Ezekiel's wife (Ezek 24:16–18); and Esther's mother (Esth 2:7), with allusions to subsequent mortuary rites only in the stories of Rachel (Gen 35:20) and Jezebel (2 Kgs 9:34).
3. On Judg 19:28 as recording the death of the *pîlegeš*, see Chapter 4, n. 61.
4. Technically speaking, no account of canine devastation is found in 2 Kgs 9:35–37, but commentators overwhelmingly assume that we are to envision dogs as devouring Jezebel's corpse, a fate that had been prophesied by Elijah in 1 Kgs 21:23 (see also 2 Kgs 9:36) and again by an unnamed prophet in 2 Kgs 9:10.
5. We know much more about funerary and mortuary rites that women took responsibility for enacting on others' behalf. See Ackerman, *Women and the Religion of Ancient Israel*, 242–46 (especially for mourning rites), and Sonia, *Caring for the Dead*, 146–50, 152–54 (for rites concerning proper burial and the deceased's ongoing care).
6. Olyan, *Biblical Mourning*, 28, n. 1. See also, for dirges sung to mourn someone's death, 2 Sam 1:17–27 and 2 Chr 35:25.
7. See also Job 21:32, which implies that a dead body is carried in some sort of procession to the grave. This text was brought to my attention by Suriano, *History of Death*, 44, who suggests that transporting a corpse to the tomb on a bier "served as a type of public viewing."
8. On rubbing dust into one's skull, see also 1 Sam 4:12 and 2 Sam 1:2, as well as Olyan, *Biblical Mourning*, 30, n. 20, who takes Jer 6:26 to imply that covering one's entire body with ashes or dust is a mourning gesture enacted upon the death of an only son. From elsewhere in the Near East, see *KTU* 1.5.6.14–16, where the god El, while engaging in a long series of mourning behaviors upon hearing of the death of the storm god Baal, rubs dirt (paralleled by dust) on his head. Likewise in Mesopotamian tradition, those who mourned the mother of Nabonidus "scattered [dust] upon their heads"; see Oppenheim, "Mother of Nabonidus," 561–62 (this reference was brought to my attention by Pham, *Mourning*, 23). On this practice in Egypt, see Ritner, "Household Religion in Ancient Egypt," 173, and for evidence from Homeric Greece, see Ackerman, *Under Every Green Tree*, 85, n. 141.

9. See 2 Sam 13:31; Isa 47:1; and Ezek 26:16; see also *KTU* 1.5.6.12–14, where the god El retires from his throne to sit on a low stool and, in the parallel colon, the ground itself when he hears of the death of the storm god Baal. Note as well the Jewish custom of sitting *shiva* after a death, which continues until this day.
10. See Chapter 2, n. 40.
11. See Gen 37:34; 2 Sam 3:31; 14:2; Ps 30:12 [30:11 in most English translations]; Isa 22:12; 32:11; Jer 6:26; 48:37; 49:3; Ezek 27:31; and Amos 8:10; see also *KTU* 1.5.6.16–17 and *KTU* 1.5.6.31, in which the god El and the goddess Anat, respectively, don sackcloth as part of the mourning rituals they undertake upon hearing of the death of the storm god Baal. For further discussion, see Ackerman, *When Heroes Love*, 270, n. 112.
12. See Lev 19:28; 21:5; Hos 7:14; Jer 16:6; 41:5; 47:5; 48:37; and 49:3; see also *KTU* 1.5.6.17–22 and *KTU* 1.6.1.2–5, in which the god El and the goddess Anat, respectively, cut their cheeks, chins, arms, chests, and backs as part of their ritual mourning over the death of the storm god Baal; see likewise *KTU* 1.19.4.9–10, 21–22, regarding the mourning rites enacted at the death of Dan'il's son, Aqhat. For further discussion, see Ackerman, *Under Every Green Tree*, 85 and n. 142 on that page.
13. See Lev 19:27; 21:5; Isa 15:2; 22:12; Jer 7:29; 16:6; 41:5; 48:37; Ezek 27:31; Amos 8:10; Mic 1:16; and Job 1:20. See also the Epic of Gilgamesh, Tablet VIII, line 63 (following here the enumeration of George, *Babylonian Gilgamesh Epic* 1), where Gilgamesh tears out his hair while mourning the death of his beloved companion Enkidu. For further discussion, see Ackerman, *Under Every Green Tree*, 85–86, and n. 143 on p. 86; eadem, *When Heroes Love*, 270, n. 112; Olyan, *Biblical Mourning*, 111–23; and idem, "What Do Shaving Rites Accomplish?," 611–22, especially 616–17.
14. Technically speaking, as Matthew J. Suriano points out, in *History of Death*, 194, a single horse (Suriano takes it to be Jehu's) trampled Jezebel's body after her blood splattered on "the horses" (plural). In ibid., 195, Suriano also notes that Jehu specifically instructs his men to attend to Jezebel's body because she is a king's daughter (2 Kgs 9:34). That is, according to Suriano, it is Jezebel's royal birth as a Phoenician princess (1 Kgs 16:31) that motivates Jehu to require that her body be properly cared for, not the courtesy that might be due any dead person nor her marital status as Ahab's wife. See also Lewis, *Cults of the Dead*, 121; Sonia, *Caring for the Dead*, 150–51; and my comments on the mortuary rites to be accorded to royal daughters in Ackerman, "Just Who Is Coming to Dinner?," 304–5.
15. See Deut 26:14; Hos 9:4; Job 21:25; and Suriano, *History of Death*, 154–72.
16. Lewis, *Cults of the Dead*, 121.
17. Lewis, *Cults of the Dead*, 53, citing Bayliss, "Cult of Dead Kin," 116. See, more recently. Suriano, *History of Death*, 179–83.
18. Suriano, *History of Death*, 191.
19. Nonkin surrogates often take responsibility for the funerary and mortuary rites enacted on behalf of royal personages and other elites, as does Jehu upon the death of Jezebel; as does David on behalf of Abner (2 Sam 3:31–37), on behalf of Ishbaal (by sending his head for proper burial; 2 Sam 4:12), also on behalf of Saul and Jonathan (more on this below); and as do David's followers on behalf of David's nephew Asahel (also discussed below). For other examples of nonkin playing this role, see n. 30; also, Ackerman, "Just Who Is Coming to Dinner?," 304–6, and Olyan, "Roles of Kin and Fictive Kin," 259–61.
20. Note also Exod 20:12 and Deut 5:16, where a son (if we take seriously the masculine singular forms used in these verses) is commanded to "honor" his father and mother, which could mean honoring them in death (for *kibbēd*, "honor," used in this way, see 2 Sam 10:3 [// 1 Chr 19:3], as pointed out by Sonia, *Caring for the Dead*, 144 and n. 37 on that page).
21. Our archaeological evidence for Judahite burials is much more abundant than is evidence from the Northern Kingdom: see Franklin, "Tombs of the Kings of Israel," 1–2, and Yezerski, "Iron Age Burial Customs," 72.
22. Bloch-Smith, *Judahite Burial Practices*, 65. As Bloch-Smith points out in "From Womb to Tomb," 124, osteological analyses primarily date "from before the mid-1980s CE, after which time religious considerations impeded study."
23. Bloch-Smith, *Judahite Burial Practices*, 68.
24. Bloch-Smith, *Judahite Burial Practices*, 69.
25. Bloch-Smith, "From Womb to Tomb," 123.
26. Osborne, "Secondary Mortuary Practice," 35. In "Cult of the Dead," 217, Elizabeth Bloch-Smith reports that in Judah, "the total number of reported tombs are 24 cave tombs and 81 bench

tombs from the tenth through the third quarter of the eighth century BCE, and 17 cave and 185 bench tombs from the late eighth through the first quarter of the sixth century BCE." See also the numerical data compiled by Bloch-Smith in *Judahite Burial Practices*, 60–62.
27. Bloch-Smith, *Judahite Burial Practices*, 69.
28. Many scholars have noted the general similarities between the physical layout and the grave assemblages found in Judean bench tombs and the architecture and material culture assemblages that characterize the typical Israelite four-room, or pillared, or pillar-courtyard house and have argued that these similarities suggest that the occupants of a tomb were once the family members and affiliates who occupied a kin-based homestead. See, e.g., Bloch-Smith, "Death and Burial," 366–67; Hallote, *Death, Burial, and Afterlife*, 38–41; Osborne, "Secondary Mortuary Practice," 50–52 (with related discussion on pp. 48–49); and Suriano, *History of Death*, 93–96. Still, as Sonia, *Caring for the Dead*, 57, reminds us, "the genetic relationship of the individuals buried in some tombs remains unclear." See also the comments of Bloch-Smith, "Cult of the Dead," 217; eadem, "Death and Burial," 367; and eadem, "From Womb to Tomb," 125.
29. In addition to the standard lexica, dictionaries, and encyclopedias, I have found helpful the foundational studies of Gerleman, "Nutzrecht und Wohnrecht," 313–25; Horst, "Zwei Begriffe für Eigentum (Besitz)," 135–56, especially 145–49; Lewis, "Ancestral Estate," 598–99, 605–7, with extensive references; and Malamat, "Mari and the Bible," 147–50.
30. Also in 2 Kgs 9:28, the servants of Ahaziah, after he is killed in battle during Jehu's coup, transport his body from Megiddo for burial in a tomb with his "fathers" in Jerusalem, and in 2 Kgs 14:20, the unspecified "they" who have conspired against King Amaziah bring his body back from Lachish, where he was killed, to Jerusalem, again so that he might be buried in a tomb with "his fathers." In 2 Kgs 23:30, too, the servants of Josiah transport his body from the site of his death in Megiddo to Jerusalem for burial—albeit in an individual versus ancestral tomb. Reflected in these three passages is the conviction that, for the members of the Davidic royal line, Jerusalem had replaced the Davidic ancestral homestead, or *naḥălâ*, in Bethlehem as the landholding to which they sought to lay claim through, among other means, locating their tombs there. Indeed, this claim is stressed through the reference to Jerusalem as the "city of *David*" in the burial accounts in 2 Kgs 9:28 and 14:20. Northern kings likewise sought to use tombs to assert their claims to the royal landholdings they had established as their capital cities: see 1 Kgs 22:37, where the body of an unnamed Israelite king killed in battle (usually taken to be Ahab) is brought to Samaria for burial. For discussion, see Olyan, "Some Neglected Aspects of Israelite Interment Ideology," 603, and also my comments below on the role a family's ancestral tomb plays in securing its claim to its *naḥălâ*.
31. According to King and Stager, *Life in Biblical Israel*, 186, "a day's journey in biblical times averaged between twenty-seven and thirty-seven kilometers [17–23 miles]."
32. Reading here *b'yrw bgl'd*, based on the LXX, as opposed to the MT *b'ry gl'd*.
33. The Tola, Ibzan, and Abdon references were brought to my attention by Russell, "Ideologies of Attachment," 35, and the 1 Sam 25:1 reference was brought to my attention by Lewis, "Ancestral Estate," 608. Lewis also cites, in addition to the references I have catalogued, 1 Kgs 2:34.
34. For further discussion, see Olyan, "Some Neglected Aspects of Israelite Interment Ideology," 604–6; Suriano, *History of Death*, 212–14.
35. Stavrakopoulou, *Land of Our Fathers*, 9–10.
36. Bloch-Smith, "Cult of the Dead," 222.
37. Van der Toorn, *Family Religion*, 199.
38. As Stavrakopoulou rather pithily puts it, in *Land of Our Fathers*, 17: "Without the dead . . . in place, the living have no claim to space."
39. Lewis, "The Ancestral Estate," *passim*. On *ʾĕlōhîm* with the meaning "deceased spirit(s)," see, in addition to 2 Sam 14:16, 1 Sam 28:13; Isa 8:19; Num 25:2, as cited in Ps 106:28; and probably Exod 21:6. On the interpretation of Exod 21:6, see van der Toorn and Lewis, "*tᵉrāpîm*," 783, and the references cited there. On Num 25:2 as cited in Ps 106:28, see Ackerman, "Who Is the Baal of Peor?," 180–82; Lewis, *Cults of the Dead*, 167; and idem, "Ancestral Estate," 602. On 1 Sam 28:13, see Hutter, "Religionsgeschichtliche Erwägungen zu *ʾlhjm*," 32–36, and Lewis, *Cults of the Dead*, 115–16, but cf. Schmidt, *Israel's Beneficent Dead*, 210–20, and idem, "'Witch' of En-Dor," 120–26.
40. Note, my emphasis on the *primary* males of a patriline, for while 1 Sam 31:11–13 describes the men of Jabesh-Gilead recovering and tending to the bodies of Saul and his three sons, David's concern, in 2 Sam 21:12–14, is only reburying the bones of Saul and his firstborn Jonathan (those who Suriano, *History of Death*, 30, calls the "meaningful dead") in the Saulides' family tomb.

41. This terminological difference is perceptively pointed out by Suriano, *Politics of Dead Kings*, 112, and idem, *History of Death*, 106 and n. 21 on that page. Note, however, that *qĕbûrâ* can occasionally be used to refer to a multigenerational group tomb: see Gen 47:30 and 2 Kgs 9:28.
42. On the location of Ephrath (in southern Benjamin? synonymous with Bethlehem?), see Cox and Ackerman, "Rachel's Tomb," 136–37.
43. Bloch-Smith, *Judahite Burial Practices*, 115. To be sure, Olyan, "Some Neglected Aspects of Israelite Interment Ideology," 606, notes other examples of individual interments that take place at or near the site of the individual's demise and shortly after death: e.g., the burial of Absalom in 2 Sam 18:17. But in each case that Olyan cites, the burial is "dishonorable," as the corpse, for example, is "thrown" (*hišlîk*) into a pit or similar burial place, which is "clearly a ritual act of disrespect and disregard." Conversely, Moses and Aaron—whatever the anomalies of their interments and whatever the misdeeds that brought about these anomalous burials (see further below)—were buried honorably. Indeed, each was mourned for an atypically long period (thirty days; see Num 20:29 and Deut 34:8), so great was the esteem accorded to them at death.
44. Ussishkin, *Village of Silwan*, 328. As pointed out by Suriano (*History of Death*, 106), such edifices can be described as a *qĕbûrâ*, just as are the tombs of Deborah and Rachel (above, n. 41).
45. Ackerman, "Just Who Is Coming to Dinner?," 302–7.
46. For further discussion, and how to make sense of the biblical account of, especially, Moses's death, see Ackerman, "Moses' Death," 103–17.
47. Cox and Ackerman, "Rachel's Tomb," 140–48.
48. Scurlock, "Baby-Snatching Demons," 135.
49. C. Meyers, *Discovering Eve*, 112–13; eadem, "Family in Early Israel," 28; and see as well as similar references cited in Chapter 5, nn. 135–37.
50. Above, nn. 25 and 27.
51. Cross-cultural evidence suggests that just as women who die tragically in childbirth can be denied a standard burial, normal burial practices can be suspended for men who die a tragic death (e.g., due to suicide, fatal sorcery, infectious disease, or accidental death, particularly from drowning). The Liberian Kpelle, e.g., bury those dead by suicide in the same sort of atypically shallow grave they use for a woman dead in childbirth: see Welmers, "Secret Medicines, Magic, and Rites," 242. But this does not seem to be the case in Israel. Rather, Samson's family, as we have seen, goes to great trouble to ensure that his body is recovered from the Philistines and is properly buried in the tomb of his father Manoah after Samson declares "Let me die with the Philistines" and kills himself by pulling the pillars of the temple of the god Dagon down upon himself and everyone else gathered there (Judg 16:30). David likewise goes to great trouble to recover the bones of King Saul and bury them in the tomb of his father Kish (2 Sam 21:12–14), despite the fact that Saul, according to 1 Sam 31:4, killed himself by falling upon his own sword after his three sons had died in battle against the Philistines and he himself was badly wounded. Ahithophel, one of the counselors of David's rebel son Absalom, was also buried in the tomb of his father after he hanged himself (2 Sam 17:23). Still, biblical tradition does indicate that nonnormative burials could be accorded to enemy agents or covenant violators: see Olyan, "Some Neglected Aspects of Interment Ideology," 606, and n. 43 above.
52. Van der Toorn and Lewis, "*tᵉrāpîm*," 777–89; see also Lewis, *Cults of the Dead*, 178; idem, "Ancestral Estate," 603; idem, "Teraphim," 844–50; and idem, "Divine Images and Aniconism," 43–44; van der Toorn, "Nature of the Biblical Teraphim," 203–23; idem, *Family Religion*, 218–25; and idem, "Recent Trends," 228–29.
53. Cox and Ackerman, "Micah's Teraphim," 10–16.
54. Although even here, the matter is confused, since this seemingly singular *tĕrāpîm* has a wig placed *mĕraʾăšōtâw*, literally "at its heads" (1 Sam 19:13, 16), as pointed out by van der Toorn, *Family Religion*, 219, n. 59.
55. Cox and Ackerman, "Micah's Teraphim," 22–24.
56. Görg, "Terafim," 15–17.
57. Vriezen, "Archaeological Traces of Cult," 66.
58. Albright, *From the Stone Age to Christianity*, 311; Gray, *I and II Kings*, 677; and May, *Material Remains of the Megiddo Cult*, 27. All these references were brought to my attention by Lewis, "Teraphim," 847.
59. Cf., however, Edelman, "Adjusting Social Memory," 122, who understands 1 Sam 19:11–17 to describe a healing ritual in which the *tĕrāpîm* of vv 13 and 16 are "figurines representing the ancestral spirits of the mother and father of the sick person."

60. Schmitt, "Elements of Domestic Cult," 61.
61. Malamat, "King Lists of the Old Babylonian Period," 173, n. 29.
62. Sonia, *Caring for the Dead*, 54.
63. Noegel, "Maleness, Memory, and the Matter of Dream Divination," 72–74 and n. 44 on p. 74; see also, on the meanings of *zikkārôn* and *yād*, Ackerman, *Under Every Green Tree*, 106–7, n. 14, and Lewis, *Cults of the Dead*, 150.
64. Van der Toorn, *Family Religion*, 229.
65. Van der Toorn, "Family Religion in Second Millennium West Asia," 27.
66. Van der Toorn, "Family Religion in Second Millennium West Asia," 28; Stol, *Women in the Ancient Near East*, 631.
67. Further on the *nadītu*, with references, see Ackerman, "Women and the Religious Culture of the Ancient Levant's State Temples," 271–72, revised and republished as "Priestesses, Purity, and Parturition" in *Gods, Goddesses, and the Women Who Serve Them*, 133–34; see also Stol, *Women in the Ancient Near East*, 587–607.
68. Van der Toorn, "Family Religion in Second Millennium West Asia," 28, 29.
69. Finkelstein, "Genealogy of the Hammurapi Dynasty," 95–118; Stol, *Women in the Ancient Near East*, 630.
70. Van der Toorn, "Family Religion in Second Millennium West Asia," 28.
71. On the meaning "deceased spirit" for *ʾēl* and *ʾĕlōhîm*, see above, n. 39.
72. Van der Toorn, "Ancestors and Anthroponyms," 6.
73. Van der Toorn, "Ancestors and Anthroponyms," 7.
74. E.g., as I discussed in Chapter 4, marriage rites within Greek tradition rely heavily on funeral traditions.
75. Suriano, *History of Death*, 2; see also ibid., 40.
76. Van der Toorn, "Ancestors and Anthroponyms," 5.
77. Van Gennep, *Rites of Passage*, 3.
78. Stavrakopoulou, *Land of Our Fathers*, 9.
79. Suriano, *History of Death*, 47.
80. Suriano, *History of Death*, 42.
81. Metcalf and Huntington, *Celebrations of Death*, 81, as cited in Osborne, "Secondary Mortuary Practice," 35.
82. Osborne, "Secondary Mortuary Practice," 40. See also the data reported in Bloch-Smith, "From Womb to Tomb," 124, who writes that "tombs in use for ca. 50–100 years held from 50 [this seems to be a typographical error for 15; see p. 128] to 100 bodies, with most accommodating 50 [again, this seems a typographical error for 15] to 30 individuals of varying ages." See in addition Bloch-Smith, "Cult of the Dead," 217, and eadem, "Death and Burial," 368.
83. Osborne, "Secondary Mortuary Practice," 40–41.
84. See Osborne, "Secondary Mortuary Practice," 38, and the references cited in nn. 18–23 there.
85. Hertz, "Contribution à une etude sur la representation collective de la mort," 48–137; English translation: "Contribution to the Study of the Collective Representation of Death," 27–86.
86. V. Turner, "Betwixt and Between," 93–111.
87. See Leach, "Review of *The Rites of Passage*," 173–74. In *Rites of Passage*, 190, van Gennep in fact acknowledges that "I am certainly not the first to have been struck by the resemblances among various components of the ceremonies discussed here," and among his predecessors, he notes that Hertz, in "Contribution à une etude sur la representation collective de la mort," 104, 117, and 126–27, "pointed out similarities among certain ceremonies of birth, marriage, and funerals." Van Gennep also cites Hertz's allusions, in ibid., 130, n. 5, "to what he called the 'transitory stage'—the period that lasts from marriage to the birth of the first child and that corresponds to the 'transitory stage' of the dead in Indonesia."
88. Deflem, "Ritual, Anti-Structure, and Religion," 7–8, paraphrasing V. Turner, "Betwixt and Between," 94.
89. Suriano, *Politics of Dead Kings*, 16.
90. The best expositions of this analysis in print are by Osborne, "Secondary Mortuary Practice," 38–47, and Suriano, *History of Death*, 20–22, 41–55; see also Suriano, *Politics of Dead Kings*, 8–10, 12–21, and the brief comments of Stavrakopoulou, *Land of Our Fathers*, 9–10 and n. 33 on those pages. But I first saw these ideas put forward in 2007, by my student Benjamin D. Cox in his remarkable Dartmouth College senior honors thesis, "Gathered to Their Fathers: Reconstructing the Folk Deathways of Iron Age Israel," and it is a pleasure to be able to

acknowledge here both the extraordinary quality of Ben's work and the enormous impact it has had on my thinking.
91. Hertz, "Contribution to the Study of the Collective Representation of Death," 83.
92. Suriano, *History of Death*, 34.
93. Genesis 25:8, 17; 35:29; 49:29, 33; Num 20:24; 27:13; 31:2; Deut 32:50.
94. On Exod 19:15, see also Bird, "Images of Women," 50, and, on both Exod 19:15 and Jer 44:24, see eadem, "Women's Religion," 286, n. 9. On Num 25:1, see Ackerman, "Who Is the Baal of Peor?," 184; on Josh 5:5, see eadem, *Women and the Religion of Ancient Israel*, 242.
95. Osborne, "Secondary Mortuary Practice," 45; see similarly Hallote, *Death, Burial, and Afterlife*, 49; E. M. Meyers, "Secondary Burials in Palestine," 15; and, for discussion of this point of view, Suriano, *Politics of Dead Kings*, 36–40. For Suriano's own interpretation, see ibid., 46–49. See also Osborne, "Secondary Mortuary Practice," 45, n. 66, for references to the interpretations of other scholars, who also include Cook, "Death, Kinship, and Community," 112–13, and Stavrakopoulou, *Land of Our Fathers*, 9, n. 32.
96. Malamat, "King Lists of the Old Babylonian Period," 173, n. 29.
97. Suriano, *Politics of Dead Kings*, 16; see also idem, *History of Death*, 49.
98. Suriano, *History of Death*, 28.
99. Van der Toorn, "Family Religion in Second Millennium West Asia," 28.
100. Quoting, as above, n. 88, Deflem, "Ritual, Anti-Structure, and Religion," 7–8, paraphrasing V. Turner, "Betwixt and Between," 94.
101. "'Immortality,'" Nancy Jay writes in *Throughout Your Generations Forever*, 39, "is commonly a masculine privilege. It is through fathers and sons, not through mothers and daughters, that 'eternal' social continuity is maintained."
102. Cox and Ackerman, "Rachel's Tomb," 147.

Epilogue

1. Van der Toorn, *From Her Cradle to Her Grave*, translated from *Van haar wieg tot haar graf*.
2. J. R. Ebeling, *Women's Lives in Biblical Times*, 4.
3. Gerstenberger and Schrage, *Woman and Man*, 25–63, translated from "Das Lebenskreis" in *Frau und Mann*, 20–52; Borowski, "Life Cycles," in *Daily Life in Biblical Times*, 80–84; Schmitt, "Rites and Rituals Associated with the Cycle of Human Life," in "Rites of Family and Household Religion," 388–99; C. Meyers, *Rediscovering Eve*, 157–61.
4. J. R. Ebeling, *Women's Lives in Biblical Times*, 3. See also Ebeling's comments in ibid., 4, 6–8.
5. See, by way of example, my "Afterword" in Ackerman, *Warrior, Dancer*, 288–92, and my "Epilogue" in eadem, *Women and the Religion of Ancient Israel*, 349–53; see also, in ibid., 208–16.
6. See Chapter 9 and the references cited in n. 95 there.
7. Exum, *Fragmented Women*, 9.

Bibliography

Abraham, Kathleen. "The Dowry Clause in Marriage Documents from the First Millennium B.C.E." Pages 311–20 in *La circulation des biends, des personnes et des idées dans la Proche-Orient ancien: Actes de la XXXVIIIe Rencontre Assyriologie Internationale (Paris, 8–10 juillet 1991)*. Edited by D. Charpin and F. Joannes. Paris: Éditions Recherche sur les Civilisations, 1992.

Abravanel, Isaac. *Commentary on the Torah*. Jerusalem: Beit Arbel, 1964.

Ackerman, Susan. "Asherah, the West Semitic Goddess of Spinning and Weaving?" *JNES* 67 (2008): 1–30.

Ackerman, Susan. "At Home with the Goddess." Pages 455–68 in *Symbiosis, Symbolism, and the Power of the Past: Canaan, Ancient Israel, and Their Neighbors from the Late Bronze Age through Roman Palaestina*. Edited by William G. Dever and Seymour Gitin. Winona Lake, IN: Eisenbrauns, 2003.

Ackerman, Susan. "The Blind, the Lame, and the Barren Shall Not Come into the House." Pages 29–45 in *Disability Studies and Biblical Literature*. Edited by Candida R. Moss and Jeremy Schipper. New York: Palgrave Macmillan, 2011.

Ackerman, Susan. *Gods, Goddesses, and the Women Who Serve Them*. Grand Rapids, MI: Eerdmans, 2022.

Ackerman, Susan. "Illnesses and Other Crises: Syria-Canaan." Pages 459–60 in *Religions of the Ancient World: A Guide*. Edited by Sarah Iles Johnston. Cambridge, MA: Harvard University Press, 2004.

Ackerman, Susan. "Just Who Is Coming to Dinner? Fostering Relationships with the Dead through Ritual Meals." Pages 297–312 in *With the Loyal You Show Yourself Loyal: Essays on Relationships in the Hebrew Bible in Honor of Saul M. Olyan*. Edited by T. M. Lemos, Jordan D. Rosenblum, Karen B. Stern, and Debra Scoggins Ballentine. AIL 42. Atlanta: SBL Press, 2021.

Ackerman, Susan. "Moses' Death." Pages 103–17 in *Myth and Scripture: Contemporary Perspectives on Religion, Language, and Imagination*. Edited by Dexter E. Callender, Jr. RBS 78. Atlanta: Society of Biblical Literature, 2014.

Ackerman, Susan. "The Queen Mother and the Cult in Ancient Israel." *JBL* 112 (1993): 385–401.

Ackerman, Susan. "The Queen Mother and the Cult in the Ancient Near East." Pages 179–209 in *Women and Goddess Traditions: In Antiquity and Today*. Edited by Karen L. King. Studies in Antiquity and Christianity. Minneapolis: Fortress, 1997.

Ackerman, Susan. *Under Every Green Tree: Popular Religion in Sixth-Century Judah*. HSM 46. Atlanta: Scholars Press, 1992.

Ackerman, Susan. *Warrior, Dancer, Seductress, Queen: Women in Judges and Biblical Israel*. AYBRL 17. New York: Doubleday, 1998.

Ackerman, Susan. *When Heroes Love: The Ambiguity of Eros in the Stories of Gilgamesh and David*. Gender, Theory, and Religion 2. New York: Columbia University Press, 2005.

Ackerman, Susan. "Who Is the Baal of Peor?" Pages 171–91 in *Mighty Baal: Essays in Honor of Mark S. Smith*. Edited by Stephen C. Russell and Esther J. Hamori. HSS 66. Leiden: Brill, 2020.

Ackerman, Susan. "Why Is Miriam Also among the Prophets? (And Is Zipporah among the Priests?)." *JBL* 121 (2002): 47–80.

Ackerman, Susan. *Women and the Religion of Ancient Israel*. AYBRL. New Haven, CT: Yale University Press, 2022.
Ackerman, Susan. "Women and the Religious Culture of the State Temples of the Ancient Levant, Or: Priestesses, Purity, and Parturition." Pages 259–89 in *Temple Building and Temple Cult: Architecture and Cultic Paraphernalia of Temples in the Levant (2.–1. Mill. B.C.E.)*. Edited by Jens Kamlah. Abhandlungen des Deutschen Palästina-Vereins 41. Wiesbaden: Harrassowitz, 2012.
Ackerman, Susan. "Women and the Worship of Yahweh in Ancient Israel." Pages 189–97 in *Confronting the Past: Archaeological and Historical Essays on Ancient Israel in Honor of William G. Dever*. Edited by Seymour Gitin, J. Edward Wright, and J. P. Dessel. Winona Lake, IN: Eisenbrauns, 2006.
Ackerman, Susan. See also Cox, Benjamin D.
Adams, Samuel L. *Social and Economic Life in Second Temple Judea*. Louisville, KY: Westminster John Knox, 2014.
Agadjanian, Victor. See Chae, Sophia.
Aharoni, Yohanan. *Excavations at Ramat Raḥel: Seasons 1959 and 1960*. Rome: Centro di Studi Semitici, 1962.
Aharoni, Yohanan. *Excavations at Ramat Raḥel: Seasons 1961 and 1962*. Rome: Centro di Studi Semitici, 1964.
Ahearne-Kroll, Patricia. "Joseph and Aseneth." Pages 2525–80 in *Outside the Bible: Ancient Jewish Writing Related to Scripture* 3. Edited by Louis H. Feldman, James L. Kugel, and Lawrence H. Schiffman. Philadelphia: The Jewish Publication Society, 2013.
Albertz, Rainer. *A History of Israelite Religion in the Old Testament Period 1: From the Beginnings to the End of the Monarchy*. OTL. Louisville, KY: Westminster/John Knox, 1994.
Albertz, Rainer. "Introduction." Pages 1–20 in Rainer Albertz and Rüdiger Schmitt, *Family and Household Religion in Ancient Israel and the Levant*. Winona Lake, IN: Eisenbrauns, 2012.
Albertz, Rainer. "Personal Names and Family Religion." Pages 245–386 in Rainer Albertz and Rüdiger Schmitt, *Family and Household Religion in Ancient Israel and the Levant*. Winona Lake, IN: Eisenbrauns, 2012.
Albright, William F. *The Archaeology of Palestine and the Bible*. New York: F. H. Revell, 1932.
Albright, William F. "Astarte Plaques and Figurines from Tell Beit Mirsim." Pages 107–20 in *Mélanges syriens offerts à Monsieur René Dussaud: secrétaire perpétuel de l'Académie des inscriptions et belles-lettres* 1. Paris: P. Geuthner, 1939.
Albright, William F. *The Excavation of Tell Beit Mirsim III: The Iron Age*. AASOR 21–22. New Haven, CT: American Schools of Oriental Research, 1943.
Albright, William F. *From the Stone Age to Christianity*. 2nd ed. Baltimore: Johns Hopkins University Press, 1957.
Alexander, T. Desmond. "Genesis 22 and the Covenant of Circumcision." *JSOT* 25 (1983): 17–22.
Allan, Robert. "Now That Summer's Gone: Understanding *qẓ* in KTU 1.24." *SEL* 16 (1999): 19–25.
Allen, James P. *The Art of Medicine in Ancient Egypt*. New Haven, CT: Yale University Press, 2005.
Altenmüller, Hartwig. *Die Apotropaia und die Götter Mittelägyptens: Eine Typologische und religionsgeschichtliche Untersuchung der sogenannten "Zaubermesser" des Mittleren Reichs* 1–2. Dissertation, Ludwig-Maximilians-Universität zu München, 1965.
Alter, Robert. *The Art of Biblical Narrative*. New York: Basic Books, 1981.
American Academy of Pediatrics, Committee on Nutrition. *Pediatric Nutrition Handbook*. Edited by Ronald E. Kleinman. 5th ed. Elk Grove Village, IL: American Academy of Pediatrics, 2003.
Amundsen, Darrel W., and Carol Jean Diers. "The Age of Menopause in Classical Greece and Rome." *Human Biology* 42 (1970): 79–86.
Andersen, T. David. "Renaming and Wedding Imagery in Isaiah 62." *Bib* 67 (1986): 75–80.

Anderson, Burton R. See Scurlock, JoAnn.
Anderson, Siwan. "The Economics of Dowry and Brideprice." *Journal of Economic Perspectives* 21 (2007): 151–74.
Angel, J. Lawrence. "Ecology and Population in the Eastern Mediterranean." *World Archaeology* 4 (1972): 88–105.
Antoine, Katja. See Bolin, Anne.
Archer, Léonie J. *Her Price Is Beyond Rubies: The Jewish Woman in Greco-Roman Palestine*. JSOTSup 60. Sheffield, UK: Sheffield Academic Press, 1990.
Archi, Alfonso. "Jewels for the Ladies of Ebla." *ZA* 92 (2002): 161–99.
Arnette, Marie-Lys. "Purification du post-partum et rites des relevailles dans l'Égypte ancienne." *Bulletin de l'Institut français d'archéologie orientale* 114 (2015): 19–72.
Arnette, Marie-Lys. See also Austin, Anne.
Asher-Greve, Julia M. "Decisive Sex, Essential Gender." Pages 11–26 in *Sex and Gender in the Ancient Near East: Proceedings of the 47th Rencontre Assyriologique Internationale, Helsinki, July 2–6, 2001*. Edited by Simo Parpola and Robert M. Whiting. Helsinki: Neo-Assyrian Text Corpus Project, 2002.
Asher-Greve, Julia M. "From La Femme to Multiple Sex/Gender." Pages 15–50 in *Studying Gender in the Ancient Near East*. Edited by Saana Svard and Agnès Garcia-Ventura. University Park, PA: Eisenbrauns, 2018.
Attridge, Harold W., and Robert A. Oden, Jr. *Philo of Byblos: The Phoenician History: Introduction, Critical Text, Translation, Notes*. Catholic Biblical Quarterly Monograph Series 9. Washington, DC: The Catholic Biblical Association of America, 1981.
Audouit, Clémentine. "Women's Intimacy: Blood, Milk, and Women's Conditions in the Gynecological Papyri of Ancient Egypt." Pages 381–93 in *Women in Ancient Egypt: Revisiting Power, Agency, and Autonomy*. Edited by Mariam F. Ayad. Cairo and New York: American University in Cairo Press, 2022.
Austen, Jane. *Pride and Prejudice*. Oxford World's Classics. Oxford: Oxford University Press, 1990, 1998.
Austin, Anne, and Marie-Lys Arnette. "Of Ink and Clay: Tattooed Mummified Human Remains and Female Figurines from Deir el-Medina." *JEA* 108 (2022): 63–80.
Avalos, Hector. *Illness and Health Care in the Ancient Near East: The Role of the Temple in Greece, Mesopotamia, and Israel*. HSM 54. Atlanta: Scholars Press, 1995.
Avalos, Hector. "Illnesses and Other Crises: Israel." Pages 460–61 in *Religions of the Ancient World: A Guide*. Edited by Sarah Iles Johnston. Cambridge, MA: Harvard University Press, 2004.
Avery, L. Creighton. "Coming of Age in the Roman Empire: Exploring the Physical and Social Transformations of *Adulescentia* (Adolescence)." PhD diss., McMaster University, 2022.
Avigad, Nahman. "Two Ammonite Seals Depicting the *Dea Nutrix*." *BASOR* 225 (1977): 63–66.
Bachvarova, Mary R. "Hurro-Hittite Stories and Hittite Pregnancy and Birth Rituals." Pages 284–318 in *Women in the Ancient Near East*. Edited by Mark V. Chavalas. Routledge Sourcebooks for the Ancient World. London: Routledge, 2014.
Bachvarova, Mary R. "Successful Birth, Unsuccessful Marriage: Aeschylus' *Suppliants* and Mesopotamian Birth Incantations." *NIN: Journal of Gender Studies in Antiquity* 2 (2001): 49–90.
Backhouse, Joanne. "'Scènes de gynécées' Figured Ostraca: Their Relationship to the Material Culture of New Kingdom Egypt." PhD diss., University of Liverpool, 2016.
Bailey, Emoke. "Circumcision in Ancient Egypt." *The Bulletin of the Australian Centre for Egyptology* 7 (1996): 15–28.
Bailey, Wilma Ann. "Baby Becky, Menarche and Prepubescent Marriage in Ancient Israel." *Journal of the Interdenominational Theological Center* 37 (2011): 113–37.
Bal, Mieke. *Death and Dissymmetry: The Politics of Coherence in the Book of Judges*. Chicago: University of Chicago Press, 1988.

Barber, E. J. W. "The Peplos of Athena." Pages 103–17 in *Goddess and Polis: The Panathenaic Festival in Ancient Athens*. Edited by Jenifer Neils. Hanover, NH: Dartmouth College, Hood Museum of Art; Princeton, NJ: Princeton University Press, 1992.

Baumgarten, Joseph M. "Purification after Childbirth and the Sacred Garden in 4Q265 and Jubilees." Pages 3–10 in *New Qumran Texts and Studies: Proceedings of the First Meeting of the International Organization for Qumran Studies, Paris 1992*. Edited by George Brooke and Florentino García Martínez. STDJ 15. Leiden: Brill, 1994.

Bayliss, Miranda. "The Cult of Dead Kin in Assyria and Babylon." *Iraq* 35 (1973): 115–25.

Beavis, Mary Ann. "A Daughter in Israel: Celebrating Bat Jephthah (Judg 11:39d–40)." *Feminist Theology* 13 (2004): 11–25.

Beck, Pirhiya. "Catalogue of Cult Objects and Study of the Iconography." Pages 27–197 in *Ḥorvat Qitmit: An Edomite Shrine in the Biblical Negev*. Edited by Itzhaq Beit-Arieh. Monograph Series of the Institute of Archaeology, Tel Aviv University 11. Tel Aviv: Institute of Archaeology of Tel Aviv University, 1995.

Beck, Pirhiya. "The Drawings and Decorative Designs." Pages 143–204 in Ze'ev Meshel, *Kuntillet 'Ajrud (Ḥorvat Teman): An Iron Age II Religious Site on the Judah-Sinai Border*. Jerusalem: Israel Exploration Society, 2012.

Becking, Bob. "Then Zipporah Took a Flint . . . Circumcision as a Rite of Passage in Exod 4, 24–26." *SJOT* 37 (2023): 3–16.

Beckman, Gary M. "Birth and Motherhood among the Hittites." Pages 319–28 in *Women in Antiquity: Real Women across the Ancient World*. Edited by Stephanie Lynn Budin and Jean MacIntosh Turfa. Rewriting Antiquity. London: Routledge, 2016.

Beckman, Gary M. *Hittite Birth Rituals*. 2nd rev. ed. Studien zu den Boğazköy-Texten 29. Wiesbaden: Harrassowitz, 1983.

Beit-Arieh, Itzhaq. "The Western Quarter." Pages 412–24 in Ze'ev Herzog and Lily Singer-Avitz, *Beer-Sheba III: The Early Iron IIA Enclosed Settlement and the Late Iron IIA–Iron IIB Cities*. Monograph Series of the Sonia and Marco Nadler Institute of Archaeology, Tel Aviv University 34. Tel Aviv: Emery and Claire Yass Publications in Archaeology; Winona Lake, IN: Eisenbrauns, 2016.

Bell, Catherine. *Ritual: Perspectives and Dimensions*. New York: Oxford University Press, 1997, 2009.

Bell, Rudolph M. See Weinstein, Donald.

Belmont, Nicole. *Arnold Van Gennep: The Creator of French Ethnography*. Chicago: University of Chicago Press, 1979.

Benjamin, Don C. See Matthews, Victor H.

Bergmann, Claudia D. *Childbirth as a Metaphor for Crisis: Evidence from the Ancient Near East, the Hebrew Bible, and 1QH XI, 1–18*. BZAW 382. Berlin: de Gruyter, 2008.

Bergmann, Claudia D. "Infant Israel Growing Up: The Theme of Breastfeeding in the Hebrew Bible." *Bib* 102 (2021): 161–81.

Bergmann, Claudia D. "Turning Birth into Theology: Traces of Ancient Obstetric Knowledge within Narratives of Difficult Childbirth in the Hebrew Bible." Pages 17–34 in *Children in the Bible and the Ancient World: Comparative and Historical Methods in Reading Ancient Children*. Edited by Shawn W. Flynn. Studies in the History of the Ancient Near East. London: Routledge, 2019.

Berlejung, Angelika. See Gertz, Jan Christian.

Beyene, Yewoubdar. See Sperling, Susan.

Bickerman, Elias. *Four Strange Books of the Bible: Jonah/Daniel/Koheleth/Esther*. New York: Schocken, 1967.

Biggs, R. D. "Conception, Contraception, and Abortion in Ancient Mesopotamia." Pages 1–14 in *Wisdom, Gods and Literature: Studies in Assyriology in Honour of W. G. Lambert*. Edited by A. R. George and I. L. Finkel. Winona Lake, IN: Eisenbrauns, 2000.

Bird, Phyllis. "Images of Women in the Old Testament." Pages 44–88 in *Religion and Sexism: Images of Women in the Jewish and Christian Traditions*. Edited by Rosemary Radford Ruether. New York: Simon & Schuster, 1974.

Bird, Phyllis. "The Place of Women in the Israelite Cultus." Pages 397–419 in *Ancient Israelite Religion: Essays in Honor of Frank Moore Cross*. Edited by Patrick D. Miller, Paul D. Hanson, and S. Dean McBride. Philadelphia: Fortress, 1987.

Bird, Phyllis. "Women (OT)." Pages 351–57 in *ABD* 6.

Bird, Phyllis. "Women's Religion in Ancient Israel." Pages 283–98 in *Women's Earliest Records from Ancient Egypt and Western Asia*. Edited by Barbara S. Lesko. BJS 166. Atlanta: Scholars Press, 1989.

Black, Jeremy, and Anthony Green. *Gods, Demons, and Symbols of Ancient Mesopotamia: An Illustrated Dictionary*. Austin: University of Texas Press, 1992.

Blank, Sheldon H. "The Curse, Blasphemy, the Spell, and the Oath." *HUCA* 23 (1950/51): 73–95.

Blenkinsopp, Joseph. "The Family in First Temple Israel." Pages 48–103 in Leo G. Perdue, Joseph Blenkinsopp, John J. Collins, and Carol Meyers, *Families in Ancient Israel*. The Family, Religion, and Culture. Louisville, KY: Westminster/John Knox, 1997.

Blenkinsopp, Joseph. "Life Expectancy in Ancient Palestine." *SJOT* 11 (1997): 44–55.

Bloch-Smith, Elizabeth. "Acculturating Gender Roles: Goddess Images as Conveyers of Culture in Ancient Israel." Pages 1–18 in *Image, Text, Exegesis: Iconographic Interpretation and the Hebrew Bible*. Edited by Izaak J. de Hulster and Joel M. LeMon. London: Bloomsbury, 2014.

Bloch-Smith, Elizabeth. "The Cult of the Dead in Judah: Interpreting the Material Remains." *JBL* 111 (1992): 213–24.

Bloch-Smith, Elizabeth. "Death and Burial in Eighth-Century Judah." Pages 365–78 in *Archaeology and History of Eighth-Century Judah*. Edited by Zev I. Farber and Jacob L. Wright. ANEM 23. Atlanta: SBL Press, 2018.

Bloch-Smith, Elizabeth. "From Womb to Tomb: The Israelite Family in Death as in Life." Pages 122–31 in *The Family in Life and in Death: The Family in Ancient Israel: Sociological and Archaeological Perspectives*. Edited by Patricia Dutcher-Walls. LHBOTS 504. New York: T&T Clark, 2009.

Bloch-Smith, Elizabeth. *Judahite Burial Practices and Beliefs about the Dead*. JSOTSup 123. JSOT/ASOR Monograph Series 7. Sheffield, UK: Sheffield Academic Press, 1992.

Bloch-Smith, Elizabeth. "Judean Pillar Figurines, 8th century BCE." Published online by the Center for Online Judaic Studies, at https://cojs.org/judean_pillar_figurines-_8th_century_bce/.

Bloch-Smith, Elizabeth. See also Smith, Mark S.

Block, Daniel I. *The Book of Ezekiel: Chapters 1–24*. NICOT. Grand Rapids, MI: Eerdmans, 1997.

Block, Daniel I. "Marriage and Family in Ancient Israel." Pages 33–102 in *Marriage and Family in the Biblical World*. Edited by Ken M. Campbell. Downers Grove, IL: InterVarsity Press, 2003.

Blyth, Caroline. *The Narrative of Rape in Genesis 34: Interpreting Dinah's Silence*. Oxford: Oxford University Press, 2010.

Boedeker, Deborah. "Family Matters: Domestic Religion in Classical Greece." Pages 229–47 in *Household and Family Religion in Antiquity*. Edited by John Bodel and Saul M. Olyan. Oxford: Blackwell, 2008.

Bohmbach, Karla G. "Names and Naming in the Biblical World." Pages 33–39 in *WIS*.

Bolin, Anne, Patricia Whelehan, Muriel Vernon, and Katja Antoine. "Sexuality through the Life Stages, Part II: Puberty and Adolescence." Pages 231–78 in *Human Sexuality: Biological, Psychological, and Cultural Perspectives*. 2nd ed. London: Routledge, 2021.

Boling, Robert G. *Judges: A New Translation with Introduction and Commentary*. AYB 6A. Garden City, NY: Doubleday, 1975.

Bonaventure. "The Life of Saint Francis." Pages 177–327 in *Bonaventure: The Soul's Journey into God; The Tree of Life; The Life of St. Francis*. Translated by Ewert H. Collins. Mahwah, NJ: Paulist Press, 1978.

Borghouts, Joris Frans. *Ancient Egyptian Magical Texts: Volume Nine*. Religious Texts Translation Series Nisaba 9. Leiden: Brill, 1978.

Borghouts, Joris Frans. *The Magical Texts of Papyrus Leiden I 348*. Leiden: Brill, 1971.

Borowski, Oded. *Daily Life in Biblical Times*. ABS 5. Atlanta: Society of Biblical Literature, 2003.

Bottéro, Jean. *The Oldest Cuisine in the World: Cooking in Mesopotamia*. Chicago: University of Chicago Press, 2004.

Bourdieu, Pierre. *Language and Symbolic Power*. Edited and introduced by John B. Thompson. Translated by Gino Raymond and Matthew Adamson. Cambridge, MA: Harvard University Press, 1991.

Bourdieu, Pierre. "The Work of Time." Pages 135–47 in *The Gift: An Interdisciplinary Perspective*. Edited by Aafke E. Komter. Amsterdam: Amsterdam University Press, 1996.

Bowen, Nancy R. "The Daughters of Your People: Female Prophets in Ezek 13:17–23." *JBL* 118 (1999): 417–33.

Bowen, Nancy R. *Ezekiel*. Abingdon Old Testament Commentaries. Nashville, TN: Abingdon, 2010.

Boyd, Samuel. *Language Contact, Colonial Administration, and the Construction of Identity in Ancient Israel: Constructing the Context for Contact*. HSM 66. Leiden: Brill, 2021.

Bradshaw, Karen D. "Diagnosing and Treating Precocious Puberty." *Hospital Medicine* 33/9 (September 1997): 40–51.

Bradshaw, Karen D. See also Kakarla, Nirupama.

Braun, Hans-Joachim. See Shiferaw, Bekele.

Bremmer, Jan N. "Rites of Passage: Introduction." Pages 438–39 in *Religions of the Ancient World: A Guide*. Edited by Sarah Iles Johnston. Cambridge, MA: Harvard University Press, 2004.

Brettler, Marc Zvi. "Gender in the Bible." Pages 2177–84 in *The Jewish Study Bible*. Edited by Adele Berlin and Marc Zvi Brettler. 2nd ed. New York: Oxford University Press, 2014.

Brettler, Marc Zvi. "A Woman's Voice in the Psalter: A New Understanding of Psalm 113." Pages 155–70 in *Built by Wisdom, Established by Understanding: Essays on Biblical and Near Eastern Literature in Honor of Adele Berlin*. Edited by Maxine L. Grossman. Bethesda, MD: CDL, 2013.

Brettler, Marc Zvi. "Women and Psalms: Toward an Understanding of the Role of Women's Prayer in the Israelite Cult." Pages 25–56 in *Gender and Law in the Hebrew Bible and the Ancient Near East*. Edited by Victor H. Matthews, Bernard M. Levinson, and Tikva Frymer-Kensky. JSOTSup 262. Sheffield, UK: Sheffield Academic Press, 1998.

Bridge, Edward J. "A Mother's Influence: Mothers Naming Children in the Hebrew Bible." *VT* 64 (2014): 389–400.

Brownlee, William H. *Ezekiel 1–19*. WBC 28. Waco, TX: Word Books, 1986.

Brunner-Traut, Emma. "Gravidenflasche: Das Salben des Mutterleibes." Pages 35–48 in *Archäologie und altes Testament: Festschrift für Kurt Galling*. Edited by A. Kuschke and E. Kutsch. Tübingen: J. C. B. Mohr, 1970.

Brunner-Traut, Emma. "Die Wochenlaube." *Mitteilungen des Instituts für Orientforschung* 3 (1955): 11–30.

Bruyère, Bernard. *Rapport sur les fouilles de Deir el Médineh* 16. Cairo: Institut français d'archéologie orientale, 1939.

Bryan, Betsy M. "In Women Good and Bad Fortune are on Earth: Status and Roles of Women in Egyptian Culture." Pages 25–46 in *Mistress of the House, Mistress of Heaven: Women in Ancient Egypt*. Edited by Anne K. Capel and Glenn E. Markoe. New York: Hudson Hills, in conjunction with the Cincinnati Art Museum, 1996.

Burchard, Christoph, assisted by Carsten Burfeind and Uta Barbara Fink. *Joseph und Aseneth*. Pseudepigrapha Veteris Testamenti Graece 5. Leiden: Brill, 2003.
Burfeind, Carsten. See Burchard, Christoph.
Burkert, Walter. *The Orientalizing Revolution: Near Eastern Influence on Greek Culture in the Early Archaic Age*. Cambridge, MA: Harvard University Press, 1992.
Burnette-Bletsch, Rhonda. "Women after Childbirth (Lev 12:1–8)." Page 204 in *WIS*.
Burney, C. F. *The Book of Judges*. London: Rivingtons, 1920.
Burrows, Millar. *The Basis of Israelite Marriage*. AOS 16. New Haven, CT: American Oriental Society, 1938.
Bynum, Caroline Walker. "Women's Stories, Women's Symbols: A Critique of Victor Turner's Theory of Liminality." Pages 27–51 in Caroline Walker Bynum, *Fragmentation and Redemption: Essays on Gender and the Human Body in Medieval Religion*. New York: Zone Books, 1991. Originally published as pages 105–25 in *Anthropology and the Study of Religion*. Edited by Robert L. Moore and Frank E. Reynolds. Chicago: Center for the Scientific Study of Religion, 1984.
Canaan, Tawfīq. "The Child in Palestinian Arab Superstition." *Journal of the Palestine Oriental Society* 7 (1927): 159–86.
Capel, Anne K. "8a Statuette of Woman Dressing Hair of Nursing Mother" and "8b Relief of Woman and Child Between Trees (Tomb of Mentuemhat)." Pages 59–60 in *Mistress of the House, Mistress of Heaven: Women in Ancient Egypt*. Edited by Anne K. Capel and Glenn E. Markoe. New York: Hudson Hills, in conjunction with the Cincinnati Art Museum, 1996.
Carley, Keith W. *The Book of the Prophet Ezekiel*. CBC. Cambridge, UK: Cambridge University Press, 1974.
Carsten, Janet. "The Process of Childbirth and Becoming Related among Malays in Pulau Langkawi." Pages 20–46 in *Coming into Existence: Birth and Metaphors of Birth*. Edited by Göran Aijmer. Göteborg, Sweden: Institute for Advanced Studies in Social Anthropology, 1992.
Cassuto, Deborah. See McKinny, Chris.
Cassuto, Umberto. *A Commentary on the Book of Genesis, Part 2: From Noah to Abraham*. Jerusalem: Magnes, 1964.
Chae, Sophia, Victor Agadjanian, and Sarah R. Hayford. "Bridewealth Marriage in the 21st Century: A Case Study from Rural Mozambique." *Journal of Marriage and Family* 83.2 (2021): 409–27.
Chapman, Cynthia R. *The Gendered Language of Warfare in the Israelite-Assyrian Encounter*. HSM 62. Winona Lake, IN: Eisenbrauns, 2004.
Chapman, Cynthia R. *The House of the Mother: The Social Roles of Maternal Kin in Biblical Hebrew Narrative and Poetry*. AYBRL. New Haven, CT: Yale University Press, 2016.
Chapman, Cynthia R. "'Oh that you were like a brother to me, one who had nursed at my mother's breasts': Breast Milk as a Kinship-Forging Substance." *JHS* 12 (2012): 1–41.
Chapman, David W. "Marriage and Family in Second Temple Judaism." Pages 183–239 in *Marriage and Family in the Biblical World*. Edited by Ken M. Campbell. Downers Grove, IL: InterVarsity Press, 2003.
Cherry, Russell Thomas, III. "Paronomasia and Proper Names in the Old Testament: Rhetorical Function and Literary Effect." PhD diss., The Southern Baptist Theological Seminary, 1988.
Cheung, Neky Tak Ching. *Women's Ritual in China: Jiezhu (Receiving Buddhist Prayer Beads) Performed by Menopausal Women in Ninghua, Western Fujian*. New York: Edwin Mellen, 2008.
Civil, Miguel. "Enlil and Ninlil: The Marriage of Sud." *JAOS* 103 (1983): 43–64.
Civil, Miguel. "Medical Commentaries from Nippur." *JNES* 33 (1974): 329–38.
Civil, Miguel. See also Landsberger, Benno.
Cogan, Mordechai. *I Kings: A New Translation with Introduction and Commentary*. AYB 10. New York: Doubleday, 2001.

Cogan, Mordechai. "A Lamashtu Plaque from the Judean Shephelah." *Israel Exploration Journal* 45 (1995): 155–61.
Cogan, Mordechai. "A Technical Term for Exposure." *JNES* 17 (1968): 133–35.
Cohen, Margaret. "Diet and Nutrition." Pages 335–49 in *The T&T Clark Handbook of Food in the Hebrew Bible and Ancient Israel*. Edited by Janling Fu, Cynthia Shafer-Elliott, and Carol Meyers. London: T&T Clark, 2022.
Cohen, Shaye J. D. "Menstruants and the Sacred in Judaism and Christianity." Pages 273–98 in *Women's History and Ancient History*. Edited by Sarah Pomeroy. Chapel Hill, NC: University of North Carolina Press, 1991.
Cohen, Shaye J. D. *Why Aren't Jewish Women Circumcised? Gender and Covenant in Judaism*. Berkeley: University of California Press, 2005.
Coleson, Joseph E. "Israel's Life Cycle from Birth to Resurrection." Pages 237–59 in *Israel's Apostasy and Restoration: Essays in Honor of Roland K. Harrison*. Edited by Avraham Gileadi. Grand Rapids, MI: Baker Books, 1988.
Collins, Billie Jean. "Rites of Passage: Anatolia." Page 444 in *Religions of the Ancient World: A Guide*. Edited by Sarah Iles Johnston. Cambridge, MA: Harvard University Press, 2004.
Collins, John J. "Marriage, Divorce, and Family in Second Temple Judaism." Pages 104–62 in Leo G. Perdue, Joseph Blenkinsopp, John J. Collins, and Carol Meyers, *Families in Ancient Israel*. The Family, Religion, and Culture. Louisville, KY: Westminster/John Knox, 1997.
Colson, F. H., translator. *Philo VII: The Decalogue; On Special Laws Books I–III*. Loeb Classical Library. Cambridge, MA: Harvard University Press, 1937.
Cook, Stephen L. "Death, Kinship, and Community: Afterlife and the ḥsd Ideal in Israel." Pages 106–21 in *The Family in Life and in Death: The Family in Ancient Israel: Sociological and Archaeological Perspectives*. Edited by Patricia Dutcher-Walls. LHBOTS 504. New York: T&T Clark, 2009.
Cooke, G. A. *A Critical and Exegetical Commentary on the Book of Ezekiel* 1. ICC. New York: Charles Scribner's Sons, 1937.
Cooper, Jerrold S. "Virginity in Ancient Mesopotamia." Pages 91–112 in *Sex and Gender in the Ancient Near East: Proceedings of the 47th Rencontre Assyriologique Internationale, Helsinki, July 2–6, 2001*. Edited by Simo Parpola and Robert M. Whiting. Helsinki: Neo-Assyrian Text Corpus Project, 2002.
Corbier, Mireille. "Child Exposure and Abandonment." Pages 68–89 in *Childhood, Class and Kin in the Roman World*. Edited by Suzanne Dixon. London: Routledge, 2001.
Cox, Benjamin D., and Susan Ackerman. "Micah's Teraphim." *JHS* 12 (2012): 1–37.
Cox, Benjamin D., and Susan Ackerman. "Rachel's Tomb." *JBL* 128 (2009): 135–48.
Cranz, Isabel. "Naaman's Healing and Gehazi's Affliction: The Magical Background of 2 Kgs 5." *VT* 68 (2018): 540–55.
Crapanzano, Vincent. *Recapitulations*. New York: Other Press, 2015.
Crapanzano, Vincent. "Rite of Return: Circumcision in Morocco." Pages 15–36 in *The Psychoanalytic Study of Society* 9. Edited by Werner Muensterberger and L. Bryce Boyer. New York: Psychohistory Press, 1981.
Cross, Frank Moore. *Canaanite Myth and Hebrew Epic: Essays in the History of the Religion of Israel*. Cambridge, MA: Harvard University Press, 1973.
Dalley, Stephanie. "Erra and Ishum." Pages 404–16 in *COS* 1.
Dalley, Stephanie. *Myths from Mesopotamia: Creation, the Flood, Gilgamesh, and Others*. Oxford: Oxford University Press, 1991.
Dalley, Stephanie. "Old Babylonian Dowries." *Iraq* 42 (1980): 53–74.
Darby, Erin. *Interpreting Judean Pillar Figurines: Gender and Empire in Judean Apotropaic Ritual*. FAT 69. Tübingen: Mohr Siebeck, 2014.
Darby, Erin. "Judean Pillar Figurines and the Making of Female Piety in Ancient Israelite Religion." Pages 193–214 in *Gods, Objects, and Ritual Practice*. Edited by Sandra Blakely. Studies in Ancient Mediterranean Religions 1. Columbus, GA: Lockwood Press, 2017.

Darby, Erin. "Judean Pillar Figurines (JPFs)." Pages 401–14 in *Archaeology and History of Eighth-Century Judah*. Edited by Zev I. Farber and Jacob L. Wright. ANEM 23. Atlanta: SBL Press, 2018.

Darby, Erin. "Seeing Double: Viewing and Re-viewing Judean Pillar Figurines through Modern Eyes." *Occasional Papers in Coroplastic Studies* 1 (2014): 13–26.

Darby, Erin. "Sex in the City? Judean Pillar Figurines and the Archaeology of Jerusalem." Pages 178–214 in *Iron Age Terracotta Figurines from the Southern Levant in Context*. Edited by Erin D. Darby and Izaak J. de Hulster. CHANE 125. Leiden: Brill, 2021.

Dasen, Véronique. "Childbirth and Infancy in Greek and Roman Antiquity." Pages 291–314 in *A Companion to Families in the Greek and Roman Worlds*. Edited by Beryl Rawson. Chichester, UK: Wiley-Blackwell, 2011.

Dasen, Véronique. *Dwarfs in Ancient Egypt and Greece*. Oxford Monographs on Classical Archaeology. Oxford: Clarendon, 1993.

Dasen, Véronique. "Probaskania: Amulets and Magic in Antiquity." Pages 177–203 in *The Materiality of Magic*. Edited by Dietrich Boschung and Jan N. Bremmer. Paderborn: Wilhelm Fink, 2015.

David, Rosalie. *Religion and Magic in Ancient Egypt*. London: Penguin, 2002.

Davies, Graham I. "An Archaeological Commentary on Ezekiel 13." Pages 108–25 in *Scripture and Other Artifacts: Essays on the Bible and Archaeology in Honor of Philip J. King*. Edited by Michael D. Coogan, J. Cheryl Exum, and Lawrence E. Stager. Louisville, KY: Westminster/John Knox, 1994.

Davis, Natalie Z. "The Reasons of Misrule." Pages 97–123 in Natalie Z. Davis, *Society and Culture in Early Modern France*. Stanford, CA: Stanford University Press, 1975.

Davis, Natalie Z. "Women on Top." Pages 124–51 in Natalie Z. Davis, *Society and Culture in Early Modern France*. Stanford, CA: Stanford University Press, 1975.

Day, Linda. "Rhetoric and Domestic Violence in Ezekiel 16." *BibInt* 8 (2000): 205–30.

Day, Peggy L. "From the Child Is Born the Woman: The Story of Jephthah's Daughter." Pages 109–24 in *Gender and Difference in Ancient Israel*. Edited by Peggy L. Day. Minneapolis: Fortress, 1989.

Day, Peggy L. "Jephthah's Daughter." Pages 465–66 in *DDD*.

DeBloois, Nanci. "Rape, Marriage, or Death? Gender Perspectives in the Homeric *Hymn to Demeter*." *Philological Quarterly* 76 (1997): 245–62.

Deflem, Mathieu. "Ritual, Anti-Structure, and Religion: A Discussion of Victor Turner's Processual Symbolic Analysis." *Journal for the Scientific Study of Religion* 30 (1991): 1–25.

Demand, Nancy. *Birth, Death, and Motherhood in Classical Greece*. Baltimore: Johns Hopkins University Press, 1994.

DeMaris, Richard E., and Carolyn S. Leeb. "Judges—(Dis)Honor and Ritual Enactment: The Jephthah Story: Judges 10:16–12:1." Pages 177–90 in *Ancient Israel: The Old Testament in its Social Context*. Edited by Philip F. Esler. Minneapolis: Fortress, 2006.

Dempsey, Carol J. "The 'Whore' of Ezekiel 16: The Impact and Ramifications of Gender-Specific Metaphors in Light of Biblical Law and Divine Judgment." Pages 57–78 in *Gender and Law in the Hebrew Bible and the Ancient Near East*. Edited by Victor H. Matthews, Bernard M. Levinson, and Tikva Frymer-Kensky. JSOTSup 262. Sheffield, UK: Sheffield Academic Press, 1998.

Deresiewicz, William. "Community and Cognition in *Pride and Prejudice*." *ELH* 64 (1997): 503–35.

Dettwyler, Katherine A., and Claudia Fishman. "Infant Feeding Practices and Growth." *Annual Review of Anthropology* 21 (1992): 171–204.

Dever, William G. *Did God Have a Wife? Archaeology and Folk Religion in Ancient Israel*. Grand Rapids, MI: Eerdmans, 2005.

Dever, William G. "Iron Age Epigraphic Material from the Area of Khirbet el-Kôm." *HUCA* 40/41 (1969–70): 139–204.

Dever, William G. *The Lives of Ordinary People in Ancient Israel: Where Archaeology and the Bible Intersect.* Grand Rapids, MI: Eerdmans, 2012.

Dewey, Kathryn. *Guiding Principles for Complementary Feeding of the Breastfeed Child.* Washington, D.C.: Division of Health Promotion and Protection, Food and Nutrition Program, Pan American Health Organization and the World Health Organization, n.d.

Diers, Carol Jean. See Amundsen, Darrel W.

Dijk, J. van. "Incantations accompagnant la naissance de l'homme." *Or* 44 (1975): 52–79.

Dijk, J. van, A. Goetze, and M. I. Hussey. *Early Mesopotamian Incantations and Rituals.* Yale Oriental Series, Babylonian Texts 11. New Haven, CT: Yale University Press, 1985.

Dijk-Hemmes, Fokkelien van. "Traces of Women's Texts in the Hebrew Bible." Pages 17–109 in Athalya Brenner and Fokkelien van Dijk-Hemmes, *On Gendering Texts: Female and Male Voices in the Hebrew Bible.* Biblical Interpretation Series 1. Leiden: Brill, 1993.

Dijkstra, Meindert. "Astral Myth of the Birth of Shahar and Shalim (KTU 1.23)." Pages 265–87 in *"Und Mose schrieb dieses Lied auf": Studien zum Alten Testament und zum alten Orient. Festschrift für Oswald Loretz zur Vollendung seines 70. Lebensjahres mit Beiträgen von Freunden, Schülern und Kollegen.* Edited by Manfried Dietrich and Ingo Kottsieper. AOAT 250. Münster: Ugarit-Verlag, 1998.

Dillmann, August. *Die Bücher Exodus und Leviticus.* 3rd ed. Leipzig: S. Hirzel, 1897.

Dinarès Solà, Rosa. See Onstine, Suzanne.

Dolansky, Shawna. "Interpreting Iconography: A Polysemic and Multivalent Approach to Understanding Judean Pillar Figurines." Pages 150–66 in *Epigraphy, Iconography, and the Bible.* Edited by Meir and Edith Lubetski. Hebrew Bible Monographs 98. Sheffield, UK: Sheffield Phoenix Press, 2022.

Dolansky, Shawna. "Re-Figuring Judean 'Fertility' Figurines: Fetishistic Functions of the Feminine Form." Pages 5–30 in *Between Israelite Religion and Old Testament Theology: Essays on Archaeology, History, and Hermeneutics.* Edited by Robert D. Miller II. Contributions to Biblical Exegesis and Theology. Leuven: Peeters, 2016.

Dor, Yonina. "The Rite of Separation of the Foreign Wives in Ezra-Nehemiah." Pages 173–88 in *Judah and the Judeans in the Achaemenid Period: Negotiating Identity in an International Context.* Edited by Oded Lipschits, Gary N. Knoppers, and Manfred Oeming. Winona Lake, IN: Eisenbrauns, 2011.

Dornemann, Rudolph Henry. *The Archaeology of the Transjordan in the Bronze and Iron Ages.* Milwaukee: Milwaukee Public Museum, 1983.

Douglas, Mary. *Purity and Danger: An Analysis of the Concepts of Pollution and Taboo.* London: Ark Paperbacks, 1966.

Douglas, Mary. "Victor Turner, 1920–1983." Accessed at https://www.therai.org.uk/archives-and-manuscripts/obituaries/victor-turner.

Driver, Samuel R. *Exodus.* Cambridge Bible for Schools and Colleges. Cambridge, UK: Cambridge University Press, 1911.

Driver, Samuel R. *Notes on the Hebrew Text and the Topography of the Books of Samuel, with an Introduction on Hebrew Paleography and the Ancient Versions and Facsimiles of Inscriptions and Maps.* 2nd ed. Oxford: Clarendon, 1913.

Droogers, André. "Symbols of Marginality in the Biographies of Religious and Secular Innovators." *Numen* 27 (1980): 105–21.

Dumermuth, Fritz. "Zu Ez. XIII 18–21." *VT* 13 (1963): 228–29.

Duncan, Christopher J. See Scott, Susan.

Dupont-Sommer, André, and Jean Starcky. "Les inscriptions araméennes de Sfiré (Stèles I et II)." *Mémoires présentés à l'académie des inscriptions et belles-lettres* 15 (1960; appeared in 1958): 197–351.

Dupras, Tosha L., Henry P. Schwarcz, and Scott I. Fairgrieve. "Infant Feeding and Weaning Practices in Roman Egypt." *AJPA* 115 (2001): 204–12.

Dupras, Tosha L., and Matthew W. Tocheri. "Reconstructing Infant Weaning Histories at Roman Period Kellis, Egypt Using Stable Isotope Analysis of Dentition." *AJPA* 134 (2007): 63–74.

Dupras, Tosha L., Sandra M. Wheeler, Lana Williams, and Peter Sheldrick. "Birth in Ancient Egypt: Timing, Trauma, and Triumph? Evidence from the Dakhleh Oasis." Pages 53–65 in *Egyptian Bioarchaeology: Humans, Animals, and Their Environment*. Edited by Salima Ikram, Jessica Kaiser, and Roxie Walker. Leiden: Sidestone Press, 2015.

Duveiller, Etienne. See Shiferaw, Bekele.

Ebeling, E. *Keilschrifttexte aus Assur religiösen Inhalts*. 2 vols. Leipzig 1919–1923.

Ebeling, Jennie R. *Women's Lives in Biblical Times*. London: T&T Clark, 2010.

Ebeling, Jennie R., and Yorke M. Rowan. "The Archaeology of the Daily Grind: Ground Stone Tools and Food Production in the Southern Levant." *NEA* 67 (2004): 108–17.

Edelman, Diana. "Adjusting Social Memory in the Hebrew Bible: The Teraphim." Pages 115–42 in *Congress Volume Stellenbosch 2016*. Edited by Louis C. Jonker, Gideon R. Kotzé, and Christl M. Maier. VTSup 177. Leiden: Brill, 2017.

Eichrodt, Walther. *Ezekiel: A Commentary*. OTL. Philadelphia: Westminster, 1970.

Eilberg-Schwartz, Howard. *The Savage in Judaism: An Anthropology of Israelite Religion and Ancient Judaism*. Bloomington: Indiana University Press, 1990.

Emmerson, Grace I. "Women in Ancient Israel." Pages 371–94 in *The World of Ancient Israel: Sociological, Anthropological, and Political Perspectives: Essays by Members of the Society for Old Testament Study*. Edited by R. E. Clements. Cambridge, UK: Cambridge University Press, 1989.

Emmett, Pauline M. See Rogers, Imogen S.

Eng, Milton. *The Days of Our Years: A Lexical Semantic Study of the Life Cycle in Biblical Israel*. New York: T&T Clark, 2011.

Erbele, Dorothea. "Gender Trouble in the Old Testament: Three Models of the Relation Between Sex and Gender." *SJOT* 13 (1999): 131–41.

Erbele-Küster, Dorothea. "'She Shall Remain (in Accordance to) Her Blood-of-Purification': Ritual Dynamics of Defilement and Blood Purification in Leviticus 12." Pages 59–70 in *Sacrificial Cult and Atonement in Early Judaism and Christianity: Constituents and Critique*. Edited by Henrietta L. Wiley and Christian A. Eberhart. RBS 85. Atlanta: SBL Press, 2017.

Eskenazi, Tamara Cohn. *Ezra: A New Translation with Introduction and Commentary*. AYB 14A. New Haven, CT: Yale University Press, 2023.

Evans, John F. "Death-Dealing Witchcraft in the Bible? Notes on the Condemnation of the 'Daughters' in Ezekiel 13:17–23." *Tyndale Bulletin* 65 (2014): 57–84.

"Exchange." *Dictionary of the Social Sciences*. Edited by Craig Calhoun. Oxford: Oxford University Press, 2002. Accessed at https://www-oxfordreference-com.dartmouth.idm.oclc.org/display/10.1093/acref/9780195123715.001.0001/acref-9780195123715-e-575?rskey= r0s9Pw&result = 576.

Exum, J. Cheryl. *Fragmented Women: Feminist (Sub)versions of Biblical Narratives*. Valley Forge, PA: Trinity Press International, 1993.

Eyben, Emiel. "Antiquity's View of Puberty." *Latomus* 31 (1972): 677–97.

Eyben, Emiel. *Restless Youth in Ancient Rome*. London: Routledge, 1993.

Fairgrieve, Scott I. See Dupras, Tosha L.

Faraone, C. A., B. Garnand, and C. López-Ruiz. "Micah's Mother (Judg. 17:1 4) and a Curse from Carthage (*KAI* 89): Canaanite Precedents for Greek and Latin Curses against Thieves?" *JNES* 64 (2005): 161–86.

Farber, Walter. *Lamaštu: An Edition of the Canonical Series of Lamaštu Incantations and Rituals and Related Texts from the Second and First Millennia B.C.* MC 17. Winona Lake, IN: Eisenbrauns, 2014.

Farber, Walter. *Schlaf, Kindchen, Schlaf! Mesopotamische Baby-Beschworungen und -Rituale*. MC 2. Winona Lake, IN: Eisenbrauns, 1989.

Farber, Zev. "Biological Explanation 2: Cold Females and Cleansing the Womb." In "Postpartum Impurity: Why Is the Duration Double for a Girl?" TheTorah.com (2020), at https://thetorah.com/article/postpartum-impurity-why-is-the-duration-double-for-a-girl.

Feder, Yitzhaq. "The Defilement of Dina: Uncontrolled Passions, Textual Violence, and the Search for Moral Foundations." *BibInt* 24 (2016): 281–309.

Feinstein, Eve Levavi. *Sexual Pollution in the Hebrew Bible*. Oxford: Oxford University Press, 2014.

Feucht, Erika. "Birth." Pages 192–93 in *OEAE* 1.

Feucht, Erika. "Childhood." Pages 261–64 in *OEAE* 1.

Feucht, Erika. *Das Kind im Alten Ägypten: die Stellung des Kindes in Familie und Gesellschaft nach altägyptischen Texten und Darstellungen*. Frankfurt: Campus, 1995.

Feucht, Erika. "Motherhood in Pharaonic Egypt." Pages 204–17 in *Women in Antiquity: Real Women across the Ancient World*. Edited by Stephanie Lynn Budin and Jean MacIntosh Turfa. Rewriting Antiquity. London: Routledge, 2016.

Feucht, Erika. "Der Weg ins Leben." Pages 33–53 in *Naissance et petite enfance dans l'Antiquité: actes du colloque de Fribourg, 28 novembre–1er décembre 2001*. Edited by Véronique Dasen. OBO 203. Fribourg: Academic Press; Göttingen: Vandenhoeck & Ruprecht, 2004.

Fink, Uta Barbara. See Burchard, Christoph.

Finkel, Irving R. "The Crescent Fertile." *Archiv für Orientforschung* 27 (1980): 37–52.

Finkelstein, J. J. "The Genealogy of the Hammurapi Dynasty." *JCS* 20 (1966): 95–118.

Fisher, Daniel. "Review of *Marriage Gifts and Social Change in Ancient Palestine: 1200 BCE to 200 CE*, by T. M. Lemos." *BASOR* 365 (2012): 88–90.

Fishman, Claudia. See Dettwyler, Katherine A.

Fitzmyer, Joseph A. *The Aramaic Inscriptions of Sefire*. Rome: Pontifical Biblical Institute, 1967.

Fitzmyer, Joseph A. *The Gospel According to Luke: Introduction, Translation, and Notes*. AYB 28. Garden City, NY: Doubleday, 1981.

Fleishman, Joseph. "Biblical Laws of Marriage vis-à-vis Seduction and Rape: Exodus 22:15–16 and Deuteronomy 22:28–29." Pages 87–129 in *Looking at the Ancient Near East and the Bible through the Same Eyes. Minha LeAhron: A Tribute to Aaron Skaist*. Edited by Kathleen Abraham and Joseph Fleishman. Bethesda, MD: CDL Press, 2012.

Fleishman, Joseph. "A Daughter's Demand and a Father's Compliance: The Legal Background to Achsah's Claim and Caleb's Agreement (Joshua 15, 16–19; Judges 1, 12–15)." *ZAW* 118 (2006): 354–73.

Fleishman, Joseph. "Did a Child's Legal Status in Biblical Israel Depend upon his being Acknowledged?" *ZAW* 121 (2009): 350–68.

Fleishman, Joseph. "Exodus 22:15–26 and Deuteronomy 22:28–29—Seduction and Rape? Or Elopement and Abduction Marriage?" Pages 59–73 in *The Jerusalem 2002 Conference Volume*. Edited by H. Gamoran. Jewish Law Studies Association 14. Binghamton, NY: Global Academic Publishing, 2004.

Fleming, Erin E. "Children: Ancient Near East." Pages 25–31 in *The Oxford Encyclopedia of the Bible and Gender Studies* 1. Edited by Julia M. O'Brien. Oxford: Oxford University Press, 2014.

Flusser, David, and Shmuel Safrai. "Who Sanctified the Beloved in the Womb?" *Immanuel* 11 (1980): 46–55.

Flynn, Shawn W. "Birthing New Life: Israelite and Mesopotamian Values and Visions of the Preborn Child." Pages 75–92 in *Life and Death: Social Perspectives on Biblical Bodies*. Edited by Francesca Stavrakopoulou. The Hebrew Bible in Social Perspective. London: T&T Clark, 2021.

Flynn, Shawn W. *Children in Ancient Israel: The Hebrew Bible and Mesopotamia in Comparative Perspective*. Oxford: Oxford University Press, 2018.

Fokkelman, J. P. *Narrative Art and Poetry in the Books of Samuel: A Full Interpretation Based on Stylistic and Structural Analyses* 4: *Vow and Desire (I Sam. 1–12)*. Studia Semitica Neerlandica. Assen: Van Gorcum, 1993.
Foster, Benjamin R. *Before the Muses: An Anthology of Akkadian Literature*. 3d ed. Bethesda, MD: CDL Press, 2005.
Foster, Benjamin R. *The Epic of Gilgamesh: A New Translation, Analogues, Criticism and Response*. 2nd ed. New York: W. W. Norton, 2019.
Fox, Michael V. *Proverbs 10–31: A New Translation with Introduction and Commentary*. AYB 18B. New Haven, CT: Yale University Press, 2009.
Fox, Michael V. "The Sign of the Covenant: Circumcision in the Light of the Priestly 'ôt Etiologies." *RB* 81 (1974): 557–96.
Franklin, Norma. "The Tombs of the Kings of Israel: Two Recently Identified Ninth-Century Tombs from Omride Samaria." *Zeitschrift des Deutschen Palästina-Vereins* 119 (2003): 1–11.
Friedman, Florence. "Aspects of Domestic Life and Religion." Pages 95–117 in *Pharaoh's Workers: The Villagers of Deir el-Medina*. Edited by Leonard H. Lesko. Ithaca, NY: Cornell University Press, 1994.
Frisch, Rose E. "Fatness, Puberty, and Fertility: The Effects of Nutrition and Physical Training on Menarche and Ovulation." Pages 29–49 in *Girls at Puberty: Biological and Psychosocial Perspectives*. Edited by Jeanne Brooks-Gunn and Anne C. Petersen. New York: Plenum Press, 1983.
Fritschel, Ann. "Women and Magic in the Hebrew Bible." PhD diss., Emory University, 2003.
Frymer-Kensky, Tikva. *In the Wake of the Goddesses: Women, Culture, and the Biblical Transformation of Pagan Myth*. New York: Free Press, 1992.
Frymer-Kensky, Tikva. "Virginity in the Bible." Pages 79–96 in *Gender and Law in the Hebrew Bible and the Ancient Near East*. Edited by Victor H. Matthews, Bernard M. Levinson, and Tikva Frymer-Kensky. JSOTSup 262. Sheffield, UK: Sheffield Academic Press, 1998.
Fuchs, Esther. "Marginalization, Ambiguity, Silencing: The Story of Jephthah's Daughter." *JFSR* 5 (1989): 35–45.
Fuchs, Esther. "Structure and Patriarchal Functions in the Biblical Betrothal Type-Scene: Some Preliminary Notes." *JFSR* 3 (1987): 7–13.
Fuhs, Hans Ferdinand. *Ezechiel 1–24*. Neue Echter Bibel. Würzburg: Echter-Verlag, 1984.
Galambush, Julie. *Jerusalem in the Book of Ezekiel: The City as Yahweh's Wife*. SBLDS 130. Atlanta: Scholars Press, 1992.
Galpaz-Feller, Pnina. "Pregnancy and Birth in the Bible and Ancient Egypt (Comparative Study)." *BN* 102 (2000): 42–53.
Ganzel, Tova, and Risa Levitt Kohn. "Ezekiel's Prophetic Message in Light of Leviticus 26." Pages 1075–84 in *The Formation of the Pentateuch: Bridging the Academic Cultures of Europe, Israel, and North America*. Edited by Jan Christian, Gertz, Bernard M. Levinson, Dalit Rom-Shiloni, and Konrad Schmid. Tübingen: Mohr Siebeck, 2016.
Garland, Robert. "Children in Athenian Religion." Pages 207–26 in *The Oxford Handbook of Childhood and Education in the Classical World*. Edited by Judith Evans Grubbs and Tim Parkin. New York: Oxford University Press, 2013.
Garland, Robert. *The Greek Way of Life, From Conception to Old Age*. Ithaca, NY: Cornell University Press, 1990.
Garnand, Brien K. See Faraone, C. A.
Garnand, Brien K., Lawrence E. Stager, and Joseph A. Greene. "Infants as Offerings: Palaeodemographic Patterns and Tophet Burials." *SEL* 29–30 (2012–2013): 193–222.
Garroway, Kristine Henriksen. "Children and Religion in the Archaeological Record of Ancient Israel." *JANER* 17 (2017): 116–39.
Garroway, Kristine Henriksen. *Children in the Ancient Near Eastern Household*. Explorations in Ancient Near Eastern Civilizations 3. Winona Lake, IN: Eisenbrauns, 2015.
Garroway, Kristine Henriksen. "The Construction of 'Child' in the Ancient Near East: Towards an Understanding of the Legal and Social Status of Children in Biblical Israel and

Surrounding Cultures." PhD diss., Hebrew Union College-Jewish Institute of Religion, 2009.
Garroway, Kristine Henriksen. "Enculturating Children in Eighth-Century Judah." Pages 415–29 in *Archaeology and History of Eighth-Century Judah*. Edited by Zev I. Farber and Jacob L. Wright. ANEM 23. Atlanta: SBL Press, 2018.
Garroway, Kristine Henriksen. "Failure to Marry: Girling Gone Wrong." Pages 59–74 in *Children in the Bible and the Ancient World: Comparative and Historical Methods in Reading Ancient Children*. London: Routledge, 2019.
Garroway, Kristine Henriksen. "Gendered or Ungendered? The Perception of Children in Ancient Israel." *JNES* 71 (2012): 95–114.
Garroway, Kristine Henriksen. "Gendering a Child with Ritual." TheTorah.com (2019), at https://thetorah.com/article/gendering-a-child-with-ritual.
Garroway, Kristine Henriksen. *Growing Up in Ancient Israel: Children in Material Culture and Biblical Texts*. ABS 23. Atlanta: SBL Press, 2018.
Garroway, Kristine Henriksen. "Methodology: Who Is a Child and Where Do We Find Children in the Ancient Near East?" Pages 67–90 in *T&T Clark Handbook of Children in the Bible and the Biblical World*. Edited by Sharon Betsworth and Julie Faith Parker. London: T&T Clark, 2018.
Garroway, Kristine Henriksen. "Rattle and Hum: A Reassessment of Closed-Form Rattles in the Southern Levant." *JAOS* 143 (2023): 173–94.
Geller, Markham J. "The Elephantine Papyri and Hosea 2, 3." *Journal for the Study of Judaism* 8 (1977): 139–48.
George, Andrew R. *The Babylonian Gilgamesh Epic: Introduction, Critical Edition and Cuneiform Texts*. 2 vols. Oxford: Oxford University Press, 2003.
Gerleman, Gillis. "Nutzrecht und Wohnrecht: Zur Bedeutung von 'ḥzh and nḥlh." *ZAW* 89 (1977): 313–25.
Gerstein, Beth. "A Ritual Processed: A Look at Judges 11:40." Pages 175–93 in *Anti-Covenent: Counter-Reading Women's Lives in the Hebrew Bible*. Edited by Mieke Bal. JSOTSup 81. Bible and Literature Series 22. Sheffield, UK: Almond, 1989.
Gerstenberger, Erhard S. *Theologies in the Old Testament*. New York: T&T Clark, 2002.
Gerstenberger, Erhard S., and Wolfgang Schrage. *Woman and Man*. Translated by Douglas W. Stott. Biblical Encounters Series. Nashville: Abingdon, 1981. Originally published as *Frau und Mann*. Kohlhammer Taschenbücher Band 1013: Biblische Konfrontationen. Stuttgart: Kohlhammer, 1980.
Gertz, Jan Christian, Angelika Berlejung, Konrad Schmid, and Markus Witte. *T&T Clark Handbook of the Old Testament*. London: T&T Clark, 2012.
Ghalioungui, Paul. *The Ebers Papyrus: A New English Translation, Commentaries and Glossaries*. Cairo: Academy of Scientific Research and Technology, 1987.
Gibson, John C. L. *Genesis*. 2 vols. The Daily Study Bible [Old Testament]. Philadelphia: Westminster, 1981–1982.
Gibson, John C. L. *Textbook of Syrian Semitic Inscriptions*. 3 vols. Oxford: Clarendon, 1971–1982.
Gilbert-Peretz, Diana. "Ceramic Figurines." Pages 29–41 in *Excavations at the City of David, 1978–1985, Directed by Yigal Shiloh* 4. Edited by Donald T. Ariel and Alan de Groot. Qedem 35. Jerusalem: The Institute of Archaeology, the Hebrew University of Jerusalem, 1996.
Gilchrist, Roberta. "Archaeological Biographies: Realizing Human Lifecycles, -Courses and -Histories." *World Archaeology* 31 (2000): 325–28.
Gilchrist, Roberta. "Archaeology and the Life Course: A Time and Place for Gender." Pages 142–60 in *A Companion to Social Archaeology*. Edited by Lynn Meskell and Robert W. Preucel. Oxford: Blackwell, 2004.
Gilchrist, Roberta. *Gender and Archaeology: Contesting the Past*. London: Routledge, 1999.
Gilchrist, Roberta. *Medieval Life: Archaeology and the Life Course*. Woodbridge, UK: Boydell Press, 2012.

Glassner, J.-J. "Rites of Passage: Mesopotamia." Pages 440–41 in *Religions of the Ancient World: A Guide*. Edited by Sarah Iles Johnston. Cambridge, MA: Harvard University Press, 2004.
Gluckman, Max. "Les Rites de Passage." Pages 1–52 in Daryll Forde, Meyer Fortes, Max Gluckman, and Victor W. Turner, *Essays on the Ritual of Social Relations*. Edited by Max Gluckman. Manchester: Manchester University Press, 1962.
Goelet, Ogden. *The Egyptian Book of the Dead: The Book of Going Forth by Day*. San Francisco: Chronicle Books, 1994.
Goetze, A. See Dijk, J. van.
Golden, Mark. "Names and Naming at Athens: Three Studies." *Echos du Monde Classique/Classical Views* 30 (1986): 245–69.
Golding, Jean. See Rogers, Imogen S.
Gonzalez, Hervé, and Lionel Marti. "Miscarriage: Ancient Near East and Hebrew Bible/Old Testament." Pages 359–66 in *Encyclopedia of the Bible and Its Reception* 19. Edited by Constance M. Fury, et al. Berlin: de Gruyter, 2021.
Goody, Esther N., with Jack Goody. "The Circulation of Women and Children in Northern Ghana." Pages 91–109 in Esther N. Goody, *Parenthood and Social Reproduction: Fostering and Occupation Roles in West Africa*. Cambridge Studies in Social Anthropology 35. Cambridge, UK: Cambridge University Press, 1982.
Goody, Jack. "Bridewealth and Dowry in Africa and Eurasia." Pages 1–58 in *Bridewealth and Dowry*. Edited by Jack Goody and Stanley J. Tambiah. Cambridge Papers in Social Anthropology 7. Cambridge, UK: Cambridge University Press, 1973.
Goody, Jack. *The Oriental, the Ancient, and the Primitive: Systems of Marriage and the Family in the Pre-Industrial Societies of Eurasia*. Studies in Literacy, Family, Culture, and the State. Cambridge, UK: Cambridge University Press, 1971.
Goody, Jack. *Production and Reproduction: A Comparative Study of the Domestic Domain*. Cambridge Studies in Social and Cultural Anthropology 17. Cambridge, UK: Cambridge University Press, 1976.
Goody, Jack. *The Social Organization of the LoWiili*. London: H. M. Stationery Office, 1956.
Goody, Jack. See also Goody, Esther N.
Görg, Manfred. "Ein verkanntes Wort für die 'Hebamme' in Ez 16, 4." *BN* 58 (1991): 13–16.
Görg, Manfred. "Terafim: tragbare Göttinnenfiguren." *BN* 101 (2000): 15–17.
Goudsouzian, Chrystal Elaine. "Becoming Isis: Myth, Magic, Medicine, and Reproduction in Ancient Egypt." PhD diss., The University of Memphis, 2012.
Granqvist, Hilma. *Birth and Childhood among the Arabs: Studies in a Muhammadan Village in Palestine*. Helsinki: Söderström & Co., 1947.
Granqvist, Hilma. *Marriage Conditions in a Palestinian Village*. Societas Scientiarum Fennica. Commentationes Humanarum Litterarum III.8. Helsinki: Akademische Buchhandlung; Leipzig: Harrassowitz, 1931.
Grant, E. *The People of Palestine*. Philadelphia: J. B. Lippincott, 1921.
Graves-Brown, Carolyn. *Dancing for Hathor: Women in Ancient Egypt*. London: Continuum, 2010.
Gray, John. *I and II Kings: A Commentary*. OTL. London: SCM Press, 1964.
Green, Anthony. See Black, Jeremy.
Greenberg, Moshe. *Ezekiel 1–20: A New Translation with Introduction and Commentary*. AYB 22. Garden City, NY: Doubleday, 1983.
Greenberg, Moshe. *Understanding Exodus*. New York: Behrman House for the Melton Research Center of the Jewish Theological Seminary of America, 1969.
Greene, Joseph A. See Garnand, Brien K.
Greengus, Samuel. "Bridewealth in Sumerian Sources." *HUCA* 61 (1990): 25–88.
Greengus, Samuel. *Laws in the Bible and in Early Rabbinic Collections: The Legal Legacy of the Ancient Near East*. Eugene, OR: Cascade, 2011.
Greengus, Samuel. "Legal and Social Institutions of Ancient Mesopotamia." Pages 469–84 in *CANE* 1–2.

Greengus, Samuel. "Old Babylonian Marriage Ceremonies and Rites." *JCS* 20 (1966): 55–72.
Greengus, Samuel. "The Old Babylonian Marriage Contract." *JAOS* 89 (1969): 505–32.
Greengus, Samuel. "Redefining 'Inchoate Marriage' in Old Babylonian Contexts." Pages 123–39 in *Riches Hidden in Secret Places: Ancient Near Eastern Studies in Memory of Thorkild Jacobsen*. Edited by Tzvi Abusch. Winona Lake, IN: Eisenbrauns, 2002.
Grimes, Ronald L. *Deeply into the Bone: Re-Inventing the Rites of Passage*. Berkeley: University of California Press, 2000.
Grosz, Katarzyna. "Bridewealth and Dowry in Nuzi." Pages 193–206 in *Images of Women in Antiquity*. Edited by Averil Cameron and Amélie Kuhrt. London: Routledge, 1983, 1993.
Grosz, Katarzyna. "Dowry and Brideprice in Nuzi." Pages 161–82 in *Studies on the Civilization and Culture of Nuzi and the Hurrians: In Honor of Ernest R. Lacheman on his Seventy-fifth Birthday, April 29, 1981*. Edited by Martha A. Morrison and David I. Owen. Winona Lake, IN: Eisenbrauns, 1981.
Grosz, Katarzyna. "Some Aspects of the Position of Women in Nuzi." Pages 167–80 in *Women's Earliest Records, from Ancient Egypt and Western Asia*. Edited by Barbara S. Lesko. BJS 166. Atlanta: Scholars Press, 1989.
Gruber, Mayer I. "Breast-Feeding Practices in Biblical Israel and in Old Babylonian Mesopotamia." Pages 69–107 in Mayer I. Gruber, *The Motherhood of God and Other Studies*. SFSHJ 57. Atlanta: Scholars Press, 1992.
Gruber, Mayer I. "Nursing Mothers (Isa 49:15, 23)." Pages 321–22 in *WIS*.
Gruber, Mayer I. "Private Life in Canaan and Ancient Israel." Pages 633–48 in *CANE* 1–2.
Gruber, Mayer I. "Women in the Cult According to the Priestly Code." Pages 49–68 in Mayer I. Gruber, *The Motherhood of God and Other Studies*. SFSHJ 57. Atlanta: Scholars Press, 1992.
Gubel, Eric. "Phoenician and Aramaean Bridle-Harness Decoration: Examples of Cultural Contact and Innovation in the Eastern Mediterranean." Pages 111–47 in *Crafts and Images in Contact: Studies on Eastern Mediterranean Art of the First Millennium BCE*. Edited by Claudia E. Suter and Christoph Uehlinger. OBO 210. Fribourg: Academic Press; Göttingen: Vandenhoeck & Ruprecht, 2005.
Guillebaud, John. See McVeigh, Edna.
Gunkel, Hermann. *Genesis*. Translated by Mark E. Biddle from the 3rd ed. (1910). Macon, GA: Mercer University Press, 1997.
Gunn, David M. *Judges*. Blackwell Bible Commentaries. Oxford: Blackwell, 2005.
Gurney, O. R., and P. Hulin. *The Sultantepe Tablets*. 2 vols. BIAA Occasional Monograph Series 7. London: The British Institute of Archaeology at Ankara, 1957–1964.
Gursky, Marjorie D. "Reproductive Rituals in Biblical Israel." PhD diss., New York University, 2001.
Hadley, Judith M. *The Cult of Asherah in Ancient Israel and Judah: Evidence for a Hebrew Goddess*. University of Cambridge Oriental Publications 57. Cambridge, UK: Cambridge University Press, 2000.
Hague, Rebecca. "Marriage Athenian Style." *Archaeology* 41/3 (May/June 1988): 32–36.
Hallo, W. W. "Isaiah 28:9–13 and the Ugaritic Abecedaries." *JBL* 77 (1958): 324–38.
Hallote, Rachel S. *Death, Burial, and Afterlife in the Biblical World: How the Israelites and Their Neighbors Treated the Dead*. Chicago: Ivan R. Dee, 2001.
Halperin, David J. *Seeking Ezekiel: Text and Psychology*. University Park, PA: Pennsylvania State University Press, 1993.
Halperin, David M. *One Hundred Years of Homosexuality*. New York: Routledge, 1990.
Hamilton, Richard. "Sources for the Athenian Amphidromia." *Greek, Roman, and Byzantine Studies* 25 (1984): 243–51.
Hamilton, Victor P. "Marriage (OT and ANE)." Pages 559–69 in *ABD* 4.
Hammons, Meredith Burke. "Before Joan of Arc: Gender Identity and Heroism in Ancient Mesopotamian Birth Rituals." PhD diss., Vanderbilt University, 2008.
Hamori, Esther J. *Women's Divination in Biblical Literature: Prophecy, Necromancy, and Other Arts of Knowledge*. AYBRL. New Haven, CT: Yale University Press, 2015.

Hansen, Wendy F., Deborah Hubbard, and Jennifer R. Niebyl. "Mastitis." Pages 376–79 in *Protocols for High-Risk Pregnancies.* 4th ed. Edited by John T. Queenan, John C. Hobbins, and Catherine Y. Spong. Oxford: Blackwell, 2005.

Haran, Menahem. "Ezekiel, P, and the Priestly School." *VT* 58 (2008): 211–18.

Harris, Rivkah. *Gender and Aging in Mesopotamia: The* Gilgamesh Epic *and Other Ancient Literature.* Norman, OK: University of Oklahoma Press, 2000.

Hartley, John E. *Leviticus.* WBC 4. Dallas, TX: Word Books, 1992.

Hayford. Sarah R. See Chae, Sophia.

Hays, Christopher B. "'Lest Ye Perish in the Way': Ritual and Kinship in Exodus 4:24–26." *Hebrew Studies* 48 (2007): 39–54.

Helle, Sophus. "Weapons and Weaving Instruments as Symbols of Gender in the Ancient Near East." Pages 105–15 in *Fashioned Selves: Dress and Identity in Antiquity.* Edited by Megan Cifarelli. Oxford: Oxbow Books, 2019.

Heltzer, Michael. *The Internal Organization of the Kingdom of Ugarit.* Wiesbaden: Reichert, 1982.

Hendel, Ronald. *Genesis 1–11: A New Translation with Introduction and Commentary.* AYB 1A. New Haven, CT: Yale University Press, 2024.

Herlihy, David, and Christine Klapish-Zuber. *Tuscans and Their Families.* New Haven, CT: Yale University Press, 1985.

Herrerin López, Jesús. See Onstine, Suzanne.

Herrmann, Christian. *Ägyptische Amulette aus Palästina/Israel IV: Von der Spätbronzezeit IIB bis in römische Zeit.* OBO Series Archaeologica 38. Fribourg: Academic Press; Göttingen: Vandenhoeck & Ruprecht, 2016.

Hertz, Robert. "A Contribution to the Study of the Collective Representation of Death." Pages 27–86 in Robert Hertz, *Death and the Right Hand.* Translated by Rodney and Claudia Needham. Glencoe, IL: The Free Press, 1960. Originally published as "Contribution à une etude sur la representation collective de la mort." *L'Année sociologique* 10 (1905–1906; published 1907): 48–137.

Herzog, Ze'ev. "The Southern Quarter." Pages 242–309 in Ze'ev Herzog and Lily Singer-Avitz, *Beer-Sheba III: The Early Iron IIA Enclosed Settlement and the Late Iron IIA–Iron IIB Cities.* Monograph Series of the Sonia and Marco Nadler Institute of Archaeology, Tel Aviv University 34. Tel Aviv: Emery and Claire Yass Publications in Archaeology; Winona Lake, IN: Eisenbrauns, 2016.

Hess, Richard S. *Israelite Religions: An Archaeological and Biblical Survey.* Grand Rapids, MI: Baker Academic; Nottingham, UK: Apollos, 2009.

Hess, Richard S. "Review: A Reassessment of the Priestly Cultic and Legal Texts (Review of Jacob Milgrom, *Leviticus 1–16: A New Translation and Commentary*; idem, *Leviticus 17–22: A New Translation and Commentary*; idem, *Leviticus 23–27: A New Translation and Commentary* [AYB 3, 3A, and 3B; New York, Doubleday, 1991, 2000, and 2001])." *Journal of Law and Religion* 17 (2002): 375–91.

Hiebert, Paula S. "'Whence Shall Help Come to Me?': The Biblical Widow." Pages 125–41 in *Gender and Difference in Ancient Israel.* Edited by Peggy L. Day. Minneapolis: Fortress, 1989.

Hillers, Delbert R. *Treaty Curses and the Old Testament Prophets.* Biblica et Orientalia 16. Rome: Pontifical Biblical Institute, 1964.

Himmelfarb, Martha. "Impurity and Sin in 4QD, 1QS, and 4Q512." *Dead Sea Discoveries* 8 (2001): 9–37.

Hoffman, David, and Sharon Hoffman. "Sappho and the Songs of Marriage." *Parabola* 29 (2004): 36–41.

Hoffman, Sharon. See Hoffman, David.

Hoffmann, David Zevi. *Sefer Va-Yiqra'*. Jerusalem: Mosad Ha-Rav Kook, 1954. Originally published as *Das Buch Leviticus.* Berlin: M. Poppelauer, 1905–1906.

Hoffner, Harry A., Jr. "Birth and Name-Giving in Hittite Texts." *JNES* 27 (1968): 198–203.

Hoffner, Harry A., Jr. *Hittite Myths*. SBLWAW 2. 2nd ed. Atlanta: Scholars Press, 1998.
Hoffner, Harry A., Jr. "Legal and Social Institutions of Hittite Anatolia." Pages 555–69 in *CANE* 1–2.
Hoffner, Harry A., Jr. "Paskuwatti's Ritual Against Sexual Impotence (CTH 406)." *Aula Orientalis* 5 (1987): 271–87.
Hoffner, Harry A., Jr. "Symbols for Masculinity and Femininity: Their Use in Ancient Near Eastern Sympathetic Magic Rituals." *JBL* 85 (1966): 326–34.
Holladay, John S., Jr. "Religion in Israel and Judah under the Monarchy: An Explicitly Archaeological Approach." Pages 249–99 in *Ancient Israelite Religion: Essays in Honor of Frank Moore Cross*. Edited by Patrick D. Miller, Paul D. Hanson, and S. Dean McBride. Philadelphia: Fortress, 1987.
Holland, Thomas A. "A Study of Palestinian Iron Age Baked Clay Figurines, with Special Reference to Jerusalem Cave 1." *Levant* 9 (1977): 121–55.
Holland, Thomas A. "A Typological and Archaeological Study of Human and Animal Representations in the Plastic Art of Palestine During the Iron Age." 2 vols. PhD diss., Magdalen College, University of Oxford, 1975.
Holloway, Steven W. "Distaff, Crutch or Chain Gang: The Curse of the House of Joab in 2 Samuel III 29." *VT* 37 (1987): 370–75.
Honeyman, A. M. "The Salting of Shechem." *VT* 3 (1953): 192–95.
Hopkins, David C. "Life on the Land: The Subsistence Struggles of Early Israel." *BA* 50 (1987): 178–91.
Homburg, Roy. See McVeigh, Edna.
Hornung, Erik. *Idea into Image: Essays on Ancient Egyptian Thought*. New York: Timken, 1992.
Horst, Friedrich. "Zwei Begriffe für Eigentum (Besitz): *naḥălâ* und *'aḥuzzâ*." Pages 135–56 in *Verbannung und Heimkehr: Beiträge zur Geschichte und Theologie Israels im 6. und 5. Jahrhundert v. Chr.: Wilhelm Rudolph zum 70. Geburtstage*. Edited by Arnulf Kuschke. Tübingen: J. C. B Mohr, 1961.
Houtman, Cornelis. "Exodus 4:24–26 and its Interpretation." *JNSL* 11 (1983): 81–105.
Howarth, William J. "The Influence of Feeding on the Mortality of Infants." *Lancet* 166, no. 4273 (1905): 210–13.
Hubbard, Deborah. See Hansen, Wendy F.
Hugenberger, Gordon Paul. *Marriage as a Covenant: A Study of Biblical Law and Ethics Governing Marriage Developed from the Perspective of Malachi*. VTSup 52. Leiden: Brill, 1994.
Hulin, P. See Gurney, O. R.
Huntington, Richard. See Metcalf, Peter.
Hurvitz, Avi. *A Linguistic Study of the Relationship between the Priestly Source and the Book of Ezekiel: A New Approach to an Old Problem*. Cahiers de la Revue biblique 20. Paris: J. Gabalda, 1982.
Hussey, M. I. See Dijk, J. van.
Hutter, Manfred. "Religionsgeschichtliche Erwägungen zu *'lhjm* in 1 Sam 28:13." *BN* 21 (1983): 32–36.
Ilan, Tal. *Integrating Women into Second Temple History*. Tübingen: Mohr Siebeck, 1999.
Imparati, Fiorella. "Private Life Among the Hittites." Pages 571–86 in *CANE* 1–2.
Isaac, Erich. "Circumcision as a Covenant Rite." *Anthropos* 59 (1964): 444–56.
Jackson, Bernard S. "The 'Institutions' of Marriage and Divorce in the Hebrew Bible." *Journal of Semitic Studies* 56 (2011): 221–51.
Jackson, Bernard S. *Wisdom-Laws: A Study of the* Mishpatim *of Exodus 21:1–22:16*. Oxford: Oxford University Press, 2006.
Jacobsen, Thorkild. "Notes on Nintur." *Or* 42 (1973): 274–98.
Janssen, Jac. J. "Absence from Work by the Necropolis Workmen of Thebes." *Studien zur altägyptischen Kultur* 8 (1980): 127–52.
Janssen, Jac. J. "Gift-Giving in Ancient Egypt as an Economic Feature." *JEA* 68 (1982): 253–58.

Janssen, Rosalind M., and Jac. J. Janssen. *Growing Up and Getting Old in Ancient Egypt.* London: Golden House Publications, 2007.

Jauhiainen, Heidi. "'Do Not Celebrate Your Feast without Your Neighbours:' A Study of References to Feasts and Festivals in Non-Literary Documents from Ramesside Period Deir el-Medina." PhD diss., University of Helsinki, 2009.

Jay, Nancy. *Throughout Your Generations Forever: Sacrifice, Religion, and Paternity.* Chicago: University of Chicago Press, 1992.

Jenkins, Ian. "Is There Life after Marriage? A Study of the Abduction Motif in Vase Paintings of the Athenian Wedding Ceremony." *Bulletin of the Institute of Classical Studies* 30 (1983): 137–45.

Jenks, Alan W. *The Elohist and North Israelite Traditions.* Missoula, MT: Society of Biblical Literature, 1977.

Jonckheere, Fr. "Un chapitre de pédiatrie égyptienne: l'allaitement." *Æsculape* 36 (1955): 203–23.

Jones. Richard N. See Wright, David P.

Joseph, Alison B. "'Is Dinah Raped?' Isn't the Right Question: Genesis 34 and Feminist Historiography." In Shawna Dolansky and Sarah Shectman, eds., "Gendered Historiography: Theoretical Considerations and Case Studies." *JHS* 19 (2019): 27–37.

Jost, Renate. "Die Töchter deines Volkes prophezeien." Pages 59–65 in *Für Gerechtigkeit streiten: Theologie im Alltag einer bedrohten Welt.* Edited by Dorothee Sölle. Gütersloh: Chr. Kaiser/Gütersloher, 1994.

Jost, Renate, and Elke Seifert. "Ezekiel: Male Prophecy with Female Imagery." Pages 345–60 in *Feminist Biblical Interpretation: A Compendium of Critical Commentary on the Books of the Bible and Related Literature.* Edited by Luise Schottroff and Marie-Theres Wacker. Grand Rapids, MI: Eerdmans, 2012.

Joyce, Paul M. *Ezekiel: A Commentary.* LHBOTS 482. New York: T&T Clark, 2007, 2009.

Kajanto, Iiro. "Women's praenomina Reconsidered." *Arctos: Acta Philologica Fennica* 7 (1972): 13–30.

Kakarla, Nirupama, and Karen D. Bradshaw. "Disorders of Pubertal Development: Precocious Puberty." *Seminars in Reproductive Medicine* 21 (2003): 339–51.

Kamionkowski, S. Tamar. "Gender Ambiguity and Subversive Metaphor in Ezekiel 16." PhD diss., Brandeis University, 2000.

Kamionkowski, S. Tamar. *Gender Reversal and Cosmic Chaos: A Study of the Book of Ezekiel.* JSOTSup 368. London: Sheffield Academic Press, 2003.

Kamionkowski, S. Tamar. "The Savage Made Civilized: An Examination of Ezekiel 16:8." Pages 124–36 in *"Every City Shall Be Forsaken": Urbanism and Prophecy in Ancient Israel and the Near East.* Edited by Lester L. Grabbe and Robert D. Haak. JSOTSup 330. Sheffield, UK: Sheffield Academic Press, 2001.

Kamrada, Dolores G. "The Sacrifice of Jephthah's Daughter and the Notion of Ḥērem: (A Problematic Narrative against its Biblical Background)." Pages 57–85 in *With Wisdom as a Robe: Qumran and other Jewish Studies in Honour of Ida Fröhlich.* Hebrew Bible Monographs 21. Edited by Károly Dániel Dobos and Miklós Köszeghy. Sheffield, UK: Sheffield Phoenix Press, 2008.

Kaplan, Lawrence. "'And the Lord Sought to Kill Him' (Exod 4:24): Yet Once Again." *HAR* 5 (1981): 65–74.

Keefe, Alice A. *Woman's Body and the Social Body in Hosea.* JSOTSup 338. Gender, Culture, Theory 10. London: Sheffield Academic Press, 2001.

Keel, Othmar, and Christoph Uehlinger. *Gods, Goddesses, and Images of God in Ancient Israel.* Minneapolis: Fortress, 1998.

Kemberling, Sidney R. See Stini, William A.

Kemp, Barry J. "Wall Paintings from the Workmen's Village at el-'Amarna." *JEA* 65 (1979): 47–53.

Kertzer, David I. "Introduction." Pages vii–xliii in Arnold van Gennep, *The Rites of Passage*. Translated by Monika B. Vizedom and Gabrielle L. Caffee. 2nd ed. Chicago: University of Chicago Press, 2019.

Kessler, R. "Benennung des Kindes durch die israelitische Mutter." *Wort und Dienst* 19 (1987): 113–23.

Keuken, Karlheinz. "Richter 11.37f.: Rite de Passage und Ubersetzungsprobleme." *BN* 19 (1982): 41–42.

Kim, Daewook. "*kstwt, msphwt*, and *npšwt* (Ezek 13:17–23)." *ZAW* 132 (2020): 301–5.

Kimball, Solon T. "Introduction." Pages v–xix in Arnold van Gennep, *The Rites of Passage*. Translated by Monika B. Vizedom and Gabrielle L. Caffee. 1st ed. Chicago: University of Chicago Press, 1960.

King, Philip J. "Circumcision: Who Did It, Who Didn't, and Why." *Biblical Archaeology Review* 32/4 (July/August 2006): 48–55.

King, Philip J., and Lawrence E. Stager. *Life in Biblical Israel*. Library of Ancient Israel. Louisville, KY: Westminster/John Knox, 2001.

Klapish-Zuber, Christine. See Herlihy, David.

Klawans, Jonathan. *Impurity and Sin in Ancient Judaism*. New York: Oxford University Press, 2000.

Klee, Deborah. "Menstruation in the Hebrew Bible." PhD diss., Boston University, 1998.

Kletter, Raz. "The Functions of Cult Stands." Pages 174–91 in Raz Kletter, Irit Ziffer, and Wolfgang Zwickel, *Yavneh I: The Excavation of the 'Temple Hill' Repository and the Cult Stands*. OBO 30. Fribourg: Academic Press; Göttingen: Vandenhoeck & Ruprecht, 2010.

Kletter, Raz. *The Judean Pillar-Figurines and the Archaeology of Asherah*. BAR International Series 636. Oxford: Tempvs Reparatvm, 1996.

Kletter, Raz. "The Typology of the Cult Stands." Pages 25–45 in Raz Kletter, Irit Ziffer, and Wolfgang Zwickel, *Yavneh I: The Excavation of the 'Temple Hill' Repository and the Cult Stands*. OBO 30. Fribourg: Academic Press; Göttingen: Vandenhoeck & Ruprecht, 2010.

Kletter, Raz, and Irit Ziffer. "Catalogues." Pages 211–68 in Raz Kletter, Irit Ziffer, and Wolfgang Zwickel, *Yavneh I: The Excavation of the 'Temple Hill' Repository and the Cult Stands*. OBO 30. Fribourg: Academic Press; Göttingen: Vandenhoeck & Ruprecht, 2010.

Klinck, Anne L. *Women's Songs in Ancient Greece*. Montreal and Kingston: McGill-Queen's University Press, 2008.

Knohl, Israel. "The Priestly Torah Versus the Holiness School: Sabbath and the Festivals." *HUCA* 58 (1987): 65–177.

Knohl, Israel. *The Sanctuary of Silence: The Priestly Torah and the Holiness School*. Minneapolis: Fortress, 1995.

Knoppers, Gary N. "Aaron's Calf and Jeroboam's Calves." Pages 92–104 in *Fortunate the Eyes That See: Essays in Honor of David Noel Freedman in Celebration of His Seventieth Birthday*. Edited by Astrid B. Beck, Andrew H. Bartelt, Paul R. Raabe, and Chris A. Franke. Grand Rapids, MI: Eerdmans, 1995.

Knuth, Deborah J. "Sisterhood and Friendship in *Pride and Prejudice*: Need Happiness Be 'Entirely a Matter of Chance'?" *Persuasions* 11 (1989): 99–109.

Koller, Aaron. "Pornography or Theology? The Legal Background, Psychological Realism, and Theological Import of Ezekiel 16." *CBQ* 79 (2017): 402–21.

Kopilovitz, Ariel. "What Kind of Priestly Writings Did Ezekiel Know?" Pages 1041–54 in *The Formation of the Pentateuch: Bridging the Academic Cultures of Europe, Israel, and North America*. Edited by Jan Christian, Gertz, Bernard M. Levinson, Dalit Rom-Shiloni, and Konrad Schmid. Tübingen: Mohr Siebeck, 2016.

Korpel, Marjo C. A. "Avian Spirits in Ugarit and Ezekiel 13." Pages 99–113 in *Ugarit, Religion, and Culture: Proceedings of the International Colloquium on Ugarit, Religion and Culture, Edinburgh, July 1994: Essays Presented in Honour of Professor John C. L. Gibson*. Edited by Nicolas Wyatt, Wilfred G. E. Watson, and Jeffrey B. Lloyd. Münster: Ugarit-Verlag, 1996.

Kosmala, Hans. "The 'Bloody Husband.'" *VT* 12 (1962): 14–28.

Kruger, Paul A. "The Hem of the Garment in Marriage: The Meaning of the Symbolic Gesture in Ruth 3:9 and Ezek. 16:8." *JNSL* 12 (1984): 79–86.
Kruger, Paul A. "Rites of Passage Relating to Marriage and Divorce in the Hebrew Bible." *JNSL* 21 (1955): 69–81.
Kudat, Ayse. "Institutional Rigidity and Individual Initiative in Marriages of Turkish Peasants." *Anthropological Quarterly* 47 (1974): 288–303.
Kunin, Seth D. "The Bridegroom of Blood: A Structuralist Analysis." *JSOT* 70 (1996): 3–16.
Laes, Christian. *Children in the Roman Empire: Outsiders Within*. Cambridge, UK: Cambridge University Press, 2011.
Laes, Christian. "Infants between Biological and Social Birth in Antiquity: A Phenomenon of the Longue Durée." *Historia* 63 (2014): 364–83.
Lafont, Sophie. *Femmes, droit et justice dans l'antiquité orientale: Contribution à l'étude du droit pénal au Proche-Orient ancient*. OBO 165. Fribourg: Academic Press; Göttingen: Vandenhoeck & Ruprecht, 1999.
La Fontaine, J. S. "Ritualization of Women's Life-Crises in Bugisu." Pages 159–86 in *The Interpretation of Ritual: Essays in Honour of A. I. Richards*. Edited by J. S. La Fontaine. London: Tavistock, 1972.
Lambert, W. G. "Appendix: Further Notes on 'Enlil and Ninlil: The Marriage of Sud.'" *JAOS* 103 (1983): 64–66.
Lambert, W. G. "A Middle Assyrian Medical Text." *Iraq* 31 (1969): 28–39.
Lambert, W. G., and A. R. Millard. *Atra-ḫasīs: The Babylonian Story of the Flood*. Oxford: Clarendon, 1969.
Landsberger, Benno. "Jungfräulichkeit: Ein Beitrag zum Thema 'Beilager und Eheschliessung.'" Pages 41–105 in *Symbolae Iuridicae et Historicae Martino David Dedicatae*. Edited by Johan Albert Ankum, Robert Feenstra, and Wilhelmus François Leemans. Leiden: Brill, 1968.
Landsberger, Benno, E. Reiner, and M. Civil. *Materialien zum sumerischen Lexikon 10: The Series HAR-ra = hubullu. Tablets XVI, XVII, XIX and Related Texts*. Rome: Pontificium Institutum Biblicum, 1970.
Lasine, Stuart. "Guest and Host in Judges 19: Lot's Hospitality in an Inverted World." *JSOT* 29 (1984): 37–59.
Lauwers, Judith, and Anna Swisher. *Counseling the Nursing Mother: A Lactation Consultant's Guide*. 4th ed. Sudbury, MA: Jones and Bartlett, 2005.
Lawrence, Ruth A. "Maternal Factors in Lactation Failure." Pages 283–91 in *Human Lactation 2: Maternal and Environmental Factors*. Edited by Margit Hamosh and Armond S. Goldman. New York: Plenum Press, 1986.
Leach, Edmund. "Anthropological Approaches to the Study of the Bible During the Twentieth Century." Pages 7–32 in Edmund Leach and D. Alan Aycock, *Structuralist Interpretations of Biblical Myth*. Cambridge, UK: Cambridge University Press and Royal Anthropological Institutes of Great Britain and Ireland, 1983.
Leach, Edmund. "Fishing for Men on the Edge of the Wilderness." Pages 579–99 in *The Literary Guide to the Bible*. Edited by Robert Alter and Frank Kermode. Cambridge, MA: Harvard University Press, 1987.
Leach, Edmund. "Review of *The Rites of Passage*. By Arnold van Gennep, translated from the French by Monika B. Vizedom and Gabrielle L. Caffee, with Introduction by Solon T. Kimball, and of *Death and The Right Hand*. By Robert Hertz, translated by Rodney and Claudia Needham, with Introduction by E. E. Evans-Pritchard." *Man* 60 (1960): 173–74.
Leeb, Carolyn S. See DeMaris, Richard E.
Leitz, Christian. *Magical and Medical Papyri of the New Kingdom*. Hieratic Papyri in the British Museum 7. London: British Museum Press, 1999.
Lemos, T. M. *Marriage Gifts and Social Change in Ancient Palestine, 1200 BCE to 200 CE*. Cambridge, UK: Cambridge University Press, 2010.

Lemos, T. M. "Were Israelite Women Chattel?" Pages 227–41 in *Worship, Women, and War: Essays in Honor of Susan Niditch*. Edited by John J. Collins, T. M. Lemos, and Saul M. Olyan. BJS 357. Providence, RI: Brown Judaic Studies, 2015.

Lemos, T. M. "Where There Is Dirt, Is There System? Revisiting Biblical Purity Constructions." *JSOT* 37 (2013): 265–94.

Lesko, Barbara S. "Household and Domestic Religion in Ancient Egypt." Pages 197–209 in *Household and Family Religion in Antiquity*. Edited by John Bodel and Saul M. Olyan. Oxford: Blackwell, 2008.

Leuchter, Mark. "'Now There Was a [Certain] Man:' Compositional Chronology in Judges–1 Samuel." *CBQ* 69 (2007): 429–39.

Leuchter, Mark. *Samuel and the Shaping of Tradition*. Biblical Refigurations. Oxford: Oxford University Press, 2013.

Levenson, Jon D. *The Death and Resurrection of the Beloved Son: The Transformation of Child Sacrifice in Judaism and Christianity*. New Haven, CT: Yale University Press, 1992.

Levine, Amy-Jill. "Introduction and Annotations to Luke." Pages 96–151 in *The Jewish Annotated New Testament: New Revised Standard Version Bible Translation*. Edited by Amy-Jill Levine and Marc Zvi Brettler. New York: Oxford University Press, 2011.

Levine, Baruch A. *Leviticus: The Traditional Hebrew Text with the New JPS Translation*. The JPS Torah Commentary. Philadelphia: The Jewish Publication Society, 1989.

Levine, Baruch A. *Numbers 1–20: A New Translation with Introduction and Commentary*. AYB 4. New York: Doubleday, 1993.

Levine, Baruch A. *Numbers 21–36: A New Translation with Introduction and Commentary*. AYB 4A. New York: Doubleday, 2000.

Levitt Kohn, Risa. See Ganzel, Tova.

Lewis, Theodore J. "The Ancestral Estate (*naḥălat ʾĕlōhîm*) in 2 Samuel 14:16." *JBL* 110 (1991): 597–612.

Lewis, Theodore J. *Cults of the Dead in Ancient Israel and Ugarit*. HSM 39. Atlanta: Scholars Press, 1989.

Lewis, Theodore J. "Divine Images and Aniconism in Ancient Israel" (Review article of Tryggve Mettinger, *No Graven Image? Israelite Aniconism in Its Ancient Near Eastern Context* [ConBOT, 42; Stockholm: Almqvist & Wiksell International, 1995]). *JAOS* 118 (1998): 36–53.

Lewis, Theodore J. "Family, Household, and Local Religion at Late Bronze Age Ugarit." Pages 60–88 in *Household and Family Religion in Antiquity*. Edited by John Bodel and Saul M. Olyan. Oxford: Blackwell, 2008.

Lewis, Theodore J. "The Identity and Function of Ugaritic Shaʿtiqatu: A Divinely Made Apotropaic Figure." *JANER* 14 (2014): 1–28.

Lewis, Theodore J. *The Origin and Character of God: Ancient Israelite Religion through the Lens of Divinity*. New York: Oxford University Press, 2020.

Lewis, Theodore J. "The Shaʿtiqatu Narrative from the Ugaritic Story about the Healing of King Kirta." *JANER* 13 (2013): 188–211.

Lewis, Theodore J. "Teraphim." Pages 844–50 in *DDD*.

Lewis, Theodore J. See also Toorn, Karel van der.

Lichtheim, Miriam. *Ancient Egyptian Literature*. 3 vols. Berkeley: University of California Press, 1975–1980.

Liebermann, Rosanne. "For-Profit Prophets? Ezekiel 13:17–23 and the Threat of Female Intermediaries." *Hebrew Studies* 61 (2020): 213–34.

Lincoln, Bruce. *Emerging from the Chrysalis: Rituals of Women's Initiation*. Cambridge, MA: Harvard University Press, 1981; 2nd ed. New York: Oxford University Press, 1991.

Lincoln, Bruce. "Initiation: Women's Initiation." Pages 4484–88 in *The Encyclopedia of Religion* 7. 2nd ed. Edited by Lindsay Jones. Detroit: Macmillan Reference USA, 2005.

Lincoln, Bruce. "The Initiatory Paradigm in Anthropology, Folklore and History of Religions." Pages 241–54 in *Initiation in Ancient Greek Rituals and Narratives: New Critical Perspectives*. Edited by David B. Dodd and Christopher A. Faraone. London: Routledge, 2003.

Lipiński, Edward. "Aḫat-milki, reine d'Ugarit, et la guerre du Mukiš." *Orientalia Lovaniensia Periodica* 12 (1981): 79–115.

Lipiński, Edward. "*mōhar*." Pages 142–49 in *TDOT* 8.

Lipka, Hilary B. *Sexual Transgression in the Hebrew Bible*. Hebrew Bible Monographs 7. Sheffield, UK: Sheffield Phoenix Press, 2006.

Liston, Maria A., and Susan I. Rotroff. "Babies in the Well: Archaeological Evidence for Newborn Disposal in Hellenistic Greece." Pages 62–82 in *The Oxford Handbook of Childhood and Education in the Classical World*. Edited by Judith Evans Grubbs and Tim Parkin. New York: Oxford University Press, 2013.

Ljung, Inger. *Silence or Suppression: Attitudes Towards Women in the Old Testament*. Stockholm: Almqvist & Wiksell, 1989.

Locher, Clemens. *Die Ehre Frau in Israel: Exegetische und rechtsvergleichende Studien zu Deuteronomium 22, 13–21*. OBO 70. Fribourg: Academic Press; Göttingen: Vandenhoeck & Ruprecht, 1986.

Lods, Adolphe. *Israel: From Its Beginnings to the Middle of the Eighth Century*. New York: Knopf, 1932.

Logan, Alice. "Rehabilitating Jephthah." *JBL* 128 (2009): 665–85.

Lohfink, Norbert. "The Cult Reform of Josiah of Judah: 2 Kings 22–23 as a Source for the History of Israelite Religion." Pages 459–75 in *Ancient Israelite Religion: Essays in Honor of Frank Moore Cross*. Edited by Patrick D. Miller, Paul D. Hanson, and S. Dean McBride. Philadelphia: Fortress, 1987.

Lonsdale, Steven H. *Dance and Ritual Play in Greek Religion*. Baltimore: Johns Hopkins University Press, 1993.

López-Ruiz, C. See Faraone, C. A.

Lorenzen, Søren. *Spoken into Being: Self and Name(s) in the Hebrew Bible*. FAT 2/137. Tübingen: Mohr Siebeck, 2022.

Lutkehaus, Nancy C. "Gender Metaphors: Female Rituals as Cultural Models in Manam." Pages 183–204 in *Gender Rituals: Female Initiation in Melanesia*. Edited by Nancy C. Lutkehaus and Paul B. Roscoe. London: Routledge, 1995.

Lyons, Michael A. *From Law to Prophecy: Ezekiel's Use of the Holiness Code*. LHBOTS 507. New York: T&T Clark, 2009.

Lyons, Michael A. "How Have We Changed? Older and Newer Arguments about the Relationship between Ezekiel and the Holiness Code." Pages 1055–74 in *The Formation of the Pentateuch: Bridging the Academic Cultures of Europe, Israel, and North America*. Edited by Jan Christian, Gertz, Bernard M. Levinson, Dalit Rom-Shiloni, and Konrad Schmid. Tübingen: Mohr Siebeck, 2016.

Macalister, R. A. S. *The Excavation of Gezer, 1902–1905 and 1907–1909*. 3 vols. London: John Murray. 1911–1912.

Maccoby, Hyam. "Holiness and Purity: The Holy People in Leviticus and Ezra–Nehemiah." Pages 153–70 in *Reading Leviticus: A Conversation with Mary Douglas*. Edited by John F. A. Sawyer. JSOTSup 227. Sheffield, UK: Sheffield Academic Press, 1996.

MacDonald, Nathan. *Not Bread Alone: The Uses of Food in the Old Testament*. Oxford: Oxford University Press, 2008.

MacDonald, Nathan. *What Did the Ancient Israelites Eat? Diet in Biblical Times*. Grand Rapids, MI: Eerdmans, 2008.

Magonet, Jonathan "'But if it is a Girl, She is Unclean for Twice Seven Days . . .': The Riddle of Leviticus 12.5." Pages 144–52 in *Reading Leviticus: A Conversation with Mary Douglas*. Edited by John F. A. Sawyer. JSOTSup 227. Sheffield, UK: Sheffield Academic Press, 1996.

Maiden, Brett. "Counterintuitive Demons: Pazazu and Lamaštu in Iconography, Text, and Cognition." *JANER* 18 (2018): 86–110.

Maier, Christl M. *Daughter Zion, Mother Zion: Gender, Space, and the Sacred in Ancient Israel.* Minneapolis: Fortress, 2008.
Malamat, Abraham. "King Lists of the Old Babylonian Period and Biblical Genealogies." Pages 163-73 in *Essays in Memory of E. A. Speiser.* Edited by William W. Hallo. AOS 53. New Haven. CT: American Oriental Society, 1968.
Malamat, Abraham. "Mari and the Bible: Some Patterns of Tribal Organization and Institutions." *JAOS* 82 (1972): 143-50.
Malul, Meir. "Adoption of Foundlings in the Bible and Mesopotamian Documents: A Study of Some Legal Metaphors in Ezekiel 16:1-7." *JSOT* 46 (1990): 97-126.
Malul, Meir. *Studies in Mesopotamian Legal Symbolism.* AOAT 221. Kevelaer: Butzon & Bercker; Neukirchen-Vluyn: Neukirchener, 1988.
Marcus, David. "The Betrothal of Yarikh and Nikkal-Ib." Pages 215-18 in *Ugaritic Narrative Poetry.* Edited by Simon B. Parker. SBLWAW 9. Atlanta: Scholars Press, 1997.
Marcus, David. *Jephthah and His Vow.* Lubbock, TX: Texas Tech University Press, 1986.
Marriott, McKim. "The Feast of Love." Pages 201-12 in *Krishna: Myths, Rites and Attitudes.* Edited by Milton B. Singer. Honolulu: East-West Center Press, 1966.
Marshall, Amandine. *L'enfant et la mort en Égypte ancienne.* Belberaud, France: Mondes Antiques, 2018.
Marshall, Amandine. *Motherhood and Early Childhood in Ancient Egypt: Culture, Religion, and Medicine.* Cairo and New York: The American University in Cairo Press, 2024.
Marshall, Amandine. "The Nurture of Children in Ancient Egypt." *Göttinger Miszellen: Beiträge zur ägyptologischen Diskussion* 247 (2015): 51-61.
Marsman, Hennie J. *Women in Ugarit and Israel: Their Social and Religious Position in the Context of the Ancient Near East.* Oudtestamentische Studiën/Old Testament Studies 49. Leiden: Brill, 2003.
Marti, Lionel. See Gonzalez, Hervé.
Martin, James D. *The Book of Judges.* CBC. Cambridge, UK: Cambridge University Press, 1975.
Martin, Michael W. "Betrothal Journey Narratives." *CBQ* 70 (2008): 505-23.
Martinez, Gladys M. "Trends and Patterns in Menarche in the United States: 1995 through 2013-2017." *National Health Statistics Reports* 146 (September 10, 2020): 1-11.
Masterman, E. W. G. "Hygiene and Disease in Palestine in Modern and in Biblical Times." *Palestine Exploration Quarterly* 50 (1918): 112-19.
"Mastitis." *Encyclopedia Britannica*, 13 June 2024, https://www.britannica.com/science/mastitis.
Matthews, Victor H. "Honor and Shame in Gender-Related Legal Situations in the Bible." Pages 97-112 in *Gender and Law in the Hebrew Bible and the Ancient Near East.* Edited by Victor H. Matthews, Bernard M. Levinson, and Tikva Frymer-Kensky. JSOTSup 262. Sheffield, UK: Sheffield Academic Press, 1998.
Matthews, Victor H. "Marriage and Family in the Ancient Near East." Pages 1-32 in *Marriage and Family in the Biblical World.* Edited by Ken M. Campbell. Downers Grove, IL: InterVarsity Press, 2003.
Matthews, Victor H., and Don C. Benjamin. *Social World of Ancient Israel: 1250-587 BCE.* Peabody, MA: Hendrickson, 1993.
Mauss, Marcel. *The Gift: The Form and Reason for Exchange in Archaic Societies.* Translated by W. D. Halls. New York: W. W. Norton, 1990. Originally published as "Essai sur le don. Forme et raison de l'échange dans les sociétés archaïques." *L'Année sociologique*, n.s., 1 (1925): 30-186.
Mauss, Marcel. "Review of A. Van Gennep, *Les rites de passage*." *L'Année sociologique* 11 (1906-1909): 200-202.
May, Herbert Gordon. *Material Remains of the Megiddo Cult.* OIP 26. Chicago: University of Chicago Press, 1935.
McCarter, P. Kyle. *1 Samuel: A New Translation with Introduction and Commentary.* AYB 8. Garden City, NY: Doubleday, 1980.

McCarter, P. Kyle. "The Sarcophagus Inscription of 'Eshmun'azor, King of Sidon (2.57)." Pages 182–83 in *COS* 2.
McClain, Carol. "Toward a Comparative Framework for the Study of Childbirth: A Review of the Literature." Pages 25–59 in *Anthropology of Human Birth*. Edited by Margarita Artschwager Kay. Philadelphia: F. A. Davis, 1982.
McKinny, Chris, Aharon Tavger, Deborah Cassuto, Casey Sharp, Matthew J. Suriano, Steven M. Ortiz, and Itzhaq Shai. "Tel Burna after a Decade of Work: The Late Bronze and Iron Ages." *NEA* 83/1 (2020): 4–15.
McMahon, Gregory. "Comparative Observations on Hittite Rituals." Pages 127–35 in *Recent Developments in Hittite Archaeology and History: Papers in Memory of Hans G. Güterbock*. Edited by K. Aslihan Yener and Harry A. Hoffner, Jr. Winona Lake, IN: Eisenbrauns, 2002.
McVeigh, Edna, John Guillebaud, and Roy Homburg. *The Oxford Handbook of Reproductive Medicine and Family Planning*. New York: Oxford University Press, 2008.
Megahed, Mohamed, and Hana Vymazalová. "Ancient Egyptian Royal Circumcision from the Pyramid Complex of Djedkare." *Anthropologie* 49 (2011): 155–64.
Meister, Natalie. See Niehoff, Arthur.
Meskell, Lynn. "Cycles of Life and Death: Narrative Homology and Archaeological Realities." *World Archaeology* 31 (2000): 423–41.
Meskell, Lynn. "Dying Young: The Experience of Death at Deir el-Medina." *Archaeological Review from Cambridge* 13/2 (1994): 35–45.
Meskell, Lynn. *Private Life in New Kingdom Egypt*. Princeton, NJ: Princeton University Press, 2002.
Metcalf, Peter, and Richard Huntington. *Celebrations of Death: The Anthropology of Mortuary Ritual*. Cambridge, UK: Cambridge University Press, 1991.
Meyers, Carol. *Discovering Eve: Ancient Israelite Women in Context*. Oxford: Oxford University Press, 1988.
Meyers, Carol. "The Family in Early Israel." Pages 1–47 in Leo G. Perdue, Joseph Blenkinsopp, John J. Collins, and Carol Meyers, *Families in Ancient Israel*. The Family, Religion, and Culture. Louisville, KY: Westminster/John Knox, 1997.
Meyers, Carol. "Food and Gender." Pages 383–98 in *The T&T Clark Handbook of Food in the Hebrew Bible and Ancient Israel*. Edited by Janling Fu, Cynthia Shafer-Elliott, and Carol Meyers. London: T&T Clark, 2022.
Meyers, Carol. "From Field Crops to Food: Attributing Gender and Meaning to Bread Production in Iron Age Israel." Pages 67–84 in *The Archaeology of Difference: Gender, Ethnicity, Class and the "Other" in Antiquity. Studies in Honor of Eric M. Meyers*. Edited by Douglas R. Edwards and C. Thomas McCullough. AASOR 60/61. Boston: American Schools of Oriental Research, 2007.
Meyers, Carol. "From Household to House of Yahweh: Women's Religious Culture in Ancient Israel." Pages 277–303 in *Congress Volume Basel 2001*. Edited by André Lemaire. VTSup 92. Leiden: Brill, 2002.
Meyers, Carol. "Guilds and Gatherings: Women's Groups in Ancient Israel." Pages 154–84 in *Realia Dei: Essays in Archaeology and Biblical Interpretation in Honor of Edward F. Campbell, Jr., at his Retirement*. Edited by Preston H. Williams, Jr., and Theodore Hiebert. Atlanta: Scholars Press, 1999.
Meyers, Carol. "Having Their Space and Eating There Too: Bread Production and Female Power in Ancient Israelite Households." *Nashim: A Journal of Jewish Women's Studies and Gender Issues* 5 (2002): 14–44.
Meyers, Carol. "Household Religion." Pages 118–34 in *Religious Diversity in Ancient Israel and Judah*. Edited by Francesca Stavrakopoulou and John Barton. London: T&T Clark, 2010.
Meyers, Carol. *Households and Holiness: The Religious Culture of Israelite Women*. Minneapolis: Fortress, 2005.
Meyers, Carol. "Material Remains and Social Relations: Women's Culture in Agrarian Households of the Iron Age." Pages 425–44 in *Symbiosis, Symbolism, and the Power of the*

Past: Canaan, Ancient Israel, and Their Neighbors from the Late Bronze Age through Roman Palaestina. Edited by William G. Dever and Seymour Gitin. Winona Lake, IN: Eisenbrauns, 2003.

Meyers, Carol. *Rediscovering Eve: Ancient Israelite Women in Context*. New York: Oxford University Press, 2013.

Meyers, Carol. "Terracottas Without Texts: Judean Pillar Figurines in Anthropological Perspective." Pages 115–30 in *To Break Every Yoke: Essays in Honor of Marvin L. Chaney*. Edited by Robert B. Coote and Norman K. Gottwald. SWBA 2/3. Sheffield, UK: Sheffield Phoenix Press, 2007.

Meyers, Carol. "Women's Daily Life" (Iron Age Israel)." Pages 488–500 in *Women in Antiquity: Real Women across the Ancient World*. Edited by Stephanie Lynn Budin and Jean MacIntosh Turfa. London: Routledge, 2016.

Meyers, Eric M. "Secondary Burials in Palestine." *BA* 33 (1970): 2–29.

Miano, David. *Shadow on the Steps: Time Measurement in Ancient Israel*. RBS 64. Atlanta: Society of Biblical Literature, 2010.

Milgrom, Jacob. "Israel's Sanctuary: The Priestly 'Picture of Dorian Gray.'" *RB* 83 (1976): 390–99.

Milgrom, Jacob. *Leviticus: A Book of Ritual and Ethics*. Continental Commentaries. Minneapolis: Fortress, 2004.

Milgrom, Jacob. *Leviticus 1–16: A New Translation with Introduction and Commentary*. AYB 3. New York: Doubleday, 1991.

Milgrom, Jacob. *Leviticus 17–22: A New Translation with Introduction and Commentary*. AYB 3A. New York: Doubleday, 2000.

Millard, A. R. See Lambert, W. G.

Miller, Patrick D. *The Religion of Ancient Israel*. Library of Ancient Israel. Louisville, KY: Westminster/John Knox, 2000.

Miller, Patrick D. "Things Too Wonderful: Prayers of Women in the Old Testament." Pages 237–51 in *Biblische Theologie und gesellschaftlicher Wandel: Für Norbert Lohfink SJ*. Edited by Georg Braulik, Walter Gross, and Sean E. McEvenue. Freiburg, Basel, and Wien: Herder, 1983.

Monroe, Lauren A. S. "Disembodied Women: Sacrificial Language and the Deaths of Bat-Jephthah, Cozbi, and the Bethlehemite Concubine." *CBQ* 75 (2013): 32–52.

Montserrat, Dominic. "Rites of Passage: Egypt." Pages 439–40 in *Religions of the Ancient World: A Guide*. Edited by Sarah Iles Johnston. Cambridge, MA: Harvard University Press, 2004.

Moor, Johannes C. de. *An Anthology of Religious Texts from Ugarit*. Nisaba 16. Leiden: Brill, 1987.

Moore, Carey A. *Esther: Introduction, Translation, and Notes*. AYB 7B. Garden City, NY: Doubleday, 1971.

Moore, George Foot. *A Critical and Exegetical Commentary on Judges*. 2nd ed. ICC 7. Edinburgh: T&T Clark, 1903.

Moorey, P. R. S. *Ancient Near Eastern Terracottas: With a Catalogue of the Collection in the Ashmolean Museum, Oxford*. Oxford: Ashmolean Museum, 2005.

Moorey, P. R. S. *Idols of the People: Miniature Images of Clay in the Ancient Near East*. The Schweich Lectures of the British Academy 2001. Oxford: Oxford University Press, for the British Academy, 2003.

Moran, William L. "Atrahasis: The Babylonian Story of the Flood." *Bib* 52 (1971): 51–61.

Morgenstern, Julian. "The 'Bloody Husband' (?) (Exod 4:24–26) Once Again." *HUCA* 34 (1963): 35–70.

Morgenstern, Julian. *Rites of Birth, Marriage, Death and Kindred Occasions Among the Semites*. Cincinnati: Hebrew Union College Press; Chicago: Quadrangle Books, 1966.

Morris, Ian. *Burial and Ancient Society: The Rise of the Greek City-State*. Cambridge, UK: Cambridge University Press, 1987.

Morris, Ian. "The Use and Abuse of Homer." *Classical Antiquity* 5 (1986): 81–138.

Mowinckel, Sigmund. *Psalmenstudien* 1. Amsterdam: P. Schippers, 1961 (reprinted edition of the 1921 publication).
Mueller, E. Aydeet. *The Micah Story: A Morality Tale in the Book of Judges*. StBibLit 34. New York: Peter Lang, 2001.
Murdock, George P., and Caterina Provost. "Factors in the Division of Labor by Sex: A Cross-Cultural Analysis." *Ethnology* 12 (1973): 203–25.
Muricho, Geoffrey. See Shiferaw, Bekele.
Musgrove, Frank. *Youth and the Social Order*. Bloomington: Indiana University Press, 1964.
Na'aman, Nadav. "Samuel's Birth Legend and the Sanctuary of Shiloh." *JNSL* 43 (2017): 51–61.
Nakhai, Beth Alpert. "Female Infanticide in Iron II Israel and Judah." Pages 257–72 in *Sacred History, Sacred Literature: Essays on Ancient Israel, the Bible and Religion in Honor of R. E. Friedman on His 60th Birthday*. Edited by Shawna Dolansky. Winona Lake, IN: Eisenbrauns, 2008.
Neifert, Marianne R., and Joy M. Scott. "Mammary Gland Anomalies and Lactation Failure." Pages 293–99 in *Human Lactation 2: Maternal and Environmental Factors*. Edited by Margit Hamosh and Armond S. Goldman. New York: Plenum Press, 1986.
Neils, Jenifer. "Children and Greek Religion." Pages 139–61 in *Coming of Age in Ancient Greece: Images of Childhood from the Classical Past*. Edited by Jenifer Neils and John H. Oakley. New Haven, CT: Yale University Press, 2003.
Neils, Jenifer. *Women in the Ancient World*. Los Angeles: The J. Paul Getty Museum, 2011.
Neufeld, E. *Ancient Hebrew Marriage Laws, with Special References to General Semitic Laws and Customs*. London: Longmans, Green and Co., 1944.
Newman, Lucille F. "The Anthropology of Birth." Pages 51–63 in Western Kentucky University Sociology, "UA68/10/1 Sociological Symposium No. 8—Childbirth & Infancy Life Cycle Series" (1972). *WKU Administration Documents*. Paper 4758. Accessed at https://digitalcommons.wku.edu/dlsc_ua_records/4758.
Nicholson, Ernest W. *The Pentateuch in the Twentieth Century: The Legacy of Julius Wellhausen*. Oxford: Clarendon, 1998.
Nicol, George G. "The Wisdom of Joab and the Wise Woman of Tekoa." *Studia Theologica* 36 (1982): 97–104.
Niditch, Susan. *Judges: A Commentary*. OTL. Louisville, KY: Westminster John Knox, 2008.
Niditch, Susan. "The Wronged Woman Righted: An Analysis of Genesis 38." *Harvard Theological Review* 72 (1979): 143–49.
Niebyl, Jennifer R. See Hansen, Wendy F.
Niehoff, Arthur, and Natalie Meister. "The Cultural Characteristics of Breastfeeding: A Survey." Pages 181–89 in *The Manner Born: Birth Rites in a Cross-Cultural Perspective*. Edited by Lauren Dundes. Walnut Creek, CA: AltaMira Press, 2003.
Nihan, Christoph L. "Ezekiel and the Holiness Legislation: A Plea for Nonlinear Models." Pages 1015–39 in *The Formation of the Pentateuch: Bridging the Academic Cultures of Europe, Israel, and North America*. Edited by Jan Christian Gertz, Bernard M. Levinson, Dalit Rom-Shiloni, and Konrad Schmid. Tübingen: Mohr Siebeck, 2016.
Nihan, Christoph L. *From Priestly Torah to Pentateuch: A Study in the Composition of the Book of Leviticus*. FAT 2/25. Tübingen: Mohr Siebeck, 2007.
Nihan, Christoph L. "Israel's Festival Calendars in Leviticus 23, Numbers 28–29 and the Formation of 'Priestly' Literature." Pages 177–231 in *The Books of Leviticus and Numbers*. Edited by Thomas Römer. Bibliotheca ephemeridum theologicarum lovaniensium 215. Leuven: Peeters, 2008.
Noegel, Scott B. "Maleness, Memory, and the Matter of Dream Divination in the Hebrew Bible." Pages 61–90 in *Perchance to Dream: Dream Divination in the Bible and the Ancient Near East*. Edited by Esther J. Hamori and Jonathan Stökl. ANEM 21. Atlanta: SBL Press, 2018.
Northup, Lesley A. "Pass-Aging Women, Jiezhu, and Life-Cycle Rituals." *Journal of Ritual Studies* 27 (2013): 1–12.

Noth, Martin. *Die israelitischen Personennamen im Rahmen der gemeinsemitischen Namengebung.* Hildesheim: Georg Olms, 1980.

Nougayrol, Jean. *Le palais royal d'Ugarit IV: Textes accadiens des archives Sud (archives internationales).* Mission de Ras Shamra 9. Paris: Imprimerie Nationale & Klincksieck, 1956.

Novick, Tzvi. "Mother and Child: Postpartum Defilement and Circumcision." TheTorah.com (2014), at https://thetorah.com/article/mother-and-child-postpartum-defilement-and-circumcision.

Oakley, John H. "Death and the Child." Pages 163–94 in *Coming of Age in Ancient Greece: Images of Childhood from the Classical Past.* Edited by Jenifer Neils and John H. Oakley. New Haven, CT: Yale University Press, 2003.

Oakley, John H., and Rebecca H. Sims. *The Wedding in Ancient Athens.* Wisconsin Studies in Classics. Madison: University of Wisconsin Press, 1993.

O'Brien, Mark A. "The Book of Deuteronomy." *Currents in Research: Biblical Studies* 3 (1995): 95–128.

Oden, Robert A., Jr. See Attridge, Harold W.

Ohnuma, Reiko. "Gift." Pages 103–23 in *Critical Terms for the Study of Buddhism.* Edited by Donald S. Lopez, Jr. Chicago: University of Chicago Press, 2005.

Olyan, Saul M. *Biblical Mourning: Ritual and Social Dimensions.* Oxford: Oxford University Press, 2004.

Olyan, Saul M. *Disability in the Hebrew Bible: Interpreting Physical and Mental Differences.* Cambridge, UK: Cambridge University Press, 2008.

Olyan, Saul M. *Rites and Rank: Hierarchy in Biblical Representations of Cult.* Princeton, NJ: Princeton University Press, 2000.

Olyan, Saul M. "The Roles of Kin and Fictive Kin in Biblical Representations of Death Rituals." Pages 251–63 in *Family and Household Religion: Towards a Synthesis of Old Testament Studies, Archaeology, Epigraphy, and Cultural Studies.* Edited by Rainer Albertz, Beth Alpert Nakhai, Saul M. Olyan, and Rüdiger Schmitt. Winona Lake, IN: Eisenbrauns, 2014.

Olyan, Saul M. "Sin, Pollution, and Purity: Syria-Canaan." Pages 501–2 in *Religions of the Ancient World: A Guide.* Edited by Sarah Iles Johnston. Cambridge, MA: Harvard University Press, 2004.

Olyan, Saul M. "Some Neglected Aspects of Israelite Interment Ideology." *JBL* 124 (2005): 601–16.

Olyan, Saul M. "What Do Shaving Rites Accomplish and What Do They Signal in Biblical Ritual Contexts?" *JBL* 117 (1998): 55–67.

Onstine, Suzanne, Jesús Herrerin López, Nataša Šarkić, Miguel Sanchez, and Rosa Dinarès Solà. "Women's Health Issues as Seen in Theban Tomb 16." Pages 395–400 in *Women in Ancient Egypt: Revisiting Power, Agency, and Autonomy.* Edited by Mariam F. Ayad. Cairo and New York: American University in Cairo Press, 2022.

Oppenheim, A. Leo. "The Mother of Nabonidus." Pages 560–62 in *Ancient Near Eastern Texts Relating to the Old Testament.* Edited by James B. Pritchard. 3rd ed. with supplement. Princeton, NJ: Princeton University Press, 1969.

Ornan, Tallay. "Chapter 14C: An Amulet of the Demon Pazazu." Pages 517–19 in Amihai Mazar, *Excavations at Tel Beth-Shean 1989–1996, vol. 1: From the Late Bronze Age IIB to the Medieval Period.* The Beth-Shean Valley Archaeological Project Publication No. 1. Jerusalem: The Israel Exploration Society and The Institute of Archaeology, The Hebrew University of Jerusalem, 2006.

Ortiz, Steven M. See McKinny, Chris.

Osborne, James F. "Secondary Mortuary Practice and the Bench Tomb: Structure and Practice in Iron Age Judah." *JNES* 70 (2011): 35–53.

Paige, Karen Ericksen. "A Bargaining Theory of Menarcheal Responses in Preindustrial Cultures." Pages 301–22 in *Girls at Puberty: Biological and Psychosocial Perspectives.* Edited by Jeanne Brooks-Gunn and Anne C. Petersen. New York: Plenum Press, 1983.

Pardee, Dennis. "Dawn and Dusk (1.87) (The Birth of the Gracious and Beautiful Gods)." Pages 274–83 in *COS* 1.
Pardee, Dennis. "Kosharoth." Pages 491–92 in *DDD*.
Pardee, Dennis. "Marzihu, Kispu, and the Ugaritic Funerary Cult: A Minimalist View." Pages 273–87 in *Ugarit, Religion, and Culture: Proceedings of the International Colloquium on Ugarit, Religion and Culture, Edinburgh, July 1994: Essays Presented in Honour of Professor John C. L. Gibson*. Edited by Nicolas Wyatt, Wilfred G. E. Watson, and Jeffrey B. Lloyd. Münster: Ugarit-Verlag, 1996.
Pardes, Ilana. *Countertraditions in the Bible: A Feminist Approach*. Cambridge, MA: Harvard University Press, 1992.
Parker, Julie Faith. *Valuable and Vulnerable: Children in the Hebrew Bible, Especially the Elisha Cycle*. BJS 355. Providence, RI: Brown Judaic Studies, 2013.
Parker, Robert. *Miasma. Pollution and Purification in Early Greek Religion*. Oxford: Clarendon, 1983.
Parker, Simon B. "The Wilderness." Pages 188–91 in *Ugaritic Narrative Poetry*. Edited by Simon B. Parker. SBLWAW 9. Atlanta: Scholars Press, 1997.
Parkin, Tim. "The Demography of Infancy and Early Childhood in the Ancient World." Pages 40–61 in *The Oxford Handbook of Childhood and Education in the Classical World*. Edited by Judith Evans Grubbs and Tim Parkin. Oxford: Oxford University Press, 2013.
Patai, Raphael. *Family, Love and the Bible*. London: Macgibbon and Kee, 1960.
Patrick, Dale. *Old Testament Law*. Eugene, OR: Wipf & Stock, 1985.
Pfeifer, Gerhard. "Entwöhnung und Entwöhnungsfest im Alten Testament: der Schlüssel zu Jesaja 28, 7–13?" *ZAW* 84 (1972): 341–47.
Pham, Xuan Huong Thi. *Mourning in the Ancient Near East and the Hebrew Bible*. JSOTSup 302. Sheffield, UK: Sheffield Academic Press, 1999.
Philip, Tarja S. *Menstruation and Childbirth in the Bible: Fertility and Impurity*. StBibLit 88. New York: Peter Lang, 2006.
Phillips, Anthony. *Ancient Israel's Criminal Law: A New Approach to the Decalogue*. Oxford: Blackwell, 1970.
Pinch, Geraldine. "Childbirth and Female Figurines at Deir el-Medina and el-'Amarna." *Or* 52 (1983): 405–14.
Pinch, Geraldine. *Magic in Ancient Egypt*. Austin, TX: University of Texas Press, 1995.
Pinch, Geraldine. "Private Life in Ancient Egypt." Pages 363–81 in *CANE* 1–2.
Pinch, Geraldine. *Votive Offerings to Hathor*. Oxford: Griffith Institute and Ashmolean Museum, 1993.
Pollock, Della. *Telling Bodies, Performing Birth*. New York: Columbia University Press, 1999.
Pope, Marvin H. "Mixed Marriage Metaphor in Ezekiel 16." Pages 384–99 in *Fortunate the Eyes That See: Essays in Honor of David Noel Freedman in Celebration of His Seventieth Birthday*. Edited by Astrid B. Beck, Andrew H. Bartelt, Paul R. Raabe, and Chris A. Franke. Grand Rapids, MI: Eerdmans, 1995.
Pope, Marvin H. "Review of Klaas Spronk, *Beatific Afterlife in Ancient Israel and in the Ancient Near East* (Kevelaer: Butzon & Bercker; Neukirchen-Vluyn: Neukirchener Verlag, 1986)." *UF* 19 (1987): 452–63.
Porter, Barbara N. *Images, Power, and Politics: Figurative Aspects of Esarhaddon's Babylonian Policy*. Philadelphia: American Philosophical Society, 1993.
Posener, G. "Sur l'attribution d'un nom à un enfant." *Revue d'Égyptologie* 22 (1970): 204–5.
Pressler, Carolyn. "The 'Biblical View' of Marriage." Pages 200–11 in *Engaging the Bible in a Gendered World: An Introduction to Feminist Biblical Interpretation in Honor of Katharine Doob Sakenfeld*. Edited by Linda Day and Carolyn Pressler. Louisville, KY: Westminster John Knox, 2006.
Pressler, Carolyn. "Sexual Violence and Deuteronomic Law." Pages 102–12 in *A Feminist Companion to Exodus to Deuteronomy*. Edited by Athalya Brenner. Feminist Companion to the Bible 6. Sheffield, UK: Sheffield Academic Press, 1994.

Pressler, Carolyn. *The View of Women Found in Deuteronomic Family Laws*. BZAW 216. Berlin: de Gruyter, 1993.
Pringle, Jackie. "Hittite Birth Rituals." Pages 128–41 in *Images of Women in Antiquity*. Edited by Averil Cameron and Amélie Kuhrt. London: Routledge, 1983, 1993.
Propp, William H. C. *Exodus 1–18: A New Translation with Introduction and Commentary*. AYB 2. New York: Doubleday, 1999.
Propp, William H. C. *Exodus 19–40: A New Translation with Introduction and Commentary*. AYB 2A. New York: Doubleday, 2006.
Propp, William H. C. "The Origins of Infant Circumcision in Israel." *HAR* 11 (1987): 355–70.
Propp, William H. C. "Symbolic Wounds: Applying Anthropology to the Bible." Pages 17–24 in *Le-David Maskil: A Birthday Tribute for David Noel Freedman*. Edited by Richard Elliott Friedman and William H. C. Propp. Biblical and Judaic Studies from the University of California, San Diego 9. Winona Lake, IN: Eisenbrauns, 2004.
Propp, William H. C. "That Bloody Bridegroom (Exodus iv 24–6)." *VT* 43 (1993): 495–518.
Provost, Caterina. See Murdock, George P.
Quick, Laura. "Spread the Hem of Your Cloak over Me (Ruth 3:9): Dress and the Body." Pages 19–46 in Laura Quick, *Dress, Adornment, and the Body in the Hebrew Bible*. Oxford: Oxford University Press, 2021.
Quirke, Steven. *Birth Tusks: The Armoury of Health in Context – Egypt 1800 BC*. Middle Kingdom Studies 3. London: Golden House Publications, 2016.
Rad, Gerhard von. *Genesis: A Commentary*. Rev. ed. Originally translated by John H. Marks (1961). OTL. Philadelphia: Westminster, 1972.
Redfield, James. "Notes on the Greek Wedding." *Arethusa* 15 (1982): 181–201.
Rehm, Rush. *Marriage to Death: The Conflation of Wedding and Funeral Rituals in Greek Tragedy*. Princeton, NJ: Princeton University Press, 1994.
Reiner, E. See Landsberger, Benno.
Reynolds, Matthew. See Shiferaw, Bekele.
Rieder, Paula M. *On the Purification of Women: Churching in Northern France, 1100–1500*. New York: Palgrave Macmillan, 2006.
Ritner, Robert K. "Household Religion in Ancient Egypt." Pages 171–96 in *Household and Family Religion in Antiquity*. Edited by John Bodel and Saul M. Olyan. Oxford: Blackwell, 2008.
Ritner, Robert K. "Magic." *OEAE*. Oxford University Press, 2005. Accessed at https://www-oxfordreference-com.dartmouth.idm.oclc.org/view/10.1093/acref/9780195102345.001.0001/acref-9780195102345-e-0424.
Roberts, J. J. M. *First Isaiah: A Commentary*. Hermeneia. Minneapolis: Fortress, 2015.
Robins, Gay. "Hair and the Construction of Identity in Ancient Egypt, c. 1480–1350 BCE." *Journal of the American Research Center in Egypt* 36 (1999): 55–69.
Robins, Gay. "Review of Rosalind M. Janssen and Jac J. Janssen, *Growing Up in Ancient Egypt*." *JEA* 80 (1994): 232–35.
Robins, Gay. "Women and Children in Peril: Pregnancy, Birth and Infant Mortality in Ancient Egypt." *KMT, A Modern Journal of Ancient Egypt* 5/4 (Winter 1994–1995): 24–35.
Robins, Gay. *Women in Ancient Egypt*. Cambridge, MA: Harvard University Press, 1993.
Robinson, Bernard P. "Zipporah to the Rescue: A Contextual Study of Exodus IV 24–6." *VT* 36 (1986): 447–61.
Roehrig, Catherine H. "Women's Work: Some Occupations of Non-Royal Women as Depicted in Ancient Egyptian Art." Pages 13–24 in *Mistress of the House, Mistress of Heaven: Women in Ancient Egypt*. Edited by Anne K. Capel and Glenn E. Markoe. New York: Hudson Hills, in conjunction with the Cincinnati Art Museum, 1996.
Rofé, Alexander. *Deuteronomy: Issues and Interpretation*. London: T&T Clark, 2002.
Rogers, Imogen S., Pauline M. Emmett, and Jean Golding. "The Growth and Nutritional Status of the Breast-Fed Infant." *Early Human Development* 49 Suppl (1997): S157–S174.

Romano, James F. "The Bes-Image in Pharaonic Egypt." 2 vols. PhD diss., New York University, 1989.
Romano, James F. "18 Vessel in the form of Bes-image." Pages 68–70 in *Mistress of the House, Mistress of Heaven: Women in Ancient Egypt*. Edited by Anne K. Capel and Glenn E. Markoe. New York: Hudson Hills, in conjunction with the Cincinnati Art Museum, 1996.
Römer, Thomas C. *The So-Called Deuteronomistic History: A Sociological, Historical, and Literary Introduction*. London: T&T Clark, 2007.
Roscoe, Paul B. "'Initiation' in Cross-Cultural Perspective." Pages 219–38 in *Gender Rituals: Female Initiation in Melanesia*. Edited by Nancy C. Lutkehaus and Paul B. Roscoe. London: Routledge, 1995.
Roscoe, Will. *Changing Ones: Third and Fourth Genders in Native North America*. New York: St. Martin's Press, 1998.
Rose, Charlotte. "Change and Continuity: Birth Practices from the Middle Kingdom through the New Kingdom." PhD diss., University of Pennsylvania, 2020.
Rose, Charlotte. "Childbirth Magic: Deciphering Bed Figurines from Ancient Egypt." *Expedition* 58/3 (2016): 38–45.
Ross. Allen P. "Paronomasia and Popular Etymology in the Naming Narratives of the Old Testament." PhD diss., St. Johns College, University of Cambridge, 1981.
Roth, Martha T. "Age at Marriage and the Household: A Study of Neo-Babylonian and Neo-Assyrian Forms." *Comparative Studies in Society and History* 29 (1987): 715–47.
Roth, Martha T. *Babylonian Marriage Agreements 7th–3rd Centuries B.C.* AOAT 222. Kevelaer: Butzon & Bercker; Neukirchen-Vluyn: Neukirchener, 1989.
Roth, Martha T. *Law Collections from Mesopotamia and Asia Minor*. SBLWAW 6. 2nd ed. Atlanta: Scholars Press, 1995.
Roth, Martha T. "Marriage and Matrimonial Prestations in First Millennium B.C. Babylonia." Pages 245–55 in *Women's Earliest Records, from Ancient Egypt and Western Asia*. Edited by Barbara S. Lesko. BJS 166. Atlanta: Scholars Press, 1989.
Roth, Martha T. "The Neo-Babylonian Widow." *JCS* 43 (1991): 1–26.
Rotroff, Susan I. See Liston, Maria A.
Rowan, Yorke M. See Ebeling, Jennie R.
Rowe, Ignacio Márquez. "Ugarit." Pages 719–35 in *A History of Ancient Near Eastern Law* 1. Edited by Raymond Westbrook. Handbook of Oriental Studies, Section 1: The Near and Middle East 72/1. Leiden: Brill, 2003.
Russell, Stephen C. "Ideologies of Attachment in the Story of Naboth's Vineyard." *Biblical Theology Bulletin* 44 (2014): 29–39.
Sachs, Abraham. "Babylonian Horoscopes." *JCS* 6 (1952): 49–75.
Safrai, Shmuel. See Flusser, David.
Salway, Benet. "What's in a Name? A Survey of Roman Onomastic Practice from 700 B.C. to A.D. 700." *Journal of Roman Studies* 84 (1994): 124–45.
Sanchez, Miguel. See Onstine, Suzanne.
Šarkić, Nataša. See Onstine, Suzanne.
Sasson, Jack M. "Circumcision in the Ancient Near East." *JBL* 85 (1966): 473–76.
Sasson, Jack M. *From the Mari Archives: An Anthology of Old Babylonian Letters*. Winona Lake, IN: Eisenbrauns, 2015.
Sasson, Jack M. *Judges 1–12: A New Translation with Introduction and Commentary*. AYB 6D. New Haven, CT: Yale University Press, 2014.
Sasson, Jack M. *Judges 13–21: A New Translation with Commentary*. AYB 6E. New Haven, CT: Yale University Press, 2025.
Sasson, Jack M. *Ruth: A New Translation with a Philological Commentary and a Formalist-Folklorist Interpretation*. The Johns Hopkins Near Eastern Studies. Baltimore: Johns Hopkins University Press, 1979.
Sasson, Jack M. "The Servant's Tale: How Rebekah Found a Spouse." *JNES* 65 (2006): 241–65.

Satlow, Michael L. *Jewish Marriage in Antiquity*. Princeton, NJ: Princeton University Press, 2001.
Satlow, Michael L. "Reconsidering the Rabbinic *Ketubah* Payment." Pages 133–51 in *The Jewish Family in Antiquity*. Edited by Shaye J. D. Cohen. BJS 289. Atlanta: Scholars Press, 1993.
Scharbert, J. "*ālâ*." Pages 261–66 in *TDOT* 1.
Schaudig, Hanspeter. *Die Inschriften Nabonidus von Babylon und Kyros' des Grossen samt den in ihrem Umfeld entstandenen Tendenzschriften: Textausgabe und Grammatik*. AOAT 256. Münster: Ugarit-Verlag, 2001.
Schearing, Linda S. "Double Time . . . Double Trouble? Gender, Sin, and Leviticus 12." Pages 429–50 in *The Book of Leviticus: Composition and Reception*. Edited by Rolf Rendtorff and Robert A. Kugler. VTSup 93. Leiden: Brill, 2003.
Schiffman, Lawrence H. "Laws Pertaining to Purification after Childbirth in the Dead Sea Scrolls." Pages 169–78 in *Strength to Strength: Essays in Honor of Shaye J. D. Cohen*. Edited by Michael L. Satlow. BJS 363. Providence. RI: Brown Judaic Studies, 2018.
Schiffman, Lawrence H. "Laws Pertaining to Women and Sexuality in the Early Stratum of the *Damascus Document*." Pages 547–69 in *The Dead Sea Scrolls and Contemporary Culture: Proceedings of the International Conference held at the Israel Museum, Jerusalem (July 6–8, 2008)*. Edited by Adolfo D. Roitman, Lawrence H. Schiffman, and Shani Tzoref. STDJ 91. Leiden: Brill, 2011.
Schmid, Konrad. See Gertz, Jan Christian.
Schmidt, Brian B. *Israel's Beneficent Dead: Ancestor Cult and Necromancy in Ancient Israelite Religion and Tradition*. Winona Lake, IN: Eisenbrauns, 1996.
Schmidt, Brian B. *The Materiality of Power: Explorations in the Social History of Early Israelite Magic*. Tübingen: Mohr Siebeck, 2016.
Schmidt, Brian B. "The 'Witch' of En-Dor, 1 Samuel 28, and Ancient Near Eastern Necromancy." Pages 111–29 in *Ancient Magic and Ritual Power*. Edited by Marvin Meyer and Paul Mirecki. Leiden: Brill, 2001.
Schmitt, Rüdiger. "Elements of Domestic Cult in Ancient Israel." Pages 57–219 in Rainer Albertz and Rüdiger Schmitt, *Family and Household Religion in Ancient Israel and the Levant*. Winona Lake, IN: Eisenbrauns, 2012.
Schmitt, Rüdiger. "Iconographic Evidence from Iconic Stamp Seals Regarding Personal Piety and Family Religion." Pages 367–86 in Rainer Albertz, "Personal Names and Family Religion." In Rainer Albertz and Rüdiger Schmitt, *Family and Household Religion in Ancient Israel and the Levant*. Winona Lake, IN: Eisenbrauns, 2012.
Schmitt, Rüdiger. *Magie im Alten Testament*. AOAT 313. Münster: Ugarit-Verlag, 2004.
Schmitt, Rüdiger. "The Ongoing Relations between the Living and the Dead: A Viewpoint from the Material Evidence." Pages 313–26 in *With the Loyal You Show Yourself Loyal: Essays on Relationships in the Hebrew Bible in Honor of Saul M. Olyan*. Edited by T. M. Lemos, Jordan D. Rosenblum, Karen B. Stern, and Debra Scoggins Ballentine. AIL 42. Atlanta: SBL Press, 2021.
Schmitt, Rüdiger. "The Problem of Magic and Monotheism in the Book of Leviticus." *JHS* 8 (2008): 2–12.
Schmitt, Rüdiger. "Rites of Family and Household Religion." Pages 387–428 in Rainer Albertz and Rüdiger Schmitt, *Family and Household Religion in Ancient Israel and the Levant*. Winona Lake, IN: Eisenbrauns, 2012.
Schmitt, Rüdiger. "Theories Regarding Witchcraft Accusations and the Hebrew Bible." Pages 181–94 in *Social Theory and the Study of Israelite Religion: Essays in Retrospect and Prospect*. Edited by Saul M. Olyan. RBS 71. Atlanta: Society of Biblical Literature, 2012.
Schneider, Tammi J. *Judges*. Berit Olam. Studies in Hebrew Narrative and Poetry. Collegeville, MN: Liturgical Press, 2000.
Schofield, Roger. "Did the Mothers Really Die? Three Centuries of Maternal Mortality in 'The World We Have Lost.'" Pages 231–60 in *The World We Have Gained: Histories of Population*

and Social Structure: Essays Presented to Peter Laslett on his Seventieth Birthday. Edited by Lloyd Bonfield, Richard M. Smith, and Keith Wrightson. Oxford: Blackwell, 1986.
Schorer, Mark. "Pride Unprejudiced." *Kenyon Review* 18 (1956): 72–91.
Schrage, Wolfgang. See Gerstenberger, Erhard S.
Schwarcz, Henry P. See Dupras, Tosha L.
Scott, Joy M. See Neifert, Marianne R.
Scott, Susan, and Christopher J. Duncan. *Demography and Nutrition: Evidence from Historical and Contemporary Populations*. Oxford: Blackwell Science, 2002.
Scurlock, JoAnn. "Baby-Snatching Demons, Restless Souls and the Dangers of Childbirth: Medico-Magical Means of Dealing with Some of the Perils of Motherhood in Ancient Mesopotamia." *Incognita* 2 (1991): 135–83.
Scurlock, JoAnn. "Medicine and Healing Magic." Pages 101–43 in *Women in the Ancient Near East*. Edited by Mark V. Chavalas. Routledge Sourcebooks for the Ancient World. London: Routledge, 2014.
Scurlock, JoAnn. "'Not Even Her Own Jewelry': Marital Property in the Middle Assyrian Laws." Pages 242–69 in *Law and (Dis)Order in the Ancient Near East: Proceedings of the 59th Rencontre Assyriologique Internationale Held at Ghent, Belgium, 15–19 July 2013*. Edited by Katrien De Graef and Anne Goddeeris. University Park, PA: The Pennsylvania State University Press, 2021.
Scurlock, JoAnn, and Burton R. Anderson. *Diagnoses in Assyrian and Babylonian Medicine: Ancient Sources, Translations, and Modern Medical Analyses*. Chicago: University of Illinois Press, 2005.
Seaford, Richard. "The Tragic Wedding." *Journal of Hellenic Studies* 107 (1987): 106–30.
Segal, J. B. *The Hebrew Passover, From Earliest Times to A.D. 70*. London: Oxford University Press, 1963.
Seifert, Elke. See Jost, Renate.
Selms, A. van. "The Best Man and Bride—From Sumer to St. John with a New Interpretation of Judges, Chapters 14 and 15." *JNES* 9 (1950): 65–75.
Seux, Marie-Joseph. *Hymnes et prières aux dieux de Babylonie et d'Assyrie*. Paris: Les Éditions du Cerf, 1976.
Shai, Itzhaq. See McKinny, Chris.
Sharp, Casey. See McKinny, Chris.
Shectman, Sarah. "Priestly Marriage Restrictions." Pages 180–93 in *Sexuality and Law in the Torah*. Edited by Hilary Lipka and Bruce Wells. LHBOTS 675. London: T&T Clark, 2020.
Shectman, Sarah. "What Do We Know about Marriage in Ancient Israel?" Pages 166–75 in *Reading a Tendentious Bible: Essays in Honor of Robert B. Coote*. Edited by Marvin L. Chaney, Uriah Y. Kim, and Annette Schellenberg. Hebrew Bible Monographs 66. Sheffield, UK: Sheffield Phoenix Press, 2014.
Sheldrick, Peter. See Dupras, Tosha L.
Shemesh, Yael. "The Sacrifice of Jephthah's Daughter (Judges 11) as a Reflection Story of the [sic] Rebecca's Betrothal and Marriage (Genesis 24)." *Jewish Studies, an Internet Journal* 15 (2019): 1–10.
Shields, Mary E. "Multiple Exposures: Body Rhetoric and Gender Characterization in Ezekiel 16." *JFSR* 14 (1998): 5–18.
Shiferaw, Bekele, Melinda Smale, Hans-Joachim Braun, Etienne Duveiller, Matthew Reynolds, and Geoffrey Muricho. "Crops that Feed the World 10. Past Successes and Future Challenges to the Role Played by Wheat in Global Food Security." *Food Security* 5 (2013): 291–317.
Shipton, Parker. *The Nature of Entrustment: Intimacy, Exchange, and the Sacred in Africa*. Yale Agrarian Studies Series. New Haven, CT: Yale University Press, 2007.
Silva, Aldina da. "The Condition of Women in Mesopotamian and Biblical Literature." Pages 51–73 in *Women Also Journeyed with Him: Feminist Perspectives on the Bible*. Translated by Madeleine Beaumont. Collegeville, MN: Liturgical Press, 2000.

Simkins, Ronald A. "Class and Gender in Early Israel." Pages 71–86 in *Concepts of Class in Ancient Israel*. Edited by Mark R. Sneed. SFSHJ 201. Atlanta: Scholars Press, 1999.
Sims, Rebecca H. See Oakley, John H.
Skinner, John. *A Critical and Exegetical Commentary on Genesis*. ICC. Edinburgh: T&T Clark, 1910.
Smale, Melinda. See Shiferaw, Bekele.
Smith, Mark S. *The Early History of God: Yahweh and the Other Deities in Israel*. San Francisco: Harper & Row, 1990; 2nd ed. Grand Rapids, MI: Eerdmans, 2002.
Smith, Mark S. *Poetic Heroes: Literary Commemorations of Warriors and Warrior Culture in the Early Biblical World*. Grand Rapids, MI: Eerdmans, 2014.
Smith, Mark S. *The Rituals and Myths of the Feast of the Goodly Gods of KTU/CAT 1.23: Royal Constructions of Opposition, Intersection, Integration, and Domination*. RBS 51. Atlanta: Society of Biblical Literature, 2006.
Smith, Mark S., and Elizabeth Bloch-Smith. "Death and Afterlife in Ugarit and Israel." *JAOS* 108 (1988): 277–84.
Soggin, J. Alberto. *Judges: A Commentary*. OTL. Philadelphia: Westminster, 1981.
Sonia, Kerry M. *Caring for the Dead in Ancient Israel*. ABS 27. Atlanta: SBL Press, 2020.
Southwood, Katherine E. "An Ethnic Affair? Ezra's Intermarriage Crisis against a Context of 'Self-Ascription' and 'Ascription of Others.'" Pages 46–59 in *Mixed Marriages: Intermarriage and Group Identity in the Second Temple Period*. Edited by Christian Frevel. LHBOTS 547. New York: Bloomsbury T&T Clark, 2011.
Southwood, Katherine E. "The Holy Seed: The Significance of Endogamous Boundaries and Their Transgression in Ezra 9–10." Pages 189–224 in *Judah and the Judeans in the Achaemenid Period: Negotiating Identity in an International Context*. Edited by Oded Lipschits, Gary N. Knoppers, and Manfred Oeming. Winona Lake, IN: Eisenbrauns, 2011.
Southwood, Katherine E. *Marriage by Capture in the Book of Judges: An Anthropological Approach*. Society for Old Testament Study Monograph Series. New York: Cambridge University Press, 2017.
Southwood, Katherine E. "The Social Dynamics Surrounding Yahwistic Women's Supposed Ritual Deviance in Ezekiel 13:17–23." *Journal for Interdisciplinary Biblical Studies* 4.2 (2002), published online at https://jibs.hcommons.org/archive/volume-4/volume-4-issue-2/.
Sperling, Susan, and Yewoubdar Beyene. "A Pound of Biology and a Pinch of Culture or a Pinch of Biology and a Pound of Culture?: The Necessity of Integrating Biology and Culture in Reproductive Studies." Pages 137–52 in *Women in Human Evolution*. Edited by Lori D. Hager. London: Routledge, 2005.
Sprinkle, Joe M. "The Rationale of the Laws of Clean and Unclean in the Old Testament." *Journal of the Evangelical Theological Society* 48 (2000): 637–58.
Spronk, Klaas. *Beatific Afterlife in Ancient Israel and in the Ancient Near East*. Kevelaer: Butzon & Bercker; Neukirchen-Vluyn: Neukirchener Verlag, 1986.
Stackert, Jeffery. *Rewriting the Torah: Literary Revision in Deuteronomy and the Holiness Legislation*. FAT 52. Tübingen: Mohr Siebeck, 2007.
Staehelin, Elizabeth. "Bindung und Entbindung. Erwägungen zu Papyrus Westcar 10,2." *Zeitschrift für Ägyptische Sprache und Altertumskunde* 96 (1970): 125–39.
Stager, Lawrence E. See Garnand, Brien K.; and King, Philip J.
Starcky, Jean. See Dupont-Sommer, André.
Stavrakopoulou, Francesca. *Land of Our Fathers: The Roles of Ancestor Veneration in Biblical Land Claims*. LHBOTS 473. New York: T&T Clark, 2010.
Stavrakopoulou, Francesca. "Making Bodies: On Body Modification and Religious Materiality in the Hebrew Bible." *Hebrew Bible and Ancient Israel* 2 (2013): 532–53.
Stavrakopoulou, Francesca. "The Materiality of Life and the Sociality of Death: An Introduction." Pages 1–23 in *Life and Death: Social Perspectives on Biblical Bodies*. Edited by

Francesca Stavrakopoulou. The Hebrew Bible in Social Perspective 2. London: T&T Clark, 2021.

Stavrakopoulou, Francesca. "Religion at Home: The Materiality of Practice." Pages 346–65 in *The Wiley Blackwell Companion to Ancient Israel*. Edited by Susan Niditch. Chichester, UK, and Malden, MA: Wiley-Blackwell, 2016.

Steinberg, Naomi. "The Problem of Human Sacrifice in War: An Analysis of Judges 11." Pages 114–35 in *On the Way to Nineveh: Studies in Honor of George M. Landes*. Edited by Stephen L. Cook and S. C. Winter. ASOR Books 4. Atlanta: Scholars Press, 1999.

Steinberg, Naomi. "Romancing the Widow: The Economic Distinctions between the 'almānâ, the 'iššâ-'almānâ, and the 'ēšet-hammēt." Pages 327–46 in *God's Word for our World* 1: *Biblical Studies in Honor of Simon John de Vries*. Edited by Deborah L. Ellens, Rolf P. Knierim, and Isaac Kalimi. JSOTSup 388. London: T&T Clark, 2004.

Steinberg, Naomi. *The World of the Child in the Hebrew Bible*. Sheffield, UK: Sheffield Phoenix Press, 2015.

Steiner, Richard C. *Disembodied Souls: The Nefesh in Israel and Kindred Spirits in the Ancient Near East, with an Appendix on the Katumuwa Inscription*. ANEM 11. Atlanta: SBL Press, 2015.

Steinert. Ulrike. "K. 263+10934, A Tablet with Recipes against the Abnormal Flow of a Woman's Blood." *Sudhoffs Archiv* 96 (2012): 64–94.

Stini, William A., Charles W. Weber, Sidney R. Kemberling, and Linda A. Vaughan. "Lean Tissue Growth and Disease Susceptibility in Bottle-fed versus Breast-fed Infants." Pages 61–80 in *Social and Biological Predictors of Nutritional Status, Physical Growth, and Neurological Development*. Edited by Lawrence S. Greene and Francis E. Johnson. New York: Academic Press, 1980.

Stökl, Jonathan. "The *mtnb'wt* in Ezekiel 13 Reconsidered." *JBL* 132 (2013): 61–76.

Stol, Marten. *Birth in Babylonia and the Bible: Its Mediterranean Setting*. Cuneiform Monographs 14. Groningen: Styx, 2000.

Stol, Marten. "Payment of the Old Babylonian Brideprice." Pages 131–67 in *Looking at the Ancient Near East and the Bible through the Same Eyes. Minha LeAhron: A Tribute to Aaron Skaist*. Edited by Kathleen Abraham and Joseph Fleishman. Bethesda, MD: CDL Press, 2012.

Stol, Marten. "Private Life in Ancient Mesopotamia." Pages 485–501 in *CANE* 1–2.

Stol, Marten. "Women in Mesopotamia." *JESHO* 38 (1995): 123–44.

Stol, Marten. *Women in the Ancient Near East*. Berlin: de Gruyter, 2016.

Stowers, Stanley K. "Greeks Who Sacrifice and Those Who Do Not: Toward an Anthropology of Greek Religion." Pages 293–333 in *The Social World of the First Christians: Essays in Honor of Wayne A. Meeks*. Edited by L. Michael White and O. Larry Yarbrough. Minneapolis: Fortress, 1995.

Stross, Brian. "Tzeltal Marriage by Capture." *Anthropological Quarterly* 47 (1974): 328–46.

Strouhal, Eugen. See Vymazalová, Hana.

Suriano, Matthew J. *A History of Death in the Hebrew Bible*. New York: Oxford University Press, 2018.

Suriano, Matthew J. *The Politics of Dead Kings: Dynastic Ancestors in the Book of Kings and Ancient Israel*. FAT 48. Tübingen: Mohr Siebeck, 2010.

Suriano, Matthew J. See also McKinny, Chris.

Swift, M. G. *Malay Peasant Society in Jelebu*. London School of Economics Monographs on Social Anthropology 29. London: Athlone Press; New York: Humanities Press, 1965.

Swisher, Anna. See Lauwers, Judith.

Tappy, Ron. "Did the Dead Ever Die in Biblical Judah?: Review of *Judahite Burial Practices and Beliefs about the Dead*, by Elizabeth Bloch-Smith." *BASOR* 298 (1995): 59–68.

Tavger, Aharon. See McKinny, Chris.

Taylor, John B. *Ezekiel*. Downers Grove, IL: Inter-Varsity Press, 1969.

Teeter, Emily. *Baked Clay Figurines and Votive Beds from Medinet Habu.* OIP 133. Chicago: The Oriental Institute of the University of Chicago, 2010.

Teeter, Emily. "Earthly and Divine Mothers in Ancient Egypt." Pages 145–67 in *Motherhood in Antiquity*. Edited by Dana Cooper and Claire Phelan. Cham, Switzerland: Palgrave Macmillan, 2017.

Thiessen, Matthew. "The Legislation of Leviticus 12 in Light of Ancient Embryology." *VT* 68 (2018): 297–319.

Thiessen, Matthew. "Luke 2:22, Leviticus 12, and Parturient Impurity." *Novum Testamentum* 54 (2012): 16–29.

Thomassen, Bjørn. *Liminality and the Modern: Living Through the In-Between*. Farnham, UK: Ashgate, 2014.

Thompson, Heather Ann. "Bloody Women: Rites of Passage, Blood and Artemis. Women in Classical Athenian Conception." PhD diss., University of St. Andrews, 1998.

Thureau-Dangin, F. "Rituel et Amulettes Contre Labartu." *Revue d'assyriologie et d'archéologie orientale* 18 (1921): 161–71.

Tocheri, Matthew W. See Dupras, Tosha L.

Toivari-Viitala, Jaana. "A Case Study of Ancient Egyptian Marriage Practices in the Workman's Community at Deir el-Medina during the Ramesside Period." Pages 613–19 in *Sex and Gender in the Ancient Near East: Proceedings of the 47th Rencontre Assyriologique Internationale, Helsinki, July 2–6, 2001*. Edited by Simo Parpola and Robert M. Whiting. Helsinki: Neo-Assyrian Text Corpus Project, 2002.

Toivari-Viitala, Jaana. "Marriage and Divorce." In *UCLA Encyclopedia of Egyptology*. Edited by Elizabeth Frood and Willeke Wendrich. Los Angeles: https://escholarship.org/uc/item/68f6w5gw.

Toivari-Viitala, Jaana. *Women at Deir el-Medina: A Study of the Status and Roles of the Female Inhabitants in the Workmen's Community during the Ramesside Period*. Egyptologische Uitgaven 15. Leiden: Nederlands Instituut voor het Nabije Oosten, 2001.

Toorn, Karel van der. "Ancestors and Anthroponyms: Kinship Terms as Theophoric Elements in Hebrew Names." *ZAW* 108 (1996): 1–11.

Toorn, Karel van der. *Family Religion in Babylonia, Syria and Israel: Continuity and Change in the Forms of Religious Life*. Studies in the History and Culture of the Ancient Near East 7. Leiden: Brill, 1996.

Toorn, Karel van der. "Family Religion in Second Millennium West Asia (Mesopotamia, Emar, Nuzi)." Pages 20–36 in *Household and Family Religion in Antiquity*. Edited by John Bodel and Saul M. Olyan. Oxford: Blackwell, 2008.

Toorn, Karel van der. "Female Prostitution in Payment of Vows in Ancient Israel." *JBL* 108 (1989): 193–205.

Toorn, Karel van der. *From Her Cradle to Her Grave: The Role of Religion in the Life of the Israelite and the Babylonian Woman*. Biblical Seminar 23. Sheffield, UK: JSOT Press, 1994. Originally published as *Van haar wieg tot haar graf: de rol van de godsdienst in het leven van de Israëlitische en de Babylonische vrouw*. Baarn: Ten Have, 1987.

Toorn, Karel van der. "Introduction: Religious Practices of the Individual and Family." Pages 423–24 in *Religions of the Ancient World: A Guide*. Edited by Sarah Iles Johnston. Cambridge, MA: Harvard University Press, 2004.

Toorn, Karel van der. "Magic at the Cradle: A Reassessment." Pages 139–47 in *Mesopotamian Magic: Textual, Historical, and Interpretative Perspectives*. Edited by Tzvi Abusch and Karel van der Toorn. Groningen: Styx, 1999.

Toorn, Karel van der. "The Nature of the Biblical Teraphim in the Light of the Cuneiform Evidence." *CBQ* 52 (1990): 203–23.

Toorn, Karel van der. "Nine Months among the Peasants in the Palestinian Highlands: An Anthropological Perspective on Local Religion in the Early Iron Age." Pages 393–410 in *Symbiosis, Symbolism, and the Power of the Past: Canaan, Ancient Israel, and Their*

Neighbors from the Late Bronze Age through Roman Palaestina. Edited by William G. Dever and Seymour Gitin. Winona Lake, IN: Eisenbrauns, 2003.

Toorn, Karel van der. "Recent Trends in the Study of Israelite Religion." Pages 223–43 in *Modern Societies and the Science of Religion: Studies in Honor of Lammert Leertouwer.* Edited by Gerard Wiegers in association with Jan Platvoet. Studies in the History of Religions 95. Leiden: Brill, 2002.

Toorn, Karel van der. "The Significance of the Veil in the Ancient Near East." Pages 327–39 in *Pomegranates and Golden Bells: Studies in Biblical, Jewish, and Near Eastern Ritual, Law, and Literature in Honor of Jacob Milgrom.* Edited by David P. Wright, David Noel Freedman, and Avi Hurvitz.

Toorn, Karel van der. "Torn between Vice and Virtue: Stereotypes of the Widow in Israel and Mesopotamia." Pages 1–13 in *Female Stereotypes in Religious Traditions.* Edited by Ria Kloppenborg and Wouter J. Hanegraaff. Numen Book Series 66. Leiden: Brill, 1995.

Toorn, Karel van der, and Theodore J. Lewis. "*tᵉrāpîm.*" Pages 777–89 in *TDOT* 15.

Töpfer, Susanne. "The Physical Activity of Parturition in Ancient Egypt: Textual and Epigraphical Sources." *Dynamis* 34 (2014): 317–35.

Trible, Phyllis. "The Daughter of Jephthah: An Inhuman Sacrifice." Pages 93–116 in Phyllis Trible, *Texts of Terror: Literary-Feminist Readings of Biblical Narratives.* Overtures to Biblical Theology 13. Philadelphia: Fortress, 1984.

Tropper, Amram. "The Economics of Jewish Childhood in Late Antiquity." *HUCA* 76 (2005): 189–233.

Turner, Edith. "Girl into Woman." *Anthropology and Humanism Quarterly* 10 (1985): 27–32.

Turner, Edith. "Prologue: From the Ndembu to Broadway." Pages 1–15 in Victor Turner, *On the Edge of the Bush: Anthropology as Experience.* Edited by Edith L. B. Turner. Tucson, AZ: University of Arizona Press, 1985.

Turner, Edith. *The Spirit and the Drum: A Memoir of Africa.* Tucson, AZ: University of Arizona Press, 1987.

Turner, Edith. "Zambia's Kankanga Dances: The Changing Life of Ritual." *Performing Arts Journal* 10 (1987): 57–71.

Turner, Judy Ann. "Hiereiai: Acquisition of Feminine Priesthoods in Ancient Greece." PhD diss., University of California, Santa Barbara, 1983.

Turner, Victor. "Are There Universals of Performance in Myth, Ritual, and Drama?" Pages 291–301 in Victor Turner, *On the Edge of the Bush: Anthropology as Experience.* Edited by Edith L. B. Turner. Tucson, AZ: University of Arizona Press, 1985.

Turner, Victor. "Betwixt and Between: The Liminal Period in *Rites de Passage.*" Pages 93–111 in Victor Turner, *The Forest of Symbols: Aspects of Ndembu Ritual.* Ithaca, NY: Cornell University Press, 1967. Originally published as pages 4–20 in *Symposium on New Approaches to the Study of Religion: Proceedings of the 1964 Annual Spring Meeting of the American Ethnological Society.* Edited by June Helm. Seattle: University of Washington Press for the American Ethnological Society, 1964.

Turner, Victor. *The Drums of Affliction: A Study of Religious Processes among the Ndembu of Zambia.* Oxford: Clarendon and the International African Institute, 1968.

Turner, Victor. *The Forest of Symbols: Aspects of Ndembu Ritual.* Ithaca, NY: Cornell University Press, 1967.

Turner, Victor. "Frame, Flow, and Reflection: Ritual and Drama as Public Liminality." Pages 94–120 in Victor Turner, *Process, Performance, and Pilgrimage: A Study in Comparative Symbology.* Ranchi Anthropology Series 1. New Delhi: Concept, 1979.

Turner, Victor. "Humility and Hierarchy: The Liminality of Status Elevation and Reversal." Pages 166–203 in Victor Turner, *The Ritual Process: Structure and Anti-Structure.* Ithaca, NY: Cornell University Press, 1969.

Turner, Victor. "Liminality and Communitas." Pages 94–130 in Victor Turner, *The Ritual Process: Structure and Anti-Structure.* Ithaca, NY: Cornell University Press, 1969.

Turner, Victor. "*Mukanda*: The Rite of Circumcision." Pages 151–279 in Victor Turner, *The Forest of Symbols: Aspects of Ndembu Ritual*. Ithaca, NY: Cornell University Press, 1967.
Turner, Victor. "Nkang'a: Part One." Pages 198–239 in Victor Turner, *The Drums of Affliction: A Study of Religious Processes among the Ndembu of Zambia*. Oxford: Clarendon and the International African Institute, 1968.
Turner, Victor. "Nkang'a: Part Two." Pages 240–68 in Victor Turner, *The Drums of Affliction: A Study of Religious Processes among the Ndembu of Zambia*. Oxford: Clarendon and the International African Institute, 1968.
Turner, Victor. *The Ritual Process: Structure and Anti-Structure*. Ithaca, NY: Cornell University Press, 1969.
Turner, Victor. *Schism and Continuity in an African Society: A Study of Ndembu Village Life*. Manchester, UK: Manchester University Press, on behalf of the Rhodes-Livingstone Institute, Northern Rhodesia, 1957.
Turner, Victor. "Three Symbols of *Passage* in Ndembu Circumcision Ritual." Pages 124–73 in Daryll Forde, Meyer Fortes, Max Gluckman, and Victor W. Turner, *Essays on the Ritual of Social Relations*. Edited by Max Gluckman. Manchester: Manchester University Press, 1962.
"Tying the Knot: Marriage in Ancient Greece." *Archaeology Odyssey* 7/5 (September/October 2004): 56.
Uehlinger, Christoph. See Keel, Othmar.
Ussishkin, David. *The Village of Silwan: The Necropolis from the Period of the Judahite Kingdom*. Jerusalem: Israel Exploration Society, 1993.
Valk, Jonathan. "'They Enjoy Syrup and Ghee at Tables of Silver and Gold': Infant Loss in Ancient Mesopotamia." *JESHO* 59 (2016): 695–749.
Van Gennep, Arnold. *The Rites of Passage*. Translated by Monika B. Vizedom and Gabrielle L. Caffee. Chicago: University of Chicago Press, 1960; 2nd ed. 2019. Originally published as *Les rites de passage*. Paris: E. Nourry, 1909.
Vaughan, Linda A. See Stini, William A.
Vaux, Roland de. *Ancient Israel: Its Life and Institutions*. Grand Rapids, MI: Eerdmans; Livonia, MI: Dove, 1997.
Vergiat, A. M. *Les Rites Secrets des Primatifs de l'Oubangui*. Paris: Payot, 1936.
Vernon, Muriel. See Bolin, Anne.
Vesco, Paolo Del. "A Votive Bed Fragment in the Egyptian Museum of Florence (Italy)." *Egitto e vicino Oriente* 32 (2009): 31–37.
Viberg, Åke. *Symbols of Law: A Contextual Analysis of Legal Symbolic Acts in the Old Testament*. Stockholm: Almqvist and Wiksell, 1992.
Vitry, Jacques de. "The Life of Marie d'Oignies." Pages 39–154 in *Two Lives of Marie d'Oignies*. Translated by Margot H. King. 4th ed. Toronto: Peregrina Publishing, 1998.
Vorderasiatische Schriftdenkmäler der Königlichen Museen zu Berlin 17 (= Johannes J. A. van Dijk, *Nicht-Kanonische Beschwörungen und sonstige Literarische Texte*). Berlin: Akademie-Verlag, 1971.
Vos, Clarence J. *Woman in Old Testament Worship*. Delft: Judels & Brinkman, 1968.
Vriezen, Karel J. H. "Archaeological Traces of Cult in Ancient Israel." Pages 45–80 in Bob Becking, Meindert Dijkstra, Marjo C. A. Korpel, and Karel J. H. Vriezen, *Only One God? Monotheism in Ancient Israel and the Veneration of the Goddess Asherah*. The Biblical Seminar 77. London: Sheffield Academic Press, 2001.
Vymazalová, Hana. See Megahed, Mohamed.
Vymazalová, Hana, and Eugen Strouhal. "Mother and Child Care." Pages 97–203 in *The Medicine of the Ancient Egyptians* 1: *Surgery, Gynecology, Obstetrics, and Pediatrics*. Cairo and New York: The American University in Cairo Press, 2010, 2014.
Wagner, Siegfred. "*dāraš*." Pages 293–307 in *TDOT* 3.
Walker, Marsha. *Breastfeeding Management for the Clinician: Using the Evidence*. Sudbury, MA: Jones and Bartlett, 2006.
Wallace, Howard N. *The Eden Narrative*. HSM 32. Atlanta: Scholars Press, 1985.

Walls, Neal H. *The Goddess Anat in Ugaritic Myth*. SBLDS 135. Atlanta: Scholars Press, 1992.
Walsh, Carey Ellen. *The Fruit of the Vine: Viticulture in Ancient Israel*. HSM 60. Winona Lake, IN: Eisenbrauns, 2000.
Warren, Michelle P. "Physical and Biological Aspects of Puberty." Pages 3–28 in *Girls at Puberty: Biological and Psychosocial Perspectives*. Edited by Jeanne Brooks-Gunn and Anne C. Petersen. New York: Plenum Press, 1983.
Weber, Charles W. See Stini, William A.
Wegner, Josef. "Decorated Birth Brick from South Abydos: New Evidence on Childbirth and Birth Magic in the Middle Kingdom." Pages 447–96 in *Archaism and Innovation: Studies in the Culture of Middle Kingdom Egypt*. Edited by David P. Silverman, William Kelly Simpson, and Josef Wegner. New Haven, CT: Department of Near Eastern Languages and Civilizations, Yale University; Philadelphia: University of Pennsylvania Museum of Archaeology and Anthropology, 2009.
Wegner, Josef. "Tradition and Innovation." Pages 119–42 in *Egyptian Archaeology*. Edited by Willeke Wendrich. Chichester, UK: Wiley-Blackwell, 2010.
Wegner, Judith Romney. "'Coming before the LORD': *lpny yhwh* and the Exclusion of Women from the Divine Presence." Pages 81–91 in *Hesed ve-Emet: Studies in Honor of Ernest S. Frerichs*. Edited by Jodi Magness and Seymour Gitin. BJS 320. Atlanta: Scholars Press, 1998.
Weiher, Egbert von. *Spätbabylonische Texte Aus Uruk* II. Ausgrabungen der Deutschen Forschungsgemeinschaft in Uruk-Warka 10. Berlin: Mann, 1983.
Weiher, Egbert von. Uruk: *Spätbabylonische Texte aus dem Planquadrat U 18* IV. Ausgrabungen in Uruk-Warka, Endberichte 12. Mainz: Philipp von Zabern, 1993.
Weinfeld, Moshe. *Deuteronomy and the Deuteronomic School*. Oxford: Clarendon, 1972.
Weinstein, Donald, and Rudolph M. Bell. *Saints and Society: The Two Worlds of Western Christendom, 1000–1700*. Chicago: University of Chicago Press, 1982.
Wells, Bruce. "First Wives Club: Divorce, Demotion, and the Fate of Leah in Genesis 29." *Maarav* 18 (2011): 101–29.
Wells, Bruce. See also Westbrook, Raymond.
Wells, Eric Ryan. "Display and Devotion: A Social and Religious Analysis of New Kingdom Votive Stelae from Asyut." PhD. diss., University of California, Los Angeles, 2014.
Welmers, William E. "Secret Medicines, Magic, and Rites of the Kpelle Tribe in Liberia." *Southwestern Journal of Anthropology* 5 (1949): 208–43.
Welton, Rebekah. "Ritual and the Agency of Food in Ancient Israel and Judah: Food Futures in Biblical Studies." *BibInt* 25 (2017): 609–24.
Wendrich, Willeke. "Entangled, Connected or Protected? The Power of Knots and Knotting in Ancient Egypt." Pages 243–69 in *Through a Glass Darkly: Magic, Dreams, and Prophecy in Ancient Egypt*. Edited by Kasia Szpakowska. Swansea, Wales: The Classical Press of Wales, 2006.
Wenham, Gordan J. "*Betûlāh* 'A Girl of Marriageable Age.'" *VT* 22 (1972): 326–48.
Wenham, Gordan J. *The Book of Leviticus*. NICOT. Grand Rapids, MI: Eerdmans, 1979.
Wenham, Gordan J. *Genesis 1–15*. WBC 1. Waco, TX: Word Books, 1987.
Wenham, Gordan J. "Marriage and Divorce in the Old Testament." *Didaskalia* 1 (1989): 6–17.
Westbrook, Raymond. "The Dowry." Pages 142–64 in Raymond Westbrook, *Property and the Family in Biblical Law*. JSOTSup 113. Sheffield, UK: Sheffield Academic Press, 1991.
Westbrook, Raymond. *Old Babylonian Marriage Law*. Archiv für Orientforschung: Beiheft 23. Horn, Austria: Ferdinand Berger, 1988.
Westbrook, Raymond, and Bruce Wells. *Everyday Law in Biblical Israel: An Introduction*. Louisville, KY: Westminster John Knox, 2009.
Westermann, Claus. *Genesis 1–11*. Translated by John J. Scullion. Minneapolis: Ausgburg, 1984.
Wevers, John. *Ezekiel*. New Century Bible Commentary. Grand Rapids, MI: Eerdmans, 1982.
Wheeler, Sandra M. See Dupras, Tosha L.
Whelehan, Patricia. See Bolin, Anne.

White, C. M. N. "Notes on the Circumcision Rites of the Balovale Tribes." *African Studies* 12 (1953): 41–56.
Whitekettle, Richard W. "Human Reproduction in the Textual Record of Mesopotamia and Syria-Palestine during the First and Second Millennia B. C." PhD diss., Yale University, 1995.
Whitekettle, Richard W. "Levitical Thought and the Female Reproductive Cycle: Wombs, Wellsprings, and the Primeval World." *VT* 46 (1996): 376–91.
Whitekettle, Richard W. "Leviticus 12 and the Israelite Woman: Ritual Process, Liminality, and the Womb." *ZAW* 107 (1995): 393–408.
Wiggerman, F. A. M. "Lamashtu, Daughter of Anu: A Profile." Pages 217–52 in Marten Stol, *Birth in Babylonia and the Bible: Its Mediterranean Setting*. Groningen: Styx, 2000.
Wilcke, Claus. "Noch einmal: *šilip rēmim* und die Adoption *ina mê-šu*. Neue und alte einschlägige Texte." *ZA* 71 (1981): 87–94.
Wilcke, Claus. "Philologische Bemerkungen zum *Rat des Šuruppag* und Versuch einer neuen Übersetzung." *ZA* 68 (1978): 196–232.
Wildberger, Hans. *Isaiah 1–12: A Commentary*. Continental Commentaries. Minneapolis: Fortress, 1991.
Willems, Harco. "A Note on Circumcision in Ancient Egypt." Pages 553–58 in *Kleine Göttergrosse Götter: Festschrift für Dieter Kessler zum 65. Geburtstag*. Edited by Mélanie C. Flossmann-Schütze, Maren Goecke-Bauer, Friedhelm Hoffmann, Andreas Hutterer, Katrin Schlüter, Alexander Schütze, and Martina Ullmann. Tuna el-Gebel 4. Vaterstetten, Germany: Patrick Brose, 2013.
Willett, Elizabeth A. "Infant Mortality and Women's Religion in the Biblical Periods." Pages 79–98 in *The World of Women in the Ancient and Classical Near East*. Edited by Beth Alpert Nakhai. Newcastle upon Tyne, UK: Cambridge Scholars Publishing, 2008.
Williams, Lana. See Dupras, Tosha L.
Williams, Ritva H. "The Mother of Jesus at Cana: A Social-Science Interpretation of John 2:1–12." *CBQ* 59 (1997): 679–92.
Williamson, H. G. M. *A Critical and Exegetical Commentary on Isaiah 1–27*. 3 vols. London: T&T Clark, 2006.
Wills, Lawrence M., editor and translator. *Ancient Jewish Novels: An Anthology*. Oxford: Oxford University Press, 2002.
Wilson, Stephen M. *Making Men: The Male Coming-of-Age Theme in the Hebrew Bible*. New York: Oxford University Press, 2015.
Wilson, Veronica. "The Iconography of Bes with Particular Reference to the Cypriot Evidence." *Levant* 7 (1975): 77–103.
Winter, Irene J. "North Syria as a Bronzeworking Centre in the Early First Millennium B.C.: Luxury Commodities at Home and Abroad." Pages 335–79 in Irene J. Winter, *On Art in the Ancient Near East Volume I: Of the First Millennium B.C.E.* CHANE 34.1. Leiden: Brill, 2010.
Witte, Markus. See Gertz, Jan Christian.
Wright, David P. "The Spectrum of Priestly Impurity." Pages 150–81 in *Priesthood and Cult in Ancient Israel*. Edited by Gary A. Anderson and Saul M. Olyan. JSOTSup 125. Sheffield, UK: JSOT Press, 1991.
Wright, David P. "Unclean and Clean (OT)." Pages 729–41 in *ABD* 6.
Wright, David P., and Richard N. Jones. "Discharge." Pages 204–7 in *ABD* 2.
Wright, Richard M. *Linguistic Evidence for the Pre-Exilic Date of the Yahwistic Source*. New York: T&T Clark, 2005.
Wyatt, Nicolas. "Circumcision and Circumstance: Male Genital Mutilation in Ancient Israel and Ugarit." *JSOT* 33 (2009): 405–31.
Wyatt, Nicolas. "The Pruning of the Vine in KTU 1.23." *UF* 24 (1992): 425–27.
Wyatt, Nicolas. *Religious Texts from Ugarit: The Words of Ilimilku and his Colleagues*. The Biblical Seminar 53. Sheffield, UK: Sheffield Academic Press, 1998.
Yamauchi, Edwin M. "Cultural Aspects of Marriage in the Ancient World." *Bibliotheca Sacra* 135 (1978): 241–52.

Yaron, R. *Introduction to the Law of the Aramaic Papyri*. Oxford: Clarendon, 1961.
Yee, Gale A. "Recovering Marginalized Groups in Ancient Israel: Methodological Considerations." Pages 10–27 in *To Break Every Yoke: Essays in Honor of Marvin L. Chaney*. Edited by Robert B. Coote and Norman K. Gottwald. SWBA 2/3. Sheffield, UK: Sheffield Phoenix Press, 2007.
Yee, Gale A. "'Take This Child and Suckle It for Me': Wet Nurses and Resistance in Ancient Israel." *Biblical Theology Bulletin* 39 (2009): 180–89.
Yezerski, Irit. "Iron Age Burial Customs in the Samaria Highlands." *Tel Aviv* 40 (2013): 72–98.
Yoder, Christine Roy. *Wisdom as a Woman of Substance: A Socioeconomic Reading of Proverbs 1–9 and 31:10–31*. BZAW 304. Berlin: de Gruyter, 2001.
Yoffee, Norman. "Rites of Marriage, Divorce, and Adoption in Old Babylonian Mesopotamia." Pages 61–72 in *Life, Death, and Coming of Age in Antiquity: Individual Rites of Passage in the Ancient Near East and Adjacent Regions*. Edited by Alice Mouton and Julie Patrier. Leiden: Nederlands Instituut voor het Nanije Oosten, 2014.
Yun, Sungduk. "Mother of Her Son: The Literary Scheme of the Adad-Guppi Stele." *Acta Orientalia Academiae Scientiarum Hungaricae* 70 (2017): 277–94.
Zevit, Ziony. *The Religions of Ancient Israel: A Synthesis of Parallactic Approaches*. London: Continuum, 2001.
Ziffer, Irit. See Kletter, Raz.
Zimmerli, Walther. *Ezekiel 1: A Commentary on the Book of the Prophet Ezekiel, Chapters 1–24*. Hermeneia. Philadelphia: Fortress, 1979.
Zorn, Jeffrey R. "The Daily Grind at Tel Dor: A Trough and Basin from an Iron Age I Kitchen." *Eretz-Israel* 29 (2009): 267*–80*.

Index of Subjects

For the benefit of digital users, indexed terms that span two pages (e.g., 52–53) may, on occasion, appear on only one of those pages.

Aaron, 247–48
Abdon, 245–46
Abigail, 92–93
Abimelech, king of Gerar, 294n.6
Abimelech, son of Gideon, 171*t*, 174
Abner, 239–40
Abraham. *See also* Isaac
  blessing of, 117
  children named by, 170, 171*t*, 194–95
  Isaac's marriage arranged by, 74, 91, 123
  marriages of, 91–92, 103–4
  Sarah buried and mourned by, 239–40, 242
  tomb of, 242–43, 247, 257
  wives and concubines of, 91–92, 121
Absalom, 234, 251–52, 311n.120
Achsah, 91, 106, 107–8
Adam, 61, 119, 170, 171*t*, 191
Adams, Samuel, 110, 275n.11
"adolescence," 43
'ādôn (lord), 127
adoption, 280n.103
agency. *See* women's agency
agrarian economy
  calories necessary within, 203–4
  children's necessity to, 112–13, 139–40, 197, 298n.1
  endogamy and, 126
Ahab, 123–24, 241–42, 321n.30
Aharoni, Yohanan, 215
Ahaziah, 321n.30
Ahithophel, 243–44, 322n.51
Akkadian loanwords, 106–7, 160, 161
Albertz, Rainer, 159, 193–94, 298n.1, 305n.4, 306n.15, 309n.67, 311n.110
Albright, William, 210, 215, 216*f*, 250–51
alcohol, at feasts, 99, 131, 138–39, 182–83
Alexander, T. Desmond, 284n.25
Allan, Robert, 72
Allen, James, 315n.95
'ām (people), 257–58, 263

el-Amarna, 152, 162–63, 176–77, 180, 182–83
Amaziah, 321n.30
Amphidromia, 3, 45, 58–59, 177–78, 181–82, 190–92
amulets, childbirth, 144–47, 148–49, 157–58, 158*f*, 162–63, 167
Anat, 152–54, 320nn.11–12
ancestral spirits, 14–15, 23, 246, 249
  communication with, 259–60
  maleness of, 258–59
  in Old Babylonian materials, 252–53, 258–59
  reintegration of, 254–55, 256, 259–60
  "remembrance" of, 241, 251–52, 258
  tĕrāpîm as representations of, 249–50, 251, 258
  theophoric names and, 253
ancient Egypt, 18–19, 20, 27
  age at marriage in, 71–72
  birthing rituals in, 147–48, 149, 150*f*
  birth scenes in, 152, 153–54
  childbirth amulets in, 144–46, 145*f*, 146*f*, 149, 157–58, 162–63
  circumcision in, 70–72
  end of birth impurity in, 182–83, 183*f*, 184–85
  fetus protection rituals in, 57–58, 63
  forecasting a newborn's fate in, 156
  infant mortality in, 274n.2
  lactation rituals in, 208–9
  locations for childbirth in, 149–50, 151–52, 153*f*
  marriage in, 295n.34
  maternal mortality in, 167–68
  midwives in, 152–55, 154*f*
  naming of children in, 176–77, 190–91, 192
  weaning in, 201, 218
  wetnurses in, 202–3
  woman-on-bed figurines from, 162–63
  women's agricultural work in, 203–4, 204*f*
  women's hair in, 148, 182–83

368 INDEX OF SUBJECTS

ancient Greece
  age at childbearing in, 66
  age at marriage in, 104, 297n.70
  age at menopause in, 317n.1
  age at puberty in, 66, 71–72
  birthing rituals in, 3, 45, 52–53, 58–59, 148, 177–78, 225–26, 279n.74
  children's gradual maturation in, 191–92
  end of birth impurity in, 181–82
  fathers accepting newborns in, 3, 45, 58–59, 177–78, 181–82, 190–91, 225
  funerals in, 138
  infant mortality in, 274n.2
  locations for childbirth in, 181–82
  maternal mortality in, 167–68
  midwives in, 178
  naming of children in, 177–78, 190–91
  textile production in, 52–53
  weddings in, 131, 136–38
  women's life-cycle rituals in, 27, 30, 79–80, 225–26
ancient Rome
  age at marriage in, 104, 281–82n.116
  age at menopause in, 317n.1
  age at puberty in, 71–72, 281n.109
  birthing rituals in, 52–53, 148, 178
  children's gradual maturation in, 191–92
  naming of children in, 58–59, 177–78, 190, 191–92, 225
Anderson, Burton, 151
Anderson, Siwan, 293n.115
Aneksi, 311n.123
Angel, J. Lawrence, 274n.2
anointing, 68–69, 99–100, 102
  at betrothal or marriage, 99, 283n.132
  at birth, 99, 283n.132
  during delivery, 149, 150*f*, 154–55, 163, 164–65, 167
  of Jerusalem, 68–69, 99
  while lactating, 209
Antoine, Katja, 281n.111
archaeological remains, 44–45, 261–62. *See also* burial; Judean pillar figurines (JPFs); *tĕrāpîm*
  of bread-making equipment, 109–10
  of communal tombs, 243–44, 244*f*, 254–55, 258
  of items related to childbirth, 144–46, 145*f*, 146*f*, 149, 150*f*, 152, 153*f*, 157–58, 162–63, 164–65
Archer, Léonie, 275n.19, 279–80n.89, 306n.15
Arnette, Marie-Lys, 184–85, 308nn.50–51, 308–9n.55, 309n.57

Arṭās, 115
Asa, 228–29, 240
Asahel, 243–44, 245
Asalluḫi, 155, 166
'ăšērâ cult object, 229, 318n.27
Asherah, 193, 229–30, 233–34
Austen, Jane, 1–3, 6
Austin, Anne, 184–85
Avery, L. Creighton, 281n.109, 281–82n.116

Baal, 152–54, 319nn.8–9, 320nn.11–12
ba'al (master), 127
Ba'anah, 241–42
Bachvarova, Mary, 147–48, 276n.27, 298n.3
bāḥûr (young man), 42–43, 103–4, 131
Bailey, Emoke, 284n.6
Bailey, Wilma Ann, 66
Bal, Mieke, 80, 81–82, 286n.46
Barber, E. J. W., 52–53
barrenness, 112–13, 114, 119–20, 122–23
Barzillai, 242–43
bathing
  birth impurity removed by, 61–62, 63, 64, 143
  Jerusalem, 61–63, 64, 67–69, 82–83, 99
  newborns, 61–63, 64, 67–68, 82–83, 99, 143, 164–65, 167
  and rubbing with salt, 62–63, 68, 143, 164–65, 167, 279n.82
Bathsheba, 92–93, 224–25
  power exerted by, 227–28, 234
  Solomon named by, 171*t*, 174
Beavis, Mary Ann, 286n.46
Beck, Pirhiya, 213, 214*f*
Beckman, Gary, 149–50, 156, 164–65, 180–81, 184, 276n.27, 279n.81, 298n.4
"begat" lists, 10–11
Bell, Catherine, 7–8
Bell, Rudolph, 28–29
bench tombs, 243–44, 244*f*, 248–49
  houses paralleling, 321n.28
  use of, 254–55, 256–57
Benjamin, Don, 94, 288n.10
Benjamin, naming of, 171*t*, 173–74, 193, 196
Benjamin, tribe of, 133–34, 245
Bergmann, Claudia, 304n.130, 316–17n.126
Bertholet, Alfred, 280n.104
Bes, 144–46, 149, 157–59, 158*f*, 183*f*
Beset, 158–59
Beth-Shean, 109–10, 157, 209–10
betrothal. *See also* bridewealth
  of "boy meets girl" type, 89–90
  and childbearing, 105, 112–17, 118, 189
  continuity for women in, 101–3, 105

INDEX OF SUBJECTS 369

discontinuity for men in, 103–5
exacerbation of liminality in, 97, 98–101
family involvement in, 90–91, 93–94
as life-cycle ritual, 97–98
liminality in, 98–99
of Ndembu girls, 14, 26
rituals associated with, 99, 283n.132
and spreading of a robe, 66–67, 98–100, 102
bĕtûlâ (young woman), 42–43, 78, 102–3
and *bāḥûr* (young man), 103
and *kallâ* (bride), 102–3
rape or seduction of, 110–12, 113–14
"betwixt and between," 8, 16–17, 58–59, 74–75, 80–81, 101, 127, 128, 168–69, 255–56
"Betwixt and Between: The Liminal Period in Rites de Passage" (Turner), 8–9, 16, 23–24, 29, 35
Beyene, Yewoubdar, 281n.109
Bible
dating, 46–47
as source, 44, 45–46, 47–48, 174–75
Bickerman, Elias, 131
Bilhah, 106, 121, 170–73, 195–96
biological sex, 40–42
Bird, Phyllis, 126
birth impurity, 143, 230, 276n.24, 276n.25, 277n.37
bathing to remove, 61–62, 63, 64, 143
celebrating end of, 182–85, 183*f*
circumcision and, 54–55
as contagious, 55–57, 60–62, 63, 168, 180–82, 191–92, 276–77n.35
in Egyptian texts, 180, 182–83
gender and, 54–59
in ancient Greece, 181–82
in Hittite texts, 54–55, 60–62, 180–81
as liminal phase, 57, 58–59
in Mesopotamian texts, 180–81
and newborn's social identity, 191–92, 278n.56
and postpartum discharge, 55, 60, 182
purification rituals for, 61–63, 64, 143, 153*f*, 164–65, 182–83, 185–86, 231
birthing stools and couches, 162–63
Blank, Sheldon, 311n.116
Blenkinsopp, Joseph, 93–94, 126, 217–18, 288n.14
Bloch-Smith, Elizabeth, 160
on burial, 243–44, 246, 247–49, 323n.82
on Judean pillar figurines (JPFs), 210, 212, 215–17
Block, Daniel, 63–64, 95–96, 100, 284n.24, 290n.37, 296n.55

bloodline purity, 124
"bloody bridegroom," 70, 73, 284–85nn.27–28
Boaz, 89–90, 98–99, 103–4
Bolin, Anne, 281n.111
Boling, Robert, 285n.39
Borowski, Oded, 206–7, 261–62, 291n.61
Bottéro, Jean, 133
Bourdieu, Pierre, 112, 189–90
Bowen, Nancy, 159, 160–61, 162, 168
boy children
cast out, 65
circumcision of, 53–55, 70, 185
dedication of firstborn, 53
Bradshaw, Karen, 281n.110
breast milk, medicinal uses of, 213–14, 315n.95
breasts, development of, 14, 15, 26, 34–35, 42–43, 65–66
breasts and breastfeeding. *See* lactation rituals; nursing
Bremmer, Jan, 156, 275n.16, 284n.24
Brettler, Marc Zvi, 41–42, 311nn.115–116
brides
abandonment of, 132–33, 135–36
adornment of, 129–30
experiencing loss, 38–39, 137, 140
grief for, 137, 138, 139–40
liminality of, 128–29, 139–40
name change of, 130
veiling of, 130
virginity of, 110–11, 132, 137, 139
bridewealth, 94–96, 114–15, 129, 139–40
in Africa, 112, 114
"brideservice," 105–6
vs. dowries, 106–9
endogamy and, 125–26
form of, 105–6
giving of, as ritual, 96–97, 105
lost labor compensated by, 108–11
naming of children and, 189
of raped or seduced *bĕtûlâ,* 110–12
time lag after giving, 112
and women's reproductive potential, 105, 112–18
women's status enhanced by, 97, 105, 115–18, 129, 179, 188–89, 200, 262
Bryan, Betsy, 295n.34
burial, 239, 240–41. *See also* bench tombs; cave tombs; funerary rituals; mortuary practices
after tragic death, 322n.51
in communal tombs, 242–44, 244*f*
dishonorable, 322n.43
by family members, 242

burial (*cont.*)
  in individual graves, 247–49, 258–59
  of infants, 278n.56
  and procession to tomb, 239–40, 319n.7
  and reburial, of men, 243–44, 245, 247, 248–49
  and reburial, of women, 247–49
  secondary, 255–57, 258, 263
  in tombs of one's "fathers," 243–47, 248–49, 251, 254–55, 256–58
  of women who die in childbirth, 248–49
Burnette-Bletsch, Rhonda, 276n.25, 276–77n.35
Burney, C. F., 131
Burrows, Millar, 94–95
Bynum, Caroline Walker
  on continuity in women's stories, 28–30
  on liminality, 10–11, 12–13, 27–30, 33, 38–39, 128, 187–88, 200
  on status elevation, 37

Cain, 170–73, 171*t*, 193, 195–96
Caleb, 91, 106, 121
the "capable wife," 52
Carley, Keith, 62, 279n.82
Carsten, Janet, 3
cave tombs, 243–44, 248–49
Chapman, Cynthia, 315n.80
Chapman, D. W., 281n.115, 292n.79
characteristics of women's life-cycle rituals, 13, 18, 25–26, 32–33, 39–40, 97. *See also* women's liminality, exacerbation of
  continuity, 21, 25–30, 38–39, 40, 101–3, 104–5, 143
  death imagery, 15, 17, 23, 77–80, 83, 84–85, 138–39, 298n.83
  focus on fertility, 12–13, 39, 40, 115–18, 188–89, 198
  liminality, generally, 18, 39–40, 97
  status elevation, 36–37, 39, 40
  tripartite structure, 16, 20–21, 39, 97
Cheung, Neky Tak Ching, 18
childbirth. *See also* birth impurity; childbirth rituals
  anxieties surrounding, 276–77n.35
  betrothal ritual and, 105, 112–17, 118, 189
  dangers of, 167–69
  of girl children, 51, 52–53, 59, 191
  liminal phase of, 6–7, 57, 168–69, 278n.56
  men excluded from, 149–52, 163–64, 168–69, 175–77, 178
  mother's isolation during, 149–52, 163–64, 168–69, 175–77, 178, 180–82

  as separation, 6–7, 57–59
  social *vs.* physical, 3, 45, 58–59, 190, 191–93, 225
  symbolism of, 8–9, 17
  as women's life-cycle ritual, 6–7, 55–56, 57–58, 167–69
childbirth demons, 144–46, 148–49, 151, 157, 168, 180, 275n.19
childbirth rituals, 3, 45, 51, 143–44, 262–63, 275n.16
  amulets, 144–47, 148–49, 157–58, 158*f*, 162–63, 167
  anointing with oil, 149, 150*f*, 154–55, 163, 164–65, 167
  flour patterns, 148–49, 154–55, 162, 167
  incantations, 51–52, 144–47, 149, 151, 155, 156, 162, 165–67
  knot magic, 146–48, 159, 160–62, 167
  and location of childbirth, 149–52, 153*f*, 181–82
  male magicians performing, 154–55, 300n.41, 300n.43, 300–1n.46
  midwives performing, 154–56, 165, 166–67
  and model couches, 162–63
  oracles, 144, 156, 167
  and pre-birth rituals, 57–58
children
  agricultural labor of, 112–13, 139–40, 197, 298n.1
  anointing of, at birth, 99, 283n.132
  bathing of, at birth, 61–63, 64, 67–68, 82–83, 99, 143, 164–65, 167, 279n.82
  as born pure, 60, 61–62
  burial of, 278n.56
  classification of, 42–43, 217–18
  decreeing the fate of, 155–56, 165
  fathers accepting, 3, 45, 58–59, 177–78, 181–82, 190–91, 225
  gemstones associated with, 51
  and infant mortality, 205, 207, 274n.2, 299n.12
  as liminal at birth, 58–59, 64
  nurses for, 56, 61, 164–65, 201, 202–3
  prophets healing, 161
  protection of, 51, 63, 144–46, 155, 157, 165, 167, 208–9
  rubbed with salt, at birth 62–63, 68, 143, 164–65, 167, 279n.82
  stages in life of, 42–43, 217–18
  "thrown out," 63–65
childwealth, 114
China, 281n.109

INDEX OF SUBJECTS 371

circumcision, 3–4, 25–26. *See also Mukanda* ritual
  in ancient Egypt, 70–72
  and birth impurity, 54–55
  of boy children, 3–4, 53–54, 70, 185, 225–26
  and death of male offspring, 73
  of grown men, in biblical texts, 70
  and marriage, 53–54, 70–74
  as near-death ordeal, 22, 73–74, 263
  as postpartum ritual, 185
  in Priestly (P) source, 53–54, 70, 185
  social identity and, 278n.56
cities as female, 63. *See also* Jerusalem
Civil, Miguel, 300n.43
Cogan, Mordechai, 63–64, 157
Cohen, Shaye, 72–73
Collins, Billie Jean, 180–81, 184
"comity of comrades," 8–9, 13, 23–24
communitas, 9
Cooper, Jerrold, 288n.14
corpse contamination, 55, 59
cosmetics, 153*f,* 182
court jesters, 9–10
Cox, Benjamin, 249–50, 259–60, 323–24n.90
Crapanzano, Vincent, 3–4, 43–44, 72–73, 225–26
cult images, 229–30, 232–34
cyclical and calendrical rituals, 35–36, 59

Dakhleh Oasis, 201
Dalley, Stephanie, 287n.71
danger of women's life-cycle rituals, 23, 83, 100, 140, 167–69
Dan'il, 294n.6
Darby, Erin, 212–13, 214–17
Dasen, Véronique, 274n.2, 312n.11
"daughters who prophesy," 159–62
David
  and Abigail, 92–93
  and Bathsheba, 92–93
  and Michal, 89–90, 91, 98, 105–6, 113–14, 119–20
  naming by, 171*t,* 174
  and Philistine foreskins, 70, 105–6, 113–14, 283n.3, 292–93n.93
  Rechab and Ba'anah killed by, 241–42
  Saul and Jonathan reburied by, 243–44, 245, 247, 322n.51
  and *tĕrāpîm,* 249–50
  and wise woman of Tekoa, 234–35
David, Rosalie, 283–84n.4
Davis, Natalie, 11–12
Day, Linda, 282n.126
Day, Peggy, 77–80, 81–82

dea nutrix, 210
death. *See also* burial; funerary rituals; mortuary practices
  childbirth complications and, 167–68, 193, 196, 248–49
  liminal phase of, 255–56
  symbolic, 8–9, 14–15, 17, 22, 23–24, 38, 77–80, 84–85, 117–18, 138–39, 298n.83
  as transition, 246, 254–55
Deborah. *See* Rebekah, wetnurse of
debt slavery, 94–95, 110
Deir el-Bahri, 182–83
Deir el-Medina, 18–19, 27, 149, 152, 153*f,* 162–63, 176–77, 180, 182–83, 183*f,* 202–3
DeMaris, Richard, 286n.46
Demeter and Persephone myth, 30, 31–32, 79–80, 298n.83
Dempsey, Carol, 68
Dettwyler, Katherine, 207, 313–14n.51
Deuteronomic (D) tradition, 46–47, 248, 292n.75
Deuteronomistic History, 46–47, 174, 291n.64, 292n.75
Dever, William, 212
diet, Israelite 206–7
Dinah, 70, 89–90, 98, 113–14, 197–98, 224
distaff, 51–52
Dorcas, 275n.11
Douglas, Mary, 12–13, 23, 100
dowries, 106–8. *See also* bridewealth
  foreignness and, 106–7
Driver, S. R., 283n.2, 312n.9
Drums of Affliction, The (Turner), 12–13, 16
Duncan, Christopher, 205, 207, 313–14n.51
Dupont-Sommer, André, 209

Ebeling, Jennie, 261–62, 315n.80
Edelman, Diana, 322n.59
Egypt. *See* ancient Egypt
Eichrodt, Walther, 280n.104
El, 72, 73, 213–14
  Baal mourned by, 319nn.8–9, 320nn.11–12
  birth of children of, 152, 176–77
Eleazar, burial of, 245–46
Elijah, 303n.106
Elisha, 62–63, 161, 303n.106
Elkanah, wives of, 121, 122–23
Elohistic writer (E), 46, 47, 173–74, 291n.64, 292n.75, 310n.106
Emerging from the Chrysalis (Lincoln), 30, 37–38
endogamy, 123, 124–26. *See also* marriage
Eng, Milton, 103–4, 217–18

epithalamia, 137
Erbele-Küster, Dorothea, 53–54, 278n.56
Erra, 207
Esau, 91–92, 103–4, 121, 123, 170
Eshmunazor II, mother of, 226–27, 229–30, 231
Eskenazi, Tamara, 295n.14
Essenes, 66, 102–3
Esther, 130–31
Eve, 61, 170–74, 171t, 193
Exodus narrative
 circumcision in, 73
 liminality in, 74–75, 80–81
exogamy, 123–24
Exum, J. Cheryl, 84, 126–27, 264–65
Eyben, Emiel, 43
Ezekiel, wife of, 239–40, 242
Ezra, 123–24

Feinstein, Eve Levavi, 111
feminine, symbolic, 11–12
Festa das Moças Novas, 30, 79
fetuses, 52–53, 57–59, 166–67
Fisher, Daniel, 292n.76
Fishman, Claudia, 207, 313–14n.51
Fitzmyer, Joseph, 279n.74, 314n.71
Fleishman, Joseph, 291n.63
Flusser, David, 73
Forest of Symbols, The (Turner), 9
Foster, Benjamin, 166–67, 287n.71
Francis of Assisi, 28–29, 34
French carnival traditions, 11–12
Frisch, Rose, 281n.109
Frymer-Kensky, Tikva, 52, 110–11, 112–13
Fuchs, Esther, 84–85
funerary rituals, 44–45, 239, 240, 254, 261–62.
 See also burial; mortuary practices
 for criminals and enemies, 240–42
 dismemberment, 241–42
 donning sackcloth, 240, 320n.11
 family members responsible for, 242
 incising one's skin, 240, 320n.12
 for Jezebel, 241–42
 vs. mortuary practices, 319n.1
 removal of body hair, 240, 320n.13
 rubbing dust or ash, 240, 319n.8
 sitting on the ground, 240, 320n.9
 surrogates undertaking, 242, 320n.19, 321n.30
 tearing one's clothes, 240, 285n.40
 weddings similar to, 138, 139
 weeping and lamentation, 239–40, 242

Galambush, Julie, 65, 283n.131
Garland, Robert, 181–82, 297n.70, 297–98n.80

Garnand, Brien, 274n.2
Garroway, Kristine Henriksen, 41–42, 191–92, 217–19, 275n.18, 278n.56, 302n.73
Gawel, Sophia, 280nn.104–105, 281n.113
gĕbîrâ (queen, queen mother), 317n.4. *See also* queen mothers
Gemnihiamente, 311n.123
gemstones, 51
gender
 birth impurity and, 54–59
 of newborns, generally, 41–42, 51–54
 objects signifying, 51–52
 value assigned to, 55
gender binary, 41–42
genealogies, women absent from, 10–11, 218–19, 251, 252–53, 258
genitalia
 and gender, 41–42
 as wet *vs.* dry, 25–26
van Gennep, Arnold, 6–8, 72–73, 74, 97–98, 254
 on calendrical rites of passage, 35–36, 59
 on funerary and mortuary rituals, 254, 255–56
 Hertz inspiring, 255–56, 323n.87
 on Hopi birth rites, 6–7, 57–58, 184–85
 on liminality, 6–7, 8–9, 16, 19–20, 39–40, 57–58, 97
 Lincoln on, 30–33
 on marriage rites, 139–40
 Meskell on, 18–19, 20–21
 on naming, 189–90
 on other types of passage, 30–31, 35–36
 on reintegration, 38–39, 81, 184–85, 187–88
 on structure of rites of passage, 6–7, 13, 16, 18, 19–22, 39, 97, 187–88, 218, 255–56
 on territorial passages, 30–32
Gershom, naming of, 171t, 195
Gerstein, Beth, 286n.46
Gerstenberger, Erhard, 261–62
gestation and parturition, symbols of, 8–9, 15, 17, 22
Gideon, 121, 122, 174, 243–44
gift giving, 95–96, 112, 182–85. *See also* bridewealth
Gilbert-Peretz, Diana, 215
Gilchrist, Roberta, 18–21, 317n.1
Gilgamesh, 80–81, 285n.40, 320n.13
girl children. *See also* Jerusalem
 associated with left side, 52–53, 55
 impurity of, as infants, 55–57, 58–59, 60, 61–63
 lament of, at menarche, 77–78
 liminality of, 58–59, 63, 64–65, 66–67, 68, 79–81, 82–83, 84–85
 textile production and, 51–53

INDEX OF SUBJECTS   373

Gisu people, 3–4, 26–27, 225–26
Goody, Esther, 114
Goody, Jack, 107, 114
Görg, Manfred, 250–51, 304n.123
Granqvist, Hilma, 115
Gray, John, 250–51
Greece. *See* ancient Greece
Greenberg, Moshe, 63–64, 280n.104, 283n.128, 290n.38, 295n.35
Greene, Joseph, 274n.2
Grimes, Ronald, 268n.8
Grosz, Katarzyna, 96, 289n.19, 292n.76
Gruber, Mayer, 55, 312n.21, 313n.45
gunaikeion, 181–82
Gursky, Marjorie, 62–63, 307–8n.35

Hadley, Judith, 210
Hagar, 74, 121, 127, 171*t*
   Ishmael's marriage arranged by, 91
   Ishmael's name and, 194–96
Hague, Rebecca, 137
Hakka women, 18
Halloween, 35–36
Hamor, 90, 95–96
Hannah, 121, 171*t*, 194–95, 196–97, 201–2, 218–19, 223–24, 316n.115
Hathor, 156
ḥaṭṭāʾt, 185–86, 231
healing rituals, 161–62. *See also* Judean pillar figurines (JPFs); knot magic; Shaʿtiqatu
   concerning breasts and breast milk, 208–10, 213–14, 217, 315n.95
   for male impotence, 294n.6
   tĕrāpîm used in, 322n.59
Herrmann, Christian, 157–58
Hertz, Robert, 255–57
Hess, Richard, 315n.80
Hillers, Delbert, 314n.71
Himmelfarb, Martha, 61
hippies, 9–10
hišlîk (thrown out), 63–65
Hittites
   betrothal among, 106–7
   birth celebrations among, 184
   birth impurity among, 54–55, 60–62, 180–81
   birth rituals among, 51, 99, 144–46, 147–48, 149, 156, 164–65
   locations for childbirth among, 149–50
   midwives used by, 51, 152–55, 156, 164–65
   naming of children by, 177–78
   postpartum rituals of, 177–78
Hoffman, David, 136
Hoffman, Sharon, 136
Hoffner, Harry, 177

Holi, 35–36
holiness, impurity and, 56–57. *See also* birth impurity
Holiness (H) source, 46, 67–68
Holland, Thomas, 215
"holy seed," 124
homer, 291n.61
"honoring" dead, 320n.20
Hopi childbirth rites, 6–7, 57–58, 184–85
Hornung, Erik, 190–91, 192
Ḥorvat Qitmit model shrine, 213, 214*f*, 214–15
Hosea, 105–6, 311n.121
"Humility and Hierarchy" (Turner), 35–36
husband as "master," "lord," 127

Ibzan, 245–46
Ichabod, naming of, 171*t*, 194–95, 196, 310n.108
Ilan, Tal, 274n.2
Iliad, 47
individuals *vs.* groups, 93–94, 288n.10
"infant," 42
infant mortality, 205, 207, 274n.2, 299n.12
infants, burial of, 278n.56
initiation. *See Mukanda* ritual; *Nkangʾa* ritual
initiations. *See* women's life-cycle rituals
initiatory agent, sex of, 83
Initiatory Paradigm, The (Lincoln), 37–38
intermarriage. *See* marriage
Isaac
   betrothal and marriage of, 74, 91, 94, 98, 99, 102–3, 105–6, 112, 116–17, 119, 123, 127, 130
   binding of, 73–75, 220
   blessing of, 117
   children named by, 170
   circumcision of, 70, 73–74, 284n.25
   and Jacob's marriage, 91, 123
   and Jephthah's daughter, 76, 80–81, 82–85
   liminal features in story of, 74–75, 82–83
   naming of, 170, 171*t*, 194–96
   tomb of, 224, 242–43
   weaning of, 217, 219–20, 223–24
   "whole life narrative" of, 263
Isaiah, book of
   naming in, 171*t*, 174–75
   weaning in, 202
Ishmael, 219–20, 263–64
   abandonment of, 65
   blessing of, 117
   marriage of, 91, 98
   naming of, 170, 171*t*, 194–96
   Sarah and, 219–20
Isis, 176
ʿIzbet Ṣarṭah, 109–10

Jabesh-Gilead, 134–35, 240–41
Jabez, mother of, 171t, 174, 194–95, 196
Jacob, 263–64
    betrothals of, 98, 101
    blessing of, 117
    "brideservice" of, 105–6, 125–26
    burial of, 242–43, 247
    burials by, 224, 239, 242, 251–52, 258–59
    children named by, 171t, 173
    as fetus, 58, 156
    living with Laban, 119
    marriages of, 91, 94, 98, 106, 119, 121, 123, 127, 130–32, 224
Janssen, J. J., 311n.123
Janssen, R. M., 311n.123
jar burials, 278n.56
Jay, Nancy, 324n.101
Jeanmarie, Henri, 30
Jedidiah, 171t, 174
Jehu, 241–42, 251–52
Jephthah, 76–77, 83–84, 245–46
Jephthah's daughter, 264, 287n.66
    as cultural heroine, 79, 286n.46
    Isaac and, 76, 80–81, 82–85
    lament of, 77, 78, 80, 138–39
    lament, reprise of, 77–78, 138–39
    liminality of, 79–81, 82–83, 84–85
    sacrifice of, 76–77, 81–84, 102
Jeremiah, 58, 138, 286n.49
Jerusalem, 264
    anointed with oil, 68–69, 99
    Asherah images in, 229–30
    bathing of, 61–63, 64, 67–69, 82–83, 99
    betrothal of, 66–67, 68, 98–100, 102
    blood of, 65–66, 67–68, 99
    as Davidic *naḥălâ,* 321n.30
    dowry of, 106–7
    foreign lovers of, 106–7
    liminality of, 63, 64–65, 68
    marriage of, 102, 106–7, 129–30
    as menstruant, 67, 102, 277n.42
    nakedness of, 66–68, 82–83
    as newborn girl, 61–67, 68, 264
    siege of, 204–5, 277n.42
    Yahweh and, 65–68, 98–100, 102, 106–7, 129–30
Jesse, 92–93
Jesus
    circumcision of, 70
    impurity of, as infant, 60–61
    naming of, 306n.15
Jezebel, 224–25
    death of, 239, 241–42, 251–52, 258–59
    marriage of, 123–24

Jiezhu ritual, 18, 20–21
Joab, 234–35
Job, 165–67, 171t
John the Baptist, 58, 70, 306n.15
Jonathan, reburial of, 243–44, 245, 247
Joseph, 263–64
    children named by, 171t, 195
    marriage of, 103–4
    naming of, 171t, 173, 193–94
    reburial of, 245, 247
Josephus, 104
Joshua, 245–46
Josiah, 321n.30
Judah, 91–92, 171t, 173–74
Judean pillar figurines (JPFs), 44–45, 209–14, 211f, 216f
    as apotropaic, 212–14
    children depicted on, 215–17, 216f
    and lactation rituals, 44–45, 209–12, 211f, 214–17, 216f
    parallels to, 213–15, 214f
    tĕrāpîm and, 250–51
Judith, 240
Justinian, 122

Kafwana, 11–12
Kakarla, Nirupama, 281n.110
kallâ (bride), 102–3
Kamionkowski, S. Tamar, 279–80n.89, 289n.33
Keel, Othmar, 212
Kemp, Barry, 182–83
Kempe, Margery, 28
Kertzer, David, 6
Keturah, 91–92
Khirbet Qeiyafa, 109–10
Kinaaldá, 30, 31–32, 33, 36–37, 115–16
King, Philip, 45–46, 285n.37, 286n.49, 321n.31
"kin group," 124–25
kinship-based societies, 107
Klawans, Jonathan, 55
Klee, Deborah, 277n.40
Klinck, Anne, 137, 297n.70
Knohl, Israel, 46
knot magic
    in childbirth, 146–48, 159, 160–62, 167
    in lactation, 208–9
Kore, 79–80
Korpel, Marjo, 160
Kpelle people, 322n.51
Kudat, Ayse, 134–35
Kuenen, Abraham, 274n.245
Kuntillet 'Ajrûd, 158–59

Laban, 91, 94, 130–31
  Jacob residing with, 119
  maidservants given by, 106
lactation rituals
  amulets, 209–10
  Aramean, 209
  Egyptian, 208–9
  in Israel, 209–12, 211f, 214–17, 216f
  and Judean pillar figurines (JPFs), 44–45, 209–12, 211f, 214–17, 216f
  Mesopotamian, 208–9
  and ointments, 209
Laes, Christian, 177–78, 190, 191–92
La Fontaine, J. S., 3–4, 26–27
Lamaštu, 151, 157, 208–10
Lamaštu plaques, 144–46, 157
Lambert, W. G., 300n.43
Lamech, 121
Lauwers, Judith, 314n.58
Leach, Edmund, 64–65
Leah, 113–14
  burial of, 239, 242, 257
  disappearance of, 224
  marriage of, 91, 101, 105–6, 115, 121, 127, 130, 131–32
  naming children, 170–73, 171t, 193–94, 195–96, 197–98
Leeb, Carolyn, 286n.46
Lemos, T. M., 101, 107–9, 127, 290n.59
Leuchter, Mark, 318n.35
Levenson, Jon, 73–74, 84
Levine, Amy-Jill, 290n.37, 290n.57
Levine, Baruch, 60, 276–77n.35
Levite's *pîlegeš*, 121, 122, 133–34, 135–36, 239
Lewis, Theodore, 241, 246, 249–50
Lichtheim, Miriam, 299n.24
"life-course perspective," 18–20, 21
life-cycle rituals, generally, 2
  van Gennep on, 6–8, 97–98, 254
  lament and, 78, 138–39
  as more than rites of passage, 7–8
  religious context of, 44
  universality of, 2, 3, 6–8, 12
  of women *vs.* men, 4–5, 12, 13–14, 21, 25–30, 31–33, 34, 262–63, 264–65
liminality. *See also* women's liminality, exacerbation of
  anonymity and, 17
  as "anti-structure," 29
  in cyclical and calendrical rituals, 35–36, 59
  and death symbolism, 8–9, 17, 22, 78, 79–80, 138–39
  and elites, 29–30

exacerbation of, 23, 25, 40, 59, 63, 64–65, 68, 82–83, 84–85, 99–101, 129, 140, 168–69, 259, 262
  of Jephthah's daughter, 79–81, 82–83, 84–85
  of matriarchs, 126–27
  negative and positive aspects of, 8–9, 38–39
  of newborns, 57, 58–59, 63–66, 68
  as permanent way of being, 9–11, 33, 36–37, 38–39, 128, 140, 187–88
  and reintegration, 21, 38–39, 64, 81–82, 184–85, 187–88
  seclusion and, 8–9, 15, 16–17, 18, 23–25, 57, 75, 184–85
  and status elevation, 13, 35–39, 40, 97, 115–17, 118, 128–29, 187–90, 192, 198–99, 200–1, 262
  of unburied corpse, 246
"Liminality and Communitas" (Turner), 9, 11, 16
liminal periods, 6–7, 8, 16
  after death, 246, 256
  betrothal as, 101
  childbirth impurity as, 57, 58–59, 184–85
  length of, 82–83
  pregnancy as, 168–69
liminal persons, 6, 8, 12
  brides as, 129, 139–40
  "comity of comrades" among, 8–9, 13, 23–24
  invisibility or seclusion of, 8–9, 10–11, 16–17, 18, 23–25, 35, 39–40, 57, 75, 184–85
  matriarchs as, 126–27
  social identity of, 8–11, 25–26, 29–30, 31–32, 33, 40, 58–59, 115–17, 118, 128–29, 186–89, 256
  submission and humiliation of, 8–10, 11, 15, 16–17, 18, 29, 35, 38, 39–40, 83, 100–1, 127
  suffering of, 8–9, 14–15, 16–17, 18, 22, 23–24, 68, 73–75, 81–82, 83, 84–85, 100, 140
  women as, 10–13, 16, 25, 29–30, 33, 36–37, 38–39, 127–28, 140, 187–88
liminal places
  mountains as, 74–75, 80
  śādeh as, 64–65, 74–75
Lincoln, Bruce, 30–34, 79, 83, 128
  on liminality, 13, 21, 33–34, 38–39, 79–80, 128, 187–88, 200
  on nudity and clothing, 34, 115–16
  on Persephone/Kore myth, 79–80
  on status elevation, 34, 36–39, 115–16, 117–18
  on territorial passages, 30–33
Lods, Adolphe, 210
Lorenzen, Søren, 189–90

Lot, daughters of, 170–73, 171*t*
LoWiili people, 114–15
Luo people, 114
lustral day, 58–59, 190, 191–92, 225
Lutkehaus, Nancy, 3–4, 26–27
Luvale people, 22
Lydia, 275n.11

Ma'acah, 228–30, 231, 233–34
Macalister, R. A. S., 210
MacDonald, Nathan, 206–7
Magonet, Jonathan, 276–77n.35
Maier, Christl, 283n.131
Malamat, Abraham, 251, 258
Malay people, birth among, 3–4, 26–27, 225–26
Malul, Meir, 63–65, 280n.103
Manam islanders, 3–4, 26–27, 225–26
Manasseh, 121, 171*t*, 195
Manja people, 22
Manoah, wife of, 171*t*, 174
Manungal, 155
Marcus, David, 285n.39, 286n.42, 287n.75
Marie d'Oignies, 28–29
marriage, 1–4, 7, 119–20. *See also* betrothal
    age at, of men, 43–44, 103–5
    age at, of women, 42–44, 66, 102–5, 112
    by capture, 134–35
    circumcision and, 53–54, 70–74
    as civil contract, 273n.237
    in Eden narrative, 119, 120
    endogamous, 123, 124–26
    as exchange of women, 93–95
    exogamous, 123–24
    kings arranging, 92–93
    levirate, 251–52
    menstruation and, 66, 67, 102–3
    nature of, in ancient Israel, 93–97
    and near-death ordeals, 73–74
    patrilocal *vs.* uxorilocal, 119–20
    of priests, 111
    women's sexual maturity and, 66, 67, 102–3, 104–5, 139
marriage contracts, 130
marriage present. *See* bridewealth
marriage ritual. *See* weddings
Marriott, McKim, 35–36
maṣṣēbâ, 251–52, 258–59
Masterman, E. W. G., 279n.82
mastitis, 207–8
maternal mortality, 167–68
matriarchs as liminal, 126–27
Matthews, Victor, 94, 96, 288n.10
Mauss, Marcel, 95, 268n.8
May, Herbert, 250–51

McCarter, P. Kyle, 227, 312n.9
McClain, Carol, 189–90
medieval Christian Europe, 19–20, 28–29, 37
Medieval Life: Archaeology and the Life Course (Gilchrist), 19–20
Meister, Natalie, 207
men. *See also* circumcision
    age of, at marriage, 43–44, 103–5
    classification of, 40–42
    infertile, 294n.6
menarche, 42–43, 65–66, 67, 77–78, 102–3
menopause, 20–21, 262–63. *See also* queen mothers
    age at, 223, 317n.1
    definition of, in ancient Israel, 43–44
    rituals for, 18, 20–21
    social, 225, 226, 231–35
menstrual disorders, 12–13
menstruation
    and age at marriage, 66, 67, 102–5, 112
    impurity from, 55–56, 61–62, 67–68
    social identity and, 278n.56
Merab, 91
Mersure, 311n.123
Meskell, Lynn, 18–19, 20–21, 25–26, 27–28
Meskhenet, 156
Mesopotamia
    age of marriage in, 104, 281–82n.116
    betrothal in, 96, 99–100, 106–8, 114–15
    birthing rituals in, 51–53, 63–64, 99, 147, 148–49, 155, 157, 160–61, 162, 166–67, 168, 180–81
    childbirth amulets in, 144–47, 148–49, 157
    end of birth impurity in, 180–81, 184
    female ancestors in, 252–53, 258–59
    fetal development in, 57–58
    lactation rituals in, 208–10
    locations for childbirth in, 151
    marriage in, 119–20
    maternal mortality in, 167–68
    midwives in, 148–49, 151, 154–55, 162
    mortuary practices in, 241
    naming of children in, 307n.28
    weaning in, 218–19
    weddings in, 133
    wetnurses in, 201, 202, 208–9
Meyers, Carol, 261–62, 288n.10
    on bridewealth, 95–96
    on childbirth and reproduction, 112–13, 165, 167–68
    on infant mortality, 274n.2
    on Judean pillar figurines (JPFs), 212, 215–17
    on marriage, 126
    on rubbing salt on newborns, 62–63

INDEX OF SUBJECTS   377

on women's life expectancy, 167–68, 248–49
on women's work, 52, 109–10
Micah, 249–51
Micah, mother of, 127–28, 231–34, 311n.116
Michal, 89–90, 91, 98, 105–6, 119–20, 249–50
midwives
   in ancient Israel, 163–65, 166–67
   in ancient Near East, generally, 51, 148–49, 151, 152–56, 154*f*, 164–65
   child's fate foretold by, 155–56
   divine, 41, 151, 152–54, 155, 166, 180
   female family members as, 163–64
   impurity of, 56
   names given by, 170, 171*t*, 173, 175–76
   rituals performed by, 154–56, 164–67
Milgrom, Jacob, 54–55, 60, 62, 185–86, 277n.37, 279n.74
milk rituals, 14–15, 34–35
Miller, Patrick, 307–8n.35, 311n.116, 311n.120
Miriam, burial of, 247–49
miscarriage, 146–48, 167–68, 299n.12
mišpāḥâ (clan), 124–25
mišteh (feast), 131
mōhar. *See* bridewealth
môledet (relations), 123, 124–25
monastics, 9–10
monogamy, 120
Monroe, Lauren, 285n.39
Montserrat, Dominic, 295n.34
Moorey, P. R. S., 214–15
Moran, William, 308n.42
Moriah, 74–75
Morocco, circumcision in, 3–4, 72–73, 225–26
Morris, Ian, 47
mortuary practices, 44–45, 239, 241, 254, 261–62. *See also* burial; funerary rituals
   addressed to male ancestors, 251–53
   vs. funerary rituals, 319n.1
   names evoked and remembered, 191, 251–52
   offerings of food and drink, 241, 249, 252–53
   tĕrāpîm, 249–51, 258
Moses, 263–64
   abandonment of, 65
   as "bloody bridegroom," 70, 73
   burial of, 247–48
   children named by, 171*t*, 195
   circumcision of, 73
   on exogamy, 123
   father-in-law of, 288n.3
   marriage of, 89–90, 94, 98, 105–6, 119
   mother of, 65, 218–19, 223–24, 312n.8
   naming of, 170, 171*t*, 196
   weaning of, 218–19, 312n.8
   and Zelophehad's daughters, 92, 124–25

motherhood, 262–63
   adulthood marked by, 3–4, 26–27, 186, 189, 225–26, 273n.231
   and community formation, 189–90, 191, 192, 198–99
   as extended ritual complex, 143, 169, 179, 200–1, 212
   status of, 179, 186–87, 188–90, 192, 198–99, 200–1
mountains as liminal places, 74–75, 80
mudyi tree, 14–15, 22
Mukanda ritual, 21–23, 25–26, 31–32, 70–71, 73–74, 225–26, 272n.173
   comity of comrades during, 23–24, 25
   differences from *Nkang'a*, 23–26, 270n.115
   father's role in, 23–25
   frequency of, 23–24
   "guardians" of, 23–25, 287n.74
Musgrove, Frank, 43

Nabonidus, 307n.28
nādān (dowry), 106–7
naḥălâ (familial landholdings), 125, 127–28, 245–47
Nakhai, Beth Alpert, 276–77n.35
names
   changing, 79–80, 171*t*, 173, 307n.28
   of dead ancestors, 10–11, 251–53, 258
   theophoric, 159, 253, 311n.123
naming, creation and, 191
naming of children, 45, 143, 262–63, 264. *See also* naming speeches
   among the Hittites, 177–78
   assertion of agency, 179, 189–90, 198–99
   at birth, 175–76
   at circumcision, 306n.15
   conveying social identity, 179, 189–91, 192, 198–99
   by deities, 176, 311n.121
   in Egypt, 176–77, 190–91, 192
   in Greece, 177–78, 190–91
   by men, 170, 171*t*, 173–74, 177–78, 195
   in Mesopotamia, 307n.28
   by midwives, 170, 171*t*, 173, 175–76
   oracular, 171*t*, 174–75
   as postpartum proclamation, 186–87, 188
   as ritualized event, 179, 186–87, 188, 189, 198–99
   in Roman society, 58–59, 177–78, 190, 191–92, 225
   in various biblical sources, 173–75
   as status-elevating, 179, 186–87, 188–90, 192, 198–99
   by women, 170–74, 171*t*, 175–77, 179, 186–87, 188–89, 192–93

naming speeches, 192–95, 197–99
  deity in, 195–99
  by fathers vs. mothers, 195–96
  for girl children, 197–98
  pregnancy or delivery and, 192–95
Naomi, 90, 170, 171t
Navajo people, 30, 31–32, 36–37, 79, 115–16
Ndembu people, 11–13, 42–43. See also Mukanda ritual; Nkang'a ritual
  ancestral shades of, 14–15, 23
  economics of rituals of, 270n.115
  hunting and masculinity linked by, 34–35, 39
  installation rite for chiefs of, 11–12, 29, 35
  Nkula ritual of, 12–13
  reproduction and femininity linked by, 39
necromancers, 159–60
Nehemiah, 123–24
Nehushta, 318n.25
Nehy, 311n.123
Neils, Jenifer, 297n.70
Nicol, George, 319n.43
Niditch, Susan, 285n.39, 287n.75
Niehoff, Arthur, 207
Nintu, 151
Nkang'a ritual, 12–14, 21, 117–18, 271n.118
  age at, 14, 43, 281n.109
  differences from Mukanda, 23–26, 270n.115
  instructress in, 15, 16–17, 24–25, 34–35
  kunkunka stage of, 14, 15, 16–17
  kwidisha stage of, 14, 16, 34–35, 38–39, 187–88
  kwing'ija stage of, 14–15, 16
  liminality in, 16–17, 23, 24–25
  mothers absent from, 24–25
  mudyi tree and, 14–15, 22
  status elevation in, 36–37, 38–39, 116–17, 188–89, 200
  "white" vs. "red," 14
Northup, Lesley, 18, 20–21
Novick, Tzvi, 278n.69
nudity, 14–15, 28–29, 34, 66–68
nudunnû (dowry), 106–7, 160
nuptial songs, 136–37, 138–39
nursing. See also lactation rituals
  benefits of, to child, 205–7, 217
  benefits of, to mother, 313–14n.51
  end of, 217–20
  energy cost of, 203–5
  failures, 207–8
  nutrition following, 205–7
  work of, 203–4
nursing children, terminology for, 42, 217–18

Oakley, John, 167–68, 297n.70
Odyssey, 47
Olyan, Saul, 55, 56–57, 60, 185–86, 231, 322n.43

oracles, during pregnancy, 144, 156, 167
oral traditions, 47
ordeals and tests, during liminality 8, 17, 23, 24–25, 73–75, 81–82, 83, 84–85
Osborne, James, 255–56

Pardes, Ilana, 192–93, 196–98
Parker, Julia, 275n.16
Parker, S. B., 307n.23
Parkin, Tim, 274n.2, 307n.31
paternity
  fathers claiming, 3, 45, 58–59, 177–78, 181–82, 190–91
  and rape, 110–12
patrilineality, 110–11, 117–18, 120, 126, 197, 218–19, 247, 253
patrilocality, 7, 109, 117–18, 119, 122, 136, 139, 247
patrimony, 110–11, 120, 125, 127–28, 245–47, 248–49. See also naḥălâ (familial landholdings)
Paul, circumcision of, 70
Pazazu, 144–46, 157, 209–10
pîlegeš, translation of, 294–95n.7, 296n.60. See also Levite's pîlegeš
Pinch, Geraldine, 162–63, 180, 182–83
Pollock, Della, 186, 192
polygyny, 120–23
Pope, Marvin, 160
praying, 196–97
preexilic period, 4–5, 46–48
pregnancy vases, 149, 150f, 163
Pride and Prejudice (Austen), 1–3
priestly families
  marriage in, 111
  weaning in, 217, 218–20
priestly ordination, 59
Priestly (P) source, 41
  birth impurity in, 54–59, 181–82
  burial of Moses and Aaron in, 248
  circumcision in, 53–54, 70, 185
  dating of, 46, 283n.1
  menstruation in, 67–68
  naming in, 173–74, 310nn.106–107
Private Life in New Kingdom Egypt (Meskell), 20
property
  liminal persons lacking, 8, 10–11, 16–17, 29, 33, 34, 127–28, 232
  naḥălâ, 125, 127–28, 245–47
prophetic healings, 161–62
prophets, female, 159, 160–62, 163–65
Propp, William, 72–73
Puah, 164
puberty
  age at, 65–66, 71
  of boys, 43–44, 70–72

circumcision at, 70–71
 of girls, 42–44, 65–66
 in preindustrial societies, 65–66, 71
 social vs. biological, 3–4, 43–44, 70–71, 225–26
pubic hair, 65–66, 70–71
purification. See birth impurity; menstruation

qadištu (female childbirth attendant), 151
qĕbûrâ (tomb), 322n.41
qînâ (sung dirge), 239–40
queen mothers, 223, 224–25
 Bathsheba, 227–28
 deposing, 228–29
 Ma'acah, 228–29
 power wielded by, 226–30, 233–34
 as religious functionaries, 227, 229–30, 233–34
 in Sidon, 226–27
 as socially menopausal, 226, 230, 231
 in Ugarit, 226

Rachel
 burial of, 242, 247–49
 death of, 164, 167–68, 203
 lament of, in Jeremiah, 259–60
 marriage of, 91, 101, 105–6, 115, 121, 127, 130–31
 maṣṣēbâ at grave of, 251–52, 258–59
 naming children, 170–73, 171t, 193–96
 and tĕrāpîm, 249–50
von Rad, Gerhard, 310n.101
rape
 of bĕtûlâ, 110–12, 113–14
 marriage and, 134–35
Rebekah 91–92, 123
 blessing of, 117
 disappearance of, 224
 marriage of, 91, 94, 98, 99–100, 102–3, 105–6, 112, 119, 127, 130
 marriage present given for, 105–6, 112, 115–18, 198, 264
 prayer of, 311n.115
 pregnancy of, 58, 156
 status of, elevated, 115–17, 179, 198
 wetnurse of, 202, 239–40, 242, 247–49
Rechab, 241–42
red thread, used at birth 165, 167
Rehm, Rush, 138
reintegration, 6–7, 16, 21, 38–39, 64, 81–82, 84–85
 after weaning, 218, 219–20
 ancestral, 254–55, 256, 259–60
 with the holy, 185–86, 231
 and liminality, 184–85, 187–88
 of mothers following birth, 184–85
Repit, 250–51

rites of passage, 6–8. See also characteristics of women's life-cycle rituals; tripartite structure of rites of passage; women's life-cycle rituals
 in ancient Egypt, 20
 in medieval Christian Europe, 19–20
 model of, as flawed, 18–19, 21, 32–33, 38–39
 rank and role in, 8–9, 10–11, 16–17, 29–30, 33, 34–36, 127–28
 seclusion in, 8–9, 15, 16–17, 18, 23–25, 57, 75, 184–85
 submission and humiliation in, 8–10, 11, 15, 16–17, 18, 29, 35, 38, 39–40, 83, 100–1, 127
 suffering in, 8–9, 14–15, 16–18, 20, 22, 23–24, 68, 73–75, 81–82, 83, 84–85, 100, 140
 and territorial passages, 30–33
Ritner, Robert, 70–72
Ritual Process, The (Turner), 9
robe, spreading, 66–67, 98–100, 102
Robins, Gay, 274n.2, 284n.6, 295n.34
Roehrig, Catherine, 203–4
Rome. See ancient Rome
Roscoe, Paul, 26–27, 271n.128
Roth, Martha, 281–82n.116, 290n.58, 291n.72
Ruddedet, 151, 152–54, 156, 176, 180, 182–83
Ruth, 89–90, 98, 99–100, 103–4, 206
 birthing of son by, 163–64, 165
 Boaz and, 66–67, 89–90, 98–100, 103–4, 115
 reproductive potential of, 115
 son of, 163–64, 165, 170, 171t

śādeh (field, outside society), 64–65, 68, 74–75
Safrai, Shmuel, 73
salt, 62–63, 68, 143, 164–65, 167, 279n.82
Samson, 98, 103, 131–32, 171t, 174, 263–64
 burial of, 243–44, 245, 322n.51
 marriage of, 89–90, 119–20, 130–31, 132–33, 135–36, 224, 264
 riddle of, 131–33
Samuel, 263–64
 burial of, 245–46
 ghost of, 259–60
 Hannah visiting, 218–19, 223–24
 name of, 305n.4
 weaning of, 201–2, 218–20
sanctuary, impurity of, 185–86
Sarah
 Abraham mourning, 239–40, 242
 barrenness of, 121
 burial of, 242–43, 257
 disappearance of, 220, 223–24
 Isaac and, 171t, 194–96, 219
 marriage of, 103–4, 127
Sasson, Jack, 165, 282n.119
Satlow, Michael, 66, 104, 292n.79

Saul
 burial of, 240–41, 243–44, 245, 247, 322n.51
 Merab given by, 91
 Michal's marriage arranged by, 70, 90, 91, 105–6, 113–14, 292–93n.93
 name of, 305n.4
Šaušga, 184
Scharbert, J., 311n.116, 318n.38
schéma, 6–7
Schiffman, Lawrence, 61
Schmitt, Rüdiger, 251, 261–62, 304n.130
Schneider, Tammi, 319n.39
Schrage, Wolfgang, 261–62
Scott, Susan, 205, 207, 313–14n.51
Scurlock, JoAnn, 114–15, 148, 151, 167–68, 248–49
Sennacherib, 307n.28
separation, 6–7, 16, 39. *See also* liminality
 and betrothal, 97–98
 and biological death, 256
 and childbirth, 57–59
 of girls *vs.* boys, 23–24, 33
 and marriage, 38–39, 139–40
 during parturition, 149–52, 163, 168–69, 175–76, 178, 180–81
 weaning as, 218–19
Seth, naming of, 170–74, 171t, 195–96
sex, biological, 40–42
sexual maturity, generally, 2, 3–4
sexual maturity of women, 79, 281n.115. *See also* women's life-cycle rituals
 girls lamenting, 77–78
 as gradual, 3–4, 26–27, 65–66
 and marriage, 66, 67, 102–3, 104–5, 139
 at parturition only, 3–4, 27, 186, 273n.231
 in preindustrial societies, 65–66
Sha'tiqatu, 213–14
Shechem, 89–90, 95–96, 98, 105–6, 113–14
Shechemites, 70
Shemesh, Yael, 287n.77
Shiloh, maidens of, 134
Shiloh, Yigal, 215
Shiphrah, 164
Shipton, Parker, 114
shrine niches, 162–63
Shua, daughter of, 171t, 173–74
Siduri, 81
silencing, 84–85
Da Silva, Aldina, 100
Silwan tombs, 247–48
Simkins, Ronald, 114
Sims, Rebecca, 297n.70
Smith, Mark, 160
social identity
 of ancestors, 254, 256–57, 258–59
 circumcision and, 278n.56
 of liminal persons, 8–11, 25–26, 29–30, 31–32, 33, 40, 58–59, 115–17, 118, 128–29, 186–89, 256
 maternal, 168–69, 184–85, 186–89, 192, 198–99
 menstruation and, 278n.56
 naming and, 179, 189–91, 192, 198–99
 of newborn, 191–92, 278n.56
 transitions in, 31–33, 35–37, 39, 115–17, 118, 188–89, 192, 198–99
 weaning and, 191–92, 218, 219–20, 278n.56
Solomon, 263–64
 Bathsheba securing kingship of, 227–28
 naming of, 171t, 174
 and Pharaoh's daughter, 106, 121
 wives of, 121, 123–24
Sonia, Kerry, 251, 321n.28
sons, importance of, 197–98
Southwood, Katherine, 134–35, 295n.15
Sperling, Susan, 281n.109
spindle, 51–52
spirits. *See* ancestral spirits
Stager, Lawrence, 45–46, 274n.2, 285n.37, 286n.49, 321n.31
status elevation, 39, 40
 bridewealth and, 115–18, 129, 179, 188–89, 200, 262
 of medieval women, 37
 naming of children and, 179, 186–87, 188–90, 192, 198–99
 sexuality, fertility, and, 39, 40, 115–18, 188–89, 198
 as temporary, for Israelite women, 117–18, 128–29, 200–1, 220, 262
 as temporary, in *Nkang'a* ritual, 13, 36–37, 38–39, 40, 200–1
 of weaned children, 219–20
Stavrakopoulou, Francesca, 53–54, 246, 254–55, 315n.80, 321n.38
Steinberg, Naomi, 186–87, 189, 273n.231, 275n.18, 278n.56
Steiner, Richard, 160
Stökl, Jonathan, 159
Stol, Marten, 62–64, 151, 202, 288n.14, 307n.28, 311n.123
stratification, social, 107–9
Stross, Brian, 134–35
Strouhal, Eugen, 315n.95
Sukkot, 59
Suriano, Matthew, 254–55, 256–57, 258–59, 319n.7, 320n.14
Swift, M. G., 3–4, 26–27
Swisher, Anna, 314n.58
sympathetic magic, 146–48, 149

"taking" a wife, 90, 94
Tālikettukalyāṇam ritual, 30, 34, 115–16

INDEX OF SUBJECTS 381

Tadebastet, 311n.123
Tamar, 164, 165, 170, 171t, 173
tannôt (rehearse, recount), 77–78
Tappy, Ron, 3
Tawaret, 144–46
Tekoa, wise woman of, 234–35
Tel Dor, 109–10
Tell Beit Mirsim, 215, 216f
tĕrāpîm, 249–51, 258
terḫatu (brideprice), 96, 114–15
terminology, 40–44
territorial passages, 30–33
Tesserakostaion, 182, 184–85
textile production, 51–52, 109, 203
Thiessen, Matthew, 60–61, 277n.39
Thomassen, Bjørn, 6, 31
Thompson, Heather Ann, 27
Timnite bride of Samson, 89–90, 119–20, 132–33, 135–36, 224, 264
Tiv people, 30, 31–32, 33, 36–37, 115–16
Tiyyar caste, 30, 31–32, 33, 36–37, 115–16
Tobias, 131–32
"toddler," 42
Tola, 245–46
tombs. See bench tombs; cave tombs
van der Toorn, Karel, 261–62, 264
 on betrothals and weddings, 93–94, 119–20, 126, 294n.2
 on childbirth rituals, 151, 180–81
 on funerary rituals, 246
 on grinding flour, 292n.89
 on lack of son, 311n.120
 on menstrual impurity, 56, 280n.104
 on mortuary practices, 249–50, 252–53, 254, 258–59
 on naming, 191, 306n.15
 on spreading of a robe, 289n.33
 on vows, 311n.118
 on weaning, 217–18, 316n.115
tribe, 124–25
Trible, Phyllis, 76–77
tripartite structure of rites of passage, 6–7, 16, 18, 20–21, 39, 97, 218, 255–56
Tukuna people, 30, 31–32, 33, 36–37, 115–16
Turner, Edith, 13–15, 23–24, 34–35, 38
Turner, Victor, 8–10, 39–40. See also liminality; liminal persons; Mukanda ritual; Ndembu people; Nkang'a ritual; ordeals and tests, during liminality; rites of passage; status elevation
 on calendrical rites of passage, 35–36, 59
 critique of, 10–13, 25, 29–30, 35–39
 on Mukanda ritual, 21–26, 27–28
 on the Ndembu, 11, 12–14, 21–22, 34–35, 39
 on Nkang'a ritual, 12–17, 23–26, 27–28, 34–35, 36–37, 38–39, 117–18, 187–88
 on ordeals, 8, 75
 on reintegration, 16, 38–39, 184–85, 187–88
 on women's connection to children, 39, 271n.143
 on women's liminality, 11–13, 16–17, 25, 29–30, 38–39, 128

Uehlinger, Christoph, 212
Ugaritic texts
 childbirth in, 152–54, 163, 176–77, 294n.6, 303n.113
 marriage in, 72, 106–7, 136
 mortuary rituals in, 311n.120
 queen mothers in, 226
 Sha'tiqatu in, 213–14
umbilical cord, cutting, 3, 63
universality of life cycle rituals, 2, 3, 6–8
uxorilocality, 119–20

de Vaux, Roland, 72–73, 273n.237
vegetarian diets, 206–7
veiling, 130
Vergiat, A. M., 22
Vernon, Muriel, 281n.111
Vos, Clarence, 55
vows, women making, 196–97
Vriezen, Karel, 250–51
Vymazalová, Hana, 315n.95

Walsh, Carey Ellen, 316n.116
weaning, 143, 191–92, 262–63
 age at, 143, 179, 191–92, 201–2, 278n.56
 in ancient Near East, 201
 feasts celebrating, 217, 219, 316n.115
 in Israelite texts, 201–2
 mother's status elevation ending with, 200–1, 220
 nutrition following, 205–7
 in priestly families, 217, 218–20
 rituals, 217–20
 as separation, 218–19
 social identity and, 191–92, 218, 219–20, 278n.56
wedding feasts, 130–33
weddings, 129–30, 273n.237. See also brides; marriage
 attendants at, 130–31
 and funerals, parallels between, 138, 139
 liminality and, 128–29, 139–40
 location of, 119, 132–33
 nuptial songs of, 136–37, 138–39
 ritual component of, 129, 273n.237
 as sorrowful for women, 133–37, 138–39, 140
Wegner, Judith Romney, 231
Weinstein, Donald, 28–29
Wellhausen, Julius, 274n.245

Wells, Bruce, 122–23, 291n.63
wells, meeting at, 89–90
Wenham, Gordon, 55, 286n.48, 291n.63
Westbrook, Raymond, 290n.37, 291n.63
wetnurses, 56, 61, 164–65, 201, 202–3
wheat, 313n.42
Whelehan, Patricia, 281n.111
White, C. M. N., 22
Whitekettle, Richard, 278nn.62–63, 294n.6
widowhood, 288n.6
Wilcke, Claus, 151
wilderness
  in binding of Isaac, 74–75
  Jephthah's daughter in, 80–81
  śādeh as, 64–65, 68, 74–75
  of Sinai, 74–75, 80–81
Williams, Ritva, 296n.47
Winter, Irene, 315n.90
wise woman of Tekoa, 234–35
women. *See also* characteristics of women's
    life-cycle rituals; liminal persons; sexual
    maturity of women
  abduction of, 134
  acting as priests, 37
  age at marriage, 42–44, 66, 102–5, 112
  and ancestral collective, 256–57, 258–59
  ancestral spirits of, 252–53, 258–59
  biological life of, 262–63
  classification of, 40–42
  disappearance of, after weaning, 220, 223–24
  "fragmented," 264–65
  genealogical absence of, 10–11, 218–19, 251, 252–53, 258
  husband's authority over, 100, 127
  life expectancy of, 167–68, 223, 248–49
  marriage as exchange of, 93–94
  as necromancers, 159–60
  as medieval saints, 28–29
  as outsiders, 126–27
  as part of "the people," 257–58
  religious discourse of, 179, 195–98
  work of, 52, 109–10, 203–4
women's agency
  bridewealth conferring, 116–17, 179, 198
  with menopause, 230, 233–35, 262
  in naming of children, 179, 188–90, 198–99
women's fertility, rituals concerning, 12–13, 39, 40, 115–18, 188–89, 198
women's life-cycle rituals. *See also* characteristics of
    women's life-cycle rituals; Jephthah's daughter
  in Austen, 1–2
  clothing in, 19–20, 34, 115–17, 129–30, 182–83, 184
  danger during, 23, 83, 100, 140, 167–69
  van Gennep, Turner, and, 12, 18–22, 25, 27–28, 29–30, 31–33, 36–37, 38–40
  initiatory agent of, 83
  Lincoln on, 21, 30–34, 36–37, 79, 83, 115–16
  status elevation in, 13, 35–39, 40, 97, 115–17, 118, 128–29, 187–90, 192, 198–99, 200–1, 262
  territorial passages in, 32–33
women's liminality, exacerbation of, 23, 25, 40, 262
  after death, 259
  at betrothal, 97, 98–101
  at birth, 59, 63, 64–65, 68, 82–83
  during childbirth, 168–69
  at coming of age, 82–83, 84–85
  at wedding, 129, 140
women's reproductive potential, 139–40. *See also* childbirth; motherhood
  marriage presents and, 112–17, 118, 188–89
  status elevation and, 39, 40, 115–17, 118, 188–89, 198
  Yahweh's promises regarding, 112–13
"Women's Stories, Women's Symbols" (Bynum), 10, 27–28
Wyatt, Nicolas, 72

Yahweh
  co-creation with, 193
  creation and naming by, 191
  images of, 232–33
  and Jerusalem, 65–68, 98–100, 102, 106–7, 129–30
  oracles and, 156
  as patrinomial lord, 285n.37
  spirit of, 76–77
  spreading robe over Jerusalem, 66–67, 98–100, 102
  women abandoned by, 68–69, 84
Yahwistic writer (J), 46, 47, 173–74, 291n.64, 292n.75, 310n.107
Yamauchi, Edwin, 289–90n.36
Yee, Gale, 126
youth, 261–62

Zelophehad, daughters of, 92, 100–1, 124–25, 127–28
Zeraḥ, 165
Zevit, Ziony, 212
Zilpah, 106, 121, 170–73
Zimmerli, Walther, 160–61, 280n.104
Zipporah, 73, 89–90, 94, 98, 105–6, 310–11n.109

Index of Scripture and Other Ancient Sources

For the benefit of digital users, indexed terms that span two pages (e.g., 52–53) may, on occasion, appear on only one of those pages.

Hebrew Bible
Genesis
  1:27 41
  2:19–20 191
  2:23 119
  2:24 119, 120
  4:1 170–73, 193
  4:19–24 121
  4:25 170–74, 195–96
  4:26 173–74
  5:3 170, 305n.9
  11:29, 32 91–92
  12:2 117
  14:16 257–58
  15:15 257
  16:1–2 263
  16:3 91–92, 121
  16:4 263–64
  16:11 194–95, 305n.9
  16:15 170, 194–95, 263–64, 305n.9
  17:11–12 185
  17:12 70
  17:17 103–4
  17:20 117
  17:25 263–64
  18:1–15 219
  18:10 263
  19:37–38 170–73
  20:12 127
  20:17 294n.6
  21:1–7 73–74, 194–95
  21:3 170, 194–95, 305n.9
  21:4 70, 185, 263
  21:6 194–95
  21:8 217
  21:8–21 74, 219–20
  21:9 219
  21:14–15 65
  21:21 91, 98, 263–64
  21:22–34 74
  22:1–19 73–75, 80, 81–83, 84, 220, 263
  22:2 74–75, 81–82, 84
  22:2–4 74–75
  22:4 75, 82–83
  22:5 75
  22:6 73–74, 84
  22:7 73–74
  22:8 84
  22:9–10 75
  22:11–12 82–83
  22:12, 16 84
  22:17 117
  23:1 74
  23:1–2 220
  23:2 239–40, 242
  23:2–4 319n.2
  23:19 242, 257, 319n.2
  24:1–9 74, 91
  24:1–67 91, 98, 103–4, 112, 117–18, 263, 264, 292n.75
  24:3–4 123
  24:5, 6–8 119
  24:10–27 89–90
  24:15–21 102–3
  24:16 102–3
  24:32–33 102–3
  24:34–51 91
  24:50–51 102–3
  24:53 105–6, 115–16, 117
  24:54 99
  24:57–58 91
  24:58 116–17, 119, 179, 198
  24:59 164–65, 202, 242
  24:59–61 102–3
  24:60 117
  24:65 130
  24:67 94, 102–3, 263
  25:1 91–92
  25:6 121
  25:8 324n.93
  25:9–10 257
  25:10 319n.2

Genesis (cont.)
  25:17 263–64, 324n.93
  25:19–26 156
  25:20 74, 103–4
  25:21 263–64
  25:22–23 58, 156
  25:25 170
  25:26 263–64
  26:4 117
  26:10 257–58
  26:24 117
  26:34 91–92, 103–4, 121
  26:35 91–92, 123
  27:46 91–92, 123, 224
  28:1–2 123
  28:1–5 91, 98
  28:9 91–92, 121
  29:1–12 89–90
  29:15–30 91, 98, 292n.75
  29:18–20 125–26, 263–64
  29:20 105–6
  29:22 130–31, 219
  29:22–23 263–64
  29:23–24 106
  29:23–25 130
  29:27 131–32, 263–64
  29:27–28 125–26
  29:28 94, 105–6, 263–64
  29:28–29 106
  29:30 263–64
  29:32 193–94
  29:32–35 170–73
  29:32–30:24 197–98
  29:33 193–94
  30:4 121
  30:6 170, 173, 195–96
  30:8 170, 173, 196
  30:9 121
  30:11, 13 170–73
  30:18, 20 170–73
  30:21 170–73, 197–98
  30:23–24 193–94, 195–96, 263–64
  30:24 173
  31:14–16 106
  31:17–18 119
  31:19–35 249–51
  31:34 249–50
  31:38, 41 119, 224
  33:1–7 224
  33:4 224
  34:1–31 98, 292n.75
  34:2 224
  34:2–4 89–90
  34:4 90

  34:6–17 224
  34:8–12 90, 95–96
  34:10 95–96
  34:12 94, 95, 105–6, 113–14
  34:13–17 70
  34:25–26, 30 224
  35:8 164–65, 202, 239–40, 242, 247–48, 319n.2
  35:16–20 247–48, 319n.2
  35:17 164
  35:18 167–68, 173, 193, 194–95, 196
  35:19–20 242
  35:20 251–52, 319n.2
  35:27 224
  35:29 263, 324n.93
  36:2 91–92
  37:3 224
  38:2 91–92
  38:3, 4–5 173–74
  38:6, 8, 11 91–92
  38:12 319n.2
  38:14, 26 91–92
  38:28 164, 165
  38:29 170, 173
  41:45 263–64
  41:45–46 103–4
  41:51 195
  47:30 257, 322n.41
  48:4 117
  48:7 242, 319n.2
  49:25 209–10
  49:29 257, 324n.93
  49:29–32 242–44
  49:30 247
  49:31 224, 239, 242, 257, 319n.2
  49:33 263–64, 324n.93
  50:4–14 247, 263–64
  50:13 247
  50:26 263–64
Exodus
  1:15–17 275n.18
  1:15–19 164
  1:16 303n.113
  1:19 164
  1:22 65
  2:2 263–64
  2:3 65
  2:7–9 164–65
  2:10 170, 218, 223–24, 312n.8
  2:15–21 89–90, 98
  2:21 90, 91, 94, 263–64
  2:22 195
  3:1 105–6, 292n.75
  4:20 119

INDEX OF SCRIPTURE AND OTHER ANCIENT SOURCES 385

4:24–26 70, 73, 263–64
4:25 73
4:29, 31 223–24
6:20 223–24
6:24 193–94
12:48 73
13:1–2, 11–16 53
13:19 245, 247
18:3 310–11n.109
19:15 257–58
20:12 320n.20
21:7 94–95
21:10 122–23
22:15–16 94–95, 105–6, 110–12, 113–14, 292n.75
22:16 113–14
22:28 53
23:25–26 112–13
29:35 59
30:35 279–80n.89
34:11–16 123–24
34:16 124
34:20 53
Leviticus
  8:33 59
  12:1–5 306n.15, 309n.67
  12:1–8 54–59, 60–61, 63, 64–65, 68, 70, 82–83, 168, 169, 181–82, 191–92, 282n.125, 285n.35
  12:2 54, 55–56, 181, 278n.56
  12:3 70, 185
  12:4 54, 56–57, 181–82, 230
  12:5 54, 55–56, 181, 275n.18, 278n.56
  12:6 231, 278n.56
  12:6–8 185–86
  12:8 60–61
  15:14 231
  15:19 56
  15:19–24 55–56, 61–62, 282n.125
  15:21–23 56
  15:24 277n.39
  16:16 185–86
  18:19 282n.125
  20:18 282n.125
  21:13–14 111, 286n.48
  21:15 111
  23:34, 42–43 59
  27:2–7 55, 66
Numbers
  3:11–12, 40–51 53
  6:2 196–97
  8:16–18 53
  18:15–16 53
  19:11, 14, 16 59

20:1 247–48, 319n.2
20:2–13 248
20:24 324n.93
20:28–29 247–48
20:29 322n.43
25:1 257–58
26:59 223–24
27:3 92
27:13 263–64, 324n.93
30:4–16 76–77, 196–97
31:2 263–64, 324n.93
31:19 59
33:38–39 247–48
36:3 247
36:6 92, 124–25
36:7 125
36:8 247
36:8–9 125
Deuteronomy
  1:28, 37 248
  3:26 248
  4:21 248
  5:16 320n.20
  7:1–4 123–24
  7:3–4 124
  7:14 112–13, 294n.6
  20:7 100
  21:13 239–40, 242
  21:15–17 122–23
  21:22–23 240–41
  22:5 41–42
  22:13–21 132
  22:14 286n.48
  22:23–27 96, 100
  22:28–29 105–6, 110–12, 113–14, 292n.75
  22:29 125–26
  23:19 196–97
  25:5–6 251–52
  26:14 320n.15
  28:30 96
  32:50 324n.93
  34:5–6 247–48, 263–64
  34:8 322n.43
Joshua
  5:5, 8 257–58
  5:11 206
  8:29 240–41
  10:26–27 240–41
  15:13–19 91, 106, 107–8
  18:28 245
  24:30 245–46
  24:32 245, 247, 263–64
  24:33 245–46

Judges
  1:11–15 91, 106, 107–8
  2:9 245–46
  2:10 257–58
  3:5–6 123–24
  5:11 286n.43
  8:30–31 121
  8:31 174
  8:32 243–44
  10:1–2 245–46
  11:1, 29 76
  11:29–40 68–69, 76–85, 102–3, 264
  11:30–31 76–77
  11:31 81–82
  11:34, 35 76–77, 84
  11:36 76–77
  11:37 77, 78, 80–81, 102
  11:37–38 77–78
  11:39 77, 78, 81–83, 102
  11:39–40 77–78
  11:40 82–83
  12:7, 8–10, 13–15 245–46
  13:5, 7 263–64
  13:24 174, 263–64
  14:1–2 89–90
  14:1–10 98
  14:2 90, 224
  14:5 90
  14:10 90, 130–31, 219
  14:10–18 119–20, 132–33, 134–36, 138–39, 263–64
  14:15 135–36, 296nn.57–58
  14:17 132–33
  14:19 119–20
  14:20 130–31, 132–33, 135–36
  15:1–2 90, 119–20
  15:2 132–33, 135–36
  15:4–6 135–36
  16:30 322n.51
  16:30–31 263–64
  16:31 243–44, 245
  17–18 231–32, 249–51
  17:1–5 231–34
  17:2–3, 4 232–33
  17:5 232–33, 249–50, 258
  18:14, 17, 18, 20 258
  19:1–2 133–34
  19:1–10 135–36
  19:1–30 121
  19:2 297n.67
  19:3, 4 296n.60, 297n.67
  19:4–10 133–34
  19:5, 6 297n.67
  19:7 296n.60
  19:8 297n.67
  19:9 296n.60, 297n.67
  19:10 135–36, 297n.67
  19:25 135–36
  19:25–28 133–34, 319n.2
  19:28 297n.61, 319n.3
  19:29 239
  20:12–17, 35–48 133–34
  21:1, 7 94
  21:8–14 134–35
  21:12 297n.67
  21:18 94
  21:19–21 134–35
1 Samuel
  1:1–28 121, 305n.4
  1:4–8 122–23
  1:19–20 263–64
  1:20 194–95, 305n.4
  1:22–24 218–19
  1:24 201–2, 316n.115
  1:28 218, 219–20, 305n.4
  2:11 201–2
  2:19 218–19, 223–24
  2:21 223–24
  4:20 163–64, 167–68
  4:21 194–95
  4:21–22 196, 310n.108
  8:2 263–64
  8:10–18 292–93n.93
  15:12 251–52
  15:23 249–50
  17:12 92–93
  17:25 91
  18:20 89–90
  18:20–25 90, 98
  18:20–27 119–20
  18:25 70, 94–95, 105–6, 292–93n.93
  18:27 283n.3, 292–93n.93
  19:11–17 249–51, 322n.59
  19:13 249–50, 322n.59
  19:16 322n.54, 322n.59
  20:29 92–93
  22:3–4 92–93
  25:1 245–46, 263–64
  25:40 92–93
  28:3–25 259–60
  31:4 322n.51
  31:11–13 240–41, 321n.40
2 Samuel
  1:17–27 319n.6
  2:32 243–44, 245
  3:2–5 121, 294n.6

INDEX OF SCRIPTURE AND OTHER ANCIENT SOURCES 387

3:6-11 227-28
3:14 292-93n.93
3:31-37 239-40, 320n.19
3:35 240
4:2-12 241-42
4:4 164-65, 203
4:12 320n.19
5:13 92-93, 121
5:13-16 294n.6
11:27 92-93
12:24 174, 263-64
12:25 174
13:1-20 110-11
14:1-20 234-35
14:3 234-35
14:16 246
14:19 234-35
14:23 234
15:16 121
16:21-22 110-11, 121
17:23 243-44, 322n.51
18:17 322n.43
18:18 191, 251-52, 311n.120
19:38 242-44
20:3 110-11
21:12-14 243-44, 245, 247, 322n.51

1 Kings
1:5-40 224-25, 227-28
2:13-25 224-25, 227-28, 234
2:34 321n.33
3:1 92-93, 121, 263-64
9:16 106, 107-8, 121
11:1 121
11:1-3 263-64
11:1-8 123-24
11:3 121
11:4-5 124
11:43 263-64
13:22 243-44, 245-46
14:1-18 161, 162
15:1-2 228
15:1-15 228
15:9-10 228
15:13 228-29
16:31 92-93, 123-24, 320n.14
17:17-24 161, 162
20:3 121
21:3 247
21:23 241-42, 319n.4
22:37 321n.30

2 Kings
2:19, 20-21 62-63
4:8-37 161, 162

4:14 294n.6
5:1-14 161, 162
9:10 241-42, 319n.4
9:28 243-44, 321n.30, 322n.41
9:34 241, 319n.2, 320n.14
9:35 241-42
9:35-37 239, 319n.4
9:36 241-42, 319n.4
9:37 251-52
10:13 224-25
11:2 164-65, 203
11:15-16 319n.2
14:20 243-44, 321n.30
20:1-11 161, 162
22:20 257-58
23:6 229
23:24 249-50
23:30 321n.30

Isaiah
4:1 130
7:14 174-75
7:20 65-66
8:3 174-75
8:19-20 259-60
11:8 217-18
28:9-10 202
38:1-8 161, 162
40:26 191
49:1 58
49:18 129-30
56:5 251-52
57:8 251-52
61:10 129-30
62:2 130
62:5 102-3
64:5 280n.104

Jeremiah
1:4-5 58
2:32 102-3, 129-30
16:1-9 138
16:2 286n.49
16:7 242
20:15 163, 175-76
29:2 318n.25
31:15 259-60
34:5 240
44:15-19 196-97
44:24 257-58
44:25 196-97

Ezekiel
13:17-23 159-62, 163-65
13:18 160-62, 303n.96
13:19 162, 168

Ezekiel (cont.)
   13:20 160–61, 162
   13:20–21 160–61, 162
   16:4 61–63, 64, 67–68, 99, 143, 164–65, 191–92, 264
   16:4–5 64–65, 68
   16:4–6 68–69
   16:4–9 60–69, 82–83
   16:5 63–67, 68
   16:5–8 67–68, 74–75
   16:6 61–62, 65–68
   16:6–7 283n.131
   16:7 65–68, 280n.104, 283n.131
   16:7–8 67, 77–78
   16:8 66–67, 68, 98–100, 102, 106–7, 280n.104, 282n.121
   16:8–9 68–69
   16:8–12 102–3, 112
   16:9 67–68, 99–100, 102
   16:10–12 102, 129–30
   16:26–34 106–7
   16:33 106–7, 160
   18:6 282n.125
   21:26 249–50
   22:10 282n.125
   24:16 239–40
   24:16–17 242
   24:16–18 319n.2
   24:17, 22–23 240
   27:30 240
   36:17–18 282n.125
   43:8 229–30
   43:24 62–63
   44:22 111, 286n.48
Hosea
   1:6 311n.121
   1:8 313–14n.51
   2:4 130
   3:1–5 105–6
   3:2 105–6
   3:4 249–50
   9:4 320n.15
   9:14 207–8
Amos
   6:10 240
   7:13 229–30
Zechariah
   10:2 249–50
Psalms
   8:3 202
   45:14–15 129–30
   45:15 130–31
   78:63 136
   78:63–64 138–39

Proverbs
   7:14 196–97
   31:2 196–97
   31:10–31 52, 275n.10
   31:13, 19, 22, 24 52
Job
   3:1–26 165
   3:4–6 166–67
   3:10 166
   21:25 320n.15
   21:32 319n.7
Canticles
   3:11 129–30
Ruth
   1:4 290n.49
   2:14 206–7
   3:1–4 90, 98
   3:9 66–67, 98–100, 282n.121
   3:10 103–4
   4:11 115
   4:13 282n.121
   4:14–15 163–64
   4:17 163–64, 165, 170
Lamentations
   4:4 204–5
Ecclesiastes
   6:10 191
Esther
   1:3 131
   2:7 319n.2
   2:18 130–31, 219
   3:15 131
Ezra
   2:49 159
   9:1–4 123–24
   9:2, 11 124
   10:10–14 124
Nehemiah
   2:3, 5 243–44
   3:23 305n.4
   5:5 94–95, 110
   13:23–27 123–24
   13:26–27 124
1 Chronicles
   2:46, 48 121
   3:24 305n.4
   4:5 121
   4:9 174, 194–95, 196
   7:14 121
   7:16, 23 174
   8:8–9 121
   14:3 92–93
2 Chronicles
   3:1 285n.31

11:18 92–93
11:20–22 228
11:21 92–93, 121
13:1–2 228
13:21 92–93, 121
15:16 228–29
16:14 240
21:19 240
22:11 164–65, 203
24:3 121
31:16 217, 218–20
31:18 218–19
34:28 257–58
35:25 319n.6

Apocryphal/Deuterocanonical Books
Tobit
  1:9 295n.19
  2:11–12 52
  8:20 131–32
  10:7 131–32
  11:18 131–32
Judith
  8:2 295n.19
  16:24 240
1 Maccabees
  2:70 243–44
  9:19 243–44
  9:37–39 130–31
2 Maccabees
  7:27 201–2, 278n.56

Old Testament Pseudepigrapha
Joseph and Aseneth
  21:8 131–32
Jubilees
  3:8–14 61
  15:12, 14, 25–26 70, 185
  17:15–16 73–74
Testament of Issachar
  3:5 104
Testament of Levi
  11:1 104
  12:5 104

New Testament
Matthew
  21:16 202
Luke
  1:27 290n.57
  1:35 282n.121
  1:39–45 58
  1:59 70, 185, 306n.15
  2:21 70, 185, 306n.15
  2:22–24 60–61
  3:18 58
  7:12–15 239–40
John
  2:1–11 131
Acts
  9:39 275n.11
  16:14 275n.11
Philippians
  3:5 70, 185

Dead Sea Scrolls
  4Q265 7.11–17 61
  4Q266 6.ii.10–11 61

Egyptian Sources
"The Autobiography of Bakenkhonsu" 218
Book of the Dead
  Spell 17 63
Borghouts, *Ancient Egyptian Magical Texts: Volume Nine*
  Text 31 147–48
"The Doomed Prince"
  §4 156
Ebers Papyrus
  500, 788 213–14
  796 209
  803, 807 300n.37
  808, 809 209, 213–14
  810, 836, 837 209
"The Instruction of Ani"
  §7 201
"The Instruction of Ankhsheshonq"
  §11.1.7 71–72
O. Cairo CG 25521 182–83
O. Cairo CG 25597 182–83
O. IFAO 1069/O. Dem 952 180, 182–83
O. Michaelides 48 rt. 182–83
Papyrus Berlin 3027
  Text F 278n.55
  Text I 315n.95
  Text O 208–9
Papyrus Berlin 3038
  Case 13 209
Papyrus Bibliothéque Nationale
  198, II 151
Papyrus Leiden I
  Spell 30, 31 149
  Spell 33 152
Papyrus London
  No. 28–30 147–48
  No. 29, IX,14–X,1 147–48
  No. 40–42 147–48
  No. 45 147–48

Papyrus Ramesseum IV
  C, 28–30 149
"The Story of Setne Khamwas and Si-Osire (Setne II)"
  §1 144–46
"The Two Brothers"
  §18 151
Westcar Papyrus, "The Birth of the Royal Children"
  §9.23 152–54
  §10.2 148
  §10.7 151, 180
  §10.7–8 152–54
  §10.9 176
  §10.12–13 156
  §10.16 176
  §10.20–21 156
  §10. 23–24 176
  §10.26–§11.1 156
  §11.18 180, 182–83
  §12.8 182–83

Hittite Sources
"Appu and His Two Sons" 177–78
Beckman, *Hittite Birth Rituals*
  "The Ritual of Papanikri"
    IV, lines 5–6 283n.132
    IV, lines 6–7 165
    IV, lines 12–16 61–62, 164–65
  Text A
    §1–§2 301n.54
  Text B
    §2', line 8' 152–54
    §3', line 10' 155
    §6', lines 25'–27' 155
    §10″ 156, 301n.56
    §11″–§12″ 51, 184
  Text C
    §5, line 18 279n.81
    §5, line 20 61–62, 164–65
    §6, line 22 177–78
    §9' 156
  Text G
    §1–§2 155
  Text H
    §16', lines 25–26 300n.37
    §16', lines 26–27 147–48
    §18', lines 34–36, 38 149–50
    §19', line 39 149–50
  Text K
    §2 144
    §5 149–50
    §6 144

  §10–§11 60–61, 180–81, 276n.27
  §12 184
  §14–§15 144
  §16 184
  §18, §21–§22 144
  §28–§29 60–61, 180–81, 276n.27
  §30 184
  Text T
    §3 184
  Text Y 184
"The Song of Ullikummi" 177–78

Mesopotamian Sources
BAM
  235 10–16 (// 236 r. 1'–9') 147
  237 i 1'–16' 146–47
Collections of the University Museum, University of Pennsylvania
  1509 ii 9–19 147
"The Cow of Sîn" 155, 300n.38
van Dijk, Goetze, and Hussey, *Early Mesopotamian Incantations and Rituals*
  Text 86a 166
  Text 86b 208–9
E. Ebeling, *Keilschrifttexte aus Assur* 2
  223:5 148–49
"Enlil and Ninlil"
  Lines 152, 154 151
Ennigaldi-Nanna Stele
  I:20–25 307n.28
"Erra and Ishum"
  IV.120 207
Epic of Atraḫasis
  I.254–90 273n.217
  I.290 151
  I.299–300 308n.42
  Late Assyrian fragments K 3399 + 3934 41
Epic of Gilgamesh
  I.76 287n.72
  III.10, 225 287n.71
  VI.6–79 287n.72
  VII.147 80–81
  VIII.91 80–81
  IX.2, 5 80–81
  X.45, 52, 62, 64, 66, 77, 118, 125, 139, 141, 143, 154, 218, 225, 239, 241, 243 80–81
  Old Babylonian Meissner Fragment iii. 2, 12–13 81
  Old Babylonian Pennsylvania Tablet iv, 147–63 287n.72
Farber, *Schlaf, Kindchen, Schlaf!*
  §39:14 147
  §40:7–9 147

INDEX OF SCRIPTURE AND OTHER ANCIENT SOURCES   391

Foster, *Before the Muses*
   II.20.b 166, 299n.22
   IV.43 208–9
   IV.53.a, lines 15–18 166–67
Genealogy of the Hammurapi
   Dynasty 252–53
Gurney and Hulin, *Sultantepe Tablets* 2
   241:5 148–49
"Instructions of Šuruppak" 151
Laws of Eshnunna
   A iii 3–5, B ii 13–15 201
Vorderasiatische Schriftdenkmäler 17
   33, 28–30 149
von Weiher, *Spätbabylonische Texte aus Uruk* II
   113 no. 22 148–49
von Weiher, *Spätbabylonische Texte aus dem Planquadrat U 18* IV
   24 148–49
Will of Sennacherib 307n.28

Ugaritic Sources
KTU
   1.10.3.19–26 152–54, 304n.122
   1.10.3.32–36 152
   1.12.1.17--18 303n.113
   1.12.1.25–29 307n.23
   1.16.5.23–1.16.6.2 213–14
   1.17.1.25–33 311n.120
   1.17.1.36–42 294n.6
   1.23.8–11 72
   1.23.52–53 152, 176–77
   1.23.59–60 152
   1.24 136
   1.24.2–3 72
   2.11, 2.12, 2.13, 2.16, 2.24, 2.30, 2.33, 2.34 226, 227–28
RS 17.352 226

West Semitic Inscriptions
KAI
   14 228
   14.1, 3, 12–13 226–27
   14.15–18 227, 229–30
   14.18–20 226–27
Samaria Ostraca
   1:5 159

Sefire Stele I
   Lines 21–22 209

Classical Greek and Roman Sources
Aristotle, *History of Animals*
   VII.1.581a.12–14, 16–17 71
   VII.1.582a.18 71–72
   VII.1.582a.27–29 66
   VII.1.582a.33–34 71–72
   VII.5.585a 317n.1
Homeric Hymn to Demeter
   Lines 5, 79 79
Justinian, *Digesta/Pandects*
   I.7.40 71–72
   XXXIV.1.14.1 71–72
Justinian, *Institutes*
   11.14 71–72
Philo of Byblos, *Phoenician History*, as quoted in Eusebius, *Praeparatio evangelica*
   1.10.33, 44 73
Plato, *Republic*
   V.460e.4–5 66
Pliny the Elder, *Natural History*
   7.14.61 317n.1
   28.9.42 148
Plutarch, *Quaestiones Romanae*
   §102 58–59, 190, 225
Sappho, *Fragments*
   105b 137
   110a 137
   114 137
Theocritus
   Idyll 18 137

Classical Jewish Sources
Josephus
   Antiquities 2.230 312n.8
   Jewish War 2.161 66, 102–3
Philo
   De Opificio Mundi 103 104
   De Specialibus Legibus 2.126 125–26

Rabbinic Sources
   b. Niddah 31 52–53, 276n.25
   m. Niddah 5:6–8 281n.115
   b. Šabbat 134b 306n.15

www.ingramcontent.com/pod-product-compliance
Ingram Content Group UK Ltd.
Pitfield, Milton Keynes, MK11 3LW, UK
UKHW041134230426
470302UK00013B/62/J